# Lecture Notes in Artificial Intelligence 1433

Subseries of Lecture Notes in Computer Science
Edited by J. G. Carbonell and J. Siekmann

## Lecture Notes in Computer Science

Edited by G. Goos, J. Hartmanis and J. van Leeuwen

**Springer**
*Berlin*
*Heidelberg*
*New York*
*Barcelona*
*Budapest*
*Hong Kong*
*London*
*Milan*
*Paris*
*Singapore*
*Tokyo*

Vasant Honavar   Giora Slutzki   (Eds.)

# Grammatical Inference

4th International Colloquium, ICGI-98
Ames, Iowa, USA, July 12-14, 1998
Proceedings

Springer

Series Editors
Jaime G. Carbonell, Carnegie Mellon University, Pittsburgh, PA, USA
Jörg Siekmann, University of Saarland, Saarbrücken, Germany


Volume Editors

Vasant Honavar
Giora Slutzki
Iowa State University, Department of Computer Science
226 Atanasoff Hall, Ames, Iowa, 50011-1040, USA
E-mail: {honavar,slutzki}@cs.iastate.edu

Cataloging-in-Publication Data applied for


Die Deutsche Bibliothek - CIP-Einheitsaufnahme

**Grammatical inference** : 4th international colloquium ; proceedings / ICGI-98,
Ames, Iowa, USA, July 12 - 14, 1998. Vasant Honavar ; Giora Slutzki (ed.). -
Berlin ; Heidelberg ; New York ; Barcelona ; Budapest ; Hong Kong ; London ;
Milan ; Paris ; Singapore ; Tokyo : Springer, 1998
  (Lecture notes in computer science ; Vol. 1433 : Lecture notes in artificial
  intelligence)
  ISBN 3-540-64776-7


CR Subject Classification (1991): I.2, F.4.2-3, I.5.1, I.5.4, J.5

ISBN 3-540-64776-7 Springer-Verlag Berlin Heidelberg New York

© Springer-Verlag Berlin Heidelberg 1998
Printed in Germany

Typesetting: Camera ready by author
SPIN 10637663      06/3142 – 5 4 3 2 1 0     Printed on acid-free paper

# Preface

Grammatical Inference, also referred to as automata induction, grammar induction, and automatic language acquisition, is the process of learning of grammars, automata, and languages from data (examples, queries, etc.). Machine learning of grammars finds a variety of applications in syntactic pattern recognition, adaptive intelligent agents, diagnosis, computational biology, systems modelling, prediction, natural language acquisition, data mining and knowledge discovery.

Historically, grammatical inference has been studied by researchers in several research communities including: Information Theory, Formal Languages, Automata Theory, Language Acquisition, Computational Linguistics, Machine Learning, Pattern Recognition, Computational Learning Theory, Neural Networks, etc. These different communities have been largely isolated.

Perhaps one of the first attempts to bring together researchers working on grammatical inference for an interdisciplinary exchange of research results took place under the aegis of the First Colloquium on Grammatical Inference held at the University of Essex in United Kingdom in April 1993. This was followed by the (second) International Colloquium on Grammatical Inference, held at Alicante in Spain and the Third International Colloquium on Grammatical Inference, held at Montpellier in France. Following the success of these events and the Workshop on Automata Induction, Grammatical Inference, and Language Acquisition, held in conjunction with the International Conference on Machine Learning at Nashville in United States in July 1997, it was deemed appropriate to hold the Fourth International Colloquium on Grammatical Inference (ICGI '98) in United States.

ICGI '98 consisted of both refereed papers as well as two invited papers and an invited tutorial. Approximately 35 papers were received for review from Europe, United States, India, Japan, and Australia. Each submitted paper was reviewed for technical soundness, originality, clarity of presentation, and relevance by at least 2 members of the program committee. A total of 22 papers were accepted for presentation at the conference. The contributed and invited papers cover a wide range of topics in the theory as well as the applications of grammatical inference, automata induction, and language learning.

We are grateful to the members of the Technical Program Committee for reviewing the papers, and the Local Arrangements Committee and Ms. Margie Poorman and Ms. Janet Gardner of the Extended and Continuing Education Division of Iowa State University for their help with the organization of the conference. We would like to thank Professor James Vary (the Director of the Institute for Theoretical and Applied Physics (IITAP)) Professor John Mayfield (the Associate Dean of the Graduate College), and Professor Arthur Oldehoeft (the Chair of Computer Science) at Iowa State University for their support of the conference. We would like to thank Professor Laurent Miclet and Professor Colin de la Higuera for their help with many aspects of the conference. We

are grateful to Professor Jerry Feldman and Professor Alvis Brazma for kindly
agreeing to give invited talks. Professor Jack Lutz graciously agreed to give a
tutorial on Kolmogorov Complexity and its Applications. We would like to thank
the attendees for making ICGI '98 a success. We are grateful to the the editorial
staff of Springer-Verlag for putting together the conference proceedings.

July 1998

Vasant Honavar and Giora Slutzki
Program Chairs
ICGI '98.

# Organization

ICGI '98 was organized at Iowa State University (ISU) in Ames, Iowa from July 12 through July 14, 1998 by Vasant Honavar and Giora Slutzki with the assistance of the Technical Program Committee, the Local Arrangements Committee, and the staff of ISU Extended and Continuing Education Division.

ICGI '98 was held in cooperation with the American Association for Artificial Intelligence (AAAI), the IEEE Systems, Man and Cybernetics Society, and the Association for Computational Linguistics (ACL) Special Interest Group on Natural Language Learning.

ICGI '98 was cosponsored by the International Institute of Theoretical and Applied Physics (IITAP), the Iowa Computational Biology Laboratory, the Complex Adaptive Systems Group, the Artificial Intelligence Research Laboratory and the Department of Computer Science at Iowa State University.

## Program Committee

### Program Chairs

Vasant Honavar and Giora Slutzki, Iowa State University, USA

### Technical Program Committee

R. Berwick, MIT, USA
A. Brazma, European Bioinformatics Institute, Cambridge, UK.
M. Brent, Johns Hopkins University, USA
C. Cardie, Cornell University, USA
W. Daelemans, Tilburg University, Netherlands
D. Dowe, Monash University, Australia
P. Dupont, Univ. St. Etienne, France.
D. Estival, University of Melbourne, Australia
J. Feldman, International Computer Science Institute, Berkeley, USA
L. Giles, NEC Research Institute, Princeton, USA
J. Gregor, University of Tennessee, USA
C. de la Higuera, LIRMM, France
A. Itai, Technion, Israel
T. Knuutila, University of Turku, Finland
J. Koza, Stanford University, USA
M. Li, University of Waterloo, Canada
E. Makinen, University of Tampere, Finland
L. Miclet, ENSSAT, Lannion, France.
G. Nagaraja, Indian Institute of Technology, Bombay, India
H. Ney, University of Technology, Aachen, Germany
J. Nicolas, IRISA, France

R. Parekh, Allstate Research and Planning Center, USA
L. Pitt, University of Illinois at Urbana-Champaign, USA
D. Powers, Flinders University, Australia
L. Reeker, National Science Foundation, USA
Y. Sakakibara, Tokyo Denki University, Japan
C. Samuelsson, Lucent Technologies, USA
A. Sharma, University of New South Wales, Australia.
E. Vidal, U. Politecnica de Valencia, Spain

## Local Arrangements Committee

Dale Grosvenor, Iowa State University, USA.
K. Balakrishnan, Iowa State University, USA.
R. Bhatt, Iowa State University, USA
J. Yang, Iowa State University, USA.

# Table of Contents

# Results of the Abbadingo One DFA Learning Competition and a New Evidence-Driven State Merging Algorithm

Kevin J. Lang[1], Barak A. Pearlmutter[2], and Rodney A. Price[3]

[1] NEC Research Institute, 4 Independence Way, Princeton, NJ 08540,
kevin@research.nj.nec.com
[2] Comp Sci Dept, FEC 313, Univ of New Mexico, Albuquerque, NM 87131,
bap@cs.unm.edu
[3] Emtex, Milton Keynes, England, rod@emtex.com

**Abstract.** This paper first describes the structure and results of the Abbadingo One DFA Learning Competition. The competition was designed to encourage work on algorithms that scale well—both to larger DFAs and to sparser training data. We then describe and discuss the winning algorithm of Rodney Price, which orders state merges according to the amount of evidence in their favor. A second winning algorithm, of Hugues Juillé, will be described in a separate paper.

## Part I: Abbadingo
## 1 Introduction

The Abbadingo One DFA Learning Competition was organized by two of the authors (Lang and Pearlmutter) and consisted of a set of challenge problems posted to the internet and token cash prizes of $1024. The organizers had the following goals:

- Promote the development of new and better algorithms.
- Encourage learning theorists to implement some of their ideas and gather empirical data concerning their performance on concrete problems which lie beyond proven bounds, particulary in the direction of sparser training data.
- Encourage empiricists to test their favorite methods on target concepts with high Kolmogorov complexity, under strict experimental conditions that permit comparison of results between different groups by eliminating the possibility of hill climbing on test set performance.

### 1.1 The learning task

The task of the Abbadingo One competition was DFA learning from given training data consisting of both positive and negative examples. The learner was provided with a set of training strings that had been labeled by an unseen deterministic finite automaton (the target concept), and was required to predict the labels that the target would assign to a set of testing strings. All three of these—the DFA, the training strings, and the testing strings—were drawn from uniform random distributions.

| | | training set density | | | lower |
|---|---|---|---|---|---|
| | dense U.B.=IV | III | II | sparse I | bound |
| small 64 | 4456 | 3478 | 2499 | 1521 | 542 |
| target 128 | 13894 | 10723 | 7553 | 4382 | 1211 |
| size 256 | 36992 | 28413 | 19834 | 11255 | 2676 |
| large 512 | 115000 | 87500 | 60000 | 32500 | 5862 |

**Table 1.** Training set sizes for the Abbadingo One competition problems.

## 1.2 Some history

DFA learning can be very hard in the worst case. [5] proved that it is NP-hard to find a DFA that is consistent with a given set of training strings and whose size is within a polynomial factor of the size of the smallest such DFA. [4] proved that predicting the output of a DFA can be as hard as breaking cryptosystems widely believed secure.

However, DFA learning does not seem to be so hard in the average case. [1] proved that a simple state merging algorithm is guaranteed to find the smallest DFA consistent with a complete training set consisting of *all* strings out to a given length. [6] showed empirically that this same algorithm can often construct an approximately correct hypothesis from a sparse subset of a complete training set, when both the target concept and training sets are randomly chosen from uniform distributions. [8] proved the approximate learnability of DFA's with worst-case graph structure and randomly labeled states, from randomly chosen training strings.[1]

We note that many papers have been published on the application of generic methods such as neural networks and genetic search to the problem of DFA learning. Unfortunately, this literature has largely focused on tiny benchmarks (the largest target machine in the widely used "Tomita" suite contains five states), so the scalability of the proposed methods is hard to assess.

## 2 Experimental setup

Abbadingo One used random target DFA's because they have some relevance to the average case, they have high Kolmogorov complexity, and they are easy to generate in any desired size. The procedure for constructing a target concept of nominal size $n$ was: construct a random degree-2 digraph on $\frac{5}{4}n$ nodes, extract the subgraph reachable from the randomly chosen root node, and label the graph's states by flipping a fair coin.

This procedure yields graphs with a distribution of sizes centered near $n$, and a distribution of depths centered near $2\log_2 n - 2$. The size variation is of no great consequence, but the depth variation would complicate our training set construction, so it was eliminated by selecting only those graphs with a depth[2] of exactly $2\log_2 n - 2$.

A training set for a target of nominal size $n$ consisted of a random sample drawn without replacement from a uniform distribution over the collection of $16n^2 - 1$ binary

---

[1] The [8] theorem concerns a slightly different protocol, in which the learner sees the label of every state that is encountered rather than just the label of the final state.

[2] By analogy to trees, the depth of a DFA is maximum over all nodes $x$ of the length of the shortest path from the root to $x$.

strings whose length lies between 0 and $2\log_2 n + 3$ inclusively. A testing set was drawn from the remaining strings in this same collection. Training strings were labeled, while testing strings were not.

# 3 Competition design:

## 3.1 Target and training set sizes

As shown in table 1, the sixteen Abbadingo One problems represented the cross product of 4 values of a target size parameter and 4 values of a training set density parameter. Both of these parameters influenced the difficulty of the problems. Our intention was to make the target concepts large enough to challenge the empirical learning community, and the training data sparse enough to challenge the theoretical learning community.

The size parameter was simply the nominal size of the target concept. Its four values were 64, 128, 256, and 512 states.

The density parameter took on values from one to four, shown as roman numerals in the tables. A density parameter value $p$ was turned into an actual training set size $s$ by linearly interpolating between rough upper and lower bounds on sample complexity: $s = L + (p/4)(U - L)$. The lower bound $L$ came from the simple counting argument which equates $2^n n^{2n}/(n-1)!$, an estimate of the number of different $n$-state (binary alphabet) target DFA's, with $2^s$, the number of ways of labeling a training set of $s$ strings. The upper bound $U$ was determined by visually inspecting the learning curves for the Trakhtenbrot-Barzdin algorithm which appeared in [6]. In addition, some rounding was performed on the training set sizes for targets of size 512.

Because the problems in column IV were already solvable by the Trakhtenbrot-Barzdin state merging algorithm, an implementation of which we distributed before the competition, these problems were considered practice problems, not official challenge problems.

## 3.2 Testing protocol

Test set tuning is an insidious problem that afflicts even the well intentioned. The Abbadingo One testing protocol was designed to eliminate this phenomenon. The test set for each problem consisted of 1800 unlabeled strings, none of which appeared in the training set. Proposed labelings were submitted to a testing oracle provided by the Abbadingo web server at http://abbadingo.cs.unm.edu. Instead of providing a score that could be used for hill climbing, the oracle provided only 1 bit of feedback, which told whether or not the accuracy of the labeling was at least 99%. Since this was the threshold at which a problem was considered solved, the feedback bit would always be zero while a participant was working on a problem, so it carried essentially no information.

Thanks to a new cryptographic technique of Joe Kilian's, the testing oracle was implemented without storing the answers anywhere online [11]. This reduced the temptation to break into the Abbadingo web server.

## 3.3 Additional rules

Two rules governed the selection of competition winners. The priority rule stated that the first person to solve a problem (to 99% accuracy) would get the credit for solving it.

| dense | training set size | | sparse |
| | III | II | I |
| --- | --- | --- | --- |
| small 64 | Juillé-PBS | Juillé-PBS | Juillé-EDSM+search |
| target 128 | Juillé-PBS | Juillé-PBS | unsolved |
| size 256 | Price-EDSM | Juillé-EDSM | unsolved |
| large 512 | Price-EDSM | Price-EDSM | unsolved |

**Table 2.** The person and algorithm that first solved each of the twelve challenge problems. The data remains available at http://abbadingo.cs.unm.edu

The dominance rule stated that problem $A$ dominates problem $B$ when TrainingSetDensity($A$) $\leq$ TrainingSetDensity($B$) and NodeCount($A$) $\geq$ NodeCount($B$).

The winners of the competition would be participants who, at the termination of the competition, had credit for solving problems that were not dominated by other solved problems.

## 4   Competition results

According to our logs (which do not include accesses to the European mirror site), training data was downloaded from the primary Abbadingo web site by about 460 IP addresses, including many major proxy servers. Proposed test set labelings were submitted from 45 IP addresses, which we estimate corresponds to about 25 different participants.[3] Nine of the twelve challenge problems were ultimately solved. The person and algorithm that first solved each problem is shown in table 2. The order of events was as follows.

First, Hugues Juillé solved the four problems in the upper left of the table using a parallel beam search technique. Because this method was computationally expensive and didn't scale well to the larger problems, there was a lull in the competition until Rodney Price discovered an evidence driven state merging algorithm (EDSM) that handles sparse data better than previous state merging algorithms, and that has much better time complexity than the beam search method which Juillé had been using. This algorithm,[4] which is discussed in detail below, quickly polished off the problems in columns II and III. Note that according to the competition rules, these results dominated the earlier results of Juillé. However, Price's algorithm could not handle training data as sparse as that in column I. There was another lull in the competition until Juillé solved the smallest problem in column I, using EDSM augmented with some search over its initial decisions.

According to the competition's priority and dominance rules, the two winners were Rodney Price, by virtue of solving problem 512-II, and Hugues Juillé, by virtue of solving problem 64-I.

The three largest problems in column I remain unsolved.

---

[3] Participants did not necessarily submit labelings to the Oracle. They could tune their algorithms using cross-validation or their own DFAs drawn from the same distribution. We made no attempt to count such silent participants.

[4] Including a similar program which Juillé coded up after a conversation with Price.

| | | dense **training set density** sparse | | | | algorithm |
|---|---|---|---|---|---|---|
| | | IV | III | II | I | |
| | 64 | 2000.0 | 15.0 | 2.4 | 2.1 | |
| nominal | 128 | 1600.0 | 21.0 | 2.6 | 2.1 | TB-92 |
| | 256 | 850.0 | 8.1 | 2.1 | 2.0 | |
| target | 512 | 130.0 | 13.0 | 2.2 | 2.0 | |
| | 64 | 2700.0 | 900.0 | 250.0 | 2.1 | |
| size | 128 | 4500.0 | 2400.0 | 720.0 | 2.1 | EDSM-97 |
| | 256 | 6600.0 | 2500.0 | 700.0 | 2.0 | |
| | 512 | 11000.0 | 6800.0 | 2300.0 | 2.0 | |

**Table 3.** Median reciprocal error rates of two algorithms on 100 new random instances of each of the 16 Abbadingo One problems. Higher scores are better; the values 2.0 and 100.0 correspond to generalization rates of 50 percent and 99 percent respectively. The latter value is the Abbadingo threshold for considering a problem solved. TB-92 is an implementation of the Trakhtenbrot-Barzdin state merging algorithm. EDSM-97 is an earlier and worse version of the reference algorithm of section 9. It is interesting to note that EDSM is getting better as one moves to lower matrix rows, while TB is getting worse.

## 5 Post-competition work

We have done some additional work since the competition. First, we ran EDSM on new random problems lying on the Abbadingo problem grid to discover the algorithm's typical behavior. The results are summarized by table 3. EDSM works well on columns IV, III, and II, whereas Trakhtenbrot-Barzdin can only handle column IV. Both algorithms die on column I.

Second, because differing choices about small details can turn Price's basic idea into many different programs of varying performance, we decided to provide some guidance by defining an official reference version of the EDSM algorithm. This algorithm will be described in part 2 of this paper. We will also describe a couple of optimizations which make the reference algorithm practical without hurting its performance too much, plus Juillé's fast and simple implementation of EDSM using the "blue-fringe" control strategy.

## 6 Conclusion of Part I

The Abbadingo One competition had three goals. The goal of promoting the development of new and better algorithms was clearly satisfied. Both Rodney Price and Hugues Juillé made useful contributions to the state of the art in DFA induction.

Although we have heard a few amusing anecdotes, we have no solid evidence that theorists have empirically explored the limits of their algorithms in the sparse data regime, or that empiricists have carefully measured the scaling properties of their algorithms. We therefore conclude this report by repeating our call for theorists to implement their best ideas, and for experimentalists to try their ideas on problems that are hard enough to really test them.

Meanwhile, we are preparing a more flexible DFA learning challenge problem generation scheme, and considering other grammar learning tasks that might be appropriate for Abbadingo Two.

## Part II: Evidence driven state merging
## 7 Background

A simple and effective method for DFA induction from positive and negative examples is the state merging method [1, 6, 7]. This method starts with the prefix tree acceptor for the training set and folds it up into a compact hypothesis by merging compatible pairs of states.[5] Two states are compatible when no suffix leads from them to differing labels.

When a state merging algorithm is applied to sparse training data, it can almost never be sure that an apparently compatible merge is truly valid. Thus, most of the algorithm's actions are hopeful guesses, which unfortunately have serious consequences later: each merge introduces new constraints on future merges, and these new constraints will be wrong when an incorrect merge is made.

Because there is a snowballing of right or wrong decisions, it is critically important for the algorithm's early decisions to be correct, and hence a good strategy is to first perform those merges that are supported by the most evidence. [6] claimed that this consideration supported the choice of breadth-first order for candidate merges, because then the earliest merges must survive the comparison of the largest trees of suffixes.

[10] suggested that a better strategy is to look at the training data and perform merges exactly in order of the amount of evidence, rather than in a predetermined order that hopefully correlates with that quantity. While this is a very good point, the actual algorithm described in [10] does not work well on the Abbadingo challenge problems due to a couple of flaws. One was a mistake in the algorithm's control strategy that will be described in section 10. A more serious mistake was the measure of evidence that they proposed, essentially the number of labels on strings that pass through the two candidate nodes. This quantity is only a weak upper bound on evidence, since labeled nodes on one side which line up with unlabeled nodes on the other side have absolutely no value in testing whether the two candidate nodes actually represent the same mapping from suffixes to labels.

Rodney Price was able to win the Abbadingo One competition because he realized that a more accurate evidence measure is the number of labels tested during a merge.

## 8 Price's motivation for EDSM

Suppose that a state merging program does $m$ merges, and that each merge is verified by $t$ independent tests, each of which has a probability $p$ of revealing that an incorrect merge is wrong. Let $c$ be the probability that any given one of these $m$ merges is valid, and $d$ be the probability that all of them are valid. Then, $d = c^m$, $1 - c = (1 - p)^t$, and finally $t = \log(1 - d^{\frac{1}{m}}) / \log(1 - b)$ shows how many tests will suffice to ensure that the whole computation is correct with confidence $d$.

Blue-fringe state merging algorithms do at most $n(a - 1) + 1$ merges when constructing an $n$-state hypothesis over an alphabet of size $a$. Combining this fact with the calculation of the previous paragraph and the assumption that the label comparisons

---
[5] Note that state merging frequently introduces non-determinism into the hypothesis, which can then be removed by a determinization procedure that recursively merges the children of the original node. In this paper, we always do merging with determinization.

which occur during a merge are independent tests having a 50 percent chance of revealing an invalid merge, one can see that problems in the top row of the Abbadingo matrix can be solved with confidence .93 by restricting the program to merges that are supported by 10 or more label comparisons. Since the highest scoring initial merges for the top-row problems in columns III, II, and I have scores of 19, 13, and 5 respectively, one would expect this method to work for the first two problems, but not the last, which is exactly what happens.

Note that while one could write a program that is willing to do any merge whose score exceeds the threshold computed above, better performance can be obtained by ignoring the threshold and simply doing the highest scoring merge in all cases.

# 9 Reference algorithm

Here we describe a post-competition version of EDSM. Compared to the programs that were used during the competition, this algorithm produces a slightly better distribution of generalization rates on random problems (see section 11).

## 9.1 Definition of a merge's score

We award one point for each state label which, as a result of a merge, undergoes an identity check and turns out to be okay. Any mismatch results in a negative overall score. Details appear in section 9.4.

## 9.2 Initial hypothesis

The initial hypothesis is the prefix tree acceptor directly embodying the training set.

## 9.3 Outer loop

The key insight of EDSM is that bad merges (which can't be directly detected when the training data is very sparse) can often be avoided if we instead do high scoring merges that have passed many tests and hence are likely to be correct. To have the best chance of finding a high-scoring merge to perform at any given moment, we need the largest possible pool of candidate merges. Thus, we would like to consider the possibility of merging every pair of hypothesis nodes, as in the following outer loop:

1. For every pair of nodes in the hypothesis, compute the score for merging that pair.
2. If any merge is valid, perform the highest scoring one, otherwise halt.
3. Go to step 1.

Note that this outer loop requires us to be able to merge nodes that are the roots of arbitrary subgraphs of the hypothesis, not just nodes that are the roots of trees. In the next section we show how to do this.

```
(define (compute-classes hypo        ; current hypothesis DFA (not modified)
                         ufer        ; union-find data structure (modified)
                         input-set)  ; list of nodes asserted to be equivalent
  (when (> (length input-set) 1)
    (let ((learned-something-new? #f)
          (guy1 (car input-set)))
      (dolist (guy2 (cdr input-set))
        (when (not (uf-same-class? ufer guy1 guy2))
          (uf-unify-classes ufer guy1 guy2)
          (set! learned-something-new? #t)))
      (when learned-something-new?
        (dotimes (i alphabet-size)
          (compute-classes hypo ufer
            (delete-duplicates-and-undefineds
              (map (lambda (node) (get-child hypo node i))
                   (uf-get-members-of-guys-class ufer guy1)))))))))
```

**Fig. 1.** Scheme code for working out which states are combined by a given merge.

## 9.4 Merging and scoring

To merge a pair of nodes, we must work out the partition of hypothesis nodes into equivalence classes which is implied by the assertion that the two candidate nodes are equivalent, plus the determinization rule which states that the children of equivalent nodes must be equivalent. Note that we can perform this computation regardless of whether the merge is valid, since validity depends on state labeling, whereas the equivalence classes only depend on the transition function.

Once we have determined the set of equivalence classes, it is trivial to consult the labels and compute a merge score, and, if the merge is in fact valid, to construct a new hypothesis reflecting the merge.

**Computing equivalence classes** Figure 1 shows the Scheme language subroutine `compute-classes`, which works out the equivalence classes implied by a merge and the determinization rule. It employs a union-find data structure to keep track of sets of states that are known to be equivalent.

To assert that a particular set of states is equivalent, we call `compute-classes` on that set. The procedure checks the union-find data structure to determine whether the assertion is new information. If not, the routine returns immediately. Otherwise, it unifies the equivalence classes associated with all the members of the input set, and then calls itself recursively on each of the sets of $i^{th}$ children of members of the newly unified equivalence class.

When considering a merge, we initiate the computation by calling `compute-classes` on the set consisting of the two nodes that we are thinking of merging. We also pass in a fresh union-find data structure that has been initialized with a singleton set for each state in the pre-merge hypothesis.

Note that the computation terminates because recursive calls only occur when separate classes have actually been unified, and the number of states in the hypothesis is an upper bound on the number of times this can happen.

**Scoring** A merge's score is the sum over equivalence classes of the following quantity: if there are conflicting labels in the class, minus infinity; if there are no labels in the class, zero; otherwise, the number of labels minus one. We subtract one because the first label in the class establishes the correct label for the class, but is not checked.

**Constructing a merged hypothesis** Once a candidate merge has been shown valid by a non-negative score, and we have decided to actually perform the merge, we can construct an updated hypothesis from the equivalence classes as follows. The new hypothesis has one state per equivalence class.

Let $C_1$ be an equivalence class, and $i$ be an input symbol. Let $s_1$ be any state in $C_1$ that has a defined transition for $i$. Let $s_2$ be the target of that transition, and let $C_2$ be the class of $s_2$. Then $i$ takes us from $C_1$ to $C_2$. If no state in $C_1$ has a defined transition for $i$, then $C_1$'s transition for $i$ is undefined.

Let $s_3$ be any state in $C_1$ that has a defined label. The label of $s_3$ becomes the label for $C_1$. If no state in $C_1$ has a defined label, then $C_1$'s label is undefined.

## 10 Blue-fringe algorithm

Because the algorithm of section 9 performs merges in arbitary order, both nodes in a merge can be the roots of arbitrary subgraphs of the hypothesis. It turns out that by placing a restriction on merge order (described below), one can guarantee that one of the two candidate nodes is always the root of a tree, resulting in a very simple algorithm for merging two nodes (see figure 2).

Much previous work has employed a restriction of this type, including the papers of [6, 7, 10]; and the Abbadingo competition programs of Price and Juillé. Note that the restriction shrinks the pool of merge candidates, so it increases the failure rate of the algorithm as compared to the unrestricted algorithm of section 9. However, the idea is well worth describing.

As usual, we start with the prefix tree acceptor. The root is colored red. Its children are blue, and all other nodes are white. We maintain the following invariants:

- There is an arbitrary connected graph of mutually unmergeable red nodes.
- All non-red children of red nodes are blue.
- Blue nodes are the roots of isolated trees.

We restrict ourselves to the following actions:

- Compute the score for merging a red/blue pair.
- Promote a blue node to red if it is unmergeable with any red node.
- Merge a blue node with a red node.[6]

This basic framework of invariants and actions can be turned into different algorithms of widely varying performance, depending on the details of the policy for choosing which action to perform when. A particularly good policy is described in [12]:

---

[6] Note that the last two actions might also require some white nodes to be recolored blue.

```
(define (merge-and-compute-score red-cand blue-cand)
  (make-blue-guys-father-point-to-red-guy red-cand blue-cand)
  (set! score 0)                      ; using global variable for simplicity here
  (merging-walk-it red-cand blue-cand)
  score)

(define (merging-walk-it r b)
  (let ((r-label (get-label r))(b-label (get-label b)))
    (when (defined? b-label)
      (if (defined? r-label)
          (if (= r-label b-label)             ; compare labels
              (set! score (+ score 1))
              (set! score -infinity))
          (set-label! r b-label))))           ; copy in missing label
  (dotimes (i alphabet-size)
    (let ((r-child (get-child r i))(b-child (get-child b i)))
      (when (defined? b-child)
        (if (defined? r-child)
            (merging-walk-it r-child b-child)
            (set-child! r i b-child)))))))     ; splice in missing branch
```

**Fig. 2.** Code for performing and scoring a merge in the blue-fringe framework.

1. Evaluate all red/blue merges.
2. If there exists a blue node that cannot be merged with any red node, promote the shallowest such blue node to red, then goto step 1.
3. Otherwise (if no blue node is promoteable), perform the highest scoring red/blue merge that we know about, then goto step 1.
4. Halt.

Note that the algorithm of [10] has the priority of steps 2 and 3 reversed, which drastically reduces its effectiveness.[7] It is important to not start merging until many merge candidates have accumulated, so that one with a high score is likely to be available.

# 11  A comparison of two EDSM implementations

We have described two implementations of EDSM. A table (like table 3) could be made for either one showing that it scales well,[8] and that it can usually solve problems at density level II but not density level I. In this section we put aside the question of scaling and focus on the question of how well the two versions can generalize on problems that lie halfway between columns II and I, that is, near the edge of typical solvability for the EDSM method.

Table 4 shows the results of a comparison on a set of 1000 such problems. Clearly, both implementations of EDSM are much more powerful than the plain Trakhtenbrot-Barzdin program. The reference program is slightly more effective than the blue-fringe program. We attribute this to its larger pool of candidate merges.

---

[7] On a set of 100 problems like the ones in section 11 but with 2500 training strings, the median generalization error rate for Juillé's policy is .004. Reversing the priority of steps 2 and 3 increases this to .39, which is nearly as bad as the value of .44 for the plain Trakhtenbrot-Barzdin algorithm.

[8] The reference algorithm needs some speedups to be practical. See the appendix.

| algorithm | median generalization rate | number of solutions (out of 1000) |
|---|---|---|
| Trakhtenbrot-Barzdin | .537 | 26 |
| blue-fringe EDSM (Juillé) | .809 | 311 |
| reference EDSM | .934 | 379 |
| combination of the previous two | .955 | 423 |

**Table 4.** A comparison of two implementations of EDSM on 1000 random problems. Each problem had 2000 training strings of length 0-15, and a depth-10 target DFA with about 64 states. Solutions are hypotheses with a generalization rate of .99 or better.

We also mention that there is a strong stochastic component to the behavior of both EDSM programs,[9] and that there are many problem instances where the reference program fails and the blue-fringe program succeeds. Given the somewhat uncorrelated failures of the two programs, it is natural to combine them by running both and then choosing the smaller of the two resulting DFA's. Table 4 shows that this combined approach works better than either program alone. In fact, the combined performance level is well into the range reported by [12] for the search-intensive SAGE system.

## 12 Notes on run time

The run time of Trakhtenbrot-Barzdin is upper bounded by $PH^2$, where $P$ is the size of the inital PTA, and $H$ is the number of nodes in the final hypothesis. The bound for the blue-fringe algorithm is $PH^3$. We don't have a tight upper bound on the run time of the reference algorithm, but we conjecture that it would be closer to $P^3H$ than to $P^4H$.

## 13 Conclusion of Part II

We have described two versions of a polynomial time DFA learning algorithm that works very well on randomly generated problems. While the algorithm can be defeated by a malicious adversary, we believe that it will degrade gracefully as one moves gradually away from the average case. We recommend that anyone faced with a DFA learning task give this algorithm a try.

## Acknowledgements

We thank Hugues Juillé for sending us code and an early draft of [12], which is the source of the blue-fringe control policy described in section 10.

---

[9] This is due to randomness in the training data and the fact that even high scoring merges can be wrong.

# Appendix: speedups for the reference algorithm

For the experiment of section 11, we sped up the reference algorithm by only considering merges between nodes that lie within a distance w of the root on a list of nodes created by a breadth-first traversal of the hypothesis. This change hurts performance by causing the algorithm to miss the (relatively rare) high scoring merges involving deep nodes. Note that while the existence of the new w parameter appears to make the algorithm less general by requiring prior knowledge of the size of the target DFA, one can use the standard doubling trick to eliminate this requirement. However, in our section 11 experiment on size-64 DFA's, we simply used a w value of 256.

We also employed the following optimizations, which don't change the behavior of the algorithm except to make it faster. Whenever the deeper of a pair of candidate nodes is the root of an isolated tree, the blue fringe scoring routine of figure 2 is used to cheaply compute the same score that would be returned by the expensive general-purpose code of section 9.4. Also, before finally resorting to the general-purpose code, we first do a quick walk looking for labeling conflicts; if one is found, we can immediately return a score of minus infinity.

# References

1. B. Trakhtenbrot and Ya. Barzdin'. (1973) *Finite Automata: Behavior and Synthesis*. North-Holland Publishing Company, Amsterdam.
2. D. Angluin. (1978) *On the Complexity of Minimum Inference of Regular Sets*. Information and Control, Vol. 39, pp. 337-350.
3. L. Veelenturf. (1978) *Inference of Sequential Machines from Sample Computations*. IEEE Transactions on Computers, Vol. 27, pp. 167-170.
4. M. Kearns and L. Valiant. (1989) *Cryptographic Limitations on Learning Boolean Formulae and Finite Automata*. STOC-89.
5. L. Pitt and M. Warmuth. (1989) *The Minimum DFA Consistency Problem Cannot be Approximated Within any Polynomial*. STOC-89.
6. Kevin J. Lang. Random DFA's can be Approximately Learned from Sparse Uniform Examples. In *Proceedings of the Fifth Annual ACM Workshop on Computational Learning Theory*, pp 45-52, July 1992.
7. J. Oncina and P. Garcia. Inferring Regular Languages in Polynomial Updated Time. In *Pattern Recognition and Image Analysis*. pp. 49-61, World Scientific, 1992.
8. Yoav Freund, Michael Kearns, Dana Ron, Ronitt Rubinfeld, Robert Schapire, and Linda Sellie. *Efficient Learning of Typical Finite Automata from Random Walks*, STOC-93, pp. 315-324.
9. P. Dupont, L. Miclet, and E. Vidal. What is the search space of the regular inference? In *Proceedings of the International Colloquium on Grammatical Inference ICGA-94*, Lecture Notes in Artificial Intelligence 862, pp. 25-37, Springer-Verlag, 1994.
10. C. de la Higuera, J. Oncina, and E. Vidal. Identification of DFA: Data-Dependent Versus Data-Independent Algorithms. In *Proceedings of the International Colloquium on Grammatical Inference ICGA-96* Lecture Notes in Artificial Intelligence 1147, pp. 313-325, Springer-Verlag, 1996.
11. Joe Kilian and Kevin J. Lang. (1997) A Scheme for Secure Pass-Fail Tests. NECI Technical Note 97-016N.
12. Hugues Juillé and Jordan B. Pollack. (1998) SAGE: a Sampling-based Heuristic for Tree Search. Submitted to *Machine Learning*.

# Learning $k$-Variable Pattern Languages Efficiently Stochastically Finite on Average from Positive Data

Peter Rossmanith[1] and Thomas Zeugmann[2]

[1] Institut für Informatik, Technische Universität München, 80290 München, Germany
rossmani@in.tum.de
[2] Department of Informatics, Kyushu University, Kasuga 816-8580, Japan
thomas@i.kyushu-u.ac.jp

**Abstract.** The present paper presents a new approach of how to convert Gold-style [4] learning in the limit into *stochastically finite* learning with *high confidence*. We illustrate this approach on the concept class of all pattern languages. The transformation of learning in the limit into stochastically finite learning with high confidence is achieved by first analyzing the Lange–Wiehagen [7] algorithm with respect to its average-case time behavior until convergence. This algorithm learns the class of all pattern languages in the limit from positive data. The expectation of the total learning time is analyzed and *exponentially* small tail bounds are established for a large class of probability distributions. For patterns containing $k$ different variables Lange and Wiehagen's algorithm possesses an expected total learning time of $O\big((1/\alpha)^k(\log_{1/\beta}(k))E[\Lambda]\big)$, where $\alpha$ and $\beta$ are two easily computable parameters from the underlying probability distribution, and $E[\Lambda]$ is the expected example string length.
Finally, we show how to arrive at stochastically finite learning with high confidence.

## 1 Introduction

Suppose you have to deal with a learning problem of the following kind. On the one hand, it is known that the problem is not solvable within the PAC model unless you achieve the needed breakthrough in complexity theory. On the other hand, your learning problem has been proved to be learnable within Gold's [4] learning in the limit model. Here, a learner is successively fed data about the concept to be learned and is computing a sequence of hypotheses about the target object. However, the only knowledge you have about this sequence is its convergence in the limit to a hypothesis correctly describing the target concept. Therefore, you never know whether the learner has already converged. Such an uncertainty may not be tolerable in many applications. In general, there may be no way to overcome this uncertainty. But part of the problem is caused by the fact that learning in the limit has to be successful from all possible data sequences. It is intuitively clear that there are data sequences that contain huge amounts of redundant data before successful learning can take place. But such sequences may be rare in practice.

What we would like to present in this paper is a rather general method to overcome the difficulties described above. This method is based on an average-case analysis of known limit learners with respect to their time complexity including tail bounds. Assuming a certain amount of knowledge concerning the underlying probability distributions, we can put it all together and arrive at *stochastically finite learning with high confidence*. This learning model may be considered as a variant of PAC-learning. The major differences are easily explained. First, stochastically finite learning with high confidence is not completely distribution independent. Thus, from that perspective, this variant is weaker than the PAC-model. But the hypothesis computed is *probably exactly correct*. Moreover, the learner is fed positive data only, while the correctness of its final hypothesis is measured with respect to both positive and negative data.

Second, it should be emphasized that our approach is applicable in a rather general context. Suppose you have a PAC-learner for the concept class you want to learn. In that case, additional knowledge about the underlying probability distributions directly yields better hypotheses, i.e., *probably correct* ones instead of *probably approximately correct* ones. But its main advantage is achieved when dealing with situations as described above, i.e., in those cases where it is highly unlikely to obtain a PAC-learner. Now, instead of facing all the disadvantages of limit learning additional knowledge about the underlying probability distributions nicely buys a learner that is even more reliable than a PAC-learner.

In the following, we exemplify this approach by dealing with the learnability of the well-known pattern languages (*PAT* for short), a prominent and important language family that can be learned from positive data (cf. [1, 10, 12]). There are also numerous interesting applications for pattern language learners (cf., e.g., [12] and the references therein).

Nevertheless, despite its importance there is still a bottleneck concerning efficient learning algorithms. Kearns and Pitt [5], Ko, Marron and Tzeng [6] and Schapire [11] intensively studied the learnability of pattern languages in the PAC–learning model. In particular, Schapire [11] proved that the class *PAT* is not PAC-learnable regardless of the representation used by the learning algorithm, provided only that the learner is requested to output a polynomial-size hypothesis that can be evaluated in polynomial time, unless $\mathcal{P}_{/poly} = \mathcal{NP}_{/poly}$. However, the class *Pat* of all patterns is not a polynomial time representation for *PAT*, since the membership problem for *PAT* with respect to *Pat* is $\mathcal{NP}$-complete [1]. In contrast, we show *Pat* to be stochastically finite learnable with high confidence with respect to *Pat* (cf. Theorem 9). On the other hand, Kearns and Pitt [5] designed a polynomial-time PAC-learner for the set of all $k$-variable pattern languages ($k$ arbitrarily fixed) if only product distributions are allowed. But the constant in the running time achieved depends *doubly exponentially* on $k$, and thus, their algorithm becomes rapidly impractical when $k$ increases.

In contrast, our stochastically finite learner achieves a running time whose constant depends only exponentially on the number $k$ of different variables occurring in the target pattern and is otherwise *linearly* bounded in the expected length of sample strings fed to the learner (cf. Corollary 1). The price paid is rather small. We restrict the class of all probability distributions to a subclass that has an arbitrary but fixed bound on two parameters arising naturally. In essence, that means at least two letters from the underlying probability distribution have a *known* lower bound on their probability.

We use the Lange–Wiehagen [7] algorithm (LWA for short) as the basic ingredient for achieving our goal. The LWA learns the class of all pattern languages in the limit from positive data. That means the learner is fed successively example strings and its previously made hypothesis, and it computes from these input data a new pattern as its hypothesis. The sequence of all hypotheses stabilizes to a single pattern which generates the target pattern language. First, we *generalize* and *improve* the average-case analysis of the same algorithm performed by Zeugmann [14] for its expected *total learning time*. The time taken by a learner for computing a single hypothesis from its input data is usually called *update time*. The total learning time is the time taken by the learner until convergence, i.e., the sum of all update times until successful learning. Note that it is a highly non-trivial task to define an appropriate complexity measure for learning in the limit (cf. [8]). The total learning time has been introduced by Daley and Smith [3]. As Pitt [8] pointed out, allowing the total learning time to depend on the length of the examples seen so far is unsatisfactory, since the learner may delay convergence until a sufficiently long example appears so that the algorithm may meet the wanted polynomial time bound. We therefore measure the total learning time *only* in dependence on the length of the target pattern.

Second, we show how the improved analysis can be used to establish *stochastically finite learnability*. The basic idea can be described as follows. Based on exponentially shrinking tail bounds obtained from our average case analysis for the expected *total learning time*, the new learner takes as input a randomly generated text and a *confidence parameter* $\delta$. It then computes internally hypotheses until the confidence bound is met and outputs exclusively its last guess (cf. Section 4, Definition 2).

Owing to lack of space some results and most proofs could not be included into this extended abstract; they can be found in the full paper (cf. [9]).

## 2 Preliminaries

Let $N = \{0, 1, 2, \ldots\}$ be the set of all natural numbers, and let $N^+ = N \setminus \{0\}$.

Following Angluin [1] we define patterns and pattern languages as follows. Let $\mathcal{A} = \{0, 1, \ldots\}$ be any non-empty finite alphabet containing at least two elements. By $\mathcal{A}^*$ we denote the set of all strings over $\mathcal{A}$ and by $\mathcal{A}^+ = \mathcal{A}^* \setminus \varepsilon$ all non-null strings. By $|\mathcal{A}|$ we denote the cardinality of $\mathcal{A}$. Furthermore, let $X = \{x_i \mid i \in N\}$ be an infinite set of variables such that $\mathcal{A} \cap X = \emptyset$. *Patterns* are non-empty strings over $\mathcal{A} \cup X$, e.g., 01, $0x_0111$, $1x_0x_00x_1x_2x_0$ are patterns. The length of a string $s \in \mathcal{A}^*$ and of a pattern $\pi$ is denoted by $|s|$ and $|\pi|$, respectively. A pattern $\pi$ is in *canonical form* provided that if $k$ is the number of different variables in $\pi$

then the variables occurring in $\pi$ are precisely $x_0, \ldots, x_{k-1}$. Moreover, for every $j$ with $0 \leq j < k - 1$, the leftmost occurrence of $x_j$ in $\pi$ is left to the leftmost occurrence of $x_{j+1}$ in $\pi$. The examples given above are patterns in canonical form. In the sequel we assume, without loss of generality, that all patterns are in canonical form. By $Pat$ we denote the set of all patterns in canonical form.

Let $\pi \in Pat$, $1 \leq i \leq |\pi|$; we use $\pi(i)$ to denote the $i$-th symbol in $\pi$. If $\pi(i) \in \mathcal{A}$, then $\pi(i)$ is a *constant*, otherwise $\pi(i) \in X$ is a *variable*. Analogously, by $s(i)$ we denote the $i$-th symbol in $s$ for $s \in \mathcal{A}^+$. By $\#\mathrm{var}(\pi)$ we denote the number of different variables occurring in $\pi$, and by $\#_{x_i}(\pi)$ we denote the number of occurrences of variable $x_i$ in $\pi$. If $\#\mathrm{var}(\pi) = k$, then we refer to $\pi$ as to a *k-variable pattern*. Let $k \in \mathbb{N}$, by $Pat_k$ we denote the set of all *k-variable patterns*. Furthermore, let $\pi \in Pat_k$, and let $u_0, \ldots, u_{k-1} \in \mathcal{A}^+$; then we denote by $\pi[x_0/u_0, \ldots, x_{k-1}/u_{k-1}]$ the string $w \in \mathcal{A}^+$ obtained by substituting $u_j$ for each occurrence of $x_j$, $j = 0, \ldots, k - 1$, in the pattern $\pi$. For example, let $\pi = 0x_0 1x_1 x_0$. Then $\pi[x_0/10, x_1/01] = 01010110$. The tuple $(u_0, \ldots, u_{k-1})$ is called a *substitution*. Furthermore, if $|u_0| = \cdots = |u_{k-1}| = 1$, then we refer to $(u_0, \ldots, u_{k-1})$ as to a *shortest substitution*. Now, let $\pi \in Pat_k$, and let $S = \{(u_0, \ldots, u_{k-1}) \mid u_j \in \mathcal{A}^+, j = 0, \ldots, k - 1\}$ be any finite set of substitutions. Then we set $S(\pi) = \{\pi[x_0/u_0, \ldots, x_{k-1}/u_{k-1}] \mid (u_0, \ldots, u_{k-1}) \in S\}$, i.e., $S(\pi)$ is the set of all strings obtained from pattern $\pi$ by applying all the substitutions from $S$ to it. For every $\pi \in Pat_k$ we define the *language generated by pattern $\pi$* by $L(\pi) = \{\pi[x_0/u_0, \ldots, x_{k-1}/u_{k-1}] \mid u_0, \ldots, u_{k-1} \in \mathcal{A}^+\}$. By $PAT_k$ we denote the set of all *k-variable pattern languages*. Finally, $PAT = \bigcup_{k \in \mathbb{N}} PAT_k$ denotes the set of all pattern languages over $\mathcal{A}$. Note that for every $L \in PAT$ there is precisely one pattern $\pi \in Pat$ such that $L = L(\pi)$ (cf. [1]).

We are interested in *inductive inference*, which means to gradually learn a concept from successively growing sequences of examples. If $L$ is a language to be identified, a sequence $(s_1, s_2, s_3, \ldots)$ is called a *text* for $L$ iff $L = \{s_1, s_2, s_3, \ldots\}$ (cf. [4]). However, in practical applications, the requirement to exhaust the language to be learned will be hardly fulfilled. We therefore *omit* this restriction here. Instead, we assume that the sequence $t = s_1, s_2, s_3, \ldots$ contains "enough" information to recognize the target pattern. As for the LWA, "enough" can be made precise by requesting that sufficiently many shortest strings appear in the text. We shall come back to this point when defining admissible probability distributions.

An *inductive inference machine* (IIM) is an algorithm that takes as input larger and larger initial segments of a text and outputs, after each input, a hypothesis from a prespecified *hypothesis space* (cf. [4]). In the case of pattern languages the hypothesis space is $Pat$.

**Definition 1.** $PAT$ is called learnable in the limit from text iff there is an IIM $M$ such that for every $L \in PAT$ and every text for $L$,

(1) for all $n \in \mathbb{N}^+$, $M(t_n)$ is defined,
(2) there is a pattern $\pi \in Pat$ such that $L(\pi) = L$ and for almost all $n \in \mathbb{N}^+$, $M(t_n) = \pi$.

It is well-known that pattern languages are learnable in the limit from text (cf. [1]).

Whenever one deals with the average case analysis of algorithms one has to consider probability distributions over the relevant input domain. For learning from text, we have the following scenario. Every string of a particular pattern language is generated by a substitution. Therefore, it is convenient to consider probability distributions over the set of all possible substitutions. That is, if $\pi \in Pat_k$, then it suffices to consider any probability distribution $D$ over $\mathcal{A}^+ \times \cdots \times \mathcal{A}^+$ ($k$ times). For $(u_0, \ldots, u_{k-1}) \in \mathcal{A}^+ \times \cdots \times \mathcal{A}^+$ we denote by $D(u_0, \ldots, u_{k-1})$ the probability that variable $x_0$ is substituted by $u_0$, variable $x_1$ is substituted by $u_1$, ..., and variable $x_{k-1}$ is substituted by $u_{k-1}$.

In particular, we mainly consider a special class of distributions, i.e., *product distributions*. Let $k \in \mathbb{N}^+$, then the class of all product distributions for $Pat_k$ is defined as follows. For each variable $x_j$, $0 \leq j \leq k - 1$, we assume an arbitrary probability distribution $D_j$ over $\mathcal{A}^+$ on substitution strings. Then we call $D = D_0 \times \cdots \times D_{k-1}$ product distribution over $\mathcal{A}^+ \times \cdots \times \mathcal{A}^+$, i.e., $D(u_0, \ldots, u_{k-1}) = \prod_{j=0}^{k-1} D_j(u_j)$. Moreover, we call a product distribution *regular* if $D_0 = \cdots = D_{k-1}$. Throughout this paper, we restrict ourselves to deal with *regular* distributions. We therefore use $d$ to denote the distribution over $\mathcal{A}^+$ on substitution strings, i.e, $D(u_0, \ldots, u_{k-1}) = \prod_{j=0}^{k-1} d(u_j)$. As a special case of a regular product distribution we sometimes consider the *uniform* distribution over $\mathcal{A}^+$, i.e., $d(u) = 1/(2 \cdot |\mathcal{A}|)^\ell$ for all strings $u \in \mathcal{A}^+$ with $|u| = \ell$.

Note, however, that most of our results can be generalized to larger classes of distributions. Finally, we can provide the announced specification of what is meant by "enough" information. We call a regular distribution *admissible* provided $d(a) > 0$ for at least two different elements $a \in \mathcal{A}$.

Following Daley and Smith [3] we define the total learning time as follows. Let $M$ be any IIM that learns all the pattern languages. Then, for every $L \in PAT$ and every text $t$ for $L$, let $Conv(M, t)$ be the least number $m \in \mathbb{N}^+$ such that $M(t_n) = M(t_m)$ for all $n \geq m$, denotes the *stage of convergence* of $M$ on $t$. Moreover, by $T_M(t_n)$ we denote the time to compute $M(t_n)$. We measure this time as a function of the length of the input and call it *update time*. Finally, the total learning time taken by the IIM $M$ on input $t$, one string at a time, is defined as

$$TT(M, t) =_{df} \sum_{n=1}^{Conv(M,t)} T_M(t_n).$$

Assuming any fixed admissible probability distribution $D$ as described above, we aim to evaluate the *expectation* of $TT(M, t)$ with respect to $D$ which we call *total average learning time*.

The model of computation as well as the representation of patterns we assume is the same as in Angluin [1]. We assume a random access machine that performs a reasonable menu of operations each in unit time on registers of length $O(\log n)$ bits, where $n$ is the input length.

Finally, we recall the LWA. The LWA works as follows. Let $h_n$ be the hypothesis computed after reading $s_1, \ldots, s_n$, i.e., $h_n = M(s_1, \ldots, s_n)$. Then $h_1 = s_1$

and for all $n > 1$:

$$h_n = \begin{cases} h_{n-1}, & \text{if } |h_{n-1}| < |s_n| \\ s_n, & \text{if } |h_{n-1}| > |s_n| \\ h_{n-1} \cup s_n, & \text{if } |h_{n-1}| = |s_n| \end{cases}$$

The algorithm computes the new hypothesis only from the latest example and the old hypothesis. If the latest example is longer than the old hypothesis, the example is ignored, i.e., the hypothesis does not change. If the latest example is shorter than the old hypothesis, the old hypothesis is ignored and the new example becomes the new hypothesis. Hence, the LWA is quite simple and the update time will be very fast for these two possibilities.

If, however, $|h_{n-1}| = |s_n|$ the new hypothesis is the *union* of $h_{n-1}$ and $s_n$. The union $\varrho = \pi \cup s$ of a canonical pattern $\pi$ and a string $s$ of the same length is defined as

$$\varrho(i) = \begin{cases} \pi(i), & \text{if } \pi(i) = s(i) \\ x_j, & \text{if } \pi(i) \neq s(i) \ \& \ \exists k < i : [\varrho(k) = x_j, \ s(k) = s(i), \ \pi(k) = \pi(i)] \\ x_m, & \text{otherwise, where } m = \#var(\varrho(1) \ldots \varrho(i-1)), \end{cases}$$

where $\varrho(0) = \varepsilon$ for notational convenience. The resulting pattern is canonical.

Obviously, the union operation can be computed in quadratic time. We finish this section by providing a linear-time algorithm computing the union operation. The only crucial part is to determine whether there is some $k < i$ with $\varrho(k) = x_j$, $s(k) = s(i)$, and $\pi(k) = \pi(i)$. The new algorithm uses an array $I = \{1, \ldots, |s|\}^{\mathcal{A} \times (\mathcal{A} \cup \{x_0, \ldots, x_{|\pi|-1}\})}$ for finding the correct $k$, if any, in *constant* time. The array $I$ is *partially* initialized by writing the first position into it at which $s(i), \pi(i)$ occurs. Then, for each position $i$, the algorithm checks whether $I_{s(i),\pi(i)} = i$. Suppose it is, thus $s(i), \pi(i)$ did not occur left to $i$. Hence, it remains to check whether or not $\pi(i) = s(i)$ and $\varrho(i)$ can be immediately output. If $I_{s(i),\pi(i)} \neq i$, then $s(i), \pi(i)$ did occur left to $i$. Hence, in this case it suffices to output $\varrho(j)$ where $j = I_{s(i),\pi(i)}$.

**Theorem 1.** *The union operation can be computed in linear time by Algorithm 1.*

## Algorithm 1

**Input:** A pattern $\pi$ and a string $s \in \mathcal{A}^+$ such that $|\pi| = |s|$.
**Output:** $\pi \cup s$
for $i = 1, \ldots, |s|$ do $I_{s(i),\pi(i)} \leftarrow i$ od; $m \leftarrow 0$;
for $i = 1, \ldots, |s|$ do $j \leftarrow I_{s(i),\pi(i)}$;
    if $i = j$ then
        if $\pi(i) = s(i)$ then $\varrho(i) = \pi(i)$
        else $\varrho(i) \leftarrow x_m$; $m \leftarrow m + 1$ fi
    else $\varrho(i) = \varrho(j)$ fi
od

The correctness of this algorithm can be easily proved inductively by formalizing the argument given above. We omit the details.

# 3 Results of the Analysis

Following [14] we perform the desired analysis in dependence on the number $k$ of different variables occurring in the target pattern $\pi$. If $k = 0$, then the LWA immediately converges. Therefore, in the following we assume $k \in \mathbf{N^+}$, and $\pi \in Pat_k$. For analyzing the *average-case* behavior of the LWA, in the following we let $t = s_1, s_2, s_3, \ldots$ range over all randomly generated texts with respect to some arbitrarily fixed admissible probability distribution $D$. Then the stage of convergence is a random variable which we denote by $C$. Note that the distribution of $C$ depends on $\pi$ and on $D$. We introduce several more random variables. By $\Lambda_i$ we denote the length of the example string $s_i$, i.e., $\Lambda_i = |s_i|$. Since all $\Lambda_i$ are independent and identically distributed, we can assume that the random variable has the same distribution as $\Lambda$. We shall use $\Lambda$ when talking about the length of an example when the number of the example is not important. Particularly, we will often use the expected length of a random example $E[\Lambda]$.

Let $T = \Lambda_1 + \Lambda_1 + \ldots + \Lambda_C$ be the *total length* of examples processed until convergence. Whether the LWA converges on $s_1, \ldots, s_r$ depends only on those examples $s_i$ with $s_i \in L(\pi)_{min} = \{ w \mid w \in L(\pi), |w| = |\pi| \}$. It should be mentioned that *without* seeing a single *shortest* string, $k$-variable pattern languages *cannot* be *learned* provided $k > 1$. This is easily seen if one looks at patterns $x_0 \cdots x_k$ and $x_0 \cdots x_k x_{k+1}$. The languages they generate are identical except for strings of length $k$. Using a result from Zeugmann [14], this negative result extends to arbitrary $k$ and $k + 1$ variable patterns, respectively. Moreover, as we shall see, waiting for one shortest strings takes almost the same time as waiting for all the shortest strings needed to converge.

Let $r \in \mathbf{N^+}$; by $M_r$ we denote the number of minimum length examples among the first $r$ strings, i.e., $M_r = |\{ i \mid 1 \le i \le r$ and $\Lambda_i = |\pi| \}|$. In particular, $M_C$ is the number of minimum length examples read until convergence. We assume that computing $\varrho \cup s$ takes at most $c \cdot |\varrho|$ steps, where $c$ is a constant that depends on the implementation of the union operation.

We express all estimates with the help of the following parameters: $E[\Lambda]$, $c$, $\alpha$ and $\beta$. To get concrete bounds for a concrete implementation one has to obtain $c$ from the algorithm and has to compute $E[\Lambda]$, $\alpha$, and $\beta$ from the admissible probability distribution $D$. Let $u_0, \ldots, u_{k-1}$ be independent random variables with distribution $d$ for substitution strings. Whenever the index $i$ of $u_i$ does not matter, we simply write $u$ or $u'$.

The two parameters $\alpha$ and $\beta$ are now defined via $d$. First, $\alpha$ is simply the probability that $u$ has length 1, i.e., $\alpha = \Pr(|u| = 1) = \sum_{a \in A} d(a)$. Second, $\beta$ is the conditional probability that two random words that get substituted into $\pi$ are identical under the condition that both their length are 1, i.e.,

$$\beta = \Pr\big(u = u' \mid |u| = |u'| = 1\big) = \sum_{a \in A} d(a)^2 \Big/ \Big(\sum_{a \in A} d(a)\Big)^2.$$

The parameters $\alpha$ and $\beta$ are therefore quite easy to compute even for complicated distributions since they depend only on $|A|$ point probabilities. We can also compute $E[\Lambda]$ for a pattern $\pi$ from $d$ quite easily. Let $\hat{\alpha} = 1/\alpha$.

**Theorem 2.** $E[TT] = O\bigl(\hat{\alpha}^k (\log_{1/\beta}(k)) E[\Lambda]\bigr)$.

Next, we insert the parameter for the uniform distribution into Theorem 2. For the uniform distribution we get $\hat{\alpha} = 2$, $\beta = 1/|\mathcal{A}|$, and $E[\Lambda] \leq 2|\pi|$.

**Theorem 3.** $E[TT] = O(2^k |\pi| \log_{|\mathcal{A}|}(k))$ *for the uniform distribution.*

Often time is the most precious resource, but the number of examples until convergence can also be interesting, if the gathering of examples is expensive.

**Theorem 4.** $E[C] = O(\hat{\alpha}^k \cdot \log_{1/\beta}(k))$.

We can even get a better understanding of the behavior if we examine the union operations by themselves. Is it worthwhile to optimize the computation of $w \cup \pi$? Let $U$ be the number of union operations and $V$ be the time spent in union operations.

**Theorem 5.**

(1) $E[U] = O(\hat{\alpha}k + \log_{1/\beta}(k))$
(2) $E[V] = O(\hat{\alpha}kE[\Lambda] + \log_{1/\beta}(k)|\pi|)$ *if the union operation is performed by Algorithm 1,*
(3) $E[V] = O(\hat{\alpha}kE^2[\Lambda] + \log_{1/\beta}(k)|\pi|^2)$ *if the union operation is performed by the naïve algorithm.*

Consequently, in most cases we can use the simple, quadratic algorithm for union operations, since they make only a small contribution to the overall running time. The proof of this counterintuitive result is unfortunately very long and can be found in the full paper (cf. [9]).

## 3.1 Tail Bounds

Finally we have to ask whether the expected value of the total learning time is sufficient for judging the LWA. The expected value of a random variable is only one aspect of its distribution. In general we might also be interested on how often the learning time exceeds the average substantially. Again this is a question motivated mainly by practical considerations. Equivalently we can ask, how good the distribution is concentrated around its expected value. Often this question is answered by estimating the *variance*, which enables the use of Chebyshev's inequality. If the variance is not available, Markov's inequality provides us with (worse) tail bounds: $\Pr(X \geq t \cdot E[X]) \leq 1/t$. The Markov inequality is quite general but produces only weak bounds. The next theorem gives better tail bounds for a large class of learning algorithms including the LWA. A learner is set-driven, if its outputs depends only on the range of its input (cf. [13]). Conservative learners maintain their actual hypotheses at least as long as they have not seen data contradicting them (cf. [2]).

**Theorem 6.** *Let $X$ be the sample complexity of a conservative and set-driven learning algorithm. Then $V[X] \leq 20E[X]^2$ and $\Pr(X \geq t \cdot E[X]) \leq 2^{-t/2}$ for all $t \in \mathbb{N}$.*

Theorem 6 holds also for conservative, *rearrangement independent* learners, which means that each hypothesis must not depend on the order of the examples.

## 3.2 The Sample Complexity

In this section we estimate the sample complexity. While being of interest itself, whenever acquiring examples is expensive, $E[C]$ is also an important ingredient in the estimation of the total learning time.

**Lemma 1.** $\Pr(M_C > m) = \Pr(C > r \mid M_r = m) \leq \binom{k}{2}\beta^m + k\beta^{m/2}$ *for all* $m, r \in \mathbb{N}^+$ *with* $r \geq m$.

*Proof.* Without loss of generality, let $S_r = \{s_1, \ldots, s_m\}$, i.e., $m = r$. Additionally, we can make the assumption that all strings $s_i \in S_r$ have length $k$, since we need to consider only shortest words for $M_C$ and we can assume that $\pi = x_0 x_1 \ldots x_{k-1}$ (cf. [14]). For $1 \leq j \leq k$ let $c_j = s_0(j)s_1(j)\ldots s_{m-1}(j)$ be the $j$th *column* of a matrix whose rows are $s_1, \ldots, s_m$.

The algorithm computes the hypothesis $\pi$ on input $S_r$ iff no column is constant and there are no identical columns. The probability that $c_j$ is constant is at most $\beta^{m/2}$, since $m/2$ pairs have to be identical, but this short argument works only for even $m$. A slightly more complicated proof shows that the same bound holds also for odd $m$. The probability that at least one of the $k$ columns is constant is then at most $k\beta^{m/2}$.

The probability that $c_i = c_j$ is $\beta^m$ if $i \neq j$. The probability that some columns are equal is therefore at most $\binom{k}{2}\beta^m$. The probability that there is a constant column *or* that there are identical columns is at most $\binom{k}{2}\beta^m + k\beta^{m/2}$.

Inserting the above tail bounds into the definition of the expected value yields an upper bound on $E[M_C]$.

**Lemma 2.** $E[M_C] \leq (2\ln(k)+3)/(\ln(1/\beta))+2 \leq 7\log_{1/\beta}(k)+2 = O(\log_{1/\beta}(k))$.

*Proof.* $M_C$ is the number of shortest words read until convergence. By Lemma 1 we have $\Pr(M_C > m) \leq \binom{k}{2}\beta^m + k\beta^{m/2}$ and thus $E[M_C]$ is

$$\sum_{m=0}^{\infty} \Pr(M_C > m) \leq \ell + \sum_{m=\ell}^{\infty}\left(\binom{k}{2}\beta^m + k\beta^{m/2}\right) = \ell + \binom{k}{2}\frac{\beta^\ell}{1-\beta} + k\frac{\sqrt{\beta}^\ell}{1-\sqrt{\beta}}$$

for each natural number $\ell$. We choose $\ell = \lceil 2\log_{1/\beta}(k)\rceil + 1$, which yields when inserted in above inequality $E[M_C] \leq \ell + \frac{\beta}{1-\beta} + \frac{\sqrt{\beta}}{1-\sqrt{\beta}}$. The lemma now follows from the inequality $\frac{\beta}{1-\beta} + \frac{\sqrt{\beta}}{1-\sqrt{\beta}} \leq 3/\ln(1/\beta)$, which can be proved by standard methods from calculus.

Our next major goal is to establish an upper bound on the overall number of examples to be read on average by the LWA until convergence.

**Theorem 7.** $E[C] = \hat{\alpha}^k E[M_C] \leq \hat{\alpha}^k(7\log_{1/\beta}(k) + 2) = O(\hat{\alpha}^k \log_{1/\beta}(k))$.

*Proof.* The LWA converges after reading exactly $C$ example strings. Among these examples are $M_C$ many of minimum length. Prior to these minimum length words come $M_C$ possibly empty blocks of words whose length is bigger than

$|\pi|$. Let us call the numbers of those words in the $i$th block $G_i$. Then $C = G_1 + G_2 + \cdots + G_{M_C} + M_C$. It is easy to compute the distribution of $G_i$:

$$\Pr(G_i = m) = \Pr(\Lambda > |\pi|)^m \Pr(\Lambda = |\pi|) = (1 - \alpha^k)^m \alpha^k \qquad (1)$$

Of course, all $G_i$ are identically distributed and independent. The expected value of $C$ is therefore

$$E[C] = E[M_C] + E[G_1 + \cdots + G_{M_C}]$$

$$= E[M_C] + \sum_{m=0}^{\infty} E[G_1 + \cdots + G_m \mid M_C = m] \cdot \Pr(M_C = m)$$

$$= E[M_C] + \sum_{m=0}^{\infty} m \cdot E[G_1] \cdot \Pr(M_C = m) = E[M_C] + E[M_C] \cdot E[G_1] \qquad (2)$$

The expected value of $G_1$ is

$$E[G_1] = \sum_{m=0}^{\infty} m \cdot \Pr(\Lambda > |\pi|)^m \cdot \Pr(\Lambda = |\pi|) = \frac{\Pr(\Lambda > |\pi|)}{\Pr(\Lambda = |\pi|)} = \frac{1 - \alpha^k}{\alpha^k} \qquad (3)$$

Now combine (2) and (3) with $E[M_C] \le 7 \log_{1/\beta}(k) + 2$ from Lemma 2.

### 3.3 The Length of the Text until Convergence

When we use the linear time algorithm for union operations, then the total learning time is $O(T)$, so the length of the text until convergence is an important number. In the following we analyze its expected value.

**Lemma 3.** Let $m \ge 1$. Then $E[\Lambda_1 \mid G_1 = m] = (E[\Lambda] - \alpha^k)/(1 - \alpha^k)$.

**Theorem 8.** $E[T] = E[M_C] \cdot \left(|\pi| + \hat{\alpha}^k(E[\Lambda] - 1)\right)$
$\le (7 \log_{1/\beta}(k) + 2)\left(|\pi| + \hat{\alpha}^k(E[\Lambda] - 1)\right) = O\left(\hat{\alpha}^k(\log_{1/\beta}(k))E[\Lambda]\right)$.

*Proof.* We can write the length of text read until convergence as $T = T_1 + T_2 + \cdots + T_{M_C} + |\pi|M_C$. Exactly $M_C$ strings of length $|\pi|$ are read; all other strings are longer and are contained in blocks in front of those minimum length strings. The $i$th block contains $G_i$ strings and we denote the total length of these $G_i$ strings by $T_i$ (these are different $T_i$'s than in [14]). In order to get $E[T]$ we start by computing $E[T_1]$.

$$E[T_1] = \sum_{m=0}^{\infty} E[\Lambda_1 + \cdots + \Lambda_m \mid G_1 = m] \cdot \Pr(G_1 = m)$$

$$= \sum_{m=1}^{\infty} m \cdot E[\Lambda_1 \mid G_1 = m] \cdot \Pr(G_1 = m)$$

$$= \sum_{m=1}^{\infty} m \cdot \frac{E[\Lambda] - \alpha^k}{1 - \alpha^k} \cdot (1 - \alpha^k)^m \alpha^k \quad \text{(by Lemma 3 and (1))}$$

$$= (E[\Lambda] - \alpha^k)\alpha^k \sum_{m=1}^{\infty} m(1 - \alpha^k)^{m-1} = \hat{\alpha}^k E[\Lambda] - 1$$

Now it is easy to estimate $E[T]$. We use that $T_1$ and $M_C$ are independent.

$$E[T] - |\pi|E[M_C] = E[T_1 + \cdots + T_{M_C}]$$

$$= \sum_{m=0}^{\infty} m \cdot E[T_1] \cdot \Pr(M_C = m) = E[M_C] \cdot E[T_1]$$

and thus $E[T] = E[M_C](|\pi| + \hat{\alpha}^k E[\Lambda] - 1)$. Finally insert the estimation of $E[M_C]$ from Lemma 2.

## 4 Learning Stochastically Finite with High Confidence

**Definition 2.** *Let $D$ be an admissible probability distribution. PAT is called stochastically finitely learnable with high confidence from random text iff there is an IIM $M$ such that for every $L \in PAT$ and every number $\delta \in (0,1)$, $M$ outputs the single hypothesis $\pi$, $L(\pi) = L$, with probability at least $\delta$, and stops thereafter, when fed a random text according to $D$ and $L$.*

Note that the learner in the definition above takes $\delta$ as additional input and that the definition immediately generalizes to arbitrary concept classes.

Next, we show how the LWA can be transformed into a stochastically finite learner that identifies all the pattern languages with high confidence provided we have a bit of prior knowledge about the class of admissible distributions that may actually be used to generate the information sequences.

**Theorem 9.** *Let $\alpha_*$, $\beta_* \in (0,1)$. Assume $\mathcal{D}$ to be a class of admissible probability distributions over $\mathcal{A}^+$ such that $\alpha \geq \alpha_*$, $\beta \geq \beta_*$ and $E(d)$ finite for all distributions $d \in \mathcal{D}$. Then PAT is stochastically finitely learnable with high confidence from random text for all distributions $D$ generated by any $d \in \mathcal{D}$.*

*Proof.* Let $d \in \mathcal{D}$ and $\delta \in (0,1)$ be arbitrarily fixed. Note that $d$ induces an admissible probability distribution $D$. Furthermore, let $t = s_1, s_2, s_3, \ldots$ be any randomly generated text with respect to $D$ for the target pattern language. The learner $M$ uses the LWA as a subroutine. Additionally, it has a counter for the number of examples already seen. We exploit the fact that the LWA produces a sequence $(\tau_n)_{n \in \mathbf{N}^+}$ of hypotheses such that $|\tau_n| \geq |\tau_{n+1}|$ for all $n \in \mathbf{N}^+$.

The learner runs the LWA until for the first time $C$ many examples have been processed, where $C = 2\log(1/(1-\delta))(7\hat{\alpha}_*^{|\tau|} + 2)\log_{1/\beta_*}(|\tau|)$ and $\tau$ is the current output made by the LWA. By Theorem 6 and 7, it follows that after processing

$$2\log(1/(1-\delta))(7\hat{\alpha}^k + 2)\log_{1/\beta}(k) \tag{A}$$

examples the LWA converges with probability at least $\delta$. The number $C$ is bigger since $|\tau| \geq k$. If we are learning $PAT_k$ instead of $PAT$, we can replace $|\tau|$ in $(A)$ by $k$ to get a better bound.

If we fix $k$ in advance to learn only $PAT_k$ then we arrive at a stochastically finite linear-time learner for $PAT_k$. This is a major improvement, since the constant depending on $k$ grows only exponentially in $k$ in contrast to the doubly exponentially growing constant in Kearns and Pitt's [5] algorithm.

**Corollary 1.** *Let* $\alpha_*$, $\beta_* \in (0,1)$. *Assume* $\mathcal{D}$ *to be a class of admissible probability distributions over* $\mathcal{A}^+$ *such that* $\alpha \geq \alpha_*$, $\beta \geq \beta_*$ *and* $E(d)$ *finite for all distributions* $d \in \mathcal{D}$. *Furthermore, let* $k \in \mathbb{N}^+$ *be arbitrarily fixed. Then there exists a learner* $M$ *such that*

(1) $M$ *learns* $PAT_k$ *stochastically finitely with high confidence from random text for all admissible probability distributions* $D$ *generated by any* $d \in \mathcal{D}$, *and*
(2) *The running time of* $M$ *is bounded by* $O\left(\hat{\alpha}^k \log(1/(1-\delta)) \log_{1/\beta}(k) E[\Lambda]\right)$.

# References

1. D. Angluin. Finding patterns common to a set of strings. *Journal of Computer and System Sciences*, 21(1):46–62, 1980.
2. D. Angluin. Inductive inference of formal languages from positive data. *Information and Control*, 45:117–135, 1980.
3. R. Daley and C.H. Smith. On the complexity of inductive inference. *Information and Control*, 69:12–40, 1986.
4. E. M. Gold. Language identification in the limit. *Information and Control*, 10:447–474, 1967.
5. M. Kearns and L. Pitt. A polynomial-time algorithm for learning $k$-variable pattern languages from examples. In R. Rivest, D. Haussler and M.K. Warmuth, editors, *Proc. 2nd Annual ACM Workshop on Computational Learning Theory* pp. 57–71, 1991, Morgan Kaufmann Publishers Inc., San Mateo.
6. Ker-I Ko, A. Marron and W.G. Tzeng. Learning string patterns and tree patterns from examples. In B.W. Porter and R.J. Mooney, editors, *Proc. 7th International Conference on Machine Learning*, pp. 384–391, 1990, Morgan-Kaufmann Publishers Inc., San Mateo.
7. S. Lange and R. Wiehagen. Polynomial-time inference of arbitrary pattern languages. *New Generation Computing*, 8:361–370, 1991.
8. L. Pitt. Inductive inference, DFAs and computational complexity. In K.P. Jantke, editor, *Proc. Analogical and Inductive Inference*, Lecture Notes in Artificial Intelligence 397, pp. 18–44, Berlin, 1989, Springer-Verlag.
9. P. Rossmanith and T. Zeugmann. Learning $k$-variable pattern languages efficiently stochastically finite on average from positive data, DOI Technical Report DOI-TR-145, Department of Informatics, Kyushu University, January 1998.
10. A. Salomaa. Patterns & Return to patterns. (The Formal Language Theory Column). EATCS Bulletin, 54:46–62 and 55:144–157, 1994.
11. R.E. Schapire. Pattern languages are not learnable. In M.A. Fulk and J. Case, editors, *Proc. 3rd Annual ACM Workshop on Computational Learning Theory*, pp. 122 – 129, 1990. Morgan Kaufmann Publishers Inc., San Mateo.
12. T. Shinohara and S. Arikawa. Pattern inference. In K. P. Jantke and S. Lange, editors, *Algorithmic Learning for Knowledge-Based Systems*, Lecture Notes in Artificial Intelligence 961, pp. 259–291, Berlin, 1995. Springer-Verlag.
13. K. Wexler and P. Culicover. *Formal Principles of Language Acquisition*. MIT Press, Cambridge, MA, 1980.
14. T. Zeugmann. Lange and Wiehagen's pattern learning algorithm: An average-case analysis with respect to its total learning time. *Annals of Mathematics and Artificial Intelligence*, 1998. To appear.

# Meaning Helps Learning Syntax[*]

Isabelle Tellier

LIFL and Université Charles de Gaulle-lille3 (UFR IDIST)
59 653 Villeneuve d'Ascq Cedex, FRANCE
Email : tellier@univ-lille3.fr

**Abstract.** In this paper, we propose a new framework for the computational learning of formal grammars with positive data. In this model, both syntactic and semantic information are taken into account, which seems cognitively relevant for the modeling of natural language learning. The syntactic formalism used is the one of Lambek categorial grammars and meaning is represented with logical formulas. The principle of compositionality is admitted and defined as an isomorphism applying to trees and allowing to automatically translate sentences into their semantic representation(s). Simple simulations of a learning algorithm are extensively developed and discussed.

## 1 Introduction

Natural language learning seems, from a formal point of view, an enigma.

As a matter of fact, every human being, given nearly exclusively positive examples ([25]), is able at the age of about five to master his/her mother tongue. Though every natural language has at least the power of context-free grammars ([22]), this class is not computationally learnable with positive data in usual models ([9, 24]).

How can a formal theory of learning give account of such a success ? Various solutions have been proposed. Following the Chomskian intuitions ([4, 5]), it can be admitted that natural languages belong to a restricted family and that the human mind includes an *innate knowledge* of the structure of this class. For example, context-sensitive grammars become learnable with positive data if the learner knows a bound on the number of rules in the grammar ([24]).

Another approach consists in putting structural, statistical or complexity constraints on the *examples proposed to the learner*, making his/her induction easier ([15, 21]). This solution formalizes the help provided by a professor ([6]). A particular family of research, more concerned with the cognitive relevance of its models, considers that learning a natural language is very different from learning a formal language, because in *natural* situations, examples are always provided with semantic and pragmatic information ([10, 2, 14, 11]). This approach may be seen as

---

[*]This research was partially supported by "Motricité et cognition" : contrat par objectifs de la région Nord/Pas de Calais and basic ideas of this paper were presented at the Workshop on Paradigms and Grounding in Language Learning of the conference Computational Natural Language Leaning 98.

another interpretation of the previous ones. As a matter of fact, it implies that natural languages belong to the restricted family of languages with which *semantics compatible with our world* can be associated (even if this class is hardly characterizable), and it also assumes that examples provided to the learner are those which are semantically coherent. This is the family our research belongs to.

A fundamental property of natural languages is then taken into account here : their *meaningfulness*. But this property is computationally tractable only if we have at our disposal a theory that precisely articulates syntax and semantics. The strongest possible articulation is known as the Fredge's *principle of compositionality*, which states that the meaning of a sentence only depends on the meaning of its constituents and of their mode of combination. This principle has acquired an explicit formalization with the works of Richard Montague ([16, 7]) and his inheritors.

In this paper, we will first expose an up-to-date version of this syntactico-semantic framework, based on a type of grammars called *categorial grammars*, and we will then show how it can been used in a formal theory of natural language learning.

## 2 Syntactic analysis with categorial grammars

In categorial grammars, each member of the vocabulary is associated with a finite set of categories characterizing its combinatorial potentialities.

The syntax only depends on the information associated with each word. This strong lexicalization is well adapted to natural languages ([18]).

### 2.1 General definition of categorial grammars

A categorial grammar G is a 4-tuple G=<V, C, f, S> where :
   - V is the finite alphabet (or vocabulary) of G;
   - C is the finite set of basic categories of G;
   We define the set of all possible categories of G, noted C', as the closure of C for the fractional operators noted / and \. C' is the smallest set of categories verifying :
      * $C \subseteq C'$;
      * if $X \in C'$ and $Y \in C'$ then $X/Y \in C'$ and $Y\backslash X \in C'$;
   - f is a function : V—>P(C') where P(C') is the set of finite subsets of C', which associates each element v in V with the finite set $f(v) \subseteq C'$ of its categories;
   - $S \in C$ is the axiomatic category of G.

The operators / and \ can be considered as oriented fractions. In this framework, the set of syntactically correct sentences is the set of finite concatenations of elements of the vocabulary for which there exists an assignment of categories that can be *reduced* to the axiomatic category S. There are different classes of categorial grammars according to the admitted *reduction rules*. We will use the most general one, called L-grammars.

## 2.2 L-grammars (from [13])

A Lambek grammar (or L-grammar) is a categorial grammar for which admitted reduction rules are all the valid sequents of the Lambek-Gentzen calculus defined by :
- an infinite number of axioms : for every category X in C', X —> X (A) is valid;
- two couples of inference rules among sequents, written in the Gentzen style (i.e. if the sequent(s) above the line is (are) valid, then the one under is also valid) :

$$* \frac{\Gamma . X \longrightarrow Y}{\Gamma \longrightarrow Y/X} \ (R/) \qquad\qquad \frac{X . \Gamma \longrightarrow Y}{\Gamma \longrightarrow X\backslash Y} \ (R\backslash)$$

$$* \frac{\Gamma \longrightarrow X \qquad \Delta . Y . \Phi \longrightarrow Z}{\Delta . Y/X . \Gamma . \Phi \longrightarrow Z} \ (L/) \qquad \frac{\Gamma \longrightarrow X \qquad \Delta . Y . \Phi \longrightarrow Z}{\Delta . \Gamma . X\backslash Y . \Phi \longrightarrow Z} \ (L\backslash)$$

where X, Y and Z are in $\in$ C' and $\Delta$, $\Phi$ and $\Gamma$ are concatenations of categories ($\Gamma \neq \varnothing$).
The language L(G) defined by G is then :
$$L(G) = \{ w \in V^*; \ \exists n \in N \ \forall i \in \{1,..., n\} \ w_i \in V, \ w = w_1...w_n, \ \exists C_i \in f(w_i), \ C_1...C_n \text{—}^* \text{—>} S \}.$$

### Useful valid sequents :
The most simple valid sequents, for any categories X and Y are the following :
R1 : X/Y . Y —> X                    R'1 : Y . Y\X —> X

These rules straightforwardly follow from (L/) and (L\) and explain, if the concatenation of categories is assimilated to a multiplication, the nature of / and \ (we use the notational variant of [17]). Other interesting valid sequents are ([17]) :

- R2 : X/Y . Y/Z —> X/Z                   R'2 : Z\Y . Y\X —> Z\X
- R3 : (Y\X)/Z —> Y\(X/Z)                  R'3 : Y\(X/Z) —> (Y\X)/Z
- R4 : X —> Y/(X\Y)                        R'4 : X —> (Y/X)\Y

### Example grammar :
Let us define a L-grammar for the analysis of a small subset of natural language.

The vocabulary is V={a, every, man, woman, John, Paul, runs, loves, meets, is...}. The set of usual basic categories needed here is C={S, T, CN}. In this set, S is the axiomatic category, T stands for *term* and is assigned to proper names, while intransitive verbs receive the category T\S and transitive ones the category (T\S)/T. CN means *common noun* and determiners like *a* and *every* receive two categories : (S/(T\S))/CN and ((S/T)\S)/CN, depending on their position as a subject or as a direct object. This grammar allows to analyze simple sentences as seen in Fig. 1.

$$\frac{CN \longrightarrow CN\ (A) \quad \dfrac{T\backslash S \longrightarrow T\backslash S\ (A) \quad S \longrightarrow S\ (A)}{S/(T\backslash S) . T\backslash S \longrightarrow S\ (L/)}}{\dfrac{S/(T\backslash S))/CN . CN . T\backslash S \longrightarrow S\ (L/)}{a \qquad man\ runs}}$$

$$\frac{T \longrightarrow T\ (A) \quad \dfrac{T \longrightarrow T\ (A) \quad T . T\backslash S \longrightarrow S\ (L\backslash)}{T . (T\backslash S)/T . T \longrightarrow S\ (L/)}}{John \quad is \quad Paul}$$

**Fig. 1.** analysis trees of simple sentences

### Formal properties of L-grammars :
L-grammars have been deeply studied. The main results about them are :
- The Lambek-Gentzen calculus is decidable. As a matter of fact, in each of its inference rules, there is one more operator / or \ under the line than there are above. To decide if a given sequent is valid, one only has to test on it each possible inference

rule in backward chaining, eliminating its operators one after the other, until only axioms (if the sequent is valid) are left.

- It is impossible to define a finite set of valid sequents (for example, rules R1 to R'4) equivalent with the complete Lambek-Gentzen calculus ([26]).

- The class of languages defined by L-grammars is the class of context-free languages ([19]) and the membership problem can be solved in polynomial time ([8]).

# 3 From syntax to semantics

The key idea of Montague's work ([16]) was to define an isomorphism between syntactic trees and semantic ones.

This definition is the formal expression of the principle of compositionality. It allows to automatically translate sentences in natural language into logical formulas.

## 3.1 The semantic representation

The logic we will use, called IL, is a simplified version of the intensional logic defined by Montague ([16, 7]). It generalizes first order predicate logic by including typed lambda-calculus.

- IL is a typed language : the set I of all possible types of IL includes
   * elementary types : $e \in I$ (type of *entities*) and $t \in I$ (type of *truth values*);
   * for any types $u \in I$ and $v \in I$, $<u,v> \in I$ ($<u,v>$ is the type of functions taking an argument of type u and giving a result of type v).

- semantics : a denotation set $D_w$ is associated with every type $w \in I$ as follows :
   * $D_e = E$ where E is the denumerable set of all entities of the world;
   * $D_t = \{0,1\}$;
   * $D_{<u,v>} = D_v^{D_u}$ : the denotation set of a composed type is a function.
IL also includes usual quantifiers and lambda-expressions.

## 3.2 Translation as an isomorphism

Each analysis tree produced by a L-categorial grammar can be *translated* into IL :
- translation of the categories into logical types (function $k : C' \longrightarrow I$) :
   * basic categories : $k(S)=t$ and in our example : $k(T)=e$, $k(CN)=<e,t>$;
   * derived categories : for any $X \in C'$ and $Y \in C'$, $k(X/Y)=k(Y\backslash X)=<k(Y),k(X)>$.
- translation of the words (function $q : V \times C' \longrightarrow IL$) : each couple (v,U) where $v \in V$ and $U \in f(v) \subseteq C'$ is associated with a logical formula q(v,U) of IL of type $k(U) \in I$.
The most usual and useful translations are :
   * $q(a,(S/(T\backslash S))/CN)=q(a,((S/T)\backslash S)/CN)=\lambda P\lambda Q\exists x[P(x)\wedge Q(x)]$
   $q(every,S/(T\backslash S))/CN)=q(every,((S/T)\backslash S)/CN)=\lambda P\lambda Q\forall x[P(x)\rightarrow Q(x)]$
   where x and y are variables of type e, P and Q variables of type $<e,t>$.
   * the verb *to be*, as a transitive verb is translated by
   $q(be,(T\backslash S)/T)=\lambda x\lambda y[y=x]$ with x and y variables of type e.

* Every other word w is translated into a logical constant noted w'.
- translation of the rules of the Lambek-Gentzen calculus :
* the axioms X —> X are translated by the identity function : $\lambda x.x$;
* the inference rules are respectively translated by rules applying to IL formulas :

$$\frac{t \cdot x \longrightarrow y}{t \longrightarrow \lambda x[y]} \qquad \frac{x \cdot t \longrightarrow y}{t \longrightarrow \lambda x[y]}$$

$$\frac{t \longrightarrow x \qquad u \cdot f(x) \cdot v \longrightarrow z}{u \cdot f \cdot t \cdot v \longrightarrow z} \qquad \frac{t \longrightarrow x \qquad u \cdot f(x) \cdot v \longrightarrow z}{u \cdot t \cdot f \cdot v \longrightarrow z}$$

As all rules Ri ($1 \leq i \leq 4$) can be proved in the Lambek calculus, the corresponding translation rules called Wi can be deduced from our translations ([17]) :

- W1 : f . a —> f(a)                    W'1 : a . f —> f(a)
- W2 : f . g —> $\lambda a[f(g(a))]$     W'2 : g . f —> $\lambda a[f(g(a))]$
- W3 : f —> $\lambda a \lambda b[(f(b))(a)]$   W'3 : f —> $\lambda a \lambda b[(f(b))(a)]$
- W4 : a —> $\lambda f[f(a)]$            W'4 : a —> $\lambda f[f(a)]$

**Examples**
Fig. 2 displays the translation of the first tree of Fig. 1. The unknown translation of the sentence is first noted M. From the isomorphism, we obtain :
$M=\lambda P \lambda Q \exists x[P(x) \wedge Q(x)](man')(run')=\lambda Q \exists x[man'(x) \wedge Q(x)](run')$
$$=\exists x[man'(x) \wedge run'(x)]$$

$$\frac{\frac{T\backslash S \longrightarrow T\backslash S \ (A) \quad S \longrightarrow S \ (A)}{CN \longrightarrow CN \ (A) \quad S/(T\backslash S).T\backslash S \longrightarrow S \ (L/)} \quad \frac{run' \longrightarrow b \quad \lambda P \lambda Q \exists x[P(x) \wedge Q(x)](a)(b) \longrightarrow M}{man' \longrightarrow a \quad P \lambda Q \exists x[P(x) \wedge Q(x)](a).run' \longrightarrow M}}{(S/(T\backslash S))/CN . CN . T\backslash S \longrightarrow S \ (L/) \quad => \quad \lambda P \lambda Q \exists x[P(x) \wedge Q(x)].man'.run' \longrightarrow M}$$

a        man   runs

**Fig. 2.** translation of the first analysis tree of Fig. 1

Similarly, the second tree of Fig. 1 is translated into : [John'=Paul']. This system gives account of ambiguities : ambiguous sentences give rise to several different trees translated into several different formulas.

# 4 First approach to the learning model

Our purpose is to provide a computational model of natural language learning. Now that the linguistic framework is given, it remains to fix what is supposed to be known by the learner and what is to be learned, under which conditions.

## 4.1 Innate knowledge and concepts to be learned

When a human being learns a natural language, we suppose that he has at his disposal sentences syntactically correct and semantically relevant.

The corresponding situation in our model is an algorithm which takes as inputs a syntactically correct sentence together with its logical translation into IL.

The innate knowledge supposed is reduced to the inference rules of the Lambek calculus and the corresponding translation rules. As opposed to usual semantic-based methods of learning, *no word meaning is supposed to be initially known.*

Finally, what does the learner have to learn ? In our linguistic framework, all syntactic and semantic information are attached to the members of the vocabulary. More precisely, the knowledge to be learned can be represented as a finite list of triplets of the form (v,U,w) where v∈V, U∈f(v)⊆C' and w=q(v,U)∈IL.

**Example :**

Learning the example grammar of 2.2 and its logical translation means learning the following set :

{ (a, (S/(T\S))/CN, λPλQ∃x[P(x)∧Q(x)]), (a, ((S/T)\S)/CN, λPλQ∃x[P(x)∧Q(x)]),
 (man, CN, man'), (woman, CN, woman'), (John,T,John'), (Paul,T,Paul'),
 (runs,T\S,run'),(meets,(S\T)/T,meet'),(is,(S\T)/T,λxλy[y=x])...}

Fig. 3. shows the components of our model.

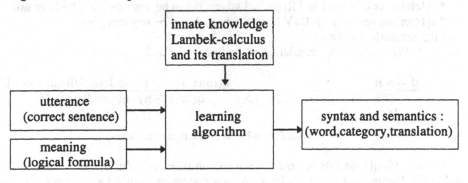

**Fig. 3.** the learning model

## 4.2 The learning algorithm

The learning strategy we propose is the following one :

- current hypothesis := ∅;
- For every couple <p, l> where p is a sentence and l is a logical formula do :
  - For every word in p do :
    * if it belongs to the current hypothesis, affect it the corresponding category;
    * else affect it the categories allowing the analysis of p;
  - For every possible analysis tree for p do :
    - for every couple (word category) in this tree do :
      * if it belongs to the current hypothesis, affect it the corresponding translation
      * else, find the simplest translation allowing to provide l
  - Update the current hypothesis.

### 4.3 Simulation of the algorithm

Let us suppose that the first given example is : <John runs, run'(John')>.

- the syntactic hypotheses : as both words of p are unknown, we call A the category associated with *John* and B the one associated with *runs*. As p is a correct sentence, we know that A . B ——> S and we want to infer values for A and B. The only applicable rules in backward chaining are (L/) and (L\), as shown in Fig. 4 :

$$\frac{\boxed{B \longrightarrow V} \quad \boxed{U \longrightarrow S}}{A=U/V . B \longrightarrow S \quad (L/)} \qquad \frac{\boxed{A \longrightarrow V} \quad \boxed{U \longrightarrow S}}{A . B=V\backslash U \longrightarrow S \quad (L\backslash)}$$

**Fig. 4.** the syntactic hypothesis

In these trees, sequents inside rectangles can only be axioms (because the category on the right side is a basic one) and there are ovals around sequents that could be developed further by decomposing the right side category and by applying rules (R/) or (R\), but which are cut at this level. So, the two possible solutions are :

* f(John)=A=U/V=S/B and f(runs)=B where B can be any category, basic or not;
* f(John)=A and f(runs)=B=V\U=A\S where A can be any category.

- the semantic translation :

    * Fig. 5 shows the translation of the first hypothesis

$$\frac{B \longrightarrow B \qquad S \longrightarrow S}{S/B . B \longrightarrow S \quad (L/)} \Rightarrow \frac{q(runs,B) \longrightarrow a \quad q(John,S/B)(a) \longrightarrow M}{q(John,S/B) . q(runs,B) \longrightarrow M}$$
$$\text{John \quad runs}$$

**Fig. 5.** translation of the first hypothesis

From M=q(John,S/B)(a)=q(John,S/B)(q(run,B))=run'(John') we infer that q(John,S/B)=run' and q(run,B)=John'. Another solution would be : q(run,A\S)=run' and q(John,S/B)=λP[P(John')] but we strictly stick to the simplest solution.

    * Fig. 6 shows the translation of the second hypothesis

$$\frac{A \longrightarrow A \qquad S \longrightarrow S}{A . A\backslash S \longrightarrow S \quad (L\backslash)} \Rightarrow \frac{q(John,A) \longrightarrow a \quad q(runs,A\backslash S)(a) \longrightarrow M}{q(John,A) . q(runs,A\backslash S) \longrightarrow M}$$
$$\text{John \quad runs}$$

**Fig. 6.** translation of the second hypothesis

Similarly, we infer that q(runs,A\S)=run' and q(John,A)=John'.

At this stage, we have no reason to prefer one hypothesis to the other. The current hypothesis is then :

H={(John,S/B,run'),(runs,B,John')} OR {(John,A,John'),(runs,A\S,run')}.

Now, let us suppose that a second given example is <Paul runs, run'(Paul')>. The same process applies, except that *runs* now belongs to the current hypothesis.

- the syntactic hypotheses :

* if *runs* is assigned the category B, then *Paul* must receive S/B;

* if *runs* is assigned the category A\S, then *Paul* can receive either A or S/(A\S). But the sequent A ——> S/(A\S) is valid in the Lambek-Gentzen calculus (see rule R4), so S/(A\S) is in fact a particular case of A and is not to be taken into account.

- the semantic translation :

* the translation of the first tree, similar to the one of Fig. 6, gives rise to : M=q(Paul,S/B)(John')=run'(Paul') which is an equation without solution. So, the first subset of the current hypothesis is given up. It can be noticed that the hypothesis concerning *John* in this subset is also given up, although it was not concerned by the new example. A similar conclusion would have followed if the second example had been <John sleeps, sleeps'(John')>. Any other example sentence including one of the words concerned by the current hypothesis is enough to discard the wrong subset.

* the translation of the second tree, similar to the one of Fig. 7, gives rise to : M=run'(q(Paul,A))=run'(Paul') and allows to infer q(Paul,A)=Paul'.

The new current hypothesis is then :

H={(John,A,John'),(runs,A\S,run'),(Paul,A,Paul')}.

Without semantics, it would have been impossible to decide between the two initial possibilities. The only reason why *runs* must receive a fractional category is that its translation behaves like a function, a predicate.

In the appendix is given the analysis of <a man runs, $\exists x[man'(x) \wedge run'(x)])$> given as a new example. There are eleven syntactical possibilities, reduced to six really different ones. The semantic translation allows to abandon three of them and only four syntactico-semantic hypotheses are built, among which three will clearly be discarded very easily at the next repetition.

### 4.4 Treatment of polymorphism :

How can our algorithm assign several different categories to a unique word (as it seems necessary for determiners) ? A special module needs to be added. It becomes active when a new sentence example contains no new word but is impossible to analyze with the current hypothesis.

In this case, each word in the sentence, one after the other, should be treated as if it were the only one unknown so as to find out its other possible categories. Nevertheless, heuristics can help us chose the words more likely to be assigned several different categories :

- grammatical words, easy to recognize because they are the ones translated by lambda expressions (whereas lexical words are nearly always translated by a logical constant) are treated in priority.

- even if a word needs several categories, most of the time a unique logical translation is enough for all of them : this is true for determiners but also for pathological ambiguous words like *fly*, which can be either a common noun or a verb but is in both cases translated by *fly'*.

Further experiments, varying the order in which the examples are proposed, need to be performed to test if they are enough to treat every case of polymorphism.

## 5 Evaluation and conclusion

The algorithmic complexity of our algorithm is clearly exponential. More complex sentences would have entailed the multiplication of hypotheses and could have been intractable. More precisely, our model seems to be particularly sensitive to the complexity of a new example *relatively to the current hypothesis*. This complexity can be measured by the number of new words appearing in an example. To master this complexity, we suggest to put *a priori* a bound on the number of new words appearing in a new sentence. An example which does not respect this bound is not treated but saved so as to be treated later, when the current hypothesis is developed enough. It is reasonable to think that children also learn from simple examples to more complex ones.

But our work also provides new insights on previous ones.

First, categorial grammars seem to be particularly adapted to the learning process. Recent research has found conditions under which the syntax of these grammars is learnable with positive examples ([3, 1, 12]). But, in these frameworks, only a simpler version of categorial grammars (restricted to rules R1 and R'1) is considered. The main interest of L-categorial grammars is that they allow to restrict the number of different categories associated with each word. This number is a crucial parameter for the complexity of the syntactic analysis and for the treatment of polymorphism. Furthermore, in most previous work ([3, 12]), tree structures are provided as input data. In our model, thanks to the tree isomorphism, the semantics translation plays a similar role but in a weaker and more cognitively relevant fashion, as the functional structure of the logical formula gives indication about the functional syntactic structure of the sentence. Adriaans ([1]) also proposed a learning algorithm for categorial grammars using both syntax and semantics but he treated them separately : the semantic learning only started when the syntax learning was achieved instead of helping it as we propose.

Learning a natural language is certainly not equivalent to learning a formal grammar. *Natural* words and sentences *refer to things and situations* and can only be learned in their presence. Cognitive models built in this spirit ([10, 2, 14, 11]) already assumed this, but the syntaxes considered were more traditional and the semantic representations used were too close to syntactic structures ([21]) : they failed to represent complex logical relations like quantification or Boolean operators. Logical languages are more powerful and *a priori* independent from linguistic structures. Our model suggests that the acquisition of a conceptual representation of the world is necessary *before* the acquisition of the syntax of a natural language can start.

Fundamentally, what makes natural languages learnable in our model is the presupposition that *there exists an isomorphism between the syntax of sentences and their semantics*. This strong principle of compositionality is contested by linguists working on discourse phenomena but remains an interesting approximation. The *graph deformation condition* used in [2] was a weaker version of it.

The work presented here is more a program of research than a full achievement, but seemed interesting enough to be exposed because our choices have theoretical, linguistic and cognitive motivations. The algorithm is being implemented and the search for a characterization of the languages it allows to learn is being explored.

# References

1. P. W. Adriaans, *Language Learning from a Categorial Perspective*, Ph.D. thesis, University of Amsterdam, 1992.

2. J. R. Anderson, "Induction of Augmented Transition Networks", *Cognitive Science* 1, p125-157, 1977.
3. W. Buszkowski, G. Penn, "Categorial grammars determined from linguistic data by unification", *Studia Logica* 49, p431-454, 1990.
4. N. Chomsky, *Aspects of the Theory of Syntax*, Cambridge, MIT Press.
5. N. Chomsky, *Language and Mind*, Brace & World, 1968.
6. F. Denis, R. Gilleron, "PAC learning under helpful distributions", Proceedings of the 8th ACM Workshop on Computational Learning Theory, p132-145, 1997.
7. D. R. Dowty, R. E. Wall, S. Peters, *Introduction to Montague Semantics*, Reidel, Dordrecht, 1989.
8. A. Finkel, I. Tellier : "A polynomial algorithm for the membership problem with categorial grammars", *Theoretical Computer Science* 164, p207-221, 1996.
9. E. M. Gold, "Language Identification in the Limit", *Information and Control* 10, P447-474, 1967.
10. H. Hamburger, K. Wexler, "A mathematical Theory of Learning Transformational Grammar", *Journal of Mathematical Psychology* 12, p137-177, 1975.
11. J. C. Hill, "A computational model of language acquisition in the two-year-old", *Cognition and Brain Theory* 6(3), p287-317, 1983.
12. M. Kanazawa, "Identification in the Limit of Categorial Grammars", *Journal of Logic, Language & Information*, vol 5, n°2, p115-155, 1996.
13. J. Lambek, "The mathematics of Sentence Structure", *American Mathematical Monthly*, n°65, p154-170, 1958.
14. P. Langley, "Language acquisition through error discovery", *Cognition and Brain Theory* 5, p211-255, 1982.
15. M. Li, P. Vitanyi, "A theory of learning simple concepts under simple distributions", *SIAM J. Computing*, 20(5), p915-935, 1991.
16. R. Montague, *Formal Philosophy; Selected papers of Richard Montague*, Yale University Press, New Haven, 1974.
17. M. Moortgat, *Categorial investigations, logical and linguistic aspects of the Lambek Calculus*, Foris, Dordrecht, 1988.
18. R. T. Oehrle, E. Bach, D. Wheeler (eds.), *Categorial Grammars and Natural Language Structure*, Reidel, Dordrecht, 1988.
19. M. Pentus, "Lambek grammars are context-free", in : 8th Annual IEEE Symposium on Logic in Computer Science, Montreal, Canada, p429-433, 1992.
20. S. Pinker, "Formal models of language learning", *Cognition* 7, p217-283, 1979.
21. Y. Sakakibara, "Efficient learning of context-free grammars from positive structural examples", *Information & Computation* 97, p23-60, 1992.
22. S. Schieber, "Evidence against the context-freeness of natural languages", *Linguistics and Philosophy* 8, p333-343, 1995.
23. T. Shinohara, "Inductive inference of monotonic formal systems from positive data", p339-351 in : *Algorithmic Learning Theory*, S. Arikara, S. Goto, S. Ohsuga & T. Yokomori (eds), Tokyo : Ohmsha and New York and Berlin : Springer.
24. L. G. Valiant, "A theory of the learnable", *Communication of the ACM*, p1134-1142, 1984.
25. K. Wexler, P. Culicover, *Formal Principles of Language Acquisition*, Cambridge, MIT Press.
26. W. Zielonka, "Axiomatizability of Ajdukiewicz-Lambek calculus by means of cancellations schemes", *Zeischrift für Mathematsche Logik und grunlagen der Mathematik* 27, p215-224, 1981.

35

# APPENDIX

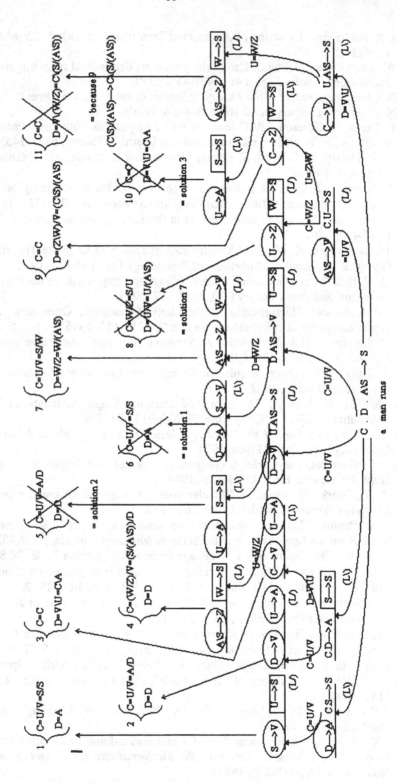

In this tree, unknown categories associated with *a* and *man* are noted C and D.

- semantic translation : let us call α=q(a, C) and β=q(man,D)

* the translation of solution 1 leads to α(run'(β))=∃x[man'(x)∧run'(x)].

The identification of both formulas imposes to define : β=x. But we forbid to introduce free variables into the logical translations of the words, so this solution is abandoned.

* the translation of solution 2 leads to run'(α(β))=∃x[man'(x)∧run'(x)].

This equation is impossible to solve, so this solution is abandoned.

* the translation of solution 3 leads to run'(β(α))=∃x[man'(x)∧run'(x)].

As in the previous case, this solution is abandoned.

* the translation of solution 4 leads to (α(β))(run')=∃x[man'(x)∧run'(x)].

To identify both formulas, we have to perform lambda-abstractions on the second one (they are only possible on logical *constants*) :

∃x[man'(x)∧run'(x)]=λP∃x[man'(x)∧P(x)](run') so α(β)=λP∃x[man'(x)∧P(x)]

and λP∃x[man'(x)∧P(x)]=λQλP∃x[Q(x)∧P(x)](man')

so the simplest solution is : α=λQλP∃x[Q(x)∧P(x)] and β=man'.

* the translation of solution 7 leads to α(β(run'))=∃x[man'(x)∧run'(x)].

with ∃x[man'(x)∧run'(x)]=λP∃x[man'(x)∧P(x)](run') we obtain two solutions :

- α=λx.x and β=λP∃x[man'(x)∧P(x)]

- α=λP∃x[man'(x)∧P(x)] and β=λx.x

(solutions using the constant function : λx.x are only considered in the cases where no other are possible, this is the reason why they were not proposed earlier).

* the translation of solution 9 leads to (β(run'))(α)=∃x[man'(x)∧run'(x)].

After abstractions, the only solution left is : α=man' and β=λPλQ∃x[Q(x)∧P(x)].

So, the hypotheses brought by this new example are :

{ (a, (S/(A\S))/D, λQλP∃x[Q(x)∧P(x)]), (man, D, man') }

OR { (a, S/W, λx.x), (man, W/(A\S), λP∃x[man'(x)∧P(x)]) }

OR { (a, S/W, λP∃x[man'(x)∧P(x)])), (man, W/(A\S), λx.x) }

OR { (a, C, man'), (man, (C\S)/(A\S), λPλQ∃x[Q(x)∧P(x)]) }.

It is obvious that only the first subset will resist to new examples using one of these words.

# A Polynomial Time Incremental Algorithm for Learning DFA

Rajesh Parekh[1], Codrin Nichitiu[2], and Vasant Honavar[3]

[1] Allstate Research and Planning Center
321 Middlefield Road, Menlo Park CA 94025, USA
rpare@allstate.com
[2] Ecole Normale Superieure de Lyon
46 Allee d'Italie, 69364 Lyon Cedex 07, France
Codrin.Nichitiu@ens-lyon.fr
[3] Department of Computer Science, Iowa State University
Ames IA 50011, USA
honavar@cs.iastate.edu
WWW home page: http://www.cs.iastate.edu/~honavar/aigroup.html

**Abstract.** We present an efficient incremental algorithm for learning deterministic finite state automata (DFA) from labeled examples and membership queries. This algorithm is an extension of Angluin's *ID* procedure to an incremental framework. The learning algorithm is intermittently provided with labeled examples and has access to a knowledgeable teacher capable of answering membership queries. The learner constructs an initial hypothesis from the given set of labeled examples and the teacher's responses to membership queries. If an additional example observed by the learner is inconsistent with the current hypothesis then the hypothesis is modified minimally to make it consistent with the new example. The update procedure ensures that the modified hypothesis is consistent with all examples observed thus far. The algorithm is guaranteed to converge to a minimum state DFA corresponding to the target when the set of examples observed by the learner includes a *live complete* set. We prove the convergence of this algorithm and analyze its time and space complexities.

## 1 Introduction

*Grammar Inference* [BF72,FB75,MQ86,Lan95] is an important machine learning problem with several applications in pattern recognition, language acquisition, bioinformatics, and intelligent agent design. It is defined as the process of learning an unknown grammar from a given finite set of labeled examples. *Regular grammars* describe languages that can be generated (and recognized) by deterministic finite state automata (DFA). Since regular grammars represent a widely used subset of formal language grammars, considerable research has focused on regular grammar inference (or equivalently, identification of the corresponding DFA). However, given a finite set of positive examples and a finite (possibly empty) set of negative examples the problem of learning a minimum state DFA equivalent to the unknown target is *NP*-hard [Gol78]. The learner's task can be simplified by requiring that the set of examples provided meet certain desired criteria (like *structural completeness* [PC78,PH96] or *characteristic sample* [OG92]), or by providing the learner with access to sources of additional information, like a knowledgeable teacher who responds to queries generated by the learner. Angluin's *ID* algorithm learns the target DFA given a *live-complete* sample and a knowledgeable teacher to answer *membership* queries posed by the learner [Ang81]. The interested reader is referred to [MQ86,Pit89,Lan95,PH98] for recent surveys of different approaches to grammar inference.

In many practical learning scenarios, a live-complete sample may not be available to the learner at the outset. Instead, a sequence of labeled examples is provided intermittently and the learner is required to construct an approximation of the target DFA based on the examples and possibly the queries answered by the teacher. In such scenarios, an online or incremental model of learning that is guaranteed to eventually converge to the target DFA in the limit is of interest. Particularly, in the case of intelligent autonomous agents, incremental learning offers an attractive framework for characterizing the behavior of the agents [CM96]. Against this background, we present a provably correct, polynomial time, incremental, interactive algorithm for learning the target DFA from *labeled examples* and *membership queries*. The proposed algorithm *IID* extends the *ID* algorithm to an incremental setting.

## 2  Preliminaries

Let $\Sigma$ be a finite set of symbols called the *alphabet*, $\Sigma^*$ be the set of strings over $\Sigma$, $\alpha, \beta, \gamma$ be strings in $\Sigma^*$, and $|\alpha|$ be the length of the string $\alpha$. $\lambda$ is a special string called the *null* string and has length 0. Given a string $\alpha = \beta\gamma$, $\beta$ is the *prefix* of $\alpha$ and $\gamma$ is the *suffix* of $\alpha$. Let $Pref(\alpha)$ denote the set of all prefixes of $\alpha$. Further if $S \subseteq \Sigma^*$ then $Pref(S) = \cup_{\alpha \in S} Pref(\alpha)$. Given two sets $S_1$ and $S_2$, the *set difference* is denoted by $S_1 \backslash S_2$ and the *symmetric difference* is denoted by $S_1 \oplus S_2$.

A *deterministic* finite state automaton (DFA) is a quintuple $A = (Q, \delta, \Sigma, q_0, F)$ where, $Q$ is a finite set of states, $\Sigma$ is the finite alphabet, $q_0 \in Q$ is the start state, $F \subseteq Q$ is the set of accepting states, and $\delta$ is the transition function: $Q \times \Sigma \longrightarrow Q$. A state $d_0 \in Q$ such that $\forall a \in \Sigma$, $\delta(d_0, a) = d_0$ is called a *dead* state. If there exists a state $q \in Q$ such that $\delta(q, a)$ is not defined for some $a \in \Sigma$ then the transition function is said to be incompletely specified. It may be fully specified by adding transitions of the form $\delta(q, a) = d_0$ when $\delta(q, a)$ is undefined. The extension of $\delta$ to handle input strings is denoted by $\delta^*$ and is defined as follows: $\delta^*(q, \lambda) = q$ and $\delta^*(q, a\alpha) = \delta^*(\delta(q, a), \alpha)$ for $q \in Q$, $a \in \Sigma$ and $\alpha \in \Sigma^*$. The set of all strings accepted by $A$ is its language, $L(A)$. $L(A) = \{\alpha | \delta^*(q_0, \alpha) \in F\}$. The language accepted by a DFA is called a *regular language*.

DFA are represented using state transition diagrams. The start state $q_0$ is indicated by the symbol $>$ attached to it. Accepting states are denoted using concentric circles. The state transition $\delta(q_i, a) = q_j$ for any letter $a \in \Sigma$ is depicted by an arrow labeled by the letter $a$ from the state $q_i$ to the state $q_j$. Fig. 1 shows the state transition diagram for a sample DFA.

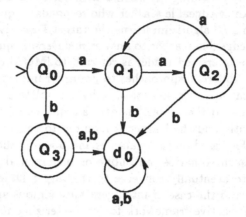

**Fig. 1.** Deterministic Finite State Automaton.

A labeled example $(\alpha, c(\alpha))$ for $A$ is such that $\alpha \in \Sigma^*$ and $c(\alpha) = +$ if $\alpha \in L(A)$ (i.e., $\alpha$ is a positive example) or $c(\alpha) = -$ if $\alpha \notin L(A)$ (i.e., $\alpha$ is a negative example). Thus, $(a, -)$, $(b, +)$, $(aa, +)$, $(aaab, -)$, and $(aaaa, +)$ are labeled examples for the DFA of Fig. 1. $S^+$ will be used to denote a set of positive examples of $A$ i.e., $S^+ \subseteq L(A)$. Similarly, $S^-$ will be used to denote a set of negative examples of $A$ i.e., $S^- \subseteq \Sigma^* \backslash L(A)$. A sample $S$ will be defined as $S = S^+ \cup S^-$. $A$ is consistent with a *sample* $S$ if it accepts all the positive examples (i.e., all examples in $S^+$) and rejects all negative examples (i.e., all examples in $S^-$).

Given any DFA $A'$, there exists a minimum state DFA (also called the *canonical DFA*) $A$, such that $L(A) = L(A')$. Without loss of generality, we will assume that the target DFA being learned is a canonical DFA. It can be shown that any canonical DFA has at most one dead state.

A state $q_i$ of a DFA $A$ is *live* if there exist strings $\alpha$ and $\beta$ such that $\alpha\beta \in L(A)$, $\delta^*(q_0, \alpha) = q_i$, and $\delta^*(q_i, \beta) \in F$. A state that is not live is called *dead*. As stated earlier, a canonical DFA can have at most one dead state and we use $d_0$ to denote this dead state. Given $A$, a finite set of strings $P$ is said to be *live complete* if for every live state $q_i$ of $A$ there exists a string $\alpha \in P$ such that $\delta^*(q_0, \alpha) = q_i$ [Ang81]. For example, $P = \{\lambda, a, b, aa\}$ is a live complete set for the DFA in Fig. 1. Any superset of a live complete set is also live complete. In order to have a representation for the start state of $A$ we assume that the string $\lambda$ is part of any live complete set. The set $P' = P \cup \{d_0\}$ represents all the states of $A$. To account for the state transitions, define a function $f : P' \times \Sigma \longrightarrow \Sigma^* \cup \{d_0\}$ as follows: $f(d_0, a) = d_0$ and $f(\alpha, a) = \alpha a$. Note that $f(\alpha, a)$ denotes the state reached upon reading an input letter $a \in \Sigma$ from the state represented by the string $\alpha \in \Sigma^*$. We will let $T' = P' \cup \{f(\alpha, a) | (\alpha, a) \in P' \times \Sigma\}$ and $T = T' \backslash \{d_0\}$.

Thus, given the live complete set $P = \{\lambda, a, b, aa\}$ corresponding to the DFA in Fig. 1 we obtain the set $T = \{\lambda, a, b, aa, ab, ba, bb, aaa, aab\}$.

## 3  The *ID* Algorithm

The *ID* algorithm for inference of the target DFA, its correctness proof, and complexity analysis are described in detail in [Ang81]. To keep the discussion that follows self-contained, we review *ID* briefly in this section.

Given a live-complete set $P$ corresponding to the target canonical DFA $A$, *ID* constructs a partition of the set $T'$ (constructed from $P$ as described above) such that elements of $T'$ that represents the same state of $A$ are grouped together in the same block of the partition. In the process a set of distinguishing strings $V$ is constructed such that no two distinct states of $A$ have the same behavior on all the strings in $V$. When the set $V$ has $i$ elements, define function $E_i : T' \longrightarrow 2^V$ as follows $E_i(d_0) = \phi$ and $E_i(\alpha) = \{v_j | v_j \in V, 0 \le j < i, \alpha v_j \in L(A)\}$. Fig. 2 describes the algorithm in detail. Step 1 performs the initialization. The set $T_0$ represents a trivial partition with all elements belonging to a single block. The first distinguishing suffix $v_0$ considered is $\lambda$. The function $E_0$ which is computed in step 2 partitions $T'$ into two blocks, representing the accepting and non-accepting states of $A$ respectively. Step 3 refines the individual blocks of the partition of $T'$ based on the behavior of the elements on the distinguishing suffixes $v_0, v_1, \ldots, v_i$. Intuitively, if two elements of $T'$, say $\alpha$ and $\beta$, have the same behavior on the current set $V$ (i.e., $E_i(\alpha) = E_i(\beta)$) then $\alpha$ and $\beta$ appear to represent the same state of the target DFA. However, if the transitions out of the states represented by $E_i(\alpha)$ and $E_i(\beta)$ on some letter of the alphabet lead to different states (i.e., $E_i(f(\alpha, a)) \ne E_i(f(\beta, a))$ for some $a \in \Sigma$) then clearly, $\alpha$ and $\beta$ cannot correspond to the same state in the target DFA. A distinguishing suffix $v_{i+1}$ is constructed to refine the partition of $T'$ such that $\alpha$ and $\beta$ appear in separate blocks of the partition. Step 3 terminates when the set $V$ contains a distinguishing suffix for each pair of elements in $T'$ that represent non-equivalent states of $A$. Step 4, finally constructs the hypothesis DFA $M$.

### 3.1  Example

We now demonstrate the use of *ID* to learn the target DFA in Fig. 1. $P = \{\lambda, a, b, aa\}$ is a live complete set and $T' = \{d_0, \lambda, a, b, aa, ab, ba, bb, aaa, aab\}$. Table 1 shows the computation of $E_i(\alpha)$ for the strings $\alpha \in T'$. The leftmost column lists the elements $\alpha$ of the set $T'$. Each successive column represents the function $E_i$ corresponding to the string $v_i$ (listed in the second row of the table).

Note that the DFA returned by the procedure is exactly the DFA in Fig. 1. Angluin [Ang81] has shown that number of membership queries needed is $O(|\Sigma| \cdot N \cdot |P|)$. Thus, *ID* runs in time polynomial in $|\Sigma|$, $N$, and $|P|$.

---

**Algorithm: ID**

**Input:**  A live complete set $P$ and a teacher to answer membership queries.
**Output:** A DFA $M$ equivalent to the target DFA $A$.

**begin**
    1)    *// Perform initialization*
        $i = 0$, $v_i = \lambda$, $V = \{\lambda\}$, $T = P \cup \{f(\alpha, b) \mid (\alpha, b) \in P \times \Sigma\}$,
        and $T' = T \cup \{d_0\}$
    2)    *// Construct function $E_0$ for $v_0 = \lambda$*
        $E_0(d_0) = \phi$
        $\forall \alpha \in T$ pose the membership query "$\alpha \in L(A)$?"
            if the teacher's response is *yes*
            then $E_0(\alpha) = \{\lambda\}$
            else $E_0(\alpha) = \phi$
            end if
    3)    *// Refine the partition of the set $T'$*
        **while** $(\exists \alpha, \beta \in P'$ and $b \in \Sigma$ such that
            $E_i(\alpha) = E_i(\beta)$ but $E_i(f(\alpha, b)) \neq E_i(f(\beta, b)))$
        **do**
            Let $\gamma \in E_i(f(\alpha, b)) \oplus E_i(f(\beta, b))$
            $v_{i+1} = b\gamma$
            $V = V \cup \{v_{i+1}\}$ and $i = i + 1$
            $\forall \alpha \in T$ pose the membership query "$\alpha v_i \in L(A)$?"
                if the teacher's response is *yes*
                then $E_i(\alpha) = E_{i-1}(\alpha) \cup \{v_i\}$
                else $E_i(\alpha) = E_{i-1}(\alpha)$
                end if
        **end while**
    4)    *// Construct the representation of the DFA $M$*
        The states of $M$ are the sets $E_i(\alpha)$, where $\alpha \in T$
        The initial state $q_0$ is the set $E_i(\lambda)$
        The accepting states are the sets $E_i(\alpha)$ where $\alpha \in T$ and $\lambda \in E_i(\alpha)$
        The transitions of $M$ are defined as follows:
            $\forall \alpha \in P'$
                if $E_i(\alpha) = \phi$
                then add self loops on the state $E_i(\alpha)$ for all $b \in \Sigma$
                else $\forall b \in \Sigma$ set the transition $\delta(E_i(\alpha), b) = E_i(f(\alpha, b))$
                end if
**end**

**Fig. 2.** Algorithm *ID*.

**Table 1.** Execution of ID.

| $i$ | 0 | 1 | 2 | 3 |
|---|---|---|---|---|
| $v_i$ | $\lambda$ | $b$ | $a$ | $aa$ |
| $E(d_0)$ | $\phi$ | $\phi$ | $\phi$ | $\phi$ |
| $E(\lambda)$ | $\phi$ | $\{b\}$ | $\{b\}$ | $\{b, aa\}$ |
| $E(a)$ | $\phi$ | $\phi$ | $\{a\}$ | $\{a\}$ |
| $E(b)$ | $\{\lambda\}$ | $\{\lambda\}$ | $\{\lambda\}$ | $\{\lambda\}$ |
| $E(aa)$ | $\{\lambda\}$ | $\{\lambda\}$ | $\{\lambda\}$ | $\{\lambda, aa\}$ |
| $E(ab)$ | $\phi$ | $\phi$ | $\phi$ | $\phi$ |
| $E(ba)$ | $\phi$ | $\phi$ | $\phi$ | $\phi$ |
| $E(bb)$ | $\phi$ | $\phi$ | $\phi$ | $\phi$ |
| $E(aaa)$ | $\phi$ | $\phi$ | $\{a\}$ | $\{a\}$ |
| $E(aab)$ | $\phi$ | $\phi$ | $\phi$ | $\phi$ |

## 4   *IID* – An Incremental Extension of *ID*

We now present an incremental version of the *ID* algorithm. As stated earlier, this algorithm does not require that the live complete set of examples be available to the learner at the start. Instead the learner is intermittently presented with labeled examples. The learner constructs a model of the target DFA based on the examples it has seen and gradually refines it as new examples become available. Our learning model assumes the availability of a teacher to answer membership queries. Let $M_t$ denote the DFA that corresponds to the learner's current model after observing $t$ examples. Initially, $M_0$ is a *null* automaton with only one state (the dead state) and it rejects every string in $\Sigma^*$. Clearly, every negative example encountered by the learner at this point is consistent with $M_0$. Without loss of generality we assume that the first example seen by the learner is a positive example. When the first positive example is seen $M_0$ is modified to accept the positive example. For each additional labeled example ($\alpha$) that is observed, it is determined whether $\alpha$ is consistent with $M_t$. If $\alpha$ is consistent with $M_t$ then $M_{t+1} = M_t$. Otherwise $M_t$ is suitably modified such that $\alpha$ is consistent with the resulting DFA, $M_{t+1}$. A detailed description of the algorithm appears in Fig. 3.

### 4.1   Example

We now demonstrate how the incremental algorithm learns the target DFA of Fig. 1. The learner starts with a model $M_0$ equivalent to the *null* DFA accepting no strings. Suppose the example $(b, +)$ is encountered. The following actions are taken. $P_0 = \{\lambda, b\}$ and $P_0' = \{d_0, \lambda, b\}$, $T_0 = \{\lambda, a, b, ba, bb\}$, and $T_0' = \{d_0, \lambda, a, b, ba, bb\}$. The computation of the functions $E_i$ is shown in Table 2. At this point the learner constructs a model $M_1$ of the target DFA (Fig. 4).

Suppose the next example observed by the learner is $(a, -)$. Since, $M_1$ correctly rejects $a$, $M_2 = M_1$ and the learner waits for additional examples. Let $(aa, +)$ be the next observed example. Since $aa \notin L(M_2)$ the learner takes the following steps to update $M_2$. $P_1 = \{\lambda, a, b, aa\}$, $P_1' = \{d_0, \lambda, a, b, aa\}$, $T_1 =$

---

**Algorithm: IID**

**Input:** A stream of labeled examples and a teacher to answer
membership queries.
**Output:** A DFA $M_t$ consistent with all $t$ examples observed by the learner.

**begin**
1)  // *Perform initialization*
    $i = 0$, $k = 0$, $t = 0$, $P_k = \phi$, $T_k = \phi$, $V = \phi$
    Initialize $M_t$ to the *null DFA*
2)  // *Process the first positive example*
    Wait for a positive example $(\alpha, +)$
    $P_0 = Pref(\alpha)$ and $P_0' = P_0 \cup \{d_0\}$
    $T_0 = P_0 \cup \{f(\alpha, b)|(\alpha, b) \in P_0 \times \Sigma\}$ and $T_0' = T_0 \cup \{d_0\}$
    $v_0 = \lambda$ and $V = \{v_0\}$
    $E_0(d_0) = \phi$
    $\forall \alpha \in T_0$ pose the membership query "$\alpha \in L(A)$?"
            if the teacher's response is *yes*
            then $E_0(\alpha) = \{\lambda\}$
            else $E_0(\alpha) = \phi$
            end if
3)  // *Refine the partition of the set $T_k'$* (as described in step 3 of Fig. 2)
4)  // *Construct the current representation $M_t$ of the target DFA*
    (as described in step 4 of Fig. 2)
5)  // *Process a new labeled example*
    Wait for a new example $(\alpha, c(\alpha))$
    if $\alpha$ is consistent with $M_t$
    **then**
            $M_{t+1} = M_t$
            $t = t + 1$
            **goto** step 5
    **else**
            $P_{k+1} = P_k \cup Pref(\alpha)$ and $P_{k+1}' = P_{k+1} \cup \{d_0\}$
            $T_{k+1} = T_k \cup Pref(\alpha) \cup \{f(\alpha, b)|(\alpha, b) \in (P_{k+1} \backslash P_k) \times \Sigma\}$
            and $T_{k+1}' = T_{k+1} \cup \{d_0\}$
            $\forall \alpha \in T_{k+1} \backslash T_k$ fill in the values of $E_i(\alpha)$ using membership queries:
                $E_i(\alpha) = \{v_j | 0 \leq j < i, \alpha v_j \in L(A)\}$
            $k = k + 1$
            $t = t + 1$
            **goto** step 3
        **end if**
**end**

---

**Fig. 3.** Algorithm *IID*.

**Table 2.** Execution of *IID* $(k = 0)$.

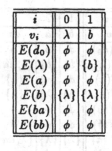

| $i$ | 0 | 1 |
|---|---|---|
| $v_i$ | $\lambda$ | $b$ |
| $E(d_0)$ | $\phi$ | $\phi$ |
| $E(\lambda)$ | $\phi$ | $\{b\}$ |
| $E(a)$ | $\phi$ | $\phi$ |
| $E(b)$ | $\{\lambda\}$ | $\{\lambda\}$ |
| $E(ba)$ | $\phi$ | $\phi$ |
| $E(bb)$ | $\phi$ | $\phi$ |

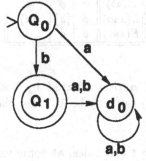

**Fig. 4.** Model $M_1$ of the Target DFA.

$\{\lambda, a, b, aa, ab, ba, bb, aaa, aab\}$, and $T_1' = \{d_0, \lambda, a, b, aa, ab, ba, bb, aaa, aab\}$. The function $E_1$ is extended to cover the new elements belonging to $T_1 \backslash T_0$. The resulting computation of the various $E_i$'s is depicted in Table 3.

The revised model of the target DFA ($M_3$) is exactly the DFA we are trying to learn (Fig. 1). Note also that at this time the set $P_1$ is live complete with respect to the target DFA.

### 4.2 Correctness Proof

The correctness of *IID* is a direct consequence of the following two theorems.

**Theorem 1.** *IID converges to a canonical representation of the target DFA when the set $P_k$ includes a live complete set for the target as a subset.*

*Proof.* Consider an execution of *ID* given a live complete set $P_l$: First we demonstrate that the execution of *ID* can be made to track that of *IID* in that the set $V$ generated during the execution of both the algorithms is the same and hence $\forall \alpha \in T_l$ the values $E_i(\alpha)$ are the same. We prove this claim by induction.

**Base Case:**
Both *ID* and *IID* start with $v_0 = \lambda$. At $k = 0$, *IID* has the set $P_0 \subseteq P_l$ available to it. Clearly, for all strings $\alpha, \beta \in P_0$ such that $E_0(\alpha) = E_0(\beta)$ but $E_0(f(\alpha, b)) \neq E_0(f(\beta, b))$ in the case of *IID* it is also the case that the same strings $\alpha, \beta \in P_l$ for *ID* such that $E_0(\alpha) = E_0(\beta)$ but $E_0(f(\alpha, b)) \neq E_0(f(\beta, b))$.

**Table 3.** Execution of *IID* ($k = 1$).

| $i$ | 1 | 2 | 3 |
|---|---|---|---|
| $v_i$ | $b$ | $a$ | $aa$ |
| $E(d_0)$ | $\phi$ | $\phi$ | $\phi$ |
| $E(\lambda)$ | $\{b\}$ | $\{b\}$ | $\{b, aa\}$ |
| $E(a)$ | $\phi$ | $\{a\}$ | $\{a\}$ |
| $E(b)$ | $\{\lambda\}$ | $\{\lambda\}$ | $\{\lambda\}$ |
| $E(ba)$ | $\phi$ | $\phi$ | $\phi$ |
| $E(bb)$ | $\phi$ | $\phi$ | $\phi$ |
| $E(aa)$ | $\{\lambda\}$ | $\{\lambda\}$ | $\{\lambda, aa\}$ |
| $E(ab)$ | $\phi$ | $\phi$ | $\phi$ |
| $E(aaa)$ | $\phi$ | $\{a\}$ | $\{a\}$ |
| $E(aab)$ | $\phi$ | $\phi$ | $\phi$ |

Assume that one such pair $\alpha, \beta$ is selected by both *ID* and *IID*. The string $\gamma \in E_0(f(\alpha, b)) \oplus E_0(f(\beta, b))$ can only be $\lambda$. Thus, the string $v_1 = b\gamma$ is the same for both the executions.

**Induction Hypothesis**:

Assume that after observing $t$ examples, at some value of $k$ ($0 \leq k < l$), when $P_k \subseteq P_l$ is available to *IID*, the sequence of strings $v_0, v_1, \ldots, v_i$ and $\forall \alpha \in T_k$ the values $E_i(\alpha)$ are the same for the executions of both *ID* and *IID*.

**Induction Proof**:

We now show that the same string $v_{i+1}$ is the generated by both *ID* and *IID*. Following the reasoning presented in the base case, and given the induction hypothesis, we can state that for all strings $\alpha, \beta \in P_k$ such that $E_i(\alpha) = E_i(\beta)$ but $E_i(f(\alpha, b)) \neq E_i(f(\beta, b))$ in the case of *IID* it is also the case that the same strings $\alpha, \beta \in P_l$ for *ID* such that $E_i(\alpha) = E_i(\beta)$ but $E_i(f(\alpha, b)) \neq E_i(f(\beta, b))$.

Assume that one such pair $\alpha, \beta$ is selected by both executions. By the induction hypothesis $E_i(f(\alpha, b)) \oplus E_i(f(\beta, b))$ is identical for both. Thus, given that the same string $\gamma \in E_i(f(\alpha, b)) \oplus E_i(f(\beta, b))$ is selected, the string $v_{i+1} = b\gamma$ is identical for both executions. When the live complete set $P_l$ is available to *IID*, $\forall \alpha \in T_l$ the values of $E_i(\alpha)$ are exactly the same as the corresponding values of $E_i(\alpha)$ for *ID*.

Given a live complete set of examples, *ID* outputs a canonical representation of the target DFA $A$ [Ang81]. From above we know that at $k = l$ the current model ($M_t$) of the target automaton maintained by *IID* is identical to one arrived at by *ID*. Thus, we have proved that *IID* converges to a canonical representation of the target DFA. $\square$

**Theorem 2.** *At any time during the execution of* IID, *all the $t$ examples observed by the learner are consistent with $M_t$, the current representation of the target.*

*Proof.* Consider an example $\alpha$ that is not consistent with $M_t$. *IID* modifies $M_t$ and constructs $M_{t+1}$ a new representation of the target. From step 5 in Fig. 3 we see that $\alpha \in P_{k+1}$ and hence $\alpha \in T_{k+1}$. $E_i$ is extended to all elements of $T_{k+1} \backslash T_k$. Thus, $\lambda \in E_i(\alpha)$ if $\alpha$ is a positive example of $A$ and $\lambda \notin E_i(\alpha)$ if $\alpha$ is a negative example of $A$. $M_{t+1}$ is constructed from $E_j$ for some $j \geq i$. Since, $E_i(\alpha) \subseteq E_j(\alpha)$ it is clear that $\alpha$ will be accepted (rejected) by $M_{t+1}$ if it a positive (negative) example of $A$. We now show that all strings $\mu$ that were consistent with $M_t$ are also consistent with $M_{t+1}$.

The set $\{E_i(\beta) \mid \forall \beta \in T_k\}$ represents the set of states of $M_t$ as shown in step 4 of the algorithm (see Fig. 3). Thus, for any string $\mu \in \Sigma^*$ and a state $q$ of $M_t$ there is a corresponding string $\beta \in T_k$ such that $\delta^*(q_0, \mu) = \delta^*(q_0, \beta) = q$. We say that $\mu$ is consistent with $M_t$ if either $\mu$ is a positive example of $A$ and $\lambda \in E_i(\beta)$ or $\mu$ is a negative example of $A$ and $\lambda \notin E_i(\beta)$. Now assume that the algorithm observes a string $\alpha$ that is not consistent with $M_t$. $T_k$ is modified to $T_{k+1}$ and the function $E_i$ is extended to the elements of $T_{k+1} \backslash T_k$. The algorithm then proceeds to refine the partition of $T_{k+1}$ by generating the distinguishing suffixes $v_{i+1}, v_{i+2}, \ldots, v_j$ and constructing the functions $E_{i+1}, E_{i+2}, \ldots, E_j$. Consider that there exists a string $\gamma \in T_{k+1}$ such that $E_l(\beta) = E_l(\gamma)$ but $E_{l+1}(\beta) \neq E_{l+1}(\gamma)$ for some $l$ where $i \leq l \leq j - 1$. Clearly, $E_{l+1}(\beta) \oplus E_{l+1}(\gamma) = v_{l+1}$. Further, $v_{l+1} \neq \lambda$ because $v_0 = \lambda$ is already chosen as the first distinguishing suffix. Thus, $\lambda \notin E_{l+1}(\beta) \oplus E_{l+1}(\gamma)$. The string $\mu$ that originally corresponded to the state represented by $\beta$ would now correspond either to the state represented by $\beta$ or to the state represented by $\gamma$. Further $\lambda$ will either belong to both $E_{l+1}(\beta)$ and $E_{l+1}(\gamma)$ or to neither depending on whether $\lambda$ was a member of both $E_l(\beta)$ and $E_l(\gamma)$ or not. Continuing with the argument we can see that there is some string $\kappa \in T_{k+1}$ where $\kappa = \beta$ or $E_j(\beta) \oplus E_j(\kappa) \subseteq \{v_{i+1}, v_{i+2}, \ldots, v_j\}$ such that $\mu$ corresponds to $\kappa$ in that $\delta^*(q_0, \mu) = \delta^*(q_0, \kappa) = q$ for some state $q$ in $M_{t+1}$. Further, since $\lambda \in E_j(\kappa)$ iff $\lambda \in E_j(\beta)$ or equivalently $\lambda \in E_j(\kappa)$ iff $\lambda \in E_i(\beta)$ we see that $\mu$ is consistent with $M_{t+1}$. This proves that all strings that were consistent with $M_t$ continue to be consistent with $M_{t+1}$. $\square$

## 4.3 Complexity Analysis

Assume that at some $k = l$ the set $P_l$ includes a live complete set for the target DFA $A$ as a subset. From the correctness proof of the algorithm, the current representation of the target $M_t$ is equivalent to the target $A$.

The size of $T_l$ is at most $|\Sigma| \cdot |P_l| + 1$. Also, the size of $V$ is no more than $N$ (the number of states of $A$). Thus, the total number of membership queries posed by the learner is $O(|\Sigma| \cdot |P_l| \cdot N)$. Searching for a pair of strings $\alpha, \beta$ to distinguish two states in the current representation of the target takes time that is $O(T_l^2)$. Thus, the incremental algorithm runs in time polynomial in $N$, $|\Sigma|$, and $|P_l|$. Since the size of $T_l$ is at most $|\Sigma| \cdot |P_l| + 1$ and the size of $V$ is no more than $N$, the space complexity of the algorithm is $O(|\Sigma| \cdot |P_l| \cdot N)$.

# 5 Discussion

Incremental or online learning algorithms play an important role in situations where all the training examples are not available to the learner at the start. We have proposed an incremental version of Angluin's *ID* algorithm for identifying the target DFA from a set of labeled examples and membership queries. The algorithm is guaranteed to converge to the target DFA and has polynomial time and space complexities.

Angluin's $L^*$ algorithm for learning the target DFA is based on *membership* and *equivalence* queries [Ang87]. The equivalence queries can be replaced by a polynomial number of calls to an oracle that supplies labeled examples to give an efficient PAC algorithm for learning DFA. The *IID* algorithm differs from $L^*$ in the following respects: *IID* is guaranteed to converge to the target DFA using only labeled examples and membership queries whereas $L^*$ makes use of equivalence queries in addition to labeled examples and membership queries to guarantee convergence. In contrast, the PAC version of $L^*$ guarantees that with very high probability the DFA output by the algorithm would make very low error (when compared to the unknown target).

Parekh and Honavar's algorithm for regular inference [PH96] searches a lattice of FSA generated by successive state mergings of a *prefix tree automaton* (PTA) for a set of positive examples of the target grammar. The lattice is represented compactly as a version space and is searched using membership queries. In the incremental framework they assume that the positive examples (needed to construct a *structurally complete* set) are provided intermittently. The algorithm augments the version space as needed in response to these new positive examples. Assuming that the examples are provided in increasing order by length, convergence to the target FSA is guaranteed when a structurally complete set of positive examples has been processed. Though provably correct, this algorithm has practical limitations because the size of the lattice grows exponentially with the number of states of the PTA.

The incremental version of the *regular positive and negative inference* (RPNI) algorithm [OG92] for regular grammar inference [Dup96] is also based on the idea of a lattice of partitions of the states of a PTA for a set of positive examples. It uses information from a set of negative examples to guide the ordered search through the lattice. It requires storage of all the examples seen by the learner to ensure that each time the representation of the target is modified, it stays consistent with all examples seen previously. The algorithm runs in time that is polynomial in the sum of lengths of the positive and negative examples and is guaranteed to converge to the target DFA when the set of examples seen by the learner include a *characteristic sample* (see [OG92]) for the target automaton as a subset.

Porat and Feldman's incremental algorithm for learning automata uses a *complete ordered sample* [PF91]. A complete ordered sample includes all the strings in $\Sigma^*$ in strict lexicographic order. The algorithm maintains a current hypothesis which is updated upon seeing a counter example and is guaranteed to converge in the limit provided the examples appear in strict lexicographic order. The algorithm needs only a finite working storage. However, it is based on an ordered presentation of examples and requires a consistency check with all the previous examples when the hypothesis is modified.

Our framework for incrementally learning a target DFA from labeled examples does not require storage of all the examples. Only those examples that are inconsistent with the current representation of the target are required to be stored (implicitly) by the learner. The algorithm does not require any specific ordering of the labeled examples. Furthermore, the incremental modification of learner's representation of the target DFA is guaranteed to be consistent with all the examples processed by the learner at any stage during learning and no explicit consistency check is needed. The reader should note that like the *ID* algorithm, this incremental version also avails of a knowledgeable teacher capable of answering membership queries.

The learner's reliance on the teacher to provide accurate responses to membership queries poses a potential limitation in applications where a reliable teacher is not available. We are exploring the possibility of learning in an environment where the learner does not have access to a teacher. The algorithms due to Dupont [Dup96] and Porat & Feldman [PF91] operate in this framework. Some open problems include whether the limitations of these algorithms (e.g., need for storage of all the previously seen examples and complete lexicographic ordering of examples) can be overcome without sacrificing efficiency and guaranteed convergence to the target. Porat and Feldman proved a strong negative result stating that there exists no algorithm which when operating with finite working storage can incrementally learn the target DFA from an arbitrary presentation [PF91]. In this context, it is of interest to explore alternative models of learning that: relax the convergence criterion (for example, allow PAC style approximate learning of the target within a given error bound); provide for some additional hints to the learning algorithm (like a bound on the number of states of the target DFA); include a helpful teacher that carefully guides the learner perhaps by providing *simple* examples first (for example see [PH97]).

## Acknowledgements

The authors are grateful to the Department of Computer Science at Iowa State University (where a major portion of this research was undertaken) for the research and computing facilities made available to them. Rajesh Parekh is thankful to the Allstate Research and Planning Center for the research support provided to him. Codrin Nichitiu's visit to Iowa State University during the summer of 1996 was made possible by the financial support from Ecole Normale Superieure de Lyon. Vasant Honavar's research was partially supported by the National Science Foundation (through grants IRI-9409580 and IRI-9643299) and the John Deere Foundation.

## References

[Ang81] D. Anguluin. A note on the number of queries needed to identify regular languages. *Information and Control*, 51:76–87, 1981.

[Ang87] D. Angluin. Learning regular sets from queries and counterexamples. *Information and Computation*, 75:87–106, 1987.

[BF72] A. Biermann and J. Feldman. A survey of results in grammatical inference. In S. Watanabe, editor, *Frontiers of Pattern Recognition*, Academic Press, pages 31–54, 1972.

[CM96] D. Carmel and S. Markovitch. Learning models of intelligent agents. In *Proceedings of the AAAI-96 (vol. 1)*, AAAI Press/MIT Press, pages 62 – 67, 1996.

[Dup96] P. Dupont. Incremental regular inference. In L. Miclet and C. Higuera, editors, *Proceedings of the Third ICGI-96*, Montpellier, France, *Lecture Notes in Artificial Intelligence 1147*, Springer-Verlag, pages 222–237, 1996.

[FB75] K. S. Fu and T. L. Booth. Grammatical inference: Introduction and survey (part 1). *IEEE Transactions on Systems, Man and Cybernetics*, 5:85–111, 1975.

[Gol78] E. M. Gold. Complexity of automaton identification from given data. *Information and Control*, 37(3):302–320, 1978.

[Lan95] P. Langley. *Elements of Machine Learning*. Morgan Kauffman, Palo Alto, CA, 1995.

[MQ86] L. Miclet and J. Quinqueton. Learning from examples in sequences and grammatical inference. In G. Ferrate *et al*, editors, *Syntactic and Structural Pattern Recognition*, NATO ASI Series Vol. F45, pages 153–171, 1986.

[OG92] J. Oncina and P. García. Inferring regular languages in polynomial update time. In N. Pérez *et al*, editors, *Pattern Recognition and Image Analysis*, World Scientific, pages 49–61, 1992.

[PC78] T. Pao and J. Carr. A solution of the syntactic induction-inference problem for regular languages. *Computer Languages*, 3:53–64, 1978.

[PF91] S. Porat and J. Feldman. Learning automata from ordered examples. *Machine Learning*, 7:109–138, 1991.

[PH96] R. G. Parekh and V. G. Honavar. An incremental interactive algorithm for regular grammar inference. In L. Miclet and C. Higuera, editors, *Proceedings of the Third ICGI-96*, Montpellier, France, *Lecture Notes in Artificial Intelligence 1147*, Springer-Verlag, pages 238–250, 1996.

[PH97] R. G. Parekh and V. G. Honavar. Learning dfa from simple examples. In *Proceedings of the Eighth International Workshop on Algorithmic Learning Theory (ALT'97)*, Sendai, Japan, *Lecture Notes in Artificial Intelligence 1316*, Springer-Verlag, pages 116–131, 1997. Also presented at the *Workshop on Grammar Inference, Automata Induction, and Language Acquisition* (ICML'97), Nashville, TN. July 12, 1997.

[PH98] R. G. Parekh and V. G. Honavar. Grammar inference, automata induction, and language acquisition. In R. Dale, H. Moisl, and H. Somers, editors, *Handbook of Natural Language Processing*. Marcel Dekker, 1998. (To appear).

[Pit89] L. Pitt. Inductive inference, dfas and computational complexity. In *Analogical and Inductive Inference, Lecture Notes in Artificial Intelligence 397*, Springer-Verlag, pages 18–44, 1989.

# The Data Driven Approach
# Applied to the OSTIA Algorithm*

José Oncina

Universidad de Alicante,
Departamento de Lenguajes y Sistemas informticos,
E-03071 Alicante (Spain)
oncina@dlsi.ua.es

**Abstract.** The OSTIA (Onward Subsequential Transducer Inference Algorithm) is an algorithm for inferring mappings between languages from input-output pairs, wich identifies in the limit any total subsequential function. It has been applied over a wide number of machine translation problems with great success. Incorporating the suggestions made in De la Higuera, Vidal and Oncina [dOV96] for automata inference, the DD-OSTIA (Data Driven OSTIA) is presented here. The experiments show a great reduction of the size of the training set needed for obtaining good models.

## 1 Introduction

The problems of Machine Translation (MT), when considered in their vast generality, are far from being satisfactorily solved. However, many MT tasks of interest to industry and business have limited domains; that is, lexicons are small in size and the universe of discourse is limited: reservation of flights, hotels, etc.; in tourist guide talks; broadcast of weather reports; etc.

Although natural languages are complex, the mappings defined by translations between them can be comparatively much simpler, specially when these languages are close each other as many European languages, and corpus-based (CB) techniques can be applied. There are some works that directly aim at placing Machine Translation (MT) within the CB framework ([BPPM93], [OGV91] and [VPL93]). Among these works, we will focus on one which is based on learning formal transducers. A formal transducer is a device that

---

* Work partially supported under grant TIC97-0941

accepts sentences from a given input and produces associated sentences of an output language. Formal transducers very seldom appear as components of MT systems. In fact, input-output relationships underlying natural language translation are very complex and the manual building of a transducer to account for these relationships, even in limited domain tasks, would be a too difficult or impossible task. However, some results in Transducer Learning have shown that this manual work can be avoided if a particular class of transducers is used, namely subsequential transducers. The *Onward Subsequential Transducer Inference Algorithm* (OSTIA) allows for the automatic learning of the structure of a (possibly very complex) transducer from a (perhaps large) set of training data consisting of input-output sentences [OGV91]. The performance of OSTIA can be significantly improved using the suggestions made in [dOV96] for learning Deterministic Finite Automata.

## 2   The algorithm

Formal descriptions of the OSTIA appeared elsewhere [Onc91] [OGV91] and here only an informal outline will be given.

A subsequential transducer is a finite-state network in which each edge has an *input symbol* and an *output string* associated to it. Each state may also have an output string associated to it. One of the states is the *initial state* and all the states can be *final* or *accepting*. For each state there is at most an outgoing edge for each symbol. An input string is *accepted* if its sequence of symbols matches the associated input symbols of a sequence of edges starting from the initial state. Every time an input string $s$ is accepted, an output string is produced which consists on the concatenation of the output strings associated to the edges and the string associated to the last state used to accept $s$.

Two subsequential transducers are equivalent if they perform the same input-output mapping. For any subsequential transducer it is always possible to find an equivalent transducer that has the output strings assigned to the edges and states in such a way that they are as "close" to the initial state as they can be. This is called the *Onward Subsequential Transducer*.

In order to learn a subsequential transducer, OSTIA takes a finite training set of input-output pairs of sentences, $T$, as input, and proceeds in tree stages:

1. A prefix tree representation of all the input sentences of $T$ is built. Then, null strings are assigned as output strings to both the internal nodes and the edges of this tree, while every output sentence of $T$ is associated as a whole to the corresponding leaf of the tree. The result is called *Tree Subsequential Transducer* (TST).
2. By systematically moving the longest common prefixes of the output strings, level by level, from the leaves of the tree towards the root, an *Onward Tree Subsequential Transducer (OTST)*, equivalent to the TST is obtained.
3. Starting from the root, all pairs of states of the OTST are orderly considered, level by level, and they are (recursively) merged if this merging is *acceptable*; i.e., if the resulting transducer is subsequential and is not in contradiction with $T$. This can be checked by testing some conditions on the edges and states involved in the merge and their associated input symbols and output strings. Sometimes, "pushing back" some output strings toward the leaves of the tree is required in order to try to make a state merging acceptable.

All these operations can be very efficiently implemented, yielding a very fast algorithm that can easily handle huge sets of training data. At the end of the process, an Onward Subsequential Transducer which is a compatible generalization of $T$ is obtained. It has been shown formaly that such strategy converges in the limit (that is, as the number of training pairs is sufficiently large) to the target subsequential transduction [Onc91].

Subsequential transducers and OSTIA have been successfully used so far in a variety of simple applications, some of which are quite contrived, such as learning to translate Roman numbers into their decimal representation, numbers written in English into their Spanish spelling, etc. [Onc91]. They have also been successfully applied to limited-domain language understanding, both in pseudo-natural and natural tasks like ATIS [CVO93], [PLV93]. Finally, some of these results have been extended by applying OSTIA to learn to translate (pseudo-natural) Spanish sentences describing simple visual scenes into corresponding English and German [CGV94].

The DD-OSTIA (Data Driven OSTIA) is inspired in the suggestion made by de la Higuera [dOV96] of substituting the order of considering the merge of states from the lexicogrphic order (by levels) to a heuristic order based on some measure of the equivalence of the states.

In the DD-OSTIA two mutual excluding subsets of states are defined in the OTST. In the beginning, the consolidated ($C$) subset only contains the initial state, and the frontier ($F$) subset contains all the states (not in $C$ because the OTST is a tree) that are directly reachable (using an edge only) from a state in $C$.

Only pairs of states $(c, f)$ such that $c \in C$ and $f \in F$ are considered. Given a state $f \in F$ such that there is no $c \in C$ such that $c$ and $f$ can be merged, then $f$ is added to $C$ and all the states directly reachable from $f$ (using one edge only) are added to $C$. Otherwise, the pair of states $(c, f)$ that maximizes the equivalence measure are merged.

This process is repeated until $F = \emptyset$. The equivalence measure that we have chosen is the reduction on the number of output symbols in the representation of the transducer if a tentative merge of both states is computed.

## 3   Experiments

The algorithm has been tested with an extension [CGV94] of a pseudo-natural task proposed by Feldman et al. [FLSW90]. The original task consisted of descriptions of simple two-dimensional visual scenes involving a few geometric objects with different shape, shade and size, and located in different relative positions.

The original language of this task was extended to cover the possibility of adding or removing objects to or from a scene, and the task was adapted to Language Translation experimentation [CGV94], [CVO93]. Nowadays this corpus is becoming a benchmark for testing language translation techniques. Some examples of sentences of this corpus can be seen in fig. 1.

For the Spanish to English task Lozano [Loz96], using a grammar association [VPL93] with Markov Models technique reported a

| |
|---|
| *Spanish:* un cuadrado grande y un circulo oscuro estan muy a la derecha de un triangulo mediano y oscuro y un circulo<br>*English:* a large square and a large circle are far to the right of a medium dark triangle and a circle |
| *Spanish:* se elimina el circulo oscuro que esta debajo del circulo y del triangulo<br>*English:* the dark circle which is bellow the circle and the triangle is removed |
| *Spanish:* se añade un circulo pequeño y oscuro muy por encima del circulo mediano y oscuro y del circulo mediano<br>*English:* a small dark circle is added far above the medium dark circle and the medium circle |

**Fig. 1.** Some pair of sentences for the Spanish to English translation from the Extended Feldman task.

22% of correct transduction using a training set of 1.000 pairs. This rate grows to 58% using 10.000 pairs. Using a grammar association technique with an association matrix the rates where 20% and 85% for 1.000 and 10.000 pairs respectively. Castaño and Casacuberta [CC97], using recurrent neural networks reported 53.1% and 98.4% for 500 and 3.000 pairs respectively. Prat [Pra98], using a grammar association technique [VPL93] reports, using 3.000 training pairs and using an improvement of the original technique a 81.6%, using the model 1 of IBM a 85.6%, using a multilayer perceptron a 95.% and using the Loco-C techniques a 95.8%.

In this section we perform these experiments for the Spanish to English translation. A series of increasing size random training sets, each including the previous one plus 100 new pairs, were used. Every set was submitted to the OSTIA and the DD-OSTIA and each subsequential transducer was used to translate 10.000 independent sentences. The results of the experiments appear in fig. 2.

It can be seen that using 3.000 training pairs the success ratio is 94.52%. Moreover, other sort of techniques (restrictions in the domain and range [OMV96]) can be applied in order to improve this rates.

# 4 Conclusions and future work

The use of a data driven strategy has shown to be fruitful when applied to the inference of subsequential transducers using OSTIA.

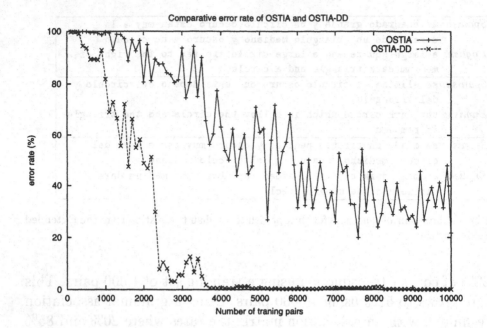

**Fig. 2.** Comparison of the error rates of the OSTIA and the DD-OSTIA when translating from Spanish to English within the extended Feldman task

One gets a dramatic reduction on the training set in order to obtain accurate models.

This technique can be merged with a technique of domain and range restriction [OMV96]. Other equivalence functions will be explored.

*Acknowledgements:* I thank M. Forcada and R.C.Carrasco for coments.

# References

[BPPM93] P. F. Brown, S.A. Della Pietra, V.J. Della Pietra, and R.L. Mercer. The mathematics of statistical machine translation: Parameter estimation. *Computational Linguistics*, 19:263–311, 1993.

[CC97] M. A. Castaño and F. Casacuberta. A connectionist approach to machine translation. In *Proceedings of the EuroSpeech'97*, volume 1, pages 91–94, Rodas, Greece, 1997. EuroSpeech'97.

[CGV94] A. Castellanos, I. Galiano, and E. Vidal. Applications of ostia to machine translation tasks. In *Grammatical Inference and Applications*, Lecture Notes in Artificial Intelligence, pages 93–105, Campello, Alicante, Spain, september 1994. 2nd International Colloquium on Grammatical Inference, Springer-Verlag.

[CVO93]    A. Castellanos, E. Vidal, and J. Oncina. Language understanding and subsequential transducer learning. In *1nd International Colloquium on Grammatical Inference*, pages 11/1–11/10, Clochester, England, 1993.

[dOV96]    C. de la Higuera, J. Oncina, and E. Vidal. Identification of dfa: Data-dependent versus data-independent algorithms. In *Grammatical Inference: Learning Syntax from Sentences*, Lecture Notes in Artificial Intelligence, pages 313–325, Montpellier, France, september 1996. 3rd International Colloquium on Grammatical Inference, Springer-Verlag.

[FLSW90]   J. A. Feldman, G. Lakoff, A. Stolke, and S. H. Weber. Miniature language acquisition: A touchstone for cognitive science. Technical Report TR-90-009, Internationa Computer Science Institute, Berkeley, CA, USA, 1990.

[Loz96]    M. Lozano. Asociación de gramaticas mediante modelos ocultos de markov. Master's thesis, Facultad de Informática, Universidad Politécnica de Valencia, Valencia, Spain, 1996.

[OGV91]    J. Oncina, P. Gracia, and E. Vidal. Learning subsequential transducers for pattern recognition interpretation tasks. *IEEE Transactions on Pattern Analysis and Machine Intelligence*, 13(3):252–264, March 1991.

[OMV96]    J. Oncina and 96 M.A. Varó. Using domain information during the learning of a subsequential transducer. In *Grammatical Inference: Learning Syntax from Sentences*, Lecture Notes in Artificial Intelligence, pages 301–312, Montpellier, France, september 1996. 3rd International Colloquium on Grammatical Inference, Springer-Verlag.

[Onc91]    J. Oncina. *Aprendizaje de lenguajes regulares y transducciones subsecuenciales*. PhD thesis, Universidad Politécnica de Valencia, Valencia, Spain, 1991.

[PLV93]    R. Pieraccini, E. Levin, and E. Vidal. Learning how to understand language. In *Proceedings of the EuroSpeech'93*, volume 2, pages 448–458, Berlin, Germany, September 1993. 3rd European Conference on Speech Communication and Technology.

[Pra98]    F. Prat. *Traducción automática en dominios restringidos: Algunos modelos estocásticos susceptibles de ser aprendidos a partir de ejemplos*. PhD thesis, Universidad Politécnica cd Valencia, Valencia, Spain, 1998.

[VPL93]    E. Vidal, R. Pieraccini, and E. Levin. Learning associations between grammars: A new approach to natural language understanding. In *Proceedings of the EuroSpeech'93*, volume 2, pages 1187–1190, Berlin, Germany, September 1993. 3rd European Conference on Speech Communication and Technology.

# Grammar Model and Grammar Induction in the System NL PAGE

Vlado Kešelj

Department of Computer Science, University of Waterloo,
Waterloo, Ontario N2L 3G1, Canada
vkeselj@uwaterloo.ca

**Abstract.** The input to the natural language parser generation system NL PAGE is in the form of an annotated natural language text, which is used to generate a grammar and a lexicon. This paper describes the format of the text, a new grammar model that is used in the system, and the process of grammar induction.

## 1 Introduction

Natural language processing contains two separate problems: The first is the linguistic problem of describing a natural language (NL), i.e., of creating an NL grammar and maintaining it. This includes defining an appropriate grammar formalism that can capture phenomena of a significant part of an NL and, still, can keep grammar complexity at a manageable level. The other problem is turning an NL grammar into a parser and providing a way in which the parser can be easily integrated with the rest of a system.

The system NL PAGE (Natural Language Parser Generator) is motivated by a growing need for more efficient and more sophisticated Internet information retrieval. Achieving such sophistication implies consideration of time-and-space efficiency requirements and the ability to produce parsers in various programming languages. The output routines for parsers in C and Java are developed, since C servers and Java applets acting as clients are good candidates for portable and efficient multi-agent systems for Internet information retrieval.

None of the available grammar models and parsers satisfied the requirements stated above, so a new grammar formalism, named FSGM, is defined and the system that induces grammars and generates parsers is implemented.

The FSGM grammar formalism is closely related to the affix grammars over finite lattices (AGFL's, [1]). An AGFL grammar can be easily embedded in the FSGM model. Additionally, it handles movement phenomena, and feature constraints are expressed in a way that provides direct generation of efficient, non-symbolic, low-level code.

On the other side, it is a difficult task for a grammarian to create and maintain a grammar for an NL. This general problem is well-known and a way of solving it is the subject of research in grammar induction. The various approaches to grammar induction can be distinguished depending on the underlying grammar formalisms and the level of supervision during the learning. A frequently used formalism is probabilistic context-free grammar [2], but the grammars in other models are also induced: e.g., constraint grammars [3], statistical decision trees [4], and so on.

A supervised induction method, based on the FSGM formalism, is presented. At the front end of our system, the input is provided in an easily maintainable form—a set of parse trees of sample sentences. The rules can also be explicitly given. NL PAGE extracts grammar rules and the lexicon, which are transformed into a parser. In the process of extraction of grammar rules, some rules are discarded. The process is described in Section 3.

An earlier stage in the system development was presented in [5].

## 2 Grammar model

The grammar is a context-free grammar (CFG) with binary features. These grammars are traditionally presented as a model with features that can have one of the two values: '+' or '−'. If we specify a set $F$ of all features appearing in a grammar, then instead of '+' and '−' feature values, we can associate each node in a parse tree with one *feature set* that is a subset of $F$. This subset consists of all features having value '+'.

The binary features are very convenient, since they can be efficiently handled by a computer in the form of a bit array, and they do nicely capture certain intuitive linguistic models, such as AGFL's (Affix Grammars over Finite Lattices [1]). We use only one simple type of *feature constraints*: for example, if we have a rule $X \rightarrow Y_1 Y_2 Y_3$ and if the symbols $X$, $Y_1$, $Y_2$, and $Y_3$ are associated with feature sets $F_0$, $F_1$, $F_2$, and $F_3$, respectively, then a typical feature constraint is $(F', \{2, 3\})$, where $F' \subset F$. It represents the condition $F' \cap F_2 \cap F_3 \neq \emptyset$, which has to be satisfied if the rule is to be applied. There is another type of constraint such as $(F', \{0, 2, 3\})$ that represents the same condition $F' \cap F_2 \cap F_3 \neq \emptyset$, but also gives a *feature propagation rule*: $F_0 \leftarrow F_0 \cup (F' \cap F_2 \cap F_3)$.

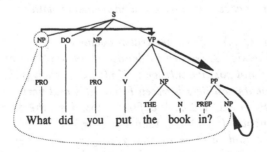

Fig. 1. Movement in our model

Our model also handles movement phenomena. Figure 1 illustrates the way we handle movement of one component: The component is "moved" during parsing along a path in the left-to-right direction, which is called *horizontal movement,* and then in the top-down direction, which is called *vertical movement.* (This is exactly the opposite direction of the movement in generation process.)

Movement in English (and many other languages) is typically handled in a left-to-right direction. Our method is also based on the assumption that the mechanism should handle unbounded movement, while the bounded movement can be handled by additional context-free rules. This solution is also justified by efficiency considerations. This method is novel—it is an intermediate solution between models that do not handle movement explicitly (e.g., GPSG) and more complex mechanisms (e.g., ATN).

Now, that we have described the intuition behind our model, we can formally define our grammar, which we call *Feature-Set Grammar with Movement (FSGM).* The FSGM semantics is explained in the example that follows definition.

**Definition 1 (FSGM).** *An FSGM is an 11-tuple $(N,T,P,S,F,\mathcal{F},f_T,f_P,h,v,g)$ where:*

- *$(N,T,P,S)$ is a CFG having set of nonterminals $N$, set of terminals $T$, set of rules $P$, and a start symbol $S \in N$. For any rule $r = X \to Y_1 \ldots Y_n \in P$, $|r|$ $(= n)$ denotes the number of symbols on the right-hand side, and we call it rule length. Having said that $(N,T,P,S)$ is a CFG, let us state that we can have two distinct rules in $P$ that are identical from the CFG perspective; however, in that case they have to differ in the relations that are defined further.*
- *$F$ is a finite set of features, which are simply some elements.*
- *$\mathcal{F} \subset 2^F$ is the set of distinguished feature sets.*
- *$f_T \subset T \times 2^{\mathcal{F}}$ defines a relation between terminals and sets of feature sets such that: $(\forall t \in T)(\exists t_f \in 2^{\mathcal{F}})\,(t,t_f) \in f_T$.*
- *$f_P \subset P \times (\mathcal{F} \times 2^{\{0,1,2,\ldots\}})$ attaches feature constraints to the rules, so that: if $(r,(F',I)) \in f_P$, for a rule $r \in P$, then $I \subset \{0,1,\ldots,|r|\}$.*
- *$h \subset P \times \{1,2,\ldots\}^2$ defines horizontal movements, so that if $(r,(i,j)) \in h$, then $i,j \in \{1,\ldots,|r|\}$ and $i < j$. For any rule $r$ and any three positive integers $i$, $j$, and $k$, $i \neq k$, we cannot have both $(r,(i,j)),(r,(k,j)) \in h$. This condition makes two horizontal movements with the same destination impossible.*
- *$v : P \to \{\bot,1,2,\ldots\}$ defines vertical movements: if $v(r) = i$, then $i =\bot$ or $1 \leq i \leq |r|$. The sign $\bot$ is used to denote absence of a movement. For any rule $r$ and positive integer $j$, if $v(r) \neq \bot$, then $(r,(j,v(r))) \notin h$. This condition prevents conflicts between horizontal and vertical movements.*
- *Finally, $g : P \to \{\bot,1,2,\ldots\}$ defines gaps, i.e., the final destinations of moved components. If $g(r) = i$, then $i =\bot$ or $1 \leq i \leq |r|$. For any rule $r$ and positive integer $j$, if $g(r) \neq \bot$, then $(r,(j,g(r))) \notin h$. For each rule $r$, at least one of $v(r)$ or $g(r)$ has to be equal $\bot$. The last two conditions prevent conflicts with horizontal and vertical movements.*

Let us use the example presented in Figure 1 to illustrate the introduced formalism and to explain semantics behind Definition 1: An underlying CFG could be defined as follows:

$$N = \{S, NP, DO, VP, PRO, V, PP, THE, N, PREP\},$$
$$T = \{What, did, you, put, the, book, in\},$$
$$P = \{r_1, r_2, \ldots, r_{12}\}$$

where

$$r_1 = S \to NP\ DO\ NP\ VP \qquad r_7 = V \to put$$
$$r_2 = NP \to PRO \qquad r_8 = NP \to THE\ N$$
$$r_3 = DO \to did \qquad r_9 = PP \to PREP\ NP$$
$$r_4 = VP \to V\ NP\ PP \qquad r_{10} = THE \to the$$
$$r_5 = PRO \to What \qquad r_{11} = N \to book$$
$$r_6 = PRO \to you \qquad r_{12} = PREP \to in,$$

and

$$S = S.$$

We want to enforce number and person agreement in the rule $r_1$. First, we define the feature set

$$F = \{sg, pl, p1, p2, p3\},$$

and we distinguish singletons and two additional subsets:

$$\mathcal{F} = \{sg, pl, p1, p2, p3, F_n, F_p\},$$

where $F_n = \{sg, pl\}$, and $F_p = \{p1, p2, p3\}$. The singleton sets are denoted by their only elements, e.g., $p1 = \{p1\}$.

Now, we define $f_T$, i.e., the terminal feature values:

$$f_T = \{(did, \{F_n, F_p\}), (you, \{F_n, p2\})\}.$$

The relation $f_T$ is interpreted as follows: If $(t, t_f) \in f_T$ for a terminal $t$, then in the parsing process we take the union of all sets in $t_f$ and the obtained feature set is attached to $t$. If there are more pairs in $f_T$ that are associated with the same terminal $t$, then the terminal $t$ is ambiguous and we can attach different feature sets to it.

In this example, the terminal 'did' can be associated with the feature set $F_n \cup F_p = F$, and there are no other possibilities.

The following set of constraints provides the necessary bottom-up feature propagation and agreement at the root:

$$f_P = \{\ (r_2, (F_n, \{0, 1\})), (r_2, (F_p, \{0, 1\})), (r_3, (F_n, \{0, 1\})), (r_3, (F_p, \{0, 1\})),$$
$$(r_6, (F_n, \{0, 1\})), (r_6, (F_p, \{0, 1\})), (r_1, (F_n, \{2, 3\})), (r_1, (F_p, \{2, 3\}))\}.$$

The interpretation of $f_P$ is: A constraint $(r, (F', I)) \in f_P$ requires that the rule $r$ can be applied only if there is a feature $f \in F'$ that belongs to all feature sets $F_i$ ($i \in I$), where $F_0$ is the feature set associated with the left-hand-side symbol of the rule $r$, and $F_1$, $F_2$, and so on are feature sets associated with right-hand-side symbols.

In our example: $(r_2, (F_n, \{0, 1\}))$ means that the rule NP $\rightarrow$ PRO can be applied if both symbols NP and PRO have at least one feature from $F_n$ in common. In practice, if we build a parse tree in the bottom-up direction, then this constraint is translated to adding all features from $F_n \cap F_1$ to $F_0$, where $F_0$ and $F_1$ are the feature sets associated with the symbols NP and PRO, respectively. We see that the index 0 is treated in a special way because the feature set of the left-hand-side symbol is evaluated according to these constraints and depending on the feature sets of the right-hand-side symbols, i.e., its children. The constraint $(r_1, (F_n, \{2, 3\}))$, for example, does not include the index 0, and it represents the constraint $F_n \cap F_2 \cap F_3 \neq \emptyset$.

Finally, let us show how the movement relations have to be defined in order to handle the movement presented in Figure 1:

$$h = \{(r_1, (1, 4))\}$$
$$v(r) = \begin{cases} 3 & \text{if } r = r_4 \\ \perp & \text{for all other rules} \end{cases}$$
$$g(r) = \begin{cases} 2 & \text{if } r = r_9 \\ \perp & \text{for all other rules} \end{cases}$$

These relation are interpreted in the following way: If the rule $r_1$ is applied, then its 1st right-hand-side component (NP) is moved horizontally to the 4th right-hand-side component (VP). When the rule $r_4$ is applied, a component is moved vertically to its $v(r_4) = $ 3rd right-hand-side component (PP). When the rule $r_9$ is applied, a component "coming" from the parent node replaces, i.e., fills gap at, the $g(r_9) = $ 2nd right-hand-side component (NP). This can be done only if the moved component has the same category as the gap, and satisfies all constraints that the gap has to satisfy.

Now, we formally define *derivation* in an FSGM (the semantic interpretation is explained after definition):

**Definition 2 (Derivation in FSGM).** *A derivation in an FSGM is similar to a CF derivation; the only difference is that each terminal and nonterminal is associated with an ordered triple* $(F', m, g) \in 2^F \times (\perp \cup (N \times 2^F)) \times \{\text{gap}, \overline{\text{gap}}\}$:

- *$F'$ is the feature set associated with the symbol,*
- *$m$ contains information about a moved component: $\perp$ means that no component is moved through this node, otherwise the component category and feature set are given, and*
- *gap denotes that the symbol is a gap filled by a component, otherwise (and more frequently) $\overline{\text{gap}}$ denotes that it is not a gap.*

*If $\alpha$ and $\beta$ are two strings of symbols from $N \cup T$ associated with such triples, then*

$$\alpha X(F_0, m_0, g_0) \beta \Rightarrow \alpha Y_1(F_1, m_1, g_1) \ldots Y_n(F_n, m_n, g_n) \beta,$$

*where* $(F_0, m_0, g_0), (F_1, m_1, g_1) \ldots (F_n, m_n, g_n)$ *are triples associated with symbols* $X, Y_1 \ldots Y_n$, *is a* derivation *if all of the following hold:*

- $g_0 = \overline{gap}$ *and there exists a rule* $p = X \to Y_1 \ldots Y_n \in P$.
- *For every terminal* $Y_i$ *there is a pair* $(Y_i, t_Y) \in f_T$ *such that* $F_i = \cup_{F' \in t_Y} F'$.
- *For all pairs* $(p, (F', I)) \in f_P$, $F' \cap (\cap_{i \in I, i \neq 0} F_i) \neq \emptyset$; *and* $F_0$ *is the union of sets* $F' \cap (\cap_{i \in I, i \neq 0} F_i)$, *for all pairs* $(p, (F', I)) \in f_P$ *such that* $0 \in I$. *If there are no such pairs, we define* $F_0 = F$.
- *For all* $(p, (i, j)) \in h$, $m_j = (Y_i, F_i)$.
- *If* $v(p) \neq \perp$, *then* $m_0 \neq \perp$ *and* $m_0 = m_{v(p)}$.
- *If* $g(p) \neq \perp$, *then* $m_0 \neq \perp$, $m_0 = (Y_{g(p)}, F_{g(p)})$, *and* $g_{g(p)} = gap$.
- *Finally, all of* $m_i$ *'s and* $g_i$ *'s,* $0 \leq i \leq n$, *that are not specified by these rules have to have values* $\perp$ *and* $\overline{gap}$, *respectively.*

**Definition 3 (Language generated by an FSGM).** *We say that an FSGM generates a language* $L \subset T^*$ *if* $L$ *is equal to the set of all strings* $w$ *such that there exists a sequence of derivations* $S(F', \perp, \overline{gap}) \Rightarrow^+ w'$, *for some nonempty* $F' \subset F$, *so that after removing symbols marked as* gap *and attached triples from* $w'$, *we obtain* $w$.

Let us illustrate derivations in FSGM using the example from Figure 1:

$S(F, \perp, \overline{gap}) \Rightarrow$

$\Rightarrow \ \mathrm{NP}(F, \perp, \overline{gap}) \, \mathrm{DO}(F, \perp, \overline{gap}) \, \mathrm{NP}(F_n \cup p2, \perp, \overline{gap}) \, \mathrm{VP}(F, (\mathrm{NP}, F), \overline{gap})$

$\Rightarrow^4 \ \mathrm{PRO}(F, \perp, \overline{gap}) \, \mathrm{did}(F, \perp, \overline{gap}) \, \mathrm{PRO}(F_n \cup p2, \perp, \overline{gap}) \, \mathrm{V}(F, \perp, \overline{gap})$
$\qquad \mathrm{NP}(F, \perp, \overline{gap}) \, \mathrm{PP}(F, (\mathrm{NP}, F), \overline{gap})$

$\Rightarrow^5 \ \mathrm{What}(F, \perp, \overline{gap}) \, \mathrm{did}(F, \perp, \overline{gap}) \, \mathrm{you}(F_n \cup p2, \perp, \overline{gap}) \, \mathrm{put}(F, \perp, \overline{gap})$
$\qquad \mathrm{THE}(F, \perp, \overline{gap}) \, \mathrm{N}(F, \perp, \overline{gap}) \, \mathrm{PREP}(F, \perp, \overline{gap}) \, \mathrm{NP}(F, \perp, gap)$

$\Rightarrow^3 \ \mathrm{What}(F, \perp, \overline{gap}) \, \mathrm{did}(F, \perp, \overline{gap}) \, \mathrm{you}(F_n \cup p2, \perp, \overline{gap}) \, \mathrm{put}(F, \perp, \overline{gap})$
$\qquad \mathrm{the}(F, \perp, \overline{gap}) \, \mathrm{book}(F, \perp, \overline{gap}) \, \mathrm{in}(F, \perp, \overline{gap}) \, \mathrm{NP}(F, \perp, gap)$.

After removing all triples and the symbol NP, since it is "marked" by 'gap', we get our sentence.

*Comparison with AGFL grammars.* Any AGFL grammar ([1]) can be directly translated to an FSGM grammar: The set of *terminal affixes* becomes $F$, *nonterminal affixes* translate to feature sets, and *consistent substitution* translates to our feature constraints. Thus, the AGFL grammar model is in a straightforward way embedded in the FSGM model. The AGFL model provides a convenient way of describing NL's for linguists [1]. Additionally, the FSGM model defines a formalism for movement phenomena and is used to define very efficient parsers.

## 3 Inducing the grammar from a parse forest

In the previous section we presented our formal grammar model. The presented definition is not very practical from a linguistic point of view. For this reason, an NL-text annotation syntax is developed, which provides a convenient way of modeling an NL. The syntax incorporates the standard parenthesized method of denoting phrase structure of a sentence. It includes some additional constructs for denoting feature constraints and movement. Instead of presenting a tedious definition of the syntax, we illustrate it using the previous example: The grammar presented in the previous example is implicitly defined in the following text:

```
\features: sg,pl,p1,p2,p3
\feature set: Fn={sg,pl}
\feature set: Fp={p1,p2,p3}

(S (NP (PRO What))
   (DO.Fn.Fp did)
   =2Fn =2Fp (NP ^Fn^Fp(PRO.Fn.p2 you))
   =1gap(VP (V put)
           (NP (THE the) (N book))
           ^gap(PP (PREP in) fgap(NP))))
```

Although used syntactically as feature sets, the 'gap' and 'fgap' words actually denote movement relations.

We can define a single CF rule with various feature constraints or movement relations in this way. These are distinct rules in FSGM. It is possible that the same CF rule can be applied under different conditions; this is especially frequent in situations with rules that might or might not include movement. However, this possibility would force us to write all feature constraints whenever we state a rule.

Let us consider the following simplified situation: We define a typical rule (S (NP...) (VP...)) and annotate it in a number of sentences before concluding that we need a feature constraint, i.e., that the rule has to be formulated as (S (NP...) =1Fn(VP...)). Now, we need to rewrite all previously annotated text, since the rule without constraints would always override the one with constraints. In a reverse situation, we may define a rule with all necessary constraints, and further on we want to annotate it (e.g., for documentation purposes) without stating the constraints and be sure that the proper constraints are attached to it.

The previous example illustrates the motive behind the idea that some of the directly generated rules should be discarded. If we have two rules: one without any feature constraints and the same rule with some feature constraints, then the former is said to be *dominated* by the latter rule and so is discarded. Before stating precisely how the rules are discarded, we define the dominance relation in FSGM's:

**Definition 4 (Dominance in FSGM's).** *Let $(N,T,P,S,F,\mathcal{F},f_T,f_P,h,v,g)$ be an FSGM. We say that a rule $r_1 \in P$ is dominated by a rule $r_2 \in P$ if and only if the following conditions are satisfied:*

*— $r_1$ and $r_2$ are identical rules in the underlying CFG,*

- *each feature constraint associated with $r_1$ by $f_P$ is a logical consequence of the constraints associated with $r_2$,*
- *for all $i, j \in \{1, 2, \ldots\}$, $(r_1, (i, j)) \in h$ if and only if $(r_2, (i, j)) \in h$,*
- *$v(r_1) = v(r_2)$, and*
- *$g(r_1) = g(r_2)$.*

Dominance is obviously a reflexive relation. In the process of grammar induction, we discard all strictly dominated rules (with their associated constraints and movement relations), i.e., we discard all rules $r_1$ such that there exists a rule $r_2$ so that $r_2$ is different from $r_1$ and $r_2$ dominates $r_1$.

The term "logical consequence" in the previous definition is ambiguous since we did not state what assumptions we can use in this logical inference. We use only the constraints associated with rules $r_1$ and $r_2$. Hence, nature of the set $F$, constraints of the other rules, contents of the distinguished feature sets, and so on, are not used.

In this way, the effective evaluation of the dominance relation is easily done, since the only inference rule is:

$$(F'_1, I_1) \text{ implies } (F'_2, I_2) \text{ if and only if } F'_1 = F'_2 \text{ and } I_1 \supset I_2.$$

There are no other inference rules, because for any set of feature constraints, such that there are no two constraints related in the above way, it is possible to construct a feature set $F$ and define the distinguished feature sets so that some arbitrarily chosen constraints are satisfied and the rest of them are not.

Due to this, it was easy to implement the dominance relation in our system, which performs well in practice. It is desirable to extend the above definition so that logical inference can be done using all available assumptions about the grammar. However, this problem is NP-complete in general. Let us show, using an example, how the 3-SAT problem can be reduced to our "dominance" problem:

Let an instance of the 3-SAT problem be the constraint satisfaction problem of the following formula:

$$(x_1 \vee \neg x_1 \vee \neg x_2) \wedge (x_2 \vee x_3 \vee x_4) \wedge (\neg x_1 \vee \neg x_3 \vee \neg x_4) \tag{1}$$

First, we define an FSGM grammar:

$N = \{S, A\}$, $T = \{t_1, t_2, t_3, t_4\}$, $S = S$, $F = \{x_1, \ldots, x_4, \overline{x}_1, \ldots, \overline{x}_4\}$,

$P = \{r_1, r_2, r_3\}$, where $r_1 = S \rightarrow A$, $r_2 = S \rightarrow A$, $r_3 = A \rightarrow t_1 t_2 t_3 t_4$,

$\mathcal{F} = \{\text{the set of all singletons}\} \cup \{F_1, F_2, F_3, F_4, G_1, G_2, G_3\}$,

   where $F_1 = \{x_1, \overline{x}_1\}$, $F_2 = \{x_2, \overline{x}_2\}$, $F_3 = \{x_3, \overline{x}_3\}$, $F_4 = \{x_4, \overline{x}_4\}$,

   $G_1 = \{x_1, \overline{x}_1, \overline{x}_2\}$, $G_2 = \{x_3, x_2, x_4\}$ $G_3 = \{\overline{x}_1, \overline{x}_3, \overline{x}_4\}$,

$f_T = \{(t_1, \{x_1\}), (t_1, \{\overline{x}_1\}), (t_2, \{x_2\}), (t_2, \{\overline{x}_2\}), (t_3, \{x_3\}), (t_3, \{\overline{x}_3\}),$

   $(t_4, \{x_4\}), (t_4, \{\overline{x}_4\})\}$,

$f_P = \{(r_1, (G_1, \{1\})), (r_1, (G_2, \{1\})), (r_1, (G_3, \{1\})), (r_2, (x_1, \{1\})),$

   $(r_2, (\overline{x}_1, \{1\})), (r_3, (F_1, \{0, 1\})), (r_3, (F_2, \{0, 2\})), (r_3, (F_3, \{0, 3\})),$

   $(r_3, (F_4, \{0, 4\}))\}$, and

$h$, $v$, and $g$ translate all rules to $\perp$.

Now, it can be verified that the constraints of the rule $r_2$ are unsatisfiable. The constraints of the rule $r_1$ are satisfiable if and only if the formula (1) is satisfiable. Hence, we see that the rule $r_1$ dominates the rule $r_2$ if and only if the formula (1) is not satisfiable. Hence, the problem of deciding the dominance relation in the most general case is NP-complete.

## 4  Parser generation part of NL PAGE

Finally, we briefly mention the generation part of NL PAGE. After a grammar and a lexicon are extracted, the system produces a parser in C or in Java. Those parsers are used in a demonstration multi-agent system for Internet information retrieval [5]. We emphasize that this grammar model is not a purely theoretical model, but it results in a generator that produces efficient NL parsers.

The experimental timing results of two produced parsers in C and Java are presented in Figure 2. The parsers are based on a grammar having 206 rules.

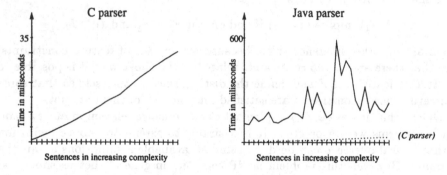

**Fig. 2.** Timing results for the generated C and Java parsers

Figure 2 gives parsing times of 31 test sentences of increasing complexity. The average parsing time is 14 ms for the C parser and 215 ms for the Java parser, on a Sun SPARCserver 670MP machine.

A training set of 15 sentences was used, and it was included in the set of 31 testing sentences. The sentence length ranges from 3 to 11 words. The generated lexicon contained 100 lexemes and there were no unknown words. All parses were correct.

The experiment is performed on a very small corpus and a very small grammar is generated. Although substantial testing remains, these preliminary results are encouraging.

## 5  Further directions

We have defined a precise grammar model in Section 2. In Section 3, we have presented an alternative notation, which is used to describe a NL. The notation provides a more flexible way of modeling a NL, leaving to the system to discard some "loose" rules. For future work, we are interested how this boundary between the exact grammar model and descriptive linguistic approach can be pushed towards the latter. The question is: How can a grammar designer to model a grammar by making localized descriptive additions without worrying about remote consequences? In this case, an FSGM would not be directly induced but it would be inferred from the provided data by the system itself. A step further is to provide the system with positive and negative examples of parse trees, and let it infer appropriate feature constraints.

Although we have shown that the general problem of evaluating the dominance relation is NP-complete, it might be useful to make the relation more general. This is a practical issue, which depends on an NL in question.

# 6 Conclusion

A novel grammar formalism and an associated grammar induction method are presented. The grammar model provides generation of efficient NL parsers, and the induction method provides a tool for creating and maintaining an NL grammar. The experimental results are encouraging, although the testing corpus is very small and larger experiments are part of the future research.

# References

1. C. H. A. Koster. Affix grammars for natural languages. In *Attribute Grammars, Applications and Systems, International Summer School SAGA,* Prague, Czechoslovakia, volume 545 of *Lecture Notes in Computer Science.* Springer-Verlag, June 1991.
2. F. Jelinek, J. D. Lafferty, and R. Mercer. Basic methods of probabilistic context-free grammars. In *Speech Recognition and Understanding: Recent Advances, Trends, and Applications. Proceedings of the NATO Advanced Study Institute,* pages 345–360, 1992.
3. Christer Samuelsson, Pasi Tapanainen, and Atro Voutilainene. Inducing constraint grammars. In *Third International Colloquium, ICGI-96,* pages 146–155, September 1996.
4. David M. Magerman. Learning grammatical structure using statistical decision-trees. In *Third International Colloquium, ICGI-96,* pages 1–21, September 1996.
5. Vlado Kešelj. Multi-agent systems for Internet information retrieval using natural language processing. Master's thesis, University of Waterloo, 1997.

# Approximate Learning of Random Subsequential Transducers *

Antonio Castellanos

Departamento de Informática, Universitat Jaume I
Campus de Penyeta Roja s/n, 12071 Castellón (Spain)
castella@inf.uji.es

**Abstract.** In this work, approximate inference of random partial Subsequential Transducers (STs) is addressed. Accessibility and distinguishability of a ST are defined and used to bound the maximum length of samples which are going to form representative sets for target STs. From these representative sets, the sample density required to obtain good approximate STs has been investigated. Dependency of the sample density on the number of states and on the accessibility and distinguishability of the target STs has been evaluated. As a general result, a decrease of the sample density has been found as these parameters increase, suggesting that accessibility and distinguishability are parameters as important as the number of states to evaluate learnability of STs.

## 1 Introduction

The problem of finding the minimum Deterministic Finite Automaton (DFA) consistent with a given sample was showed to be NP-hard [5]. Some other related problems have also been show to have similar complexity [1, 11, 12]. Nevertheless, Trakhtenbrot and Barzdin' [13] proved that in the concrete case that the sample set contains all labeled strings up to a given length, then there exists a polynomial algorithm which obtains the minimum DFA consistent with this sample set. Moreover, if this length is greater than $a + d$, then this algorithm yields the minimum DFA for the target language [13]. First parameter, $a$, is the accessibility of a DFA, which can be informally defined as the length of the longest string belonging to the set of shortest strings which allow for reaching all the states from the initial state [13]. Second parameter, $d$, is the distinguishability of a DFA and can be understood as the length of the longest string belonging to the set of shortest strings which distinguish every pair of non equivalent states [13].

More recently, Oncina and García [9] also proposed a polynomial algorithm to obtain the minimum DFA for an unknown language from samples of this language. The state merging process underlying this algorithm is essentially the same as that of the algorithm introduced in [13]. However, a significantly different proof establishes that such a state merging algorithm does not require all labeled strings up to a certain length. Only a *representative* set of samples (labeled

---

* Work partially supported by the Spanish CICYT, under grant TIC97-0745-C02-01.

strings) from an unknown language is needed to guarantee identification in the limit, yielding then the minimum DFA for the target language [9]. And, a sample set to be representative is only required to include a subset of labeled strings that fulfill two conditions on the minimum DFA and whose size is bounded by $n^2 \cdot m$ in the worst case, where $n$ is the number of states of the minimum DFA and $m$ is size of the alphabet [9]. Another property of the algorithm is that it always produces a DFA consistent with the sample, although only if the sample is representative, then it is guaranteed to be the minimum consistent DFA [9].

The result obtained by Oncina and García [9] implies that the set of all labeled strings up to length $a + d + 1$ is a representative sample. Moreover, some subsets of this set could be representative as well if they would contain appropriate labeled strings which fulfill the required conditions. This fact was empirically shown by Lang [7], whose experiments revealed that sparse fractions of the set of all labeled strings up to length $a + d + 1$ lead to exact identification of a DFA. However, at the same time, these experiments suggested that exact identification from sparse data is not possible in the average case, since such fractions remain fixed at least as the size of target DFAs is increased. On the contrary, they suggested that, in the average case, the density of sparse uniform samples required to infer an approximate DFA, which constitutes a good generalization for a target DFA, decreases as the size of the target DFA increases.

These theoretical and empirical results, mainly the last one, constitute required steps to start to really think about inference of DFAs, in particular, and any kind of finite state machines, in general, as a useful technique for some practical applications. In this work, some issues related with approximate inference of finite state machines are addressed, in an attempt to extend knowledge of their capabilities for practical applications.

Like regular languages, total subsequential functions were shown to be identifiable in the limit by a polynomial state merging algorithm [8, 10]. Subsequential functions are a subclass of rational functions that are realizable by deterministic finite state machines known as Subsequential Transducers (STs) [2]. The inference algorithm for total subsequential functions proposed by Oncina et al. [8, 10] is similar to the algorithm for inferring regular languages. That is to say, the algorithm always yields a ST which is consistent with the given sample, and if the sample is representative of a target total subsequential function, then the algorithm produces a minimum ST for this function. The size of this representative sample for a total subsequential function is also polynomially bounded, like for regular languages. More general classes of languages and functions have been shown to be non identifiable from polynomial size representative sets [6].

In this work, this algorithm has been used to obtain approximate STs for partial subsequential functions and the goodness of such an approximation has been only measured on the positive samples of the partial functions. First, accessibility and distinguishability of a ST have been defined in order to establish a relationship between the set of all samples of a total subsequential function up to a certain input string length depending on accessibility and distinguishability, and a representative set [8, 10]. In this way, the set of all positive samples of a partial subsequential function up to the input string length bounded by accessibility and distinguishability has been used as a representative set for the function, from which the sample density required to obtain good approximate STs has been investigated. Dependency of the sample density on the number of states and on the accessibility and distinguishability of the target STs has been evaluated. As a general result, a decrease of the sample density has been found as these parameters increase, suggesting that accessibility and distinguishability are as important as the number of states to evaluate learnability of STs.

## 2 Subsequential Transducers

### 2.1 Notation and Definition

Let be $\Sigma$ an alphabet and $\Sigma^*$ the free monoid over $\Sigma$. For every string $x \in \Sigma^*$, $|x|$ denotes the length of $x$ and $\epsilon$ is the symbol for the empty string. For all $x_1, x_2 \in \Sigma^*$, $x_1 x_2$ is the concatenation of $x_1$ and $x_2$. The *set of prefixes* of a string $x$ is the set $Pr(x) = \{x_1 \in \Sigma^* \mid x_1 x_2 = x,\ x_2 \in \Sigma^*\}$, and the *longest common prefix* of a set of strings, $Z \subseteq \Sigma^*$, is the substring [2, 8, 10]

$$\mu(Z) = x \ \Leftrightarrow \ x \in \bigcap_{x' \in Z} Pr(x') \wedge \forall x'' \in \Sigma^*(x'' \in \bigcap_{x' \in Z} Pr(x') \Rightarrow |x''| \le |x|).$$

The *right quotient* of a string $x \in \Sigma^*$ with regard to another string $u \in \Sigma^*$ is $u^{-1}x = v \Leftrightarrow x = uv$. If $u \notin Pr(x)$, then $u^{-1}x = \emptyset$.

A *Subsequential Transducer* (ST) [2] $\tau = (Q, \Sigma, \Delta, q_0, \delta, \lambda, \sigma)$ consists of an input alphabet $\Sigma$, an output alphabet $\Delta$, a set of states $Q$, an initial state $q_0$, two partial functions $\delta : Q \times \Sigma \to Q$ and $\lambda : Q \times \Sigma \to \Delta^*$ such that $dom(\delta) = dom(\lambda)$, and a partial function $\sigma : Q \to \Delta^*$. Functions $\delta$ and $\lambda$ are extended to $Q \times \Sigma^*$ by setting, $\forall q \in Q, \forall x \in \Sigma^*, \forall a \in \Sigma, \delta(q, \epsilon) = q, \delta(q, xa) = \delta(\delta(q, x), a), \lambda(q, \epsilon) = \epsilon, \lambda(q, xa) = \lambda(q, x)\lambda(\delta(q, x), a)$. Thus, the partial function $t_\tau : \Sigma^* \to \Delta^*$ realized by a ST $\tau$ is defined by $t_\tau(x) = \lambda(q_0, x)\sigma(\delta(q_0, x))$, $\forall x \in \Sigma^*$.

A *subsequential transduction* is a partial function realized by some ST [2].

### 2.2 Minimum Onward ST and Inference

Given a ST $\tau = (Q, \Sigma, \Delta, q_0, \delta, \lambda, \sigma)$, the *longest common output prefix* associated to a state $q \in Q$ is $\mu_\tau(q) = \mu(\{\lambda(q, x)\sigma(\delta(q, x)) \ / \ x \in \Sigma^*\})$ [3]. Then, a ST $\tau = (Q, \Sigma, \Delta, q_0, \delta, \lambda, \sigma)$ is *onward* if and only if $\forall q \in Q - \{q_0\}, \mu_\tau(q) = \epsilon$ [3, 8, 10].

For each subsequential function there exists a *family of minimum STs* (minimum number of states) whose structures of edges are identical, but whose output strings are assigned differently to the edges [3]. One of the STs of this family is onward, and thus, the *minimum onward ST* for the given function [3, 8, 10].

Total subsequential functions were shown to be identifiable in the limit [8, 10]. To this end, the *Onward Subsequential Transducer Inference Algorithm* (OSTIA) was introduced, which was guaranteed to always build an onward ST consistent with the sample it is provided [8, 10]. Afterwards, it was shown that if the sample

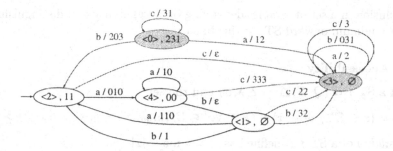

**Fig. 1.** Completely specified random ST generated by initially setting $|Q| = 5$, $|\Sigma| = 3$, $|\Delta| = 4$ and $L = 3$. Grey states and edges are useless and consequently removed. Each ST state displays its name and output substring, and each edge displays its input symbol and output substring.

is representative of the total subsequential function, then OSTIA produces the minimum onward ST for the function [8, 10]. The definition of this representative sample is presented in next section.

## 2.3 Random Generation

Random generation of STs has been based on a stochastic procedure for generating DFAs, which was also proposed by Trakhtenbrot and Barzdin' [13]. In this case, given a set of states $Q$, an input alphabet $\Sigma$, an output alphabet $\Delta$ and a predetermined maximum length $L$ for output strings, a ST is built by randomly choosing $\delta(q, x) \in Q$ and $\lambda(q, x) \in \Delta^{\leq L}$ for each $(q, x) \in Q \times \Sigma$, $\sigma(q) \in \Delta^{\leq L} \cup \{\emptyset\}$ for each $q \in Q$, and an initial state $q_0 \in Q$ [4]. Predetermined parameter $L$ is required to establish a finite space of possible STs. Symbol $\emptyset$ represents the undefined output string.

From these random assignments, useless states are removed from $Q$, and $\delta$, $\lambda$ and $\sigma$ are consequently updated. Useless states are those which cannot be reached from $q_0$ or which cannot reach a state $q$ such that $\sigma(q) \neq \emptyset$ ("accepting state"). In this way, a trim random ST is obtained with possibly less states and input and output symbols than those initially set. Figure 1 shows a completely specified random ST generated from a certain initial setting, emphasizing the final trim random ST obtained.

## 3 Identification Bound for a Subsequential Transducer

In this section, the relationship between a representative sample of a total subsequential function and accessibility and distinguishability of the minimum onward ST for this function is established. First, accessibility and distinguishability of a ST are defined. Then, a characterization of a representative sample of a total subsequential function is presented, which is intended to make easy to understand its inclusion in a set of samples depending on accessibility and distinguishability of the minimum onward ST for this function.

## 3.1 Accessibility

Given a ST $\tau = (Q, \Sigma, \Delta, q_0, \delta, \lambda, \sigma)$ and the set

$$C_{a_\tau} = \{x \in \Sigma^* \mid \delta(q_0, x) \in Q \wedge \forall x' \in \Sigma^*, \delta(q_0, x') = \delta(q_0, x) \Rightarrow |x'| \geq |x|\},$$

*accessibility* of a ST $\tau$ is defined as $a_\tau = \max\limits_{x \in C_{a_\tau}} |x|$.

The intuitive idea underlying this definition is the same as in the case of a DFA; i.e., the accessibility of a ST is the length of the longest string belonging to the set of shortest strings which allow for reaching all the states from the initial state. Moreover, provided that accessibility of a ST is only evaluated on input strings and function $\delta$, lower and upper bounds equal to those of accessibility of a DFA [13] can be stated; i.e., $\log_{|\Sigma|} |Q| - 1 \leq a_\tau \leq |Q| - 1$.

## 3.2 Distinguishability

Let $\equiv_\tau$ be an equivalence relationship on the states of a ST, such that $\forall p, q \in Q$,

$$q \equiv_\tau p \Leftrightarrow \forall x \in \Sigma^*, \sigma(\delta(q, x)) \neq \emptyset \Leftrightarrow \sigma(\delta(p, x)) \neq \emptyset \ \wedge$$
$$\mu_\tau(q)^{-1}\lambda(q, x)\sigma(\delta(q, x)) = \mu_\tau(p)^{-1}\lambda(p, x)\sigma(\delta(p, x)).$$

From this equivalence relationship, we will say that state $q$ is *equivalent* to state $p$ if $q \equiv_\tau p$. On the contrary, if $q$ is not equivalent to $p$, then $q$ is *distinguishable* from $p$. This means that $q$ and $p$ will be distinguishable if $\exists y \in \Sigma^* \mid$

$$(\sigma(\delta(q, y)) = \emptyset \ \wedge \ \sigma(\delta(p, y)) \neq \emptyset) \ \vee \ (\sigma(\delta(q, y)) \neq \emptyset \ \wedge \ \sigma(\delta(p, y)) = \emptyset) \ \vee$$
$$(\mu_\tau(q)^{-1}\lambda(q, y)\sigma(\delta(q, y)) \neq \mu_\tau(p)^{-1}\lambda(p, y)\sigma(\delta(p, y))).$$

In this case, we will say that $y$ *distinguishes* $q$ and $p$.

Therefore, given a ST $\tau = (Q, \Sigma, \Delta, q_0, \delta, \lambda, \sigma)$ and the set

$$C_{d_\tau} = \left\{ \begin{array}{l} x \in \Sigma^* \mid \exists q, p \in Q, \ x \text{ distinguishes } q \text{ and } p \ \wedge \\ \qquad \forall x' \in \Sigma^*, \ x' \text{ distinguishes } q \text{ and } p \Rightarrow |x'| \geq |x| \end{array} \right\}$$

*distinguishability* of a ST $\tau$ is defined as $d_\tau = \max\limits_{x \in C_{d_\tau}} |x|$.

In principle, the intuitive idea of this definition is also the same as that of a DFA; i.e., the distinguishability of a ST is the length of the longest string belonging to the set of shortest strings which distinguish every pair of non-equivalent states. However, there exists a significant difference. In a DFA, a string distinguishes two states if from one of them the string parsing through the DFA allows for reaching a final state while from the other does not. In a ST, two states can also be distinguishable if they produce different output strings when the same input string lead to a final state from both.

The upper bound for distinguishability of a ST is obviously the same as in the case of a DFA, $|Q| - 1$ [13]. However, lower bound for distinguishability of a ST is 0, which is obtained if values of function $\sigma$ are different among all states.

## 3.3 Identification Bound Based on Accessibility and Distinguishability

First, a characterization of a representative sample for a total subsequential function, which allows for exactly identifying the minimum onward ST for the function through OSTIA, is provided. Unlike the characterization provided by Oncina et al. [8, 10], here the representative sample is defined in terms of the minimum onward ST for the total subsequential function. This different presentation is only intended to avoid defining some more concepts on subsequential functions, which can be derived in a simple way from the minimum onward ST.

Given a subsequential function $t : \Sigma^* \to \Delta^*$ and the minimum onward ST for $t$, the *set of short prefixes* of $t$ is defined as

$$SP(t) = \{x \in \Sigma^* \ / \ \delta(q_0, x) \in Q \ \wedge \ \forall y \in \Sigma^*, \delta(q_0, x) = \delta(q_0, y) \Rightarrow x \leq y\}$$

where $\leq$ is the lexicographic order. And, the *kernel set* of $t$ is defined as

$$K(t) = \{xa \in \Sigma^* \ / \ x \in SP(t) \ \wedge \ a \in \Sigma \ \wedge \ \delta(q_0, xa) \in Q\} \cup \{\epsilon\}$$

Intuitively, the set of short prefixes constitutes a minimal set of shortest strings which allow reaching all states of the minimum onward ST. By its side, the kernel set contains the empty string and the extensions of all the strings in $SP(t)$ with all symbols in $\Sigma$ such that these extensions are prefixes of the domain of $t$.

In this way, given a total subsequential function $t : \Sigma^* \to \Delta^*$ and the minimum onward ST for $t$, $\tau = (Q, \Sigma, \Delta, q_0, \delta, \lambda, \sigma)$ a set of samples $T$ of $t$ is said to be *representative* of $t$ if and only if the following three conditions are satisfied:

1. $\forall x \in SP(t), \ \exists \ (x, \lambda(q_0, x)\sigma(\delta(q_0, x))) \in T$;
2. $\forall x \in SP(t), \forall y \in K(t), \ \delta(q_0, x) \neq \delta(q_0, y) \Rightarrow$
   $\exists \ (xw, \lambda(q_0, xw)\sigma(\delta(q_0, xw))), \ (yw, \lambda(q_0, yw)\sigma(\delta(q_0, yw))) \in T \ /$
   $\lambda(\delta(q_0, x), w)\sigma(\delta(q_0, xw)) \neq \lambda(\delta(q_0, y), w)\sigma(\delta(q_0, yw))$;
3. $\forall x \in K(t), \ \exists \ (xy, \lambda(q_0, xy)\sigma(\delta(q_0, xy))), \ (xw, \lambda(q_0, xw)\sigma(\delta(q_0, xw))) \in T \ /$
   $y \neq w \ \wedge \ \mu(\{ \ \lambda(\delta(q_0, x), y)\sigma(\delta(q_0, xy)), \ \lambda(\delta(q_0, x), w)\sigma(\delta(q_0, xw)) \ \}) \ = \ \epsilon$.

Condition 1 guarantees that all states of the minimum onward ST are implicitly represented in the sample. Second condition ensures that the sample will contain all input suffixes required to distinguish each state of the minimum onward ST represented in $SP(t)$ from all of its non-equivalent states represented in $K(t)$. Last condition forces all edges of the minimum onward ST to appear in the sample, and all of them to be able to associate the same output substring as in the minimum onward ST.

Notice that the number of samples required by condition 1 is $|SP(t)|$, by condition 2 is $(|SP(t)| - 1) \cdot |K(t)|$ and by condition 3 is $2 \cdot |K(t)|$. In this way, realizing that $|SP(t)| = |Q|$ and $|K(t)| = |Q| \cdot |\Sigma| + 1$ given a total subsequential function $t$ and its minimum onward ST, the number of samples required in a representative set of samples is $|Q|^2 \cdot |\Sigma| + |Q| \cdot |\Sigma| + 2 \cdot |Q| + 1$ at most, provided that some samples can be useful for more than one condition.

Now, next proposition establishes the existing relationship between accessibility and distinguishability of the minimum onward ST for a total subsequential function and exact identification of the function. The proof of this proposition is provided as an appendix.

**Proposition 1.** *Let be* $t : \Sigma^* \rightarrow \Delta^*$ *a total subsequential function and* $\tau = (Q, \Sigma, \Delta, q_0, \delta, \lambda, \sigma)$ *the minimum onward ST for t. The sample* $T = \{(x, y) \in t \mid |x| \leq a_\tau + d_\tau + 2\}$ *is representative.*

This proposition establishes that all transduction samples whose input string length is less than or equal to $a_\tau + d_\tau + 2$ exactly identify a total subsequential function, through OSTIA. As may be deduced from the above requirements on the size of a representative sample, some of the proper subsets of the set of samples whose input string length is $a_\tau + d_\tau + 2$ at most can also yield exact identification of the total subsequential function. However, most of these proper subsets cannot identify the function, and in this case, OSTIA produces a ST consistent with the sample $T$. This consistency mean that the ST could realize a function which can oscillate from being strictly sample $T$ up to being a close approximation for the target total subsequential function.

Random STs generated by the above procedure define not total but partial subsequential functions. In this case, from proper subsets of the set of all positive samples of the partial function whose input string length is less than or equal to $a_\tau + d_\tau + 2$, OSTIA can produce a ST which in the best case realizes a function $t'$ such that $\forall x \in dom(t)$, $t'(x) = t(x)$. Obviously, like for total subsequential functions, the ST could realize a function which is strictly sample $T$ or other functions which more or less approximate target partial subsequential function.

In subsequent experiments, OSTIA is used to obtain approximate STs for partial subsequential functions and the goodness of the approximation is measured only on the positive samples of the partial functions. In this way, the set of all positive samples of a partial subsequential function with input string length up to $a_\tau + d_\tau + 2$ is considered a representative set for the function, from which the sample density required to obtain good approximate STs is investigated.

## 4 General Experimental Setting

All random STs generated have been required that $a_\tau + d_\tau + 2 \leq 18$; otherwise, they have been discarded. They all also had 2 input and output symbols, and a maximum length of 5 for output strings. Provided that the maximum number of samples is $(|\Sigma|^{(a_\tau + d_\tau + 2) + 1} - 1)/(|\Sigma| - 1)$, $a_\tau + d_\tau + 2 \leq 18$ and $|\Sigma| = 2$ have constituted a balanced solution to make experiments computationally feasible.

On the other hand, similar to random DFA generation [7], random ST generation requires $|Q| + (1/4) \cdot |Q|$ states to have maximum probability of producing a ST with $|Q|$ effective states. In this way, only STs with 32, 64, 128, 256 and 512 effective states have been used, discarding STs with different number of states.

For each generated ST, $\tau$, all input strings accepted by $\tau$ up to length $a_\tau + d_\tau + 2$, along with their corresponding transduction strings, were obtained. In average, for all STs generated in the experiments, the size of this sample set was half of $|\Sigma^{\leq a_\tau + d_\tau + 2}|$. All these samples were randomly ordered to produce an ordered set, $M = \{m_1, \ldots, m_{|M|}\}$, which is one of all possible orders for them.

Taking the order of $M$ into account, for each predetermined success rate, the minimum number $i$ has been found such that the ordered subset $\{m_1, \ldots, m_i\}$ allows to infer an approximate ST which yield the given rate, and then, the quotient $i/|M|$ is the minimum density searched. Predetermined success rates were: 95.00%, 99.00%, 99.90% and 99.99%. In order to evaluate this success rate, the sorted total set $M$ is used as the test set. Obviously, this test set is not independent, but it is considered as *representative* for the function.

For each generated ST and for each predetermined success rate, another parameter has been measured. After finding the minimum number $i$ such that the set $\{m_1, \ldots, m_i\}$ leads to a good approximate ST, the relationship between the numbers of states of the approximate ST and generated ST has been computed.

With the purpose of studying the minimum density of training samples required to infer approximate STs which yield a predetermined success rate, two experiments have been carried out. In the first one, the evolution of the minimum density depending on the number of states of the target random STs has been evaluated. In the second one, the behavior of the minimum density has been analyzed with regard to the sum $a_\tau + d_\tau + 2$ for each number of states.

## 5 Minimum Density Depending on the Number of States

For each number of effective states in $\{32, 64, 128, 256, 512\}$, 100 STs have been generated which complied with the above conditions, and for each ST, the above procedures have been applied. Figure 2 shows averaged results of the experiment.

Minimum density of training samples decreases for all predetermined success rates when the number of states of target random STs increases (Fig. 2a). Nevertheless, in the last number of states (512), all minimum densities tend to become stable. In Fig. 2b an increase of the relationship between the sizes of learned approximate STs and target random STs can be observed, for predetermined success rate 95.00%. A similar behavior appears for the rate 99.00%, but from a greater number of states and more slightly. The other two rates, show a very slight decrease of the relationship between sizes when the number of states is increased, but on values close to 1.

## 6 Minimum Density Depending on Accessibility and Distinguishability

With the purpose of analyzing the dependency of the learned approximate STs from the sum $a_\tau + d_\tau + 2$, for each number of effective states the possible range of values of this sum such that $a_\tau + d_\tau + 2 \leq 18$ have been considered. These ranges are also strongly affected by the other fundamental experimental condition ($|\Sigma| = 2$). Thus, the different ranges considered depending on the number of effective states have been:

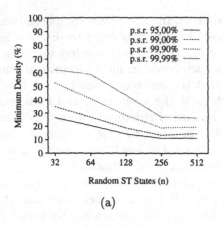 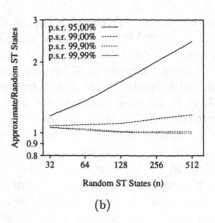

(a)                  (b)

**Fig. 2.** Averaged results of learning approximate STs for 100 random STs for each $|Q| \in \{32, 64, 128, 256, 512\}$, with $a_\tau + d_\tau + 2 \leq 18$, $|\Sigma| = 2$, $|\Delta| = 2$ and $L = 5$. From each random ST, $\tau$, a randomly sorted set of all positive samples up to input string length $a_\tau + d_\tau + 2$, $M = \{m_1, \ldots, m_{|M|}\}$, is produced. Within each $M$, minimum numbers $i_{psr}$ are searched, in such a way that $M_{i_{psr}} = \{m_1, \ldots, m_{i_{psr}}\}$ lead to approximate STs, $\tau_{psr}$, which yield each predetermined success rate (p.s.r.) on test set $M$. (a) Minimum Density: $(|M_{i_{psr}}|/|M|) \cdot 100$. (b) Approximate/Random ST States: $|Q_{\tau_{psr}}|/|Q_\tau|$.

| | | |
|---|---|---|
| **32** : 9, 10, 11, 12, 13, 14, 15, 16, 17, 18. | **256** : 15, 16, 17, 18. |
| **64** : 11, 12, 13, 14, 15, 16, 17, 18. | **512** : 17, 18. |
| **128** : 13, 14, 15, 16, 17, 18. | |

These ranges have been experimentally obtained from the observed values of the sum $a_\tau + d_\tau + 2$ in 500 random STs for each number of effective states [4].

For each number of effective states in $\{32, 64, 128, 256, 512\}$ and for each value of its possible range of the sum $a_\tau + d_\tau + 2 \leq 18$, 50 STs which complied with the above conditions have been generated. For each of them, the above procedures have been applied. Complete results of this experiment are detailed in [4]. Figure 3 presents averaged results for 128 effective states.

In Fig. 3a, an outstanding reduction of the minimum density of training samples for increasing values of $a_\tau + d_\tau + 2$ is observed, for all success rates. Similar behavior appears for the other number of states (32, 64, 256 and 512).

With regard to the relationship between the sizes of learned approximate STs and target random STs, the curves for predetermined success rate 95.00% tend to progressively start more separated from the value 1 as the number of states grows. At the same time, for 128, 256 and 512 states, these curves significantly increase as the sum $a_\tau + d_\tau + 2$, for each number of states, increases. For rate 99.00%, from the chart for 256 states a clear separation of the relationship from the value 1 can be observed, and for 512 states, an increase of the curve appears as the values of the sum $a_\tau + d_\tau + 2$ increase. The other two rates show more or less stabilized curves with values close to 1, in all cases.

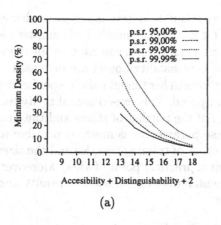
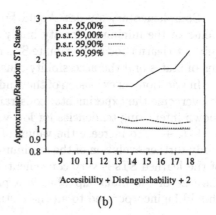

(a)                                          (b)

**Fig. 3.** Averaged results of learning approximate STs for 50 random STs for each $a_\tau + d_\tau + 2 \in \{13, 14, 15, 16, 17, 18\}$, with $|Q| = 128$, $|\Sigma| = 2$, $|\Delta| = 2$ and $L = 5$. From each random ST, $\tau$, a randomly sorted set of all positive samples up to input string length $a_\tau + d_\tau + 2$, $M = \{m_1, \dots, m_{|M|}\}$, is produced. Within each $M$, minimum numbers $i_{psr}$ are searched, in such a way that $M_{i_{psr}} = \{m_1, \dots, m_{i_{psr}}\}$ lead to approximate STs, $\tau_{psr}$, which yield each predetermined success rate (p.s.r.) on test set $M$. (a) Minimum Density: $(|M_{i_{psr}}|/|M|) \cdot 100$. (b) Approximate/Random ST States: $|Q_{\tau_{psr}}|/|Q_\tau|$.

# 7 Discussion and Future Work

Results presented in Sect. 5 show that the increase of the number of states of target random STs decreases the minimum density of training samples required to learn approximate STs, which can constitute good generalizations for target random STs. This decrease appears to be more important as the required goodness of the approximate STs is increased. Final stabilization of these decreases can be explained as a side effect of the experimental condition $a_\tau + d_\tau + 2 \leq 18$. As the number of states of target random STs grows, the possible ranges for $a_\tau + d_\tau + 2$ is being reduced, which make greater numbers of states to include random STs with low values of $a_\tau + d_\tau + 2$, increasing the average density such as results of Sect. 6 show.

The sum $a_\tau + d_\tau + 2$ for target random STs is demonstrated to strongly affect the minimum density of training samples required to learn approximate STs. The increase of this sum, for a given number of states, yield significant decrements of the minimum density. Moreover, this parameter appears to be as important as the number of states for determining the minimum density required to learn good approximations for a target ST. Note, for instance, that inferring an approximate ST for a target random ST with 32 states and $a_\tau + d_\tau + 2 = 18$ requires much less minimum density of samples than inferring an approximate ST for a target random ST with 128 states and $a_\tau + d_\tau + 2 = 13$. Results in Sect. 5 show that this should not be the expected behavior if only the number of states is considered. Clearly, the probability distribution of random STs with a given number of states, with regard to $a_\tau + d_\tau + 2$ influence these results.

Complementary studies should be carried out to determine if these decrements of the minimum density imply that the absolute number of samples required to learn good approximate STs remains more or less constant, as the number of states and the accessibility plus distinguishability bound are increased.

In addition, an extension of the study presented here should also be performed to overcome the experimental constrains imposed. This experimental study has shown interesting tendencies for low values of the number of states and the sum $a_\tau + d_\tau + 2$. To increase the values of these parameters as much as possible to study further evolution of the minimum density of training samples and the sizes of the learned STs is very convenient, from a practical point of view. Moreover, the size of the input alphabet is a parameter that can affect the results and should be incorporated to all these studies.

# References

1. D. ANGLUIN. "On the Complexity of Minimum Inference of Regular Sets", *Information and Control*, Vol. 39, pp. 337–350. 1978.
2. J. BERSTEL. *Transductions and Context-Free Languages*. Teubner, Stuttgart. 1979.
3. A. CASTELLANOS. "Funciones y Transductores Subsecuenciales", Technical Report, UPI 01-03/98, Universitat Jaume I, Castellón, Spain. 1998. (In Spanish)
4. A. CASTELLANOS. "Aprendizaje Aproximado de Transductores Subsecuenciales Aleatorios", Technical Report, UPI 02-03/98, Universitat Jaume I, Castellón, Spain. 1998. (In Spanish)
5. E. M. GOLD. "Complexity of Automaton Identification from Given Data", *Information and Control*, Vol. 37, pp. 302–320. 1978.
6. C. DE LA HIGUERA. "Characteristic sets for polynomial grammatical inference", in *LNAI (1147): Grammatical Inference. Learning Syntax from Sentences*, L. Miclet and C. de la Higuera (eds.), Springer-Verlag. Berlin, Germany. pp. 59–71. 1996.
7. K. J. LANG. "Random DFA's can be Approximately Learned from Sparse Uniform Examples", in Proceedings of the *5th ACM Workshop on Computational Learning Theory*, pp. 45–52. 1992.
8. J. ONCINA, P. GARCÍA. "Inductive Inference of Subsequential Functions", Technical Report DSIC-II/34/91, Univ. Politécnica de Valencia, Spain. 1991.
9. J. ONCINA, P. GARCÍA. "Inferring Regular Languages in Polynomial Update Time", in *Series in Machine Perception and Artificial Intelligence (1): Pattern Recognition and Image Analysis*, N. Pérez de la Blanca, A. Sanfeliu and E. Vidal (eds.), World Scientific, pp. 49–61. 1992.
10. J. ONCINA, P. GARCÍA, E. VIDAL. "Learning Subsequential Transducers for Pattern Recognition Interpretation Tasks", *IEEE Transactions on Pattern Analysis and Machine Intelligence*, Vol. 15, pp. 448–458. 1993.
11. L. PITT. "Inductive Inference, DFAs, and Computational Complexity", in *Lecture Notes in Artificial Intelligence (397): Analogical and Inductive Inference*, K. P. Jantke (ed.), Springer-Verlag, pp. 18–44. 1989.
12. L. PITT, M. K. WARMUTH. "The Minimum Consistent DFA Problem Cannot be Approximated within any Polynomial", *Journal of the Association for Computing Machinery*, Vol. 40, pp. 95–142. 1993.
13. B. A. TRAKHTENBROT, YA. M. BARZDIN'. *Finite Automata: Behavior and Synthesis*. North Holland Publ. Co., Amsterdam. 1973.

# Appendix: Proof of Proposition 1

In the following proof, note that the subsequential function $t$ is total and the ST $\tau$ is onward ($\forall q \in Q, \mu_\tau(q) = \epsilon$). In this case, the set $\mathcal{C}_{d_\tau}$ can be rewritten as

$$\mathcal{C}_{d_\tau} = \left\{ \begin{array}{l} x \in \Sigma^* \ / \ \exists q, p \in Q, \ (\ \lambda(q, x)\sigma(\delta(q, x)) \neq \lambda(p, x)\sigma(\delta(p, x)) \ \wedge \\ \forall x' \in \Sigma^*, \ (\ \lambda(q, x')\sigma(\delta(q, x')) \neq \lambda(p, x')\sigma(\delta(p, x')) \ \Rightarrow \ |x'| \geq |x| \ ) \ ) \end{array} \right\}$$

*Proof.* The set of samples $T$ is going to be shown to include all the samples required by the three conditions, which makes $T$ a representative sample.

1) By definition, $SP(t) = \{x \in \Sigma^* \ / \ \delta(q_0, x) \in Q \ \wedge \ \forall y \in \Sigma^*, \ \delta(q_0, x) = \delta(q_0, y) \Rightarrow x \leq y\}$. And by definition of lexicographic order, if $x \leq y$ then $|x| \leq |y|$, which means that $SP(t) \subseteq \mathcal{C}_{a_\tau}$. Therefore, $\displaystyle\max_{x \in SP(t)} |x| \leq \max_{x' \in \mathcal{C}_{a_\tau}} |x'| = a_\tau < a_\tau + d_\tau + 2$, implying that $\forall x \in SP(t), \ \exists \ (x, \lambda(q_0, x)\sigma(\delta(q_0, x))) \in T$.

2) Since $\displaystyle\max_{x \in SP(t)} |x| \leq a_\tau$, by definition of $K(t)$, $\displaystyle\max_{v \in K(t)} |v| \leq \max_{x \in SP(t)} |x| + 1 \leq a_\tau + 1$.

On the other hand, if distinguishability is $d_\tau$, then $\forall q, p \in Q, \ q \neq p \Rightarrow \exists w \in \Sigma^*, \ |w| \leq d_\tau$, such that $\lambda(q, w)\sigma(\delta(q, w)) \neq \lambda(p, w)\sigma(\delta(p, w))$.

Consequently, provided that $Q = \{\delta(q_0, x) \ / \ x \in SP(t)\} = \{\delta(q_0, y) \ / \ y \in K(t)\}$,

$$\forall x \in SP(t), \ \forall y \in K(t), \ \delta(q_0, x) \neq \delta(q_0, y) \Rightarrow$$
$$\exists w \in \Sigma^*, \ |xw| \leq a_\tau + d_\tau + 1 \ \wedge \ |yw| \leq a_\tau + d_\tau + 1 \ /$$
$$\lambda(\delta(q_0, x), w)\sigma(\delta(q_0, xw)) \neq \lambda(\delta(q_0, y), w)\sigma(\delta(q_0, yw)).$$

Thus finally,

$$\forall x \in SP(t), \ \forall y \in K(t), \ \delta(q_0, x) \neq \delta(q_0, y) \Rightarrow$$
$$\exists \ (xw, \lambda(q_0, xw)\sigma(\delta(q_0, xw))), \ (yw, \lambda(q_0, yw)\sigma(\delta(q_0, yw))) \in T \ /$$
$$\lambda(\delta(q_0, x), w)\sigma(\delta(q_0, xw)) \neq \lambda(\delta(q_0, y), w)\sigma(\delta(q_0, yw)).$$

3) Provided that $\displaystyle\max_{x \in K(t)} |x| \leq a_\tau + 1$, it is easy to see that $\forall x \in K(t), \forall c \in \Sigma \cup \{\epsilon\}, \exists \ (xcz, \lambda(q_0, xcz)\sigma(\delta(q_0, xcz))) \in T$ such that $z \in \Sigma^*$ and $|xcz| \leq a_\tau + d_\tau + 2$.

For each $x \in K(t)$, let be $c_1 \in \Sigma \cup \{\epsilon\}$ such that $\forall z_1 \in \Sigma^*$, with $|xc_1 z_1| \leq a_\tau + d_\tau + 2, \forall c_2 \in \Sigma \cup \{\epsilon\}, c_2 \neq c_1$, and $\forall z_2 \in \Sigma^*$, with $|xc_2 z_2| \leq a_\tau + d_\tau + 2$,

$$\mu(\{ \ \lambda(\delta(q_0, x), c_1 z_1)\sigma(\delta(q_0, xc_1 z_1)), \ \lambda(\delta(q_0, x), c_2 z_2)\sigma(\delta(q_0, xc_2 z_2)) \ \}) = \epsilon.$$

For each $x \in K(t)$, such a $c_1$ exists in $\Sigma \cup \{\epsilon\}$ because $\tau$ is an onward ST.

In this way, for each $x \in K(t)$, take $y = c_1 z_1$ for some $z_1 \in \Sigma^*, |xc_1 z_1| \leq a_\tau + d_\tau + 2$, and take $w = c_2 z_2$, for some $c_2 \in \Sigma \cup \{\epsilon\}, c_2 \neq c_1$, and some $z_2 \in \Sigma^*$, $|xc_2 z_2| \leq a_\tau + d_\tau + 2$. Thus, it appears that

$$\forall x \in K(t), \ \exists \ (xy, \lambda(q_0, xy)\sigma(\delta(q_0, xy))), \ (xw, \lambda(q_0, xw)\sigma(\delta(q_0, xw))) \in T \ /$$
$$y \neq w \ \wedge \ \mu(\{ \ \lambda(\delta(q_0, x), y)\sigma(\delta(q_0, xy)), \ \lambda(\delta(q_0, x), w)\sigma(\delta(q_0, xw)) \ \}) = \epsilon.$$

$\square$

# Learning Stochastic Finite Automata from Experts

Colin DE LA HIGUERA,
*EURISE, Université de Saint-Etienne, France*
*www.univ-st-etienne.fr/eurise/cdlh.html*

**Abstract.** We present in this paper a new learning problem called learning distributions from experts. In the case we study the experts are stochastic deterministic finite automata (sdfa). We deal with the situation arising when wanting to learn sdfa from unrepeated examples. This is intended to model the situation where the data is not generated automatically, but in an order dependent of its probability, as would be the case with the data presented by a human expert. It is then impossible to use frequency measures directly in order to construct the underlying automaton or to adjust its probabilities. In this paper we prove that although a polynomial identification with probability one is not always possible, a wide class of automata can successfully, and for this criterion, be identified. As the framework is new the problem leads to a variety of open problems.

**Keywords:** identification with probability one, grammatical inference, polynomial learning, stochastic deterministic finite automata.

## 1   Introduction and Related Work

Inference of deterministic finite automata (dfa) or of regular grammars is a favourite subject of grammatical inference. It is well known [6], [7] that the class cannot be identified in the limit from text, *i.e.* from positive examples only. As the problem of not having negative evidence arises in practice, different options as how to deal with the issue have been proposed. Restricted classes of dfa can be identified [2], [4], heuristics have been proposed [17] and used for practical problems in speech recognition or pattern recognition [12], and stochastic inference has been proposed to deal with the problem [3], [19].

Stochastic grammars and automata have been used for some time in the context of speech recognition [15], [13]. Algorithms that (heuristically) learn a context-free grammar have been proposed (for a recent survey see [18]), and other algorithms (namely the forward-backward algorithm for Hidden Markov Models, close to stochastic finite automata or the inside-outside algorithm for stochastic context-free grammars) that compute probabilities for the rules have been realised [15], [11]. But in the general framework of grammatical inference it is important to search for algorithms that not only perform well in practice, but that provably converge to the optimal solution, using only a polynomial amount of time.

For the case of stochastic finite automata the problem has been dealt with by different authors: Stolcke and Ohomundro [19] learn stochastic deterministic finite automata through Bayes minimisation, Carrasco and Oncina [3] through state merging techniques common to classical algorithms for the dfa inference problem. Along the same line Ron *et al.* [16] learn acyclic dfa, proving furthermore that under certain restrictions the inferred automaton is Probably Approximately Correct.

In these papers (but also those from the speech recognition community) an elementary assumption is that the presentation of the examples is unordered (or at least the algorithms do not use this information), and that strings with high probability can appear many times in the learning multisample. If for instance some string has probability 1/3, it is expected that one third of the sample is occupied by this string. This can be justified by practical reasons: when learning from a set where sampling has been done automatically, strings will be repeated according to their probability.

But let us deal with the case where it is not so, and suppose that the protocol does not allow for multiple presentation of data. This is intended to model the situation where the learning data is given to us by a human expert who will certainly not give us repeatedly the same string. Nevertheless the same expert will give us the strings accordingly to the distribution they follow. We can thus consider the expert as a black box containing the distribution to be learned. When requested the expert computes (accordingly to the distribution) a new example and adds it with a label to the learning set, and increases the label.

The expert acts as follows:
    *rank*←0
    Do *n* times (or less if less than *n* strings have non null probability)
        1. Generate an unseen example *u*
        2. Add (*u, rank*) to the learning set
        3. *rank*←*rank*+1

The problem of learning from examples delivered by such a black box will be called *learning from an expert* (as opposed to *multisample learning*) in the sequel.

In this paper the expert will be a sdfa. Usual techniques that infer sdfa by using the frequencies will not be able to learn from an expert generated sample. But we will prove that for restricted classes of sdfa the structure of the automaton can be learned, and the probabilities estimated. Furthermore the algorithms to do so are polynomial in the overall length of the data and convergence can be obtained with probability one.

In section 2 we provide the elementary definitions and techniques. The problem of learning sdfa involves two different matters: learning the structure or topology of the underlying automaton and estimating the probabilities. In the usual framework of multisample learning both problems are dealt with simultaneously. Two passes are needed in learning from an expert. In section 3 we study the easier of the two problems: estimating the probabilities given a structure. In section 4 we give our results concerning the inference of the structure. We conclude with a first list of open problems concerning this new model.

# 2 Preliminaries

An alphabet is a finite non empty set of distinct symbols. For a given alphabet $X$, the set of all finite strings of symbols from $X$ is denoted by $X^*$. The empty string is denoted by $\lambda$. A language $L$ over $X$ is a subset of $X^*$. Given $L$, $\overline{L}$ is the complementary of $L$ in $X^*$.

A *stochastic deterministic finite automaton (sdfa)* $A = <X, Q, q_0, P, \delta>$ consists of an alphabet $X$, set of terminal symbols, a set $Q$ of states, with $q_0$ the initial state, a partial transition function $\delta: Q \times X \to Q$ and $P$ a probability function $Q \times X \copyright \{\lambda\} \to \mathbb{Q}$, such that:

$$\forall q \in Q, \quad \sum_{x \in X \cup \{\lambda\}} P(q, x) = 1$$

We define recursively:

$$\delta(q_i, x.w) = \delta(q_{\delta(q_i, x)}, w)$$

And the probability for a string to be generated by $A$ is defined recursively by:

$$P(q_i, x.w) = P(q_i, x).P(q_{\delta(q_i, x)}, w)$$

The language generated by the automaton is defined as $L = \{w \in X^* : p(w) \neq 0\}$

In case the sdfa contains no useless nodes it generates a distribution over $X^*$. We can then also define recursively:

$$P(q_i, x.wX^*) = P(q_i, x).P(q_{\delta(q_i, x)}, wX^*)$$

$$P(q_i, X^*) = 1$$

The class of stochastic regular languages consists of all languages generated by stochastic non deterministic finite automata. Although not all stochastic regular languages can be generated by sdfa, we will concentrate on the deterministic case: indeed determinism plays a central part in grammatical inference, and by doing so we are following the same line as related work [3], [16], [19]

Two sdfa are equivalent if they provide identical probability distribution over $X^*$, *i.e.* if every string over $X$ has equal probability for both distributions.

A sample is a finite presentation of examples, *i.e.* a subset $S$ of $X^*$, and a rank function $\rho: S \to \mathbb{N}$ giving the rank of each element of $S$.

The main tool to compare distributions given a sample is to use the fact that given strings appear before others in the sample. This will be done through the following lemma:

**Lemma 1**

Let $A = <X, Q, q_0, P, \delta>$ be a sdfa, $S$ a sample and $w, w'$ two strings appearing in $S$ such that $w = uv$, $w' = u'v$ and $\delta(q_0, u) = \delta(q_0, u')$.

Then $\Pr(\rho(w) < \rho(w')) = \dfrac{P(q_0, uX^*)}{P(q_0, uX^*) + P(q_0, u'X^*)}$

**Proof**

$$\Pr(\rho(w) < \rho(w')) = \frac{P(q_0, w)}{P(q_0, w) + P(q_0, w')} =$$

$$\frac{P(q_0, uX^*) \cdot P(q_{\delta(q_0, u)}, v)}{P(q_0, uX^*) \cdot P(q_{\delta(q_0, u)}, v) + P(q_0, u'X^*) \cdot P(q_{\delta(q_0, u')}, v)} =$$

$$\frac{P(q_0, uX^*)}{P(q_0, uX^*) + P(q_0, u'X^*)}$$

◊

# 3 Learning the Probabilities

In this section we suppose that the actual structure (the automaton) is given, and the problem is to infer from the data the probabilities of the automaton. Thus we are given an automaton $A=<X, Q, q_0, P, \delta>$, and a sample $S$.

In the case of repeated data the results for the problem are two fold. On one hand the backward-forward algorithm performs well in practice [11], or alternatively Alergia [3] can compute the probabilities. On the other hand negative results [1], [10] show that if the size of the alphabet is allowed to increase no polynomial algorithm can achieve identification.

We start this section with a counter-example showing that in general the probabilities are hard to learn:

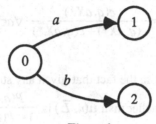

**Figure 1.**

When learning from an expert from the automaton of figure 1 a set of learning examples can contain at most 3 examples, and the 6 possible orderings or rank functions for these 3 examples will only allow us to learn 6 different distributions. Therefore a necessary condition for learning to be possible is that an infinite number of examples is available. This condition has to hold for all probabilities we wish to compute hence it is sufficient (but also necessary) that the automata has to accept an infinity of strings re-entering at least once into the initial state. Technically:

**Definition 1**
A sdfa is left infinite if $|\ \{u \in X^*\colon \delta(q_0, u)=q_0 \wedge \exists v \in X^*\ P(uv)>0\}\ | = \infty$

In order to learn the probability distributions we need the following notations:
given $q \in Q$, a language $L$ over $X$ and a string $u \in X^*$,
$$\mu(u, L)=\min\ \{\rho(uv)\colon v \in L\}$$
$$c(q, L)=|\ \{w \in X^*\colon \delta(q_0, w)=q \wedge \mu(w, L)<\mu(w, \bar{L})\}|$$
where if $\mu(w, L)$ is undefined then it is incomparable and so is not counted.

**Example** : given the following (indexed) presentation of examples on alphabet $X=\{a, b\}$: $[bb, \lambda, b, bbbabab, ba, ababaa, bbb, baabb, bbbaaa, bbbabbb, bababaaaaaaaaaaaabb, bbabb, aab, bbbabbbababaaabaaaabbb, abb, abbaaababbab, a, bbbb, baaabbbaa, bbaaab, bba, bbaa, abababab]$
and the automaton of figure 2,

$$\mu(\lambda, \{\lambda\})=1, \qquad\qquad \mu(\lambda, \overline{\{\lambda\}})=0$$
$$c(q_0, \{\lambda\})=3 \qquad\qquad c(q_0, \overline{\{\lambda\}})=4$$

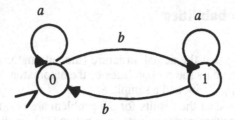

**Figure 2.**

**Proposition 1**

1 when $n \to \infty$, $P(q, \lambda) = \dfrac{c(q, \{\lambda\})}{c(q, \{\lambda\}) + c(q, \overline{\{\lambda\}})}$

2 when $n \to \infty$, $P(q, a) = \dfrac{c(q, aX^*)}{c(q, aX^*) + c(q, \overline{aX^*})}$ $\forall a \in X$

**Proof**

This follows by lemma 1 from the fact that given any string $u$ such that $\delta(q_0, u) = q$ the probability that $\mu(u, L)$ is smaller than $\mu(u, \overline{L})$ is $\dfrac{P(q, x)}{1 - P(q, x)}$ where $x = \lambda$ if $L = \{\lambda\}$, or $x = a \in X$ if $L = aX^*$. The $\mu(u, L) < \mu(u, \overline{L})$ correspond to the outcome of independent Bernoulli trials, and hence as the number of examples grows, we have the following convergence:

$$\frac{c(q, \{\lambda\})}{c(q, \overline{\{\lambda\}})} \text{ to } \frac{P(q, \lambda)}{1 - P(q, \lambda)} \text{ and } (\forall a \in X) \ \frac{c(q, aX^*)}{c(q, \overline{aX^*})} \text{ to } \frac{P(q, a)}{1 - P(q, a)}.$$

◊

This gives us a formula to estimate the different quantities $P(q, x)$ for each state $q$. The estimation of the probabilities converges if the automaton is left-infinite, *i.e.* if an unbounded amount of data is available.

Without formalising the computations, all this can be done in polynomial time. From a finite set of examples the probabilities will presumably not add up. It is therefore necessary at the end of the process to adjust the probabilities *via* :

$$P'(q, x) = \frac{P(q, x)}{\sum\limits_{y \in X \cup \{\lambda\}} P(q, y)}$$

Following with the example, we have:

$c(q_1, \{\lambda\}) = 1$ $\quad c(q_1, \overline{\{\lambda\}}) = 2$ $\quad c(q_0, aX^*) = 2$ $\quad c(q_0, \overline{aX^*}) = 6$ $\quad c(q_0, bX^*) = 3$

$c(q_0, \overline{bX^*}) = 2$ $\quad c(q_1, aX^*) = 2$ $\quad c(q_1, \overline{aX^*}) = 4$ $\quad c(q_1, bX^*) = 3$ $\quad c(q_1, \overline{bX^*}) = 3$

$P(q_0, \lambda) = 3/7$ $\quad P(q_0, a) = 1/4$ $\quad P(q_0, b) = 3/5$

$P(q_1, \lambda) = 1/3$ $\quad P(q_1, a) = 1/3$ $\quad P(q_1, b) = 1/2$

After adjusting we get :

$$P(q_0, \lambda)=60/179 \qquad P(q_0, a)=35/179 \qquad P(q_0, b)=84/179$$
$$P'(q_1, \lambda)=2/7 \qquad P'(q_1, a)=2/7 \qquad P'(q_1, b)=3/7$$

giving the following sdfa:

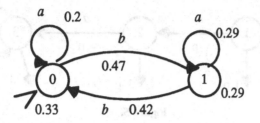

**Figure 3.**

# 4 Learning the Structure

In this section we aim at learning the topology of the automaton, given a finite ranked set of examples. In the context of learning from a multisample this is dealt with at the same time as the computation of the probabilities takes place [3], [16], [5]. When learning from an expert this cannot be so as and a first pass is needed to construct the underlying automaton. As in the previous section we start with an example showing that for arbitrary automata the topology cannot be inferred. This will lead to defining a restrictive class of sdfa for which we sketch a learning algorithm. The condition we give is sufficient but finding a necessary condition remains an open problem.

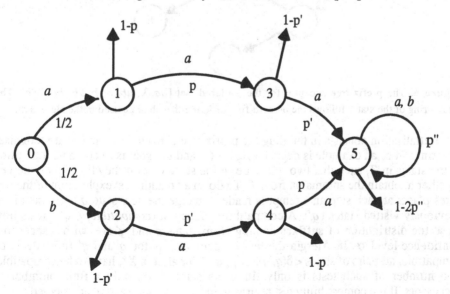

**Figure 4.**

Now notice that for all sdfa based on figure 4 such that p.p' is constant the distributions over all strings but { a, aa, b, ba} are equal. Thus only a finite number of strings would separate the distribution from the one given by the automaton depicted figure 5, making identification impossible.

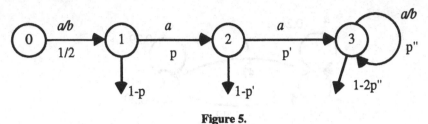

**Figure 5.**

The algorithm for learning the structure of a sdfa from an expert is based on Alergia, the algorithm inferring sdfa from multisamples [3].

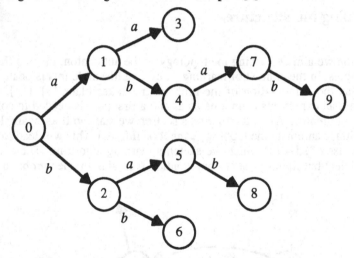

**Figure 6.** The prefix tree acceptor for the (ordered) set [aa, λ, abab, b, bb, bab, ab]. The numbering of the states follows the breadth-first ordering that shall be used in the algorithm.

Initialisation consists in building the prefix tree $T$ from $S$ (the tree that recognises all strings in $S$, an example is depicted figure 6), and the goal is to compute a partition of the states in $T$, such that two states are in the same class if they have to be merged together to obtain the automaton from $T$. To do so a breadth-first exploration of the tree takes place; at each step an attempt is made to merge the new state $q$ with one of the previously visited states ($q'$). A compatibility function (*compatible*($q$, $q'$)) tests how close the distribution of suffixes coming from states $q$ and $q'$ are, with respect to a confidence level $\alpha$. In Alergia the test is recursive, as for $q$ and $q'$ to be declared compatible, all pairs of states $<\delta(q, u), \delta(q', u)>$, for all $u$ in $X^*$, have to be compatible. The number of such tests is only finite, as state $q$ has only a finite number of successors. If the compatibility test returns value true, states $q$ and $q'$ are merged.

**Algorithm learn-by-merging**
    input : a sample $S$, a confidence level $\alpha$.
    output : a sdfa
    begin
        $A$= Prefix Tree acceptor from S.
        for $j = 1$ to $|T|$-1 do
                for $i$=0 to $j$ do
                        if compatible $(q_i, q_j)$ then
                                merge $(A, q_i, q_j)$
                                determinise($A$)
                                exit ($i$-loop)
                        end if
                end-for
        end-for
        return $A$
    end algorithm

The backbone of the algorithm is identical to that of state merging techniques inferring dfa from positive and negative data [14] This enables the algorithm to be modified to take into account quantitative information about the data, thus modifying the exploration order [5], [8].

In the case of learning from experts a compatibility test remains to be proposed. To do so it is necessary to translate the order preserving properties into Bernoulli trials. We turn to lemma 1 and define the following:

$$minrank(q,v) = \min\{\rho(uv) : \delta(q_0, u) = q\}$$

$$m(q,q',L) = |\{v \in L : minrank(q,v) < minrank(q',v)\}|$$

And using Hoeffding bounds [9] we have:

$$\left|P(q,q',L) - \frac{f}{n}\right| < \sqrt{\frac{1}{2n}\log\frac{2}{\alpha}} \quad \text{with probability larger than 1-}\alpha.$$

where $P(q, q', L)$ is the probability that given any string $v$ in $L$, a string $uv$ (with $\delta(q_0, u)=q$) appears before the first string $u'v$ (with $\delta(q_0, u')=q'$) in a sample of $L(A)$;
    and where $f= m(q, q', L)$, $n=m(q, q', L)+m(q', q, L)$

As the actual probability is unknown we can use the bound to compare two frequencies. We will use a base frequency ( the estimation of $P(q, q', X^*)$) to which shall be compared, for each prefix $v$ the frequency corresponding to the value $P(q, q', vX^*)$. This is possible by the following lemma:

**Lemma 2**
Let $L$ be a language over $X$. If $q$ and $q'$ are in the same class then:
$$P(q, q', X^*)=P(q, q', L)$$

**Proof**

$$\frac{\sum\limits_{u:\delta(q_0,u)=q} P(q_0,uv)}{\sum\limits_{u:\delta(q_0,u)=q'} P(q_0,uv)} = P(q,q',\{v\})$$

We have $(\forall v \in X^*)$:  . The result follows.

◊

If the difference between frequencies is more than the sum of the confidence ranges the states $q$ and $q'$ will be declared incompatible. The actual test is the following:

$$\left| \frac{m(q,q',L_1)}{n_1} - \frac{m(q,q',L_2)}{n_2} \right| < \sqrt{\frac{1}{2} \log \frac{2}{\alpha}} \cdot \left( \frac{1}{\sqrt{n_1}} + \frac{1}{\sqrt{n_2}} \right)$$

with $n_i = m(q, q', L_i) + m(q', q, L_i)$.

We now have the different elements to write our compatibility algorithm.

**Algorithm compatible**
    input : $q,\ q'$ : states
    output : Boolean
    begin
        $n_1 \leftarrow m(q,q',X^*) + m(q',q,X^*)$

        $val \leftarrow \dfrac{m(q,q',X^*)}{n_1}$

        do (for all $v \in X^*$ s. t. there exists in $S$ a string $uvw$ with $\delta(q_0, u) = q$)
        $n_2 \leftarrow m(q,q',vX^*) + m(q',q,vX^*)$

        if $\left| val - \dfrac{m(q,q',vX^*)}{n_2} \right| < \sqrt{\dfrac{1}{2} \log \dfrac{2}{\alpha}} \cdot \left( \dfrac{1}{\sqrt{n_1}} + \dfrac{1}{\sqrt{n_2}} \right)$ return false

        end do
        return true
    end algorithm.

**Convergence of the algorithm.**

It is clear that if $q$ and $q'$ belong to the same class, compatibility will be detected. But what of the opposite ? Can two states be merged due to a wrong result of the compatibility test ? Clearly, through our initial example the answer is positive. We can nevertheless give a sufficient condition so that two states belonging to two different classes be declared (in probability) incompatible:

**Definition 2**

Given a sdfa $A$, two states $q$ and $q'$ are *order-distinguishable* if $\exists\, u,\ v \in X^*$ / $P(q, q', uX^*)$  $P(q, q', vX^*)$ and all sets $\{w' \in X^*: \exists w \in X^*\ \delta(q_0, w) = \gamma \wedge P(wyw')\, 0\}$ (for $\gamma \in \{q, q'\}$ and $y \in \{u,\ v\}$) are infinite.

A sdfa is *order-distinguishable* if every pair of states in $A$ are order-distinguishable.

It follows that if two states corresponding to two order-distinguishable (classes of) states are tested for compatibility, given sufficient data (which is possible because the amount of possible data is unbounded), the test will return a negative answer. Furthermore the number of calls to function compatible is bounded by $|T| \cdot |T+1|/2$, where $|T|$ is the size of $T$. And inside each call only $|T_q|$ "$v$" will be used for tests, where $T_q$ is the sub-tree of $T$ at node $q$.

## Conclusion

The results in this paper are two-fold. We first present a new learning paradigm, that we call learning from an expert. Instead of learning a distribution from a multisample we use the order of appearance of the data to do so. We provide the techniques to learn stochastic deterministic finite automata in this context, although to do so we have to restrict technically the class. The derived algorithms are polynomial in the size of the learning sample, and they allow for identification with probability one. They do not (it is also the case with multisample learning algorithms [3], [5]) assure us to identify correctly from a polynomial quantity of data. There are several open questions to be dealt with. First the condition of order-distinguishability is obviously a very strong condition, and if a less restrictive one (or a more descriptive one) for which polynomial identification can be obtained it would be of interest. A second problem is, as in [16] to give sufficient conditions for only a polynomial (in the size of the sdfa) amount of data to be necessary even if this requires restricting further the class of automata. Finally a third trend of research would be to see how having access to more than one expert can help the learning. Perhaps even a second expert can help : one can use the amount of times experts agree on the ordering of specific strings as a compatibility test.

## References

1. [AW92] Abe, N. & Warmuth, M.K. (1992): On the Computational Complexity of Approximating Distributions by Probabilistic Automata. Machine Learning 9, pp. 205-260.

2. [Ang82] Angluin, D. (1982): Inference of reversible languages. Journal of the ACM 29 (3), pp. 741-765

3. [CO94] Carrasco, R.C. & Oncina J. (1994): Learning Stochastic Regular Grammars by means of a State Merging Method. Proceedings of the International Colloquium on Grammatical Inference ICGI-94 (pp. 139-152). Lecture Notes in Artificial Intelligence 862, Springer-Verlag.

4. [GV90] García, P. & Vidal, E. (1990): Inference of k-testable languages in the strict sense and application to syntactic pattern recognition. IEEE Transactions on Pattern Analysis and Machine Intelligence 12 (9), pp. 920-925.

5.  [GBE96] Goan, T., Benson, N. & Etzioni, O. (1996): A Grammar Inference Algorithm for the World Wide Web. In Proceedings of the 1996 AAAI Spring Symposium on Machine Learning in Information Access (MLIA '96), Stanford, CA, AAAI Press.

6.  [Gol67] Gold, E.M. (1967): Language identification in the limit. Inform.&Control. 10, pp. 447-474.

7.  [Gol78] Gold, E.M. (1978): Complexity of automaton identification from given data. Information and Control 37, pp. 302-320.

8.  [HOV96] de la Higuera, C., Oncina, J. & Vidal, E. (1996): Identification of dfa : data-dependant Vs data-independent algorithms. Proceedings of the International Colloquium on Grammatical Inference ICGI-96 (pp. 313-326). Lecture Notes in Artificial Intelligence 1147, Springer-Verlag.

9.  [Hoe63] Hoeffding, W. (1963): Probability inequalities for sums of bounded random variables. American Statistical Association Journal 58, pp. 13-30.

10. [K&al94] Kearns, M., Mansour, Y., Ron, D., Rubinfeld, R., Shapire, R.E. & Sellie, L. (1994): On the learnability of discrete distributions. In Proceedings of the 24th Annual ACM Symp. on Theory of Computing.

11. [LY90] Lari, K. & Young, S.J. (1990): The estimation of stochastic context free grammars using the inside outside algorithm, Comput. Speech. Language 4, pp 35-56.

12. [L&al94] Lucas, S., Vidal, E., Amiri, A., Hanlon, S. & Amengual, J.C. (1994): A comparison of syntactic and statistical techniques for off-line OCR. Proceedings of the International Colloquium on Grammatical Inference ICGI-94 (pp. 168-179). Lecture Notes in Artificial Intelligence 862, Springer-Verlag.

13. [N95] Ney, H. (1995): Stochastic grammars and Pattern Recognition. In Speech Recognition and Understanding, edited by P. Laface and R. de Mori, Springer-Verlag, pp. 45-360.

14. [OG92] Oncina, J. & García, P. (1992): Inferring regular languages in polynomial time. In Pattern Recognition and Image Analysis, World Scientific.

15. [RJ93] Rabiner, L. &Juang, B. H. (1993): Fundamentals of Speech Recognition. Prentice-Hall.

16. [RST95] Ron, D., Singer, Y. & Tishby, N. (1995): On the Learnability and Usage of Acyclic Probabilistic Finite Automata. Proceedings of COLT 1995, pp 31-40.

17. [RV87] Rulot, H. & Vidal, E. (1987): Modelling (Sub)string-Length-Based Constraints through a grammatical Inference Method. In Pattern Recognition : Theory and Applications. Eds: Devijver and Kittler, pp.451-459, Springer Verlag.

18. [Sak97] Sakakibara, Y. (1997): Recent Advances of grammatical inference. Theoretical Computer Science 185, pp. 15-45.

19. [SO94] Stolcke, A. & Omohundro, S. (1994): Inducing Probabilistic Grammars by Bayesian Model Merging. In Proceedings of the International Colloquium on Grammatical Inference ICGI-94 (pp. 106-118). Lecture Notes in Artificial Intelligence 862, Springer-Verlag.

# Learning a Deterministic Finite Automaton with a Recurrent Neural Network

* Laura Firoiu, Tim Oates, and Paul R. Cohen

Computer Science Department, University of Massachusetts at Amherst
lfiroiu,oates,cohen@cs.umass.edu

**Abstract.** We consider the problem of learning a finite automaton with recurrent neural networks from positive evidence. We train an Elman recurrent neural network with a set of sentences in a language and extract a finite automaton by clustering the states of the trained network. We observe that the generalizations beyond the training set, in the language recognized by the extracted automaton, are due to the training regime: the network performs a "loose" minimization of the *prefix DFA* of the training set, the automaton that has a state for each prefix of the sentences in the set.

## 1 Introduction

### 1.1 The Problem of Inducing a Deterministic Finite Automaton(*DFA*)

Our interest in *DFA* inference is partly induced from the larger goal of explaining how humans learn the grammar rules of their native language. There have been debates on whether children learn in an unsupervised mode, just by listening to other language speakers, or if they have innate knowledge of language. Therefore, it is an interesting problem to see what can be learned just by "listening to others", that is, from a set of grammatically correct sentences. While the complex syntactic rules of natural language cannot be encoded efficiently as regular grammar productions, fragments of language can be represented by finite automata. Thus this representation, which we prefer due to its simplicity, is adequate for some language fragments. Throughout the paper we will call the symbols of the alphabet "words" and the strings over the alphabet "sentences".

### 1.2 Deterministic Finite Automata and Recurrent Neural Networks

The problem of learning finite automata is difficult. Gold ([7]) showed that if the language is not known to be finite, then learning from positive evidence is

---

* This research is supported by DARPA/AFOSRF and DARPA under contracts No. F49620-97-1-0485 and No. N66001-96-C-8504. The U.S. Government is authorized to reproduce and distribute reprints for governmental purposes notwithstanding any copyright notation hereon.The views and conclusions contained herein are those of the authors and should not be interpreted as necessarily representing the official policies or endorsements either expressed or implied, of the or the U.S. Government.

not always possible, even from infinite sequences of words. Some other hardness (NP-complete) results concern finding the minimum, or a polynomial approximation of the automaton consistent with a finite sample([11]). In this work we study the problem of using simple recurrent neural networks ($RNN$) to induce a regular grammar that is consistent with a *training set* of sentences from the language, i.e. from positive evidence only. We use an Elman recurrent network to induce a $DFA$, and are interested in understanding what the network learns. The contribution of this paper is in informally characterizing the automaton extracted from the network states as a "loose" minimization of the *prefix DFA* (the automaton that has a state for each prefix of the sentences in the set). The absence of negative examples renders the problem of learning a $DFA$ underspecified and may lead to one of two extreme assumptions. One assumption is that negative examples do not exist, so the language consists of all the sentences over the alphabet and the minimum $DFA$ that represents the language is the automaton with just one state. The other assumption is that the negative examples are all the sentences that are not in the training set. The language is then the training set and it is accepted by the *prefix DFA*. This $DFA$ has a unique state for each prefix of the sentences in the training set and can be constructed and minimized in polynomial time(on the size of the training set). We call the minimized automaton the *training set DFA*. Since we do not make any explicit assumptions about the target language, the problem setting resembles the conditions of Gold's theorem on the impossibility of language learning from positive evidence, with the provision that the sequence of examples cannot be infinite.

Recurrent neural networks and deterministic finite automata are both state devices. It has been shown (see [13]) that there is an immediate encoding of a $DFA$ with $n$ states and $m$ input symbols into a simple recurrent neural network with $mn$ state units and integer weights. A $DFA$ can be easily extracted from such an $RNN$. Because neural networks can be trained with the backpropagation algorithm they have been a natural choice for the tasks of $DFA$ induction. For accepting automata, the network target output can be either the word following the current input, i.e. (*the prediction task*) ([4], [2]), or if both positive and negative examples are present, a value encoding the membership in the language of the current string ([6]). As in [2] and [4] we use an Elman recurrent network trained on the prediction task to induce a $DFA$, and are interested in understanding what the network learns. In section 2 we describe in more detail the setting of the learning task, the experiments and the results. In section 3 we observe that the network learns an approximation of the *training set DFA* of the training set and conclude that this network architecture and training regime are biased towards the extreme case where the training set is the entire language.

## 2   The Learning Task

### 2.1   The Grammar and the Training Sets

We wrote a small context free grammar ($CFG$), that generates natural-sounding sentences, similar to the one used in [5].From this CFG we obtained regular grammars by expanding the start symbol with all possible productions, up to arbitrary depths in the derivation trees. The resulting regular grammars can generate only subsets of the original language. These regular grammars are used to generate sentences with bounded length to obtain the training sets. The training sets are denoted "elm_rm_dn", where $m$ is the depth of the CFG expansion and $n$ is the maximum sentence length. The language generated by the CFG can be seen as the intended target lannguage.

## 2.2 Network Architecture and Training

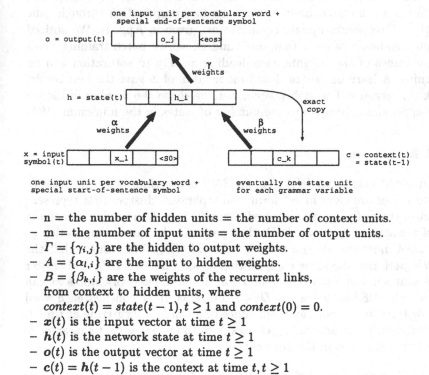

- n = the number of hidden units = the number of context units.
- m = the number of input units = the number of output units.
- $\Gamma = \{\gamma_{i,j}\}$ are the hidden to output weights.
- $A = \{\alpha_{l,i}\}$ are the input to hidden weights.
- $B = \{\beta_{k,i}\}$ are the weights of the recurrent links,
  from context to hidden units, where
  $context(t) = state(t-1), t \geq 1$ and $context(0) = 0$.
- $x(t)$ is the input vector at time $t \geq 1$
- $h(t)$ is the network state at time $t \geq 1$
- $o(t)$ is the output vector at time $t \geq 1$
- $c(t) = h(t-1)$ is the context at time $t, t \geq 1$

**Fig. 1.** Elman network architecture and notation.

We use Elman recurrent neural networks, with the architecture and notations as in Fig. 1. The activation function of the hidden and output nodes is the sigmoid $\sigma(x) = 1/(1 + exp(-x))$. The network is trained with the backpropagation through time algorithm and with the cross-entropy error function. All sentences in the training set are presented to the network, one word at each time step. There is one input unit for each word of the alphabet. An extra symbol, "start_of_sentence", marks the beginning of each sentence. Because the network state is set to 0 at the beginning of each sentence, this additional input unit provides the initial context and plays the role of the starting state of the automaton. The (approximately) periodic reset and the fact that sentences are short help avoid the state instability mentioned by Kolen in [8]. Thus, we avoid the solution proposed by Giles in [10] that relies on large weights and biases, since these large values hinder network training. The network is trained for the prediction task: the word following the input word in the current sentence represents the target output. There is also one output unit for each word in the alphabet, and a special marker "end_of_sentence". The cost to be optimized by the network is the cross-entropy error function. As described in [12], the cross-entropy function makes the network learn the probability distribution over the next words, conditioned on the input symbol and the network: $P(x(t+1) \mid \mathcal{N}, x(t))$. The network weights are updated on-line, with the backpropagation through time algorithm([14]). The weight update equations are given in App. A. We noticed that for input sequences of more than one hundred words, batch training yields large update values of the weights, thus leading quickly to saturation and no further learning. A learning rate of .1 and momentum of .9 gave the best results for network convergence. For each training set, we chose the number of hidden units to be approximately equal to the number of states in the minimum $DFA$.

## 2.3  $DFA$ Extraction

One method used to extract a $DFA$ from an $RNN$ is to assume that the network states whose values are close in $R^n$ form well separated clusters that represent the automaton states ([6]). Casey showed that this is a valid method, since the structure of the state space of an $RNN$ that performs the same computation as a minimal $DFA$ must encode the states of the $DFA$([1]). We assume that the trained $RNN$ performs the same computation as an unknown $DFA$ and cluster the network states in order to extract the $DFA$. From the network states we can identify either the $DFA$ states or the $DFA$ transitions. If we consider each word occurrence distinct and denote $w_t$ an instance of a word $w$ occurrring at time $t$, then this identification means finding classes of word instances that characterize either states or transitions in the automaton:

- state identification: the $RNN$ state $h(t)$ identifies the $DFA$ state $q_t$; the set $\{w_{t_i}\}$ associated with a cluster $\{h(t_i)\}$ forms a class of word instances that transition to the same $DFA$ state: the class identifies the state.
- transition extraction: the pair $\langle h(t-1), h(t)\rangle$ identifies a transition between the states $q_{t-1}$ and $q_t$; the set $\{w_{t_i}\}$ associated with a cluster $\{h(t_i-1), h(t_i)\}$ forms a class of word instances that occur only between a pair of $DFA$ states: the class identifies the transition.

Clustering of network vectors, $\{h(t)\}$ for states and $\{\langle h(t-1), h(t)\rangle\}$ for transitions is thus equivalent with clustering of word instances $\{w_t\}$. Because we use different vectors for state identification and transition identification, the resulting partitions may be different. Once the classes of word instances are found the

*DFA* extraction is easy. If the classes characterize *DFA* states then the productions are immediately identified by following the sentences in the training set. If the classes characterize transitions then the inference algorithm is the same as that for *Szilard* [1] languages of regular grammars. As described in [9], this kind of language has an inference algorithm that induces the grammar from a set of positive examples and runs in polynomial time on the sample size. We cluster the

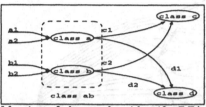
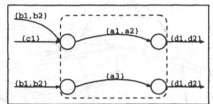

Merging of classes that identify *DFA* states: classes $\{a_1, a_2\}$ and $\{b_1, b_2\}$ are merged.

Merging of classes that identify *DFA* transitions: classes $\{a_1, a_2\}$ and $\{a_3\}$ are merged.

**Fig. 2.** Merging tests.

vectors hierarchically into a binary tree, as in [4], but then selectively merge tree nodes in order to obtain the word instance classes. The initial classes are formed by the instances associated with the leaves of the tree, where a leaf contains identical network vectors. Sibling leaf nodes are then merged if their associated classes satisfy a statistical *distributional criterion*. This criterion is necessary for two reasons: first, to stop the merging process from reaching the root of the tree, thus yielding a one-state automaton, and second to correct eventual "network errors", that is, states that have close values but cannot encode the same *DFA* state. When *DFA* states are identified we test for the similarity of the distributions over the next classes, since if two classes have identical distributions, then their states are equivalent in the *DFA* extracted from the current classes. For *DFA* transition identification the distribution similarities over the preceding classes are tested as well, because two classes cannot belong to the same transition unless they are preceded by the same classes and followed by the same classes. If we tested for equality instead of statistical similarity of the distributions, then generalizations might not take place. Fig. 2 illustrates the merging process. We use the G statistic, which has a $\chi^2$ distribution ([3]), to test if there is a statistically significant difference between two probability distributions. At the beginning of merging, because there are too many degrees of freedom (the number of states), and each state is usually preceded and followed by only one state, respectively, the statistical test is not effective at distinguishing the distributions. But as merging proceeds, irrespective of the distributional criterion, the

---

[1] A Szilard language of a regular grammar is generated by a finite automaton with the property that a terminal may appear on an arc only, thus uniquely labeling it (with the exception that transitions to the final state may share "labels").

number of states in each class increases, while the number of degrees of freedom decreases and the G statistic becomes effective and eventually stops the merging.

## 2.4 Results

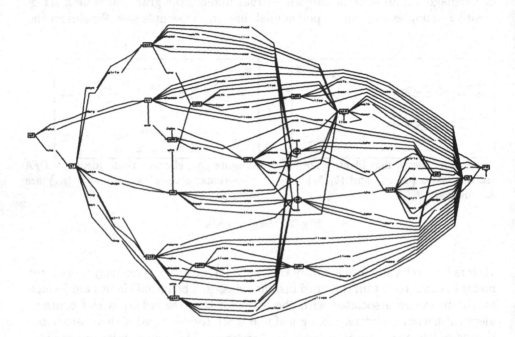

**Fig. 3.** Extracted *state DFA* for the training set "elm_r2_d5".

We trained the network with each of the chosen sub-languages and extracted the automaton by identifying either *DFA* states or transitions. The extracted automata were then minimized with a classical minimization algorithm. The induced automata are denoted *state DFA* and *Szilard DFA*. In Table 1 we list the results from an arbitrary trial for the training sets "elm_r1_d4" and "elm_r2_d5" and compare the induced automata with the corresponding minimized *training set DFA*. The results in Table 1 show that while for the smaller language the *training set DFA* is recovered (no generalization occurs), for the larger language the resulting automaton generates many more sentences than there are in the training set. While some of these sentences are in the language of the original CFG and represent correct generalizations, the majority of them is not. Many of the sentences not in the original language are generated by cycles in the induced *DFA*. Fig. 3 shows the extracted *state DFA* for "elm_r2_d5".

## 3  What *DFA* Is Extracted from the Trained Network ?

If the network always starts in the same state at the beginning of the sentence, then the *RNN* will reach the same state for all unique prefixes of the sentences

| language | hidden layer | # it. | state DFA states & sentences | Szilard DFA states & sentences |
|---|---|---|---|---|
| elm_r1_d4 7 states 56 sent. | 7 units | 16 | 7 states 56 (elm_r1_d4) 36 err. | 10 states 56 (elm_r1_d4) 36 err. |
| | | 32 | 7 states 56 (elm_r1_d4) 0 err. | 11 states 56 (elm_r1_d4) 32 err. |
| | | 64 | 7 states 56 (elm_r1_d4) 0 err. | 9 states 56 (elm_r1_d4) 32 err. |
| | | 128 | 7 states 56 (elm_r1_d4) 0 err. | 9 states 56 (elm_r1_d4) 0 err. |
| elm_r2_d5 22 states 512 sent. | 25 units | 16 | 22 states 512 (elm_r2_d5) 224 (elm_r2_d6) 64 (elm_r2_d7) 3942 err. | 22 states 512 (elm_r2_d5) 312 (elm_r2_d6) 64 (elm_r2_d7) ) 10000 err. |
| | | 32 | 19 states 512 (elm_r2_d5) 152 (elm_r2_d6) 624 err. | 23 states 512 (elm_r2_d5) 248 (elm_r2_d6) 384 (elm_r2_d7) 6064 err. |

**Table 1.** The original and induced automata for two increasingly complex sub-languages of the CFG grammar. The notation "384 (elm_r2_d7)" means that 384 sentences recognized by the induced *DFA* are also in the language elm_r2_d7. The sentences recognized by the induced automata were generated by imposing a soft limit of $d + 1$ words on the sentence length, where $d$ is the sentence length bound in the training set.

in the training set. For example, the two occurrences of the prefix "a b" in the sentences "a b c ." and "a b d ." will lead the network to the same state. Because network states belong to a continuous space, albeit computer representation of real numbers, it is not likely that two states corresponding to two different prefixes will be identical, unless the weights are adapted to encode precisely such an equality. So, for random weights, we can assume a one-to-one mapping between the set of sentence prefixes and the network states, and name each state with its associated prefix. It follows that the *RNN* will construct the prefix tree of the training set, as it can be seen in Fig. 4. This implies that the network tries to learn the probability distribution over the next words conditioned on the current prefix : $P(x(t + 1) \mid N, x(t)) = P(x(t + 1) \mid h_w, x(t)) = P(x(t + 1) \mid h_w)$ For the simple example in Fig. 4 the network states are: $\{h_0, h_a, h_{ab}, h_{ac}, h_{ab.}, h_{ac.}\}$. The states in a finite automaton are also defined by the strings of words that label the paths that lead to them from the start state. For example, in Fig. 4, state $q_1$ is defined by "a", while $q_2$ is defined by the set $\{$"a b", "a c"$\}$. It follows that the network states can be partitioned into groups that correspond to the states of the training set DFA. For the example in Fig. 4 the network states $\{h_{ab}, h_{ac}\}$ correspond to the *DFA* state $q_2$. Due to the cross-entropy error

**Fig. 4.** The prefix tree of the training set {"a b .", "a b ."} and the *DFA* that represents it.

function, the training process will adapt the network weights such that each state will describe the probability distribution over next words. For a prefix $w$, this constraint is described by the equation $\sigma(\Gamma * h_w) = P(next\_word \mid w)$. Because the sigmoid function $\sigma$ is injective, if two strings $w_1$ and $w_2$ have the same distributions over the next words, then the network will ideally assign two states $h_{w_1}$ and $h_{w_2}$ such that $\Gamma * h_{w_1} \approx \Gamma * h_{w_2}$. It follows that a possible solution is $h_{w_1} \approx h_{w_2}$. So, the network will eventually assign similar values for the states associated with prefixes that can be followed by the same words. This approximate merging is reminiscent of the classical *DFA* minimization algorithm. The difference is that while the *DFA* minimization algorithm, according to the definition of equivalent states, considers entire paths from each state to the final state, the network is trained only with the words immediately following the two states and thus has a different criterion for merging. This criterion, i.e. the probability distribution over next words, is weaker than the finite automaton state equivalence criterion, because it relies on less information. It follows that it can lead to mergings of states which are not equivalent in the *DFA* of the training set and thus to generalizations. For some training sets, for example like that in Fig. 4, the two criteria are equivalent: the first word of the path following a state uniquely identifies the path. For such cases, the network training process can converge to an approximate encoding of the training set *DFA*: the network states $\{h_{w_i}, h_{w_j}, \ldots\}$ corresponding to one *DFA* state might converge to values close in metric space. On the other hand, because the backpropagation algorithm may find only a local optimum of the cost function, it can happen that not all the states with the same probability distribution over next words are assigned similar values. Thus, states that are equivalent in the training set *DFA* might not get close values and are not merged. For the training set {"a b .", "a c ."} Fig. 5 shows how the encodings in the hidden layer of the states $\{h_{ab}, h_{ac}\}$ and $\{h_{ab.}, h_{ac.}\}$ converge towards the same values for a network with two hidden units. For this network the evolution of states during learning can be traced by examining the weight update equations. In order to explain, for example, how the values of the first hidden unit for the prefix states $h_{ab}$ and $h_{ac}$, which have the same probability distribution over next words, vary together in time, we look at the weights $\alpha_{c,1}$ and $\alpha_{b,1}$. The prefix states occur at time steps 2 and 4. Because these states are preceded by the same state $h_a$ , the difference in their activation values is given only by the difference of the two weights. It follows that the two weights, $\alpha_{c,1}$ and $\alpha_{b,1}$ must also have the same variation in time.

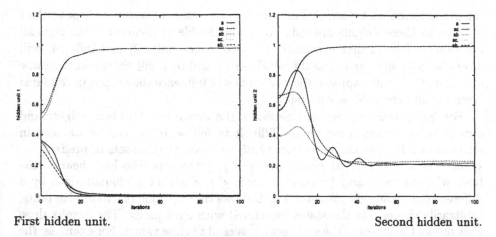

First hidden unit.                                                    Second hidden unit.

The values of the hidden units after 20000 iterations, for all the prefixes in the training set:

| prefix(time): | "a" (1) | "ac" (2) | "ac." (3) | "a" (4) | "ab" (5) | "ab." (6) |
|---|---|---|---|---|---|---|
| hidden unit 1 | 0.054 | 1.000 | 0.001 | 0.054 | 1.000 | 0.001 |
| hidden unit 2 | 0.062 | 0.123 | 1.000 | 0.062 | 0.123 | 1.000 |

**Fig. 5.** Convergence of the network states to an encoding of the states of the *DFA* that represents the training set for a network with two states.

From the fact that the network is reset at time 3 and from the update equations in App. A (infl is also defined there) it follows that the updates of these weights for one iteration in the training set are :

$$\Delta\alpha_{c,1} \propto \underbrace{h_1(2)[1 - h_1(2)]}_{positive}\underbrace{\{\text{infl}_{h_1}(2) + \sum_{a=1}^{n}\beta_{1,a}h_a(3)[1 - h_a(3)]\text{infl}_{h_a}(3)]\}}_{part2}$$

$$\Delta\alpha_{b,1} \propto \underbrace{h_1(4)[1 - h_1(4)]}_{positive}\underbrace{\{\text{infl}_{h_1}(4) + \sum_{a=1}^{n}\beta_{1,a}h_a(5)[1 - h_a(5)]\text{infl}_{h_a}(5)]\}}_{part2}$$

If we consider that at the beginning of training the weights are small, the second term can be ignored in both equations. Thus, the more important terms are $\text{infl}_{h_1}(2)$ and $\text{infl}_{h_1}(4)$. Because the two prefix states are followed by the same symbol, '.', the two terms become : $\text{infl}_{h_1}(2) = \gamma_{1,.} - \sum_{j=1}^{m}\gamma_{1,j}o_j(2)$ and $\text{infl}_{h_1}(4) = \gamma_{1,.} - \sum_{j=1}^{m}\gamma_{1,j}o_j(4)$ .

The values of the output units for the two states are:

- $h_{ab} : o_j(2) = \sigma(\sum_{i=1}^{n}\gamma_{i,j}\sigma(\alpha_{c,i} + const(B, context)))$
- $h_{ac} : o_j(4) = \sigma(\sum_{i=1}^{h}\gamma_{i,j}\sigma(\alpha_{b,i} + const(B, context)))$

From the above formulas it follows that $o_j(2)$ and $o_j(4)$ cannot be far apart, because the weights $\alpha_{c,i}$ and $\alpha_{b,i}$ , which are the only non-equal quantities in the above formulas, are small. Furthermore, the differences in the output values induced by these weights are reduced by the double application of the sigmoid function. It follows that eventually the two values $\mathrm{infl}_{h_1}(2)$ and $\mathrm{infl}_{h_1}(4)$ will have the same sign, and thus the weights $\alpha_{c,1}$ and $\alpha_{b,1}$ will change in the same direction. Once this happens, these weights will influence the output in the same direction and the process continues.

For larger training sets and networks the evolution of states, weights and output values becomes even more difficult to follow, but it can be watched in experiments. For the language "elm_r2_d5" we look at three sets of prefixes: { "the cats who hear", "the boys who see"}, { "the cats who hear hear", "the boys who see see"} and { "Mary", "the boy"}. Each set is characterized by a different probability distribution. Fig. 6 shows the evolution of two hidden units, arbitrarily chosen, for the states associated with each prefix. The graphs show that not all the states in the same set converged to close values. For example, the states "the boy" and "Mary" get different representations for those two units, despite their common next word probability distribution. On the other hand, the states of the first two sets do get similar values although they should be distinguished.

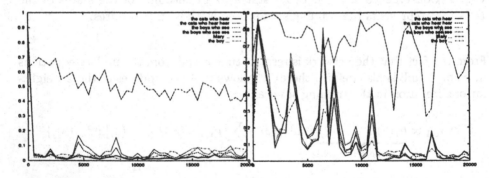

**Fig. 6.** Evolution of hidden units 9 and 17 over 20000 iterations of the states associated with prefixes { "the cats who hear", "the boys who see" }, { "the cats who hear hear", "the boys who see see"} and { "Mary", "the boy"}.

## 4  Conclusions

In the experiments conducted, simple recurrent neural networks were trained with sets of sentences from a regular language. The results indicate that the network is biased towards encoding the minimum automaton of the training set. For a very small network, an informal analysis of the learning process supports this finding. This bias is more evident for smaller training sets and networks, where it is more likely that the next words distinguish the paths to the final correctly minimize the *training set DFA*, mainly because the network minimization criterion, the similarity of probability distributions over next words, is less likely to yield the same results as the finite automata state equivalence criterion. This "incorrect" minimization may lead sometimes to good generalizations but also to many sentences not in the intended language.

## A  The Update Equations for Batch Training for Backpropagation Through Time and Cross-Entropy Cost Function

The following formulas use the notations and apply to the network described in section 2.2. As in [12], the cost function for a set of $T$ input-output vector pairs $\{\langle x(t), d(t)\rangle, 1 \leq t \leq T\}$ is: $C = \prod_{t=1}^{T} C_t = \prod_{t=1}^{T} P(d(t) \mid x(t), N(t))$. If the output units are seen as encoding the probability $o_j(t) = P(d_j(t) = 1 \mid x(t), N(t))$ then the logarithm of the cost function is:

$$\ln C = \sum_{t=1}^{T} \sum_{j=1}^{m} d_j(t) \ln o_j(t) + [1 - d_j(t)] \ln[1 - o_j(t)] .$$

For the prediction task, $\{d(t), d(t+1), \ldots\}$ are independent, given the network state, because this state encodes the prefix at each time step. The partial derivative of the $C_t$ component of this function to a parameter $\eta$ is:

$$\frac{\partial C_t}{\partial \eta} = \sum_{j=1}^{m} [d_j(t) - o_j(t)] * \frac{\partial net_{o_j}(t)}{\partial \eta} , \text{ where } net_{o_j}(t) \text{ is the net activation of}$$

output unit $j$.

The weight changes are : $\Delta \eta \propto \sum_{t=1}^{T} \frac{\partial C_t}{\partial \eta}$, with $\eta \in \{\gamma_{i,j}, \alpha_{l,i}, \beta_{k,i}\}$.

By applying the chain rule, the weight changes at a time step $t$ are:

- The weights from hidden to output units: $\frac{\partial C_t}{\partial \gamma_{i,j}} = [d_j(t) - o_j(t)] h_i(t)$

- Let $\text{infl}_{h_i}(t) = \sum_{j}^{m} \gamma_{i,j} [d_j(t) - o_j(t)]$. Let $\delta_{i,a}$ be the function that is 1 when $a = i$ and 0 otherwise.

- The weights from input to hidden units: $\frac{\partial C_t}{\partial \alpha_{l,i}} = \sum_{a=1}^{n} h_a(t)[1 - h_a(t)] \text{infl}_{h_a}(t) \frac{\partial net_{h_a}(t)}{\partial \alpha_{l,i}}$

- The recurrent weights from context to hidden units:

$$\frac{\partial C_t}{\partial \beta_{k,i}} = \sum_{a=1}^{n} h_a(t)[1 - h_a(t)] \text{infl}_{h_a}(t) \frac{\partial net_{h_a}(t)}{\partial \beta_{k,i}}$$

The derivatives of the net activations $\{net_a\}$ are defined iteratively:

- $t = 0 : h_a(0) = 0$ and $\frac{\partial net_{h_a}}{\partial \eta} = 0$

- $\frac{\partial net_{h_a}(t)}{\partial \alpha_{l,i}} = \delta_{i,a} x_l(t) + \sum_{b=1}^{n} \beta_{b,a} h_b(t)[1 - h_b(t)] \frac{\partial net_{h_b}(t-1)}{\partial \alpha_{l,i}}$

$$- \frac{\partial net_{h_a}(t)}{\partial \beta_{k,i}} = \delta_{i,a} k_k(t-1) + \sum_{b=1}^{n} \beta_{b,a} h_b(t)[1 - h_b(t)] \frac{\partial net_{h_b}(t-1)}{\partial \beta_{k,i}}$$

From the above equations it follows that:

$$- t = 1 : \frac{\partial net_{h_a}(t)}{\partial \beta_{k,i}} = 0 \;,\; \frac{\partial net_{h_a}(t)}{\partial \alpha_{l,i}} = \delta_{i,a} x_l(1)$$

$$- t = 2 : \frac{\partial net_{h_a}(t)}{\partial \beta_{k,i}} = \delta_{i,a} h_k(1)$$

$$\frac{\partial net_{h_a}(t)}{\partial \alpha_{l,i}} = \delta_{i,a} x_l(2) + \beta_{i,a} h_i(1)[1 - h_i(1)] x_l(1)$$

$$- t = 3 : \frac{\partial net_{h_a}(t)}{\partial \beta_{k,i}} = \delta_{i,a} h_k(2) + \beta_{i,a} h_i(1)[1 - h_i(1)] h_k(1)$$

$$\frac{\partial net_{h_a}(t)}{\partial \alpha_{l,i}} = \delta_{i,a} x_l(3) + \beta_{i,a} h_i(2)[1 - h_i(2)] x_l(2) + \sum_{b=1}^{n} \beta_{b,a} h_b(2)[1 - h_b(2)] \beta_{i,b} h_i(1)[1 - h_i(1)] x_l(1)$$

# References

1. M. Casey. The dynamics of discrete-time computation, with application to recurrent neural networks and finite state machine extraction. *Neural Computation*, 8:1135–1178, 1996.
2. A. Cleeremans, D. Servan-Schreiber, and J.L. McClelland. Finite state automata and simple recurrent networks. *Neural Computation*, 1:372–381, 1989.
3. P. R. Cohen. *Empirical Methods for Artificial Intelligence*. The MIT Press, 1995.
4. J. L. Elman. Finding structure in time. *Cognitive science*, 14:179–211, 1990.
5. J. L. Elman. Distributed representations, simple recurrent networks, and grammatical structure. *Machine Learning*, 1992.
6. C. L. Giles, C. B. Miller, D. Chen, G. Z. Sun, H. H. Chen, and Y. C. Lee. Extracting and learning an *unknown* grammar with recurrent neural networks. In *Advances in Neural Information Processing Systems 4*. 1992.
7. E. M. Gold. Language identification in the limit. *Information and control*, 10:447–474, 1967.
8. John F. Kolen. Fool's gold: Extracting finite state machines from recurrent network dynamics. In *Advances in Neural Information Processing Systems 6*, 1994.
9. E. Makinen. Inferring regular languages by merging nonterminals. Technical Report A-1997-6, Department of Computer Science, University of Tampere, 1997.
10. Christian W. Omlin and C. Lee Giles. Constructing deterministic finite-state automata in recurrent neural networks. *Journal of the ACM*, 45(6):937, 1996.
11. Leonard Pitt and Manfred K. Warmuth. The minimum consistent dfa problem cannot be approximated within any polynomial. *Journal of the ACM*, 40(1):95–142, 1993.
12. D. E. Rumelhart, R. Durbin, R. Golden, and Y. Chauvin. Backpropagation: The basic theory. In *Backpropagation: Theory, architectures, and applications*. Erlbaum, 1993.
13. H. T Siegelmann. *Theoretical Foundations of Recurrent Neural Networks*. PhD thesis, Rutgers, 1992.
14. P. N. Werbos. *The roots of backpropagation*. John Wiley & Sons, Inc., 1994.

# Applying Grammatical Inference in Learning a Language Model for Oral Dialogue

Jacques Chodorowski and Laurent Miclet

ENSSAT - IRISA ** {chodorow, miclet}@enssat.fr

**Abstract.** We present an application of the ECGI algorithm to the learning of a language model for Speech Recognition. Results are given on a real dialogue corpus. Integrating this technique in a Speech Recognizer is discussed.

**Key Words :** *Grammatical Inference, Speech Recognition*

## 1 Grammatical Inference and Natural Language Processing

### 1.1 Natural Language Learning

It is only recently that the two main domains of Artificial Intelligence : Machine Learning (ML) and Natural Language Processing (NLP) have crossed paths. This encounter has given birth to what is currently called Natural Language Learning (NLL). Although several pioneering works can be quoted, it was only in the mid-nineties [DvdBW97], [WRS96] that the systematic study of the possibilities of cross-fertilization between these two domains appeared.

The variety and the practical interest of NLP applications to which ML could be useful are quite vast : they span from automatic text tagging to learning of prosody for speech synthesis, from the discovery of syntactic rules in the sequencing of dialogue acts to the research of information through Internet by means of written requests, etc. It is important to note that NL data can represent either written language or oral language, the latter case implying a Signal Processing phase leading to low-level problems, such as word recognition, which is frequently ignored by written language.

Language data are basically sequences of events, hence obliging the classical ML algorithms to match this particular knowledge representation. Fortunately, learning paradigms exist which are especially devised to produce generating models of sequences : simple probabilistic models (bigrams, n-grams), sophisticated ones (multigrams, Hidden Markov Models, ...), Grammatical Inference, Recurrent Artificial Neural Networks. Other general ML techniques, such as Decision Trees, feedforward Neural Networks, Inductive Logic Programming, Lazy Learning ..., have also been employed (with some adaptation) to Natural Language applications [Mic97].

** This research is supported by France-Telecom (CNET) under the contract 97-1B-004

## 1.2  Learning Language Models for Speech Recognition

A Speech Recognition system is classically built by integrating two levels of knowledge : an acoustic decoder and a language model [RJ92]. The acoustic decoder is generally based on a hierarchy of Hidden Markov Models (HMM). The language model is often a simple statistical tool, e.g. a bigram matrix.

**Pure statistical models** A bigram model learns transition probabilities between events, for example between words (*bigrams*) or word categories (*biclass*) from a labelled corpus of data. They are therefore able to assign probabilities to alternative labellings and/or taggings of an unknown text. Although it is a simple technique, technical problems quickly appear, mainly due to the precision of the estimation, even on large corpora, in particular when one is interested in enlarging the window from two words (bigrams) to three (trigrams). One also has to deal with words that have never appeared during the learning phase, to which it would obviously be impossible to affect a null probability [Cha93] [JLM92].

To improve the quality of the compromise between the decrease of precision of the estimation and the increase of the context, attempts have been made to use a variable size context, according to the frequency of the event in the learning corpus [DYB96].

**Grammatical Inference** From as early as in the fifties [CM57], Grammatical Inference was already conceived as a technique used to learn syntax from example sentences. In practical NLL, its applications are still few, although this problem has been extensively studied from various points of view [ICG94], [ICG96]. Most of the research efforts are concentrated on the learning of finite automata (i.e. regular grammars). In NLL, it has recently spread from morphology to syntax ("light parsing", chunking [RS97]) and to CFG approximation, and also been applied to information extraction. It is nevertheless worth noticing that efficient heuristic methods require negative data, which are seldom found in NL corpora.

The inference of probabilized regular (e.g. : [SO94], [Vid94]) or context-free (e.g. : [JLM92]) grammars is certainly a good issue, since stochastic automaton and bigram models have proved to be equivalent, in theory. Nevertheless, it may be interesting to tackle the learning problem keeping in mind the direct research of grammatical rules, hence starting from the grammatical inference point of view to help statistical modelling.

Recent work on grammatical inference, including applications to NLP, will be found in [ICG94], [ICG96].

## 2  The Practical Problem

### 2.1  Inserting a language model into a Speech Recognition System

The integration of the acoustic models and the language model in a Speech Recognition system is based on a bayesian assumption. Denoting :

- $P(X)$ the probability of observing the sequence $X$ of acoustic data,
- $P(X|W)$ the estimation of the probability (computed by the acoustic HMM models) that the sequence of words $W$ has been pronounced,
- $P(W)$ the probability of the word sequence $W$,

we can decide that the best sequence of words is that maximizing the term :

$$P(W|X) = \frac{P(X|W)P(W)}{P(X)}$$

Here, we are only interested in $P(W)$, the language model. When a bigram model is chosen, denoting $W_{1...k}$ any prefix of $W$ and $W_j$ the $j$th element of this prefix, we simplify the language model down to :

$$P(W_{1...k}) = P(W_1) \cdot \prod_{j=2}^{k} P(W_j|W_{j-1})$$

We therefore have to estimate $P(W_j|W_{j-1})$ for any possible pair of words in the lexicon. This can be done by corpus-based methods, on the basis of estimating a probability by a frequency counting.

When using symbolic language models, the integration into such a Pattern Recognition equation is less straightforward. It is relatively easy to conceive how a regular grammar (under the representation of a finite-state automaton) can be transformed into a bigram equation : the value $P(W)$ is set to 1 when the sequence of words $W$ is accepted by the automaton, to 0 in the other case. This can be extended for stochastic automata, which can affects a recognition probability to any sentence. If the language model is a context-free grammar (possibly stochastic), the process is more complex [Dup96] [Cha93].

An open question is the merging of the statistical acoustic decoding with high-level symbolic grammatical description, such as unification-based grammars. They are commonly used in written Natural Language Processing, where no prior decision has to be made on the nature of the lexical items.

In practical terms, for an oral language problem, considering that

- the inferred model has to be integrated into a speech recognition system
- Grammatical Inference presently gives its best results on regular languages

it is natural to try to infer a regular grammar.

## 2.2 The data

This work has been conducted within the scope of a contract with France-Telecom, which develops vocal servers integrating a real dialogue with the user [Sad94]. The aim is to compare bigram models, as already working in the system, with language models issued from grammatical inference techniques. The data on which we have to learn a grammar are real transcriptions of dialogues through a speech recognition device, uttered by about 20 different speakers [SFC+96]. A short example of sentences found in dialogue is as follows :

- le Calvados
- et les autres départements en Normandie
- mais encore
- la Normandie
- oh je vous remercie au_revoir
- au_revoir
- je voudrais connaître les numéros de téléphone des serveurs concernant la météo dans la région de Rennes
- est-ce_que vous pouvez me répéter les numéros s'il-vous-plaît
- non c'est bon merci
- je voudrais connaître le numéro de téléphone du serveur du journal l' Express
- concernant les annonces
- oui

One can summarize the characteristics of the raw data, as provided by France-Telecom, in the table 1:

| Number of sentences | Size of the lexicon | Average number of words per sentence |
|---|---|---|
| 5845 | 1041 | 4.21 |

**Table 1.** Characteristics of the original France-Telecom corpus

A few preliminary remarks can be made:

- the size of the vocabulary is very large for a grammatical inference problem : usual benchmarks [LP97] use sentences composed on alphabets of 2 or 3 letters ; a few real world experiments have been made with vocabularies of the same magnitude [CGV94]
- consequently, although the total size of the corpus may seem high, each word appears on average only 10 or 11 times
- the average length of the sentences is short ; this is not aproppriate for detecting regularities, as most regular inference algorithms do.

## 3 The Grammatical Inference Experiment

### 3.1 Choosing an inference algorithm

As in many Language Processing problems, a characteristic of our corpus is that it is solely composed of *examples*, with no *counter-examples*. This implies two different issues in inferring regular grammars [Gre94] :

– either choose a *characterizable* method. This would mean assuming that the underlying language to be discovered is, say, k-testable or k-reversible. In that case, we know that adequate algorithms can identify in the limit the language we are looking for.
– or select an *empirical* method, possibly able to infer any regular language, but with no theoritical framework and only heuristics to stop the generalization process.

We have abandoned the first possibility, considering that the algebraic structure of the language we had to infer was not a good bias for choosing an algorithm. Nevertheless, considering the brevity of the sentences, we decided to assume that no recursivity had to be looked for in the data. In other terms, that a sentence such as : "errr give give me the number..." has not to be generalized into the regular expression : "errr (give)* me the number".

This was a major reason for choosing the Error-Correcting Grammatical Inference (ECGI) algorithm [RPV89]. But it has more interesting characteristics for our problem :

– As mentioned above, it does not look for repetitions of the same sub-sentence in the data, but is more adequate to discover the common sub-sentences in different parts of the examples.
– It is based on a metrics between the letters of the alphabet. In our case, it is reasonable to think of using an a priori knowledge to propose a similarity between words (e.g., indicate that two city names are more similar one with respect to the other than a verb and an adjective). It is also possible to extract such a metrics from the learning corpus itself (two words that often occur in the same context are likely to be syntactically similar).
– ECGI has already been succesfully used on real-size corpora [LVA+94].

## 3.2  The ECGI inference method

**An informal presentation**  This algorithm, proposed and used by Rulot and Vidal [RV88,RPV89] infers from positive examples a non-deterministic loop-free finite automaton. Consequently, the inferred language is of finite size.

It works in an incremental fashion : for each new example $x$, the current automaton $A$ tries to recognize $x$. If this is not possible, $A$ is modified for accepting $x$, by adding new states and new transitions. The crucial point is that the number of such modifications is minimized by computing the Levenshtein distance [Lev66] between $A$ and $x$ according to the metrics between letters [1]. A dynamic programming algorithm ensures this optimality.

At the end of the process, the inferred automaton accepts all the examples, but not only the examples : it has generalized to a (finite) language, grossly

---

[1] Levenshtein distance between $A$ and $x$ is defined as following :

$$d_{Levenshtein}(A, x) = \min_{y \in L(A)} (d_{Levenshtein}(y, x))$$

speaking, composed of sentences resulting of concatenations of sub-sentences of the examples.

The inferred automaton is non-deterministic, with the extra property that all the transitions leading to the same state are labelled by the same letter.

**A formal presentation** Let $G = (V, \Sigma, P, S)$ be a regular grammar. The *error rules* of $G$ can be defined as follows :

**Definition 1.** *For each rule in $P$, each $a, b \in \Sigma$, define the error rules associated to $P$ by :*

> *Insertion (of $a$) :*
> $A \to aA, \forall (A \to bB) \in P, \quad A \to ab, \forall (A \to b) \in P$ ;
> *Substitution (of $a$ by $b$) :*
> $A \to aB, \forall (A \to bB) \in P, \quad A \to a, \forall (A \to b) \in P$ ;
> *Deletion (of $b$) :*
> $A \to B, \forall (A \to bB) \in P, \quad A \to \epsilon, \forall (A \to b) \in P.$

**Definition 2.** *The* extended grammar $G' = (V, \Sigma, P', S)$ *de $G$ is obtained by adding the error rules to $P$.*

**Definition 3.** *The* optimal corrective derivation *of $x \in \Sigma^*$ is the derivation $D_{G'}(x)$ of $x$ using the minimal number of error rules in $P'$.*

The inner loop of the following procedure [RV88] computes the optimal corrective derivation of a sentence with respect to a grammar. The whole procedure infers a grammar which depends on the order of the examples.

**Algorithm** ECGI

**input** $I_+$
**output** A grammar $G$ accepting $I_+$

**begin**

$a \leftarrow I_+^1 (= a_1 .. a_i .. a_n)$;
$V \leftarrow \{A_0, .., A_n - 1\}$;
$\Sigma \leftarrow \{a_1, .., a_n\}$;
$P \leftarrow \{A_{i-1} \to a_i A_i), i = 1, ..., i = n\} \cup \{A_{n-1} \to a_n\}$;
$S \leftarrow A_0$;
$G \leftarrow (V, \Sigma, P, S)$; // current grammar
**for** $i \leftarrow 2$ **until** $|I_+|$ // taking a new example
    $b \leftarrow I_+^i$;
    $D \leftarrow D_G(b)$;
    $G \leftarrow G \cup \{D\}$; // Adding the corrective rules to the current grammar
**end for**
**return** $G$;

**end** ECGI

Adding the corrective rules to the current grammar follows a procedure that we shall not detail here, but rather illustrate on the example of the next section.

This algorithm runs in $\mathcal{O}(|\Sigma| \cdot \|I_+\|^2)$ [Dup96]. Its results depend on the ordering of the examples.

**An example** Let the set of examples be : $I_+ = \{aab, abb, ab, baab\}$

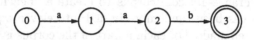

**Fig. 1.** Initialisation with 'aab'

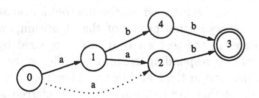

**Fig. 2.** Parsing 'abb' and replacing $a$ by $b$

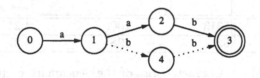

**Fig. 3.** Parsing 'ab' and deleting $a$

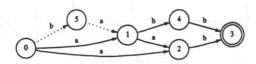

**Fig. 4.** Parsing 'baab' and inserting $b$

On this simple example, a generalisation to the sentence 'bbab' has been realized.

## 4 Results

### 4.1 Creating the benchmark

We have used the France-Telecom corpus to create a "benchmark" in the following manner : it has been randomly divided into eleven equal parts. Eleven experiments have been made. For each, a part of the corpus is used as a test set, while the union of the ten others is taken as the learning set. The results have been averaged on these eleven experiments.

The characteristics of our benchmark are as follows :

| Corpus | Number of sentences | Size of the lexicon | Average number of words per sentence |
|---|---|---|---|
| Learning corpus | 5313 | 1008 | 4.21 |
| Test corpus | 532 | 398 | 4.21 |

**Table 2.** Characteristics of the benchmark corpus

### 4.2 Generalization results

The ECGI algorithm has been run eleven times on the learning sets, then each corresponding test set has been tested on the inferred automaton.

To measure the generalization power of the algorithm, we firstly give the percentage of sentences in the test set that are recognized by the Prefix Tree Acceptor ($PTA$) of the corresponding learning set. This is the ratio of sentences in the test set that are also in the learning set. Then we give the percentage of sentences in the test set that are recognized by the inferred automaton $A$. We give also the number of states and transitions of the $PTA$, of $A$ and of $DA$, the automaton obtained by determinizing $A$.

All results are averaged on the eleven experiments.

| #sentences | #unknown words | A% | PTA % | #states A | #tr A | #states DA | #tr DA |
|---|---|---|---|---|---|---|---|
| 532 | 32.7 | 65.7% | 55.3% | 5494 | 7589 | 3690 | 17516 |

**Table 3.** Results

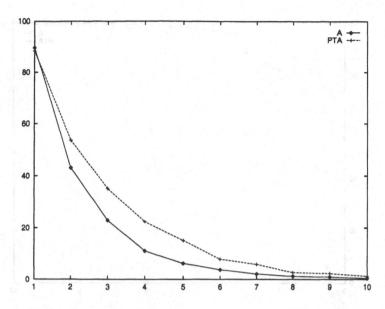

**Fig. 5.** Distance between the test sentences and $A$ or $PTA$

## 4.3 Evaluating the generalization

Figure 5 gives the average number of test sentences that are not recognized by the inferred automaton $A$, with respect to the Levenshtein distance to $A$ (solid line) and $PTA$ (dashed line).

On Figures 5 and 6, one can check that about 95% of the test sentences are at a Levenshtein distance 3 or less from $A$, and at a distance 6 or less from the $PTA$.

In average, the distance of a test sentence is 1.67 to the $PTA$ and 1.00 to $A$.

## 4.4 Integrating an automaton inferred by ECGI in a speech recognition system

As mentioned in section 1, the probability of recognizing a given sentence $W$ would be 0 or 1 if we straightforwardly use an automaton as a language model. But in speech recognition, rather than deciding whether a given sentence is recognized or not, the problem is actually to select among *several* sentences the one with the highest probability $P(X|W) \cdot P(W)$.

For that purpose we could directly reuse the ECGI basic process in computing the Levenshtein distance between all the possible sentences (as proposed by the acoustic decoder)and the inferred automaton, and make profit of this distance to estimate $P(W)$. But this computation would be expensive (even if it realized through a dynamic programming scheme) : its complexity is $\mathcal{O}(N_A * |x|)$, where $N_A$ is the number of states of the automaton $A$ et $|x|$ the length of the sentence

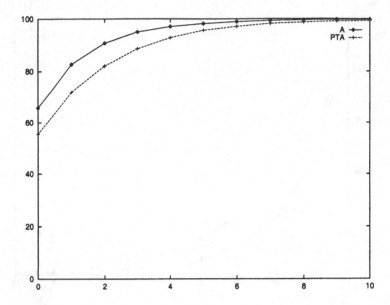

**Fig. 6.** Cumulated distribution of the average distance between a test sentence and $A$ or $PTA$

$x$. Choosing the closest sentence to the automaton in a set of $n$ sentences is in $\mathcal{O}(n * N_A * \bar{L})$, where $\bar{L}$ is the average length of the sentences in the set.

We can reduce this computational cost in organizing the data structure of the acoustic output. We can represent the set of lexical hypotheses as a directed acyclic graph (DAG) with a number $N_G$ of states. This data structure can easily be output from the acoustic decoding, with no extra cost. Considering that $A$ is itself a DAG, we can use an algorithm ([KS83]) that extracts the couple of closest paths in a couple of DAGs with a complexity of $\mathcal{O}(N_A * N_G)$.

## 5    Conclusion and Perspectives

We envisage to extend the application of ECGI to the inference of syntactic models in natural language along several paths :

- A straightforward stochastic version of ECGI has already been proposed [RV88]. It is easy to implement by counting the frequency of using each rule during the corrective analysis process. This would be interesting to compare with the bigram model or a stochastic automaton inferred with another method from the same data.
- An important amelioration would be to implement a meaningful metrics between the words of the lexicon. We are currently testing two possibilities :
  - extracting from the corpus a similarity matrix between lexical items. Assume that, in a vocabulary $\Sigma = \{a, b, c, d, e\}$ the word $a$ occurs $N_{cd}^a$

times in a sequence *...cad...*, the word $b$ occurs $N_{da}^{b}$ times in a sequence *...dba...*, etc ... A context similarity between the words $a$ and $b$ can easily be derived from the frequency distributions $N_{\cdot\cdot}^{a}$ and $N_{\cdot\cdot}^{b}$.

- A counting, as proposed by Rulot, can be used to estimate the similarity matrix between item. Then, in a EM-like manner, a new automaton can be inferred. Even if the convergence of this method seems difficult to establish, preliminary experiments have been promising.
- Finally, we are working on the reduction of the number of terminals. The context similarity matrix can be used to compute a hierarchical bottom-up clustering, grouping words into categories induced by the corpus itself. This technique has already been used for example by Powers [Pow96] and Brown [BDPdS+92].

# References

[BDPdS+92] Brown (P.), Della-Pietra (V.), de Souza (P.), Lai (J.) et Mercer (R.). – Class-based n-gram models of natural language. *Computational Linguistics, Vol 18*, 1992, pp. 467–479.

[CGV94] Castellanos (A.), Galliano (I.) et Vidal (E.). – Application of ostia to machine translation tasks. *ICGI'94*, 1994, pp. 93–105.

[Cha93] Charniak (E.). – *Statistical Language Learning.* – The MIT Press, 1993.

[CM57] Chomsky (N.) et Miller (G. A.). – *Pattern conception.* – Rapport technique, AFCRC-TN-5757, 1957. (ASTIA Document AD 110076).

[Dup96] Dupont (P.). – *Utilisation et apprentissage de modèles de langages pour la reconnaissance de la parole continue.* – Thèse de PhD, ENST, 1996.

[DvdBW97] Daelemans (W.), van den Bosch (A.) et Weijters (T.). – Empirical learning of natural language processing tasks. *In: Proceedings of 9th European Conference on Machine Learning, Workshop on Empirical Learning of Natural Language Processing Tasks.* – 1997.

[DYB96] Deligne (S.), Yvon (F.) et Bimbot (F.). – Introducing statistical dependencies and structural constraints in variable-length sequence models. *Grammatical inference and Applications, ICGI'96*, 1996, pp. 156–167.

[Gre94] Gregor (J.). – Data-driven inductive inference of finite-state automata. *Intenationnal Journal of Pattern Recognition and Artificial Intelligence*, vol. 8, n° 1, 1994, pp. 305–322.

[ICG94] *Grammatical Inference and Applications.* – September 1994. Springer-Verlag.

[ICG96] *Grammatical Inference : Learning Syntax from Sentences.* – 1996. Springer-Verlag.

[JLM92] Jelinek (F.), Lafferty (J.) et Mercer (R. L.). – Basic methods of probabilistic context-free grammars. *In: Speech Recognition and Understanding : Recent advances, Trends and Applications.* pp. 345–360. – Nato ASI Series, 1992. Springer Verlag.

[KS83] Kruskal (J. B.) et Sankoff (D.). – *Time Warps, String Edits, and Macromolecules : the Theory and Practice of Sequence Comparaison.* – Addison-Wesley, 1983.

[Lev66] Levenshtein (V. I.). – Binary codes capable of correcting deletions, insertions and reversals. *Cybernetics and Control Theory*, vol. 10, 1966, pp. 707–710.

[LP97]    Lang (K.) et Pearlmutter (B.). – Abbadingo one competition, 1997.
          http://abbadingo.cs.unm.edu/.

[LVA⁺94]  Lucas (S.), Vidal (E.), Amiri (A.), Hanlon (S.) et Amengual (J. C.). – A
          comparison of syntaxic and statistical techniques for off-line ocr. *ICGI'94*,
          vol. Lecture Notes in Artificial Intelligence 862, 1994, pp. 168–180.

[Mic97]   Miclet (L.). – Machine learning (including grammatical inference) and
          natural language processing : a short introduction to the bibliography.
          *Workshop on Automata Induction, Grammatical Inference and Language
          acquisition*, 1997.

[Pow96]   Powers (D.). – *Unsupervised learning of linguistic structure. An empiri-
          cal evaluation.* – Rapport technique, Department of Computer Science,
          Faculty of Science and Engineering, The Flinders University of South
          Australia, 1996.

[RJ92]    Rabiner (L.) et Juang (B. H.). – *Fundamentals of speech recognition.* –
          Prentice-Hall, 1992.

[RPV89]   Rulot (H.), Prieto (N.) et Vidal (E.). – Learning accurate finite-state
          structural models of words: the ecgi algorithm. *In: ICASSP'89*, pp. 643–
          646. – 1989.

[RS97]    Roche (E.) et Schubes (Y.). – *Finite-State Language Processing.* – MIT
          Press, 1997.

[RV88]    Rulot (H.) et Vidal (E.). – An efficient algorithm for the inference of
          circuit-free automata. *Syntactic and Structural Pattern Recognition*, 1988,
          pp. 173–184.

[Sad94]   Sadek (D.). – Communication theory = rationality principles + com-
          municative act models. *In: AAAI Workshop on Planning for Interagent
          Communication*, pp. 100–106. – 1994.

[SFC⁺96]  Sadek (D.), Ferrieux (A.), Cozannet (A.), Bretier (P.), Panaget (F.) et
          Simonin (J.). – Effective human-computer cooperative spoken dialogue :
          the ags demonstrator. *In: Proceedings of ICSLP*, pp. 542–545. – 1996.

[SO94]    Stolke (A.) et Omohundro (S.). – Inducting probabilistic grammars by
          bayesian model merging. *In: International Colloquium on Gramatical In-
          ference*, éd. par in Artificial Intelligence (Lecture Notes). ICGI'94, pp.
          106–118. – 1994.

[Vid94]   Vidal (E.). – Language learning, understanding and translation. *Progress
          ond Prospects of Speech Research and Technology. Proceedings of the
          CRIM/FORWISS Workshop*, September 1994.

[WRS96]   Wermter (S.), Riloff (E.) et Scheler (G.). – *Connectionnist, Statistical
          and Symbolic approaches to Learning for Natural Language Processing.* –
          Springer-Verlag, 1996.

# Real Language Learning

Jerome A. Feldman

ICSI, Berkeley CA 94704, USA,
jfeldman@icsi.berkeley.edu,
WWW home page: http://www.icsi.berkeley.edu/jfeldman.htm

**Abstract.** Formal studies of learning abstract grammars have, for decades, yielded deep results, some practical applications and quite a lot of fun. But no one believes that children learn the grammar of their native language independent of meaning (semantics) and use (pragmatics). Recent results suggest that is now possible, although still very difficult, to build computational and formal models of how children learn language. This paper will review some recent developments in computational modeling of language acquisition and suggest how they might be extended to grammatical inference.

## 1   Introduction

Formal studies of learning abstract grammars have, for decades, yielded deep results, some practical applications and quite a lot of fun. But no one believes that children learn the grammar of their native language independent of meaning (semantics) and use (pragmatics). The problem is that, until recently, there has been no way to tackle the more general and natural language learning problem. Recent results suggest that is now possible, although still very difficult, to build computational and formal models of how children learn language. This paper will review some recent developments in computational modeling of language acquisition and suggest how they might be extended to grammatical inference. I will focus on work in our NTL group, more fully described on the web site: www.icsi.berkeley.edu/NTL/.

The starting point for this effort, about a decade ago, was a challenge problem on learning natural languages from examples. For almost a decade, the Neural Theory of Language (NTL) group at ICSI and UC Berkeley has sought computational insight into this question by asking it of structured connectionist systems, rather than the physical neural systems of the brain [Feldman et al., 1996]. The basic questions of neural and cognitive development have been receiving increasing attention from the connectionist perspective. But despite considerable theoretical and modeling work on the acquisition of syntax, there does not appear to be any detailed theory of lexical development comparable to the NTL project.

One critical empirical finding from studies of language acquisition is that the child's first words label not only things, but also relationships, actions and internal states [Tomasello, 1995]. Clearly, embodiment is central to all of these. Early lexical development thus provides an ideal task for studying embodied cognition, since we can isolate linguistically and conceptually simple situations for which to construct and test detailed models.

Our first major effort was the dissertation work of Regier (1996), a computational model of how some lexical items describing spatial relations might develop in different languages. Since languages differ radically in how spatial relations are conceptualized, there was no obvious set of primitive features to build into the program. The key to Regier's success came directly from embodiment: all people have the same visual system from which all visual concepts must arise. By including a simple visual system model, Regier's program was able to learn spatial terms from labeled example movies for a wide range of languages, using conventional back-propagation techniques.

Though embodied and deeply semantic, Regier's system only learned individual words. A parallel project by Andreas Stolcke used Bayesian model merging to induce stochastic context free grammars over the same domain [Stolcke, 1994]. Although it was strictly formal, Stolcke's system did take a first step towards semantics in that it could learn a simple form of (stochastic) attribute grammar rather than just context free systems. There is currently a large amount of work along these lines in the statistical language learning community [Collins, 1996], where learning lexicalized and otherwise augmented grammars is popular. There is no obvious link between this work and the embodied semantic approach that will be described here. In fact, most of the researchers and all of the funding agencies in statistical language learning explicitly reject semantics and understanding as technical goals. We will return to the question of semantics-based grammatical inference after describing more carefully the current state of our efforts in modeling concepts and their acquisition.

Our semantic acquisition models made a major advance with Bailey's dissertation [Bailey, 1997,Bailey et al., 1997], a computational model that learns to produce verb labels for actions and also carry out actions specified by verbs that it has learned. A shortcoming of the standard view of lexical acquisition is that it provides no account of how a child learns to *make use* of the concepts she learns and the words that label them. This same weakness appears as a technical consequence of using back-propagation in Regier's work and in PDP models: even when the network learns perfectly how to classify a domain, it has no mechanism for executing the action. Bailey's work addresses this shortcoming by employing learning algorithms that produce usable representations of actions. After training on examples of action-word pairs, the system can produce an appropriate label for a particular motor action based on features of both the action and the world state. In addition, however, the learned verb representation also functions as a command interface that allows the system to carry out the meaning of a given verb.

Cross-linguistic experiments with both Regier's spatial relations network and Bailey's verb-learning system reveal both strengths and weaknesses of the current state of development. We believe that the basic principle that early word learning across languages can be modeled very well by embodiment-based structured connectionist models has been established. On the other hand, it is clear that our systems must incorporate much richer models of the neural substrate to handle even the early lexical development of children. To better estimate what is required, the group is beginning to study the full range of early word learning, rather than continuing to focus on isolated sub-vocabularies.

The original name of the project, *L0*, was chosen because zero was the approximate percentage of language we were attempting to cover. The current effort is still concerned with only a tiny fraction of the complexity of language learning, but because we are now grappling with all of a child's first (say) 200 words, we have presumptuously renamed the project NTL. In this paper, we outline plans for expanding our detailed connectionist modeling to cover all early lexical acquisition. As always, the theories and systems are intended to apply to all natural languages.

## 2 Representational mechanisms

To bridge the gap from embodied experience to its expression as abstract symbols in language, we have found it necessary to work at multiple levels of description. Regier's work, for instance, linked the connectionist and cognitive levels, with the neural level implicit. Subsequent more complicated domains have required us to add a computational level as an abstraction from the connectionist level. Although the focus of this paper is this computational level, the NTL papers in the 1997 Conference of the Cognitive Science Society spanned all five levels:

| | |
|---|---|
| cognitive: | words, concepts |
| computational: | f-structs, x-schemas (see below) |
| connectionist: | structured models, learning rules |
| computational neuroscience: | detailed neural models |
| neural: | [still implicit] |

Our computational level is analogous to Marr's and comprises a mixture of familiar notions like feature structures and a novel representation, executing schemas, described below. Apart from providing a valuable scientific language for specifying proposed structures and mechanisms, these representational formalisms can be implemented in simulations to allow us to test our hypotheses. They also support computational learning algorithms so we can use them in experiments on acquisition. Importantly, these computational mechanisms are all reducible to structured connectionist models so that embodiment can be realized.

The most novel computational feature of our current effort is our representation of actions, **executing schemas** (**x-schemas** for short), so named to distinguish them from other notions of schema and to remind us that they are intended to execute when invoked. We represent x-schemas using an extension of a computational formalism known as Petri nets [Murata, 1989]. A Petri net is a bipartite graph containing **places** (drawn as circles) and **transitions** (rectangles). Places hold **tokens** and represent predicates about the world state or internal state. Transitions are the active component. When all places pointing into a transition contain an adequate number of tokens (usually 1), the transition is enabled and may fire, removing its input tokens and depositing a new set of tokens in its output places. X-schemas cleanly capture sequentiality, concurrency and event-based asynchronous control; with our extensions they also model hierarchy and parameterization. Our extensions to the basic Petri net formalism include typed arcs, hierarchical control, durative transitions, parameterization, typed (individual) tokens and stochasticity.

The bottom third of Figure 1 depicts an example x-schema for sliding an object on a tabletop. The SLIDE x-schema captures the fact that people shape the hand while moving the arm to an object and that large and small objects are handled differently. It includes a loop that continues motion when not yet at the goal and a separate little schema for tightening the grip if slip is detected.

To keep things minimal, our models use only one other computational mechanism— **feature structures** (f-structs for short, drawn as a row of double-boxes). F-structs are used for static knowledge representation, parameter setting, and binding. They have been chosen to be compatible with the "f-structures" in the literature on unification grammars, and are similar to well-known AI slot-filler mechanisms. From these simple constructs, a wide variety of modeling structures can be built.

## 3 Bailey's verb learning model

An overview of Bailey's verb learning system is given in Figure 1. In this model a special **linking f-struct** (center of Figure 1) plays an important role as the sole interface between language and action. It maintains bidirectional connections to the x-schemas: an x-schema receives bindings from f-structs and produces additional bindings during its execution. In this way, actions can be translated to and from semantic features. More generally, we claim that the requirements of parameterizing x-schemas are the principal determiner of which semantic features get encoded in a language. One critical linking feature is the name of the x-schema generating the action. Others include motor parameters such as force, elbow joint motion, and hand posture. Some world state features are also relevant, such as object shape.

Each sense of a verb is represented in the model by an f-struct whose feature values are probability distributions. Features are presumed independent and the representation is conjunctive or gestalt-like in nature. The top third of Figure 1 shows several word senses for the verbs *push* and *shove*. The upper left ellipse gives f-structs for two senses of *push*. The top sense is a hand motion that invokes the SLIDE x-schema. The ellipse on the upper right shows that *shove* also codes for the SLIDE x-schema but specifies high acceleration.

In execution mode, a verbal command is interpreted by choosing the sense that best matches the current world state. This sense is in turn used to set the linking f-struct, thus determining which x-schema is to execute and with what parameters. For example, *shove* specifies both a SLIDE x-schema and high

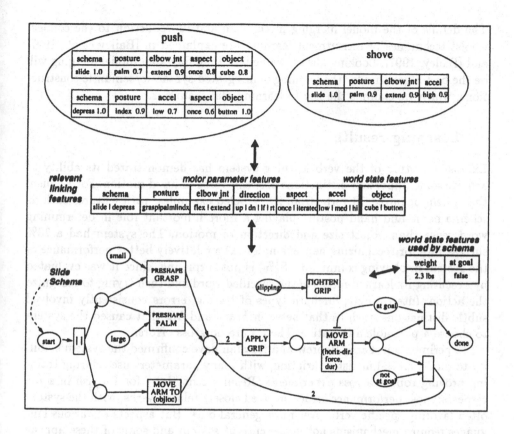

**Fig. 1.** An overview of the verb-learner at the computational level, showing details of the SLIDE x-schema, some linking features, and two verbs: *push* (with two senses) and *shove* (with one sense).

acceleration, but the force required depends (at least) on the size of the object involved, which is not specified in the utterance.

The verb learning model assumes that the child (or agent) has already acquired various x-schemas for the actions of one hand manipulating an object on a table, and that an informant labels actions that the agent is performing. As in Regier's work, we avoid some hard but, we feel, separable issues by assuming that the informant supplies just the verb. The problem faced by the model (and the child) is thus to learn how the verbs relate to its actions and goals. Interestingly, the basic learning methodology used in this semantic system is the same Bayesian model merging that was used in Stolcke's syntax learning program [Stolcke, 1994]. The algorithm starts by assuming that each instance (e.g. of a word sense) is a new category and then proceeds to merge these until a total information criterion (like Minimum Description Length) no longer improves.

The details of the model merging mechanism and its reduction to the connectionist techniques of recruitment learning are explained in [Bailey et al., 1997] and [Bailey, 1997]. Looking ahead, we believe that Bayesian model merging will be the best algorithm for the learning of integrated syntactic/semantic constructions, which we claim is the key to learning real grammar.

## 4 Learning results

Extensive testing of the verb learning system has demonstrated its ability to acquire some important distinctions between verbs of hand motion. For English, the system acquired 18 verbs from 200 labeled examples, with features such as schema name and hand posture playing a more important role in determining word sense than object size and direction of motion. The system had a 78% success rate for recognizing new examples. The relatively better performance of the system in obeying commands (81%) is not surprising, since it was evaluated by executing its learned model of the specified word and then trying to recognize the action. Interestingly, for both types of testing, errors consistently involved subtle distinctions, such as that between *heave* and *lift*, that caused the system to choose a plausible alternative. There were no gross errors.

Experiments in Farsi, Hebrew and Russian have confirmed the system's ability to model cross-linguistic variation, with many parameters used during training proving robust across experiments. Results echo those for English in some respects: most performance errors involved closely related verbs, with the system often favoring specific verbs over more general ones. But aspects of various languages require mechanisms not in the current system and some of these appear to help grammar learning as well. One crucial idea is the ability to model the simulated execution of X-schemas.

## 5 An x-schema simulation environment

In recent work [Narayanan, 1997], Narayanan has extended the basic x-schema representation to model domain theories, with the same mechanism used for acting and reasoning about actions in a dynamic environment. We assume that people can execute x-schemas with respect to f-structs that are not linked to the body and the here and now. In this case, x-schema actions are not carried out directly but instead trigger simulations of an imagined situation. It is easy to imagine, for instance, sliding King Kong up to the top of the Empire State Building and to predict what happens upon letting go. The NTL model for such mechanical planning assumes that the SLIDE x-schema can run with respect to a world model with simple qualitative physics. Physical models that people normally use appear to be simple enough to fit our paradigm fairly well, and some elementary ones have been implemented. We model the physical world as independent x-schemas with links to the x-schema representing the planned action. A simplified simulation of the dropping of an object and the corresponding world simulation, depicted in Figure 2, illustrates the central ideas.

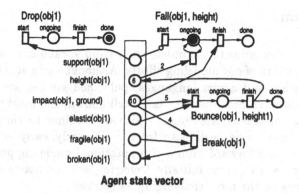

**Fig. 2.** X-schema simulation of DROP, resulting in the object falling and either breaking or bouncing.

On the left of Figure 2, we have an x-schema corresponding to the important control transitions of the underlying DROP x-schema [Narayanan, 1997]. On the right are x-schemas corresponding to the agent's simulation of the world. Both the agent's actions and the world's simulated evolution affect the agent's mental state. At the start of the simulation, the object is supported by an agent who then withdraws support as as result of the DROP action, consuming the token at the place labeled supported(obj1) and, through an inhibitory link, triggers the FALL x-schema. FALL simulates the decreasing height of the object until it hits the ground.[1] Once the object hits the ground, it may bounce back to some new height, depending on the impact force and the object's elasticity. If the object is brittle (like a vase), it does not bounce but will instead break.

In our simulation framework, whenever an executing x-schema makes a control transition, it potentially modifies state, leading to asynchronous and parallel triggering or inhibition of other x-schemas. We believe such a system design supports a broad notion of action, in that the same active representation can be used for monitoring, control and inference. The notion of state as a graph marking is inherently distributed over the network, so the working memory of an x-schema-based inference system is distributed over the entire set of x-schemas and f-structs.

This x-schema simulation framework has already proven useful in modeling metaphoric reasoning about event descriptions in abstract domains such as international economics. A crucial aspect of the implemented model is its capacity to exploit domain knowledge of spatial motion and manipulation (implemented as x-schema simulations) for real-time simulative inference. Results of applying Narayan's model to discourse fragments from newspaper stories in international economics show that crucial facts about abstract plans, goals, resources and intent can be expressed by projections from embodied concepts. Further details of this work can be found in [Narayanan, 1997].

---

[1] To simplify exposition, we leave out the relationship computed between the initial height and impact strength.

# 6 Extensions

In this section, we examine the complete early child vocabulary and its implications for the direction of our modeling efforts. Although early vocabularies differ widely both within and across languages, published studies are sufficient for identifying the most common words. As is well known, the most frequent word types (although not tokens) are nouns, which we continue to view as relatively unproblematic cases to be dealt with later. [2] Similarly, early adjectives seem comparatively straightforward from a computational modeling perspective and moreover are not very common initially. Deferring work on nouns and adjectives allows us to focus on the more challenging early words.

For concreteness, let us consider the 49 words used by the most children in the Bloom (1993) preschool study. Half of these are nouns or names of sounds like *boom*, *moo* or *woof*. When we consider the other words, several issues come to the fore. In particular, two methodological issues come prior to any detailed modeling: First, it is known that children often use a word very differently from how an adult would. For example, *down* and *more* from the right hand column in Table 1 are often initially requests. This is closely related to the second, more general issue: any serious modeling must be based on the physical and intentional context in which the child is using a given word. The literature is not complete in this regard, but it is good enough to get us started.

Several of the 23 words in the table that are not nouns or names of sounds (shown in bold) appear to be covered by our previous efforts to model the acquisition of spatial relation terms (Regier) or verbs of personal movement (Bailey), although really learning even these words involves some rather deep issues to which we will return later in this section. With this proviso, we can count four

| 7 | 8 | 9 | 10 | 11 | 12 | 13 | 14 |
|---|---|---|----|----|----|----|----|
| box | cookie | | | | | | |
| choo-choo | door | | | | | | |
| get | eye | banana | | | | | |
| girl | go | boom | | | | | |
| hammer | here | bottle | apple | | | | |
| horse | moo | cow | boy | | | | baby |
| in | no more | daddy | that | | | mommy | ball |
| out | on | shoe | this | bead | bye | no | down |
| sit | truck | spoon | uhoh | open | hi | oh | juice |
| two | woof | there | whee | yes | yum | up | more |

Number of children

Table 1. Words learned by 7 or more children, reproduced from Bloom (1993).

verbs of action (*get*, *sit*, *go* and *open*) and five spatial relation words (*in*, *out*, *on*, *up* and *down*) as understood.

Beyond the cases arguably covered by our previous models, the remaining lexemes again cluster into a small number of basic kinds. There are four that appear to be express emotion: *uhoh*, *whee*, *oh* (surprise) and *yum*. For our pur-

---

[2] Of course, to really implement an object naming system would require solving the computer vision problem.

poses, these present no basic problems; we assume that the child learns parents' labels for her emotions. The meanings of the remaining items all depend on conversational context or reference. There are two greetings, *hi* and *bye*, and four general communication terms: *yes*, *no*, *more* and *no more*. Also, there are two adult spatial adverbs, *here* and *there*, which again rely crucially for their meanings on the physical context of the conversation.

Both *this* and *that* similarly have referential potential only in conversational context. Note also that in adult speech they are each members of two closed classes: articles and pronouns. As such they play important functions at both the discourse level and the sentence-syntactic level (since articles are associated with an extremely restricted range of syntactic environments and thus are good predictors of the syntactic class of the next item). Beyond their semantic dependence on conversational setting, then, the development of specific grammatical functions for these lexical items is a question of central interest in our new effort to expand from word learning to grammatical inference. Following the idea that early words label existing functionality, demonstratives can be seen as labeling known communication actions.

As this sampling demonstrates, many early lexemes depend on conversational context and thus present the same basic challenge to the NTL paradigm: modeling other people. We can simplify this task by assuming that these lexemes originally label or augment pre-verbal communication acts. Children develop communication patterns with their parents well before they speak; there are patterns of shared eye movements and other physical and vocal gestures [Foster, 1990] that form an obvious possible substrate for the deictic articles *this* and *that*. And no parent needs to be told about *no*.

Under the assumption that pre-linguistic communication routines are a necessary precursor to learning communication terms, the challenge to the NTL paradigm becomes one of modeling the interaction of the child's own mental representations with its representations of other agents. This simulation of other agents is a direct extension of the general x-schema simulation environment described earlier. Instead of passive x-schemas representing the physical world as in Figure 2, we use x-schemas that model the other agent. The interactions between the model's plans and the anticipated response of the other agent are computationally the same as in the case of physical simulation, although models of other agents must be much richer, including models of both their actions and their beliefs.

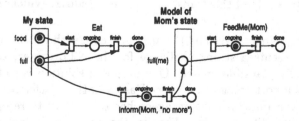

**Fig. 3.** Depiction of child's own state and model of her mother's state in a context in which the child might say *no more* to halt feeding.

Figure 3 illustrates one context in which the phrase *no more* might be used. The simplified x-schemas and state representations depict both the child's own actions (EAT, INFORM) and her model of her mother's FEED ME action. The EAT schema on the left is enabled by the presence of food and continues until the child is full. The figure models a point when the child, having eaten her fill, is using the phrase *no more* to informing her mother that she is full, which she knows will stop her mother's feeding process. This communicative act presumably replaces or augments earlier gestural x-schemas.

This approach accommodates many simple cases in which a lexeme labels some action in the child's mental model of (conversational) context. But more complicated semantic distinctions will require additional mechanisms. Let us return to the four action verbs and five spatial relation words that appear to be explained by previous NTL models. The previous models took a fixed perspective with respect to which all words were learned. Regier's spatial term network takes what we call the **observer** perspective; the learning agent views scenarios that are then labeled. Bailey's action verb learner assumes what we call the **agent** perspective; the learning agent receives labels for its own actions. Regier gave no hint how an agent who learns to label a scene as *into* would know how to apply this label to its own actions. Bailey is similarly silent on how an agent who learns that one of its actions can be called *push* would recognize the same action when carried out by others. The situation is even more complex than this — there is at least one additional basic perspective, which we call the **experiencer**. Being pushed is experientially quite distinct from either pushing or observing some third party pushing. Similarly, it is quite different to put a toy *in* your mouth, see milk put *in* the refrigerator or be put *in* your bath.

As is clear from the words of our sample, children's initial word meanings may take any of the three basic perspectives of agent, experiencer or observer. Most nouns are, of course, learned by observation, although some (*eye*, *boy*) might be learned first as part of one's own body or as a reference to oneself. Emotion words and actions like *sit* (and Bailey's examples) are normally learned first from the agent perspective. At least for American middle class children, words like *up* and *down* are first used in the experiencer perspective — the child is picked up or put down when the word is used. It isn't terribly important which perspective comes first for some lexeme for a given child — the question is how all of these come to be associated with the same term. Crucially, can a term learned from one perspective be understood and used from the others? We know of no systematic study of this transfer, but the anecdotal evidence suggests that it is common.

The multiple perspectives and the apparent ease with which children transfer among them presents a strong challenge for the NTL project of constructing detailed, neurally plausible models. Our proposed solution is to further extend x-schemas to support recognition as well as execution. Referring once again to Figure 1, one can imagine that an agent has the ability to recognize someone else carrying out a SLIDE action. That is, the x-schema formalism can also be used as an active template to recognize actions as well as carry them out.

This solution is computationally elegant and has some experimental basis, but it is still very speculative. In fact, there have been connectionist models that work exactly this way. The most relevant is Goddard's thesis system (1992) that recognizes human gaits from stick figure movie input. Goddard found that the best way to recognize a motion was to have an x-schema-like active representation that was brought into synchronization with the incoming visual data. In a good match, the simulation predicted the input stream and the visual recognition became easy. Alternative models competed in the usual connectionist way to provide the best match for a data stream.

The idea of using x-schemas for execution, inference and recognition might also help with another major shortcoming of Bailey's verb learning paradigm. Bailey's system learns only the most concrete embodiment of a word like *push*. But there is a more general, abstract meaning as well. This might be glossed as moving an object away from a deictic center using force directed through the object. Much of the cognitive linguistics literature is concerned with these general image-schematic [Lakoff, 1987] and force-dynamic [Talmy, 1988] semantic representations. In our Bloom data, three of the four verbs of action are the general forms: *get*, *go* and *open*, but these might refer to specific actions; *get* might refer to a pulling action representable directly in Figure 1. While it is still not known whether children develop the general meanings early, the model must allow for the possibility that they do.

Our current idea is to allow the embodied semantics for early action words to have both specific and general components. In this formulation, the SLIDE x-schema of Figure 1 would be accompanied by a general x-schema for achieving the goal of moving a physical object to a desired place. In learning *push* the child might associate the word with either the specific action, the general goal achievement or both. Recent work by C. Johnson (1997) suggests that early word learning might conflate specific and general meanings, such as *view* and *know* for *see*. This early conflation may serve as the basis for later metaphorical mappings in a manner that fits very well with the NTL paradigm.

The claim is that these mechanisms can be realized and that they provide a semantic basis for language learning that can be cleanly extended to incorporate syntax as well as word learning. There is quite a lot of information on the order in which children learn syntactic constructions [Foster, 1990] and one striking fact from these studies is that it takes several years for children to acquire full adult grammar. The key to our approach to grammar learning is to explicitly exploit the idea that children learn linguistic constructions that carry both semantic and syntactic structure [Goldberg, 1995]. The full construction grammar story includes phonological structures as well, but these do not appear in our current treatments. What we can do is study how children learn their early syntactic/semantic constructions and attempt to build models and theories of this process. Even from the very early examples in this paper, some issues are highlighted. One central role of early grammar is to help control the communication process itself. The other current focus is argument structure; this is early and important and is marked very differently in various languages. The Bayesian model-merging techniques that we have been for formal grammar learning and for verb learning appear to be very promising in this context as well.

# References

[Bailey, 1997] Bailey, D. R. (1997). *When Push Comes to Shove: A Computational Model of the Role of Motor Control in the Acquisition of Action Verbs.* PhD thesis, Computer Science Division, EECS Department, University of California at Berkeley.

[Bailey et al., 1997] Bailey, D. R., Feldman, J. A., Narayanan, S., and Lakoff, G. (1997). Modeling embodied lexical development. *Proceedings of the 19th Cognitive Science Society Conference.*

[Collins, 1996] Collins, M. (1996). A new statistical parser based on bigram lexical dependencies. *Proceedings of the 34th Annual Meeting of the ACL.*

[Feldman et al., 1996] Feldman, J. A., Lakoff, G., Bailey, D. R., Narayanan, S., Regier, T., and Stolcke, A. (1996). *L0*—the first five years of an automated language acquisition project. *AI Review,* 10:103–129. Special issue on Integration of Natural Language and Vision Processing.

[Foster, 1990] Foster, S. (1990). *The communicative competence of young children : a modular approach.* Longman.

[Goddard, 1992] Goddard, N. (1992). *The Perception of Articulated Motion: Recognizing Moving Light Displays.* PhD thesis, University of Rochester.

[Goldberg, 1995] Goldberg, A. E. (1995). *Constructions: A Construction Grammar Approach to Argument Structure.* University of Chicago Press.

[Johnson, 1997] Johnson, C. (1997). Learnability and the acquisition of multiple senses: Source reconsidered. *Proc. 22nd Annual Meeting of the Berkeley Linguistics Society.*

[Lakoff, 1987] Lakoff, G. (1987). *Women, Fire, and Dangerous Things: What Categories Reveal about the Mind.* University of Chicago Press.

[Murata, 1989] Murata, T. (1989). Petri nets: Properties, analysis and applications. *Proceedings of IEEE,* 77(4):541–580.

[Narayanan, 1997] Narayanan, S. (1997). *Knowledge-based Action Representations for Metaphor and Aspect (KARMA).* PhD thesis, Computer Science Division, EECS Department, University of California at Berkeley.

[Regier, 1996] Regier, T. (1996). *The Human Semantic Potential.* MIT Press.

[Stolcke, 1994] Stolcke, A. (1994). *Bayesian Learning of Probabilistic Language Models.* PhD thesis, University of California, Berkeley.

[Talmy, 1988] Talmy, L. (1988). Force dynamics in language and thought. *Cognitive Science,* 12:49–100.

[Tomasello, 1995] Tomasello, M. (1995). *Beyond Names for Things: Young Children's Acquisition of Verbs.* Lawrence Erlbaum Associates, Hillsdale, NJ.

# A Stochastic Search Approach
# to Grammar Induction

Hugues Juillé and Jordan B. Pollack

Computer Science Department, Brandeis University
Waltham, Massachusetts 02254-9110, USA
hugues,pollack@cs.brandeis.edu

**Abstract.** This paper describes a new sampling-based heuristic for tree search named SAGE and presents an analysis of its performance on the problem of grammar induction. This last work has been inspired by the Abbadingo DFA learning competition [14] which took place between Mars and November 1997. SAGE ended up as one of the two winners in that competition. The second winning algorithm, first proposed by Rodney Price, implements a new evidence-driven heuristic for state merging. Our own version of this heuristic is also described in this paper and compared to SAGE.

## 1 Introduction

In the field of Artificial Intelligence, important efforts are devoted to the design of efficient search algorithms. Among those approaches, stochastic search algorithms benefit from several interesting properties. First, they often admit an efficient implementation on distributed architectures because they use a limited central control strategy. Secondly, they offer a general purpose procedure when little knowledge is available about the intrinsic properties of the problem or when this knowledge is difficult to introduce in a search procedure. In particular, techniques like Genetic Algorithms (GAs) [8], Genetic Programming (GP) [12], Evolutionary Programming (EP) [5] or Evolutionary Strategies (ES) [2] have had some recent success to tackle some problems with ill-defined search space. Basically, those algorithms sample the state space in order to gather information about the distribution of solutions. Then, this information is used to control the focus of the search.

This paper describes a new algorithm named Self-Adaptive Greedy Estimate (SAGE) search procedure whose underlying heuristics are similar to the ones implemented in those evolutionary algorithms. However, this algorithm has been designed for the search of trees or directed graphs (DAG). Indeed, problems for which the natural representation of the state space is a tree of a DAG are usually not amenable to evolutionary search. So far, random sampling techniques on search trees have been used essentially to predict the complexity of search algorithms [11, 3], but never as a heuristic to control the search. We believe our algorithm to be the first to exploit that knowledge. The work presented in this paper tests this search algorithm on a *grammar induction* problem. This application originated from the Abbadingo DFA learning competition [14] which took place between March and November 1997. This competition proposed a set of difficult instances for the problem of DFA learning as a challenge to the machine learning community and to encourage the development of new algorithms for grammar induction. Our motivation for using a search intensive approach came from a first insight that there might be no simple heuristic to address the problems proposed in that competition. The outcome of the competition proved us wrong on that point since an evidence-driven heuristic discovered by Rodney Price appears to be very adapted for that task, improving very significantly over the Trakhtenbrot-Barzdin algorithm. Because of the requirement in computing resource, SAGE was not able to address problems with large target DFA. For that reason, it was defeated by the evidence-driven heuristic on the problems with average density training sets. However, by solving one problem from the set of challenges with sparse training data, SAGE ended up as a co-winner of that competition.

The paper is organized as follows: Section 2 presents an overview of the SAGE search algorithm. Section 3 describes the DFA learning task and the Abbadingo competition. Then, the implementation of SAGE is described in section 4 along with an implementation of the evidence-driven heuristic. Experimental results are presented in section 5. In this last section, an analysis also compares the performance of SAGE to the Trakhtenbrot-Barzdin algorithm and to the evidence-driven heuristic.

## 2 Description of the SAGE Search Algorithm

The central component for SAGE is a problem-specific *construction procedure*. This construction procedure is designed such that it always terminates and outputs a feasible solution for the problem under consideration. The construction procedure is an iterative algorithm which makes an ordered sequence of decisions, each decision being selected among a list of valid extensions given the current partial solution. Therefore, this procedure defines the search space as a tree. Solutions correspond to the leaves of that tree while internal nodes represent partial solutions. Eventually, the search space can be a directed acyclic graph (DAG) if there are equivalent nodes in the tree.

There is a well-known AI algorithm for search in DAGs and trees called *Beam search*. Beam search examines in parallel a number of nearly optimal alternatives (the *beam*). This search algorithm progresses level by level in the tree of states and it moves downward only from the best $w$ nodes at each level. Consequently, the number of nodes explored remains manageable: if the branching factor in the tree is at most $b$ then there will be at most $wb$ nodes under consideration at any depth. SAGE is similar to this algorithm in the sense that it implements a multi-threaded search. More precisely, SAGE is composed of a population of *processing elements*. Each of them plays the role of an elementary search algorithm and is seen as one alternative in the beam. However, there are two important differences between SAGE and Beam search. First, Beam search uses an evaluation function to score the different alternatives in order to select alternatives that are most promising. The design of such an evaluation function involves some problem-specific knowledge in order to exploit some properties about the problem under consideration that have been identified. When such knowledge is not available, this approach might not be appropriate. The heuristic exploited by SAGE to address this issue consists in estimating the score of internal nodes by performing a random sampling. That is, the construction procedure selects at random a valid extension at each step until a leaf (or valid solution) is reached. Then, the score of this solution is directly computed with respect to the problem objective function and it is assigned to the initial node. Secondly, the control strategy implemented by Beam search to focus the search simply selects the best $w$ alternatives among the current set of partial solutions. In the case of SAGE, the control strategy involves two mechanisms. The first one implements a model of local competition among the processing elements, which allows the algorithm to allocate more "resources" (i.e., processing elements) to the most promising alternatives in a self-adaptive manner. The motivation for this approach is to allow a scalable system in which the number of elements can be increased easily in order to augment (hopefully) the performance of the algorithm. The second one is a greedy strategy which controls the depth in the search tree of the current alternatives represented by the population of processing elements. This control strategy is discussed in little more details in the following paragraphs.

Put in another way, SAGE is an iterative search procedure for which each iteration is composed of two phases, a *construction* phase and a *competition* phase. SAGE implements a population of elementary randomized search algorithms and a *meta-level heuristic* which controls the search procedure by distributing the alternatives under consideration among this population of processing elements. For any iteration, all the alternatives represented in the population have the same depth in the search tree and they are represented by a number of processing elements which depends on their relative performance. At the beginning of the search, this depth is null and it increases with the number of iterations according to a strategy implemented by the meta-level heuristic. At each iteration, the construction phase is performed, followed by the competition phase. The following operations are performed during those two phases:

- *construction phase*: each processing element calls the construction procedure. This procedure starts the construction from the partial solution represented by the calling processing element and thereafter makes each decision by randomly selecting one choice from the list of valid extensions available at each step. Each random selection is performed with respect to a uniform probability distribution. This phase ends when all the processing elements have constructed a complete solution.
- *competition phase*: the purpose of this phase is to focus the search on most promising alternatives by assigning more representatives to them. This result is achieved by assigning better alternatives to the processing elements that are representative of poor alternatives. A model of local competition between

the different processing elements implements this mechanism. Such a model allows a very efficient implementation on different distributed architectures.

In summary, SAGE is a population-based model in which each processing element is the representative of one alternative for the current level of search in the tree. That alternative determines the initial node from which the random sampling is performed by that processing element during the construction phase. Then, SAGE controls the exploration of the search space according to the following strategy:

1. Initially, the search is restricted to the first level of the tree and each processing element in the population randomly selects one of the first-level nodes.
2. Each processing element scores its associated node (or alternative) by performing a random sampling. This is the construction phase.
3. Then, the competition phase is operated. The purpose of this phase is to focus the search on most promising alternatives.
4. A test is performed by the meta-level heuristic and the result determines whether the level of search is increased by one or not. In the affirmative, each processing element selects uniformly randomly one of the children of its associated node in the search tree and this node becomes the new alternative assigned to the processing element.
5. The search stops if no new node can be explored (because the search reached the leaves of the tree); otherwise it continues with step 2.

In the SAGE model, the level of search in the tree is called the *commitment degree* since it corresponds to a commitment to the first choices of the incremental construction of the current best solution.

A complete description of the search algorithm can be found in [10].

# 3 Induction of DFAs

## 3.1 Presentation

The aim of inductive inference is to discover an abstract model which captures the underlying rules of a system from the observation of its behavior and thus to become able to give some prediction for the future behavior of that system. In the field of grammar induction, observations are strings that are labeled "accepted" or "rejected" and the goal is to determine the language that generates those strings. An excellent survey of the field is presented in [1], covering in particular the issue of computational complexity and describing some inference methods for inductive learning. Several representations have been proposed to describe the abstract models used for grammar induction like deterministic finite state automata, boolean formula or propositional logic. More recently, Pollack [16] proposed dynamical recognizers as an interesting alternative to those symbolic approaches, leading to a wide range of Recurrent Neural Network (RNN) architectures [18, 19, 4, 6] that have been employed for similar tasks. However, none of them could compete in the Abbadingo competition because of the proposed problems size.

## 3.2 The Abbadingo Competition

The Abbadingo competition (organized by Lang and Pearlmutter [14]) is a challenge proposed to the machine learning community in which a set of increasingly difficult DFA induction problems have been designed. Those problems are supposed to be just beyond the current state of the art for today's DFA learning algorithms and their difficulty increases along two dimensions: the size of the underlying DFA and the sparsity of the training data. Gold [7] has shown that inferring a minimum finite state automaton compatible with given data consisting of a finite number of labeled strings is NP-complete. However, Lang [13] empirically found out that the average case is tractable. That is, randomly generated target DFAs are approximately learnable even from sparse data when this training data is also generated at random. One of the aims of the Abbadingo competition is to estimate an empirical lower bound for the sparsity of the training data for which DFA learning is still tractable on average.

**Competition Setup** A set of DFAs of various size has been randomly constructed. Then, a training set and a test set have been generated from each of those DFAs. Only the labeling for the training sets have been released. Training sets are composed of a number of strings which varies with the size of the target DFA and the level of sparsity desired. The goal of the competition is to discover a model for the training data that has a predictive error rate smaller than one percent on the test set. Since the labeling for the test sets has not been released, the validity of a model can be tested only by submitting a candidate labeling to an "Oracle" implemented on a server at the University of New Mexico [14] which returns a "pass/fail" answer. Table 1 presents the different problems that compose this competition. The size and the depth of the target DFA are provided as a piece of information to estimate how close a DFA hypothesis is from the target.

### Procedure for Generation of Problems

- *Generation of target DFAs*: To construct a random DFA of nominal size $n$, a random digraph with $\frac{5}{4}n$ nodes is constructed, each vertex having two outgoing edges. Then, each node is labeled "accept" or "reject" with equal probability, a starting node is picked, nodes that can't be reached from that starting node are discarded and, finally, the Moore minimization algorithm is run. If the resulting DFA's depth isn't $\lfloor (2\log_2 n) - 2 \rfloor$, the procedure is repeated. This condition for the depth of DFAs corresponds to the average case of the distribution. It is a design constraint which allows the generation of a set of problems whose relative complexity remains consistent along the dimension of target size.
- *Generation of training and testing sets*: A training set for a $n$-state target DFA is a set drawn without replacement from a uniform distribution over the set of all strings of length at most $\lfloor (2\log_2 n) + 3 \rfloor$. The same procedure is used to construct the testing set but strings already in the training set are excluded.

**Table 1.** Abbadingo data sets.

| Problem name | Target DFA size | Target DFA depth | Training set size |
|---|---|---|---|
| 1 | 63 | 10 | 3478 |
| 2 | 138 | 12 | 10723 |
| 3 | 260 | 14 | 28413 |
| R | 499 | 16 | 87500 |
| 4 | 68 | 10 | 2499 |
| 5 | 130 | 12 | 7553 |
| 6 | 262 | 14 | 19834 |
| S | 506 | 16 | 60000 |
| 7 | 65 | 10 | 1521 |
| 8 | 125 | 12 | 4382 |
| 9 | 267 | 14 | 11255 |
| T | 519 | 16 | 32500 |

**Results of the Competition** The description of the development of the competition is presented in details in [15]. The two-dimensional ranking of problems with respect to target size and training data density allowed multiple winners. In fact, two algorithms ended up as co-winners in the competition. The first one used an evidence driven heuristic discovered by Rodney Price. This algorithm outperformed SAGE by being able to solve the largest problems from the first and second group in table 1 (i.e. problems R and S). However, SAGE has later been able to solve problem 7 (the smallest of the problems with sparse training data) and ended up as the second co-winner in the competition.

## 4 Implementation

### 4.1 Construction Procedure for SAGE

The construction procedure makes use of the state merging method described in [17]. It takes as input the prefix tree acceptor constructed from the training data. Then, a finite state automaton is iteratively constructed, one transition at a time until a valid DFA is generated (i.e., until every state has a "0" and a "1" outgoing transition).

In the construction procedure two cases are possible when considering a transition: either it goes to an existing state or it goes to a newly created state. As the hypothesis DFA is constructed, states are mapped with nodes in the prefix tree and transitions between states are mapped with edges. When a transition is created going to an existing state, corresponding nodes in the prefix tree are merged. When two nodes in the prefix tree are merged, the labels in the tree are updated accordingly and the merging of more nodes can be recursively triggered so that the prefix tree reflects the union of the labeled string suffixes that are attached to those nodes. Thus, as the DFA is constructed, the prefix tree is collapsed into a graph which is an image of the final DFA when the construction procedure terminates. This merging procedure provides the mechanism to test whether a transition between two existing states is consistent with the labeling and should be considered as a potential choice in the construction procedure. The pseudo-code describing this construction procedure is given in figure 1.

Begin with a single state mapped to the root of the prefix tree
The list $\mathcal{L}$ of unprocessed states consists of that state
**do**
    Pick randomly a state $S$ from $\mathcal{L}$
    Compute the set $T_0$ of valid transitions on "0" from state $S$
    Pick randomly a transition $t_0$ from $T_0$
    **if** ($t_0$ goes to an existing state) **then**
        Merge corresponding nodes in the prefix tree
    **else**
        Create a new state, map it to the corresponding
            node in the prefix tree and add it to $\mathcal{L}$
    **endif**

    Compute the set $T_1$ of valid transitions on "1" from state $S$
    Pick randomly a transition $t_1$ from $T_1$
    **if** ($t_1$ goes to an existing state) **then**
        Merge corresponding nodes in the prefix tree
    **else**
        Create a new state, map it to the corresponding
            node in the prefix tree and add it to $\mathcal{L}$
    **endif**
**until** ($\mathcal{L}$ is empty)
/* The output is a DFA consistent with the training data */

**Fig. 1.** Randomized construction procedure for DFA learning.

## 4.2 The Evidence-Driven Heuristic

The state merging method implemented in [17] considers a breadth-first order for merging nodes, with the idea that a valid merge involving the largest sub-trees in the prefix tree has a higher probability of being correct than other merges. The evidence-driven heuristic doesn't follow that intuition and considers instead the number of labeled nodes that are mapped over each other and match when merging sub-trees in the prefix tree. Different control strategies can be designed to explore the space of DFA constructions exploiting this heuristic. Our implementation maintains a list of valid destinations for each undecided transition for the current partial DFA and, as a policy, always gives priority to "forced" creation of new states over merge operations. The pseudo-code for this algorithm is presented in figure 2.

Begin with a single state mapped to the root of the prefix tree
The list $S$ of existing states in the DFA construction consists of that state
The list $T$ of unprocessed transitions consists of the two outgoing transitions
        from that state, on "0" and "1"
For each $t \in T$, compute:
      . the subset $S_{dest}(t)$ from $S$ of valid destinations for $t$
      . the merge count for each destination in $S_{dest}(t)$
**do**
    Construct the subset $T_0$ of transitions $t \in T$ for which $S_{dest}(t) = \emptyset$
    /* Transitions in $T_0$ cannot go to any existing state */
    **if** ($T_0$ is not empty) **then**
        Select $t_0 \in T_0$ outgoing from the shallowest node (break ties at random)
        Remove $t_0$ from $T$
        Create a new state $S_0$ mapped to the destination node for $t_0$ in the prefix tree
        Add $S_0$ to $S$
        Add the two outgoing transitions from $S_0$, $t'_0$ and $t'_1$, to $T$
        Compute $S_{dest}(t'_0)$ and $S_{dest}(t'_1)$ along with the corresponding merge counts
        For each transition $t \in T$, add $S_0$ to $S_{dest}(t)$ if it is a valid destination for $t$
            and compute its merge count
    **else**
        /* Operate a merge */
        Select $t_0 \in T$ with the highest merge count (break ties at random)
        Merge the destination node for $t_0$ in the prefix tree with the destination
            state corresponding to this highest merge count
        Remove $t_0$ from $T$
        For each $t \in T$, update $S_{dest}(t)$ and the merge counts
    **endif**
**until** ($T$ is empty)

**Fig. 2.** A construction procedure using the evidence-driven heuristic.

## 5 Experimental Results

### 5.1 Problems in the Abbadingo Competition

In a first stage, we used a sequential implementation of SAGE since small populations were enough to solve the smallest instances of the Abbadingo competition. Then, we used a network of workstations to scale the population size and address the most difficult problem instances in the competition. In particular, the solution to problems 5 and 7 involved around 16 workstations on average. This parallel implementation is composed of a server that manages the population of partial solutions and distributes the work load among several clients. This architecture presents the advantage that clients can be added or removed at any time.

SAGE has been able to solve problems 1, 2, 4, 5 and 7 from table 1. To solve problem 7, we proceeded in two steps. First, the construction procedure described previously has been extended with the evidence-driven heuristic in order to prune the search tree. The construction procedure switches to this heuristic when the number of states in the current DFA has reached a given size. Before that threshold size is reached, the construction procedure remains unchanged. After about 10 runs, a DFA with 103 states has been discovered very early. Then, in a second step, more experiments were performed using the original construction procedure but starting with the same first few choices as those that had been made for the 103-state DFA. This resulted in a DFA of size 65. This second step uses SAGE for local search, starting from a good prefix for the DFA construction. The appropriate size for the prefix has been determined experimentally. It is clear from those experiments that the density for the training data available for problem 7 is at the edge of what SAGE can manage. This observation is confirmed by the analysis presented in the following section.

Table 2 presents the population size, the size of the DFA hypothesis and an estimate of the computation time for the different problems that SAGE has been able to solve. We decided to report in that table the values when each problem was solved for the first time. Parameters could be tune to improve the execution time (on average up to a fourfold factor). Experiments for problems 1, 2 and 4 have been performed on a Pentium PC 200MHz. For problems 5 and 7, a network of Pentium PCs and SGI workstations has been used. The evidence-driven heuristic can solve all the problems in the first and the second group in table 1 except problem 5 on which it fails.

**Table 2.** Experimental results for the SAGE search algorithm applied to problems 1, 2, 4, 5 and 7 of the Abbadingo competition.

| Problem name | 1 | 2 | 4 |
|---|---|---|---|
| Population size | 64 | 64 | 256 (+ best of 2 samples) |
| Size of DFA model | 63 states | 150 states | 71 states |
| Execution time | 1 hour (sequential) | 40 hours (sequential) | 4 hours (sequential) |

| Problem name | 5 | 7 (step 1) | 7 (step 2) |
|---|---|---|---|
| Population size | 576 (+ best of 8 samples) | 1024 | 4096 |
| Size of DFA model | 131 states | 103 states | 65 states |
| Execution time | 40 hours (parallel) | 2 hours (parallel) | 4 hours (parallel) |

**Comparative Performance Analysis.** In a comparative study, the performance of the three approaches: Trakhtenbrot-Barzdin (T-B) algorithm, evidence-driven heuristic and SAGE has been evaluated against a set of random problem instances generated using the procedure described in the previous section. For each target DFA, the three algorithms were evaluated across a range of density for the training data in order to observe the evolution of each approach when working with sparser data. For the first two algorithms, 1000 problems were used while only 100 problems were used to evaluate SAGE because of the requirement in computational resources. This comparison has been performed for three values of the population size for SAGE: 64, 256 and 1024 and for two values of the targets nominal size: 32 and 64 states (figures 3 and 4 respectively).

In those experiments, the performance is the ratio of problems for which the predictive ability of the model constructed by the algorithm is at least 99% accurate. This threshold is the same as the success criterion for solving problems in the Abbadingo competition. Figures 3 and 4 show the dependence of SAGE on the population size for its performance. Indeed, a larger population results in a better reliability for the control of the focus of the search because of a larger sample. For the set of problems generated for the purpose of this analysis, SAGE and the evidence-driven heuristic clearly outperform the T-B algorithm. With a population size large enough, SAGE also exhibits a performance consistently better than the evidence-driven heuristic. However, it is difficult to compare those two approaches since SAGE is a general purpose search algorithm using very little knowledge about the problem (i.e., the one introduced in the construction procedure) while the other is a greedy algorithm using a strong problem-specific heuristic. For this reason, SAGE doesn't scale up as well as the evidence-driven heuristic (or the T-B algorithm) for larger target DFAs. The introduction of problem-specific heuristics in the construction procedure becomes necessary for SAGE to address this scaling issue.

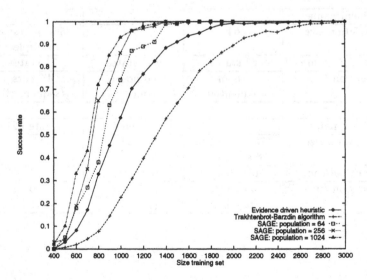

**Fig. 3.** Comparison of performance for target DFAs of nominal size 32.

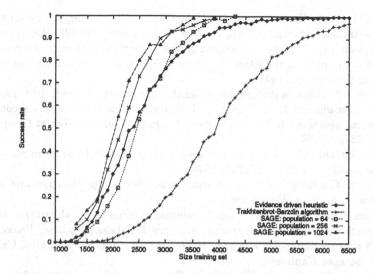

**Fig. 4.** Comparison of performance for target DFAs of nominal size 64.

# 6 Conclusion

One property of the state merging approach for DFA learning is that early merges play a very important role since they propagate constraints that control the future merges. This property is exploited by the underlying heuristics implemented in SAGE. Indeed, the random sampling strategy used to evaluate partial solutions is likely to return a better score (that is a smaller DFA hypothesis) on average if the early merges implemented in those partial solutions are correct.

The comparative analysis presented in this paper shows that for average size target DFAs (on the order of 64 to 128 states) SAGE compares favorably to the well-known Trakhtenbrot-Barzdin algorithm and to a new evidence-driven heuristic. However, as the size of the target DFA increases, SAGE doesn't scale up and requires a prohibitive amount of computer resource. To search such a large state space, the introduction of problem-specific heuristics becomes necessary.

DFA induction is not the only field of application for SAGE. In a previous work, we applied SAGE to the construction of sorting networks with a minimum number of comparators [9].

# References

[1] Dana Angluin and Carl H. Smith. Inductive inference: Theory and methods. *Computing Surveys*, 15:237–269, september 1983.
[2] Thomas Bäck, Frank Hoffmeister, and Hans-Paul Schwefel. A survey of evolution strategies. In Richard K. Belew and Lashon B. Booker, editors, *Proceedings of the Fourth International Conference on Genetic Algorithms*, pages 2–9, San Mateo, California, 1991. Morgan Kaufmann.

[3] Pang C. Chen. Heuristic sampling: a method for predicting the performance of tree searching programs. *SIAM Journal on Computing*, 21:295–315, april 1992.

[4] S. Das and M. C. Mozer. A unified gradient-descent/clustering architecture for finite state machine induction. In *Neural Information Processing Systems*, volume 6, pages 19–26, 1994.

[5] Lawrence J. Fogel. Autonomous automata. *Industrial Research*, 4:14–19, 1962.

[6] M. L. Forcada and R. C. Carrasco. Learning the initial state of a second-order recurrent neural network during regular-language inference. *Neural Computation*, 7(5):923–930, 1995.

[7] E. Mark Gold. Complexity of automaton identification from given data. *Information and Control*, 37:302–320, 1978.

[8] David E. Goldberg. *Genetic Algorithms in Search, Optimization and Machine Learning*. Addison-Wesley, 1989.

[9] Hugues Juillé. Evolution of non-deterministic incremental algorithms as a new approach for search in state spaces. In Larry J. Eshelman, editor, *Proceedings of the Sixth International Conference on Genetic Algorithms*, San Mateo, California, 1995. Morgan Kaufmann.

[10] Hugues Juillé and Jordan B. Pollack. Sage: a sampling-based heuristic for tree search. 1998. Submitted to Machine Learning.

[11] Donald E. Knuth. Estimating the efficiency of backtracking programs. *Math. Comp.*, 29:121–136, 1975.

[12] John R. Koza. *Genetic Programming: On the Programming of Computers by Means of Natural Selection*. MIT Press, 1992.

[13] Kevin J. Lang. Random dfa's can be approximately learned from sparse uniform examples. In *Proceedings of the Fifth Annual ACM Workshop on Computational Learning Theory*, pages 45–52, 1992.

[14] Kevin J. Lang and Barak A. Pearlmutter. Abbadingo one: Dfa learning competition. http://abba–dingo.cs.unm.edu, 1997.

[15] Kevin J. Lang, Barak A. Pearlmutter, and Rodney Price. Results of the abbadingo one dfa learning competition and a new evidence driven state merging algorithm. 1998. Submitted to Machine Learning.

[16] Jordan B. Pollack. The induction of dynamical recognizers. *Machine Learning*, 7:227–252, 1991.

[17] B. A. Trakhtenbrot and Ya M. Barzdin. *Finite Automata: Behavior and Synthesis*. North Holland Publishing Company, 1973.

[18] R. L. Watrous and G. M. Kuhn. Induction of finite state languages using second-order recurrent networks. *Neural Computation*, 4(3):406–414, 1992.

[19] Z. Zeng, R. M. Goodman, and P. Smyth. Learning finite state machines with self-clustering recurrent networks. *Neural Computation*, 5(6):976–990, 1994.

# Transducer-Learning Experiments on Language Understanding *

David Picó ** and Enrique Vidal

Institut Tecnològic d'Informàtica
Universitat Politècnica de València
València, Spain
{dpico, evidal}@iti.upv.es

**Abstract.** The interest in using Finite-State Models in a large variety
of applications is recently growing as more powerful techniques for learning them from examples have been developed. Language Understanding
can be approached this way as a problem of language *translation* in
which the target language is a *formal* language rather than a natural
one. Finite-state transducers are used to model the translation process,
and are automatically learned from training data consisting of pairs of
natural-language/formal-language sentences. The need for training data
is dramatically reduced by performing a two-level learning process based
on lexical/phrase categorization. Successful experiments are presented
on a task consisting in the "understanding" of Spanish natural-language
sentences describing dates and times, where the target formal language
is the one used in the popular Unix command *"at"*.

## 1 Introduction

Language Understanding (LU) has been the focus of much research work in
the last twenty years. Many classical approaches typically consider LU from a
linguistically motivated, generalistic point of view. Nevertheless, it is interesting
to note that, in contrast with some general-purpose formulations of LU, many
applications of interest to industry and business have *limited domains*; that is,
lexicons are of small size and the semantic universe is limited.

Under the *limited-domain* framework, the ultimate goal of a system is to *drive
the actions* associated to the meaning conveyed by the sentences issued by the
users. Since actions are to be performed by machines, the understanding problem
can then be simply formulated as *translating* the *natural language* sentences
into *formal sentences* of an adequate (computer) command language in which
the actions to be carried out can be specified. For example, "understanding"
natural language (spoken) queries to a database can be seen as "translating"

---

* Work partially supported by EuTRANS, European Union ESPRIT LTR Project
30268, and the Spanish CICYT under grant TIC–0745–CO2.
** Author supported by a FPI grant from the Conselleria d'Educació i Ciència of Va-
lencian Government.

these queries into appropriate computer-language code to access the database. Clearly, under such an assumption, LU can be seen as a possibly simpler case of Language Translation in which the output language is *formal* rather than *natural*.

Nevertheless, even in limited domain LU situations, this kind of mapping can actually be very complex and it is often argued that correspondingly complex devices should be required for its implementation. While this is essentially true, one should take into account that, from an engineering point of view, all what is required is just an approriate (simple) *model* that would give a suitable *approximation* to the possibly contrived underlying mapping. To this end, *Finite State Models* often prove adequate in many cases of interest.

The capabilities of Finite-State Models (FSM) have been the object of much debate in the past few years. On the one hand, in the Natural Language (NL) community, FSMs have often been ruled out for many NL processing applications, including LU, even in limited domains. On the other hand, in Speech Recognition, the use of N-Gram models, which are just among the simplest types of FSMs [26, 11, 27], is firmly established nowadays as a state-of-the-art technique for Language Modeling, even for open-domain applications. Recently, many NL and Computational Linguistic researchers are (re-)considering the interesting features of FSMs for their use in NL processing Applications [13].

Simple as they are, FSMs generally need to be huge in order to be useful approximations to complex languages. Consequently, building them by some procedure of automatical learning from large enough sets of training data becomes a must [11, 23, 17, 24, 26].

The present work continues a line of research centered in language understanding and subsequential transducer learning [6, 20, 21, 24]. Here, more powerful techniques are being tested on a complex, useful task of practical interest.

## 2 Subsequential Transduction Learning

The *Finite-State* or *Rational Transductions* are simple models of mappings between languages, that have been extensively studied [4]. An interesting subclass of these are *Subsequential Transductions*, which properly contains the class of *Sequential Transductions*. A Sequential Transduction in one that preserves the increasing length prefixes of input-output strings. While this can be considered as a rather "natural property" of transductions, there are many real-world situations in which such a strict sequentiality is clearly inadmissible. The class of Subsequential Transductions makes this restriction milder, therefore allowing for its application in many practical situations of interest. Apart for this flexibility of subsequential transducers, perhaps more important is the fact that these mappings have been proved *learnable* from positive presentation of input-output examples, by making use of the so-called *Onward Subsequential Transducer Inference Algorithm* (OSTIA), by Oncina [16, 17].

A *Subsequential Transducer* (SST) is a six-tuple $\tau = (Q, X, Y, q_0, E, \sigma)$, where $Q$ is a finite set of states, $X, Y$ are input and output alphabets, $q_0 \in Q$

140

is an initial state, $E \subset Q \times X \times Y^* \times Q$ is a set of edges and $\sigma : Q \to Y^*$ is a partial *state output function* [4]. Additionally, all states must be accepting and must fulfill all the conditions for determinism. The (subsequential) transduction associated by $\tau$ to an input string, $x$, is obtained by concatenating the output strings of the edges of $\tau$ that are used to parse the successive symbols of $x$, together with $\sigma(q)$, where $q$ is the last state reached with the input $x$. Examples of SSTs are shown in Fig.1.

Two SSTs are equivalent if they perform the same input-output mapping. Among equivalent SSTs there always exists one that is *canonical*. This transducer always adopts an *"onward"* form [17], in which the output substrings are assigned to the edges in such a way that they are as "close" to the initial state as they can be. On the other hand, any finite (training) set of input-output pairs of strings can be properly represented as a *Tree Subsequential Transducer* (TST), which can then be easily converted into a corresponding *Onward Tree Subsequential Transducer* (OTST). Fig.1 (left and center) illustrates these concepts (and construction), which are the basis of the so-called *Onward Subsequential Transducer Inference Algorithm (OSTIA)*, by Oncina [16, 17].

Given an input-output training sample $T$, the OSTI Algorithm works by *merging states* in the $OTST(T)$ as follows [17]: All pairs of states of $OTST(T)$ are orderly considered level by level, starting at the root, and, for each of these pairs, the states are tentatively merged. If this results in a non-deterministic state, then an attempt is made to restore determinism by recursively pushing-back some output substrings towards the leaves of the transducer (i.e., partially undoing the onward construction), while performing the necessary additional state merge operations. If the resulting transducer is subsequential, then (all) the merging(s) is (are) accepted; otherwise, a next pair of states is considered in the previous transducer. A transducer produced by this procedure from the OTST of Fig.1 (center) is shown in Fig.1 (right). All these operations can be very efficiently implemented, yielding an extremely fast algorithm that can easily handle huge sets of training data. It has formally been shown that OSTIA always converges to any target subsequential transduction for a sufficiently large number of training pairs of this transduction [17].

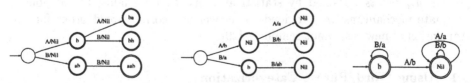

**Fig. 1.** Learning a Subsequential Transducer from the input-output sample T={(A,b), (B,ab), (AA,ba), (AB,bb), (BB,aab)}. *Left*: Tree Subsequential Transducer $TST(T)$; *Center*: Onward Tree Subsequential Transducer $OTST(T)$; *Right*: transducer yield by OSTIA. Each state contains the output string that the function $\sigma$ associates to this state.

The learning strategy followed by OSTIA tries to generalize the training pairs as much as possible. This often leads to very compact transducers that accurately translate *correct* input text. However, this compactness often entails excessive *over-generalization* of the input and output languages, allowing nearly meaningless input sentences to be accepted, and translated into even more meaningless output! While this is not actually a problem for perfectly *correct text* input, it leads to dramatic failures when dealing with not exactly correct text or (even "correct") *speech* input.

A possible way to overcome this problem is to limit generalization by imposing adequate Language Model (LM) constraints: the learned SSTs should *not* accept input sentences or produce output sentences which are not consistent with given LMs of the input and output languages. These LMs are also known as *Domain* and *Range* models [19]. Learning with Domain and/or Range constraints can be carried out with a version of OSTIA called OSTIA-DR [18, 19]. This version was used in the work presented in this paper. Here, we have adopted the well-known bigrams [11] among many possibilities for (finite-state) modeling the input and output languages. Bigrams can be easily learned from the same (input and output) training sentences used for OSTIA-DR.

Subsequential Transducers and the OSTI (or OSTI-DR) Algorithm have been very successfully applied to learning several quite contrived (artificial) translation tasks [17]. Also, it has recently been applied to Language Translation [25, 12, 1] and Language Understanding. This work extends previous results [6, 12] in this last application.

## 3 Reducing the Demand for Training Data

The amount of training data required by OSTIA(-DR)–learning is directly related with the size of the vocabularies and the amount of input-output *asynchrony* of the translation task considered. This is due to the need of using states and transitions to "delay" the output until enough input has been seen. In the worst case, the number of states required by a SST to achieve this delaying mechanism can grow as much as $O(n^k)$, where $n$ is the number of (functionally equivalent) words and $k$ the length of the delay [29].

Techniques to reduce the impact of $k$ were studied in [29]. These techniques rely on *reordering* the words of the (training) output sentences on the base of *partial alignments* obtained by statistical translation methods [5]. Obviously, adequate mechanisms are provided to recover the correct word order for the translation of new test input sentences [29].

### 3.1 Using Word/Phrase Categorization

On the other hand, techniques to cut down the impact of vocabulary size were studied in [28] and [1]. The basic idea was to substitute words or groups of words by labels representing their syntactic (or semantic) *category* within a limited rank of options. Learning was thus carried out with the categorized sentences, which involved a (much) smaller effective vocabulary. As proposed in [1], introducing lexical categories in the learning and transducing processes begin with category identification and categorization of the corpus. Once a categorized corpus is available, it can be used for training the *"base transducer"*. Also, for each category, a simple transducer is built: its *"category transducer"*, which accounts for the "local" input-output mapping associated with the corresponding category. Finally, category expansion is needed for obtaining the final sentence-transducer: the arcs in the base transducer associated to the different categories are expanded using the corresponding category transducers.

Note that, while all the transducers learned by OSTIA-DR are subsequential and therefore deterministic, this embedding of categories generally results in final transducers that are no longer subsequential and often they can be ambiguous. Consequently, translation can not be performed through deterministic parsing and Viterbi-like Dynamic Programming is required. Ambiguities in transduction can be dealt with by extending the transducer stochastically, in such a way that the probability distribution of appearance of sentences in the training corpus is reflected. Rule probabilities may be estimated in a straight-forward manner, by estimating the base-transducer and category-transducers probabilities by maximum likelihood through the frequency of rules, and combining them adequately to obtain the final sentence-transducer [1]. Better estimation appraches exist, though they have not been used in this work [8, 9]

Obviously, categorization has to be done for input/output *paired clusters*; therefore adequate techniques are needed to represent the actual identity of input *and* output words in the clusters and to recover this identity when parsing test input sentences. This recovering is made by keeping referencies between category labels and then solving them with a postprocess filter. This method is explained in detail in [1].

## 3.2 Coping with Undertraining through Error Correcting

The performance achieved by a SST model (and for many other types of models whatsoever) tends to be poor if the input sentences do not strictly comply with the syntactic restrictions imposed by the model. This is the case of syntactically incorrect sentences, or correct sentences whose precise "structure" has not been exactly captured because it was not present in the training data.

Both of these problems can be approached by means of Error-Correcting Decoding (ECD) [3, 29]. Under this approach, the input sentence, $x$, is considered as a *corrupted* version of some sentence, $\hat{x} \in L$, where $L$ is the domain or input language of the SST. The corruption process is modeled by means of an Error Model that accounts for insertion, substitution and deletion *"edit errors"*. In practice, these "errors" should account for likely vocabulary variations, word disappearances, superfluous words, repetitions, and so on. Recognition can then be seen as an ECD process: given $x$, find a sentence $\hat{x}$ in $L$ such that the distance form $\hat{x}$ to $x$, measured in terms of edit operations (insertions, deletions and substitutions) is minimum. Stochastic ECD is similarly formulated with a stochastic transducer and a probabilistic error model, and where sentence $\hat{x}$ in

$L$ is to be found for which the probability that $x$ is a corrupted version of $\hat{x}$ is maximum [2].

Given the finite-state nature of SST Models, Error Models can be *tightly* integrated, and combined error-correcting decoding and translation can be performed very efficiently using fast ECD beam-search, Viterbi-based techniques such as those proposed in [3].

# 4  Experiments

The chosen task in our experiments was the translation from Spanish sentences specifying times and dates into sentences of a formal semantic language. This is in fact an important subtask that is common to many real-world LU applications of much interest to industry and society. Examples of this kind of applications are flight, train or hotel reservations, appointment schedules, etc. [10, 14, 15]. Therefore, having an adequate solution to this subtask can significantly simplify the building of successful systems for these applications (see [7] for an independent work on a similar date/time understanding subtask).

The chosen formal language has been the one used in UNIX command "at". This simple language allows both absolute and relative descriptions of time. From these descriptions, the "at" interpreter can be directly used to obtain date/time interpretations in the desired format. The correct syntax of "at" commands is described in the standard Unix documentation (see, e.g. [30]). Figure 2 shows some training pairs that have been selected from the training material.

| ("dos minutos después de la una y media", 01 : 30 + 2 MINUTE) |
| *(two minutes after one thirty)* |
| ("dentro de tres horas", NOW + 3 HOUR) |
| *(in three hours)* |
| ("el martes, a la hora del té, más un minuto", TEATIME TUE + 1 MINUTE) |
| *(on thursday, at teatime plus one minute)* |
| ("el catorce de octubre del año dos mil tres, a las diecisiete horas |
| y cinco minutos", 17 : 05 OCT 14 , 2003) |
| *(on october the first, year two thousand and three, at seventeen hours* |
| *and five minutes)* |

**Fig. 2.** Sample of selected training pairs for the date specification task.

Starting from the given context-free-style syntax description of the "at" command [30], and knowledge-based patterns of typical ways of expressing dates and times in natural, spontaneous Spanish, a large corpus of pairs of "natural-language"/at-language sentences was artificially constructed. This was intended to be the first step in a bootstrapping development. On-going work on this task is aimed at (semi-automatically) obtaining additional corpora produced by real user interaction. The corpus generation procedure incorporated 11 different "category labels", such as *hour, month, day of week*, etc. We have used a similar process for defining and generating subcorpora in which every input and its corresponding semantic coding belong to the different categories. We finally have obtained an uncategorized version of the categorized corpus, by means of randomly instantiating the category marks in the samples. The examples found on Fig. 2 come from this uncategorized corpus, while Fig. 3 shows the corresponding categorized pairs.

| |
|---|
| ("**inc-number** minutos después de **h24 mm**", h24 : mm + **inc-number** MINUTE) |
| ("dentro de **inc-number** horas", NOW + **inc-number** HOUR) |
| ("el **day-of-week** , a **t-dest** , mas un minuto", t-dest day-of-week + 1 MINUTE) |
| ("el **day-txt** de **month-name** del año **year-name**, a h24 mm", h24 : mm month-name day-txt , year-name) |

**Fig. 3.** Sample of categorized pairs for the date specification task.

We have generated a training corpus of 48353 different, uncategorized translation pairs, and a *disjoint* test set with 1331 translation pairs. We have presented the OSTIA-DR with 8 training subsets of sizes increasing from 1817 up to 48353. We also have presented OSTIA-DR with the same, but categorized, training subsets. In this case, the number of different pairs went from 1384 up to 12381. Figure 4 shows the size of categorized corpora vs. uncategorized corpora. The input language vocabulary has 108 words, and the output language has 125 semantic symbols.

In the categorized experiments, the procedure described in Sect. 3.1 was followed. The sizes of the inferred transducers are shown on Fig. 5. Non-categorized transducers increase their sizes much faster than categorized transducers as the training corpus grows larger.

Performance has been measured in terms of both semantic-symbol error and full-sentence matching rates. The translation of the test set inputs has been computed using both the standard Viterbi algorithm and the Error Correction techniques, outlined on Sects. 3.1 and 3.2. In all cases, the translation procedure did not make use of the transducer or error-model probabilities. Take into account that experiments using Viterbi algorithm have had error rates computed by considering rejected sentences as if the output had been the empty string. Experiments using Error Correction have no rejected sentences, since an output is always produced for any possible input. The results are shown in Fig. 6.

A big difference in performance between the uncategorized and categorized training procedures can be observed. Semantic-symbol error rates are much lower in the categorized experiments than in the uncategorized ones. We can also appreciate a remarkable decrease in semantic-symbol error rates of Error Correcting with respect to Viterbi translations, specially for smaller training corpus. The

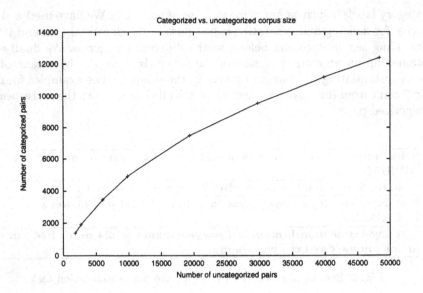

**Fig. 4.** Corpora size before and after categorization.

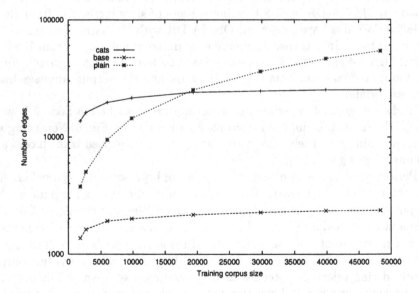

**Fig. 5.** Size of the inferred transducers (number of edges): "base" stands for the categorized sentence transducer, while "cats" stands for the final sentence-transducer obtained by embedding the (small) category-transducers into the "base" one; "plain" stands for the uncategorized sentence-transducer.

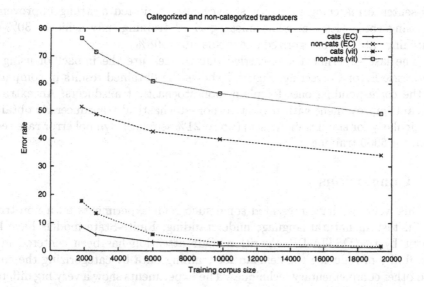

**Fig. 6.** Comparison between semantic-symbol error rates for categorized ("cats") and non-categorized ("non-cats") transducers, with and without Error Correcting ("EC" and "vit", respectively).

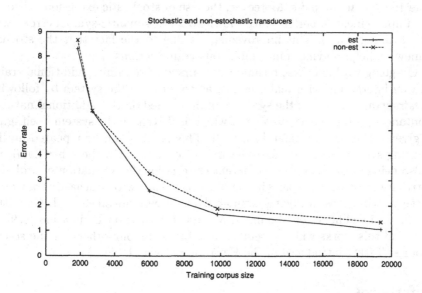

**Fig. 7.** Comparison between semantic-symbol error rates for stochastic ("est") and non-stochastic ("non-est") Error Correcting transductions.

full-sentence matching rate (not shown) also exhibited a strong improvement by using categorization: while uncategorized training only achieves 30%-40% matching rate, the categorized one yields up to 98%.

The last experiment was carried out to measure the impact of using full *stochastic* Error Correcting. Figure 7 shows the obtained results in comparison to the corresponding ones for plain, non-stochastic transducers. An extra significant improvement with respect to non-stochastical transducers is obtained, particularly for small training-sets (up to 21% semantic-symbol error rate reduction, for 6000 training pairs).

## 5 Conclusions

In this work, we have presented some successful experiments on a non-trivial, useful task in natural language understanding. Finite-State models have been learnt by the OSTIA-DR algorithm. Our attention has been centered in the possibility of reducing the demand for training data by categorizing the corpus and other complementary techniques. The experiments show a very big difference in performance between the categorized and plain training procedures. In this task, we only obtain useful results if we use categories.

The Error Correcting technique for translation also permits reducing the size of corpora and still obtain useful performance. In our task, we got a 3.2% semantic-symbol error rate for a training set of approximately 6000 pairs, while for the same level of performance using the standard Viterbi algorithm requires some 10000 training pairs. Moreover, the use of stochastic extensions yields further improvement in performance (down to 2.6% semantic-symbol error rate for 6000 training pairs). This improvement is due to the fact that the stochastic framework helps solving some ambiguous transductions.

On-going work on these techniques is aimed at obtaining additional training data by interaction with real users, so as to improve the system by following a *bootstrapping* procedure: the system will be trained on this additional natural or spontaneous data, the acquisition of which is driven by the system itself, guided by given task-relevant semantic stimuli. This process can be repeated until the resulting system exhibits a satisfactory performance. On the other hand, work is also being done on applying different criteria for the estimation of probability distributions of sentence pairs in the training corpus with stochastic transducers. These distributions are being estimated by Maximum-Likelihood, Conditional Maximum-Likelihood, or Maximum Mutual Information Estimation [8,9]. The results of this works will be useful as a subtask, among others, of the so-called "Tourist Task", introduced in the EuTrans project [1,25].

## References

1. J.C AMENGUAL, J.B.BENEDÍ, F.CASACUBERTA, A. CASTAÑO, A. CASTELLANOS, D. LLORENS, A. MARZAL, F. PRAT, E. VIDAL AND J.M.VILAR: "Using Categories in the Eutrans System". *ACL-ELSNET Workshop on Spoken Language Translation*, Madrid, Spain, pp. 44-52. (1997)

2. J.C. AMENGUAL, E. VIDAL. *Two Different Approaches for Cost-efficient Viterbi Parsing with Error Correction*. Proc. of the SSPR'96, IAPR International Workshop on Structural and Syntactical Pattern Recognition, August 20–23, 1996, Leipzig. To be published in the Proceedings.

3. J.C. AMENGUAL, E. VIDAL AND J.M. BENEDÍ. "Simplifying Language through Error-Correcting Decoding". *Proceedings of the ICSLP96 (IV International Conference on Spoken Language Processing)*. To be published. October, 1996.

4. J. BERSTEL. *Transductions and Context-Free Languages*. Teubner, Stuttgart. 1979.

5. P.F.BROWN ET AL.. "A Statistical Approach to Machine Translation". *Computational Linguistics*, Vol. 16, No.2, pp.79-85, 1990.

6. A.CASTELLANOS, E.VIDAL, J.ONCINA. "Language Understanding and Subsequential Transducer Learning". *1st International Colloquium on Grammatical Inference*, Colchester, England. proc., pp. 11/1-11/10. April, 1993.

7. J.G.BAUER, H.STAHL, J.MLLER: "A One-pass Search Algorithm for Understanding Natural Spoken Time Utterances by Stochastic Models". *Proc. of the EUROSPEECH'95*, Madrid, Spain, vol.I, pp. 567-570. (1995)

8. F. CASACUBERTA: "Maximum Mutual Information and Conditional Maximum Likelihood Estimations on Stochastic Regular Syntax-Directed Translation Schemes", *Lecture notes in Artificial Intelligence*, vol.1147, pp. 282-291, Springer-Verlag. (1996)

9. F. CASACUBERTA: "Growth Transformations for Probabilistic Functions on Stochastic Grammars", *International Journal of Pattern Recognition and Artificial Intelligence*, vol. 10, n. 3, pp. 183-201, Word Scientific Publishing Company. (1996)

10. C.T.HEMPHILL, J.J.GODFREY, G.R.DODDINGTON. "The ATIS Spoken Language Systems, pilot Corpus". *Proc. of 3rd DARPA Workshop on Speech and Natural Language*, pp. 102-108, Hidden Valley (PA), June 1990.

11. F. JELINEK: "Language Modeling for Speech Recognition". In [13] (1996).

12. V.JIMENEZ, A.CASTELLANOS, E.VIDAL. "Some results with a trainable speech translation and understanding system". In *Proceedings of the ICASSP-95*, Detroit, MI (USA), 1995

13. A.KORNAI (ED.); *Proceedings of the ECAI'96 Workshop: Extended Finite State Models of Language*. Budapest, 1996.

14. A.LAVIE, A.WAIBEL, L.LEVIN, M.FINKE, D.GATES, M.GAVALDÀ, T.ZEPPENFELD AND P.ZHAN: "JANUS-III: Speech-to-speech Translation in Multiple Languages", Proc. of the ICASSP'97, Munich, Germany, vol. I, pp. 99-102. (1997)

15. E. MAIER AND S. MCGLASHAN: "Semantic and Dialogue Processing in the VERBMOBIL Spoken Dialogue Translation System", In *Proceedings in Artificial Intelligence: CRIM/FORWISS Workshop on Progress and Prospects of Speech Research and Technology*, H. Niemann, R. de Mori and G. Hanrieder (eds.), Infix, pp. 270–273. (1994)

16. J.ONCINA. "Aprendizaje de Lenguages Regulares y Funciones Subsecuenciales". Ph.D. diss., Universidad Politecnica de Valencia, 1991.

17. J.ONCINA, P.GARCIA, E.VIDAL. "Learning Subsequential Transducers for Pattern Recognition Interpretation Tasks". *IEEE Transactions on Pattern Analysis and Machine Intelligence*, Vol.15, No.5, pp.448-458. May, 1993.

18. J.ONCINA, A.CASTELLANOS, E.VIDAL, V.JIMENEZ. "Corpus-Based Machine Translation through Subsequential Transducers". *Third Int. Conf. on the Cognitive Science of Natural Language Processing*, proc., Dublin, 1994

19. J.ONCINA, M.A.VAR. "Using domain information during the learning of a subsequential transducer". In Laurent Miclet and Colin de la Higuera, editors, *Grammatical Inference: Learning Syntax from Sentences, Lecture Notes in Computer Science*, vol. 1147, pp. 301-312. Springer-Verlag. 1996

20. R. PIERACCINI, E. LEVIN. "Stochastic Representation of Semantic Structure for Speech Understanding". EUROSPEECH'91, Proc., Vol. 2, pp.383-386. Genoa Sept, 1991.

21. R. PIERACCINI, E. LEVIN, E. VIDAL. "Learning How To Understand Language". EUROSPEECH'93, proc., Vol.2, pp. 1407-1412. Berlin, Sept, 1993.

22. N.PRIETO, E.VIDAL. "Learning Language Models through the ECGI method". Speech Communication, No.11, pp.299-309. 1992.

23. K.SEYMORE, R.ROSENFELD. "Scalable Backoff Language Models". *ICSLP-96, proc..* pp.232-235. Philadelfia, 1996.

24. E. VIDAL: "Language Learning, Understanding and Translation", In *Proc. in Art. Intell.: CRIM/FORWISS Workshop on Progress and Prospects of Speech Research and Technology*, H. Niemann, R. de Mori and G. Hanrieder (eds.), pp. 131–140. Infix, (1994).

25. E. VIDAL: "Finite-State Speech-to-speech Translation", Proc. of the ICASSP'97, Munich, Germany, vol.I, pp. 111-122. (1997)

26. E.VIDAL, F.CASACUBERTA, P.GARCIA. "Grammatical Inference and Automatic Speech Recognition". In *Speech Recognition and Coding. New Advances and Trends*, J.Rubio and J.M.Lopez, Eds. Springer Verlag, 1994.

27. E.VIDAL, D.LLORENS. "Using knowledge to improve N-Gram Language Modeling through the MGGI methodology". In *Grammatical Inference: Learning Syntax from Sentences*, L.Miclet, C.De La Higuera, Eds. LNAI (1147), Springer-Verlag, 1996.

28. J.M. VILAR, A. MARZAL, E. VIDAL: "Learning Language Translation in Limited Domains using Finite-State Models: some Extensions and Improvements". *Proceedings of the EUROSPEECH-95*, Madrid, Spain, pp. 1231-1234. (1995)

29. J.M. VILAR, E. VIDAL AND J.C. AMENGUAL: "Learning Extended Finite State Models for Language Translation". *Proceedings of the ECAI96* (12th European Conference on Artificial Intelligence). August (1996).

30. Linux system documentacion, at directory "/usr/doc/at" (Debian distribution). Also, see "man at" on a Unix system.

# Locally Threshold Testable Languages in Strict Sense: Application to the Inference Problem

José Ruiz, Salvador España, Pedro García

Depto. de Sistemas Informáticos y Computación.
Universidad Politécnica de Valencia. Valencia (Spain).
jruiz@dsic.upv.es
sespana@iti.upv.es
pgarcia@dsic.upv.es

**Abstract.** The aim of this paper is to define a new family of regular languages, the *Locally Threshold Testable Languages in Strict Sense* (*LTTSS*). This family includes the well known family of locally testable languages in strict sense (*LTSS*) and is included in the family of locally threshold testable languages (*LTT*). Membership of a word to a *LTTSS* language can be decided by means of local scanning, using a sliding window of a fixed length $k$, although in this case, we have to care that the number of occurrences of certain segments of length $\leq k$ in the words is not greater than a level of restriction, less than a threshold $r$. As *LTTSS* languages may be of interest in disciplines such as Pattern Recognition and specially in Speech Recognition, an inference algorithm that identifies the family of $(k, r)$-*TTSS* languages from positive data in the limit is proposed. Finally we also report some results aiming to reflect the evolution of the behavior of this algorithm for different values of $k$ and $r$ when it is used in a handwritten digits recognition task.

## 1 Introduction

One of the families of languages that has received more attention in the literature is the family of *Locally Testable Languages* (*LT*). Membership of a word to a *LT* language is determined by the set of factors of a fixed length $k$ and by the prefixes and suffixes of length less than $k$ of the word. The number of occurrences of the factors in the word or the order in which they appear are not relevant. Local languages, known either by their ability to generate the family of regular languages by means of morphisms [12] or by Chomsky-Schützemberger's theorem for Context Free Languages, are included in the family of *LT*. In fact they constitute a particular instance of the so called Locally Testable Languages in Strict Sense (*LTSS*).

The words of a *LTSS* language $L$, for a given value of $k \geq 1$, are defined by means of three finite sets: A set $A$ of prefixes of length $< k$, a set $B$ of suffixes of length $< k$ and a set $C$ of segments of length $k$ not allowed to appear in its strings. Membership of a word to a *LTSS* language, for a given value of $k$ ($k$-*TSS*) can be decided exploring the word through a sliding window of length

$k$ and testing if its prefix belongs to $A$, its suffix belongs to $B$ and also that it does not contain any segment of length $k$ in $C$.

An extension of the family of $LT$ languages is the family of locally threshold testable languages $(LTT)$. $LTT$ languages are defined in a similar way as $LT$ languages are, with the difference that in this case, frequency of factors of length $\leq k$ are count up to a threshold $r \geq 1$ ($LT$ are a particular instance of $LTT$, the case $r = 1$). If a word $x$ belongs to a $LTT$ language $L$ for given values of $k$ and $r$, any word $y$ will also belong to $L$ iff it meets the three following conditions:

1. Begins and ends with the same segments of length $k - 1$ that $x$.
2. The frequency of each segment of length $\leq k$ in $y$ is the same as in $x$, if this number is less than $r$.
3. If the frequency of a factor of length $\leq k$ in $x$ is $\geq r$, then the frequency of that factor in $y$ is also $\geq r$.

It seems natural, in this context, to define the family of *Locally Threshold Testable Languages in Strict Sense* $(LTTSS)$, which, on one hand, is a restriction the family of $LTT$ and, on the other, is an extension of $LTSS$ languages. We define $LTTSS$ languages by means of the sets of prefixes and suffixes of length $< k$ and by a set of *restricted segments* of length $\leq k$. Each segment in the set of restricted segments is associated with a level of restriction, which is less than a fixed threshold $r$. The segments for which this level is zero are forbidden. The language defined this way contains the words that begin and end with elements of the indicated sets and such that none of the restricted segments appears in them a number of times beyond its level of restriction. For each value of $k$, if we set $r$ to 1 we obtain the family of $k$-Testable Languages in Strict Sense $(k$-$TSS)$. The family of $LTTSS$ languages has been algebraically characterized by means of a property of the idempotents of their syntactic semigroup (see [6] for further details).

Besides its theoretical interest, another reason to study $LTTSS$ languages is the possibility of being used in Pattern Recognition $(PR)$ [5], [9]. Stochastic $LTSS$ languages, also known as $N$-*grams*, are frequently used in $PR$, particularly in Speech Recognition, both in Acoustic-Phonetics Decoding as in Language Modeling [14]. We show in this work that, like $k$-$TSS$ languages [7], $(k,r)$-$TTSS$ languages are learnable from positive data, and we present some results obtained by using learned $(k,r)$-$TTSS$ languages for handwritten digits classification task. The main goal of the experiments is to show the evolution of the classification rates when $k$ and $r$ vary.

## 2 Preliminaries and Notation

### 2.1 Formal Languages

We assume that the reader is familiar with the rudiments of formal language theory. Any concept not mentioned here can be found in [10].

Let $\Sigma$ be a finite alphabet and $\Sigma^*$ the free monoid generated by $\Sigma$ with concatenation as the binary operation and $\lambda$ as neutral element. A *language* $L$ over $\Sigma$ is a subset of $\Sigma^*$, its elements will be referred as *words*. The set of all words of length $k$ will be represented as $\Sigma^k$, also $\Sigma_1^k = \bigcup_{i=1}^k \Sigma^i$. Given $x \in \Sigma^*$, if $x = uvw$ with $u, v, w \in \Sigma^*$, then $u$ (resp. $w$) is called *prefix* (resp. *suffix*) of $x$, while $v$ (also $u$ and $w$) is said to be a *factor* or *segment* of $x$. $\mathrm{Pr}(L)$ (resp. $\mathrm{Suf}(L)$) denotes the set of prefixes (resp. suffixes) of $L$. The *length* of a word $x$ is represented by $|x|$. The frequency of appearance of a word $w$ as a segment of $x$ (its number of occurrences in $x$) is written as $|x|_w$. Given $u \in \Sigma^*$ and $L \subseteq \Sigma^*$, $u^{-1}L = \{v \in \Sigma^* : uv \in L\}$. Also, if $R \subseteq \Sigma^*$ is a finite set, $|R|$ denotes its cardinal.

A Deterministic Finite-state Automaton $(DFA)$ is a 5-tuple $A = (Q, \Sigma, \delta, q_0, F)$ where $Q$ is a finite set of states, $\Sigma$ is a finite alphabet, $q_0 \in Q$ is the initial state, $F \subseteq Q$ is the set of final states and $\delta$ is a partial function, mapping $Q \times \Sigma$ to $Q$ that can be extended to words defining $\delta(q, \lambda) = q$ and $\delta(q, xa) = \delta(\delta(q, x), a)$, $\forall q \in Q$, $\forall x \in \Sigma^*$, $\forall a \in \Sigma$. A word $x$ is accepted by $A$ if $\delta(q_0, x) \in F$. The set of words accepted by an automaton $A$ is denoted by $L(A)$.

Given $R \subset \Sigma^*$, $PTA(R)$ denotes the prefix tree acceptor for $R$, that is $PTA(R) = (Q, \Sigma, \delta, q_0, F)$, being $Q = \mathrm{Pr}(R)$, $q_0 = \lambda$, $F = R$ and $\forall u, ua \in \mathrm{Pr}(R)$, $\delta(u, a) = ua$. Given $A_0 = PTA(R)$, if $\sim$ is an equivalence relation defined in $Q$, $A_0/\sim$ denotes the quotient automaton (obtained by merging equivalent states).

## 2.2 Language inference from positive presentation

A *positive sample* of a language $L$ is any finite subset of $L$. A *positive presentation* of $L$ is any enumeration of $L$. Let $\mathcal{L}$ a family of languages over $\Sigma$, a *class of representations* $\mathcal{H}$ for the languages in $\mathcal{L}$ must accomplish that for any $L \in \mathcal{L}$ there exists at least $h \in \mathcal{H}$ such that $L(h) = L$. For example, if $\mathcal{L}$ is a family of regular languages, $\mathcal{H}$ can be taken as the set of $DFA$ over $\Sigma$. An *inference algorithm* for $\mathcal{L}$ from positive samples and representations in $\mathcal{H}$ is an algorithm $\mathcal{A}$ that, with input of a finite set $R \subset \Sigma^*$, outputs a hypothesis $h \in \mathcal{H}$. If $L \in \mathcal{L}$ and $< x_1, x_2, \ldots >$ is a positive presentation of $L$, we denote as $t_k$ the finite sequence $< x_1, x_2, \ldots x_k >$. $\mathcal{A}$ identifies the family $\mathcal{L}$ with respect to $\mathcal{H}$ from positive samples in the limit if for any $L \in \mathcal{L}$ and any positive presentation $< x_1, x_2, \ldots >$ of $L$ there exists a natural number $n_0$ such that for $n \geq n_0$, $h_n = h_{n_0}$ and $L(h_n) = L$, where $h_n = \mathcal{A}(t_n)$. A family $\mathcal{L}$ is identifiable with respect to $\mathcal{H}$ in the limit if there exists an algorithm $\mathcal{A}$ that identifies $\mathcal{L}$ [8], [2].

Let $R$ a positive sample of $L$ and $A$ a $DFA$ such that $L(A) = L$. We say that $R$ is *structurally complete* for $A$ iff every transition of $A$ is used in the acceptance by $A$ of some of the words of $R$.

A well known technique in regular language inference is the one known as *state clustering* [4], [2]. It is basically carried out, given a finite set $R \subset \Sigma^*$, obtaining $A_0 = PTA(R)$, defining an equivalence relation $\sim$ in $\mathrm{Pr}(R)$, and outputting $A_0/\sim$.

A class $\mathcal{L}$ is learnable in the limit from positive data with conjectures updated in polynomial time if there exists an algorithm $\mathcal{A}$ for $\mathcal{L}$ such that $\mathcal{A}(t_i) = M_i$ and there exists a polynomial $P$ such that $\forall L \in \mathcal{L}$, the time used by $\mathcal{A}$ between receiving the sample $x_i$ and outputting the hypothesis $M_i$ is $P(n, m_1 + ... + m_i)$, where $m_j = |x_j|$ and $n$ is the number of states of the minimal automaton accepting $L$.

# 3 Locally Threshold Testable Languages in Strict Sense

Given positive integers $k$ and $r$. The equivalence relation $\approx_{k,r}$ over $\Sigma^*$ is defined as follows:

- If $|x| < k$, then $x \approx_{k,r} y$ iff $x = y$.
- Otherwise $x \approx_{k,r} y$ iff:
  1. $\mathrm{Pr}(x) \cap \Sigma^{k-1} = \mathrm{Pr}(y) \cap \Sigma^{k-1}$.
  2. $Suf(x) \cap \Sigma^{k-1} = Suf(y) \cap \Sigma^{k-1}$.
  3. $\forall w \in \Sigma_1^k(|x|_w = |y|_w < r \vee (|x|_w > r \wedge |y|_w > r))$.

The relation $\approx_{k,r}$ is a congruence of finite index. A language is $(k, r)$-TT iff it is saturated by $\approx_{k,r}$. A language $L$ is *Locally Threshold Testable* (*LTT*) if there exist integers $k, r \geq 1$ such that $L$ is $(k, r)$-TT . If $r = 1$ this family coincides with the well known family of Locally Testable Languages (*LT*).

A subclass of the *LT* languages is the class of Locally Testable Languages in Strict Sense (*LTSS*). A language $L$ over $\Sigma$ is *LTSS* iff there exists an integer $k \geq 1$ and sets $A, B \subseteq \Sigma^{k-1}$ and $C \subseteq \Sigma^k$ such that

$$\Sigma^{k-1}\Sigma^* \cap L = A\Sigma^* \cap \Sigma^*B - \Sigma^*C\Sigma^*$$

We are going to define a new family of languages, called *Locally Threshold Testable Languages in Strict Sense* (*LTTSS*) that are related to *LTT* languages in the same way as *LTSS* are related to *LT*. The case $r = 1$ constitutes the family of *LTSS* languages.

Given an alphabet $\Sigma$ and integers $k, r \geq 1$ we define the 4-tuple $(I_k, F_k, T_{k,r}, g)$ where

- $I_k, F_k \subseteq \Sigma^{k-1}$, which are respectively the sets of prefixes and suffixes of length $k - 1$.
- $T_{k,r} \subseteq \Sigma_1^k$, the set of restricted factors of length $k$.
- $g : T_{k,r} \to \{0, 1, ...r - 1\}$, a function that defines the level of restriction of each of the restricted factors.

We say that $L$ is a *k-Testable Language in Strict Sense with Threshold r* (in the sequel this family will be referred as *(k,r)-TTSS*) iff

$$\Sigma^{k-1}\Sigma^* \cap L = I_k\Sigma^* \cap \Sigma^*F_k - \left( \bigcup_{w \in T_k} \{x \in \Sigma^* : |x|_w > g(w)\} \right)$$

$L$ is obviously regular. Language $L$, except for a finite number of words of length less than $k$, is the set of all words that:

- begin with a prefix of length $k - 1$ in $I_k$,
- end with a suffix of length $k - 1$ in $F_k$ and,
- if they contain segments of length $k$ belonging to $T_{k,r}$, the number of occurrences of these segments is less than or equal to the level of restriction given by the function $g$.

*Example 1.* The language $a^+ba^+b \cup a^+b$ is (2,3)-*TTSS*, as it fulfils the definition with $I_2 = \{a\}$, $F_2 = \{b\}$, $T_{k,r} = (b, ab, ba, bb)$ with $g(b) = 2$, $g(ab) = 2$, $g(ba) = 1$, $g(bb) = 0$.

A language $L$ is threshold locally testable in strict sense (*LTTSS*) if there exist two positive integers $k$ and $r$ such that $L$ is $(k, r)$-*TTSS*.

$\forall k, r \geq 1$, the family of $(k, r)$-*TTSS* languages is included in the family of $(k, r)$-*TT*. From the definition of $(k, r)$-*TTSS* languages, it follows that any language belonging to that family is saturated by the relation $\approx_{k,r}$, so $LTTSS \subset LTT$. It is easily seen that this inclusion is strict from the fact that $(k, r)$-*TTSS* languages are not closed under boolean operations.

# 4 Smallest $(k, r)$-*TTSS* Language That Contains a Positive Sample $S$

Given $x \in \Sigma^*$ we define the initial and final segments of $x$ of length $\leq k$ as follows:

$$i_k(x) = \begin{cases} x & if \ |x| < k \\ u \in \Sigma^k : x = uv, v \in \Sigma^* & if \ |x| \geq k \end{cases}$$

$$f_k(x) = \begin{cases} x & if \ |x| < k \\ v \in \Sigma^k : x = uv, u \in \Sigma^* & if \ |x| \geq k \end{cases}$$

Let $S$ be a positive sample of $L$, that is, $S \subset L$ finite. $\forall w \in \Sigma^k$ we define $n_{S,k}(w) = \max_{x \in S} |x|_w$, and let

- $I_k(S) = \{i_{k-1}(x) : x \in S\}$.
- $F_k(S) = \{f_{k-1}(x) : x \in S\}$.
- $T_{k,r}(S) = \{w \in \Sigma_1^k : n_{S,k}(w) < r\}$ and the function
- $g : T_{k,r}(S) \to \{0, 1, ...r - 1\}$ such that $g(w) = n_{S,k}(w)$.

It is evident that the language $(k, r)$-*TTSS* defined by $(I_k(S), F_k(S), T_{k,r}(S), g)$ is the smallest $(k, r)$-*TTSS* language that contains $S$. It will be denoted as $L_{k,r}(S)$.

## 4.1 Properties of $L_{k,r}(S)$.

The following properties follow directly from the definition of $L_{k,r}(S)$:

1. $S \subseteq S' \Rightarrow L_{k,r}(S) \subseteq L_{k,r}(S')$.
2. $k \leq k' \lor r \leq r' \Rightarrow L_{k',r'}(S) \subseteq L_{k,r}(S)$.
3. $r > \max_{x \in S} |x| - k + 1 \Rightarrow L_{k,r}(S) = \Pr(S) \cap \Sigma^* F_k(S)$.
4. $k > \max_{x \in S} |x| - r + 1 \Rightarrow L_{k,r}(S) = S$.

## 4.2 Automaton accepting the smallest $(k,r)$-$TTSS$ language that contains a positive sample $S$

The following automaton recognizes $L_{k,r}(S)$, the smallest $(k,r)$-$TSS$ language that contains a positive sample $S$.

Given the sample $S$ we obtain the 4-tuple $(I_k(S), F_k(S), T_{k,r}(S), g)$. In the sequel $\mathbf{0}$ will represent the $|T_{k,r}(S)|$-dimensional null vector. Vectors $\mathbf{v}$ have also dimensión $|T_{k,r}(S)|$.

Let $A = (Q, \Sigma, \delta, q_0, F)$ with

- $Q = \{[u, \mathbf{0}] : u \in \mathrm{Pr}(I_k(S))\} \cup$
  $\{[v, \mathbf{v}] : v \in \Sigma^{k-1}, \mathbf{v}_w \le g(w), \forall w \in T_{k,r}(S)\}$.
- $q_0 = [\lambda, \mathbf{0}]$.
- $F = \{[v, \mathbf{v}] \in Q : v \in F_k(S)\}$.
- The transition function $\delta$ defined as follows:

  1. $\forall u, ua \in \mathrm{Pr}(I_k(S)), |u| < k - 1, \delta([u, \mathbf{0}], a) = [ua, \mathbf{0}]$.
  2. $\forall aub \in T_{k,r}(S)$, where $a, b \in \Sigma$
     - $\delta([au, \mathbf{v}], b) = \emptyset$ if $\mathbf{v}_{aub} = g(aub)$
     - $\delta([au, \mathbf{v}], b) = [ub, \mathbf{v}']$ if $\mathbf{v}_{aub} < g(aub)$ where $\mathbf{v}'_{aub} = \mathbf{v}_{aub} + 1$ and $\mathbf{v}'_w = \mathbf{v}_w \forall w \in T_{k,r}(S) - \{aub\}$.
  3. $\forall aub \in \Sigma^k - T_{k,r}(S), \delta([au, \mathbf{v}], b) = [ub, \mathbf{v}]$.

**Lemma 1.** *The transition function $\delta$ defined above can be extended to the words of $S$, that is, $\forall x \in \mathrm{Pr}(L_{k,r}(S)), \delta([\lambda, \mathbf{0}], x) = [f_{k-1}(x), \mathbf{v}]$, with $\mathbf{v}_w = |x|_w, \forall w \in T_{k,r}(S)$.*

*Proof.* We proceed by induction in $|x|$.

For $x = \lambda$ it evidently holds.

Let us suppose that the proposition is true $\forall x \in \mathrm{Pr}(L_{k,r}(S))$ with $|x| = m$ and let $x = ya$ with $|y| = m$,

1. If $m < k - 1$,
   $\delta([\lambda, \mathbf{0}], ya) = \delta(\delta([\lambda, \mathbf{0}], y), a) = \delta([y, \mathbf{0}], a) = [ya, \mathbf{0}] = [f_{k-1}(ya), \mathbf{0}]$
2. If $m \ge k - 1, \delta([\lambda, \mathbf{0}], ya) = \delta(\delta([\lambda, \mathbf{0}], y), a) = \delta([f_{k-1}(y), \mathbf{v}], a)$, with $\mathbf{v}_w = |y|_w, \forall w \in T_{k,r}(S)$

   (a) If $f_{k-1}(ya) \in \Sigma^k - T_{k,r}(S)$, it follows that $\delta([f_{k-1}(y), \mathbf{v}], a) = [f_{k-2}(y)a, \mathbf{v}] = [f_{k-1}(ya), \mathbf{v}]$ and the proposition holds, as these words don't modify the associated vector of any of the segments of length $k$, that is, $\forall w \in T_{k,r}(S), |ya|_w = |y|_w$.

   (b) If $f_{k-1}(ya) \in T_{k,r}(S)$ it follows that $|y|_{f_{k-1}(y)a} < g(f_{k-1}(y)a)$, otherwise $ya \notin \mathrm{Pr}(L_{k,r}(S))$. Then $\delta([f_{k-1}(y), \mathbf{v}], a) = [f_{k-1}(ya), \mathbf{v}']$, with
   $$\begin{cases} \mathbf{v}'_{f_{k-1}(y)a} = |y|_{f_{k-1}(y)a} + 1 = |ya|_{f_{k-1}(y)a} \\ \mathbf{v}'_w = |ya|_w = |y|_w \quad \forall w \in T_{k,r}(S) : w \ne f_{k-1}(y)a \end{cases}$$

$\square$

**Proposition 1.** $L_{k,r}(S) = L(A)$.

*Proof.* – If $x \in L_{k,r}(S)$, then $x \in \mathrm{Pr}(L_{k,r}(S)) \cap \Sigma^* F_k(S)$, that is, $f_{k-1}(x) \in F_k(S)$ and by lemma 1 $\delta([\lambda, 0], x) = [f_{k-1}(x), \mathbf{v}] \in F$, therefore $x \in L(A)$.

– Let $x \in L(A)$. It can be shown by induction in $|x|$ that $\forall x \in \mathrm{Pr}(L(A))$, $\delta([\lambda, 0], x) = [f_{k-1}(x), \mathbf{v}(x)]$. It follows that $[f_{k-1}(x), \mathbf{v}(x)] \in F$, and by the definition of $A$, this implies that $f_{k-1}(x) \in F_k(S)$. By the definition of $Q$, $\mathbf{v}_w(x) \leq \mathbf{v}_w(S)$. Moreover $\delta([\lambda, 0], i_{k-1}(x)) = [i_{k-1}(x), 0]$, therefore $i_{k-1}(x) \in I_k(S)$ and then $x \in L_{k,r}(S)$.

$\square$

## 5 Inference of $(k, r)$-$TTSS$ Languages from Positive Data

The class of regular languages is not identifiable from positive data in the limit [8]. Even though, interesting subclasses of the family of regular languages that can be inferred this way [3], [7], [13]. Conditions for language identifiability can be found in [2], [11].

Given $k, r \geq 1$, the family of $(k, r)$-$TTSS$ languages is identifiable from positive data in the limit. That comes from the fact that, given an alphabet $\Sigma$, the family of $(k, r)$-$TTSS$ languages is finite.

Let $L$ an unknown $(k, r)$-$TTSS$ language and $S$ a positive sample for $L$. An algorithm that, on input of $k$, $r$ and $S$ outputs a finite automaton accepting the smallest $(k, r)$-$TTSS$ language that contains $S$, converge in el limit to an automaton accepting $L$. In this sense, section 4 provides an algorithm that identifies in the limit the family of $(k, r)$-$TTSS$ languages. The main disadvantage of that algorithm is its high computational cost.

In this section we propose a new algorithm, less expensive in time, and though it needs more data to converge, it identifies the family of $(k, r)$-$TTSS$ languages also. It is a states-merging algorithm and is shown in Figure 1. We will refer it as $(k,r)$-$TTSSI$ algorithm.

```
INPUT:   S ⊆ Σ*, k ≥ 1, r ≥ 1
OUTPUT: AFD A_{k,r} compatible with S (S ⊆ L(A_{k,r}))
METHOD: Obtain T_{k,r}(S)
         A_0 = (Q, Σ, δ, q_0, F) the PTA(S)
         A'_0 = (Q, Σ, δ, q_0, F') with
         F' = {u ∈ Pr(S) : ∃x ∈ S, f_{k-1}(u) = f_{k-1}(x)}
         Compute ∼, the equivalence in Q = Pr(S), defined:
         ∀u, v ∈ Pr(S), u ∼ v ⟺
         f_{k-1}(u) = f_{k-1}(v) ∧ ∀w ∈ Σ_1^k(w ∈ T_k(S) ⇒ |u|_w = |v|_w)
         A_{k,r} := A'_0/ ∼
End.
```

**Fig. 1.** Algorithm $(k, r)$-$TTSSI$ for inference of the family of $(k,r)$-$TTSS$ languages.

It is easy to see that $L(A_{k,r}) \subseteq L_{k,r}(S)$. Moreover, the automaton $A_{k,r}$ is a subautomaton of the one defined in section 4. It is evident that if $S$ is structurally complete with respect to the automaton of section 4, we have that $L(A_{k,r}) = L_{k,r}(S)$. So $(k,r)$-$TTSSI$ algorithm identifies the family of $(k, r)$-$TTSS$ languages in the limit.

As far as its application to Pattern Recognition tasks is concerned, the variation of parameters $k$ and $r$ permits a double control of the degree of generalization obtained from the sample, which may be interesting for that purpose. It is easily seen that for any fixed value of $k$ and $r$,

1. $L(A_{k+1,r}) \subseteq L(A_{k,r})$.
2. $L(A_{k,r+1}) \subseteq L(A_{k,r})$.

On the other hand, the algorithm can be implemented so that it works in an incremental way, that is, if a new input is considered, the new hypothesis can be obtained only from the current hypothesis and from this new input.

### 5.1 Example of run

Let $k = 2$, $r = 2$ and $S = \{aababa, abaaba\}$. Then, $I_2(S) = F_2(S) = \{a\}$, $T_{2,2}(S) = \{aa, bb\}$, with $g(aa) = 1$ and $g(bb) = 0$.

Figure 2 shows the automaton $A_0'$ for the sample $S$. Observe that $A_0'$ has the same set of states that $PTA(S)$, the only difference between them is the set of final states.

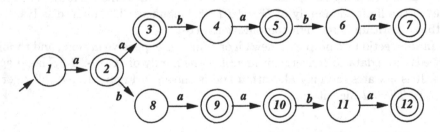

**Fig. 2.** Automaton $A_0'$ obtained from sample $S = \{aababa, abaaba\}$

Table 1 summarizes the values of $[f_{k-1}(\Pr(S)), \mathbf{v}]$ for the states of $A_0'$ and the values $k = 2, r = 2$ in order to obtain $A_0'/\sim$. The resulting automaton is shown in Figure 3(A). Figure 3(B) shows the automaton obtained from the same input data for the values $k = 2$ and $r = 1$.

### 5.2 Time complexity.

Let us suppose that $(k, r)$-$TTSSI$ algorithm has obtained automaton $A_{i-1}$ from the sample $w_1...w_{i-1}$ and receives $w_i = w_{i_1} w_{i_2}...w_{i_{n_i}}$ as input. For each symbol

**Table 1.** Values $[f_{k-1}(Pr(S)), v]$ of the states of $A_0'$

| State | 1 | 2 | 3 | 4 | 5 | 6 | 7 | 8 | 9 | 10 | 11 | 12 |
|---|---|---|---|---|---|---|---|---|---|---|---|---|
| $f_{k-1}(Pr(S))$ | $\lambda$ | $a$ | $a$ | $b$ | $a$ | $b$ | $a$ | $b$ | $a$ | $a$ | $b$ | $a$ |
| $\|v\|_{aa}$ | 0 | 0 | 1 | 1 | 1 | 1 | 1 | 1 | 0 | 0 | 1 | 1 |
| $\|v\|_{bb}$ | 0 | 0 | 0 | 0 | 0 | 0 | 0 | 0 | 0 | 0 | 0 | 0 |

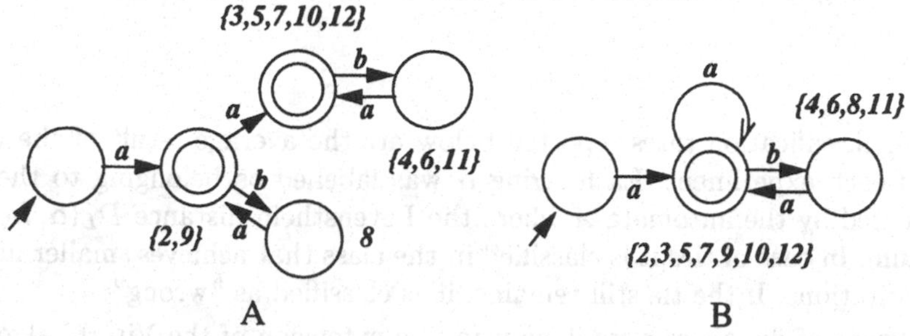

**Fig. 3.** Quotient automaton $A_0'/\sim$ obtained after merging states in $A_0'$: (A) for $k = 2$, $r = 2$. (B) for $k = 2$, $r = 1$. Numbers in the states correspond to the states merged in $A_0'$.

$w_{i_j}$ of $w_i$ the algorithm has to decide if the state that corresponds to the prefix $w_{i_1} w_{i_2} ... w_{i_j}$ has already been created and, if this is not the case, it has to construct it. Afterwards, it has to update the transitions table. With convenient data structures this opperation can be attained in $k \log |\Sigma| + |\Sigma|^k \log r$ steps for each symbol in the worst case, so the total cost of obtaining automaton $A_i$ from $A_{i-1}$ is $(k \log |\Sigma| + |\Sigma|^k \log r)|w_i|$ steps.

## 6 Experiments with Handwritten Digits

We present the results of an experiment aiming to show the behavior of the algorithm in a classification task for different values of $k$ and $r$. In the experiment, a database with 2400 images of handwritten digits has been used. It was composed of 240 repetitions of each digit written by 12 different writers. The images were processed and an eight-symbol chaincode was achieved following the contour of the image from the left end superior point. As the original chaincodes were long and with great amount of information, the resolution was decreased using separation grids of 6 and 10 pixels. In the sequel they will referred as $G6$ and $G10$. Examples of this representation for several digits are shown in Figure 4.

As the amount of samples in the database is small, in order to obtain significant results, twelve different runs of each experiment for different values of $k$ and $r$ were carried out using the *leaving $k$-out* (with $k = 2$) scheme. So, in each run, the database was split into two sets: one (with 200 images of each digit) for learning and the other (with 40 images of each digit) for testing. Therefore,

```
0: 10212222223334565666666770
   011022123222334464656666666677
1: 32222222224666766663376760
   222222222224666676642476766
2: 12233333200002444457777767644433470770
   102332333200070244443467767776644443770
```

**Fig. 4.** Two randomly chosen digits from some of the 10 classes.

the well classification rates reported below are the average result of the twelve runs of each experiment. Each string $\alpha$ was labelled as belonging to the class represented by the automata $A$ where the Levensthein distance $D_L(\alpha, L(A))$ is minimum. In case of ties it is classified in the class that achieves smaller number of substitutions. If the tie still remains, it is classified as "wrong".

Calculus of distances were done using an extension of the Viterbi algorithm that finds a minimum cost path through a general directed cyclic graph [1].

The confusion matrix for the 12 runs of the experiment with a separation grid of 6 pixels and values $k = 3$ and $r = 3$ are described in Table 2. The column labeled as "W" shows the number of ties for each digit. One should observe the special behavior of the digit "8", which has been classified as "0" 115 times, while digit "0" has been classified as "8" only 10 times. This situation is a constant in most of the experiments (either digit "0" is classified as "8" or digit "8" is classified as "0", but not both in the same experiment).

We have also observed that the number of ties of each experiment decreases as $k$ or $r$ increase. In case of a tie between two or more classes, one of them is the correct class in more than 98% of the cases.

**Table 2.** Confusion matrix of the experiment with grid 6, $k = 3$ and $r = 3$

|   | 0 | 1 | 2 | 3 | 4 | 5 | 6 | 7 | 8 | 9 | W | % |
|---|---|---|---|---|---|---|---|---|---|---|---|---|
| 0 | 459 | 0 | 0 | 0 | 8 | 0 | 0 | 0 | 10 | 2 | 1 | 95.6 |
| 1 | 0 | 465 | 3 | 0 | 2 | 0 | 0 | 3 | 0 | 0 | 7 | 96.9 |
| 2 | 2 | 0 | 474 | 0 | 0 | 0 | 0 | 0 | 4 | 0 | 0 | 98.8 |
| 3 | 0 | 0 | 6 | 456 | 2 | 1 | 0 | 3 | 2 | 8 | 2 | 95.0 |
| 4 | 0 | 17 | 0 | 0 | 448 | 0 | 0 | 2 | 0 | 6 | 7 | 93.3 |
| 5 | 1 | 0 | 0 | 3 | 0 | 475 | 0 | 0 | 0 | 0 | 1 | 99.0 |
| 6 | 1 | 0 | 0 | 0 | 0 | 0 | 477 | 0 | 2 | 0 | 0 | 99.4 |
| 7 | 0 | 26 | 4 | 0 | 8 | 0 | 0 | 421 | 0 | 15 | 6 | 87.7 |
| 8 | 115 | 2 | 4 | 1 | 3 | 0 | 5 | 8 | 316 | 9 | 17 | 65.8 |
| 9 | 2 | 5 | 0 | 15 | 10 | 0 | 0 | 0 | 0 | 446 | 2 | 92.9 |

The well classification rates for values of $k$, $2 \leq k \leq 5$ and $r$, $1 \leq r \leq 5$ are summarized in Table 3.

**Table 3.** Correct classification rates of the experiment for different values of $k$ and $r$.

| G10 | | $k$ | | |
|---|---|---|---|---|
| | 2 | 3 | 4 | 5 |
| 1 | 0.67 | 31.00 | 77.12 | 87.90 |
| 2 | 23.06 | 84.17 | 88.31 | 89.06 |
| $r$  3 | 71.92 | 87,50 | 89.23 | 89.94 |
| 4 | 82.92 | 88.87 | 89.27 | 90.00 |
| 5 | 86.18 | 88.52 | 89.27 | 90.44 |

| G6 | | $k$ | | |
|---|---|---|---|---|
| | 2 | 3 | 4 | 5 |
| 1 | 0.31 | 20.27 | 63.15 | 80.83 |
| 2 | 15.52 | 61.17 | 94.56 | 94.56 |
| $r$  3 | 26.44 | 92.44 | 95.44 | 95.04 |
| 4 | 73.00 | 93.62 | 96.24 | 95.73 |
| 5 | 84.06 | 95.11 | 96.41 | 95.81 |

We can observe that:

- As $k$, $r$ (or both) increase, the correct classification rates become greater too, with only one exception (the case $k = 3$ and $r = 5$ in grid 10).
- The classification rates increase faster when using grid 10 (shorter chains containing less information) than with grid 6 for small values of $k$ and $r$, but the later achieves better classification rates than the former for greater values of $k$ and $r$.

Some partial experiments have been done using stochastic automata. The methodology for those experiments was essentially the same except that in each run, the set of 200 images used before to learn the automata was split into two sets: 120 images to learn the stochastic automata and 80 images to estimate the probability of the error rules. In this case each string was classified as belonging to the class that maximizes the a posteriori probability.

The classification rates achieved by stochastic automata are much better for the values $k = 2, 3$, but decrease with respect to non stochastic when $k = 4, 5$ and $r > 2$ (this can be explained from the fact that each stochastic automata was learned from 120 images, while non stochastic were learned from 200 images).

## 7  Conclusions

A new family of regular languages, the *Locally Threshold Testable Languages in Strict Sense* has been introduced. This family includes the family of locally testable languages in strict sense (for each value of $k$, they constitute the case $r = 1$) and is included in the family of locally threshold testable languages. An algorithm for inference of $(k,r)$-$TTSS$ languages from positive data in the limit and some experiments that show the evolution of the learning process as $k$ and $r$ vary have also been presented.

# References

1. Amengual, J.C. and Vidal E. *Two different approaches for Cost-efficient Viterbi Parsing with Error Correction*. LCNS (1121): Advances in Structural and Syntactic Pattern Recognition. Percier, Wang and Rosenfeld (Eds.) Springer Verlag. pp 30-39, 1996.
2. Angluin, D. *Inductive inference of formal languages from positive data*. Information and Control, 45. pp. 117-135, 1980.
3. Angluin, D. *Inference of reversible languages*. Journal of the ACM 29 (3). pp. 7741-765, 1982.
4. Biermann A.W. and Feldman, J.A. *On the synthesis of finite state machines from samples of their behavior*. IEEE Trans. on Computers, C-21:592-597, 1972.
5. Fu, *K*. S. *Syntactic Pattern Recognition and Applications*. Prentice Hall, 1982.
6. García, P. and Ruiz, J. Locally Threshold Testable Languages in Strict Sense. Research Report DSIC-II/36/96. Univ Politécnica de Valencia. 1996.
7. García, P. and Vidal, E. *Inference of k-testable Languages in the Strict Sense and application to Syntactic Pattern Recognition*. IEEE Trans. Pattern Analysis and Machine Intelligence, Vol. PAMI-12 pp.920-925, 1990.
8. Gold, E.M. *Language identification in the limit*. Information and Control, 10. pp. 447-474, 1967.
9. González R.C. and Thomason, M.G. *Syntactic Pattern Recognition: An Introduction*. Addison Wesley, 1978.
10. Hopcroft, J. Ullman, J. *Introduction to Automata theory, Languages and Computation*. Addison-Wesley. 1979.
11. Kapur, S. and Bilardi, G. *Language learning without overgeneralization*. Theoretical Computer Science 141, pp. 151-162, 1995.
12. Medvedev, Y. T. *On the Class of Events Representable in a Finite Automaton*. Sequential Machines-Selected Papers, ed. E. F. Moor, Addison-Wesley, pp.227-315, 1964.
13. Ruiz, J. and García, P. *Learning k-Piecewise Testable Languages from Positive Data*. Proc. of the 3rd Intern. Conference on Grammatical Inference. LNCS 1147 Springer Verlag, pp. 203-210. 1996.
14. Vidal, E., Casacuberta, F and García, P. *Grammatical Inference and Automatic Speech Recognition*. In Speech Recognition and Coding. Springer Verlag, pp.175-191. 1995.

# Learning a Subclass of Linear Languages from Positive Structural Information[*]

José M. Sempere[1] and G. Nagaraja[2]

[1] DSIC, Universidad Politécnica de Valencia, Valencia 46071 (Spain)
email: jsempere@dsic.upv.es
[2] DCSE, Indian Institute of Technology, Powai, Mumbai 400 076 (India)
email: gn@cse.iitb.ernet.in

**Abstract.** A method to infer a subclass of linear languages from positive structural information (i.e. *skeletons*) is presented. The characterization of the class and the analysis of the time and space complexity of the algorithm is exposed too. The new class, Terminal and Structural Distinguishable Linear Languages (TSDLL), is defined through an algebraic characterization and a pumping lemma. We prove that the proposed algorithm correctly identifies any TSDL language in the limit if structural information is presented. Furthermore, we give a definition of a characteristic structural set for any target grammar. Finally we present the conclusions of the work and some guidelines for future works.

**Keywords** : Formal languages, grammatical inference, characterizable methods, structural information.

## 1 Introduction

Linear languages [Ha78] form a language class known to be properly included in the class of context-free languages which properly includes regular languages and even linear languages [AP64]. Within this class, there are some unsolvable problems such as the equivalence problem between linear grammars [Ro72] or the characteristic set problem for grammatical inference [Hi97]. Anyway, some formal language classes which include linear languages or intersect with them have been proposed to be learned from positive strings or positive and negative strings or structural (*skeletons*) information. Specifically, parenthesis linear grammars can be learned by using a reduction to regular languages [Ta88a], even linear languages can be learned by a reduction to regular languages [Ta88b,SG94] and some subclasses of even linear languages can be learned from positive strings [KMT97,Ra87,RN88,Ma96]. Takada has proposed a hierarchy in which some reductions can be performed by using control sets [Ta95] and within this hierarchy, some linear languages and some context-sensitive languages can be learned.

---

[*] Part of this work was carried out during a visit of J. Sempere to Prof. G. Nagaraja at IIT, Mumbai. The visit was granted by the Área de Programas Internacionales (API) of the Universidad Politécnica de Valencia

Mäkinen has proposed a method to learn the Szilard language of linear grammars [Ma90].

On the other hand, structural information (*skeletons*) has been used as data source in learning context-free languages. Sakakibara [Sa90,Sa92] has proposed two different methods to learn context-free grammars by using queries and positive information. Mäkinen [Ma92b] has pointed out a different way of taking advantage of structural information in learning context-free grammars by using Szilard languages while Ruiz and García [RG94] have presented some preliminary comparative results in using Sakakibara's algorithm or a method to infer $k$-testable tree sets proposed by García [Ga93]. Mäkinen [Ma92a] has proposed a grammar class to be learned from structural information (*type invertible grammars*), this work is highly related to Sakakibara's algorithm [Sa90]. Radhakrishnan and Nagaraja [Ra87,RN87] have presented a method to infer a subclass of regular languages, *Terminal Distinguishable Regular Languages* (TDRL), from the structural information induced by positive data. They have proposed a similar method [Ra87,RN88] to infer a subclass of even linear languages, *Terminal Distinguishable Even Linear Languages* (TDELL), from positive strings. Sempere and Fos [SF96] proposed a heuristic technique, based on the previous methods by Radhakrishnan and Nagaraja, to work with positive linear skeletons.

In this paper, we present a characterizable method which infers linear grammars from positive structural information (i.e. linear skeletons). The learned class, *Terminal and Structural Distinguishable Linear Languages* (TSDLL), is characterizable by terminal distinguishability and, which is a necessary condition, by distinguishable subskeletons.

The paper has the following sections : in section 2, we give some basic definitions from formal language theory which help to formalize the results and to understand the proposed inference method. An algebraic definition of TSDL languages together with a pumping lemma is presented in section 3 to define the formal framework in which the method will work. The inference method is proposed and we give some features of the method such as convergence property and complexity analysis. We will present a complete example to understand the method. Finally, we present some conclusions and suggestions for future work related to the results of this paper.

## 2  Basic definitions and notation

We introduce some basic concepts about formal language theory and formal grammars. Most of them can be found in any introductory book on the subject such as [Ha78].

In what follows, $\Sigma$ denotes an alphabet and $\Sigma^*$ the universal language over $\Sigma$, that is the set of all possible strings over $\Sigma$. Given an alphabet $\Sigma$ and a string $x \in \Sigma^*$, we denote by $|x|$ the length of $x$. $\lambda$ denotes the empty string with $|\lambda| = 0$.

$G = (N, \Sigma, P, S)$ is a *context-free* grammar, where $N$ is an alphabet of auxiliary symbols, $\Sigma$ is an alphabet of terminal symbols with $\Sigma \cap N = \emptyset$, $P$ is a set of productions where every production is a pair $(A, \beta)$ with $A \in N$ and $\beta \in \{N \cup \Sigma\}^*$, it can be denoted as $A \to \beta$, and $S \in N$ is the axiom of the grammar.

Given a grammar $G = (N, \Sigma, P, S)$, and two strings $x, y \in \{N \cup \Sigma\}^*$, we can say that $x$ *derives to* $y$, denoted by $x \overset{*}{\underset{G}{\Rightarrow}} y$, if $y$ can be obtained by applying to $x$ a finite set of productions of $P$. The language generated by the grammar $G$ is denoted as $L(G)$ and is defined as the set $L(G) = \{x \in \Sigma^* \mid S \overset{*}{\underset{G}{\Rightarrow}} x\}$.

**Definition 1.** *Let $G = (N, \Sigma, P, S)$ be a grammar. $\forall A \in N$, the set $L(G, A)$ is defined as $\{x \in \Sigma^* \mid A \overset{*}{\underset{G}{\Rightarrow}} x\}$. Obviously, $L(G, S) = L(G)$, and we denote $L(G, A)$ as $L(A)$ whenever $G$ is understood.*

**Definition 2.** *Let $G = (N, \Sigma, P, S)$ be a context-free grammar. A derivation tree in $G$ is a tree which can be defined by the following rules:*

1. *Every node of the tree can be labeled with a (terminal or auxiliary) symbol of the grammar or with the empty string $\lambda$.*
2. *The root of the tree is labeled with $S$.*
3. *The internal nodes of the tree are always labeled with auxiliary symbols.*
4. *If an internal node is labeled with $A$ and its sons are labeled with symbols $X_1, X_2, \cdots X_n$ then $A \to X_1 X_2 \cdots X_n \in P$.*
5. *If a node is labeled with $\lambda$ then it is the only son of its father.*

The *result* of a derivation tree is the string obtained by looking over all its leaves from left to right. It is obvious that every string of $L(G)$ admits at least one derivation tree.

A grammar $G$ is said to be *ambiguous* if there exists a string $x \in L(G)$ such that there exist more than one derivation tree with result $x$. A derivation $A$-tree is a derivation tree with root label $A$.

**Definition 3.** *Let $G = (N, \Sigma, P, S)$ be a context-free grammar. A skeleton in $G$ is a derivation tree in which the internal nodes are not labeled.*

In Figure 1, a grammar together with a derivation tree and the corresponding skeleton are given for a string $x = abbd$.

**Definition 4.** *Let $G = (N, \Sigma, P, S)$ be a grammar. We will say that $G$ is linear if every production in $P$ takes one of the following forms*

- *$A \to uBv$, where $A, B \in N$ and $u, v \in \Sigma^*$.*
- *$A \to u$, where $A \in N$ and $u \in \Sigma^*$.*

Every linear grammar $G = (N, \Sigma, P, S)$ admits the following normal form in its productions $A \to aB \mid Ba \mid a \mid \lambda$ where $A, B \in N$ and $a \in \Sigma$

From now on, we will deal with linear grammars in this normal form. Furthermore, we can omit the production $A \to \lambda$, given that it is only necessary in such languages where $\lambda \in L(G)$. In such case we can easily extend the results and formalization that we are going to carry out.

$S \rightarrow AB$

$A \rightarrow aAb \mid b$

$B \rightarrow cBd \mid d$

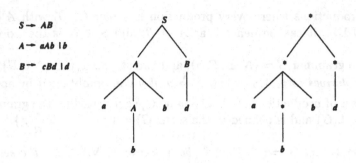

**Fig. 1.** A context-free grammar together with a derivation tree and the associated skeleton for a string $x = abbd$.

**Definition 5.** *Let $G$ be a linear grammar in normal form, $x \in L(G)$ and $sk$ a skeleton with result $x$ according to grammar $G$. Then, for every internal node $n$ of $sk$ the frontier of $n$ can be defined as the result of the subskeleton rooted at $n$, the head of $n$ can be defined as the left result of the skeleton up to $n$ and the tail of $n$ can be defined as the right result of the skeleton up to $n$. Given an internal node $n$, the tuple $(head(n), frontier(n), tail(n))$ denotes its structural information.*

In Figure 2, the *frontier*, *head* and *tail* of a skeleton internal node is shown. It is obvious that, given a skeleton $sk$ and one of its internal nodes $n$, then the result of the skeleton, denoted by $result(sk)$, is equal to $head(n) \cdot frontier(n) \cdot tail(n)$.

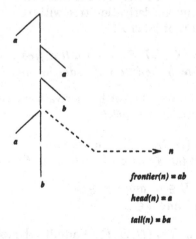

$frontier(n) = ab$

$head(n) = a$

$tail(n) = ba$

**Fig. 2.** A skeleton and *head, tail* and *frontier* of an internal node.

**Definition 6.** *Given a linear grammar $G$ in normal form, a skeleton $sk$ according to $G$ and an internal node $n$ of $sk$, we define the structural head of $n$,* denoted by *headstr(n)* and the *structural tail* of *n* denoted by *tailstr(n)* as the strings obtained by including in *head(n)* and *tail(n)* the symbol ∗ which denotes the absence of left or right son in the ancestral nodes.

In Figure 2, given the internal node $n$ of the skeleton, then $headstr(n) = a**$ and $tailstr(n) = ba*$.

**Definition 7.** *Let $w \in \Sigma^*$. We denote by $ter(w)$ the set of symbols of $\Sigma$ which appear in $w$. That is, $ter(w) = \{a \in \Sigma \mid \exists w_1, w_2 \in \Sigma^* : w = w_1 \cdot a \cdot w_2\}$. Obviously, $ter(\lambda) = \emptyset$.*

*Given a grammar $G = (N, \Sigma, P, S)$ and $A \in N$, we denote by $ter(A) = \bigcup_{w \in L(A)} ter(w)$.*

# 3 Algebraic and structural characterization of TSDL languages

Radhakrishnan and Nagaraja [Ra87,RN87,RN88] have proposed different regular and even linear language classes which can be inferred from positive strings. Furthermore, they have proposed a structural definition for the new classes. In what follows, we propose an extension from their methods to enlarge the class, and we focus on linear languages. One of the most important problems to deal with linear languages is the *ambiguity* problem, that is different skeletons with the same result. In order to obtain an efficient method to recognize similar structures we need to impose a condition which we have named *strong backward determinism* and we define it as follows.

**Definition 8.** *Let $G = (N, \Sigma, P, S)$ be a linear grammar in normal form. $G$ is said to be a strongly backward deterministic grammar if $\forall w \in \Sigma^*$, $A \underset{G}{\overset{*}{\Rightarrow}} w$ and $B \underset{G}{\overset{*}{\Rightarrow}} w$ implies that $A = B$. Moreover, the A-tree with result $w$ is unique.*

Obviously, every *strongly backward deterministic* grammar is an unambiguous grammar.

**Definition 9.** *Let $G = (N, \Sigma, P, S)$ be a linear grammar in normal form. $G$ is said to be a Terminal and Structural Distinguishable Linear (TSDL) grammar if the following conditions are fulfilled:*

1. *$G$ is strongly backward deterministic.*
2. *$\forall A, B, C \in N$ such that*

$$(A \to aB \ \land \ A \to aC \in P) \lor (A \to Ba \ \land \ A \to Ca \in P)$$

*then $ter(B) \neq ter(C)$.*

A language $L$ is *Terminal and Structural Distinguishable Linear* (TSDL) if there exists a TSDL grammar $G$ such that $L = L(G)$.

We can give the following pumping lemma, which characterizes TSDL languages, by using some substring properties from the definition that we have given before.

**Lemma 1.** *Let $L$ be a TSDL language over $\Sigma^*$. Then $\forall u_1, v_1, u_2, v_2, w, z \in \Sigma^*$ the following result holds*

$$u_1 w v_1, \quad u_2 w v_2 \in L \Rightarrow (u_1 z v_1 \in L \Leftrightarrow u_2 z v_2 \in L).$$

*Proof.*

Let us suppose that $L = L(G)$ with $G$ a TSDL grammar. The derivation trees for $u_1 w v_1$ and $u_2 w v_2$, according to $G$, are the following ones

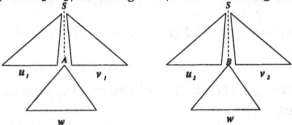

Since $G$ is a TSDL grammar it is strongly backward deterministic, and $A = B$ in the previous derivation trees. Hence, $u_1 z v_1$ and $u_2 z v_2$ are or are not in $L$ depending on the existence of the derivation $A \stackrel{*}{\underset{G}{\Rightarrow}} z$.

$\square$

*Example 1.* The following languages are not TSDL languages. Observe that we propose examples of finite, regular, even linear and linear languages which are not TSDL languages and we prove it by applying the previous lemma.

- $\{aab, aaabb, aabb\}$. In this case it is enough to take $u_1 = a$, $v_1 = \lambda$, $u_2 = aa$, $v_2 = b$, $w = ab$ and $z = abb$
- $\{aab\} \cup aaab^*$. By taking $u_1 = a$, $v_1 = \lambda$, $u_2 = aa$, $v_2 = b$, $w = ab$ and $z = abb$, a contradiction appears against the lemma.
- $\{a^{2n+1}b^{2n}\} \cup \{a^{2n}b^{2n+1}\}$. Here we take $u_1 = aa$, $v_1 = bb$, $u_2 = a$, $v_2 = bbb$, $w = aaabb$ and $z = aabbb$.
- $\{a^n b^{2n+1}\} \cup \{a^{n+1} b^{2n}\}$. In this case $u_1 = aa$, $v_1 = bbb$, $u_2 = aaa$, $v_2 = bb$, $w = abbbb$ and $z = aabbb$.

$TSDL$ languages form a class which intersect with finite languages, regular languages, even linear languages and linear languages, but do not properly contain any of them. We have given some examples which prove the non proper inclusion property. In Figure 3 we show the relationships between $TSDL$ languages and other formal language classes.

## 4 Inference method

Once we have defined the $TSDL$ language class, we propose an inference method. In the first place, we propose an equivalence relationship between the internal nodes of the skeletons. Later, the proposed algorithm calculates the equivalence classes according to the previous relationship and then induces a $TSDL$ grammar from the equivalence classes.

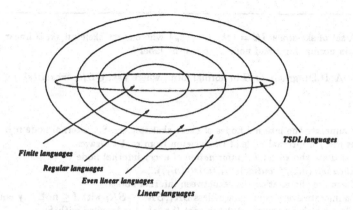

**Fig. 3.** TSDL languages in relationship with other formal language families.

**Definition 10.** *Let G be a TSDL grammar and SK a nonempty set of skeletons according to G. We can define an equivalence relationship between the internal nodes of the skeletons as follows:*

*n ≡ m if and only if one of the following conditions is fulfilled:*

1. *frontier(n) = frontier(m).*
2. *headstr(n) = headstr(m) ∧ tailstr(n) = tailstr(m) ∧ ter(frontier(n)) = ter(frontier(m)).*

In Figure 4 we propose the inference method and we give the following example to apply it

*Example 2.* Let us take the language $\{a^i b^{2i} : i \geq 1\}$. We provide the following skeletons to the learning algorithm as input data:

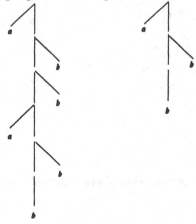

In the first step, the algorithm enumerates the internal nodes as follows:

**Input :** A set of skeletons $SK = \{sk_1, \cdots, sk_n\}$ where every skeleton $sk_i$ is linear in normal form and none contains the label $\lambda$.

**Output :** A TSDL grammar $G$ in normal form, where $\forall sk_i \in SK$, $result(sk_i) \in L(G)$.

**Method :**

    **(1)** Enumerate the internal nodes of every skeleton $sk_i$. So, internal node $n_{ij}$.
        is the $j$th internal node of $i$th skeleton from root to leaves.

    **(2)** Calculate the *structural information* of every internal node
        $(headstr(n_{ij}), frontier(n_{ij}), tailstr(n_{ij}))$.

    **(3)** Calculate the relationship $\equiv$ between internal nodes.

    **(4)** Enumerate every equivalence class $SK_1, SK_2 \cdots SK_l$ with $l \leq n$. Every equivalence
        class which contains a skeleton root (i.e. $sk_{i1}$) is labelled with $S$.

    **(5)** Substitute every internal node by its equivalence class
        (every skeleton is transformed into a derivation tree).

    **(6)** Obtain a grammar $G$ from the derivation trees.

**endMethod**

**Fig. 4.** TSDL languages inference method.

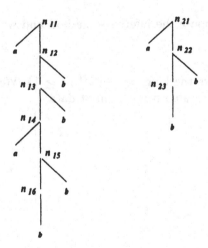

Then, the structural information of every internal node is showed in the next table.

| | headstr | tailstr | frontier | ter(frontier) |
|---|---|---|---|---|
| $n_{11}$ | $\lambda$ | $\lambda$ | $aabbbb$ | $\{a,b\}$ |
| $n_{12}$ | $a$ | $*$ | $abbbb$ | $\{a,b\}$ |
| $n_{13}$ | $a*$ | $b*$ | $abbb$ | $\{a,b\}$ |
| $n_{14}$ | $a**$ | $bb*$ | $abb$ | $\{a,b\}$ |
| $n_{15}$ | $a**a$ | $*bb*$ | $bb$ | $\{b\}$ |
| $n_{16}$ | $a**a*$ | $b*bb*$ | $b$ | $\{b\}$ |
| $n_{21}$ | $\lambda$ | $\lambda$ | $abb$ | $\{a,b\}$ |
| $n_{22}$ | $a$ | $*$ | $bb$ | $\{b\}$ |
| $n_{23}$ | $a*$ | $b*$ | $b$ | $\{b\}$ |

The equivalence classes induced by the relationship are

$$SK_1 = \{n_{11}, n_{21}, n_{14}\}$$
$$SK_2 = \{n_{16}, n_{23}\}$$
$$SK_3 = \{n_{22}, n_{15}\}$$
$$SK_4 = \{n_{12}\}$$
$$SK_5 = \{n_{13}\}$$

So, we can make the following replacement in order to label the auxiliary symbols $SK_1 = S, SK_4 = A, SK_5 = B, SK_3 = C$ and $SK_2 = D$. The output grammar is the following one:

$$S \to aA \mid aC$$
$$A \to Bb$$
$$B \to Sb$$
$$C \to Db$$
$$D \to b.$$

## 4.1 Convergence and identification in the limit

Once we have presented the inference algorithm, we are going to prove that it converges to the target grammar if enough information is presented. Here, the information presentation is structural. Under this protocol, we prove that the proposed algorithm identifies any $TSDL$ grammar in the limit [Go64]. The proof is based on the existence of a structural characteristic set for any $TSDL$ grammar in normal form. We give the construction algorithm for such a set by the following lemma

**Lemma 2.** *Let $G$ be a $TSDL$ grammar and $L = L(G)$. Then there exists a finite set of skeletons according to $G$ such that if it is given as input to the proposed inference algorithm the output is a grammar $G'$ which is isomorphic to $G$.*

*Proof.*

Let $G = (N, \Sigma, P, S)$. For every auxiliary symbol $A \in N$, its minimal structural information can be calculated as follows:

- Take the minimal derivation path in which $A$ appears. That is $S \overset{*}{\underset{G}{\Rightarrow}} \alpha A \beta \overset{*}{\underset{G}{\Rightarrow}} w$ with $w \in \Sigma^*$ and it is the shortest derivation path.
- Construct the derivation tree according to the previous derivation.
- Calculate $headstr(A)$, $tailstr(A)$ and $frontier(A)$ as in skeletons.

Since $G$ is TSDL, so it is strongly backward deterministic, then the set of skeletons induced by the derivation trees have the property that if internal nodes $n_i$ and $n_j$ are labeled with different auxiliary symbols, then

1. $frontier(n_i) \neq frontier(n_j)$, and
2. $headstr(n_i) = headstr(n_j) \ \wedge \ tailstr(n_i) = tailstr(n_j) \Rightarrow$
   $\Rightarrow ter(frontier(n_i)) \neq ter(frontier(n_j))$.

If

$$S \underset{G}{\Rightarrow} \alpha_1 A_1 \beta_1 \underset{G}{\Rightarrow} \cdots \underset{G}{\Rightarrow} \alpha_n A_n \beta_n \underset{G}{\Rightarrow} \alpha A \beta \overset{*}{\underset{G}{\Rightarrow}} \alpha w \beta$$

and

$$S \underset{G}{\Rightarrow} \alpha_1 A_1 \beta_1 \underset{G}{\Rightarrow} \cdots \underset{G}{\Rightarrow} \alpha_n A_n \beta_n \underset{G}{\Rightarrow} \alpha B \beta \overset{*}{\underset{G}{\Rightarrow}} \alpha w' \beta$$

are derivations with $A \neq B$, then $ter(w) \neq ter(w')$ and $A$ and $B$ are not related under $\equiv$.

So, the algorithm correctly distinguishes two different internal nodes associated to two different auxiliary symbols.

On the other hand, let us suppose that, in the skeleton set, two different internal nodes, $n_i$ and $n_j$, are labeled by the same auxiliary symbol. Then one of the following conditions is fulfiled:

1. $frontier(n_i) = frontier(n_j)$. This condition can be true given that we have selected the shortest derivations for every symbol.
2. $\exists n_k : n_k \equiv n_i \ \wedge \ n_k \equiv n_j$. So $n_i \equiv n_j$.

From the previous conditions we can affirm that the algorithm correctly relates those internal nodes induced by one auxiliary symbol.

We can conclude that if the skeleton set we have defined is given as input data then every auxiliary symbol in the grammar is represented and the algorithm correctly distinguishes each of them.

□

From Lemma 2, we can conclude that the algorithm identifies any $TSDL$ grammar in the limit. Here, the proof is trivial given that if every skeleton string is presented then sooner or later the algorithm will work with a characteristic set as input data and, from Lemma 2, it will output the target grammar. Hence, we have the following theorem

**Theorem 1.** *The proposed algorithm identifies any $TSDL$ language in the limit if structural information is presented.*

## 4.2 Complexity analysis

Let us suppose that the language to be identified is defined over the alphabet $\Sigma$, with $|\Sigma| = n$. The size of an input sample $SK$ is defined by the number of internal nodes that it contains. In linear languages the number of internal nodes of a skeleton is equal to the length of its result. So, we can establish

$$|SK| = \sum_{sk_i \in SK} |frontier(sk_i)| = m.$$

Let $k$ be the size of the maximum length string in the input data.

We can establish the time complexity of the algorithm step by step as follows:

1. **Step 1**. The enumeration of every internal node takes as much time as reading all the skeletons. So the time complexity is $\mathcal{O}(m)$.
2. **Step 2**. As in the previous step, here the algorithm only needs reading all the skeletons once. Observe that we can store the *headstr* and *tailstr* of every internal node by reading the skeleton. Later, the calculation of every *frontier* and its terminals can be established by applying the definition we have given in section 2. In this case the time complexity is $\mathcal{O}(m)$.
3. **Step 3**. The relationship $\equiv$ is established by comparing the structural information of every internal node. The algorithm makes at most $m \times m$ comparisons. For every comparison, the strings *tailstr*, *headstr* and *frontier* have $k$ as maximum length and $ter(frontier)$ has $n$ as maximum size, so the time complexity is $\mathcal{O}(m^2(k+n))$.
4. **Step 4**. As in step 1, this takes time complexity $\mathcal{O}(m)$ given that the number of equivalence classes is less than or equal to $m$.
5. **Step 5**. Again, as in step 4, it has time complexity $\mathcal{O}(m)$.
6. **Step 6**. As in steps 1, 4 and 5, the time complexity is $\mathcal{O}(m)$.

The space complexity takes into account the necessary space to storage the structural information of every internal node. Let $l$ be the number of skeletons to be processed, then the necessary space of a skeleton $sk$ is

$$\sum_{i=1}^{|frontier(sk)|} i.$$

This space is $\mathcal{O}(k^2)$. So, the total space is $\mathcal{O}(k^2 l)$.

**Theorem 2.** *Let $SK$ be a set of skeletons given to the proposed algorithm as input and defined over an alphabet with $n$ symbols. Let $m$ be the size of $SK$, let $k$ be the size of the maximum length string in $SK$ and let $l$ be the number of skeletons in $SK$. The proposed algorithm has time complexity $\mathcal{O}(m^2(k+n))$ and space complexity $\mathcal{O}(k^2 l)$.*

# 5  Conclusions and future work

We have presented a new language class which can be inferred from positive structural information. We think that the proposed method can be applied to other classes and our future work will focus on this. The main advantage of the method is that it doesn't need negative data, this is important when working with non regular languages and structural information, given that the meaning of negative examples can be taken as good strings with bad skeletons or simply bad strings.

The complexity of the method and the method itself makes its implementation relatively easy. It is important for real tasks as picture description languages [RN88] or transduction tasks in which left and right linear productions can be taken as input/output strings.

## Aknowledgements

The initial ideas in this paper were formulated during the visit of G. Nagaraja to UPV in July 1997 on the invitation of Prof. Enrique Vidal under a grant from Iberdrola which is gratefully acknowledged. G. Nagaraja is also grateful to IIT Bombay for permission to visit UPV.

J. Sempere is grateful to Dr. Pedro García for helpful discussions about this work.

The authors gratefully acknowledge the suggestions and corrections of the anonymous referee.

## References

[AP64]  V. AMAR, G. PUTZOLU *On a Family of Linear Grammars*. Information and Control **7** (1964) 283–291.

[Ga93]  P. GARCÍA *Learning k-Testable Tree Sets from positive data*. Departamento de Sistemas Informáticos y Computación. Universidad Politécnica de Valencia. Technical report DSIC-II/46/93. 1993.

[Go64]  E. MARK GOLD *Language Identification in the Limit*. Information and Control, **10** (1969) 447–474.

[Ha78]  M. HARRISON *Introduction to Formal Language Theory*. Addison-Wesley Publishing Company. 1978.

[Hi97]  C. DE LA HIGUERA *Characteristic Sets for Polynomial Grammatical Inference*. Machine Learning **27** (1997) 125–138.

[KMT97]  T. KOSHIBA, E. MÄKINEN, Y. TAKADA *Learning deterministic even linear languages from positive examples*. Theoretical Computer Science **185** (1997) 63–97.

[Ma90]  E. MÄKINEN *The grammatical inference problem for the Szilard languages of Linear Grammars*. Information Processing Letters **36** (1990) 203–206.

[Ma92a]  E. MÄKINEN *On the structural grammatical inference problem for some classes of context-free grammars*. Information Processing Letters **42** (1992) 1–5.

[Ma92b]  E. MÄKINEN *Remarks on the structural grammatical inference problem for context-free grammars*. Information Processing Letters **44** (1992) 125–127.

[Ma96] E. MÄKINEN *A note on the grammatical inference problem for even linear languages.* Fundamenta Informaticae **25**, No. 2 (1996) 175–181.

[Ra87] V. RADHAKRISHNAN *Grammatical Inference from Positive Data : An Effective Integrated Approach.* Ph.D. Thesis. Department of Computer Science and Engineering. IIT Bombay. 1987.

[RN87] V. RADHAKRISHNAN AND G. NAGARAJA *Inference of Regular Grammars via Skeletons.* IEEE Trans. on Systems, Man and Cybernetics, **17**, No. 6 (1987) 982–992.

[RN88] V. RADHAKRISHNAN AND G. NAGARAJA *Inference of Even Linear Languages and Its Application to Picture Description Languages.* Pattern Recognition, **21**, No. 1 (1988) 55–62.

[Ro72] G. ROZENBERG *Direct Proofs of the Undecidability of the Equivalence Problem for Sentential Forms of Linear Context-Free Grammars and the Equivalence Problem for 0L Systems.* Information Processing Letters **1** (1972) 233–235.

[RG94] J. RUIZ AND P. GARCÍA *The algorithms RT and k-TTI : A first comparison.* Proceedings of the Second International Colloquium, ICGI-94. LNAI Vol. 862, pp 180–188. 1994.

[Sa90] Y. SAKAKIBARA *Learning context-free grammars from structural data in polynomial time.* Theoretical Computer Science **76** (1990) 223–242.

[Sa92] Y. SAKAKIBARA *Efficient Learning of Context-Free Grammars from Positive Structural Examples.* Information and Computation **97** (1992) 23–60.

[SG94] J.M. SEMPERE AND P. GARCÍA *A Characterization of Even Linear Languages and its Application to the Learning Problem.* Proceedings of the Second International Colloquium, ICGI-94. LNAI Vol. 862, pp 38–44. Springer-Verlag. 1994.

[SF96] JOSÉ M. SEMPERE AND ANTONIO FOS *Learning linear grammars from Structural Information.* Proceedings of the Third International Colloquium, ICGI-96. LNAI Vol. 1147, pp 126–133. Springer-Verlag. 1996.

[Ta88a] Y. TAKADA *Inferring Parenthesis Linear Grammars Based on Control Sets.* Journal of Information Processing, **12**, No. 1 (1988) 27–33.

[Ta88b] Y. TAKADA *Grammatical Inference for Even Linear Languages based on Control Sets.* Information Processing Letters. **28**, No. 4 (1988) 193–199.

[Ta95] Y. TAKADA *A hierarchy of languages families learnable by regular language learning.* Information and Computation, **123(1)** (1995) 138–145.

# Grammatical Inference in Document Recognition

Alexander S. Saidi[1,2], Souad Tayeb-bey[1]

1- Laboratoire de Reconnaissance de Formes et Vision
INSA de Lyon- Bât. 403
20 Ave. Albert Einstein 69621 Villeurbanne
2- Dépt. Mathématiques, Informatique et Systèmes
Ecole Centrale de Lyon
B.P. 163. 69131 Ecully
saidi@cc.ec-lyon.fr, tayebbey@rfv.insa-lyon.fr

**Abstract.** In this paper, we consider the Pattern Recognition applied to paper documents based on the grammatical inference (GI) for classes of structured documents like summaries, dictionaries, bibliographic data basis, encyclopaedias and so on. In this task, the inference engine takes as input a set of individual examples of these documents and outputs a set of rules that recognise similar documents. We place GI in an algebraic framework in which rewrite rules will define the process of generalisation. The implementation algorithm discussed here is used in a current document handling project in which paper documents are typographically tagged and then recognised. One of the current applications in this project is to extract the physical and the logical structures of a given set of paper documents and then reorganise them in a machine readable form like HTML code.

## I- Introduction

In order to recognise a paper document and extract its hierarchical structure and content, we apply the process of grammatical inference to a set of production rules. These rules represent the logical structure of these documents (i.e. text and images organised in titles, chapters, sub-chapters and so on) and are defined for each element of the sample set. The inference engine then generalise these rules and produce a representative context-free grammar that will reorganise texts and images content in their respective contexts. In this paper, the problem of grammatical inference is considered for such classes of structured documents as for summaries, dictionaries, scientific reports, bibliographic basis, encyclopaedias and so on from examples. We propose an algorithm that can identify the class of regular languages from positive examples. This is the usual case in the grammatical inference for classes of documents whose structures are learned from examples.

In the proposed method, we infer a regular grammar which generalise the Prefix-tree of a given positive sample of documents. Although negative examples can be considered, the usual situation in this kind of document recognition is to deal only with the positive representation. These examples are structured representation of documents which are collected by optical typographic recognition techniques ([1]).

It is known that any algorithm that would construct a DFA (deterministic finite automaton) with a minimum number of states compatible with all the data already processed can identify any regular language in the limit ([2]). The search space being a lattice, we develop in this paper an algebraic framework for the grammatical inference and show a function on the lattice that characterise the construction of partitions over the Prefix-tree of the representation.

In this framework, an initial algebra $A_G$ is assigned to the Prefix-tree of the strings in the sample. Then the main result is that a quotient automaton of the Prefix-tree denotes a quotient algebra $A'_G$ whose terms are obtained by the application of a uniquely defined homomorphism from $A_G$ to $A'_G$. The corresponding function induced by this homomorphism is then defined by an algorithm. We also discuss an alternative view of GI problem base on the construction of a table of successor and predecessors of any element of the alphabet. Then the relation between this table and the above algorithm is discussed.

The proposed algorithms are used for GI in a project on paper document processing whose one application is the translation of the document into HTML text.

## II- Inductive and Grammatical Inference

The Inductive Inference paradigm is the basis of the automatic learning problem ([1]). Besides, in the Syntactical Pattern Recognition framework, there exist many grammatical inference algorithms that can be used in the learning step of pattern recognition tasks ([3],[4],[5],[6], [7]).

This is a fact that the class of regular languages can not be correctly identified from only positive examples. Hence, any recursively enumerable class of language is identifiable using a complete representation with positive and negative data ([14]). However, the usual situation in (paper) document recognition is to infer a regular grammar from only positive data.

For example, from scientific reports, we may have :

report --> abstract, acknowledgement, outline, chapter, chapter, references.

report --> abstract, outline, chapter, subchapter, chapter, references, index.

report --> abstract, acknowledgement, outline, figure-table, chapter, chapter, index.

Although one can propose some negative examples (for instance, express that there is no report without any chapter or no report without outline), the general case is the unsupervised inference where the negative information is not available.

In this paper, first we give some basic definitions for reference. Then, in section IV, an algebraic view of GI problem is given in details. In section V, some practical issues and the implementation of the proposed algorithm are reported. An alternative view of GI based on tables are presented in section VI. Then, some relationships with other works in the field is recalled in the section VII.

# III- Basic Definitions

We give some basic definitions used in the rest of the paper but assume the reader is familiar with context-free grammars, regular grammars and regular expressions ([15]).

Let $\Sigma$ be a finite alphabet. The set of all finite strings of symbols from $\Sigma$ is denoted $\Sigma^*$. The empty string is denoted by $\varepsilon$. The concatenation of two strings u and v is denoted uv. If a string is u=vw then v is a *prefix* of u and w a *suffix* of u. A *language* denoted by $L$ is any subset of $\Sigma^*$.

A *finite automaton* (FA) A is a quintuplet $(Q, \Sigma, \delta, q_0, F)$ where Q is the set of states, $\Sigma$ is the set of input symbols, $\delta : Q \times \Sigma^* \to 2^Q$ is the transition function, $q_0 \in Q$ is the start state and $F \subseteq Q$ is the set of final states.

For an automaton A, the (regular) language accepted by A is denoted by $L(A)$.

An automaton A is *deterministic* (DFA) if for all $q \in Q$ and for all $a \in \Sigma$, $\delta(q,a)$ has at most one (state) element. A language is *regular* iff it is accepted by a FA.

If $A=(Q, \Sigma, \delta, q_0, F)$ is a FA and $\pi$ a *partition* of Q, $B(q,\pi)$ is the only block that contains q and we denote the quotient set by $Q/\pi$ as the set of all partitions $\{B(q,\pi) \mid q \in Q\}$. If A is a FA and a partition $\pi$ over Q, the *quotient* (or derived) *automaton* $A/\pi$ = $\{Q/\pi, \Sigma, \delta', B(q_0,\pi), \{B_i \in Q/\pi \mid \exists q \in B_i, q \in F\}$ where $\delta'$ is defined by $\forall B, B' \in Q/\pi$, $\forall a \in \Sigma$, $B' \in \delta'(B,a)$ iff $\exists q, q' \in Q, q \in B, q' \in B' : q' \in \delta(q,a)$.

It is easy to see that for a partition $\pi$ over Q, $L(A) \subseteq L(A/\pi)$. The set of all automata derived from A is a (language inclusion) lattice Lat(A).

If r and s are *regular expressions*, then (r|s), (rs), (r*) are regular expressions. An optional regular expression r is denoted by $[r]=(r \mid \varepsilon)$ and $(r+) = r^* r$.

A *context-free grammar* (CFG) is denoted by G=(N, T, P, S) where N and T are finite sets of *non terminals* and *terminals* and P is a finite set of productions. The special non terminal S is called the start symbol.

A (right) *regular grammar* is a context-free grammar whose the productions rules are of the form A --> $\alpha$. or A --> $\alpha$ B. where $\alpha \in T$, A,B $\in$ N.

The *language* L(G) is any string $\omega \in T^*$ such that there is a derivation from S to $\omega$ (denoted by S =>*w). By extension, the language of any non terminal A$\in$N is any string $\upsilon \in T^*$ such that for $\tau, \sigma \in T^*$, S =>* $\tau A \sigma$ =>* $\tau \upsilon \sigma$.

Given $I_+$ the positive representation from a regular language L, $I_+$ is said to be *structurally complete* if all transitions of (the unknown) automaton A(L) are used in the acceptance of strings in $I_+$. If A(L) is the *canonical automaton* of a language L, then A is a DFA accepting L and has the minimal number of states. The *maximal canonical automaton* MCA with respect to $I_+$ (where $I_+$ is structurally complete) is the automaton whose language is L and has the largest number of states. One can define the *prefix tree* acceptor of $I_+$ denoted by $PT(I_+)$ from the MCA by merging states sharing the same prefix. $PT(I_+)$ accepts only the strings of $I_+$.

It is well known that if $I_+$ is a structurally complete sample of a regular language L, then there exists a partition $\pi$ over the states of $PT(I_+)$ such that $PT(I_+)/\pi$ is isomorphic to A(L).

The aim of this paper is to give an algebraic specification of the state partitions of $PT(I_+)$ in order to formally characterise a function on $PT(I_+)$. This is done by the

definition of a function over the terms of an algebra associated to $PT(I_+)$ that produces a quotient-algebra whose terms are (by construction) isomorphic to those of $PT(I_+)$.
The following theorems delimit the search space of $L(A)$ ([8]):
If $I_+$ is a positive sample, the set $\Gamma$ of automata such that $I_+$ is structurally complete with any automaton in $\Gamma$ is **Lat(MCA($I_+$))**.
If $I_+$ is a positive sample, L the target language and $I_+$ is structurally complete with respect to $A(L)$, then $A(L)$ is an element of **Lat(PT($I_+$))**.
The automaton $A(L)$ is learnable as a partition $PT(I_+)/\pi$ isomorphic to $A(L)$ in the lattice of all possible partitions of $PT(I_+)/\pi$. The main aim of grammatical (regular) inference is to characterise this lattice and to guide a search in it. Note that this search space grows exponentially with the size of the state set in $PT(I_+)$ and therefore with the size of $I_+$. The automata we will construct in the sequel are constrained automata [9] : some kind of conditional automata where transitions are constrained to fulfil some conditions. For example, a transition $\delta$ (p, $\alpha/\beta$) means that the transition takes place if the symbol $\alpha \in \Sigma^+$ is followed by $\beta \in \Sigma^+$. By this means, one can constrain the context (left and right) of a symbol in the automaton.

## IV- The Algebra

We use here the relation between an initial many sorted algebra and grammars [goguen-77-78]. This relation over context-free grammars is easily extended to regular grammars. Such a grammar is used as a specification (rewrite) system to define an algebra. The major property is that the defined algebra is initial in a given category. To construct the algebra associated to a context-free grammar G, each non terminal of G is assigned to a class of derivation tree. Consequently, the non terminals of G are sorts of a many sorted algebra whose operations are defined by the production of G. The derivation tree (and hence the language) of any non terminal X denote the carriers of the sort X.
Let $G=(N,T,P,S)$ be a non ambiguous context-free grammar and L be its language (we do not use variables in the sequel; the algebraic representation of grammatical programming is detailed in [11], [12]). Let $L_G$ be the terms (strings represented by their derivation tree) of G. Let the algebra $A_G$-algebra be associated to G whose signature is $((N \cup T), P')$ where P' is the set of names given to the productions in P. The terms of this algebra are derivation trees starting from any non terminal of G.
The terms of the $A_G$-algebra are constructed by using the names of the productions of G. Constants (0-air operators of $A_G$-algebra) are elements of T in the grammar G. By *equivalence*, we mean an equivalence relation over the sorts of $A_G$. Two strings will be equivalent if their derivation tree (terms of $A_G$-algebra) are equivalent. Since the non terminals N are sorts of $A_G$-algebra, any string $\omega$ such that $X \in N$, $X ==>^* \omega$ is typed by X, particularly when $\omega \in L(G)$ where for the start non terminal $S ==>^* \omega$.
Note that the terms of $L_G$ are strings whose derivation tree are the terms of $A_G$.
An $A_G$-algebra is initial in a category C if for all algebra B of C, there exist a unique homomorphism $h_G : A_G --> B$.

By the initiality of $A_G$, we have a homomorphism $h_G : A_G \text{ --> } sem$ where *sem* denotes any algebra of C. One can consider the language generated by a context-free (or regular) grammar as an example of sem and hence to associate a *string semantics* to the terms of $A_G$. One can also define another algebra assigned to another context-free grammar G' and then define a homomorphism from G to G'. This function will be a syntax-directed translation function. Here, we are interested by $h : A_G \text{ --> } L_G$. We may note that by initiality, $h$ always exists and is defined uniquely. $h$ is surjective and if the grammar G is not ambiguous, then $h$ is also injective. In this case, $h$ will be an isomorphism from $A_G$ to $L_G$. For any partition of $PT(I_+)$ where some states are considered *equivalent* (merged by some function), the generated language is a super set of $I_+$. We will show that there exists a uniquely defined homomorphism $h$ from the derivations in $PT(I_+)$ to the derivations in any partition of $PT(I_+)$. We also show that for some function induced by $h$, terms of $PT(I_+)/\pi$ are homomorphic to those of $PT(I_+)$. Thus, we will characterise different DFA of the lattice $Lat(PT(I_+)/\pi$ by the application of this function to the terms of the $A_G$-algebra.

Let $PT(I_+)$ and its automaton (a regular grammar) G, a partition $PT(I_+)/\pi$ from $PT(I_+)$ and its automaton G'. Let $A_G$ and $A'_G$ be the algebra assigned to G and G'. Note that $A_G$ and $A'_G$ have the same signature and $A'_G$ is a quotient algebra of $A_G$. Suppose further that the sorts p and p' of $A_G$ are equivalent (p≡p' are in the same block of $PT(I_+)/\pi$). Let [p] denote the equivalence class of p.

*Lemma-1* : the value of a derivation tree Z in $A'_G$ is the equivalence class of derivation tree of Z in $A_G$. That is : $(A'_G)(Z) = [A_G (Z)]$
proof : this is an immediate consequence of the quotient algebra $A'_G$ of $A_G$.
In other words, if p≡p'∈ [p], then the derivation trees of $A_G$ whose root are p and p' are equivalents terms in $A'_G$. One can define i : $A_G \text{ --> } \Sigma^*$ a homomorphism from $PT(I_+)$ to L (or j : $A'_G \text{ --> } \Sigma^*$) and show that all strings of L whose derivation tree root is [p] are equivalents.

Let $V=(N \cup T)$ be the set sort of the algebra $A_G$ and $A'_G$ and $h : A_G \text{ --> } A'_G$.
Let $\equiv_h = (\equiv_{hv})$ $v \in V$, be a family of relations on $A_G$ defined by : a $\equiv_h$ a' iff h(a)=h(a') with a, a'∈ V. $\equiv_h$ is called the congruence relation induced by the homomorphism $h$.
The main problem of grammatical inference is to define $h : A_G \text{ --> } A'_G$ and to assign it a function. This function is defined by f : $PT(I_+) \text{ --> } PT(I_+)/\pi$. Let us define the properties of h (and f).

*Lemma-2* : Let $A_G$ and $A'_G$ be the algebra assigned to $PT(I_+)$ and $PT(I_+)/\pi$. Furthermore, let $h : A_G \text{ --> } A'_G$ be a homomorphism and $\equiv_h$ be the congruence relation induced by h. If the homomorphism h is surjective, then $A_{G/\equiv h} \approx A'_G$.
Proof : according to the theorem of homomorphism [13];
Let f : $A_{G/\equiv h} \text{ --> } A'_G$ be the family of functions defined by f([a])=h(a), a is of a sort of $A_G$. We have [a]=[a'] implies that h(a)=h(a').
    To show that f is an isomorphism :
- f is bijective : as h is surjective by assumption, then f is surjective. Further, if f([a])=f([a']), then h(a)=h(a') and consequently [a]=[a']. Hence f is injective.
- f is a homomorphism : let (r : p <-- α q) be an operation of $A_G$. The homomorphism condition may be satisfied by

$f((A_{(i,nb)}) r([\alpha], [q])) = f([(A_G)( \alpha, q)])$
$= h((A_G) (\alpha, q))$

$$= (A'_G)(h(\alpha) , h(q)) \text{ and by homomorphism condition}$$
$$= (A'_G)(f([\alpha]) , f([q]))$$

Informally, this means that given $h$ and f the function induced by $h$, if the states p≡p' under some conditions, then for every derivation in $PT(I_+)/\pi$, there is a derivation in $PT(I_+)$. Note that we have seen that the inverse is true in the lattice $L(PT(I+))$. The term $[\alpha]$ denotes the equivalence class of the terminal $\alpha$ which is $\alpha$ in the simplest case (see section VI).

# V- Definition of the Homomorphism h

Below, we will give an algorithm (infer) that corresponds to the function f. The function *infer* induced by the homomorphism $h$ is parametered by an integer k>0. A derivation tree in $A_G$ is of the form p0(a1/a2, p1(a2/a3, p3(a3/a4,p4(.......))...))) where ai/aj means that ai is followed by aj.

Informally speaking, if one can find two derivations

$$p0(a1/a2/.../ak, p1(a2/a3/...ak+1, p3(a3/a4/.../ak+2,p4(.......))...)))$$
and $$q0(b1/b2/.../bk, q1(b2/b3/.../bk+1, q3(b3/b4/.../bk+2,q4(.......))...)))$$
where for i=1..k-1, j=i+1, ai/aj=bi/bj, then for l=0..k-1, pl≡ql.

Note that k>0 defines the extent of the function *infer* below where. for k=0, the language of the generated partition is $\Sigma^*$. The more k is great, the "lower" is $PT(I+)/\pi$ in the lattice whose bottom element is $PT(I+)$ and whose top element is $\Sigma^*$. It is straightforward to see that for $0 < i^2 j$, $L(PT(I+)/\pi, i) \subseteq L(PT(I+)/\pi, j)$. Hence, the value of the parameter k defines the depth of the search in the lattice.

The function infer induced by the homomorphism $h$ is defined as follows :

Given an integer value $k^3 1$, consider every string $I_+$. The inference process starts with $infer(<q0, \omega>, \{\}, k)$, $\omega \in I_+$, $q_0$ the start symbol (initial state). The function infer will generate a set of conditional rules for $I_+$ if k>1. Let the call $infer(<q,\omega>, G, k)$ be the general case. A state variable is a state like $q_i$ where i is an unknown natural number to be defined at the end of each step.

```
Function infer(<q,ω>, G₁ , k) returns Gₖ₊₁ =
    if <q,ω> = <_,ε> return Gᵢ;
    if |ω|<k then let k= |ω| -- for this last turn !
    if there exists a rule <p,υ> <-- <p',γ> in Gᵢ where
        υ=α₁,...,αₖ ρ and ω=α₁,...,αₖ φ and unify(q,p,Gᵢ)          (1)
    then return infer(<p', α₂,...,αₖ φ>, Gᵢ)
    else  create a rule r : <p, ω > <-- <p',α₂,...,αₖ φ>   -- p' of the form q , i will
        return infer(<p',α₂,...,αₖ φ>, Gᵢ ∪ {r});          -- be defined later.
    end if;
end infer;
```

Each example been processed, different variables states of the grammar $G_n$ of the current step are assigned natural numbers beginning from the least natural not yet used. Note that merges are done in infer function at (1).

The unify function sets the relations between states.

```
Function unify(q, p, G) returns Boolean =
        if q = p then return true;
```

```
            else      if one of (or both) p and q is a state variable (say p)
                      then set (p=q) in Gi; return true;
                      else return false;
                      end if;
            end if;
     end unify;
```

## V-1- A simple example

We consider the following simple positive set for $I_+ : I^* = \{$abbbcde, abccdee, abcde$\}$
Let K=2. Then consider the first example " abbbcde ". The $A_G$ term corresponding to this example is (x/y means "x" followed by "y") :
p0(a/b, **p1**(b/b, **p2**(b/b, **p3**(b/c, p4(c/d, p5(d/e, p6(e/ε))))))) depicted by the following path in PT($I_+$) :

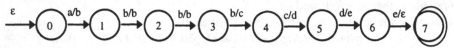

Following *infer* function, the states with the same prefix of length K are merged from 1..k-1. Here the states 2 and 3 are merged and give the following automata:

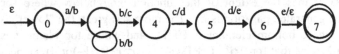

In other words, we had $\delta(p1, b/b) = p2$ and $\delta(p2, b/b) = p3$. Then p1, p2 and p3 are merged.
One may note that merging prefixes is done in other situations in an automaton : when designing an automaton, every derivation begins from $q_0$ where we want that every example of $I_+$ begins with $q_0$.
The set of rules of **G1** obtained from this example analysis is :

<p0, "ab".ω> --> <$p_1$, "b". ω>          ;          <$p_1$, "bb".ω> --> <$p_1$, "b". ω>
<$p_1$, "bc".ω> --> <$p_4$, "c". ω>          ;          <$p_4$, "cd".ω> --> <$p_5$, "d". ω>
<$p_5$, "de".ω> --> <$p_6$, "e". ω>          ;          <$p_6$, "e">    --> <>

The regular expression associated to G1 is :          **L(G1) = a b\* c d e**
Note that we apply a usual generalisation rule applied in the Grammatical Inference where every v+, v ∈ Σ* is generalised to v*.
The call infer(<p0, "abccdee">, G1, 2) for the next example adds two more rules to G1

<$p_4$, "cc".ω> --> <$p_4$, "c". ω> ;  <$p_6$, "ee".ω> --> <$p_6$, "e". ω>

Then **G2** is :

| | | |
|---|---|---|
| <$p_0$, "ab".ω> --> <$p_1$, "b". ω> ; | <$p_1$, "bb".ω> --> <$p_1$, "b". ω> |
| <$p_1$, "bc".ω> --> <$p_4$, "c". ω> ; | <$p_4$, "cd".ω> --> <$p_5$, "d". ω> |
| <$p_2$, "cc".ω> --> <$p_2$, "c". ω> ; | <$p_5$, "de".ω> --> <$p_6$, "e". ω> |
| <$p_6$, "ee".ω> --> <$p_6$, "e". ω> ; | <$p_6$, "e">    --> <> |

The third example "abcde" is accepted by G2 and does not change the grammar. The final DFA is :

The regular expression associated to G2 is $L(G2) = ab^*c^*de^*$

## V-2- Generating a Constraint Logic Program for G1

The grammar G2 can be immediately prototyped by a (constraint) logic program. We implemented the grammatical inference by a logic program which is parametered by the value of K. The (constraint) logic program $\mathbf{Prg}^{std}$ associated to G2 where K=2 is given by the predicate $aut^{std}$ :

$$aut^{std}(['a', 'b' \mid L], p0) \quad <-- \quad aut^{std}(['b' \mid L], p1).$$
$$aut^{std}(['b', 'b' \mid L], p1) \quad <-- \quad aut^{std}(['b' \mid L], p1).$$
$$aut^{std}(['b', 'c' \mid L], p1) \quad <-- \quad aut^{std}(['c' \mid L], p4).$$
$$aut^{std}(['c', 'd' \mid L], p4) \quad <-- \quad aut^{std}(['d' \mid L], p5).$$
$$aut^{std}(['c', 'c' \mid L], p4) \quad <-- \quad aut^{std}(['c' \mid L], p4).$$
$$aut^{std}(['d', 'e' \mid L], p5) \quad <-- \quad aut^{std}(['e' \mid L], p6).$$
$$aut^{std}(['e', 'e' \mid L], p6) \quad <-- \quad aut^{std}(['e' \mid L], p6).$$
$$aut^{std}(['e', \varepsilon \mid L], p6) \quad <-- \quad aut^{std}([\varepsilon \mid L], p7).$$
$$aut^{std}([\varepsilon], p7).$$

The query $<-aut^{std}(\omega, p0)$ submitted to $Prg1^{std}$ will succeed if $\omega \in L(G2)$.
In order to apply an ascending evaluation procedure, the initial state $p_0$ should appear in a basic clause (not in the query). For this sake, the above programme is then transformed to a *dual* one. Then we obtain a logic program on which we would apply the immediate consequence operator ([18]). The least fix-point of this operator is defined by $T\!\uparrow = \cup_{j \geq 0} T\!\uparrow^j$ denoted by $T\!\uparrow^\omega$ where $T\!\uparrow^0 = \{aut^{dual}(p0)\}$ and $T\!\uparrow^{j+1} = T\!\uparrow^j$. $T\!\uparrow^\omega$ characterise the set of available states of the automaton. Furthermore, for an automaton $A=(Q, \Sigma, \delta, p_0, F)$, $aut(f) \in T\!\uparrow^\omega$, $f \in F$, if there exists a valid string (starting from q0) which ends to the final state f. Details of the transformation and the extraction of the properties of the dual program are out of the scope of this paper (see e.g. [9] for details).

## V-3- Another example

Let us consider the following example of final research reports. We apply the function *infer* for K=1 and K=2.

Content --> Title, Intr, Abs, Ack, Oln, Chap, Chap, Ref, Ind.
Content --> Title, Abs, Oln, Chap, Chap, Chap, Ref, Anx, Anx.
Content --> Title, Intr, Abs, Oln, Chap, SChap, Chap, SChap, Ref, Ind, Anx.
Content --> Title, Intr, Oln, Chap, SChap, Chap, SChap, Chap, SChap, Ref.
Content --> Title, Oln, Chap, SChap, Chap, SChap, Chap, SChap, Ref.

For the sake of simplicity, we abbreviated symbols as follows :

Intr :Introduction  Abs :Abstract  SChap :subchapter  Ack : Acknowledgement  Chap : Chapter
Ref : Reference  Ann : Annexes  Oln :Outline  Ind : Index

The set of rules generated for K=1:

| | | |
|---|---|---|
| <p0 , "Title".ω> | --> | <p7 , ω> |
| <p1 , "Anx".ω> | --> | <p2 , ω> |
| <p1 , 'ε' > | --> | <> |
| <p2 , "Anx".ω> | --> | <p2 , ω> |
| <p2 , "Ind".ω> | --> | <p1 , ω> |
| <p2 , 'ε' > | --> | <> |
| <p3 , "SChap".ω> | --> | <p3 , ω> |
| <p3 , "Chap".ω> | --> | <p3 , ω> |
| <p3 , "Ref".ω > | --> | <p2 , ω> |
| <p4 , "Oln".ω > | --> | <p3 , ω> |
| <p5 , "Oln".ω > | --> | <p3 , ω> |
| <p5 , "Ack".ω > | --> | <p4 , ω> |
| <p6 , "Oln".ω > | --> | <p3 , ω> |
| <p6 , "Abs".ω > | --> | <p5 , ω> |
| <p7 , "Oln".ω > | --> | <p3 , ω> |
| <p7 , "Abs".ω > | --> | <p4 , ω> |
| <p7 , "Intr".ω > | --> | <p6 , ω> |

The language of this automaton is :

L = Title [Intr [Abs [Ack]] | Abs] (SChap | Chap)* Ref ([Ind] Anx)* [Ind]

It is easy to note that for K=1, the language accepted by the automaton is a larger set over Σ* than the one for K=2 (see also the next section). The set of rules generated for K=2 is given in the next page. Note that the recursive part of the language for K=2 is on the Chapter × Sub_Chapter part. The associated language to this automaton is

L     = Title (Abs | Intr [Abs [Ack]]) L1               where
L1     = Oln (Chap SChap)* (Chap SChap | Chap*) L2; L2 = Ref [Anx Anx | Ind [Anx]]

**The set of rules generated for K=2 :**

<p0, "Title"."Oln".ω> → <p5, "Oln".ω>
<p0, "Title"."Intr".ω> → <p8, "Intr".ω>;
<p1, "Ind"> → <>
<p2, "Ref"."Ind".ω> → <p1, "Ind".ω >
<p3, "Chap"."Chap".ω> → <p3, "Chap".ω>
<p4, "Chap"."SChap".ω> → <p12, "SChap".ω>
<p5, "Oln"."Chap".ω> → <p4, "Chap".ω>
<p7, "Abs"."Oln".ω> → <p5, "Oln".ω>
<p8, "Intr"."Oln".ω> → <p5, "Oln".ω>
<p9, "Anx"> → <>
<p11, "Abs"."Oln".ω> → <p5, "Oln".ω>
<p12, "SChap"."Ref".ω> → <p2, "Ref".ω>

<p0, "Title"."Abs".ω> → <p11, "Abs".ω>
<p1, "Ind"."Anx".ω> → <p9, "Anx".ω>
<p2, "Ref"."Anx".ω> → <p10, "Anx".ω>
<p2, "Ref"> → <>
<p3, "Chap"."Ref".ω> → <p2, "Ref".ω>
<p4, "Chap"."Chap".ω> → <p3, "Chap".ω>
<p6, "Ack"."Oln".ω> → <p5, "Oln".ω>
<p7, "Abs"."Ack".ω> → <p6, "Ack".ω>
<p8, "Intr"."Abs".ω> → <p7, "Abs".ω>
<p10, "Anx"."Anx".ω> → <p9, "Anx".ω>
<p12, "SChap"."Chap".ω> → <p4, "Chap".ω>

## VI- The Table of Contexts : An Alternative View of the Generalisation

We give here an alternative construction of the result of *infer* and give the related automaton. We believe that this representation is a suitable alternative for the GI problem with a set of positive examples. This is done by the construction of a table where every symbol of $\Sigma$ is given with its successor and predecessor. For the above example, we have :

| Symbol $\alpha \in \Sigma$ | P= Predecessor of $\alpha$ | S= Successor of $\alpha$ |
|---|---|---|
| Title | $\varepsilon$ | Intr, Abs, Oln |
| Intr | Title | Abs, Oln |
| Abs | Intr, Title | Ack, Oln |
| Ack | Abs | Oln |
| Oln | Ack, Abs, Intr, Title | Chap |
| Chap | Oln, Chap, SChap | Chap, Ref, SChap |
| Ref | Chap, SChap | Ind, Anx, $ |
| Anx | Ref, Ind, Anx | Anx, $ |
| SChap | Chap | Chap, Ref |
| Ind | Ref | Anx, $ |

Note that the P=predecessor and the S=Successeur column of a symbole $\alpha$ constitute the equivalence class of P and S denoted by $[P]_\alpha$ and $[S]_\alpha$. The special symbol '$' denotes the end of a string (a final state of the automaton; the '$' symbol is added to the end of each string before analysing) while $\varepsilon$ denote the empty string at the beginning of a string. In fact, the table shows that some symbol of $\Sigma$ can be followed (resp. preceded) by a set of other symbols in $\Sigma$. The canonical automaton associated to this table is :

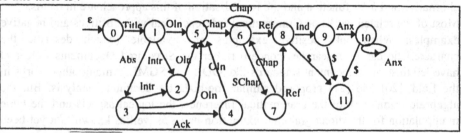

Note that there are three recursive parts on the nodes 6, 6-7-6, and 10.

In order to generalise the examples of $I_+$, the context in which the symbol $\alpha \in \Sigma$ is present can be "forgotten" and let the symbol $\alpha$ be followed by its successor anywhere in a string whatever be the predecessor of $\alpha$.

Let a symbol $\alpha \in \Sigma$, P the set of its predecessors and S the set of its successors. Consider also the (language inclusion) lattice(PT($I_+$)) whose top element is $\Sigma^*$ and whose bottom is PT($I_+$).

An interesting use of this table is based on the well known but yet simple generalisation rule in Inductive Learning ([19]) which "forgets" the context of a sequence. Consequently, in the case of the above table, we can :

1- Allow $\alpha \in \Sigma$ to be followed by **an** element of $[S]_\alpha$ and preceded by **an** element of $[P]_\alpha$ according to $I_+$. This corresponds to K=3 in function *infer*. For example, if $\alpha$="Abs", the only possible triplets of the form $\beta$."Abs".$\delta$ are <Intr, Abs, Ack>, <Title, Abs, Oln> and <Intr, Abs, Oln>.

2- Allow $\alpha \in \Sigma$ to be followed by **any** element of $[S]_\alpha$ and preceded by **any** element of $[P]_\alpha$. This gives a good degree of generalisation. This is a special case of *infer* with K=2. For $\alpha$="Abs", the possible cases are : {"Intr", "Title"} x "Abs" x {"Ack", "Oln"} which makes 4 possibilities (generalisation).

3- Allow a∈ Σ to be preceded and followed by **any** element of Σ*. This is a special case of infer with K=0. This gives the Top element of the lattice. For α="Abs", the possible cases are β x "Abs" x δ with δ,β∈ Σ.

Other configurations are possible which correspond to K=1 : allowing α to be only followed (resp. preceded) by any symbol of $[S]_\alpha$ (resp. $[P]_\alpha$) and free for the rest. However, during our experimentation on paper documents, the case (2) above showed to be a reasonable configuration. While an automaton specifies rules to construct sequences of, say characters, the choices above (variations of K) let generate strings with various degree of constraints. Note that if negative examples are present, more constraints must be verified and the precedence table alone will not suffice.

## VII- Conclusion

A new algorithm for GI has been presented which is immediately prototyped by a constraint logic program. The algebraic specification allows to show that the homomorphism h exists and we gave an implementation of it by the *infer* function. An alternative view of GI based on the construction of the table of successors and predecessors of any symbol in Σ* has been outlined. The relationship between this alternative and *infer* function and the formalisation of this approach are in hands.

Most of the related works on Grammatical Inference deal with positives and negative examples. When only positive examples are available (which describe the characteristic cases), researches concern rather the Structured Documents field and have led to several document standards like ODA and SGML. Among other works in the field, [20] and [21] proposed similar methods for document analysis. But the algebraic framework of the grammatical Inference, the logical aspects and the table manipulation for the direct grammar extraction have, as well as known, not yet been investigated.

This work is developed inside a paper document processing project where GI results are used to classify and then translate documents into machine readable form. The generated logic program is augmented to handle some attributes of the logical structure of paper documents such as typographic attributes.

Many non GI methods for document conversion exist. In a much broader sense we might regard the transformation task as an information retrieval and a classification (discrimination) with respect to some criteria. Among others we may mention the use of tectonics like fuzzy logic and weight values, mixed use of dynamic programming searching, neural network self-organizing maps, grammar based ones, etc. The reader may consult ([22], [23]) for a survey of related transformation and knowledge acquisition systems. As far as the paper document conversion with a priori unknown structure is concerned, grammatical (syntactic) methods are of the well developed but still, we believe, easy to understand area. Once the information is structured with a set of production rules, any homomorphism from the associated algebra to another algebra (specially a language) of the category is a matter of specification. The resulting system is likely parametered by an algebra to realize a new conversion. One application we test is to realize a PS to HTML (as in [24]) where we may extract graphic primitives from PS files and convert them to HTML format. Ps conversion to Tex (or Latex) are other case studies we currently work on.


# VIII- References

[1] S. Tayeb-Bey, A. S. Saidi "Grammatical Formalism for Document Understanding System : From Document towards HTML Text". BSDIA'97, November 1997, Brasilia.

[2] E.M. Gold. "Language identification in the limit". Inf. and Control, 10(5)- 1967.

[3] H.S. Fu and T. Booth : "Grammatical Inference: Introduction and Survey". parts 1 & 2. IEEE Trans. Sys. man and Cyber. SMC-5: 95-11.

[4] R. C. Gonzalez and M. G. Thomason. "Syntactic Pattern Recognition, an Introduction" . Addison Wesley. Reading Mass. 1978.

[5] H.S. Fu. "Syntactic Pattern Recognition and Applications". Prentice Hall, N.Y. 1982.

[6] L. Miclet. "Grammatical Inference". Syntactic and Structural Pattern Recognition. H. Bunk and SanFeliu eds. World Scientific.

[7] J. Onica, P. Garcia. "Inferring regular Languages in Polynomial Update time". Pattern Recognition and Image Analysis. 1992.

[8] P. Dupont, L. Miclet & E. Vidal. "What is the search space of Regular Inference?". ICGI'94, Grammatical Inference and Applications. Springer-Verlag-94.

[9] L. Fribourg, M. V. Peixoto. "Automates concurrents à Contraintes". TSI.13 (6). 1994.

[10] J. A. Goguen, J.W. Tatcher, E.G. Wagner, J.B. Wright. "Initial Algebra Semantics and Continuous Algebra". JACM 24(1). 1977.

[11] A. S. Saidi : "Extensions Grammaticales de la Programmation Logique". PhD. 1992.

[12] A. S. Saidi. "On the unification of phrases". IFIP-94 .

[13] H. Ehrig, B. Mahr. " Fundamentals of Algebraic Specification". Vol-1 & 2. Springer-Verlag1985.

[14] E.M. Gold. "Complexity of automaton identification from given data"". Information and Control, 37- 1978.

[15] J. E. Hopcroft, J.D. Ullmann. "Formal Languages and their Relation to Automata". Addison-Wesley 1969.

[16] F. Bancilhon & all. "Magic Sets and Other Strange Ways to Implement Logic Programs". Proc. ACM Symp. on principles of Databases Systems. Boston 1986.

[17] F. Coste, J. Nicols : "Regular Inference as a graph coloring Problem". ICML'97. 1997.

[18] K.R. Apt, M.H. Van Emden : "Contribution to the Theory of Logic Programming". JACM. 29(3°. 1982.

[19] R.S. Michalski & all. "Machine Learning : An Artificial Intelligence Approach", vol. 1 & 2. Springer-Verlag 1984 and Morgan Kaufmann 1986.

[20] H. Ahohen, H. Mannila. "Forming Grammars for structured documents". Research report. University of Helsinki. 1994.

[21] P. Frankhauser, Y. Xu. "MarkitUp! an incremental approach to document structure recognition". Elect. Publishing-Organisation, Dissemination and Design, 6(4). 1994.

[22] G. Lindén "Structured Document Transformation". PhD Thesis. University of Helsinki. Finland june 1997.

[23] Y. Yan Tang, C. De Yan, C. Y. Suen "Document processing for Automatic Knowledge Acquisition". IEEE transactions on Knowledge and Data Engineering. 6(1). 1994.

[24] B. Poirier, M. Dagenais. "Outils d'extraction et de reconnaissance de la structure de documents". CNED'96. pp. 179-184. Nantes-France 1996.

# Stochastic Inference of Regular Tree Languages[*]

Rafael C. Carrasco, Jose Oncina and Jorge Calera

Departamento de Lenguajes y Sistemas Informáticos
Universidad de Alicante, E-03071 Alicante
E-mail: (carrasco, oncina, calera)@dlsi.ua.es

**Abstract.** We generalize a former algorithm for regular language identification from stochastic samples to the case of tree languages or, equivalently, string languages where structural information is available. We also describe a method to compute efficiently the relative entropy between the target grammar and the inferred one, useful for the evaluation of the inference.

## 1 Introduction

A common concern in the grammatical inference approach is to avoid overgeneralization. Although complete samples may be used for this purpose, representative sets of counter-examples are usually difficult to obtain. A different way to prevent overgeneralization is the use of stochastic samples. Indeed, many experimental settings involve random or noisy examples. Some algorithms for learning regular (string) languages from stochastic samples have been proposed before (Stolcke & Omohundro, 1993; Carrasco & Oncina, 1994). The last one has the interesting property that identification in the limit of the structure of the deterministic automaton (DFA) is guaranteed.

Learning context-free languages is harder, but identification is still possible if structural descriptions are available. In such case, the identification of CFG's becomes equivalent to the problem of identifying regular tree languages, and algorithms for this purpose have been proposed by Sakakibara (1992) and Oncina & García (1994). The first algorithm uses positive examples and works within the subclass of reversible tree languages. The second one uses complete samples but identifies any deterministic tree grammar (and therefore, any backwards-deterministic CFG).

In this paper, we introduce a modification of the last algorithm that can be trained with positive stochastic samples generated according to a probabilistic production scheme. The construction follows the same guidelines as the algorithm for string languages in Carrasco & Oncina (1994). We also describe a method to directly evaluate the relative entropy between the inferred language and the true grammar which avoids the generation of large test sets. The relative entropy measures the distance between languages and is usually approximated by means of numerical estimations over large samples generated with the correct

---
[*] Work partially supported by the Spanish CICYT under grant TIC97-0941.

distribution. However, this method is in general unfeasible in the case of tree languages, due to the huge number (enormous compared with the case of strings) of different trees that one has to generate. Therefore, an alternative method for such evaluation is of interest.

## 2 Regular tree languages

Ordered labeled trees will be represented using the functional notation: for instance, the functional notation for the tree shown in Fig. 1 is $a(b(a(bc))c)$. Given a finite set of labels $V$, the set of all finite-size trees whose nodes are labeled with symbols in $V$ will be denoted as $V^T$. Any symbol $a$ in $V$ is also the representation of a tree consisting of a single node labeled with $a$ and, therefore, $V \subset V^T$.

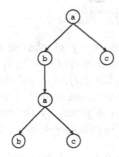

**Fig. 1.** A graphic representation of the ordered labeled tree $a(b(a(bc))c)$

Deterministic tree automata (DTA) generalize deterministic finite-state automata (DFA), which work on strings. In contrast with DFA's —where strings are processed from left to right—, in DTA's the trees are processed bottom-up and a state in the automaton is assigned to every node in the tree. This state depends on the node label and on the states associated to the descendents of the node. The state assigned to the root of the tree has to be an accepting state for the tree to be accepted by the automaton. Formally, the DTA is a 4-tuple $A = (Q, V, \delta, F)$, where

- $Q$ is a finite set of *states*;
- $V$ is a finite set of *labels*;
- $F \subset Q$ is the subset of *accepting states*;
- $\delta = \{\delta_0, \delta_1, ..., \delta_n\}$ is a set of *transition functions* of the form $\delta_k : V \times Q^k \to Q$.

If $t = f(t_1, t_2, ..., t_k)$ is a tree (or subtree) consisting of an internal node labeled $f$ which expands $k$ subtrees $t_1, t_2, ..., t_k$, the state $\delta(t)$ is $\delta_k(f, \delta(t_1), ..., \delta(t_k))$. In other words, $\delta(t)$ is recursively defined as:

$$\delta(t) = \begin{cases} \delta_k(f, \delta(t_1), ..., \delta(t_k)) & \text{if } t = f(t_1 ... t_k) \in (V^T - V) \\ \delta_0(a) & \text{if } t = a \in V \end{cases} \quad (1)$$

Every DTA defines a *regular* tree language (RTL) consisting of all trees accepted by the automaton: $L(A) = \{t \in V^T : \delta(t) \in F\}$. By convention, undefined transitions lead to an *absorption* state, i.e., to non-acceptable trees.

## 3   Stochastic tree automata

Stochastic tree automata incorporate a probability for every transition in the automaton, with the normalization that the probabilities of transitions leading to the same state $q \in Q$ must add up to one[1]. In other words, there is a collection of functions $p = \{p_0, p_1, p_2, ...p_n\}$ of the type $p_k : V \times Q^k \to [0,1]$ such that they satisfy, for all $q \in Q$,

$$\sum_{f \in V} \sum_{k=0}^{n} \sum_{\substack{q_1,...,q_k \in Q: \\ \delta_k(f,q_1,...,q_k)=q}} p_k(f, q_1, ..., q_k) = 1 \qquad (2)$$

In addition to this probabilities, every *stochastic deterministic tree automaton* $A = (Q, V, \delta, p, r)$ provides a function $r : Q \to [0,1]$ which, for every $q \in Q$, gives the probability that a tree satisfies $\delta(t) = q$ and substitutes, in the definition of the automaton, the subset of accepting states. Then, the probability of a tree $t$ in the language generated by $A$ is given by the product of the probabilities of all the transitions used when $t$ is processed by $A$, times $r(\delta(t))$:

$$p(t|A) = r(\delta(t))\, \pi(t) \qquad (3)$$

with $\pi(t)$ recursively given by

$$\pi(f(t_1, \dots, t_k)) = p_k(f, \delta(t_1), \dots, \delta(t_k))\, \pi(t_1) \cdots \pi(t_k) . \qquad (4)$$

Of course, $\pi(a) = p_0(a)$ for $t = a \in V$. The equations (3) and (4) define a probability distribution $p(t|A)$ which is consistent if

$$\sum_{t \in V^T} p(t|A) = 1. \qquad (5)$$

The condition of consistency can be written in terms of matrix analysis. Indeed, let us define the expectation elements:

$$\Lambda_{ij} = \sum_{k=1}^{n} \sum_{f \in V} \sum_{\substack{q_1,q_2,...,q_k \in Q: \\ \delta(f,q_1,...,q_k)=j}} p_k(f, q_1, q_2, ..., q_k)(\delta_{iq_1} + \delta_{iq_2} + \cdots + \delta_{iq_k}), \qquad (6)$$

where $\delta_{ij}$ is Kronecker's delta. Consistency, in the sense of Eq. (5), is preserved if the spectral radius of matrix $\Lambda$ is smaller than one (Wetherell 1980).

---

[1] This normalization makes the probabilities of all possible expansions of a tree node to add up to one.

It is important to remark that two stochastic languages are *identical* if

$$T_1 = T_2 \Leftrightarrow p(t|T_1) = p(t|T_2) \ \forall t \in V^T. \tag{7}$$

In contrast to strings, concatenation of trees requires marking the node where the attachment takes place. For this purpose, let \$ be a special symbol not in $V$. With $V_\$^T$ we denote the set of trees in $(V \cup \{\$\})^T$ with no internal node labeled \$ and exactly one leaf labeled with \$. For every $s \in V_\$^T$, and every $t \in V^T \cup V_\$^T$, the tree $s\#t$ is obtained by replacing in $s$ the node marked with \$ by a copy of $t$. For every stochastic tree language $T$ and $t \in V^T$, the *quotient* $t^{-1}T$ is a stochastic language over $V_\$^T$ defined through the probabilities

$$p(s|t^{-1}T) = \frac{p(s\#t|T)}{p(V_\$^T\#t|T)} \ . \tag{8}$$

In case $s \notin V_\$^T$ then $p(s|t^{-1}T) = 0$. On the other hand, if $p(V_\$^T\#t|T) = 0$, the quotient (8) is undefined and we will write $t^{-1}T = \emptyset$.

The Myhill-Nerode's theorem for rational languages (see Hopcroft & Ullman 1979) can be generalized for stochastic rational tree languages. If $T$ is a stochastic RTL, the number of different sets $t^{-1}T$ is finite and a deterministic tree automaton (DTA) accepting $\{t \in V^T : p(t|T) > 0\}$ can be defined. We will call it the *canonical acceptor* $M = (Q^M, V, \delta^M, F^M)$, with:

$$\begin{aligned} Q^M &= \{t^{-1}T \neq \emptyset : t \in V^T\} \\ F^M &= \{t^{-1}T : p(t|T) > 0\} \\ \delta^M(f, t_1^{-1}T, \dots, t_k^{-1}T) &= f(t_1, \dots, t_k)^{-1}T \end{aligned} \tag{9}$$

A stochastic sample $S$ of the language $T$ is an infinite sequence of trees generated according to the probability distribution $p(t|T)$. We denote with $S_n$ the sequence of the $n$ first trees (not necessarily different) in $S$ and with $c_n(t)$ the number of occurrences of tree $t$ in $S_n$. For $X \subset V^T$, $c_n(X) = \sum_{t \in X} c_n(t)$. Provided that the structure (states and transition functions) of $M$ is known, we can estimate the probability functions in the stochastic DTA from the examples in $S_n$:

$$r(t^{-1}T) = \frac{c_n(\Delta_{f(t_1,\dots,t_k)})}{n} \tag{10}$$

$$p_k(f, t_1^{-1}T, \dots, t_k^{-1}T) = \frac{c_n(V_\$^T\#f(t_1, \dots, t_k))}{c_n(V_\$^T\#\Delta_{f(t_1,\dots,t_k)})} \ . \tag{11}$$

where $\Delta_t = \{s \in V^T : \delta^M(s) = t^{-1}T\}$.

## 4 Inference algorithm

In the following, we will assume that an arbitrary total order relation has been defined in $V^T$ such that $t_1 \leq t_2 \Leftrightarrow \text{depth}(t_1) \leq \text{depth}(t_2)$. As usual, $t_1 < t_2 \Leftrightarrow t_1 \leq t_2 \wedge t_1 \neq t_2$.

```
algorithm tlips
input: A ⊂ Sub(T) such that K(T) ⊂ A
output: SSub (short subtree set)
        F (frontier set)
begin algorithm
  SSub = F = ∅
  W = V₀ ∩ A
  do ( while W ≠ ∅ )
    x = min W
    W = W − {x}
    if ∃y ∈ SSub : equivₜ(x, y) then
        F = F ∪ {x}
    else
        SSub = SSub ∪ {x}
        W = W ∪ {f(t₁, ..., tₖ) ∈ A : t₁, ..., tₖ ∈ SSub}
    endif
  end do
end algorithm
```

**Fig. 2.** Algorithm tlips.

The *subtree set* and the *short-subtree set* are respectively defined as

$$\mathrm{Sub}(T) = \{t \in V^T : t^{-1}T \neq \emptyset\}$$
$$\mathrm{SSub}(T) = \{t \in \mathrm{Sub}(T) : s^{-1}T = t^{-1}T \Rightarrow s \geq t\} \tag{12}$$

The *kernel* and the *frontier set* are defined as:

$$K(T) = \{f(t_1, ..., t_k) \in \mathrm{Sub}(T) : t_1, ..., t_k \in \mathrm{SSub}(T)\}$$
$$F(T) = K(T) - \mathrm{SSub}(T) \tag{13}$$

Note that there is exactly one tree in $\mathrm{SSub}(T)$ for every state in $Q^M$ of the canonical acceptor, while the trees in $K(T) - V_0$ correspond to the rules in the generating grammar and, therefore, both $\mathrm{SSub}(T)$ and $K(T)$ are finite.

Finally, we define a boolean function $\mathbf{equiv}_T : K(T) \times K(T) \rightarrow \{\text{true, false}\}$ such that

$$\mathbf{equiv}_T(t_1, t_2) = \text{true} \Leftrightarrow t_1^{-1}T = t_2^{-1}T. \tag{14}$$

The following theorems support the inference algorithm:

**Theorem 1.** *If* $\mathrm{SSub}(T)$, $F(T)$ *and* $\mathbf{equiv}_T$ *are known, then the structure of the canonical acceptor is isomorphic to:*

$$Q = \mathrm{SSub}(T)$$
$$\delta(f, t_1, ..., t_k) = t \tag{15}$$

*where* $t$ *is the only tree in* $\mathrm{SSub}(T)$ *such that* $\mathbf{equiv}_T(t, f(t_1, ..., t_k))$.

```
algorithm comp_n
input:x, y ∈ V^T, S_n
output:boolean
begin algorithm
  do ( ∀t, z : depth_t($) = 1 ∧ (t#z#x ∨ t#z#y) ∈ Sub(S_n) )
    if different(c_n(V_$^T#t#z#x), c_n(V_$^T#x), c_n(V_$^T#t#z#y), c_n(V_$^T#y), α) then
      return FALSE
    endif
  end do
  return TRUE
end algorithm
```

**Fig. 3.** Algorithm comp_n.

**Theorem 2.** *The algorithm in Fig. 2 outputs* $\text{SSub}(T)$ *and* $F(T)$ *with input* $\text{equiv}_T$ *plus any* $A \subset \text{Sub}(T)$ *such that* $K(T) \subset A$.

The proofs can be found in the Appendix. Note that the finite set $\text{Sub}(S_n) \subset \text{Sub}(T)$ can be used as input in the former algorithm, as $K(T) \subset \text{Sub}(S_n)$ for $n$ large enough. On the other hand, the algorithm never calls $\text{equiv}_T$ out of its domain $K(T)$ and the number of calls is bounded by $|K(T)|^2$. Thus, the global complexity of the algorithm is $\mathcal{O}(|K(T)|^2)$ times the complexity of function $\text{equiv}_T$.

## 5  Probabilistic inference

In practice, the unknown language $T$ is replaced by the stochastic sample $S$ and the equivalence test $\text{equiv}_T(x, y)$ is performed through a probabilistic function $\text{comp}_n(x, y)$ of the $n$ first trees in $S$ (i.e., of $S_n$). The algorithm will output the correct DTA in the limit as long as $\text{comp}_n$ tends to $\text{equiv}_T$ when $n$ grows.

According to (14), $\text{equiv}_T(x, y) = \text{true}$ means $x^{-1}T = y^{-1}T$. This can be checked by means of Eq. (8), but we rather check the conditional probabilities:

$$\frac{p(V_$^T#t#z#x)}{p(V_$^T#z#x)} = \frac{p(V_$^T#t#z#y)}{p(V_$^T#z#y)} \tag{16}$$

for all $z \in V_$^T$ and for all $t \in V_$^T$ such that $\$$ is at depth one in $t$.

In order to check (16) a statistical test is applied to the difference (provided that $t#z#x$ or $t#z#y$ are in $\text{Sub}(S_n)$):

$$\frac{c_n(V_$^T#t#z#x)}{c_n(V_$^T#z#x)} - \frac{c_n(V_$^T#t#z#y)}{c_n(V_$^T#z#y)}. \tag{17}$$

We have chosen a Hoeffding (1963) type test, as described in Fig. 4. This check provides the correct answer with probability greater than $(1 - \alpha)^2$, $\alpha$ being

```
algorithm different
input: f, m, f', m', α
output: boolean
begin algorithm
```
$$\text{return } |f/m - f'/m'| > \sqrt{\tfrac{1}{2m} \log \tfrac{2}{\alpha}} + \sqrt{\tfrac{1}{2m'} \log \tfrac{2}{\alpha}}$$
```
end algorithm
```

**Fig. 4.** Algorithm different.

an arbitrarily small positive number. Therefore, the algorithm $\text{comp}_n$ plotted in Fig. 3 returns the correct value with probability greater than $(1 - \alpha)^{2r}$, where $r$ is smaller than the number of different subtrees in $S_n$. Because $r$ grows slowly with $n$, we allow $\alpha$ to depend on $r$. Indeed, if $\alpha$ decreases faster than $1/r$ then $(1 - \alpha)^r$ tends to zero and $\text{comp}_n(x, y) = \text{equiv}_T(x, y)$ in the limit of large $n$. Finally, note that the complexity of $\text{comp}_n$ is at most $O(n)$. As $|K(T)|$ does not depend on $S_n$ then the global complexity of our algorithm is $O(n)$.

## 6 Relative entropy between stochastic languages

The entropy of a probability distribution $p(t|A)$ over $V^T$,

$$H(A) = - \sum_{t \in V^T} p(t|A) \log_2 p(t|A) , \tag{18}$$

bounds (within a deviation of one bit, see Cover & Thomas 1991) the average length of the string needed to code a tree in $V^T$ provided that an optimal coding scheme is used. Optimal coding implies an accurate knowledge of the source $A$. If only an approximate model $A'$ is available, the average length becomes:

$$G(A, A') = - \sum_{t \in V^T} p(t|A) \log_2 p(t|A') \tag{19}$$

The difference $H(A, A') = G(A, A') - H(A)$ is known as *relative entropy* between $A$ and $A'$ or *Kullback-Leibler distance*, a magnitude which is always a positive number: indeed, a suboptimal coding leads to larger average lengths. Note that $H(A) = G(A, A)$ and, thus, $H(A, A') = G(A, A') - G(A, A)$ and, therefore, a procedure to compute $G(A, A')$ can also be used to compute the entropy of a regular tree language or the relative entropy between two languages.

Recall from Eq. (3) that the probability that the tree $t$ is generated by the automaton $A' = (Q', V, \delta', p', r')$ is given by the product of two different factors, and $\log_2 p(t|A') = \log_2 r'(\delta'(t)) + \log_2 \pi'(t)$. On the other hand, the class of subsets $L_{ij} = \{t \in V^T : \delta(t) = i \wedge \delta'(t) = j\}$ for $i \in Q$ and $j \in Q'$ defines a partition in $V^T$. This allows one to write the contribution to $G(A, A')$ of the

$r$-terms as

$$G_r(A, A') = - \sum_{\substack{i \in Q \\ j \in Q'}} \sum_{t \in L_{ij}} p(t|A) \log_2 r'(j) = - \sum_{\substack{i \in Q \\ j \in Q'}} r(i) \eta_{ij} \log_2 r'(j) \qquad (20)$$

where $\eta_{ij}$, defined as

$$\eta_{ij} = \sum_{t \in L_{ij}} \pi(t), \qquad (21)$$

represents the probability that a node of type $i \in Q$ expands as a subtree $t$ such that $\delta'(t) = j$. It is not difficult to show (Calera & Carrasco 1998) that all $\eta_{ij}$ can be easily obtained by means of an iterative procedure:

$$\eta_{ij}^{[t+1]} = \sum_{k=0}^{n} \sum_{f \in V} \sum_{\substack{i_1, i_2, \dots, i_k \in Q: \\ \delta_k(f, i_1, i_2, \dots, i_k) = i}} \sum_{\substack{j_1, j_2, \dots, j_k \in Q': \\ \delta'_k(f, j_1, j_2, \dots, j_k) = j}}$$

$$p_k(f, i_1, i_2, \dots, i_k) \, \eta_{i_1 j_1}^{[t]} \eta_{i_2 j_2}^{[t]} \cdots \eta_{i_k j_k}^{[t]} \qquad (22)$$

with $\eta_{ij}^{[0]} = 0$. The iterative series monotonically converges to the correct values, as it can be proved straightforwardly by induction.

In order to evaluate the contribution to $G(A, A')$ of the $\pi$-terms,

$$G_\pi(A, A') = - \sum_{t \in V^T} p(t|A) \log_2 \pi'(t) , \qquad (23)$$

recall that

$$\log_2 \pi'(f(t_1, \dots t_k)) = \log_2 p'_k(f, \delta'(t_1), \dots, \delta'(t_k)) + \log_2 \pi'(t_1) + \cdots + \log_2 \pi'(t_k), \qquad (24)$$

so that the contribution of the $\pi$-terms becomes

$$G_\pi(A, A') = - \sum_{k=0}^{n} \sum_{f \in V} \sum_{j_1, \dots, j_k \in Q'} \log_2 p'_k(f, j_1, \dots, j_k) \, n'(f, j_1, \dots, j_k) \qquad (25)$$

where $n'(f, j_1, j_2, \dots, j_k)$ is the expected —according to the distribution $p(t|A)$— number of subtrees $f(t_1, t_2, \dots, t_k)$ in $t$ such that $\delta'(t_1) = j_1$, $\delta'(t_2) = j_2, \dots,$ $\delta'(t_k) = j_k$. This leads to

$$G_\pi(A, A') = - \sum_{k=0}^{n} \sum_{f \in V} \sum_{i_1, i_2, \dots, i_k \in Q} \sum_{j_1, j_2, \dots, j_k \in Q'} C_{\delta_k(f, i_1, i_2, \dots, i_k)} \times$$

$$p_k(f, i_1, i_2, \dots, i_k) \log_2 p'_k(f, j_1, j_2, \dots, j_k) \eta_{i_1 j_1} \eta_{i_2 j_2} \cdots \eta_{i_k j_k} \qquad (26)$$

where $C_q$ is the expectation number of subtrees of type $q$. This vector $\mathbf{C}$ of expectation values $C_i$ can be easily computed using the matrix $\Lambda$ defined in Eq. (6) together with vector $\mathbf{r}$ of probabilities $r(i)$. As shown in Wetherell (1980), $\mathbf{C} = (\sum_{m=0}^{\infty} \Lambda^m)\,\mathbf{r}$ and, then, $\mathbf{C} = \mathbf{r} + \Lambda\mathbf{C}$. This relationship allows a fast iterative computation:

$$C_i^{[t+1]} = r(i) + \sum_{j \in Q} \Lambda_{ij} C_j^{[t]} \tag{27}$$

with $C_i^{[0]} = 0$. As in the case of Eq. (22), it is straightforward to show that the iterative procedure converges monotonically to the correct value.

## 7 An example

The following probabilistic context-free grammar generates conditional statements:

$$
\begin{array}{ll}
statement \rightarrow \textbf{if } expression \textbf{ then } statement \textbf{ else } statement \textbf{ endif} & (0.2) \\
statement \rightarrow \textbf{if } expression \textbf{ then } statement \textbf{ endif} & (0.4) \\
statement \rightarrow \textbf{print } expression & (0.4) \\
expression \rightarrow expression \textbf{ operator } term & (0.5) \\
expression \rightarrow term & (0.5) \\
term \rightarrow \textbf{number} & (1.0)
\end{array}
$$

where variables appear in italics, terminals in bold and the number in parenthesis represents the probability of the rule. The average number of rules in the hypothesis as a function of the number of examples is plotted in Fig. 5. When the sample is small, rather small grammars are found and overgeneralization occurs. As the number of examples grows, the algorithm tends to output a grammar with the correct size, and for larger samples (above 150 examples) the correct grammar is always found. Similar behavior was observed for other grammars and experiments. On the other hand, our implementation needed very few seconds to process the sample, even when it contained thousands of examples. In Fig. 6, the relative entropy between the target grammar and the hypothesis is computed following the method described in section 6. The results are shown in the region where identification takes place and the relative entropy becomes always finite. For comparison purposes, the relative entropy between the target grammar and the sample is also plotted. It is clear from the figure that identifying the structure of the DTA makes the distance converge at a much higher rate than a mere estimation of the probabilities from the sample.

## 8 Conclusions

The algorithm `tlips` learns context-free grammars from stochastic examples of parse tree skeletons. The result is, in the limit, structurally identical to the target grammar (i.e., they generate the same stochastic set of skeletons) and is

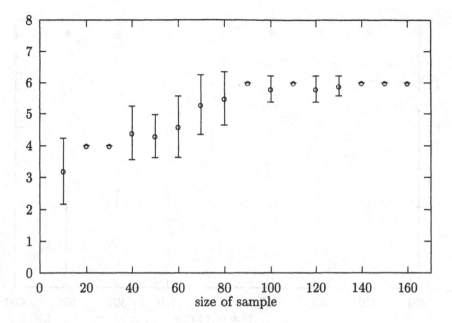

**Fig. 5.** Average number of rules in the hypothesis as a function of the number of examples. The target grammar has 6 rules.

found in linear time with the size of the sample. Experimentally, identification is reached with relatively small samples, the relative entropy between the model and the target grammar decreases very fast with the size of the sample, and the algorithm proves fast enough for application purposes.

# A    Proof of theorems.

**Theorem 1:** Let $\Phi$ be a mapping that for every language $t^{-1}T$ gives the only tree $s = \Phi(t^{-1}T)$ in SSub$(T)$ such that $s^{-1}T = t^{-1}T$. Clearly, if $t \in$ SSub$(T)$ then $\Phi(t^{-1}T) = t$. The mapping $\Phi$ is an isomorphism if

$$\delta(f, \Phi(t_1^{-1}T), ..., \Phi(t_k^{-1}T)) = \Phi\delta^M(f, t_1^{-1}T, ..., t_k^{-1}T).$$

As $t_1, ..., t_k$ are in SSub$(T)$, and $\delta^M(f, t_1^{-1}T, ..., t_k^{-1}T) = f(t_1, ..., t_k)^{-1}T$, then one can rewrite the above condition as

$$\delta(f, t_1, ..., t_k) = \Phi(f(t_1, ..., t_k)^{-1}T)$$

which holds if $\delta(f, t_1, ..., t_k)$ is the only tree $t \in$ SSub$(T)$ satisfying $t^{-1}T = f(t_1, ..., t_k)^{-1}T$. Note that $t_1, ..., t_k \in$ SSub$(T)$ implies $f(t_1, ..., t_k) \in K(T)$, and therefore, the condition can be written as equiv$_T(t, f(t_1, ..., t_k))$.

**Theorem 2 (sketch):** Simple induction shows that after $i$ iterations SSub$^{[i]} \subset$ SSub$(T)$, $F^{[i]} \subset F(T)$ and $W^{[i]} \subset K(T)$. On the other hand, if $t \in K(T)$ then $t \in A$ and induction in the depth of the tree shows that $t$ eventually enters the algorithm.

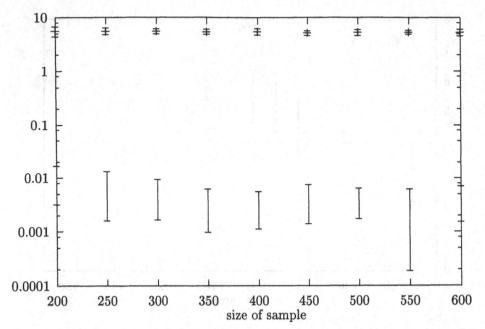

**Fig. 6.** Lower dots: relative entropy between the target grammar and the output of algorithm `tlips` as a function of the number of examples in the sample. Upper dots: relative entropy between the target grammar and the sample.

# References

- Aho, A.V. & Ullman, J.D. (1972): "The theory of parsing, translation and compiling. Volume I: Parsing". Prentice-Hall, Englewood Cliffs, NJ.
- Angluin, D. (1982): Inference of reversible languages. *Journal of the Association for Computing Machines* **29**, 741–765.
- Calera, J. & Carrasco, R.C: (1998): Computing the relative entropy between regular tree languages. Submitted for publication.
- Carrasco, R.C. (1997): "Inferencia de lenguajes racionales estocásticos". Ph.D. dissertation. Universidad de Alicante.
- Carrasco, R.C. (1998): Accurate computation of the relative entropy between stochastic regular grammars. *Theoretical Informatics and Applications*. To appear.
- Carrasco, R.C. & Oncina, J. (1994): Learning stochastic regular grammars by means of a state merging method in "Grammatical Inference and Applications" (R.C. Carrasco and J. Oncina, Eds.). Lecture Notes in Artificial Intelligence **862**, Springer-Verlag, Berlin.
- Cover, T.M & Thomas, J.A. (1991): *Elements of Information Theory*. John Wiley and Sons, New York.
- Hoeffding, W. (1963): Probability inequalities for sums of bounded random variables. *American Statistical Association Journal* **58**, 13–30.
- Hopcroft, J.E. & Ullman, J.D. (1979): "Introduction to automata theory, languages and computation". Addison Wesley, Reading, Massachusetts.

- Oncina, J. & García, P. (1994): Inference of rational tree sets. Universidad Politécnica de Valencia, Internal Report DSIC-ii-1994-23.
- Sakakibara, Y. (1992): Efficient learning of context-free grammars from positive structural examples. *Information and Computation* **97**, 23–60.
- Stolcke, A. & Omohundro, S. (1993): Hidden Markov model induction by Bayesian model merging in "Advances in Neural Information Processing Systems 5" (C.L. Giles, S.J. Hanson and J.D. Cowan, Eds.). Morgan-Kaufman, Menlo Park, California.
- Wetherell, C.S. (1980): Probabilistic Languages: A Review and Some Open Questions *ACM Computing Survey* 12 361–379

# How Considering Incompatible State Mergings May Reduce the DFA Induction Search Tree

François Coste and Jacques Nicolas

IRISA- INRIA
Campus de Beaulieu, F-35042 Cedex, France

**Abstract.** A simple and effective method for DFA induction from positive and negative samples is the state merging method. The corresponding search space may be tree-structured, considering two subspaces for a given pair of states: the subspace where states are merged and the subspace where states remain different. Choosing different pairs leads to different sizes of space, due to state mergings dependencies. Thus, ordering the successive choices of these pairs is an important issue. Starting from a constraint characterization of incompatible state mergings, we show that this characterization allows to achieve better choices, i.e. to reduce the size of the search tree. Within this framework, we address the issue of learning the set of all minimal compatible DFA's. We propose a pruning criterion and experiment with several ordering criteria. The prefix order and a new entropy based criterion have exhibit the best results in our test sets.

**keywords** Grammatical inference, DFA, constraint system, search tree.

Grammatical Inference is an important machine learning problem with applications in language processing, pattern recognition and genetics. It is defined as the process of learning a grammatical representation of a language from examples of words of this language and words that do not belong to the language. In this paper, we address the issue of learning canonical automata of regular languages. More precisely, we are concerned with the following DFA induction problem. Given a set of positive strings $I_+$ and a set of negative strings $I_-$, find the DFA's $A$ satisfying:

1. $I_+$ is *structurally complete* wrt $A$ (i. e. there exists an acceptance of $I_+$ such that every transition of $A$ is exercised and every final state of $A$ is used as an accepting state);
2. $A$ is *compatible* with $I_+$ and $I_-$ (i. e. $L(A)$, the language accepted by $A$, contains all the strings of $I_+$ and does not contain any string of $I_-$);
3. $L(A)$ is a most general language
   (i.e. no other solution $A'$ is such that $L(A) \subseteq L(A')$).

Most of the proposed algorithms focus on the production of a single solution. They proceed either with a depth first strategy (Oncina & Garcia 1992, Lang 1992), an evidence driven state merging strategy (Lang 1997, Lang & al 1998,

Juillé & Pollack 1998), a beam search strategy (Miclet & de Gentille 1994), or with an optimization method (Dupont 1994).

But these algorithms do not ensure the minimal solution. Indeed, the problem of finding the minimal compatible DFA has been proven NP-complete in the worst case (Angluin 1978,Kearns & Valiant 1989). Using an interactive or incremental process, it seems interesting to continue the search if the proposed DFA is not satisfactory. Algorithms seeking more than one solution are then needed. Furthermore, from a scientific point of view, complete algorithms producing all the solutions are also useful to better understand and characterize the search space and the solution set, before deriving more specialized algorithms.

Few algorithms seeking a set of solutions have been proposed. Miclet has proposed in Miclet & de Gentille 1994 a heuristic algorithm. An algorithm using graph coloring methods can be found in Coste & Nicolas 1997. Preliminary studies have also been attempted in the context free case (Giordano 1993, Vanlehn & Ball 1987).

Looking for all solutions is a difficult problem due to the size of the search space and, in some case, due to the solution set size itself. We present in section 2 a constraint system allowing to manage the set of all compatible DFA's in a compact and implicit representation.

Using a state merging algorithm, we show in section 3 how the knowledge of constraints reflecting incompatible mergings may help to reduce the size of the search space. It allows to define two criteria: a pruning criterion detecting dead ends in the search space and an entropy based ordering criterion.

To begin with, the next section is devoted to basic definitions, notations and theorems on regular grammatical inference.

# 1 Search space in regular grammatical inference

## 1.1 Definitions and notations

We first recall basic definitions of the field of grammatical inference.

**Definition 1.** (DFA) A finite state automaton is a quintuplet $(Q, \Sigma, \delta, q_0, F)$ where $Q$ is a finite set of states, $\Sigma$ an alphabet, $\delta$ a transition function from $Q \times \Sigma$ to $2^Q$ (extended to $Q \times \Sigma^* \to 2^Q$), $q_0$ is the initial state and $F \subseteq Q$ is the set of accepting or final states.
If $\forall q \in Q, \forall a \in \Sigma, \delta(q, a)$ has at most one element, the automaton is said deterministic and we denote DFA such an automaton.
A DFA $A$ accepts a regular language $L(A)$.

**Definition 2.** $(A(L), MCA, PTA)$ The canonical automaton of a language $L$, $A(L)$ is the DFA accepting $L$ which has the minimal number of states.
The maximal canonical automaton with respect to a set of words $I$, $MCA(I)$, is the automaton $A$ with the largest number of states such that $L(A) = I$ and $I$ is structurally complete with respect to $A$.
The prefix tree acceptor of $I$, $PTA(I)$, is obtained from $MCA(I)$ by merging states sharing the same prefixes.

The natural generality relation between languages is inclusion, corresponding to inclusion between sets of accepted words. While working on representations of languages, one has to find a compatible relation with this inclusion relation. Such a relation is known for automata (Miclet 1990,Pao & Carr 1978) : the set of finite automata may be partially ordered with a derivation relation, corresponding to the merging of states in the automata.

**Definition 3.** (Derived automaton $A/\pi$) Given an automaton $A = (Q, \Sigma, \delta, q_0, F)$ and a partition $\pi = (B_0, B_1, \ldots, B_r)$ of $Q$, the derived or quotient automaton $A/\pi = (\pi, \Sigma, \Delta, B_0, R)$ is defined as follows:

- $q_0 \in B_0$ ;
- $R = \{B_i \in \pi, \exists q \in B_i \text{ st } q \in F\}$ ;
- $B_j \in \Delta(B_i, a)$ iff $\exists q \in B_i, \exists q' \in B_j$ such that $q' \in \delta(q, a)$.

The set of all automata derived from $A$ is a lattice $Lat(A)$.

## 1.2   Search Space : a lattice of automata

We can now characterize more precisely the search space of DFA's for an inference problem (Dupont& al. 1994).

**Theorem 4.** *Let $I_+$ be a positive sample. Let $L$ be the target language. If $I_+$ is structurally complete with respect to $A(L)$, then $A(L)$ is an element of $Lat(PTA(I_+))$.*

Another way to look at this theorem is to state that every language, such that $I_+$ is structurally complete with respect to its canonical automaton, is learn-able in the lattice, and as a consequence, our search space will be this lattice in the rest of this paper:

**Corollary 5.** *Let $I_+$ be a positive sample.*
*A regular language $L$ is said to be admissible if $I_+$ is structurally complete with respect to $A(L)$, the canonical automaton of $L$. The set of canonical automata of all admissible languages is included in $Lat(PTA(I_+))$.*

As the search space of automata is finite and may be partially ordered, we can use a version space approach (Mitchell 1982) where all solutions of a learning problem are characterized using two sets: the set $S$ of maximally specific solutions and the set $G$ of maximally general solutions. An incremental approach using membership queries has been proposed within this framework (Parekh & Honavar 1993). In our case, $S$ may be built straightforwardly, using $PTA(I_+)$. $G$ is the set of all the solutions to the automata induction problem as stated in the introduction. Building $G$ (also called *Border Set*, Dupont& al. 1994) is much more difficult, due to the size of the search space and, in some case, to the size of $G$ itself. When the language of generalization consists of vectors of attribute-value pairs, several authors have proposed to manage an implicit representation of the version space (Hirsh 1992,Nicolas 1993,Sebag 1994).

We propose in the next section a compact representation of compatible DFA's set, based on the set of incompatible state mergings.

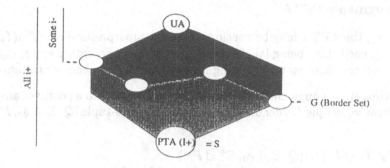

**Fig. 1.** Search Space: the set of compatible DFA's lies between $PTA(I_+)$ and $G$

# 2 Constraint characterization

In this section we propose to characterize the set of compatible DFA's, such that the positive sample is structurally complete wrt the DFA. The structural completeness condition ensures that solutions are in $Lat(PTA(I_+))$. The solutions are then the deterministic automata in the lattice accepting no string of the negative sample.

In order to further explain our approach, we need to introduce two auxiliary concepts, closely related to the search space to be explored. In section 2.1 we introduce the merging procedure for determinization allowing to stay in the space of deterministic automata. In section 2.2, we introduce the *augmented PTA* (APTA) following in this the data structure proposed in Higuera & al. 1996 and Alquézar & Sanfeliu 1995, in order to handle simultaneously the positive sample $I_+$ and the negative sample $I_-$. The set of compatible DFA's can then be characterized by a system of constraints presented in section 2.3.

## 2.1 Merging for determinization

Since the merging procedure may produce a non deterministic automaton, an extended version of the merging procedure (the merging procedure for determinization) is used by algorithms such that RPNI to consider only deterministic automata.

Such a procedure corresponds to the existence of a binary relation between pairs of states. Formally, if we denote $\rightarrow$ such a relation, we have

$$(q_1, q_2) \rightarrow (q'_1, q'_2) \; iff \; \exists a \in \Sigma \; \delta(q_1, a) = q'_1 \wedge \delta(q_2, a) = q'_2 \tag{1}$$

The merging procedure for determinization can be stated as follow: *each time $q_1$ and $q_2$ such that $(q_1, q_2) \rightarrow (q'_1, q'_2)$ are merged, merge also $q'_1$ and $q'_2$.*

The result of this procedure is a (eventually smaller) DFA in the lattice.

The transitive closure of $\rightarrow$ is denoted $\rightarrow^*$.

## 2.2 Augmented PTA

Intuitively, the APTA may be considered as the superposition of $PTA(I_+)$ and $PTA(I_-)$, each state being labeled into three classes : accepting state, rejecting state or intermediate state, accepting no positive and no negative instance.

**Definition 6.** An augmented PTA (APTA) with respect to a positive sample $I_+$ and a negative sample $I_-$, denoted $APTA(I_+, I_-)$, is a 6-tuple $(Q, \Sigma, \delta, q_0, F^+, F^-)$ where

- $PTA(I_+ \cup I_-) = (Q, \Sigma, \delta, q_0, F^+ \cup F^-)$
- $F^+$ and $F^-$ are subsets of $Q$ respectively identifying accepting states of $I_+$ and $I_-$
- $F^+$ is the set of final states of $APTA(I_+, I_-)$

We give as an illustration, the APTA of sample 1 of language 2 in our benchmark (cf section 4). In this sample, $I_+ = \{ababab\}$, $I_- = \{a, b, abaa, abbbb, ababbbba\}$.

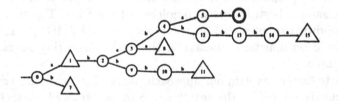

**Fig. 2.** APTA of sample 1 of language 2

States of $F^+$ are double circles and states of $F^-$ are triangles.

By construction, for a partition $\pi$ of states of the $PTA(I_+)$, we get the following property :

$$L(APTA(I_+, I_-)/\pi) = L(PTA(I_+)/\pi) \qquad (2)$$

Considering the APTA, instead of the PTA, has the advantage of explicitly propagating the consequences of merging some states in the PTA on the acceptance of negative instances.

## 2.3 Constraint system

To ensure determinism, the merging procedure will use the merging procedure for determinization presented in section 2.1.

The set of compatible DFA's can then be characterized by a constraint system on incompatible state mergings in the APTA. Intuitively, an incompatible state merging involves after a chain reaction the merging of a state accepting a positive string and a state accepting a negative string.

Such considerations can be formalized in the following constraint system:

If we denote $q_\pi$ the block in the partition of the state $q$ for a partition $\pi$, the set of compatible DFA's will be the set of automata derived from $PTA(I_+)$ such that:

$$q_\pi^+ \neq q_\pi^- \quad \forall q^+ \in F^+, \forall q^- \in F^- \tag{3}$$
$$q_{1\pi}' \neq q_{2\pi}' \Rightarrow q_{1\pi} \neq q_{2\pi} \quad \forall q_1', q_2' \in APTA(I_+, I_-)/ (q_1, q_2) \rightarrow (q_1', q_2') \tag{4}$$

Note that constraints of type 4 may be reversed in form of equality constraints $q_{1\pi} = q_{2\pi} \Rightarrow q_{1\pi}' = q_{2\pi}'$.

Moreover, the system of constraints may be simplified, applying modus ponens and discarding redundancy. The subset of constraints of type 3 (after simplifications) is called $F_{Nok}$. It represents incompatible pairs of states mergings. It may be represented as a graph on the set of states. In the next section, we propose to maintain the validity of this subset and to use it to reduce the search tree in state merging algorithms.

# 3 Reducing the search tree in state merging algorithms

## 3.1 A generalized state merging algorithm

State merging algorithm explores the PTA lattice by merging states of the PTA until the border set $G$ is reached. The search space is then a set of partitions and there is one operation, namely merging two blocks in a partition, to move from one node to another one, more general in the search space.

---

**Algorithm 1 Generalized State Merging Algorithm with incompatibilities**

GSMA($A$)
  if ($s1$, $s2$) ← ChooseStatesToMerge($A$) then
    if ($A' \leftarrow A[s1 = s2]$) /* merge states and propagates consequences */ then
      GSMA($A'$)
    end if
    /* Extension allowed by $F_{Nok}$ management */
    if ($A' \leftarrow A[s1 \neq s2]$) /* add constraint in $F_{Nok}$ and propagates consequences */
    then
      GSMA($A'$)
    end if
  else if $A$ is solution then
    Output $A$
  end if
end

main()
init_constraint_system()
GSMA($PTA(I_+)$)
end

---

As we explicitly and dynamically manage the set of incompatible mergings $F_{Nok}$, we can consider an alternative representation of this search space such that each pair of states in PTA is an attribute with two possible values : = if states are merged in the derived automaton, $\neq$ if we decide not to merge states in the derived automaton. We give the sketch of the corresponding algorithm (Algorithm 1). At each step, a pair of states is chosen and assigned successively the two possible values (= and $\neq$), the constraint system being updated accordingly. An example of search tree for this algorithm is given (figure 3.2).

Adressing now the issue of producing all minimal (in the sense of the number of states) solution DFA's, we propose two ways of reducing the search tree: a new heuristic ordering of pairs of states, based on entropy measure(section 3.2) and pruning with an incompatibility clique (section 3.3).

## 3.2 Ordering pairs of states, entropy based selection

Heuristics of every known algorithm working on the search of a single solution may be used for the selection of attributes in this tree and thus these algorithms may be naturally extended to the search of all solutions.

In Trakhenbrot & Barzdin 1973, the order in which the states are merged is not important since the presentation is complete. In algorithms such as RPNI (Oncina & Garcia 1992) or the algorithm of K. Lang (Lang 1992), the states to be merged are chosen in a breadth-first predetermined order. Recent results in the Abbadingo One competition show that better results can be obtained by considering candidate mergings in order of the amount of evidence supporting them, as claimed in Higuera & al. 1996. The most interesting order seems to be merging states according to the implied number of states merged together with the same label (Lang & al 1998).

The question is then to find the most efficient heuristic with respect to this new "all solutions" goal, and this is not a trivial task since a given algorithm may well find very quickly a first solution, taking advantage of a property of this solution, and then be laborious in finding the other ones, that do not respect this property.

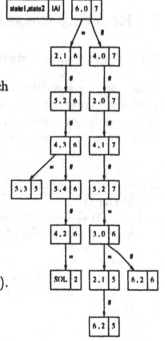

**Fig. 3.** Search tree of sample 1 of language 2, with a random order selection

We have developed an entropy based criterion (section 3.2), using the same idea of dynamically computing the evidence of a merging. However, it is no longer based on labels counts but uses instead a more abstract view of merging constraints (positive *and* negative) existing between states.

**The search tree as a decision tree** Another way of looking at the search space is to consider the search tree as a kind of decision tree, its leaves being labeled either success or failure, according as the corresponding automaton is or not an acceptable solution. Given this framework, reducing the amount of search to be done is equivalent to finding the smallest tree where all leaves contain either a single solution automaton or lead to a failure. Following the methodology TDIDT (Quinlan 1986), we have tried various criteria in order to select the best attribute at each node. However, one has to keep in mind that this is an analogy and not the usual framework, since we do not know how many solutions or failures are below a given node. All we can do is to estimate this number. Defining this estimate is the purpose of the next part of this section.

**Estimating the number of solutions** In order to estimate the number of solutions, we split the set of states into two parts. The first part, *the pseudo-clique* $(PC)$, corresponds to a set of candidates such that every other state (in the second part denoted $\overline{PC}$) is supposed to be merged with to obtain the target automaton. The name pseudo-clique refers to graph $F_{Nok}$, where states $PC$ are likely to be in relation and to form a clique (or a densest 'almost' clique).

Once a pseudo-clique is chosen, we estimate the number of solutions by considering possible relations between states in $PC$ and states in $\overline{PC}$.

Let $m$ be the size of $PC$ (i. e. the size of the target automaton), $l$ be the size of $\overline{PC}$ and $|A|$ be the number of states of the current automaton. States of the pseudo-clique $PC$ are denoted $p_i$ and states of the $\overline{PC}$ set are denoted $q_i$. Let $d_i$ be the number of states of $PC$ not related to state $q_i$ in $\overline{PC}$.

The total number of configurations (possible completions of graph $F_{Nok}$ by adding new edges) $tot$ is: $tot = \prod_{1 \leq i \leq l} 2^{d_i}$

**Fig. 4.** If the pseudo-clique found for this graph is the set of states in the grey box, then $tot = 32$, $p = 6$, $n = 11$, $u = 15$

Then, we can roughly estimate the number of solutions $p$ as the number of possible mappings of states from $\overline{PC}$ to $PC$. The number of failure configurations $n$ is the number of configurations where a state of $\overline{PC}$ can not be merged with any state of $PC$.

$$p = \prod_{1 \leq i \leq l} d_i \; ; \qquad n = tot - \prod_{1 \leq i \leq l} (2^{d_i} - 1)$$

Therefore, in this node, the number of undefined configurations is $u$:

$$u = tot - (p + n) = \prod_{1 \leq i \leq l} (2^{d_i} - 1) - p$$

Since the value of $p$ may be neglected compared to $u$ and $n$, the estimated entropy of a given node finally writes:

$$I = -(1 - r)log_2(1 - r) - rLog_2(r) \quad where \quad r = \prod_{1 \leq i \leq l} \frac{(2^{d_i} - 1)}{2^{d_i}}$$

Finally, by averaging entropies of the *left* and *right* edges of a given node in the search tree, we propose to select the attribute corresponding to the pair of states minimizing $E$:

$$E = tot_{left}I_{left} + tot_{right}I_{right}$$

### 3.3 Clique in the graph of incompatible mergings

When an upper bound of the number of states of the DFA is available (either user provided or estimated and refined or by a solution found before), the search may be pruned if there exists a clique of states in the graph of $F_{Nok}$ whose size is greater than the maximal expected size of the DFA. In this case the states of the clique cannot be merged together and the size of the resulting DFA is bigger or equal to the size of the clique.

The search of the largest clique is NP-complete. However, if the size of the clique is not too large and an approximation is sufficient, efficient algorithm are known. Our experimentation (section 4) shows good results with a greedy search. Moreover, we have observed that starting from the root of the $PTA(I_+)$ provides a good approximation of the size of the best clique.

## 4 Experimentation

### 4.1 Settings

We have used a benchmark described in Dupont 1996 for a first validation of ideas developed in this paper. Target automata are small ($< 6$ states) but structurally complex. For instance, $L_{11}$ is the language accepting an even number of $a$ and an odd number of $b$. For each language, 20 training samples have been drawn. The size of these sets of words is less than or equal to 50. The size of the words themselves varies from 1 to 40.

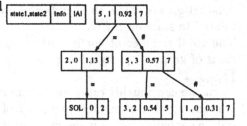

**Fig. 5.** Search tree of the entropy criterion on sample 1 of language 2.

We have used five orders to build a complete search tree of the solutions: Random order (20 trials have been made for each training set); Prefix order; RPNI order (same as Prefix order except that only pairs of states that can be merged are considered); Entropy-based order and Rlb order (Lang 1997). In each case, pseudo-cliques have been computed and used to detect failure nodes. Indeed, if a clique of size greater than $m$ is detected in $F_{Nok}$, it means that the corresponding automaton has more than $m$ states, and the search may be pruned. Using RPNI order, we have also tried experiments without clique pruning to show the influence of it. In this case, the maximal number of nodes, fixed to 150000, has often been reached. The average number of nodes have been calculated using this maximal value when the number of nodes was greater.

## 4.2 Results

| Lang. | #s/#t | #sol | APTA | #FN | #n !p | #n rpni | #n rand | #n pref | #n I | #n Rlb |
|-------|-------|------|------|-----|-------|---------|---------|---------|------|--------|
| L1 | 1/1 | 1 | 3 | 0 | 9 | 2 | 3 | 2 | 2 | 2 |
| L2 | 2/2 | 1 | 25 | 43 | >15760 | 5 | 10 | 3 | 3 | 3 |
| L3 | 4/7 | 1.75 | 180 | 998 | >133500 | 17 | 4326 | 14 | 15 | 53 |
| L4 | 3/5 | 8.5 | 102 | 192 | >115900 | 84 | 3298 | 59 | 71 | 269 |
| L5 | 4/8 | 2.1 | 65 | 218 | >150000 | 51 | 30837 | 32 | 38 | 73 |
| L6 | 3/6 | 2.45 | 40 | 108 | >106300 | 28 | 9843 | 19 | 19 | 73 |
| L7 | 4/7 | 4.75 | 85 | 545 | >150000 | 217 | 27291 | 93 | 134 | 406 |
| L8 | 2/2 | 1.25 | 19 | 43 | 393 | 3 | 4 | 3 | 3 | 3 |
| L9 | 4/7 | 1.65 | 61 | 358 | >150000 | 18 | 115 | 6 | 7 | 7 |
| L10 | 5/6 | 2.4 | 81 | 432 | >68200 | 22 | 98 | 16 | 10 | 17 |
| L11 | 4/8 | 2.85 | 65 | 215 | >150000 | 36 | 37035 | 27 | 34 | 74 |
| L12 | 3/3 | 1.5 | 38 | 120 | >23100 | 5 | 9 | 4 | 4 | 4 |
| L13 | 2/4 | 1.25 | 32 | 71 | >90521 | 6 | 476 | 6 | 6 | 6 |
| L14 | 3/4 | 1.4 | 38 | 101 | >41200 | 5 | 30 | 6 | 6 | 6 |
| L15 | 4/6 | 2.1 | 71 | 353 | >60900 | 9 | 36 | 9 | 9 | 9 |

#s/#t characterizes the size of target automata in terms of number of states and transitions, #sol is the mean number of minimal automata found in $BS$. #FN is the mean size of $F_{Nok}$ at the root node. #n !p #n rpni, #n rand, #n pref, #n Rlb, #n I are the mean number of nodes of the tree for respectively a rpni without pruning, a rpni, a random, a prefix, a Rlb, and an entropy selection of pairs of states.

First, the influence of pruning is so important that it would have been much more difficult to compare the orders without it. Results show also how important is the choice of a selection criterion for the reduction of the search space. A random selection of nodes may increase the size of the tree by several orders of magnitude, with respect to best criteria. Results are in favor of the prefix order. The refined Rlb order is not only not necessary but gives worse results in almost every case. The more expensive criterion, entropy, seems comparable or slightly worse than the prefix order.

In order to better differentiate the behavior of the best criteria, we ran a second series of experiments comparing prefix order and entropy order as the amount of samples was increasing. Ten DFA's of size 5 have been drawn from a uniform distribution (Same generation of DFA's and sample strings than for Abbadingo One Competition (Lang & al 1998)). Figure 6 shows the average number of nodes in the search tree for the ten DFA's for sample files ranging from 10 strings to 390 strings. Results are clearly in favor of the entropy order : the number of nodes is an order of magnitude smaller and less data are needed to converge towards the best ordering of mergings.

We have to temperate these observations with an important remarks : our benchmarks contain target automata of small size. Scaling effects may appear with larger DFA.

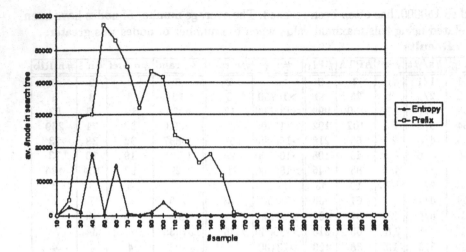

**Fig. 6.** Average number of nodes in search tree

## 5 Conclusion

We have presented a system of constraints characterizing the set of compatible DFA's. Using the corresponding knowledge on incompatible state mergings ($F_{Nok}$) allows to reduce the search tree in state merging algorithms. It is a key point since usually, automata inferring algorithms do consider possible mergings but not impossible ones.

The benchmark needs of course to be completed with more difficult problems, increasing the size of the vocabulary and the size of the target automaton. The first important result of this study is that a greedy search of clique in $F_{Nok}$ allows to prune efficiently the search tree and leads to very small search trees in our experiment. Ordering the choice of the pairs of states to be merged is also an important point when considering the "all solutions" search problem. The simple prefix order seems to be a good candidate for this search. We have studied a new entropy based criterion that behaves well, especially in our second experiment, but is expensive to compute. We expect it to be interesting in large search spaces.

## References

R. Alquézar and A. Sanfeliu, "Incremental grammatical inference from positive and negative data using unbiased finite state automata," In *Shape, Structure and Pattern Recognition*, Proc. Int. Workshop on Structural and Syntactic Pattern Recognition, SSPR'94, Nahariya (Israel), World Scientific Pub., Singapore, 291–300, 1995.

Angluin, D. On the complexity of minimum inference of regular sets. *Information and Control* 29(3):741 – 765, 1978.

Coste, F. and Nicolas, J. : Regular Inference as a Graph Coloring Problem. Workshop on Grammar Inference, Automata Induction, and Language Acquisition (ICML' 97), Nashville, TN, 1997.

Dupont, P. Regular Grammatical Inference from Positive and Negative Samples by Genetic Search : the GIG method. *ICGI'94, Grammatical inference and Applications* 236–245. Springer Verlag, 1994.

Dupont, P.; Miclet, L.; and E.Vidal. What is the search space of the regular inference ? *ICGI'94, Grammatical inference and Applications* 25–37. Springer Verlag, 1994.

Dupont, P. *Utilisation et apprentissage de modèles de langages pour la reconnaissance de la parole continue*. Ph.D. Dissertation, Ecole Nationale Supérieure des Télécommunications, 1996.

Giordano, J. Espace des versions et inférence de grammaires algébriques. In *Journées Francophones d'Apprentissage*, 1993.

Higuera (de la), C.; Oncina, J.; and Vidal, E. : Identification of DFA : data-dependent versus data-independent algorithms. Grammatical inference Learning Syntax from Sentences, ICGI'96 311–325. Springer Verlag, 1996.

Hirsh, H. Polynomial-time Learning with Version Spaces *National Conference on Artificial Intelligence*, San Jose, CA, 117–122 july 1992.

Juillé, H., and Pollack, J.B. SAGE: a Sampling-based Heuristic for Tree Search. Submitted paper.

Kearns, M., and Valiant, L. Cryptographic limitation on learning boolean formulae and finite automata. In *Proceedings of the Twenty First Annual Symposium on Theory of Computing*, 433 – 444, 1989.

Lang, K. Random DFA's can be Approximately Learned from Sparse Uniform Examples. In *proceedings of the fifth annual ACM Workshop on Computational Learning Theory* 45–52, July 1992.

Lang, K. Merge Order count NECI Tech Report, Sept26, 1997

Lang, K., and Pearlmutter, B., and Price, R. Results of the Abbadingo One DFA Learning Competition and a New Evidence Driven State Merging Algorithm. Submitted paper.

Miclet, L. Grammatical Inference. *Syntactic and Structural Pattern Recognition : Theory and Applications*, Bunke, H. and Sanfeliu, A. Eds, Singapore, World Scientific, 237–290, 1990.

Miclet, L., and de Gentille, C. Inférence grammaticale à partir d'exemples et de contre-exemples : deux algorithmes optimaux : (big et rig) et une version heuristique (brig). *JAVA94, Journées Acquisition, Validation, Apprentissage* F1–F13, Strasbourg France, 1994.

Mitchell, T. Generalization as search. *Artificial Intelligence* (18):203–226, 1982.

Nicolas, J. Une représentation efficace pour les espaces de versions. *8ièmes JFA*, Saint-Raphael, 1993.

Oncina, J., and Garcia, P. Inferring regular languages in polynomial update time. *Pattern Recognition and Image Analysis* 49 – 61, 1993.

Pao, T., and Carr, J. A solution for the syntactic induction inference problem for regular languages in *Computer Language vol3* 53 – 64, 1978.

Parekh, R., and Honavar, V. Efficient Learning of Regular Languages using Teacher Supplied Positive Examples and Learner Generated Queries. In Proceedings of the Fifth UNB Conference on AI , Fredrickton, Canada. 195–203, August 1993.

Quinlan, J.R. Induction of decision trees. *Machine Learning* (1):81–106, 1986.

Sebag, M. Une approche par contraintes de l'espace des versions. *RFIA'94* 17–25,1994.

Trakhenbrot, B. and Barzdin, Y., Finite Automata : Behavior and Synthesis *Amsterdam, North Holland Pub. Comp*, 1973.

Vanlehn, K., and Ball, W. A version space approach to learning context-free grammars. *Machine Learning* (2):39–74, 1987.

# Learning Regular Grammars to Model Musical Style: Comparing Different Coding Schemes [*]

Pedro P. Cruz-Alcázar[1], Enrique Vidal-Ruiz[2]

[1] EPSA, Universidad Politécnica de Valencia, DISCA-Alcoy, Alicante, Spain
pcruz@iti.upv.es
[2] Universidad Politécnica de Valencia, DSIC, Valencia, Spain
evidal@iti.upv.es

**Abstract.** An application of Grammatical Inference (GI) in the field of Music Processing is presented, were Regular Grammars are used for modeling musical style. The interest in modeling musical style resides in the use of these models in applications, such as Automatic Composition and Automatic Musical Style Recognition. We have studied three GI Algorithms, which have been previously applied successfully in other fields. In this work, these algorithms have been used to learn a stochastic grammar for each of three different musical styles from examples of melodies. Then, each of the learned grammars was used to stochastically synthesize new melodies (Composition) or to classify test melodies (Style Recognition). Our previous studies in this field showed the need of a proper music coding scheme. Different coding schemes are presented and compared according to results in Composition and Style Recognition. Results from previous studies have been improved.

## 1 Introduction

*Grammatical Inference* (GI) aims at learning models of languages from examples of sentences of these languages. *Sentences* can be any structured composition of primitive elements or symbols, though the most common type of composition is the *concatenation*. From this point of view, GI find applications in all those many areas in which the objets or processes of interest can be adequately represented as strings of symbols. Perhaps the most conventional application areas are Syntactic Pattern Recognition [9] and Language Modeling [18]. But there are many other areas in which GI can lead to interesting applications. One of these areas is *Music Processing*. Here, the very notion of language explicitly holds, where primitive symbols or *"notes"* are adequate descriptions of the acoustic space, and the concatenation of these symbols leads to strings that represent musical sentences.

Classical discretization/idealization of the acoustic space in music, entails

---

[*] This work has been partially supported by European Union ESPRIT LTR Project 30268 "EUTRANS".

appropriate descriptions of fundamental frequency or *pitch* of sounds and their temporal span or *duration*. These descriptions are called *"scores"*. Other features of sound, such as *timbre* and *tempo* are generally considered less essential for describing music and are often specified just as "side annotations" to the main score. The choice of a discretized, symbolic representation of pitch and duration constitutes the very essence of a musical system. Many different settings have been employed in different cultures, but modern occidental music has adopted the so-called *tempered scale*, which contains 12 symbols to represent different pitches within one *"octave"* (the range of pitch from a frequency $f$ to $2f$). The "minimal distance" between pitches is called *"halftone"*. On the other hand, the choice of a symbolic scheme to represent duration may also depend of each musical system and, in modern occidental music this leads to symbols such as *whole note, half note, quarter note*, etc. where each element describes an event whose duration is half that of the previous symbol in the scale. In order to use Grammatical Inference in Music Processing (MP), a proper method to convert scores into symbol strings must be found. In this paper different coding schemes for music are proposed and compared.

By adequately concatenating symbols of a given musical system, a musical event emerges. However, not any possible concatenation can be considered a "proper" event. Certain rules dictate what can or can not be considered an appropriate concatenation, leading to the concept of *musical style*. Main features of a musical style are *rhythm* and *melody*, which are directly related with the rules used to concatenate duration and pitch of sounds, respectively. For the sake of conciseness, in what follows, we will use just the term *"melody"* for the combination of these two features. Our aim is to find these rules for modeling a musical style by means of GI. The interest in modeling musical style resides in the use of these models in MP applications, such as *Automatic Composition* and *Automatic Musical Style Recognition*, which are the areas of our interest. Since the creation of the first computers, many experiments have been carried out on how to use them advantageously in music composition [12], obtaining results that go from anecdotic to true masterpieces. Many Artificial Intelligence techniques have been used in MP [15], being Expert Systems very popular over the past years. Very interesting results have been obtained, but these methods have a strong limitation: it is very difficult to code musical knowledge as a set of rules. This limitation restrains the action field to simple and well known musical styles, such as Bach's chorales and standard Jazz. The use of an inductive method such as GI avoids this restrictions, because musical style is learned without human participation. We have focused our work in music composition in generating pieces in a determined musical style, such as Renaissance, Baroque, etc. This leads to the need of a model for musical style. On the other hand, the field of *Automatic Musical Style Recognition* does not seem to have been studied so much. It deals with giving certain skills to a computer so that it will be able to recognize the musical style to which supplied melodies belong. It is still a field to explore and applications can be found in musicology, music teaching, etc. These areas of MP were studied using GI in a previous work [4] [5] [6], that has been extended in the work presented in this paper.

# 2 Grammatical Inference Algorithms

In this section, we concisely explain the three algorithms used in our study to infer the grammars employed for *composing* and *recognizing* musical styles. These algorithms are fairly well known in the GI community and have been proven useful in other fields.

## 2.1 The Error-Correcting Grammatical Inference (ECGI) Algorithm

ECGI is a GI heuristic that was explicitly designed to capture relevant regularities of concatenation and length exhibited by substructures of unidimensional patterns. It was proposed in [13] and relies on error-correcting parsing to build up a stochastic regular grammar through a single incremental pass over a positive training set. Let $R_+$ be this training sequence of strings. Initially, a trivial grammar is built from the first string of $R_+$. Then, for every new string that cannot be parsed with the current grammar, a standard *error-correcting* scheme is adopted to determine a string in the language of the current grammar that is error-correcting closest to the input string. This is achieved through a Viterbi-like, error-correcting parsing procedure [8] which also yields the corresponding optimal sequence of both non-error and error rules used in the parse. From these results, the current grammar is updated by adding a number of rules and (non-terminals) that permit the new string, along with other adequate generalizations, to be accepted. Similarly, the parsing results are also used to update frequency counts from which probabilities of both non-error and error rules are estimated.

## 2.2 The k-TSI Algorithm

This algorithm belongs to a family of techniques which explicitly attempt to learn which symbols or substrings tend to follow others in the target language. It is a "characterizable" method that infers *k-Testable Languages in the Strict Sense* (k-TSSL) in the limit. A k-TSSL is usually defined by means of a four-touple $Z_k = (\Sigma, I, F, T)$ where $\Sigma$ is the *alphabet*, $I$ is a set of *initial substrings* of length smaller than $k$; $F$ is a set of *final substrings* of length smaller than $k$ and $T$ is a set of *forbidden substrings* of length $k$. A language associated with $Z_k$ is defined by the following regular expression: $\mathcal{L}(Z_k) = I\Sigma^* \cap \Sigma^* F - \Sigma^* T\Sigma^*$. In other words, $\mathcal{L}(Z_k)$ consists of strings that begin with substrings in $I$, end with substrings in $F$ and do not contain any substring in $T$. Stochastic k-TSSL are obtained by associating probabilities to the rules of the grammars, and it has been demonstrated that they are equivalent to N-GRAM's with N=k [16]. The inference of k-TSSLs was discussed in [11] where the k-TSI algorithm was proposed. This algorithm consists in building the sets $\Sigma, I, F, T$ by observation of the corresponding events in the training strings. From these sets, a Finite-State automaton that recognizes the associated language is straightforwardly built.

## 2.3 The ALERGIA Algorithm

ALERGIA infers stochastic regular grammars in the limit by means of a State Merging Technique based on probabilistic criteria [3]. It builds the prefix tree acceptor (PTA) from the sample and, at every node, estimates the probabilities of the transitions associated to the node. The PTA is the canonical automaton for the training data (R+) and only recognizes L(R+). Next, ALERGIA tries to merge pairs of nodes, following a well-defined order. Merging is performed, if the tails of the states have the same probabilities within statistical uncertainties. The process ends when further merging is not possible. By merging states in the PTA the size of the recognized language is increased, and so, training samples are generalized. In order to cope with common statistical fluctuations of experimental data, state-equivalence is accepted within a confidence interval calculated from a number between 0 and 1, which is introduced by the user, and which is called accuracy ($a$). This parameter will be the responsible for the higher or lower generalization of the language recognized by the resulting automaton.

## 2.4 The Synthesis Algorithm

In this work, automata will be inferred for different musical styles (languages). "Composing" melodies in specified style amounts to synthesizing strings (melodies) from the automaton that represents the desired style. To achieve this, we use an algorithm that performs random string generation from a stochastic automaton. It randomly follows the transitions of the automaton from the initial state to some final state, according to the probabilities associated to each transition. In order to listen to the synthesized strings, we developed a program to convert them into MIDI files [14], so they can be listened to with any MIDI file player.

## 2.5 The Analysis Algorithm

As each inferred automaton represents a musical style, "recognizing" the style of a test melody consists in finding the automaton which best recognizes this melody. This can be best achieved by using an algorithm that performs stochastic Error-Correcting Syntactic Analysis through an extension of the Viterbi algorithm [8]. The probabilities of error rules (Insertion / Deletion / Substitution) can be estimated from data [1] [2]. The Analysis Algorithm returns the probability that the analyzed string (melody) is (error-correcting) generated by the automaton. By analyzing the same melody with different automata, we classified it as belonging to the musical style (language) represented by the automaton that gave the greatest probability.

# 3  How to Code Music. Different Coding Schemes

As it was mentioned in the introduction, GI algorithms work with symbol strings, so it is necessary to code music in the same way. In this section we present four different coding schemes for music that have been used in our experiments. These coding schemes were developed along with the experiments in order to improve the results. They are conversions from the traditional musical notation into simple codes that preserve the main attributes of music and are formed of symbols.

The first coding scheme we proposed [4] was called *implicit notation* because each note "length", or duration, is implicit in the coding as in a musical score. As every *melody* is characterized by the *pitch* and *length* of the sounds that compose it, we coded only these two attributes. Each note is coded as a symbol or word composed of three "fields", one to code the pitch and two for the length. A space character is used between symbols to separate them. To code the *pitch*, a number was assigned to each note of the adopted scale, beginning with the deepest sound, corresponding to number 1, and ascending progressively halftone by halftone to the highest sound, corresponding to number 43. If the note is a *rest* (a period of time with no sound), the pitch will be coded with number 0. The *note length* was coded using one or two characters after the note number. The second character is optional and we call it "*extra_length*". Thus, a note in implicit notation is coded as follows:

*Note number + length + extra_length.*

The way of coding the field *length* can be seen in Fig. 1 (left side). The field *extra_length* contains a symbol that modifies the length given by the previous field, normally increasing it. We only needed the symbols described in Fig. 1 (right side) to code the training samples, but there are more. *Tied notes* were coded with dots and it was necessary to introduce the *half dot* (which does not exist in music notation) to code notes tied with notes whose length is a quarter of their value, like a *half note* tied to an *eighth note*. An example of implicit notation of a score can be seen in Fig. 2. The idea of employing a discrete representation of the pitches and lengths has been used before by other authors, like Eberhart [7] and Todd [17] in their experiments in music composition with Neural Networks. It is a direct translation from traditional musical notation into symbol strings.

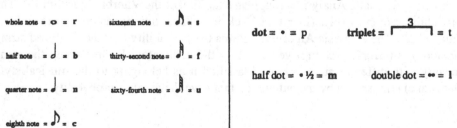

**Fig. 1.** How to code the length of notes in implicit notation (left side). How to code the "extra_length" field (right side)

After performing Automatic Composition experiments with implicit notation many results presented a non-desired effect, which we called the "*tonality problem*". The term *tonality* alludes to the set of relationships established between the sounds of a scale and the first note from this scale, which is called *tonic*. These relationships make us to consider the sounds of the scale organized by reference to a tonic sound or *fundamental note*, having the other notes from the scale a tendency towards it. Therefore, *tonal music* is the music written inside a *tonal system*, that is, the one that it has a tonal center or fundamental note.

Every musical style modeled in this work belongs to tonal music and the *tonality problem* was present when GI algorithms tried to compose in each of them. This problem can be described as follows. Since training samples have different tonalities and even can "modulate" (change the tonality) several times within the same sample, this increases the diversity of the samples and tends to "confuse" GI algorithms. So, in many compositions, modulations were observed to be incoherent in the musical style they should belong to. One of the solutions we proposed and adopted was changing the coding scheme in this way: instead of coding the absolute pitch of the notes, the *intervals* (distance in halftones) between notes, that is, the relative pitch from one note to the previous one, are coded. This coding scheme was called *differential notation* and allows us to abstract from the pitch of the notes and so, from the tonality. Given the nature of the tempered scale, the way to obtain this notation is just by subtracting the number that represents the previous note's pitch in implicit notation from the number that represents present note's pitch, leaving the length of notes coded as in implicit notation. Obviously, the first note from a score has not any note for subtracting its pitch, so its pitch will be coded with a special character 'S'. If a note to code is a *rest*, the pitch will be coded with number 99 because being a note without pitch (no sound) it can not be subtracted to next note. We do not maintain the number 0 for rests because in this notation it means that there are two notes with the same pitch. An example of this notation can be seen in Fig. 2. This idea of employing a differential representation of the pitches was also used by Todd [17].

In the two previous coding schemes, each note from the score is represented by only one symbol, that is to say, a string of characters or 'word' that globally represents both the pitch and length from the note. After performing the experiments with differential notation, it was considered that these coding schemes established a relationship between the pitch and length stronger than the one generally existing in music. So, it was decided to modify the previous notations by coding the pitch and length as separated words. These two new coding schemes were called *splitted implicit notation* and *splitted differential notation*. Results with them improved noticeably as can be seen in next section. An example of these coding schemes is shown in Fig. 2.

| Implicit Notation: | 22c 26c 24c 24c 24n 0c 24c 27c 24c 26c 27c 24c 22c 26c 22c 24c 26c 24n |
|---|---|
| Differential Notation: | Sc 4c -2c 0c 0n 99c 0c 3c -3c 2c 1c -3c -2c 4c -4c 2c 2c -2n |
| Splitted Implicit Notation: | 22 c 26 c 24 c 24 c 24 n 0 c 24 c 27 c 24 c 26 c 27 c 24 c 22 c 26 c 22 c 24 c 26 c 24 n |
| Splitted Differential Notation: | S c 4 c -2 c 0 c 0 n 99 c 0 c 3 c -3 c 2 c 1 c -3 c -2 c 4 c -4 c 2 c 2 c -2 n |

**Fig. 2.** A Gregorian style score coded with the four notations presented.

## 4  Experiments

For the present study, we chose 3 occidental musical styles from different epochs and we took 100 sample melodies from each one. These samples were 10 to 40 seconds long. The first style was *Gregorian* (Middle Ages). As a second style, we used passages from the sacred music of *J. S. Bach* (Baroque). The third style consisted of passages from *Scott Joplin* Ragtimes for piano (beginning of 20th cent.). The results in Musical Style Recognition are expected to be an indicative of the goodness of the musical style's models. So, if a model has been good for *Automatic Musical Style Recognition* it can be supposed that it will be good for *Automatic Composition*. This goodness will be further evaluated through more direct subjective listening tests with melodies automatically composed by the learned models.

### 4.1  Automatic Musical Style Recognition Experiments

We inferred three automata (one per style) with each GI algorithm, trying different values of $k$ (with k-TSI) and $a$ (with ALERGIA). Test melodies are analyzed to see which of the learned automaton can generate them with the greatest probability. Given the small size of the available corpus, *Cross-Validation* was used to measure the recognition accuracy of the different techniques. In each experiment, we took 90 melodies for training and 10 for test. Then the role of the melodies was shifted in such a way that, at the end, every melody was used for both training and testing. A *Confusion Matrix* was built with the results of each cross-validation partition. Its rows and columns denote the style of test melodies and the style in which they were classified, respectively. Then we obtained an *Average Confusion Matrix* that summarized the overall cross-validation results. The diagonal of the matrix represents the *Average Success Rate* in recognition. We also obtained the *Average Classifying Error* [4]. For the sake of simplicity, results will be summarized in tables representing the *average success rate* and *classification error*.

**Results.** In our previous work [4], experiments were performed using only *implicit notation* and tables 1-3 present the best results for each GI algorithm. Results using ECGI were good for Gregorian, but not for Bach and Joplin's styles, giving a high *average classifying error* of the 35.9 %. With k-TSI, the results were better and the best were obtained with $k=3$. K-TSI was the algorithm that best worked in style recognition with this coding scheme, achieving an average classification error of the 9.96 %. The ALERGIA results were similar to k-TSI. We tried different $a$ values covering its entire range ([0,1]) and the best results were achieved with $a=0.01$, obtaining an average classification error of the 13.3 %. It is worth noting that every algorithm obtained a 100% success rate when classifying Gregorian melodies. This will be a constant in almost every performed experiment. Clearly, Gregorian style is less complex than the others, and it is easy for the algorithms to discriminate Gregorian melodies from the rest.

Tables 1-3 also show the results for each GI algorithm using the different here proposed coding schemes. In order to summarize, only the best will be presented. Table 1 presents the results obtained with the ECGI algorithm. It can be seen that the use of *differential notation* leads to a great reduction in the classifying error (more than 50 % as compared with *implicit notation*). The use of *splitted differential notation* reduces error more than 75 %. Using *splitted implicit notation*, the classifying error is reduced drastically too, but not as much as with *splitted differential notation*. The great reduction of the classifying error using *differential notation* is specific for the ECGI algorithm as can be seen in table 1.

The k-TSI algorithm, results were much better than with ECGI for every coding scheme used. The best results were obtained with different $k$ values depending on the coding scheme employed (Table 2). The "splitted" notations needed a greater value for k because now the number of symbols needed for coding a music sample is doubled. The most important error reduction is obtained with the *splitted notations*, being over 50% with respect to *implicit notation*. The best result is obtained with the *splitted differential notation* and it is the best one achieved in this work for Musical Style Recognition. It was reached a 5% classification error and close to 100% average success rate for melodies form Bach's style. ALERGIA was the only algorithm whose results got slightly worse using *differential notation*. However, as can be noticed in Table 3, these were improved using the *splitted* notations, but not as much as with the previous algorithms. The best results were obtained with different *accuracy* ($a$) values depending on the coding scheme employed and, as with the other algorithms, the best one for our purpose was the *splitted differential notation*.

Clearly, with every algorithm the fact of separating the pitch and length from notes has been more important than changing the way of coding pitches to a *differential code*. This confirms our assumption that *implicit notation* established a relationship between the pitch and length stronger than the one generally existing in music. The best result was obtained with k-TSI algorithm, and it is worth noting that results with this coding scheme are quite good considering the small number of samples available.

| | Implicit Notation | Differential Notation | Splitted Implicit Notation | Splitted Differential Notation |
|---|---|---|---|---|
| GREGORIAN | 100 % | 100 % | 100 % | **100 %** |
| BACH | 40 % | 75 % | 82 % | **89 %** |
| JOPLIN | 52 % | 79 % | **88 %** | 86 % |
| Classif. Error | 35.9 % | 15.3 % | 11.3 % | **8.3 %** |

**Table 1.** Results for ECGI algorithm with the different coding schemes.

| | Implicit Notation (k=3) | Differential Notation (k=3) | Splitted Implicit Notation (k=5) | Splitted Differential Notation (k=4) |
|---|---|---|---|---|
| GREGORIAN | 100% | 100% | 100 % | **100%** |
| BACH | 85% | 88 % | 94 % | **96 %** |
| JOPLIN | 85% | 86 % | 89 % | **89 %** |
| Classif. Error | 9.96% | 8.6 % | 5.6 % | **5 %** |

**Table 2. Results** for k-TSI algorithm with the different coding schemes.

| | Implicit Notation (a=0.01) | Differential Notation (a=0.2) | Splitted Implicit Notation (a=0.009) | Splitted Differential Notation (a=0.009) |
|---|---|---|---|---|
| GREGORIAN | 100 % | 100 % | 100 % | **100 %** |
| BACH | 80 % | 85 % | 82 % | **86 %** |
| JOPLIN | 80 % | 69 % | **86 %** | 83 % |
| Classif. Error | 13.3 % | 15.3 % | 10.6 % | **10.3 %** |

**Table 3.** Results for ALERGIA algorithm with the different coding schemes.

## 4.2 Automatic Composition Experiments

Here, the procedure is similar to that used in Automatic Musical Style Recognition. The difference is that, once the automata are obtained, new melodies are randomly synthesized with the aim of obtaining good synthesis results. For a preliminary evaluation, the following criteria were adopted:

1.- The synthesis must make musical sense and must not be a random series of sounds.
2.- It must sound similar to the Musical Style that it is meant to (Gregorian, Bach, etc.).
3.- It must have the characteristics of a proper melody (beginning, development, and end).
4.- It must be different from any of the training melodies.

In order to assess the quality of the synthesis, a secondary evaluation was carried out by the first author following his own (subjective) musical criteria. This quality evaluation was made according to the following classification: very good, good, not very good, bad. A synthesis was considered *bad*, if it did not satisfy all of the above four criteria. If it did satisfy them all, then it was classified according to quality level of the composition as *very good*, *good* or *not very good*. We consider a synthesis as *very good* when it can be taken as an original piece from the current style without being a copy or containing evident fragments from samples, and the remaining qualifying adjectives explain themselves.

**Results.** In our previous work [4], experiments were performed using only the *implicit notation* coding scheme and the best results were obtained with ECGI and K-TSI (with *k*=3,4) algorithms. These results ranged from *good* to *very good* for Gregorian and from *bad* to *not very* good for the styles of Bach and Joplin. ALERGIA's results were not so good, so it was decided not to use it in future studies unless a larger number of samples were available. Many compositions synthesized using *implicit notation* showed what we called the *"tonality" problem*, which was explained in section 3. For solving this problem alternative coding schemes were proposed. To this end, only *differential notation* has been tested so far, leaving the rest of coding schemes for future studies.

With the ECGI algorithm, *differential notation* results in Bach's and Joplin's styles are improved, increasing the number of *good* syntheses, but not obtaining still any *very good* one. An example of ECGI compositions in Gregorian style using *differential notation* can be seen in Fig. 3. With the K-TSI algorithm, results have been enhanced in every style, specially in Gregorian style, but still *very good* melodies are not obtained for the other styles (in the opinion of the authors). Best *k* values were, as with *implicit notation*, *k*= 3 and *k*=4. . The best results in *Automatic Composition* have been obtained with this algorithm, like in *Automatic Musical Style Recognition*.

As a whole, results have been improved in every experiment, but not as much as we expected. The *tonality problem* has been partially solved, because now the synthesized melodies have more continuity (tonally speaking) but another not desired effect derived from the coding has appeared: if two or more musical fragments that follow a descending/ascending scale are concatenated while creating a synthesis, as the pitch encoding is always relative to the previous note, the synthesis tends to exceed the common *tessitura* (range of pitches) in the corresponding style. This effect was observed also by Todd [17], but in his experiments it was more negative and he discarded this notation. In ours, the improvement of the results has been better than the occasional occurrences of this effect.

**Fig. 3.** Example of ECGI composition in *Gregorian* style using *differential notation*.

## 5  Conclusions and Future Trends

Two applications of Grammatical Inference to Music Processing have been presented. These *are Automatic Composition* and *Automatic Musical Style Recognition*. Different coding schemes for music have been proposed and compared according to results in Style Recognition. Preliminary Composition results with one of the newer coding schemes are also presented. Results from our previous studies in this areas have been improved, showing the need of proper music coding schemes in order to take the greatest advantage of the GI algorithms. The best results have been obtained with the k-TSI algorithm both in *Automatic Musical Style Recognition* and in *Automatic Composition.* Limitations of space and time in this paper have prevented us from discussing many aspects in a deeper way, and future trends for this work are presented next.

Several lines of study can be followed to attempt improving results. Obviously, experiments must be done with *splitted* notations in Automatic Composition, and a better protocol for the analysis of automatic compositions should be found (establishing more rules, analysis by a set of musicians, etc.). Additionally, the following lines of study are proposed. First, the amount of data used so far is insufficient and better performance is expected by increasing the number of training samples. Second, since training samples have different tonalities, this increases the diversity of the samples and tends to "confuse" GI algorithms. This was called the *tonality problem* in our previous work and it became quite apparent in Automatic Composition when using *implicit notation.* This problem has been partially solved using *differential notation,* but still has to be fixed. For this purpose one can take advantage of the flexibility offered by the MGGI methodology [10] [19] to explicitly impose tonality constraints in the learning procedure, by adequately relabeling of symbols in the training strings. Once these problems are solved, we could employ entire musical pieces as samples, and not just small fragments as was done in this study. Future studies could also be expanded to include *polyphony.* So far, GI algorithms compose *monodies;* that is, melodies without accompaniment. By changing the GI algorithms in such a way that they could accept samples formed by several strings, it might be possible to deal with samples with more than one voice. This is not a trivial task, and an easier way is to apply automatic harmonizing algorithms to the GI compositions.

# References

1. Amengual J.C., Vidal E. and Benedí J.M. October 1996. Simplifying Language through Error-Correcting Decoding. Proceedings of the ICSLP96 (IV International Conference on Spoken Language Processing), pp. 841--844, Philadelphia, PA., USA, 3-6.
2. Amengual J.C. and Vidal E. 1996. Two Different Approaches for Cost-efficient Viterbi Parsing with Error Correction. Advances in Structural and Syntactic Pattern Recognition, pp. 30-39. P. Perner, P. Wang and A. Rosenfeld (eds.). LNCS 1121. Springer-Verlag.
3. Carrasco, R.C.; Oncina, J. 1994. Learning Stochastic Regular Grammars by means of a State Merging Method. "Grammatical Inference and Applications". Carrasco, R.C.; Oncina, J. eds. Springer-Verlag, (Lecture notes in Artificial Intelligence (862)).
4. Cruz P.P. 1996. Estudio de diversos algoritmos de Inferencia Gramatical para el Reconocimiento Automático de Estilos Musicales y la Composición de melodías en dichos estilos. PFC. Facultad de Informática. Universidad Politécnica de Valencia.

5. Cruz P.P. 1997. A study of Grammatical Inference Algorithms in Automatic Music Composition. Proceedings of the SNRFAI97 (VII Simposium Nacional de Reconocimiento de Formas y Análisis de Imágenes). Vol. 1, pp. 43-48. Sanfeliu A., Villanueva J.J. and Vitrià J. Eds. Centre de Visió per Computador, Universidad Autónoma de Barcelona.

6. Cruz P.P. 1997. A study of Grammatical Inference Algorithms in Automatic Music Composition and Musical Style Recognition. Proceedings from the 'Workshop on Automata Induction, Grammatical Inference, and Language Acquisition', celebrated during the ICML97 (The Fourteenth International Conference on Machine Learning) Nashville, Tennessee. Electronic publication in the Workshop Web page (http://www.cs.cmu.edu/~pdupont/mlworkshop.html).

7. Eberhart, R.C.; Dobbins, R.W. 1990. Neural Network PC Tools. Academic Press Inc, pp. 295-312.

8. Forney, G. D. 1973. The Viterbi algorithm. IEEE Proc. 3, pp. 268-278.

9. Fu, K.S. 1982. Syntactic Pattern Recognition and Applications. Prentice Hall.

10. García P., Vidal E., Casacuberta F. 1987. Local Languages, the Successor Method, and a step towards a general methodology for the Inference of Regular Grammars. IEEE Trans. on Pattern Analysis and Machine Intelligence. Vol.PAMI-9, No.6, pp.841-844.

11. García, P.; Vidal, E 1990. Inference of K-Testable Languages In the Strict Sense and Application to Syntactic Pattern Recognition. IEEE Trans. on PAMI, 12, 9, pp. 920-925.

12. Nuñez, A. 1992. Informática y Electrónica Musical. Ed. Paraninfo.

13. Rulot, H.; Vidal, E. 1987. Modelling (sub)string-length based constraints through a Gramatical Inference method. NATO ASI Series, Vol. F30 Pattern Recognition Theory and Applications, pp. 451-459. Springer-Verlag.

14. Rumsey, F. 1994. *MIDI Systems & Control*. Ed. Focal Press.

15. Schwanauer S.M.; Levitt D.A. 1993. Machine Models of Music. The MIT Press.

16. Segarra, E. 1993. Una Aproximación Inductiva a la Comprensión del Discurso Continuo. Facultad de Informática. Universidad Politécnica de Valencia.

17. Todd P. 1989. A sequential network design for musical applications. Proc. of the 1988 Connectionist Models Summer School. Morgan Kaufmann Publishers, pp. 76-84.

18. Vidal E., Casacuberta F., García P. 1995. Grammatical Inference and Automatic Speech Recognition. In "Speech Recognition and Coding: New Advances and Trends", A.Rubio y J.M.López, Eds., Springer Verlag.

19. Vidal E., Llorens D. 1996. Using knowledge to improve N-Gram Language Modelling through the MGGI methodology. In 'Grammatical Inference: Learning Syntax from Sentences'. Proc. of 3rd ICGI. L.Miclet, C. de la Higuera (Eds.). Springer-Verlag (Lect. Notes in Artificial Intelligence, Vol.1147).

The authors wish to thank the anonymous reviewers for their proposals for the improvement of this paper.

# Learning a Subclass
# of Context-Free Languages

J.D. Emerald, K.G.Subramanian, and D.G.Thomas

Department of Mathematics
Madras Christian College
Tambaram, Madras - 600 059
India.

**Abstract.** In this paper, Apical growth Pure context-free grammars
(AGPCFG) which are a variation of the pure grammars of Maurer et
al are introduced. These grammars allow rewriting of active symbols at
the ends of a string simultaneously. They also provide a variation of another kind of grammars called filamentous systems with apical growth,
which are motivated by biological considerations. The family of languages
generated by AGPCFGs is a subclass of context-free languages. An algorithm for learning this language subclass, in the framework of identification in the limit from positive examples, is provided.

## 1 Introduction

Pure grammars introduced by Maurer et al [6] make no distinction between terminals and nonterminals. In this paper,we introduce a variation of pure grammars called Apical Growth Pure Context-free Grammars (AGPCFG). These
grammars have the following features i) there are only terminal symbols ii) the
rules are context-free in nature and iii) active rightmost and leftmost symbols
of words of length $\geq 2$ are rewritten simultaneously. Inactive rightmost/leftmost
symbols of words are not rewritten, due to absence of rules for these symbols.
These grammars also provide a variation of another kind of grammars called filamentous systems with apical growth, which are motivated by biological considerations [8, 10] and in which the rightmost and leftmost symbols are independently
rewritten.

Extensive research on the problem of learning of formal languages has been
done in the literature. Learning subclasses of regular languages in the framework of identification in the limit from positive data [1, 2, 4, 5, 9, 11, 12] gained
importance, in view of a result of Gold [3], which implies that the class of regular
languages is not identifiable in the limit from positive data.

Recently, it is shown [4, 11] that the whole class of pure context-free languages
is not inferable from positive data only.In fact, Tanida and Yokomori [11] have
introduced monogenic pure context-free grammars in which each string generated is uniquely determined by its predecessor in a derivation. They have shown
that this subclass of pure context-free languages is identifiable in the limit from
positive data.

In this paper, we provide a learning algorithm for identifying in the limit from positive data, apical growth deterministic pure context-free languages with a distinguished marker (AGDmPCFL). These languages constitute a subclass of AGPCFL. It is of interest to note that even the class of AGDmPCFL is incomparable with the class of mono-PCF languages [11] and regular languages. Application of the learning algorithm to picture classes is indicated.

## 2  Apical Growth Pure Context-Free Grammars

We first define apical growth pure context-free grammars.

**Definition 1.** *An apical growth pure context-free grammar (AGPCFG) is $G = (\Sigma, P, S)$ where $\Sigma$ is a finite alphabet; $S$ is a finite set of nonempty strings over $\Sigma$, called axioms; $P = P_1 \cup P_2$ is a finite set of productions of the form $a \to \alpha$, $a \in \Sigma$ and $\alpha \in \Sigma^*$. The rules of $P_1$ (resp. $P_2$) are called left (resp. right) rules. A left rule is denoted as $l : a \to \beta$ and a right rule as $r : a \to \gamma$. A symbol $a$ in $\Sigma$ is called active, if there is a rule for $a$ in $P_1$ or $P_2$. If there is no left (resp. right) rule for $a$, then $a$ is called left inactive (resp. right inactive). The symbol $a$ will be called inactive if it is either left inactive or right inactive.*

A string $w_1$ directly derives $w_2$, written $w_1 \implies w_2$, if and only if (i)$w_1 = xuy$, $w_2 = \alpha u \beta$ where $x, y \in \Sigma$ and $u, \alpha, \beta \in \Sigma^*$ and $x \to \alpha$ is in $P_1$, $y \to \beta$ is in $P_2$ or (ii) $w_1 = xuy$, $w_2 = xu\beta$ where $x, y \in \Sigma$, $u, \beta \in \Sigma^*$ and $y \to \beta$ is in $P_2$ and $x$ is an inactive symbol or (iii) $w_1 = xuy$, $w_2 = \alpha uy$ where $x, y \in \Sigma$, $u, \alpha \in \Sigma^*$ and $x \to \alpha$ is in $P_1$ and $y$ is an inactive symbol. (If $x$ and $y$ are both inactive, then $w_2 = w_1$). $\overset{*}{\implies}$ is the reflexive, transitive closure of $\implies$. The language generated by a AGPCF grammar $G$ is $L(G) = \{w \in \Sigma^* / s \overset{*}{\implies} w, s \text{ in } S\}$.

**Definition 2.** *A deterministic apical growth pure context-free grammar with a distinguished marker, (AGDmPCFG) is a AGPCFG, $G = (\Sigma \cup \{d\}, P, \{s\})$ such that i)$d \notin \Sigma$ ii) for each $a \in \Sigma$, there is at most one right rule $r : a \to \alpha$ and at most one left rule $l : a \to \beta$ where $\alpha, \beta \in \Sigma*$ and iii) $s \in \Sigma^+ d\Sigma^+$.*

**Definition 3.** *[11] A pure grammar $G$ is said to be monogenic if and only if, whenever $w$ is in $L(G)$ and $w \implies w'$, then there exist unique strings $w_1$ and $w_2$ such that $w = w_1 x w_2$ and $w' = w_1 y w_2$, and $x \to y$ is a production and, moreover, there is no string $w''$ such that $w'' \neq w'$ and $w \implies w''$. Thus, each string generated by a monogenic grammar is uniquely determined by its predecessor in a derivation, i.e., the production to apply and the position of application in the predecessor.*

**Example 1.** The AGDmPCF grammar $G_1 = (\{a, b\} \cup \{d\}, P, \{adb\})$ where P has the rule $l : a \to aa$ generates the language $L_1 = \{a^n db / n \geq 1\}$. Note that b is inactive.

*Example 2.* The AGDmPCF grammar $G_2 = (\{a, b\} \cup \{d\}, P, \{adb\})$ where $P$ has the rules $l : a \to aa$, $r : b \to bb$ generates the language $L_2 = \{a^n db^n / n \geq 1\}$.

*Example 3.* The AGDmPCF grammar $G_3 = (\{a, b, c, x, y\} \cup \{d\}, P, \{cxdyc\})$ where $P$ has the rules $l : c \to ca$, $r : c \to bc$ generates the language $L_3 = \{ca^n xdyb^n c / n \geq 0\}$.

**Proposition 1.** *(a) The class of AGDmPCFG is incomparable with the classes of mono-PCF languages and regular languages.*
*(b) The class of AGPCFLs is properly included in the class of CFLs.*

*Proof.* (a) The proposition is clear from the following observations:

1. The AGDmPCF language $L_1 = \{a^n db / n \geq 1\}$ in example 1 is indeed a regular language.
2. The AGDmPCF language $L_2 = \{a^n db^n / n \geq 1\}$ in example 2 is indeed a mono-PCF language generated by a mono-PCF grammar with axiom $adb$ and rules $d \to adb$.
3. The AGDmPCF language $L_3 = \{ca^n xdyb^n c / n \geq 0\}$ is neither a PCF language nor a regular language.
4. The language $L_4 = \{aba^m da^p ba / m, p \geq 0\}$ is a regular language but is not even AGPCF.
5. The language $L_5 = \{a^2 b^n db^n a^2 / n \geq 0\}$ is generated by the mono-PCF grammar with axiom $a^2 da^2$ and a rule $d \to bdb$ but it cannot be generated by even any AGPCF grammar.

(b) Inclusion is clear and proper inclusion is a consequence of the fact that the class of AGDmPCFL is incomparable with the class of regular languages. $\square$

**Proposition 2.** *[11] Every mono-PCF language L is a finite union of languages of the form $\{xu^n bv^n y / n \geq 1\}$, where $x, u, v, y$ are strings and $b$ is a symbol.*

Analogously, we have the following proposition for AGDmPCF languages.

**Proposition 3.** *The language generated by a AGDmPCFG is of the form $\{w_0, w_1, ..., w_k\} \cup \{gu^n xdyv^n h / n \geq 1\}$ where $w_i (0 \leq i \leq k), u, v, x, y \in \Sigma^*$, $g, h \in \Sigma$ and $d$ is a distinguished symbol not in $\Sigma$.*

## 3   The Identification Algorithm for AGDmPCF Languages

We refer to [12] for the concept of identification in the limit from positive examples.

We now describe an identification algorithm $A$ for learning the class of AGDmPCF languages with an axiom of length $\geq 3$ in the limit from positive data.

Let $L$ be a AGDmPCF language over $\Sigma = \{a_1, ..., a_m\} \cup \{d\}$ where $d \notin \Sigma$ and $T_i = \{w_1, ..., w_i\}$ be a finite sample set of positive examples of $L$ provided up to the i-th stage of the inference process.

Let $w_i$ be the i-th positive example provided at the i-th stage of the inference process and let $G_i = (\Sigma, P_i, S_o)$ be the conjectured AGDmPCF grammar at the i-th stage. Now, suppose that $w_i$ is not consistent with $G_{i-1}$, that is $w_i \notin L(G_{i-1})$.

## Identification algorithm $A$

**Input** : Alphabet $\Sigma \cup \{d\}$ where $d \notin \Sigma$; a positive presentation of AGDmPCF language $L$.

**Output** : A sequence of AGDmPCF grammars for AGDmPCF language $L$.

**Procedure**

let $P_1 = \{a_1 \rightarrow a_1, ..., a_m \rightarrow a_m\}$;
let $P_2 = \{a_1 \rightarrow a_1, ..., a_m \rightarrow a_m\}$;
read the first positive example $w_1$;
let $T_1 = \{w_1\}$; let $S_0 = \{w_1\}$;
output $G_1 = (\Sigma, P = P_1 \cup P_2, \{w_1\})$;
let $i = 2$;
repeat (forever)
[i-th stage]
let $G_{i-1} = (\Sigma, P, S_0)$ be the $(i - 1)st$ conjectured AGDmPCF grammar;
let $s$ be the unique element in $S_o$;
read the next positive example $w_i$;
if $w_i \in L(G_{i-1})$ then
 output $G_i(= G_{i-1})$ as the i-th conjecture
else
 begin
  if $|w_i| \leq |s|$ then
   begin
    call UPDATE $(P_1, P_2, w_i, s)$;
    $S_0 = \{w_i\}$;
   end
  else
   for all $w \in T_{i-1}$ do the following;
    begin
     if $|w_i| < |w|$ then
      UPDATE $(P_1, P_2, w_i, w)$;
     else
      UPDATE $(P_1, P_2, w, w_i)$;
    end
 end
let $T_i = T_{i-1} \cup \{w_i\}$;

output $G_i = (\Sigma, P = P_1 \cup P_2, S_0)$ as the $i$-th conjecture;
$i = i + 1$.

## 3.1 Updating production set P

In the procedure UPDATE, $|u| \leq |v|$ where $|u|$ is the length of string $u$. $lcm(u, v)$
denotes the longest common middle of $u$ and $v$ including the distinguished
marker. Then $v = xlcm(u, v)y$ where $x, y \in \Sigma^*$; $rem - pref(u, v) = x$; $rem - suf(u, v) = y$.

Now we describe the procedure "UPDATE" that, given $u, v$ and a current
production set $P = P_1 \cup P_2$, produces the new production set, where each left
rule in $P_1$ is in the form $l : \gamma \rightarrow a\delta$, $\delta \in \Sigma^*$, $|\delta| \geq 1$ and each right rule in $P_2$ is
in the form $r : \gamma \rightarrow \delta b$, $\delta \in \Sigma^*$ and $|\delta| \geq 1$.

We use the following notations in the procedures SUFMAX $(P_1, u, v)$ and
PREMAX $(P_2, u, v)$ assuming that $|u| < |v|$ : $lcs(u, v)$ denotes the longest com-
mon suffix of $u$ and $v$; $pre - suf(u, v) = \omega$ where $v = \omega lcs(u, v)$; $lcp(u, v)$
denotes the longest common prefix of $u$ and $v$; $suf - pref(u, v) = \omega'$ where
$v = lcp(u, v)\omega'$.

**Procedure UPDATE** $(P_1, P_2, u, v)$

```
let P_1 = {a_1 → t_{a_1}, ..., a_m → t_{a_m}};
let P_2 = {a_1 → t_{a_1}, ..., a_m → t_{a_m}};
let α be the first letter of u;
let β be the last letter of u;
let u = αūβ;
let rem − pref(ū, v) = α';
let u = αūβ;
let rem − suf(ū, v) = β';
if t_alpha = α in P_1 then
    replace α → α in P_1 by α → α'
else
    if α' ≠ t_α and |α'| < |t_α| then
        begin
            replace α → t_α by α → α';
            call SUFMAX (P_1, α', t_α);
        end
    else
        call SUFMAX (P_1, t_α, α');
        if t_β = β in P_2 then
            replace β → β in P_2 by β → β';
        else
            if β' ≠ t_β and |β'| < |t_β| then
                begin
                    replace β → t_β by β → β';
```

```
                        call PREMAX (P₂, β', tβ)
                 end
          else
                 call PREMAX (P₂, tβ, β');
```

**SUFMAX** $(P, u, v)$

    let $\gamma$ be the first letter of $u$;
    let $u = \gamma \bar{u}$;
    let $pre - suf(\bar{u}, v) = \delta$;
    if $t_\gamma = \gamma$ then
        replace $\gamma \to \gamma$ by $\gamma \to \delta$
    else
        if $\delta \neq t_\gamma$ and $|\delta| < |t_\gamma|$ then
            begin
                replace $\gamma \to t_\gamma$ by $\gamma \to \delta$;
                call SUFMAX $(P_1, \delta, t_\gamma)$;
            end
        else
            call SUFMAX $(P_1, t_\gamma, \delta)$;

**PREMAX** $(P, u, v)$

    let $\gamma'$ be the last letter of $u$;
    let $u = \bar{u} \gamma'$;
    let $suf - pre(\bar{u}, v) = \delta'$;
    if $t_{\gamma'} = \gamma'$ then
        replace $\gamma' \to \gamma'$ by $\gamma' \to \delta'$
    else
        if $\delta' \neq t_\gamma$ and $|\delta'| < |t_{\gamma'}|$ then
            begin
                replace $\gamma' \to t_{\gamma'}$ by $\gamma' \to \delta'$;
                call PREMAX $(P_2, \delta', t_{\gamma'})$;
            end
        else
            call PREMAX $(P_2, t_{\gamma'}, \delta')$;

The idea behind the algorithm can be informally described as follows. The technique is closely related to that of [12] as follows, but the difference is that since the leftmost and rightmost symbols of a word are rewritten in a AGDm-PCF, the procedure at any time conjectures rules for the right most and left most symbols by using two subprocedures SUFMAX and PREMAX of procedure UPDATE. This is in contrast to that of [11], wherein the rule for a single *"inner"* symbol is conjectured.

$T_i$ contains the set of positive examples read so far and $S_0$ contains the smallest positive example $s$ among the examples so far considered.

If $G_{i-1}$ is the $(i-1)$st conjectured grammar and the i-th example is $w_i$, then the output grammar $G_i = G_{i-1}$ if $w_i$ belongs to the language generated by $G_{i-1}$. Otherwise, the length of the positive example $w_i$ is compared with that of axiom $s$ of $G_{i-1}$ and if it is less than or equal to the length of $s$, then the rules are updated using procedure UPDATE $(P_1, P_2, u, v)$ where $u$ is taken as $w_i$ and $v$ as $s$. On the other hand, if the length of $w_i$ is greater than that of $s$, then the procedure UPDATE is carried out using $w_i$ and words of $T_{i-1}$.

The procedure UPDATE works by calling two subprocedures, SUFMAX which updates the left rules for symbols and PREMAX which updates the right rules for symbols.

*Remark 1.* The distinguished marker $d$ can be dispensed with in the following situation: If the set of all words $v$ obtained from the left rules in the form $l : u \to av$ and the right rules in the form $r : u \to va$, form a code set, then the code set is to be given as the input and each sample word is factored using the code set. The above algorithm can be used on similar lines without the use of the distinguished marker $'d'$.


## 3.2 Characteristic Sample

The correctness of the algorithm $A$, can be seen by considering a characteristic sample for a target AGDmPCF language.

Let $L$ be a AGDmPCF language. A finite set $C$ is called a characteristic sample of $L$ if and only if $L$ is the smallest AGDmPCF language containing $C$. We illustrate the method of forming a characteristic sample, with an example.

Consider a AGDmPCF grammar $G = (\Sigma \cup \{d\}, P, S)$ where $\Sigma = \{x, y, a, b, c, f, g, h\}$, $S = \{xdy\}$ and $P = \{l : x \to ba, r : y \to af, l : b \to cba, r : f \to abg, l : c \to bc, r : g \to gf\}$ generating a language $L = \{xdy, badaf\} \cup \{(cba)^n ada(abg)^n / n \geq 1\} \cup \{b(cba)^n ada(abg)^n f / n \geq 1\}$. We construct the characteristic sample $S_G$ by taking a finite number of strings derived from the axiom till each of the rules of the grammar finds application in one or other of the derivations of these strings. In the grammar considered here,

$$S_G = \{xdy, badaf, cbaadaabg, bcbaadaabgf\}$$

When the sample set $T_i$ contains all the elements of $S_G$, the algorithm $A$ converges to a correct AGDmPCF grammar $G$ for the target language $L$. Hence, it is clear from the manner in which the characteristic sample $S_G$ is formed that, the class of AGDmPCF languages is identifiable in the limit from positive data.

It can be seen that the algorithm $A$ takes time polynomial in the sum of the lengths of all positive examples presented.

Although, for simplicity, we have considered only one axiom in a AGDm-PCFG, we can extend the learning algorithm to a finite number of axioms.

*Remark 2.* Certain patterns described by chain codes [7] can also be learnt using the identification algorithm described earlier. For instance, the picture describing "staircases" ing Fig.1 can be encoded as a string $(ru)^4r^3lr^3(dr)^4$ where $l, r, u, d$ respectively, stand for moving one unit to the left, right, up, down from the current point in the plane. (The encoding depends on the starting point and ending point). The pictures as in Fig.1 are thus represented by elements of the language $\{(ru)^n r^m lr^m (dr)^n / n, m \geq 1\}$ where $l$ is the distinguished marker. The chain-coded language is learnt and is interpreted to give chain code pictures.

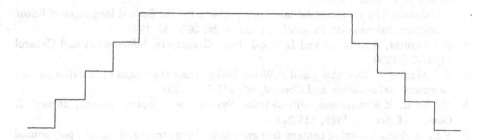

**Fig. 1.** Staircases

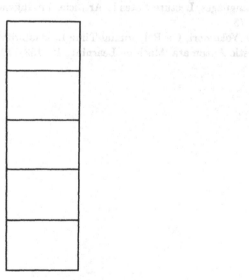

**Fig. 2.** Stack of Boxes

Similarly, the picture "Stack of boxes" in Fig.2 can be encoded as a string $(rdluurdlu)^4$ which is an element of the language $\{(rdluurdu)^{4n}/n \geq 0\}$ generated by a PPL, $G = (\{l, r, u, d\}, \{rdluurdlu\}, \{rdlu\})$.

# References

1. D.Angluin, Inference of reversible languages, J. ACM 29, 1982, 741-765.
2. J.D.Emerald, K.G.Subramanian and D.G.Thomas, Learning Code regular and Code linear languages, Proceedings of ICGI-96, Lecture Notes in Artificial Intelligence 1147, 1996, 211-221.
3. E.M.Gold, Language identification in the limit, Information and Control, 10, 447-474, 1967.
4. T.Koshiba, E.Makinen and Y.Takada, Inferring pure context-free languages from positive data, Technical Report A-1997-14, Department of Computer Science, University of Tampere, 1997.
5. E.Makinen, The grammatical inference problem for the Szilard languages of linear grammars, Information Processing Letters, 36, 203-206, 1990.
6. H.A.Maurer, A.Salomaa and D.Wood, Pure Grammars, Information and Control 44, 47-72, 1980.
7. H.A.Maurer, G.Rozenberg and E.Welzl, Using string languages to describe picture languages, Information and Control, 54, 155-185, 1992.
8. N.Nirmal, K.Krithivasan, Filamentous Systems with apical growth, Intern. J. Comp. Inf. Sci. 14, 1985, 235-242.
9. Y.Sakakibara, Learning context-free grammars from structural data in polynomial time, Theoretical Computer Science, 76(2): 223-242, 1990.
10. K.G.Subramanian, A note on regular-controlled apical growth filamentous systems, Intern. J.Comp.Inf.Sci.14, 1985, 235-242.
11. N.Tanida and T.Yokomori, Inductive Inference of Monogenic Pure Context-free languages, Lecture Notes in Artificial Intelligence, 872, Springer-Verlag, 1994, 560-573.
12. T.Yokomori, On Polynomial-Time Learnability in the Limit of Strictly Deterministic Automata, Machine Learning, 19, 153-179, 1995.

# Using Symbol Clustering to Improve Probabilistic Automaton Inference

Pierre Dupont[1] and Lin Chase[2]

[1] EURISE, Université Jean Monnet
23, rue P. Michelon
42023 Saint-Etienne Cedex – France
pdupont@univ-st-etienne.fr
[2] LIMSI/CNRS
B.P.133
91403 Orsay Cedex – France
chase@limsi.fr

**Abstract.** In this paper we show that clustering alphabet symbols before PDFA inference is performed reduces perplexity on new data. This result is especially important in real tasks, such as spoken language interfaces, in which data sparseness is a significant issue. We describe the application of the ALERGIA algorithm combined with an independent clustering technique to the Air Travel Information System (ATIS) task. A 25 % reduction in perplexity was obtained. This result outperforms a trigram model under the same simple smoothing scheme.

## 1   Introduction

Inference of deterministic finite automaton (DFA) from positive and negative data can be solved by the RPNI algorithm, proposed independently by Trakhtenbrot *et al.* [16] and by Oncina *et al.* [13]. This algorithm was used by Lang in his extensive experimental study of learning random deterministic automata from sparse samples [10]. An adapted version of this algorithm proved to be successful in the recent Abbadingo competition [9]. However the use of the RPNI algorithm and other grammatical inference techniques requires several adaptations in order to be feasible for real applications such as speech recognition interfaces.

Since most databases do not include negative information, the learning can be controlled by probabilistic information instead. Several inference algorithms for probabilistic automata are known [15, 3, 14]. In particular, the ALERGIA algorithm proposed by Carrasco and Oncina [3] is the probabilistic version of the RPNI algorithm. As the purpose of the machines built by these algorithms is not to define hard decision boundaries, the quality of learning is not estimated by classification errors on new data. Instead we use a distance measure, such as the Kullback-Leibler divergence, between the learned distribution and the target distribution. Because the target distribution is unknown in practice, this distance measure is approximated by test set perplexity (see section 2 for more details).

Another problem arises from the fact that simulated learning curves do not accurately predict the performance on actual data sets of limited size. First, learning curves usually depend on the size of the target machine which is unknown. Second, real alphabets, at least for speech applications, typically contain up to several thousand symbols instead of just a few. Thus an extremely small fraction of all strings up to the maximal length observed is actually available. This data sparseness problem is a key concern to reserarchers who deal with human language applications.

In this context, clustering alphabet symbols can lead to a denser training set at the cost of a reduced ability to discriminate between individual symbols. The present work aims at showing that the performance of the ALERGIA algorithm improves when a clustering algorithm is used before the actual inference.

## 2   Definitions and notations

A *probabilistic DFA* (PDFA) is a 6-tuple $(Q, \Sigma, \delta, q_0, \gamma, \tau)$ where $Q$ is a finite set of *states*, $\Sigma$ is an *alphabet*, $\delta$ is a *transition function*, i.e. a mapping from $Q \times \Sigma$ to $Q$, $q_0$ is the *initial state*, $\gamma$ is the *next symbol probability function*, i.e. a mapping from $Q \times \Sigma$ to $[0, 1]$ and $\tau$ is the *end of string probability function*, i.e. a mapping from $Q$ to $[0, 1]$. The probability functions must satisfy the following constraints:

$$\gamma(q, a) \qquad = 0 \text{ , if } \delta(q, a) = \emptyset$$
$$\sum_{a \in \Sigma} \gamma(q, a) + \tau(q) = 1 \text{ , } \forall q \in Q$$

The probability $P_A(x)$ of *generating* a string $x = x_1 \ldots x_n$ from a PDFA $A = (Q, \Sigma, \delta, q_0, \gamma, \tau)$ is defined as

$$P_A(x) = \begin{cases} \left( \prod_{i=1}^{n} \gamma(q^i, x_i) \right) \tau(q^n) & \text{, if } \delta(q^i, x_i) \neq \emptyset \text{ with } q^{i+1} = \delta(q^i, x_i) \\ & \qquad \text{for } 1 \leq i < n \text{ and } q^1 = q_0 \\ 0 & \text{, otherwise} \end{cases}$$

Our definition of probabilistic automaton is equivalent to a stochastic regular grammar used as string generator. Thus, $\sum_{x \in \Sigma^*} P_A(x) = 1$. Note that some works on the learning of discrete distributions use distributions defined on $\Sigma^n$ (that is $\sum_{x \in \Sigma^n} P(x) = 1$, for any $n \geq 1$), instead of $\Sigma^*$ (see for instance [1, 7]).

The probabilistic automaton $A/\pi$ denotes the automaton *derived from* the probabilistic automaton $A$ *with respect to the partition* $\pi$ of $Q$, also called the *quotient automaton* $A/\pi$. It is obtained by merging states of $A$ belonging to the same subset in $\pi$. When $q$ results from the merging of the states $q'$ and $q''$, the following equalities must hold

$$\gamma(q, a) = \gamma(q', a) + \gamma(q'', a) \text{ , } \forall a \in \Sigma$$
$$\tau(q) = \tau(q') + \tau(q'')$$

Let $PPTA(I_+)$ denote the *probabilistic prefix tree acceptor* built from a positive sample $I_+$. Let $C(q)$ denote the count of state $q$, that is the number of times the state $q$ was used while generating $I_+$ from $PPTA(I_+)$. Let $C(q, \lambda)$ denote the number of times a string of $I_+$ ended on $q$ ($\lambda$ denotes the empty string). Let $C(q, a)$ denote the count of the transition $(q, a)$ in $PPTA(I_+)$. The $PPTA(I_+)$ is the maximal likelihood estimate built from $I_+$. In particular, for $PPTA(I_+)$ the probability estimates are $\hat{\gamma}(q, a) = \frac{C(q,a)}{C(q)}$ and $\hat{\tau}(q) = \frac{C(q,\lambda)}{C(q)}$.

Let $Lat(PPTA(I_+))$ denote the lattice of automata which can be derived from $PPTA(I_+)$.

Let $A$ be a target PDFA and $\hat{A}$ a hypothesis PDFA, $D(P_A \parallel P_{\hat{A}})$ denotes the *Kullback-Leibler divergence* or *cross entropy*.

$$D(P_A \parallel P_{\hat{A}}) = \sum_{x \in \Sigma^*} P_A(x) \log \frac{P_A(x)}{P_{\hat{A}}(x)}$$

The divergence can be rewritten as follows.

$$D(P_A \parallel P_{\hat{A}}) = \sum_{x \in \Sigma^*} P_A(x) \log \frac{1}{P_{\hat{A}}(x)} + \sum_{x \in \Sigma^*} P_A(x) \log P_A(x)$$
$$= E_{P_A} \left[ \log \frac{1}{P_{\hat{A}}(x)} \right] - H(P_A)$$

The first term above denotes the expectation of $\log \frac{1}{P_{\hat{A}}(x)}$ according to the distribution $P_A$ and $H(P_A)$ denotes the entropy of $P_A$. In other words, the divergence is the additional number of bits[1] needed to encode data generated from $P_A$ when the optimal code is used for $P_{\hat{A}}$ instead of $P_A$. Note that the second term does not depend on the hypothesis. Thus the first term can be used to measure the *relative* quality of several hypotheses.

In practice, the target distribution is unknown. Instead, an independent sample $S$, which is assumed to have been drawn according to the distribution $P_A$, can be used. Let $\tilde{P}_S(x)$ denote the empirical distribution computed from the sample $S$ containing $|S|$ strings $x$ and $\|S\|$ symbols $x_i$. Letting $C_S(x)$ denote the count of the string $x$ in $S$, one can write

$$E_{P_A} \left[ \log \frac{1}{P_{\hat{A}}(x)} \right] \simeq \sum_{x \in S} \tilde{P}_S(x) \log \frac{1}{P_{\hat{A}}(x)}$$
$$= -\frac{1}{|S|} \sum_{x \in S} C_S(x) \log P_{\hat{A}}(x)$$
$$= -\frac{1}{\|S\|} \sum_{i=1}^{\|S\|} \log P_{\hat{A}}(x_i | q^i)$$

Thus the quality measure is the *average log-likelihood* of $x$ according to the distribution $P_{\hat{A}}$ computed on the sample $S$. Most commonly used is the *sample perplexity* $PP$ given by

$$2^{\left( -\frac{1}{\|S\|} \sum_{i=1}^{\|S\|} \log P_{\hat{A}}(x_i | q^i) \right)}$$

---

[1] Base 2 is assumed for the log function.

The minimal perplexity $PP = 1$ is reached when the next symbol is always predicted with probability 1 while $PP = |\Sigma|$ corresponds to random guessing from a lexicon of size $|\Sigma|$.

## 3 Probabilistic DFA Inference

**Algorithm** ALERGIA
**input**
$I_+$                                                    // A positive sample
$\alpha$                                                  // A precision parameter
**output**
a PDFA                                                   // A probabilistic DFA

**begin**

// $N$ is the number of states of $PPTA(I_+)$

$\pi \leftarrow \{\{0\}, \{1\}, \ldots, \{N-1\}\}$        // One block for each prefix in the order $<$
$A \leftarrow PPTA(I_+)$

**for** $i = 1$ **to** $|\pi| - 1$                         // Loop on the blocks of partition $\pi$
  **for** $j = 0$ **to** $i - 1$                 // Loop on the blocks of lower rank
    **if** *compatible* $(i, j, \alpha)$ **then**
      $\pi' \leftarrow \pi \backslash \{B_j, B_i\} U \{B_i U B_j\}$   // Merging of block $B_i$ and block $B_j$
      $A/\pi' \leftarrow derive(A, \pi')$
      $\pi'' \leftarrow determ\_merge \, (A/\pi')$
      $A \leftarrow A/\pi''$
      $\pi \leftarrow \pi''$
      **break**                 // Break $j$ loop
    **end if**
  **end for**                                    // End $j$ loop
**end for**                                              //End $i$ loop
**return** $A$
**end** ALERGIA

**Fig. 1.** The ALERGIA algorithm.

The ALERGIA algorithm [3] is depicted in pseudocode in figure 1. It performs an ordered search in the lattice $Lat(PPTA(I_+))$. By construction each of the states of $PPTA(I_+)$ corresponds to a unique prefix. The prefixes may be sorted according to the standard order $<$ on strings[2]. This order also applies to the prefix tree states. A partition in the state set of the $PPTA(I_+)$ consists of an ordered block set, each block receiving the rank of its state of minimal rank. The ALERGIA algorithm proceeds in $N-1$ steps, where $N = \mathcal{O}(\|I_+\|)$ is the number of states of $PPTA(I_+)$. The partition $\pi(i)$ at step $i$ is obtained by merging the

---
[2] According to the standard order, the first strings on the alphabet $\Sigma = \{a, b\}$ are $\lambda < a < b < aa < ab < ba < bb < aaa < \ldots$

two first blocks, according to the standard order, of the partition $\pi(i-1)$ at step $i-1$ such that $PTA(I_+)/\pi(i)$ is a compatible automaton.

The function *derive* $(A, \pi')$ returns the quotient automaton $A$ with respect to partition $\pi'$. The automaton $A/\pi'$ may be non-deterministic. The function *determ_merge* $(A/\pi')$ returns the partition $\pi''$ obtained by recursively merging all blocks of $\pi'$, which creates a non-determinism. If $A/\pi'$ is deterministic, the partition $\pi''$ is equal to partition $\pi'$.

The function *compatible* $(i, j, \alpha)$ controls the merging of states. It returns TRUE if the states $i$ and $j$ are compatible within the precision defined by the parameter $\alpha$ and FALSE otherwise. The compatibility measure derives from the Hoeffding bound [5]. Formally, two states $q_1$ and $q_2$ are $\alpha$-compatible ($0 < \alpha \leq 1$) if the two following conditions hold

$$\left| \frac{C(q_1, a)}{C(q_1)} - \frac{C(q_2, a)}{C(q_2)} \right| < \sqrt{\frac{1}{2} \ln \frac{2}{\alpha}} \left( \frac{1}{\sqrt{C(q_1)}} + \frac{1}{\sqrt{C(q_2)}} \right), \quad \forall a \in \Sigma \cup \lambda \quad (1)$$

$$\delta(q_1, a) \text{ and } \delta(q_2, a) \text{ are } \alpha\text{-compatible}, \forall a \in \Sigma \quad (2)$$

## 4 Clustering algorithm

At least two algorithms have been proposed to define classes automatically from data [2, 12]. Both algorithms can be shown to optimize the same criterion, the minimization of the training set perplexity of a class bigram. This is equivalent to the maximization of *average mutual information* between classes $I(g_1, g_2) = E_p \left[ \log \frac{P(g_1, g_2)}{P(g_1)P(g_2)} \right]$ (see [2] for more details). While the algorithms use the same optimization function, however, they differ in the greedy search they follow. We have chosen to use the clustering algorithm proposed by Ney *et al.* [12] which is described in figure 2.

### 4.1 Definition of a class bigram

Given a deterministic symbol to class mapping $g : x_i \to g(x_i)$ a class bigram is defined as :

$$p(x_i | x_{i-1}) \stackrel{def}{=} p(x_i | g(x_i)) \cdot p(g(x_i) | g(x_{i-1}))$$

Let $k$ denote the number of classes. The two limit cases are $k = 1$, which is equivalent to a unigram model, or $k = |\Sigma|$, which is equivalent to a bigram model at the symbol level.

### 4.2 Greedy reestimation algorithm

The objective of the clustering algorithm is to find the class mapping which minimizes the class bigram perplexity on the training set for a fixed number of classes $k$. Initially, each of the $k-1$ most frequent symbols is assigned to a 1-symbol class. All other symbols are assigned to the last class. At every iteration each symbol is moved from its original class to the class which corresponds to the local minimum of the class bigram perplexity. The reestimation is halted either when a predefined number of iterations (typically 100) is reached or when the difference between perplexities obtained at two consecutive iterations falls below a certain threshold (typically 0.01).

**Algorithm** CLUSTER
**input**
$I_+$                                                              // A positive sample
$k$                                                                // A fixed number of classes
**output**
$g$                                                                // A symbol to class mapping

**begin**
$g \leftarrow$ *Initialize_mapping* $(I_+, k)$        // Initialize symbol to class mapping
**while** (not end)
    **for all** $a \in \Sigma$                                // Loop on all symbols of the alphabet
        **for** $j = 1$ **to** $k$                       // Loop on the $k$ classes
          $g(a) \leftarrow g^j$                      // Move $a$ from $g(a)$ to $g^j$
          $PP(g^j) \leftarrow$ *perplexity* $(I_+, g)$    // Compute the resulting perplexity
        **end for**                                 // End $j$ loop
        $g(a) \leftarrow \underset{g^j}{\text{argmin}}\ PP(g^j)$

    **end for all**                                          // End loop on $\Sigma$
**end while**                                                      // Some stopping criterion is met
**return** $g$
**end** CLUSTER

**Fig. 2.** The clustering algorithm.

# 5  Infering from clustered data

Clustering the alphabet symbols allows us to reduce the alphabet size and thus to increase the training set density, relative to the set of strings defined on the class alphabet. After the symbol mapping has been performed, however, prediction of individual symbols can be more difficult. Trading off these effects one can find an optimal number of classes such that the resulting PDFA has a minimal perplexity on independent data. This is decribed in details in section 7.

The inference procedure can be summarized as follows.

1. Estimate a symbol to class mapping
2. Label the training set in terms of classes
3. Infer a PDFA from the relabeled training set
4. Expand the resulting PDFA by replacing each class by the symbols it contains
5. Interpolate the resulting PDFA with a unigram model

The first step requires choosing $k$, the number of classes. For the third step, the precision parameter $\alpha$ of the ALERGIA algorithm must be set. Expansion of the resulting PDFA consists in replacing each transition labeled with a class by a set of transitions labeled by its corresponding symbols. The probability of any transition $(q, a)$ is then given by $\gamma(q, a) = \gamma(q, g(a))P(a|g(a))$. Finally, in order to guarantee that the probability of predicting any symbol from any given state is strictly positive, the PDFA must be smoothed. We use here linear interpolation with a unigram model $P_1(x)$:

$$P(x) = \beta P_{\hat{A}}(x) + (1 - \beta)P_1(x)$$

This smoothing technique is very rudimentary but, because it is so simple, it best reflects the quality of the PDFA itself. Thus our inference procedure depends on the free parameters $k, \alpha, \beta$.

## 6 The ATIS task

The Air Travel Information System (ATIS) corpus [4] was developed under a DARPA speech and natural language program that focussed on developing language interfaces to information retrieval systems. The corpus consists of speakers of American English making information requests such as, "Uh, I'd like to go from, uh, Pittsburgh to Boston next Tuesday, no wait, Wednesday".

We use the ATIS-2 sub-corpus in the experiments reported here. This portion of the corpus was developed under a Wizard-of-Oz conditions in which a human being secretly replaced the speech recognition component of an otherwise fully automated dialogue system.

The ATIS-2 is officially defined as containing a training set and two evaluation sets. The training set, which we used for estimating classes and for infering PDFA's, contains 13,186 utterances (130,773 tokens). The observed vocabulary contains 1,294 words. We used the first evaluation set (Feb92, 980 utterances, 10636 tokens) as a development set to tune our free parameters $(k, \alpha, \beta)$. The second evaluation set (Nov92, 1002 utterances, 11703 tokens) was used as our independent test set.

## 7 Results

In the context of these experiments, alphabet symbols represent *words* from the ATIS vocabulary and strings represent *utterances*. Our experiments aim at showing that the use of classes reduces perplexity on independent data.

The first three figures describe the original ALERGIA algorithm without using classes while the last three figures illustrate the inference behavior when clustering is performed beforehand. Figure 3 shows that the size of the inferred PDFA grows with the value of $\alpha$. As $\alpha$ increases the compatibility criterion is harder to satisfy. Consequently fewer merging operations are performed.

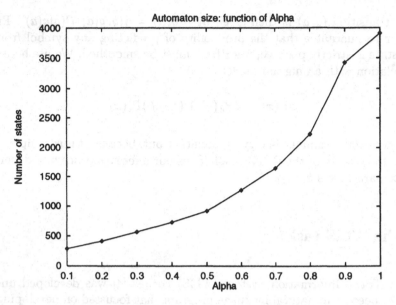

**Fig. 3.** Effect of $\alpha$ on the automaton size.

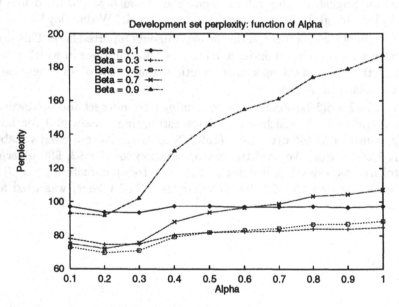

**Fig. 4.** Effect of $\alpha$ on development set perplexity with various interpolation parameters.

With the original ALERGIA algorithm the perplexity on new data depends only on the two parameters $\alpha$ and $\beta$. Figure 4 illustrates the relation between perplexity, $\alpha$ and $\beta$ as measured on the development set. Optimal values are $\alpha = 0.2$ and $\beta = 0.5$. This result is detailed at figure 5 where the development set perplexity depends on $\alpha$ (for $\beta$ fixed to its optimal value). The perplexity is minimal (PP=70) for small $\alpha$'s. However the limit case ($\alpha = 0$) results in the universal automaton which is equivalent to a unigram model. In this case the perplexity is 145.

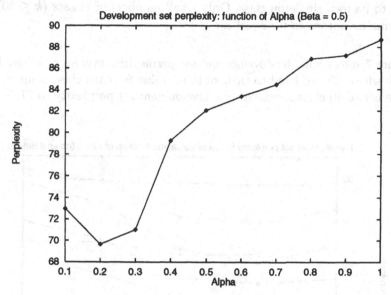

**Fig. 5.** Development set perplexity as a function of $\alpha$ with optimal interpolation ($\beta = 0.5$).

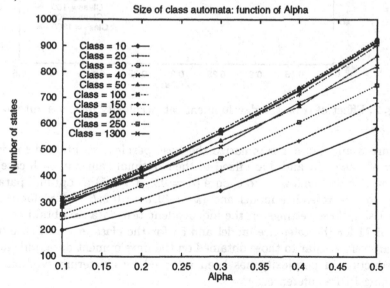

**Fig. 6.** Effect of $\alpha$ on the size of automata learned from classes.

Next we study how the use of classes modifies the previous results. In this case class-based automata refer to PDFA's obtained after expanding each class transition into its corresponding word transitions. Figure 6 shows that the size of the resulting automata follows the same dependence on $\alpha$. Here the maximal number of classes ($k = 1300$) correponds to the reference model, as each word belongs to its own singleton class. Only small numbers of classes ($k \leq 50$) give rise to smaller automata for equal $\alpha$'s.

Figure 7 shows how the development set perplexities evolves as a function of $\alpha$ and $k$ where $\beta$'s are fixed to their optimal value for each class number. Note that the use of 40 classes reduces the development set perplexity to 51.

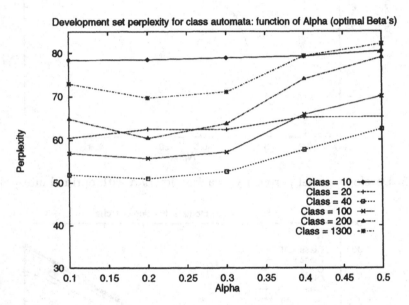

**Fig. 7.** Effect of $\alpha$ on the development set perplexity for class automata.

Figure 8 and table 1 summarize the best perplexity obtained for various number of classes ($\alpha$ and $\beta$ are fixed to their optimal values in each case). The results in this table allow us to choose ($\alpha = 0.2, \beta = 0.5$) as optimal parameter settings for the reference model and ($k = 40, \alpha = 0.2, \beta = 0.8$) for the class model. Using these settings on the independent test data we obtain perplexity values of 71 for the reference model and 53 for the class model. These figures, which are very similar to those obtained on the development data, indicate that 25% reduction in perplexity has been achieved by clustering symbols before performing PDFA inference.

As a point of comparison we repeated the experiments using a trigram model with the same smoothing technique. Interpolating the unsmoothed trigram model with the unigram model (optimal $\beta = 0.5$) resulted in a test set perplexity of 59, a figure slightly inferior to the optimal value for the class model. The best known smoothed trigram model, due to Kneser and Ney [8], yields a perplexity of 14. This difference in performance indicates clearly that smoothing will be a key issue in improving the performance of learned automata.

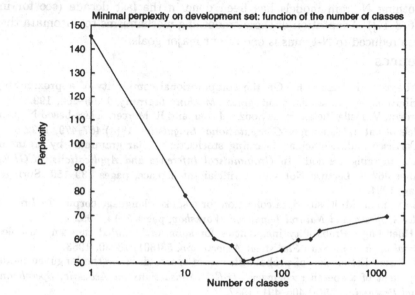

**Fig. 8.** Best development set perplexities as a function of the number of classes.

| k | α | β | PP |
|---|---|---|---|
| 1 | - | 0.0 | 145 |
| 10 | 0.1 | 0.8 | 78 |
| 20 | 0.1 | 0.8 | 60 |
| 30 | 0.1 | 0.8 | 58 |
| 40 | 0.2 | 0.8 | 51 |
| 50 | 0.1 | 0.8 | 52 |
| 100 | 0.2 | 0.7 | 56 |
| 150 | 0.2 | 0.6 | 60 |
| 200 | 0.2 | 0.6 | 60 |
| 250 | 0.2 | 0.6 | 64 |
| 1300 | 0.2 | 0.5 | 70 |

**Table 1.** Best development set perplexities depending on $k, \alpha, \beta$.

## 8 Future work

We show in this paper that clustering alphabet symbols before PDFA inference reduces perplexity on new data. Here the clustering algorithm does not depend on the inference procedure. A potential extension would use the infered PDFA to update the clustering. Indeed compatible states define sets of compatible symbols. This property would allow to iteratively adapt the clustering while adapting the precision parameter of the ALERGIA algorithm.

Clustering the alphabet symbols can be considered as a particular type of smoothing. We believe that smoothing is the central issue if we are to improve the performance of learned PDFAs, especially for tasks which face serious data sparseness problems, as in the case of human language systems. Extensive work on smoothing N-gram models has been done in the last decade (see for instance [6, 8, 11]). Adaptation of these smoothing mechamisms to automata that cannot be reduced to N-grams is one of our major goals.

## References

1. N. Abe and M. Warmuth. On the computational complexity of approximating distributions by probabilistic automata. *Machine Learning*, 9:205–260, 1992.
2. P. Brown, V. Della Pietra, P. de Souza, J. Lai, and R. Mercer. Class-based N-gram models of natural language. *Computational Linguistics*, 18(4):467–479, 1992.
3. R. Carrasco and J. Oncina. Learning stochastic regular grammars by means of a state merging method. In *Grammatical Inference and Applications, ICGI'94*, number 862 in Lecture Notes in Artificial Intelligence, pages 139–150. Springer Verlag, 1994.
4. L. Hirschman. Multi-site data collection for a spoken language corpus. In *Proc. of DARPA Speech and Natural Language Workshop*, pages 7–14, 1992.
5. W. Hoeffding. Probability inequalities for sums of bounded random variables. *Journal of the American Statistical Association*, 58(301):13–30, 1963.
6. S.M. Katz. Estimation of probabilities from sparse data for the language model component of a speech recognizer. *IEEE Transactions on Acoustic, Speech and Signal Processing*, 35(3):400–401, 1987.
7. M.J. Kearns, Y. Mansour, D. Ron, R. Rubinfeld, R.E. Schapire, and L. Sellie. On the learnability of discrete distributions. In *Proc. of the 25th Annual ACM Symposium on Theory of Computing*, pages 273–282, 1994.
8. R. Kneser and H. Ney. Improved backing-off for m-gram language modeling. In *International Conference on Acoustic, Speech and Signal Processing*, pages 181–184, 1995.
9. K. Lang. Merge order counts. Technical report, NEC Research Institute, September 1997.
10. K.J. Lang. Random DFA's can be approximately learned from sparse uniform examples. In *5th ACM workshop on Computational Learning Theory*, pages 45–52, 1992.
11. H. Ney, U. Essen, and R. Kneser. On structuring probabilistic dependences in stochastic language modelling. *Computer Speech and Language*, 8:1–38, 1994.
12. H. Ney and R. Knesser. Improved clustering techniques for class-based statistical language modelling. In *European Conference on Speech Communication and Technology*, pages 973–976, Berlin, 1993.
13. J. Oncina and P. García. Inferring regular languages in polynomial update time. In N. Pérez de la Blanca, A. Sanfeliu, and E.Vidal, editors, *Pattern Recognition and Image Analysis*, volume 1 of *Series in Machine Perception and Artificial Intelligence*, pages 49–61. World Scientific, 1992.
14. D. Ron, Y. Singer, and N. Tishby. On the learnability and usage of acyclic probabilistic automata. to appear in Journal of Computer and System Sciences.
15. H. Rulot and E. Vidal. An efficient algorithm for the inference of circuit-free automata. In G. Ferratè, T. Pavlidis, A. Sanfeliu, and H. Bunke, editors, *Advances in Structural and Syntactic Pattern Recognition*, pages 173–184. NATO ASI, Springer-Verlag, 1988.
16. B. Trakhtenbrot and Ya. Barzdin. *Finite Automata: Behavior and Synthesis*. North Holland Pub. Comp., Amsterdam, 1973.

# A Performance Evaluation of Automatic Survey Classifiers

Peter Viechnicki

Department of Linguistics,
The University of Chicago
pdviechn@midway.uchicago.edu,
WWW home page: http://student-www.uchicago.edu/users/pdviechn/

**Abstract.** A novel NLP task, automatic survey coding, is described, and two methods for performing this task are presented. The first method uses a Boolean pattern-matching strategy to code survey responses, while the second uses a vector-based (probabilistic) method. The performance of the two methods is tested and compared on three representative survey datasets. The Boolean method is shown to perform slightly better on average than the vector-based method. Linguistic factors affecting the difficulty of the coding task for each survey are discussed.

## 1 Introduction

Open-ended survey questions have long been problematic in survey research, because of the time and effort necessary to code the resulting responses. The difficulty of coding open-ended responses has resulted in a situation in which open-ended questions are either not asked, or if they are asked, their responses are under-utilized. However, if responses to open-ended questions could be easily coded, they would constitute a potentially rich source of information for survey researchers. Recently, development of new technologies in natural language processing (NLP) and information retrieval (IR) has brought the previously intractable task of automatic survey coding into the realm of possibility.

The survey classification (coding) task can be defined as follows: take a set of textual responses to an open-ended survey question, and assign each response to a category drawn from a set of pre-defined coding categories. Since the goal is to take a set of pre-existing categories and apply them to survey responses as accurately as possible, survey classification is by definition a 'top-down', or 'concept-driven' process. This process can also be referred to as *category assignment,* and is distinguished here from bottom-up processes such as text clustering [17], which force categories to emerge from data. Once the classifier has assigned all the responses to appropriate categories, it should ideally be able to report the accuracy level of its assignments, so that a confidence factor can be established for further quantitative analysis of the coding results. At the same time, the classifier must be flexible enough so that it can be used on other datasets, or be used differentially on the same dataset as different categorization needs arise.

To the author's knowledge, the domain of automatic survey classification has not yet been elucidated, though some preliminary attempts in this direction have been made, e.g. [11], [12]. Though this task has not received a satisfactory solution as yet, it can be approached using the methods of other, better-understood tasks which it resembles. For example, survey classification shares certain important similarities with IR [14], [2] and document routing [16]. For a full discussion of the relationship between survey categorization and other similar tasks, see [18]. But which methods from IR and document routing are best suited to survey classification? In particular, this paper asks, which classification algorithm is more successful on survey data, a Boolean classification algorithm, or a vector-based algorithm? In Boolean classification, a response is assigned to a category IFF the category's logical definition is true for that resp onse. In vector-based classification, a distance is computed between a response and each coding category, and the response is assigned to the closest category. Comparisons of Boolean and vector-based (probabilistic) retrieval strategies have been extensively discussed in the IR literature [7], [15]. Though the issue is by no means solved, the consensus within the IR field seems to be that vector-based retrieval strategies offer more flexibility and better performance for most users than Boolean strategies do; for a concise review of the factors involved, see [2]. The question is worth asking again for survey classification, because of the different nature of the task as well as differences in the input data [18]. This paper reports the results of testing Boolean and vector-based classification algorithms against each other on representative survey datasets.

## 2 Description of Automatic Classification Algorithms

The two automatic classification methods to be compared are the Boolean method, exemplified by SPSS's TextSmart version 1.1, and the weighted vector-based method, exemplified by Solomon.

### 2.1 Boolean Classification: TextSmart 1.1

TextSmart is a commercial application for PC's specifically designed to categorize survey responses. TextSmart processes a set of responses to a survey question in the following way. A set of indexing terms is created from the set of all unique stems in the response set, minus a standard stop-list of function words, enriched by a small custom thesaurus. Each response can then be represented as a vector of ones and zeroes, corresponding to the presence or absence of the indexing terms in that response. Within TextSmart, category assignment proceeds as follows. The response categories are defined by user-selected key words, linked together by the Boolean operators AND, OR, or NOT. Once the categories have been defined, each response vector is compared to a category definition, and if that category definition is true for that response, then the response is assigned to that category. In cases where more than one Boolean category definition is true for a response, that response is assigned to the first category in the sequential list of categories. In cases where no category definition is true for a response, the response is assigned to a default category OTHER.

## 2.2 Weighted Vector-based Classification: Solomon

The weighted vector-based classifier, Solomon, is implemented in PERL on a UNIX mainframe running SunOS, and is loosely modeled on the SMART system [14]. It classifies survey responses as follows. First, it represents all responses as weighted vectors of positive real numbers, whose bits correspond to the weights of each indexing term in the response. The indexing terms used to create the vectors are the set of all unique word-stems in the response set, minus the same stop list used by TextSmart, minus stems whose total frequency in the response collection is 1, and minus stems whose 'Inverse Document Frequency' (IDF) is less than 1.5 [15], where $IDF_k$, the Inverse document frequency of term $k$ is defined as follows:

$$IDF_k = \ln(n) - \ln(DOCFREQ_k) + 1 \tag{1}$$

where $n$ is the number of responses in the survey, and $DOCFREQ_k$ is the number of responses in which term $k$ appears. The vector for each response is formed of the weighted value for each indexing term in succession, where the weighted value is the product of the term's $IDF$ and its frequency in the particular response. Vectors for each classification category are formed in the same way, from the user-defined query strings.

The distance between each response and each category vector is calculated as a function of the cosine of the angle between the two vectors, where the distance between a response vector $\mathbf{r}$ and a category vector $\mathbf{c}$ is defined as follows:

$$DISTANCE_{rc} = \frac{(1 - \cos\theta)}{2} \tag{2}$$

where $\cos\theta$ is the inner product of the two vectors divided by the product of their lengths. Once distances have been produced between each response and each coding category, each response is then assigned to the category which is located the shortest distance away. If no category vector is closer than a threshold $\epsilon$, then the response is assigned to the default OTHER category.

The key difference between the two algorithms is that the Boolean classifier treats each category definition as either true or false for a given response; conflicts where multiple Boolean categories are true for a single response are resolved by assigning the response to the first category in the ordered list of categories. The vector-based algorithm, on the other hand, computes a numerical distance from each category to each response. It then selects the closest category for a response, and assigns the response to that category, as long as the smallest distance is less than the threshold $\epsilon$.

# 3   Testing Methods

Tests were performed on three survey datasets to determine which classification algorithm was more effective, the Boolean algorithm or the vector-based algorithm.

## 3.1   Datasets

The datasets used for testing were chosen to be representative of typical mid-size social science surveys. The three datasets were taken from the National Opinion Research Center's (NORC) General Social Survey (GSS); details of data collection procedures can be found in [4]. Since the datasets had been hand-coded by NORC's professional survey researchers, the accuracy of the machine codes for each dataset could be adequately assessed by comparing them to NORC's codes. The first dataset used is derived from a survey conducted in 1996, and comprises a set of 367 responses to the question:

> If you have ever anticipated a nervous breakdown, what did you do about it? [4]

NORC classified these responses according to what source of help the respondent mentioned first for dealing with his/her nervous breakdown, using the following categories:

*Classification Categories for Breakdown Dataset*

**Family**  Family is source of help ($n = 57$).

**Friend**  Source of help is non-family, non-professional, including friends, neighbors, and co-workers ($n = 33$).

**Group**  Source of help is a group such as Alcoholics Anonymous or other self-help group ($n = 2$).

**Clergy**  Source of help is a professional, but not a mental health specialist; this category includes clergymen, family doctors and other non-specialist physicians, nurses, and teachers ($n = 55$).

**Psychiatrist**  Source of help is a professional mental health specialist, such as a therapist, a psychiatrist, a psychologist, or a counselor ($n = 56$).

**Agency**  Source of help is a professional agency such as a hospital, social service agency, or rehabilitation center ($n = 16$).

**Other**  Source of help does not fit any of the above categories ($n = 148$).

This dataset will be referred to as the *Breakdown* dataset.

In the second survey, also performed in 1996, 1370 respondents were asked the following question:

> Within the past month, think about the last time you felt really angry, irritated or annoyed. Could you describe in a couple of sentences what made you feel that way - what the situation was? [4]

The NORC coders classified the 1370 responses according to nature of the situation which the respondent described, using the following categories:

### Classification Categories for Angry_At Dataset

**Angrywrk** Situation involved work ($n = 345$).
**Angryfam** Situation involved family ($n = 275$).
**Angrygvt** Situation involved government or government officials ($n = 74$).
**Wrk&Fam** Situation involved both work and family ($n = 27$).
**Wrk&Gvt** Situation involved both work and government ($n = 8$).
**Fam&Gvt** Situation involved both family and government ($n = 16$).
**Other** Situation did not fit the above categories ($n = 625$).

This set of responses will be referred to as the *Angry_At* dataset.

The third dataset is a subset of responses from the *Angry_At* dataset, coded using different categories; the intention was to test the effects of applying different category schemes to the same set of responses. The dataset contains 460 responses, which the NORC coders grouped into the following categories, according to why the respondent had gotten angry: [4]

### Classification Categories for Angry_Why Dataset

**Self** Respondent angry at self because of something he/she did ($n = 29$).
**Prevented** Respondent angry at another person who kept him/her from doing something he/she wanted to do ($n = 36$).
**Critical** Respondent angry at someone who was critical, insulting, or disrespectful (must be some direct and overt action) ($n = 88$).
**Demanding** Respondent angry at someone who demanded too much from him/her ($n = 60$).
**Expect** Respondent angry at someone who failed to do something they were supposed to do ($n = 196$).
**Other** Situation does not fit into above categories ($n = 51$).

This subset of responses will be referred to as the *Angry_Why* dataset.

## 3.2 Testing Procedures

Each dataset was imported into TextSmart, and Boolean category definitions were created using suggestions from the NORC codebook as keywords. Additional terms which were high in frequency were added to the category definitions to improve coding accuracy.[1] Responses were then assigned to that category whose Boolean definition was true for the response text , and responses which fit into no category were assigned to OTHER. If multiple category definitions were true for a single response, then the response was assigned to the first true

---

[1] For example, the Boolean query which defined the category ANGRYWRK in the *Angry_At* dataset was: 'boss' OR 'job' OR 'coworker(s)' OR 'co-worker(s)' OR 'company' OR 'office' OR 'partner' OR 'working'.

category in the sequential list of categories. Codes for each response were then exported to the mainframe for scoring.

Next, each survey was processed by Solomon. The survey responses were automatically indexed as described in **2.2** above. Natural-language category definitions were then generated using the same keywords as were used for TextSmart's Boolean category definitions (expanded to include synonyms from TextSmart's thesaurus).[2] Solomon then created vectors for each category definition as described in **2.2** above, and assigned each response to the closest category vector. Codes for each response were then exported for scoring. Because the same keywords in were used in Solomon's categories as in TextSmart's categories, the only relevant differences between the two programs are their different representations of responses and categories, and their different category assignment algorithms.

## 3.3 Accuracy Scoring

Because there is no standard way of evaluating text classifiers [10], a method was developed to fit the needs of this task.[3] Scoring proceeded as follows. Two diagnostic measures were calculated for each dataset, error rate and agreement coefficient. Error rate is the most typical measure for assessing the performance of different classifiers [6], and can be determined empirically by running the classifiers on test sets of data. Here, error rate of each classification algorithm as compared to the human codes was calculated as a simple percentage of responses incorrectly categorized. In order to derive a confidence factor for the error rate, its variance and standard deviation were calculated by splitting each dataset into five random samples, and comparing the error rate for each of those samples to the overall error rate.

The second measure of classifier accuracy presented in this study is Cohen's $\kappa$ agreement coefficient [3], which measures the correlation between the codes of two independent raters classifying the same categorical data. Agreement is measured by $0 < \kappa < 1$; $\kappa = 0$ indicates chance agreement; and $\kappa = 1$ indicates perfect agreement. Cohen's $\kappa$ is more informative of classifier performance than simple error rate because an objective psychometric scale for Cohen's $\kappa$ can be defined [9], which allows the two classification algorithms to be evaluated according to what their respective $\kappa$ scores are. A further advantage of Cohen's $\kappa$ for this test is that Cohen's $\kappa$ is not based on the assumption that the codes generated by one rater are objectively 'correct'. (For a fuller discussion of the different evaluation metrics, see [18].) In this test, Cohen's $\kappa$ is presented for each classification algorithm for each of the three surveys, calculated by comparing TextSmart's and Solomon's codes against NORC's codes.

---

[2] For example, Solomon's query for the category ANGRYWRK in the *Angry_At* dataset was: 'Give me responses for people who are angry at situations involving their boss or job or coworker or co-worker or coworkers or something that happened at their company or office, or involving a partner while working.'

[3] Because the categories used for these datasets were exhaustive and mutually exclusive, evaluation metrics based on the concepts 'recall' and 'precision' (e.g. [10]) will not work here.

A question that arises is, what kind of agreement can be expected given the nature of the data? When two people code the same survey, how closely do they agree? Preliminary data calculated from surveys similar to the ones used in this test indicate an average agreement coefficient of $\kappa = 0.81$ for multiple human raters. If either classification algorithm were able to achieve a comparable score, then it would be functioning with approximately the same level of accuracy as a human coder on these surveys.

## 4 Results

Results for Boolean and Vector-based classification algorithms are presented for each dataset in **4.1** through **4.3**. The results are summarized in **4.4**.

### 4.1 Breakdown Dataset

Results for the two classification algorithms on the *Breakdown* dataset are presented in Table 1 below:

**Table 1.** Results for Breakdown dataset

|  | Boolean | Vector-based |
|---|---|---|
| Error rate (%) | 25.34 | 35.42 |
| variance | 41.36 | 60.72 |
| st.deviation | 6.43 | 7.79 |
| Cohen's $\kappa$ | 0.668 | 0.544 |

**Discussion** The Boolean classification algorithm was quite successful on this dataset: its error rate was only 25.34%, and its Cohen's $\kappa$ score of 0.668 indicates 'substantial' agreement with the NORC codes, according to Landis and Koch's psychometric scale [9]. The vector-based algorithm was slightly less successful, but still achieved an error rate of only 35.42% and a 'moderate' level of agreement, $\kappa = 0.544$. For both the Boolean and the vector-based methods, the variance and standard deviation of the error rate are comparatively small, indicating that the error rate is well-representative of the whole dataset.

Errors made by TextSmart fall into two broad categories: cases where multiple categories were true for a single response, and cases where respondents used unexpected words in their reponse, instead of TextSmart's expected keywords. A response from the first class is shown below, coded by NORC as PSYCHIATRIST, but assigned by TextSmart to GROUP:

'Went for individual therapy, then group therapy.'

This response fit the Boolean definition both for GROUP and for PSYCHIATRIST; TextSmart resolved the conflict by assigning the response to the first category in order, which was GROUP. Without more advanced conflict resolution procedures, these sorts of mistakes will continue to occur.

The second class of mistakes made by TextSmart is exemplified by the following response, which NORC coded as CLERGY, but TextSmart assigned to OTHER:

> 'First, I got about 6 valiums and I went to my ob-gyn and she told me I didn't need the valium, she told me to talk to everyone and anyone and it worked. It took about 2 months.'

TextSmart was unable to identify 'ob-gyn' as an example of a non-mental health doctor, hence the error. This category CLERGY was difficult to learn because its definition ('non-mental health professionals') was somewhat vague, and could be referred to using a variety of words. A more highly-developed thesaurus might have avoided some of these problems.

The errors made by Solomon on this dataset are cases in which Solomon was unable to assign appropriate weightings to multiple indexing terms within the same response. For example, the following response was coded by NORC as OTHER, but by Solomon as FAMILY:

> 'I accepted the responsibility. I can't let my family down. My wife had to quit work. She's expecting any day now.'

In this case, the respondent does mention family, but as a motivation for his course of action rather than as his source of help; Solomon, however, has no way of distinguishing between different semantic roles for family terms. Without at least a rudimentary knowledge of semantics, errors of these classes will be hard for either automatic classifier to overcome.

## 4.2 Angry_At Dataset

Results for the two classification algorithms on the *Angry_At* dataset are presented in Table 2 below:

**Table 2.** Results for Angry_At dataset

|                | Boolean | Vector-based |
|----------------|---------|--------------|
| Error rate (%) | 53.54   | 54.85        |
| variance       | 419.63  | 207.27       |
| st.deviation   | 20.48   | 14.40        |
| Cohen's $\kappa$ | 0.209 | 0.151        |

**Discussion:** Both classification algorithms had more difficulty categorizing this dataset, but both performed well over chance (defined as 86%). Their error rates are almost identical, 53.54% for the Boolean method, and 54.85% for the vector-based method. Note that the standard deviations of their respective error rates are higher in this dataset than in the previous one, indicating that the confidence factor of error rate is not as high. The different agreement coefficients are better discriminators of true classification performance on this dataset: the Boolean algorithm achieved a level of 'slight' with $\kappa = 0.209$, while the vector-based method displayed 'poor' agreement, $\kappa = 0.151$.

Where the Boolean algorithm differed significantly from the vector-based algorithm was on the category ANGRYWRK. TextSmart agreed with NORC in 38% of responses in this category, whereas Solomon agreed with NORC in only 16%, indicating that the Boolean algorithm was more sensitive to the semantics of this category than the vector-based algorithm was. A typical example where TextSmart agreed with NORC in assigning the response to ANGRYWRK but Solomon disagreed by assigning the response to OTHER is below:

> 'I was at work and I had to re-do a project because someone didn't have time.'

Even though this response contained the word 'work', its vector was still not within the threshold value for assignment into any category, so Solomon classified it as OTHER. In cases like this one, vector-based classification algorithms seem to introduce a level of uncertainty into the category assignment process which can hinder proper assignment.

## 4.3   Angry_Why Dataset

Results for the two classification algorithms on the *Angry_Why* dataset are presented in Table 3 below:

**Table 3.** Results for Angry_Why dataset

|                 | Boolean | Vector-based |
|-----------------|---------|--------------|
| Error rate (%)  | 72.83   | 78.91        |
| variance        | 105.44  | 66.99        |
| st.deviation    | 10.27   | 8.18         |
| Cohen's $\kappa$ | 0.117   | 0.076        |

**Discussion** Both classification algorithms performed poorly on this classification task. The error rate for the vector-based algorithm, at 78.91%, was only slightly above chance performance, i.e. 83%. The Boolean algorithm performed only slightly better, with 72.83% error rate. All of the categories in this dataset were difficult to learn; neither classifier agreed with NORC's codes for any category above 31%. These difficulties can be traced to two factors. First, the categories in *Angry_Why* were defined using verbs, unlike the categories for the *Breakdown* and *Angry_At* datasets, which were defined mainly using nouns (see 3.1 for category definitions). Second, since the categories in this survey shared semantic features with each other, proper assignment of responses to the categories in this dataset requires two or more semantic decisions, where other datasets require only one semantic decision to categorize each response (see **5.2** for further discussion).

## 4.4 Summary of results

Below are summarized the results for both classification algorithms for the three datasets. In each graph, dataset 1 refers to *Breakdown*, dataset 2 refers to *Angry_At*, and dataset 3 refers to *Angry_Why*.

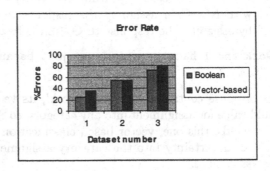

**Fig. 1.** Error rate (%) by classifier for three survey datasets

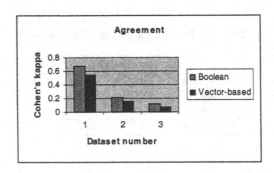

**Fig. 2.** Agreement coefficient by classifier for three survey datasets

The general pattern which emerges from these results is that the Boolean algorithm performs slightly better than the vector-based algorithm across the board. Cohen's $\kappa$ is more effective at separating the classifiers on a performance scale than is simple error rate. However, the differences between the two classification algorithms on the same dataset are far less significant than the differences between the performances of both classifiers across the three datasets. These latter differences are discussed below.

# 5 General Discussion

At least two factors can be identified as contributing to the different performance of the automatic classifiers on the different datasets: first, consistency of language employed by respondents; and second, the semantics of the category definitions themselves.

## 5.1 Consistency of Response Language

The easiest response-sets for machines to classify will be those whose language is most consistent from respondent to respondent. By consistency of language is meant the extent to which respondents choose the same words and linguistic structures to express similar concepts. Different levels of consistency can be seen in the language used in the *Breakdown* and the *Angry_At* datasets: respondents used more consistent language in the former dataset than in the latter [18]. *Breakdown* has more consistent language than *Angry_At* for a number of reasons. First, the universes which the two surveys refer to are different: when one is asked what one did about a nervous breakdown, a more limited range of answers is imaginable than when one is asked to describe a situation that made one angry. Second, respondents to *Breakdown* used more stock phrases, such as 'sought professional help', than respondents to *Angry_At* used. Conversely, respondents to *Angry_At* used freer, less formulaic language, as reflected in the greater degree of dialectal variation between responses. Third, the design of the question used in *Breakdown* was more constraining than the one used in *Angry_At*. The *Breakdown* question constrained respondents to answer by naming an action which they, the respondent, had taken, whereas the *Angry_At* question allowed respondents to describe any situation at all, so long as it had made them angry. These factors collectively make the language of *Breakdown* more consistent than that of *Angry_At*, and hence lead to better classifier performance on *Breakdown* than on *Angry_At*.

## 5.2 Effects of Semantics of Category Definitions

Another important factor affecting classifier performance is the semantics of the category codes into which the survey is to be classified. An example of this factor can be seen by comparing *Angry_Why* with *Angry_At*. These surveys used highly similar response-sets (the *Angry_Why* response set was a subset of *Angry_At*), yet both automatic classifiers performed much better on *Angry_At* than on *Angry_Why*. The difference in performance must lie in the differences between the category-sets. *Angry_At* was comparatively easy to classify because its category definitions were mainly expressed in terms of nouns such as 'work', 'boss', 'job', etc. (see **3.1** above). *Angry_Why*, on the other hand, used categories which were mainly expressed with verbs, such as 'ask', 'demand', 'criticize', 'insult'. Because verbs are more polysemous than nouns are [8], and shift their meanings more than nouns do, category definitions based on verbs will tend to be less meaningful than definitions based on nouns. As a result, automatic classifiers will perform better if their category definitions are based on nouns than on verbs.

Another factor affecting classifier performance on these two datasets is the fact that the definitions of the categories in *Angry_Why* share more semantic features with one another than do those in *Angry_At* [18]. Because the *Angry_At* categories share few semantic features with each other, they can be identified with what Rosch [13] calls 'basic-level categories', also known as 'generic' categories [1]. On the other hand the *Angry_Why* categories are best analyzed as subordinate to the basic category level [13]. It is likely that automatic classifiers will perform much better when the categories used are basic-level categories, because the greater amount of shared features within categories and fewer shared features between categories will allow the classifier to distinguish the categories more accurately. When the coding categories are subordinate-level, more semantic decisions will be necessary to disambiguate them from other categories, an d hence the classification task will be more difficult.

## 6   Conclusions

Results of tests on three datasets showed that the Boolean survey classification algorithm has a slight but consistent edge in performance over the vector-based classification algorithm. This pattern was less visible from the raw error rates of the two classifiers, and more visible from their respective agreement coefficients.

More significant than the differences between the two classification algorithms was their combined pattern of performance on different datasets, using different category-sets. Both classifiers performed well on the same datasets, and poorly on the same datasets. These differences can be traced to: 1) Differences in the consistency of response language, due to differences in question design and cultural factors; 2) Differences in the specificity-level of the categories, and the number of semantic decisions necessary to classify responses into those categories.

## References

1. Berlin, B. (1978) 'Ethnobiological classification.' In E. Rosch and B. Lloyd (eds.) *Cognition and Categorization*, pp. 9-27. Hillsdale, New Jersey: Lawrence Erlbaum.
2. Bookstein, A., (1985) 'Probability and fuzzy-set applications to information retrieval.' In M. Williams (ed.), *Annual Review of Information Science and Technology* **20**:117-151.
3. Cohen, J. (1960) 'A coefficient of agreement for nominal scales.' *Education and Psychological Measurement* **20**:37-46.
4. Davis, J., and Smith, T. (1996) *General Social Surveys, 1972-1996: Cumulative Codebook*. Chicago: National Opinion Research Center.
5. Deerwester, S., Dumais, S., Furnas, G., Landauer, T., and Harshman, R. (1990) 'Indexing by latent semantic analysis.' *Journal of the American Society for Information Science* **41(6)**.
6. Duda, R., and Hart, P. (1973) *Pattern Classification and Scene Analysis*. New York: John Wiley & Sons.

7. Ellis, D. (1990) *New Horizons in Information Retrieval*. London: Library Association.

8. Fellbaum, C. (1993) 'English verbs as a semantic net.' In G. Miller (ed.) *Five Papers on Wordnet*. http://www.cogsci.princeton.edu/~wn.

9. Landis, J., and Koch, G. (1977) 'The measurement of observer agreement for categorical data.' *Biometrics* **33**:159-174.

10. Lewis, D. (1992) 'An evaluation of phrasal and clustered representations on a text categorization task.' *ACM-SIGIR'92*, pp. 37-50.

11. Pratt, D., and Mays, J. (1989) 'Automatic coding of transcript data for a survey of recent college graduates.' *Proceedings of the Section on Survey Methods of the American Statistical Association Annual Meeting*,pp. 796-801.

12. Raud, R., and Fallig, M. (1995) 'Automating the coding process with neural networks.' http://www.monmouth.com/~rraud/autocode.html.

13. Rosch, E. (1978) 'Principles of categorization.' In E. Rosch and B. Lloyd (eds.) *Cognition and Categorization*, pp. 28-49. Hillsdale, New Jersey: Lawrence Erlbaum.

14. Salton, G. (ed.) (1971) *The SMART Retrieval System - Experiments in Automatic Document Processing*. Englewood Cliffs, New Jersey: Prentice-Hall.

15. Salton, G., and McGill, M. (1983) *Introduction to Modern Information Retrieval*. New York: McGraw-Hill.

16. Schuetze, H., Hull, D., and Pedersen, P. (1995) 'A comparison of classifiers and document representations for the routing problem.' *ACM-SIGIR'95*, pp. 229-237.

17. Thomas, T. (1994) 'Concept extraction applied to text analysis of medical records.' *Los Alamos Science* **22**:145-148.

18. Viechnicki, P. (1997) 'A comparison of classification algorithms for a survey coding task.' http://student-www.uchicago.edu/users/pdviechn/comp.html.

# Pattern Discovery in Biosequences

Alvis Brāzma[1], Inge Jonassen[2], Jaak Vilo[3], and Esko Ukkonen[3]

[1] EMBL Outstation - Hinxton, European Bioinformatics Institute
Wellcome Trust Genome Campus, Hinxton, Cambridge CB10 1SD, UK
e-mail: brazma@ebi.ac.uk
[2] Department of Informatics, University of Bergen,
HIB, N5020 Bergen, Norway
e-mail: inge@ii.uib.no
[3] Department of Computer Science, University of Helsinki
P.O.Box 26, FIN-00014 University of Helsinki, Finland
e-mail: vilo,ukkonen@cs.helsinki.fi

**Abstract.** We discuss the problem of algorithmic discovery of patterns common to sets of sequences and its applications to computational biology. We formulate a three step paradigm for pattern discovery, which is based on choosing the hypothesis space, designing the function rating a pattern in respect to the given sequences, and developing an algorithm finding the highest rating patterns. We give some examples of implementing this paradigm, and present experimental results of discovering new patterns in sets of biosequences. In these experiments the sets of given sequences are noisy, that is, many of the sequences given as belonging to the family, actually do not belong to the family. Nevertheless our algorithms have been able to identify biologically sound patterns. In particular we present novel results of discovering transcription factor binding sites from the complete set of over 6000 sequences, taken from the yeast genome upstream to the potential genes.

## 1 Introduction

The biological macromolecules DNA, RNA, and proteins are essentially chains of relatively small building blocks of fairly limited variety - four *nucleotides* for DNA and RNA, and twenty *amino acids* for proteins. Making a certain abstraction, these molecules can be considered as strings over alphabets of four or twenty letters, respectively. We will call such strings *biosequences* or simply *sequences*.

DNA sequencing projects, which aim at determining the biosequences corresponding to DNA molecules, have produced sequences of the total length of more than a billion characters. The genome, i.e., the complete DNA, of the first bacterial organism *H. Influenzae*, having roughly 1.7 million nucleotides, has been sequenced in 1995. This was followed by sequencing many other microbial organisms and the yeast *S.Cerevisiae* (12 million nucleotides). The complete human genome (3 billion nucleotides) is expected to be completed within next decade. These sequences are stored in databases and are a rich source of data for algorithmic problems.

Recently, with DNA sequencing becoming a routine, and the amount of sequence data almost doubling every year, the algorithmic methods for their analysis are becoming ever more important. Sequence data analysis frequently involves some grammar inference related tasks. Applying formal grammars for describing DNA sequences has been proposed, for instance, by David Searls [11]. Some examples of inference problems are the prediction of RNA or protein structure, prediction of genes, prediction of active sites or protein binding sites.

Biosequences can be grouped in *families*, a family being a set of sequences believed to be biologically (i.e., evolutionary, structurally, functionally, or otherwise) related. Many of the protein families have been collected in the protein family database PROSITE [4]. Finding characterizations of biosequence families is an important sequence analysis problem. If a feature common to all known sequences of a family is found, then it is likely that this particular feature is important for the biological role of the family. By a feature we mean a pattern of symbols.

Formal grammars[1] provide an obvious way of sequence family characterization - given a family, we would like to have a grammar describing this family. Such an approach has been used, for instance, in the PROSITE database, where for many families a regular expression type pattern is given such that most of the sequences in the family match this pattern. An instance of a type of patterns used in the PROSITE database is A-[CD]-x(2,3)-E. This pattern matches all the sequences containing a substring beginning by A followed by C or D, followed by from 2 to 3 arbitrary characters, followed by E.

In this paper we will describe some attempts of algorithmically finding simple grammars characterizing biosequence families from sample sequences. In the simplest case we are given a set of sequences belonging to the family (*positive examples*), and possibly another set of of sequences not belonging to the family (*negative examples*), and we wish to find a grammar approximately describing the family[2]. We prefer simpler descriptions, therefore, we will probably have to compromise between how well the grammar approximates the family, and how simple it is.

In many cases we cannot be sure that all our positive examples really belong to the family, and the negative examples are outside the family. Therefore, a more general problem is, given a set of sequences intersecting with the family, and possibly another set intersecting with the family in a lesser degree, find a grammar approximately describing the family.

Note that in general we do not know all the family members *a priori*, as we are given only examples of the family members. Consequently, unless we make

---

[1] We use the term *grammars* in a broad sense that includes different formalisms for specifying patterns in sequences.

[2] There may be various ways how to interpret "approximately describing". One possibility is to require that the ratio of the number of the sequences in the intersection of the biosequence family and the language of the grammar, divided by the number of sequences in the symmetric difference of the biosequence family and the language of the grammar, is relatively small.

certain assumptions about the family properties, the problem cannot be solved algorithmically in principle (if there are no restrictions on the possible families, we can always extend the family in the way opposite to the predictions of the chosen algorithm). The fact that the sequences in a family are biologically related puts some constraints on the family. For instance, if the family sequences are evolutionary related, we can sometimes assume that they have been generated in a certain probabilistic process by a stochastic grammar, and we can try to use the Bayesian inference to find the most probable grammar [7, 8].

Ultimately any algorithmic approach will be tested in biological applications. Therefore we can take a more pragmatic approach and try to develop algorithms which, given a set of sequences believed to be the family members, return grammars that are biologically sound for the particular family. Most of the existing approaches are based on the following three step paradigm [6]:

1. choose the class of grammars that will be used for family characterization (i.e., the hypothesis space);
2. design a rating function that, given (a) a set of positive and, possibly, negative examples, and (b) a grammar, returns the rating of this grammar in respect to the examples;
3. develop an algorithm that, given a set of examples, returns a grammar with relatively high rating (ideally with the best rating).

Choosing the class of grammars involves making a compromise between its descriptive power and the size of the hypothesis space that can be explored efficiently. The rating of the grammar should apparently increase with the number of positive examples belonging to the language defined by the grammar, and decrease with the negative ones, and also to reflect in some way our *a priori* knowledge about the family. After we have chosen the class of grammars and the rating function, we have to solve an optimization problem: given the examples, find the grammar of the highest rating. The ultimate test of the method will be the biological soundness of the discovered grammars.

In the next sections we will give a more formal definition of the problem that we are attacking and discuss in more detail the mentioned three step paradigm. We mention some of the grammars, rating functions, and algorithmic principles of the approaches studied so far. Then, we will discuss some applications and new results. We will conclude with some open problems.

## 2   Problem formulation

We will concentrate on very simple grammars, and at the same time on a nontrivial problem of discovering such grammars from rather noisy sets of examples (i.e., many of the sequences given as positive examples may actually be negative, and vice versa). Our grammars will be various subclasses of a certain generalization of regular patterns of Angluin [2] and Shinohara [29].

Let $\Sigma = \{a_1, \ldots, a_m\}$ be an alphabet called the *basic alphabet*. Biosequences (or simply sequences) are strings over this alphabet.

Let $K_1, \ldots, K_n$ be nonempty subsets of $\Sigma$, such that each subset contains more than one element. Let $\Gamma = \{b_1, \ldots, b_n\}$ be another alphabet disjoint with $\Sigma$, and let us define $L(b_i) = K_i$ $(i = 1, \ldots, n)$. Let us also assume that $L(a_i) = \{a_i\}$, for $a_i \in \Sigma$. In practice each $K_i$ is a class of in some way related amino-acids or nucleotides, and $b_i$ is the character denoting this class. The character $b_i$ standing for the whole $\Sigma$, effectively meaning the *wild-card* (or *don't-care*) character, is denoted by $x$.

We define a *flexible wild-card of length between $p$ and $q$* as an expression of the type $x(p, q)$, where $p$ and $q$ are non-negative integers and $p \leq q$. We define $L(x(p, q))$ as the set of all words over $\Sigma$ of length between $p$ and $q$, (i.e., $L(x(p, q)) = \{\alpha \in \Sigma^* \mid p \leq |\alpha| \leq q\}$). Let $X$ be the set of all flexible wild-cards $x(p, q)$ for all $0 \leq p \leq q$. Let $*$ be a character such that $* \notin \Sigma \cup \Gamma$, and let $L(*) = \Sigma^*$, (i.e., $*$ is the wild-card of unrestricted length).

We define a *generalized regular pattern* $\pi$ as a string over the alphabet $\Sigma \cup \Gamma \cup X \cup \{*\}$. We define the *language* $L(\pi)$ of pattern $\pi$, where $\pi = c_1 \ldots c_r$, and $c_i \in \Sigma \cup \Gamma \cup X \cup \{*\}$, as

$$L(\pi) = \{\zeta_1 \ldots \zeta_r \mid \zeta_1 \in L(c_1), \ldots, \zeta_r \in L(c_r)\}.$$

A pattern $\pi$ *matches* a string $\alpha$ if $\alpha \in L(\pi)$. The class of languages that can be expressed by generalized regular patterns is a subset of regular languages. From now on, by a *pattern* we will understand a generalized regular pattern. Note that the regular patterns of [29] are a subclass of our patterns (for a regular pattern, $\pi$ is a string over the alphabet $\Sigma \cup \{*\}$).

We will be frequently interested in patterns of the form $\pi = *\pi'*$, where $\pi'$ does not contain any $*$ character. If $\pi' \in \Sigma^*$, then $\pi$ is called a *substring pattern*. If $\Sigma$ is the alphabet of amino acids, and $\pi' \in (\Sigma \cup \Gamma \cup X)^*$, then the subclass effectively corresponds to the class of patterns used in PROSITE database. (The notation in the PROSITE database is slightly different. A character of the alphabet $\Gamma$ denoting a group of basic characters, say $\{A, B, C\}$ is denoted as [ABC], the initial and final $*$ are skipped, and the characters in the pattern are separated by -. The wild-cards $x(c, c)$ are abbreviated to $x(c)$.)

We define a *union of patterns* as an expression of the type $\pi_1 + \ldots + \pi_k$, where $\pi_i$ $(1 \leq i \leq k)$ is a pattern and $+ \notin \Sigma \cup \Gamma$. The language of the union is defined as

$$L(\pi_1 + \ldots + \pi_k) = L(\pi_1) \cup \ldots \cup L(\pi_k).$$

Further on by a *grammar* we will understand a pattern or a union of patterns.

Informally the problems we are attacking in this paper can be described as follows.

1. *The family characterization problem:* given a set of sequences $S$, find a grammar "characterizing" $S$.
2. *The family classification problem:* given two sets of sequences $S_+$ and $S_-$, find a grammar "distinguishing" the sequences in $S_+$ from the sequences in $S_-$.

The phrases "characterizing" and "distinguishing", are defined by introducing a *rating function* $R(\gamma, S)$ (or, $R(\gamma, S_+, S_-)$ for the classification problem), which given a pattern $\gamma$ and a set $S$ (or two sets $S_+$ and $S_-$, respectively) returns a real number rating how good the pattern $\pi$ is for the set $S$ (or the sets $S_+$ and $S_-$, respectively). The problem becomes:

> *Given a set of sequences $S$ (or two sets of sequences $S_+$ and $S_-$), find the grammar $\gamma$ from the given subclass such that the value of $R(\gamma, S)$ (or, $R(\gamma, S_+, S_-)$, respectively) is the maximal.*

In practice we are interested not only in the highest scoring grammar, but in several high scoring grammars, so that the final choice can be made by human experts.

## 3  Rating functions

Formally, any real-valued function that uses a set (two sets) of sequences and a grammar as arguments, can be used as a rating function. Nevertheless, to be meaningful for our original real-world problem, evidently the rating function should rate higher the grammars that include more positive and less negative examples in their languages. It should also in some way take into account Occam's Razor principle of rating simpler grammars higher (note that in the case of characterization problem this cannot be done in a straight-forward way). There may be many other heuristic factors that reflect our *a priori* knowledge about the properties of the family, which can be taken into account when designing a meaningful rating function. Different rating functions ranging from simple counts of number of matches in positive and negative sets, to quite complicated statistical or information theory considerations have been introduced, for instance, in [16, 18, 19, 23, 28, 32, 33, 39].

We will discuss in more detail two rating functions that we will use later. Both are designed specifically for the case when the level of noise, i.e., the number of misclassified examples, can be very high.

### 3.1  A rating function for the classification problem

This rating function is based on a ratio of the number of positive examples matching the pattern divided by the number of negative examples matching the pattern. Additionally we require that the pattern matches some minimal number of positive examples (in practice this number may be very small). Thus, the rating function depends on some threshold $t$, and can be described as

$$R_t(\pi, S_+, S_-) = \begin{cases} \frac{|S_+ \cap L(\pi)|}{|S_- \cap L(\pi)|}, & \text{if } |S_+ \cap L(\pi)| \ge t \text{ and } |S_- \cap L(\pi)| > 0 \\ \infty, & \text{if } |S_+ \cap L(\pi)| \ge t \text{ and } |S_- \cap L(\pi)| = 0 \quad (1) \\ 0, & \text{otherwise} \end{cases}$$

Note that this ratio is proportional to the conditional probability that the example is positive if it matches the pattern, divided by the conditional probability that the example is negative, if it does not match the pattern. This rating function does not use the Occam's Razor principle of rating simpler patterns higher. We can take this partially into account, by rating higher the shorter patterns, that have the same rating according to $R_t(\pi, S_+, S_-)$. We will use this simple rating function in the next section for discovering patterns involved in gene regulation from thousands of examples, simply by trying to separate the genome regions suspected to contain gene regulation elements from random regions in the same genome.

## 3.2 A rating function for the characterization problem

The second rating function that we use is for the characterization problem and is based on the Minimum Description Length (MDL) principle [20, 26], which in our context means that the best grammar is the one which minimizes the sum of

- the length (in bits) of the grammar; and
- the length (in bits) of the data when encoded with the help of the grammar.

Let us describe the application of the MDL principle in more detail for unions of substring patterns.

Let $B_1, \ldots, B_k$ be a partition of a set of sequences $S = \{\alpha_1, \ldots, \alpha_n\}$ (i.e., $B_1, \ldots, B_k$ are disjoint and their union is $S$) and let $\Pi = \{\pi_1, \ldots, \pi_k\}$ be a set of patterns such that the pattern $\pi_j$ matches all the sequences of $B_j$. We call $\Omega = \{(\pi_1, B_1), \ldots, (\pi_k, B_k)\}$ a *cover* of $S$. We call $\Pi$ the *pattern set* of $\Omega$.

For $S = \{\alpha_1, \ldots, \alpha_n\}$ we define $\|S\| = \sum_{j=1}^n |\alpha_j|$, and $|S| = n$. Let us assume that we want to transmit the set of sequences $S$ over some channel. A trivial way would be to transmit $\alpha_1, \ldots, \alpha_n$ one after another. If we abstract from the fact that some delimiters between sequences also have to be transmitted, the message length (in characters) would be $\|S\|$. Suppose that a substring pattern $*\varepsilon*$ is present in all the sequences, i.e., $\alpha_i = \delta_i \varepsilon \zeta_i$, for some $\delta_i, \zeta_i \in \Sigma^*$. Then we can compress the message by first transmitting $\varepsilon$, and then $\delta_1, \zeta_1, \ldots, \delta_n, \zeta_n$. Similarly, if $\Omega = \{(*\varepsilon_j*, B_j) | j = 1, \ldots, k\}$ is a cover of $S$ (i.e., $B_j = \{\delta_i^j \varepsilon_j \zeta_i^j | i = 1, \ldots, |B_j|\}$) , then $S$ can be transmitted using $\Omega$, as:

```
for j = 1 to k do
    send ε_j
    for i = 1 to |B_j| do
        send δ_i^j, send ζ_i^j
```

The message length obtained this way is $M(\Omega) = \|S\| - \sum_{j=1}^k (|B_j| - 1)|\varepsilon_j|$. The MDL principle suggests that the best pattern set $\Pi$ is the pattern set of a cover $\Omega$ that minimizes the message length $M(\Omega)$. The second term

$$C(\Omega) = \sum_{j=1}^k (|B_j| - 1)|\varepsilon_j|$$

in the expression can be considered as the *compression* in comparison to $\|S\|$. Minimizing $M(\Omega)$ equals maximizing $C(\Omega)$ and thus $C$ defines a rating function for pattern set $\Pi$ in respect to $S$.

For generalized regular patterns, when we take into account the frequencies of different alphabet characters and the delimiter problem, these MDL considerations lead to a rating function of the type

$$R(\Omega) = \sum_{j=1}^{k}(u_j|B_j| - w_j), \tag{2}$$

where $u_j$ and $w_j$ are parameters (positive numbers) that depend on the pattern $\pi_j$ and assumptions about various probability distributions. It has been shown in [7] and [8], that under certain Bayesian assumption this rating function maximizes the probability that the particular union of patterns is the "source" of the examples.

## 4  Pattern discovery algorithms

Shinohara [29] studied the problem of restoring regular patterns from a set of positive examples, and proved that this can be done in polynomial time in the total length of examples in the sense of inference in the limit [14]. But this result is not applicable in the case when the example set is noisy.

There are basically two different algorithmic approaches used for pattern discovery in biosequences. The first, which we call the pattern driven (PD) approach, is based on enumerating the pattern space and collecting the patterns with high rating. The PD enumeration does not have to be straight-forward, various methods of provably accurate, as well as heuristic pruning of the search space have been proposed. The second approach starts from the sequences and by "aligning" them progressively builds patterns matching as many sequences as possible. We call this a sequence driven (SD) approach. It is possible to combine both approaches, and the most efficient pruning methods in PD approaches that take into account the given sequences effectively merge them with the SP approaches.

Except for very restricted pattern classes, PD algorithms use time exponential in the pattern length. For substring patterns, low order polynomial time enumeration algorithms can be based on the same techniques as suffix tree building [21,35]. Also, when patterns contain only up to a constant number of non basic alphabet characters, polynomial time algorithms exist. In practice, this number has to be very small as it affects the order of the polynomial. The SD methods can often find patterns of unrestricted length, but if the running time is to be polynomial in the number of input sequences, they are not guaranteed to find the highest rating patterns. This is related to the NP-hardness of the multiple sequence alignment problem [38].

An example of a PD method is Smith *et al.* [30], which starts with enumerating all patterns of the form $a_1\text{-}x(d_1)\text{-}a_2\text{-}x(d_2)\text{-}a_3$, where each $a_i$ is a basic alphabet character (in practice amino acid symbol) and $x(d_i)$ is a wild-card of length $d_i$, for $d_i$ being an integer up to some maximum (in practice, 10). More advanced methods have later been proposed, for example, by Neuwald and Green [23] and Sagot *et al.* [27], who developed an algorithm for a depth-first search of the pattern space represented as a tree, and a pruning mechanism permitting to avoid exploring many patterns that are unlikely to have high fitness values. Extending the method of [23], Jonassen *et al.* [15, 16] have developed a method for the discovery of patterns covering a large subclass of patterns used in PROSITE database.

An example of an SD approach is the method proposed by Smith and Smith [31], which first finds the best pattern common to the most similar pair of sequences and gradually builds up a pattern common to the complete set of sequences. Another example is a method proposed by Vingron and Argos [37], which combines the results of all pairwise sequence comparisons. Both methods have time complexity polynomial in the number and length of the sequences, and can find long and complex patterns. On the other hand, they are not guaranteed to find the highest scoring patterns.

Existing pattern discovery methods have been developed for the analysis of smaller data sets, and cannot realistically be scaled up to analyze the available amount of data. For the analysis of the upstream regions of all genes in yeast (described in Section 5.2) we had a set of 6000 sequences of lengths between 100 and 1200. The number of occurrences for the most interesting patterns were not known a priori. We developed a pattern discovery algorithm based on the suffix tree data structure [21, 35]. The lazy suffix tree generation algorithm [12] was extended for generating the suffixes of all sequences in the set, and further, to generate only the patterns that match the sufficient number of examples. The generated patterns are maintained in a trie structure that is expanded in a systematic way. The patterns are generated simultaneously from the positive and negative examples, thus the exact counts for the occurrences of these patterns (that are essential for the ranking function) in each of the input sets are easy to obtain. The method is described in [36].

As another example let us consider the problem of discovering the set $\Pi$ of patterns that covers the example sequences as defined in Section 3.2. The set $\Pi$ (or actually the associated cover $C$) should maximize the MDL-principle based rating function $R(\Omega)$ described earlier.

Unfortunately we cannot optimize the function $R(\Omega)$ efficiently (it can be shown that it involves solving of the set cover problem [9], which is NP-hard). In many cases we can approximate the best solution within logarithmic factor. Particularly we can prove the following two theorems [8].

We denote the minimum value of $R(\Omega)$ in the given class of patterns by $R_{opt}$.

**Theorem 1.** *There exists an algorithm that, given a set of sequences $S$, finds a substring pattern cover $\Omega_s$ of $S$ such that $R(\Omega_s) \leq R_{opt} \times \log |S| + O(1)$. The running time of the algorithm is $O(|S| \cdot ||S||)$.*

Let us call a pattern a *v-pattern* if it contains no more than a given number $v$ of unlimited or flexible wild-cards.

**Theorem 2.** *There exists an algorithm that, given an integer $v$ and a set of strings $S$, finds a $v$-pattern cover $\Omega$ of $S$, such that $R(\Omega) \leq R_{opt} \times \log |S| + O(1)$. The running time of the algorithm is polynomial in $\|S\|$.*

The algorithms are similar to the well-known greedy set cover algorithm. Roughly they work as follows. Find patterns $\pi_i$ that maximize $R(\pi_i, B_i) = u_i|B_i| - w_i$, for $i = 1, \ldots, |S|$, where $B_i$ is an arbitrary subset of $S$ such that $|B_i| = i$; take the best pattern amongst $\pi_i$; exclude the sequences matching this pattern from $S$; and iterate these steps until the set of the remaining sequences is empty. In the case of substring patterns this can be done rather efficiently using suffix-tree constructions. In the case of more complicated patterns the maximization of $R(\pi_i, B_i)$ for a subset of the given size becomes a much more difficult problem. The proof of Theorem 2 is based on the fact that for patterns with up to some fixed number $v$ of wild-cards there exists only a polynomial number of them matching at least one string from the set $S$. In practice, for larger sets $S$, we cannot consider all the sizes from 1 to $|S|$, but only $i = s, s + s', s + 2s', \ldots, |S|$, for some $s$ and $s'$. Thus we introduce an additional, heuristic, approximation element. Fortunately in practice this is sufficient.

In the case of PROSITE type patterns, the (approximately) best pattern for a subset of the given size can be found, for instance, by the algorithm Pratt [15]. We implemented algorithm called MDL-Pratt by combining Pratt with the above sketched set cover algorithm. An application of this algorithm to biosequences will be described in the next section.

## 5 Applications and experiments

### 5.1 Simultaneous discovery of patterns and subfamilies

We collected a set of 31 protein sequence segments, each of which is believed to contain a chromo domain [24]. Aasland and Stewart identified two subfamilies (subsets); (1) the classical chromo domains linked to chromo shadow domains and (2) the chromo shadow domains [1]. Our sample set contained 8 members of each subfamily.

MDL-Pratt, when run on this set of 31 sequences, produced three patterns given in the Figure 1, covering subsets of sizes 7, 6, and 8 respectively (the remaining 10 sequences were included in the union individually). The first two sets produced by MDL-Pratt correspond closely to the two subfamilies[3] given in [1]. The result indicates that MDL-Pratt can be used to discover family- and subfamily-relationships in a set of sequences and to filter out the "noise".

### 5.2 Discovering gene regulatory elements from complete yeast genome

The 12 million character long complete genome of the yeast *S.Cerevisiae* is publicly available in the database MIPS [13]. It has been estimated that the yeast

---

[3] Compared to the subfamilies, one segment is missing from the first set, and two segments are missing from the second.

1. E-x(0,1)-E-E-[FY]-x-V-E-K-[IV]-[IL]-D-[KR]-R-x(3,4)-G-x-V-x-Y-x-L-K-
   W-K-G-[FY]-x-[ED]-x-[HED]-N-T-W-E-P-x(2)-N-x-[ED]-C-x-[ED]-L-[IL]
   DmHP1_A DvHP1_A HuHP1_A MoMOD1_A MoMOD2_A PcHET1_A PcHET2_A
2. L-x(2,3)-E-[KR]-I-[IL]-G-A-[TS]-D-[TSN]-x-G-[EDR]-L-x-F-L-x(2)-[FW]-
   [KE]-x(2)-D-x-A-[ED]-x-V-x-[AS]-x(2)-A-x(2)-K-x-P-x(2)-[IV]-I-x-F-Y-E
   DmHP1_B DvHP1_B HuHP1_B MoMOD1_B MoMOD2_B PcHET1_B
3. Y-x(0,2)-L-[IV]-K-W-x(6)-[HE]-x-[TS]-W-E-x(4)-[IL]
   DmPc MoMOD3 HuMG44 CfTENV FoSKPY MoCHD1_A MoCHD1_B ScYEZ4_B

**Fig. 1.** The patterns obtained when running MDL-Pratt on the 31 chromo domain sequence segments. The patterns are given in PROSITE notation, and are followed by the names of the sequences (among the initial set of 31 sequence) that matches the pattern. The remaining 10 sequences were represented by singleton sets in the cover.

contains about 6000 genes, i.e., fragments of the DNA that encode the proteins, and the putative genes (so-called open reading frames - ORFs) have been anno-tated in MIPS. Usually each gene has a particular combination of *sites* in the genome where special proteins called *transcription factors* can bind and activate or repress the expression of the gene (see for instance [22]). These sites are spe-cific DNA sequences of length from about 5 to 25 nucleic acids, and in yeast they are usually located within a few hundreds of nucleotides upstream from the gene itself. One transcription factor can bind to different DNA sequences and the set of such sequences can be consider as a sequence family. We can look for descriptions of these families, which essentially will give us the description of the binding sites for the specific transcription factor.

We have studied the upstream regions of all the genes in the yeast looking for patterns that could distinguish upstream regions from other genomic regions, and upstream regions of genes having similar expression profiles[4] from upstream regions of other genes.

We selected all sequences of length 100, 300 and 600 nucleotides upstream to every annotated gene. For each upstream region we also extracted a random region of the same length from the genome. We searched these sets of sequences for all the patterns of some restricted classes (but unrestricted length) that occur in at least some given number (in practice 10) of upstream sequences, and rated these patterns according to the rating function $R_t(\pi, S_+, S_-)$ given in equation (1), treating the random genomic regions as the negative examples. (To test the statistics of the pattern occurrences in these upstream regions we also extracted a second set of random regions, and treated it the same way as upstream regions).

The inspection of the patterns that occur substantially more frequently in upstream regions than in random regions (i.e., having a high rating $R(\pi, S_+, S_-)$)

---

[4] Expression profile of a gene shows the expression rate of that gene during some selected time-period, or essentially the production rate of the protein coded by that gene at different time-points, e.g., during a change in the environment. First such large-scale laboratory experiments have been made for the full genomes thanks to the emerging technology of DNA chips [25].

showed, that many of these can be regarded as "simple" (i.e., easily compressible) sequences (e.g., *AAAAAAATA*). (This is not unexpected, as upstream regions have higher A-T content, while genes rarely contain long simple sequences.) Among other patterns, one of the top scoring was a pattern *AAAGCGAAA*. Matching this pattern against the transcription factor database TRANSFAC [40] we found that it was similar to the binding site for the yeast transcription factor URS1 [34]. The pattern given for URS1 in TRANSFAC is *AAACGAAACGAAACGAAACTAA*. This pattern has only one match in the entire yeast genome, which means that it is probably longer than the actual binding site. The pattern *AAAGCGAAA* gives 115 matches in the upstream regions of length 600, and 254 matches in the total yeast genome.

The above studies show that, given a genome with annotated genes, some putative transcription factor binding site descriptions can be generated without any other background knowledge.

We have also used the information about the gene expression profiles to extract some small subsets of genes that potentially share similar regulation mechanisms and hence also transcription factor binding sites. We used the data from the yeast gene expression studies reported in [10][5] and clustered the genes by similarities in their expression profiles. These clusters were used for the discovery of patterns "characteristic" to the upstream regions of these clusters, i.e., patterns with high rating $R_t(\pi, S_+, S_-)$, where $S_+$ are the sequences from the cluster, and $S_-$ are the other upstream sequences. Some examples of the discovered patterns are *CCCCT* matching 64% (35 out of 55) of sequences in the respective cluster and 21% (1280 out of 5921) of remaining upstream regions (and thus getting a score of 2.95), *CxxCCCxT* (score 2.88), *TxCxxCCC* (score 2.85), and *TxAGGG* (score 2.27). Some of these patterns are similar to known binding sites for the transcription factors known to be relevant to the diauxic shift in yeast.

# 6 Open problems

In the Introduction we formulated the problem of biosequence family characterization, while later we were solving the mathematical problem of finding the highest rating grammar for the given set of sequences. Our argumentation why these two problems are related, is experimental: the computing experiments show that the grammars that we have found from the sample sequences are biologically sound for the particular families. This is partly achieved by choosing "appropriate" rating functions, although the way we designed these functions were purely heuristic. We did not use any formal principles how to choose these functions, or provide any theory why they should work. Developing such a theory might improve the understanding of the pattern discovery problem. Further on, we could assume certain constraints on the sets of sequences representing families,

---

[5] J. F. DeRisi et al. [10] have studied the relative expression rate changes of all (over 6000) genes of yeast during the diauxic shift from anaerobic (fermentation) to aerobic (respiration) metabolism.

and study what rating functions are appropriate for the particular constraints. For instance, we could assume that the family sequences are obtained in some stochastic mutation process from sequences that belong to some regular language [5], or in some other stochastic process.

The algorithms that we used for finding patterns with high rating were sufficiently efficient for our experiments. Still, for instance, when analyzing the upstream regions in the yeast genome, we had to restrict the experiments to rather simple classes of patterns. With the volume of biosequence data exponentially growing, more efficient algorithms will be needed. We consider developing such algorithms as one of the most important problems in computational biology.

In this paper we have considered discovery of only very simple grammars. Some more complicated grammars used for characterization of biosequence families are decision trees over regular patterns [3] and hidden Markov models [17]. However, the discovery of such grammars from only sequence information in presence of many misclassified sequences is very difficult because of the too large hypothesis space, as well, as the presence of noise (i.e. misclassified sequences) that can easily be incorporated into the model. The discovery of such more complicated grammars from pure sequence information in presence of noise is an important problem for future research.

# 7 Acknowledgments

A.Brazma was supported by BIOSTANDARDS project at the European Bioinformatics Institute and partially by the Research Council of Latvia. I.Jonassen was supported by grants from the Norwegian Research Council. J.Vilo was supported by grant 8745 from the Academy of Finland.

# References

1. R. Aasland and F. A. Stewart. The chromo shadow domain, a second chromo domain in heterchromatin-binding protein 1, HP1. *Nucleic Acids Research*, 23:3168–3173, 1995.
2. D. Angluin. Finding patterns common to a set of strings. *J. of Comp. and Syst. Sci.*, 21:46–62, 1980.
3. S. Arikawa, S. Miyano, A. Shinohara, S. Kuhara, Y. Mukouchi, and T. Shinohara. A Machine Discovery from Amino Acid Sequences by Decision Trees over Regular Patterns. *New Generation Computing*, pages 361–375, 1993.
4. A. Bairoch. PROSITE: a dictionary of sites and patterns in proteins. *Nucleic Acids Research*, 20:2013–2018, 1992.
5. A. Brazma and K. Cerans. Noise-tolerant inductive synthesis of regular expressions from good examples. *New Generation Computing*, 15(1):105–140, 1997.
6. A. Brazma, I. Jonassen, I.Eidhammer, and D. Gilbert. Approaches to automatic discovery of patterns in biosequences. *Journal of Computational Biology*, (2):(to appear), 1998.
7. A. Brazma, I. Jonassen, E. Ukkonen, and J. Vilo. Discovering patterns and subfamilies in biosequences. In *Proc. of Fourth International Conference on Intelligent Systems for Molecular Biology*, pages 34–43. AAAI Press, 1996.

8. A. Brazma, E. Ukkonen, and J. Vilo. Discovering unbounded unions of regular pattern languages from positive examples. In *Proceedings of 7th Annual International Symposium on Algorithms and Computation (ISAAC-96), Lect. Notes in Computer Science*, volume 1178, pages 95–104, December 1996.

9. V. Chvátal. A greedy heuristic for the set-covering problem. *Math. Oper. Res.*, 4:233–235, 1979.

10. J. L. DeRisi, V. R. Iyer, and P. O. Brown. Exploring the metabolic and genetic control of gene expression on a genomic scale. *Science*, 278:680–686, 1997.

11. S. Dong and D. B. Searls. Gene structure prediction by linguistic methods. *Genomics*, 23:540–551, 1992.

12. R. Giegerich and S. Kurtz. A comparison of imperative and purely functional suffix tree constructions. *Science of Computer Programming*, 25(2–3):187–218, 1995.

13. A. Goffeau, B. G. Barrell, H. Bussey, R. W. Davis, B. Dujon, H. Feldmann, F. Galibert, J. D. Hoheisel, C. Jacq, M. Johnston, E. J. Louis, H. W. Mewes, Y. Murakami, P. Philippsen, H. Tettelin, and S. G. Oliver. Life with 6000 genes. *Science*, 274:546–567, 1996.

14. E. M. Gold. Language identification in the limit. *Information and Control*, 10:447–474, 1967.

15. I. Jonassen. Efficient discovery of conserved patterns using a pattern graph. *Comput. Appl. Biosci.*, 13:509–522, 1997.

16. I. Jonassen, J. F. Collins, and D. G. Higgins. Finding flexible patterns in unaligned protein sequences. *Prot. Sci.*, 4(8):1587–1595, 1995.

17. A. Krogh, M. Brown, I. S. Mian, K. Sjoelander, and D. Haussler. Hidden Markov model in computational biology. Applications to protein modelling. *Journal of Molecular Biology*, 235:1501–1531, 1994.

18. R. Lathrop, T. Webster, R. Smith, P. Winston, and T. Smith. Integrating AI with sequence analysis. In L. Hunter, editor, *Artificial Intelligence and Molecular Biology*, pages 211–258. AAAI Press/The MIT Press, 1993.

19. C. E. Lawrence, S. F. Altschul, M. S. Boguski, J. S. Liu, A. F. Neuwald, and J. C. Wootton. Detecting Subtle Sequence Signals: A Gibbs Sampling Strategy for Multiple Alignment. *Science*, 262:208–214, Oct 1993.

20. M. Li and P. Vitanyi. *An introduction to Kolmogorov complexity and its applications*. Springer-Verlag, New York, 1993.

21. E. M. McCreight. A space–economical suffix tree construction algorithm. *Journal of the ACM*, 23:262–272, 1976.

22. P. J. Mitchell and R. Tijan. Transcription regulation in mammalian cells by sequence-specific DNA binding proteins. *Science*, 245:371–378, 1989.

23. A. F. Neuwald and P. Green. Detecting patterns in protein sequences. *Journal of Molecular Biology*, 239:689–712, 1994.

24. R. Paro and D. H. Hogness. The polycomb protein shares a homologous domain with a heterochromatin-associated protein of drosophila. In *Proc. Natl. Acad. Sci. USA*, pages 263–267, Jan 1991.

25. G. Ramsay. DNA chips: State-of-the-art. *Nature Biotechnology*, 16:40–44, 1998.

26. J. Rissanen. Modeling by the shortest data description. *Automatica-J.IFAC*, 14:465–471, 1978.

27. M-F. Sagot, A. Viari, and H. Soldano. Multiple sequence comparison: a peptide matching approach. In Z. Galil and E. Ukkonen, editors, *Proc. of 6th Annual Symposium on Combinatorial Pattern Matching, Lecture Notes in Computer Science 937*, pages 366–385. Springer, July 1995.

28. R. F. Sewell and R. Durbin. Method for calculation of probability of matching a bounded regular expression in a random data string. *Journal of Computational Biology*, 2:25–31, 1995.
29. T. Shinohara. Polynomial time inference of extended regular pattern languages. *Lect. Notes in Computer Science*, 147:115–127, 1983.
30. H. O. Smith, T. M. Annau, and S. Chandrasegaran. Finding sequence motifs in groups of functionally related proteins. In *Proc. Natl. Acad. Sci. USA*, pages 826–830, Jan 1990.
31. R. F. Smith and T. F. Smith. Automatic generation of primary sequence patterns from sets of related protein sequences. In *Proc. Natl. Acad. Sci. USA*, pages 118–122, Jan 1990.
32. R. Staden. Methods for calculating the probabilities of finding patterns in sequences. *CABIOS*, 5:89–96, 1989.
33. R. Staden. Methods for discovering novel motifs in nucleic acid sequences. *CABIOS*, 5(4):293–298, 1989.
34. T. G. Turi and J. C. Loper. Multiple regulatory elements control expression of the gene encoding the Saccharomyces cerevisiae cytochrome P450, lanosterol 14 alpha-demethylase (ERG11). *Journal of Biological Chemistry*, 267:2046–2056, 1992.
35. E. Ukkonen. On-line construction of suffix trees. *Algorithmica*, 14:249–260, 1995.
36. J. Vilo. Discovering frequent patterns from strings. Technical Report C-1998-9, Department of Computer Science, University of Helsinki, P. O. Bo 26, FIN-00014, University of Helsinki, May 1998.
37. M. Vingron and P. Argos. Motif Recognition and Alignment for Many Sequences by Comparison of Dot-matrices. *Journal of Molecular Biology*, 218:33–43, 1991.
38. L. Wang and T. Jiang. One the complexity of multiple sequence alignment. *Journal of Computational Biology*, 1(4):337–348, 1994.
39. M. S. Waterman, R. Arratia, and D. J. Galas. Pattern Recognition in Several Sequences: Consensus and Alignment. *Bulletin of Mathematical Biology*, 46(4):515–527, 1984.
40. E. Wingender, P. Dietze, H. Karas, and R. Knuppel. TRANSFAC: a database of transcriptional factors and their DNA binding sites. *Nucleic Acids Research*, 24:238–241, 1996.

# Author Index

# Springer
# and the
# environment

At Springer we firmly believe that an international science publisher has a special obligation to the environment, and our corporate policies consistently reflect this conviction.
We also expect our business partners – paper mills, printers, packaging manufacturers, etc. – to commit themselves to using materials and production processes that do not harm the environment. The paper in this book is made from low- or no-chlorine pulp and is acid free, in conformance with international standards for paper permanency.

 Springer

# Lecture Notes in Artificial Intelligence (LNAI)

# Lecture Notes in Computer Science

# Lecture Notes in Artificial Intelligence    4597

Edited by J. G. Carbonell and J. Siekmann

Subseries of Lecture Notes in Computer Science

Petra Perner (Ed.)

# Advances
# in Data Mining

Theoretical Aspects and Applications

7th Industrial Conference, ICDM 2007
Leipzig, Germany, July 14-18, 2007
Proceedings

 Springer

Series Editors

Jaime G. Carbonell, Carnegie Mellon University, Pittsburgh, PA, USA
Jörg Siekmann, University of Saarland, Saarbrücken, Germany

Volume Editor

Petra Perner
Institute of Computer Vision and Applied Computer Sciences (ibai)
Arno-Nitzsche-Str. 43, 04277 Leipzig, Germany
E-mail: pperner@ibai-institut.de

Library of Congress Control Number: 2007929837

CR Subject Classification (1998): I.2.6, I.2, H.2.8, K.4.4, J.3, I.4, J.6, J.1

LNCS Sublibrary: SL 7 – Artificial Intelligence

ISSN      0302-9743
ISBN-10   3-540-73434-1 Springer Berlin Heidelberg New York
ISBN-13   978-3-540-73434-5 Springer Berlin Heidelberg New York

Springer is a part of Springer Science+Business Media

springer.com

© Springer-Verlag Berlin Heidelberg 2007
Printed in Germany

Typesetting: Camera-ready by author, data conversion by Scientific Publishing Services, Chennai, India
Printed on acid-free paper      SPIN: 12086436      06/3180      5 4 3 2 1 0

# Preface

ICDM / MLDM Medaillie (limited edition)
Meissner Porcellan, the "White Gold" of King
August the Strongest of Saxonia

ICDM 2007 was the seventh event in the Industrial Conference on Data Mining series and was held in Leipzig (www.data-mining-forum.de).

For this edition the Program Committee received 96 submissions from 24 countries (see Fig. 1).

After the peer-review process, we accepted 25 high-quality papers for oral presentation that are included in this proceedings book. The topics range from aspects of classification and prediction, clustering, Web mining, data mining in medicine, applications of data mining, time series and frequent pattern mining, and association rule mining.

| Germany | 9,30% | 4,17% | China | 9,30% | 1,04% | South Korea | 6,98% | 3,13% |
|---|---|---|---|---|---|---|---|---|
| Czech Republic | 6,98% | 3,13% | USA | 6,98% | 2,08% | UK | 4,65% | 2,08% |
| Portugal | 4,65% | 2,08% | Iran | 4,65% | 2,08% | India | 4,65% | 2,08% |
| Brazil | 4,65% | 1,04% | Hungary | 4,65% | 1,04% | Mexico | 4,65% | 1,04% |
| Finland | 2,33% | 1,04% | Ireland | 2,33% | 1,04% | Slovenia | 2,33% | 1,04% |
| France | 2,33% | 1,04% | Israel | 2,33% | 1,04% | Spain | 2,33% | 1,04% |
| Greece | 2,33% | 1,04% | Italy | 2,33% | 1,04% | Sweden | 2,33% | 1,04% |
| Netherlands | 2,33% | 1,04% | Malaysia | 2,33% | 1,04% | Turkey | 2,33% | 1,04% |

**Fig. 1.** Distribution of papers among countries

Twelve papers were selected for poster presentations that are published in the ICDM Poster Proceedings Volume.

In conjunction with ICDM two workshops were run on special hot application-oriented topics in data mining. The workshop Data Mining in Life Science DMLS 2007 was held the second time this year and the workshop Data Mining in Marketing

DMM 2007 was held for first time this year. Right after ICDM, the International Conference on Machine Learning and Data Mining, MLDM 2007, was held in Leipzig (www.mldm.de)

The invited talk was given by Prof. Richter, titled "Case-Based Reasoning and the Search for Knowledge." The talk illustrated that case-based reasoning on the lower, i.e., more personal levels is quite useful, in particular in comparison with traditional information-retrieval methods.

We saw an increasing number of industrial participants at our conference in the special sessions that covered topics that are important for industry. An invited talk was given by Andrea Ahlemeyer on the topic of "How to Combine Data Mining and Market-Research Technologies?." A discussion forum that described and discussed the occupational image of the data miner was given by Prof. Gentsch from the Business Intelligence Group Inc. Special talks were given by industry staff in a marketing workshop that described the special problems of different industries.

We are pleased to announce that we gave out the best paper award for ICDM for a second time this year.

We also established an MLDM/ICDM/MDA Conference Summary Volume first the time this year, which summarizes the vision of the three conferences and the paper presentations and also provides a "Who is Who" in machine learning and data mining by giving each author the chance to present himself.

We thank members of the Institute of Applied Computer Sciences, Leipzig, Germany (www.ibai-institut.de) who handled the conference as secretariat. We appreciate the help and understanding of the editorial staff at Springer, and in particular Alfred Hofmann, who supported the publication of these proceedings in the LNAI series.

Last, but not least, we wish to thank all the speakers and participants who contributed to the success of the conference.

July 2007                                                           Petra Perner

# Industrial Conference on Data Mining, ICDM 2007

## Chair

Petra Perner            IBaI Leipzig, Germany

## Committee

| | |
|---|---|
| Klaus-Peter Adlassnig | Medical University of Vienna, Austria |
| Andrea Ahlemeyer-Stubbe | ECDM, Gengenbach, Germany |
| Klaus-Dieter Althoff | University of Hildesheim, Germany |
| Chid Apte | IBM Yorktown Heights, USA |
| Isabelle Bichindaritz | University of Washington, USA |
| Leon Bobrowski | Bialystok Technical University, Poland |
| Marc Boullé | France Télécom, France |
| Juan M. Corchado | Universidad de Salamanca, Spain |
| Da Deng | University of Otago, New Zealand |
| Peter Funk | Mälardalen University, Sweden |
| Ron Kenett | KPA Ltd., Israel |
| Eduardo F. Morales | INAOE, Ciencias Computacionales, Mexico |
| Stefania Montani | Università del Piemonte Orientale, Italy |
| Eric Pauwels | CWI Utrecht, The Netherlands |
| Rainer Schmidt | University of Rostock, Germany |
| Stijn Viaene | KU Leuven, Belgium |
| Rob A. Vingerhoeds | Ecole Nationale d'Ingénieurs de Tarbes, France |

## Additional Reviewers

| | |
|---|---|
| Fabrice Clerot | France Télécom R&D |
| Francoise Fessant | France Télécom R&D |
| Carine Hue | France Télécom R&D |
| Vincent Lemaire | France Télécom R&D |

# Table of Contents

# Web Mining

# Data Mining in Medicine

# Applications of Data Mining

# Case Based Reasoning and the Search for Knowledge

Michael M. Richter

Department of Computer Science
University of Calgary, 2500 University Dr.
Calgary, AB, T2N 1N4, Canada
mrichter@cpsc.ucalgary.ca

**Abstract.** A major goal of this paper is to compare Case Based Reasoning with other methods searching for knowledge. We consider knowledge as a resource that can be traded. It has no value in itself; the value is measured by the usefulness of applying it in some process. Such a process has info-needs that have to be satisfied. The concept to measure this is the economical term utility. In general, utility depends on the user and its context, i.e., it is subjective. Here we introduce levels of context from general to individual. We illustrate that Case Based Reasoning on the lower, i.e., more personal levels CBR is quite useful, in particular in comparison with traditional informational retrieval methods.

**Keywords:** Case Based Reasoning, Knowledge, Processes, Utility, Context.

## 1 Introduction

Our starting point is that knowledge and information is some kind of a resource that is used for making processes possible or improving them. Such processes have a certain goal and knowledge is used for achieving it. Therefore knowledge has a certain value; this value is called the utility. In general the utility cannot be defined by looking at the knowledge and the process only. It depends on the specific goal and the person or team performing the process. We refer to is as the context of the user. We distinguish three levels of contexts: A general context that applies to everybody, a group specific context and an individual context. This has an important impact on the problem which knowledge is actually useful.

A major goal of this paper is to compare Case Based Reasoning with other methods to search for knowledge. We show that it is applicable the more specific the context is. For this purpose we discuss the knowledge containers of CBR and pay special attention to similarity, what is the most distinguishing element of CBR. In order to provide relevant knowledge the role of communication between a system and a user is explained and ways towards an optimal dialog is shown. As a final result, we obtain a more sophisticated view under which conditions CBR or related methods can be useful for searching for knowledge.

P. Perner (Ed.): ICDM 2007, LNAI 4597, pp. 1–14, 2007.
© Springer-Verlag Berlin Heidelberg 2007

## 2 From Knowledge Based Systems to Knowledge Management

Knowledge based systems (also called expert systems) were fully automated systems with a strong logic orientation that could be considered that as ordinary programs, written in a declarative language. One had three more or strictly separated phases: Knowledge and requirement collection, planning and design, and execution. The search for knowledge was done by the system builder and there was no need for the user to do that at application time. Knowledge management was therefore almost not an issue for the user.

Despite many successes of such systems several limitations were known. In particular, the systems were not at all able to handle problems where the strict sequential view had to be given up. These are problem situation that demanded an interleaving of the phases, and one had to start with design and application before the knowledge acquisition was finished. If the system could not solve the problem a human could not help as a "partner". One of the most important consequences was that human and machine activities should be executed interleaved and concurrently. In engineering disciplines the term "socio-technical processes" was used for such processes, it was later on adapted by computer science. In such processes humans and machines formed a team, they were partners.

The birth of knowledge management was a process, not an event. One observed that they were not simply technical extensions of classical expert systems but demanded the development of systematic investigations. The humans played an essential role in such systems; they had the creativity and the responsibilities. The computer support concentrated (besides the use of pure computations) on providing needed knowledge "at the right time to the right agent in the needed form".

## 3 Knowledge, Processes, and Utility

In knowledge based systems one started to regard knowledge as a resource. This was no new insight; it was present long before the electronic age. One could trade, buy, and sell knowledge. Like any other resource, it was needed for some purpose. This purpose was to plan, design, and execute processes. For processes a goal and evaluation methods need to be assigned. On this basis it is possible to measure the success and the improvement of the process performance when using some resource.

### 3.1 Processes and Utilities

Processes have goal, i.e., a utility in economical terms. Utility has a relational and a functional form. The relational form is a preference relation and the functional form a real valued function. The preference relation "b is preferred over a" is denoted by a < b; a ≲ b says that a is not preferred over b and a ~ b denotes indifference.

Utility functions u operate on actions, whole processes or decisions. They assign real numbers as values to the elements of their domain A:

$$u: A \to \Re.$$

A utility function always induces a preference relation by:

$$b \text{ is preferred over } c \iff u(b) > u(c).$$

Both, utility functions and preference relations are usually complex. User preferences are easier to acquire than utility functions. In Mathematics, utility theory is an established discipline. Among the mathematical approaches the most prominent one is the von Neumann-Morgenstern theory [12]. However, it is an old insight that often utilities are not formulated in mathematical terms. Utility is rather subjective because it depends on the special situation of the person or the company. The term "subjective" is not used here in the sense of psychology; it just means that there is no model of the utility visible to the outside. A detailed discussion of subjective expected utility has been given in [19], which was a highly influential book. The rational behaviour of humans is expressed in the equation

$$subjective\ value = subjective\ probability \times subjective\ utility.$$

The subjective value has to be maximized. The subjective view becomes in particular important if knowledge is needed. The utility of knowledge is strongly influenced by the goal and by the knowledge and level of understanding the user has.

### 3.2  Processes and Knowledge

The knowledge and information units needed to perform a process are called the *info-needs* [9]. They are stored in *info-sources* as shown in Figure 1.

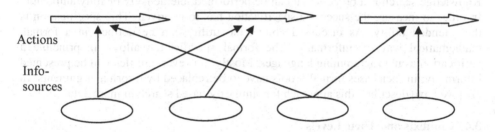

Actions

Info-
sources

**Fig. 1.** Processes, info-needs, info-sources

The agent to take care of this is usually called the knowledge manager who has two tasks:

1) To define the info-sources, to structure them, to fill them, and to apply maintenance.
2) To take care that the agent performing the process obtains the info-needs in the way needed, i.e., in the right form and at the right time.

Structuring and searching for knowledge is not for free. It has costs that can be measured in terms of money, time, inconvenience, and other units. Some financial figures are given in [10].

However, there is not always such a manager and often this agent has limited abilities. Hence, the acting agent has to search on its own for the needed info-sources.

There are basically two ways to provide knowledge. The first one is on demand. That means, a question is presented and an answer is returned. Here the answering agent knows that some knowledge is missing. Nevertheless, often the answer is not very satisfactory. This is mainly due to the fact that the query formulation is incomplete, misleading, or not understandable. The second way is pro-active. Here the knowledge manager has to act on her own; the addressee may not even know that certain knowledge is needed. In many situations, both ways are combined. For instance, a user formulates a query where not only some answer is given but additional information is provided that is useful for the user.

What has to be done is to bridge the gap between the info-needs and the knowledge delivered. As we will see, the width of that gap can be measured by a similarity measure; this is discussed in the section 5.

What has to be observed is that often knowledge search takes place when no knowledge manager is present. For instance, if I am in the process of downloading my program, who is telling me pro-actively that there is a program from another company that is a serious alternative? The best that can happen is that my company has an internal management that supports me. In addition, often it is not clear who searches for the knowledge: The one who needs it or the one who has it? This will be discussed in section 5.3 on communication.

### 3.3 Specifications and Knowledge Search

Knowledge search is a process that can be performed interactively or fully automatic. In order to measure the success a specification has to be given. This specification is the intended utility. As discussed above, the utility can be defined in a formal, mathematical way, or informally. The formal specification allows in principle a verification as in programming languages. Mostly, however, utilities will be presented informally; in such cases formal proofs have to be replaced by informal arguments. In [16] we have described this approach for similarity based search in more detail.

### 3.4 Contexts and Their Levels

In principle, there is usually an infinite amount of knowledge that has a relation to the process of interest. What is actually needed depends on the context in which the process takes place. There are various ways a goal can be missed, for instance if the knowledge is incomplete, too general, confusing, or not understandable. We distinguish external and internal contexts. The external context considers what happens around the performing agent (the specific task, the general circumstances etc.) The internal context is concerned with the knowledge and experience of the agent, its preferences etc. The context can be more or less general.

We define three *context levels* as shown in Figure 2.

1) The general level: Everybody has the same context, for instance, when one searches for the Lufthansa schedule.
2) The group level: There are groups of users and each group has a different context; for instance, different social groups look for different entertainments.
3) The individual level: The context depends on the user, for instance, when one searches for an employee with specific abilities.

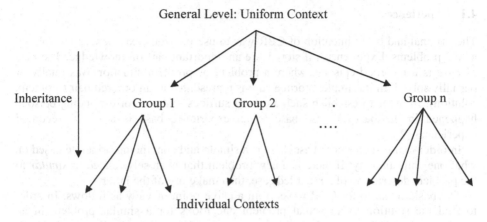

**Fig. 2.** Context Levels

Ordinarily, everybody has utility aspects from all three levels; one is an individual, belongs to one or more groups and shares also some general views. On the general level often one finds mathematical utility function; the more one goes down the more subjective the utilities play a role and the more relevant the internal context will be. There are two major problems associated with contexts:

a)  These contexts are not static, they rather change over time. The speed of change increases the more one comes down to the lower levels; on the general level the change proceeds very slowly. Each change has to be reflected in a system that provides knowledge; this is known as the maintenance task.

b)  The contexts are partially unknown. This is a little problem only on the general level. On the group level it requires, depending on the group, sometimes much effort to acquire it. On the individual level there are mainly two possibilities. The first one is to learn preferences from user's histories; what necessitates that these are recorded. The second possibility is a direct communication with the user,

At the general level general search machines and retrieval techniques are located, like those that search in the web. The more one goes down the levels the more difficulties one has with general machines. The recent activities on level three run under the name *personalization and context awareness*. This means, one is not only task-centric but at least as much user-centric.

## 4   Case Based Reasoning

Case Based Reasoning (CBR) is now an established technology. We start with a short introduction into the basic concepts. They are all concentrated around search for knowledge and it is justified to call CBR a knowledge search technology. An overview over CBR and knowledge management is given in [3].

## 4.1 Experiences

The original and basic intention of CBR was to use previous experiences for solving actual problems. Experiences, if stored, are an important part of knowledge. The idea of *case* is a recorded episode, where a problem or problem situation was totally or partially solved. In its simplest form a case is represented as an ordered pair (problem, solution). In order to establish such a case it suffices that the corresponding episode happened in the past. A case base or an experience base is a set of recorded experiences [2].

In order to use such a case base there is a simple and convincing principle based on what one calls analogy: If there is a new problem that is closely related or *similar* to the problem description of a recorded case, then make use of the latter.

The basic scenario for CBR looks from a naive point of view as follows: In order to find the solution to an actual problem one looks for a similar problem in an experience base, takes the solution from the past and uses it for finding a solution to the actual problem. This is shown in the Aamodt-Plaza-Cycle [1] in Figure 3. The cycle describes the CBR activities only superficially and in the sequel we will discuss several aspects in more detail.

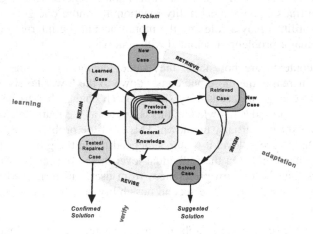

**Fig. 3.** Aamodt-Plaza Cycle

When the problem is presented to the system a search in the case base takes place. This search is more involved than a data base search because one is not looking for a specific object but rather for a "relatively useful" one. The formal concept to do this is the similarity measure that selects the most similar problem (the nearest neighbour); this is discussed in section 5.

The retrieved case is then reused. This does not mean that it is used directly as retrieved because the old solution may not quite do the job because of the difference of the old and the new problem. To take care of this, some adaptation takes place.

The solution obtained in this way is tested and verified. If the solution passes the tests, then one has a new experience that can be stored in the case base. This means, a learning step took place.

CBR as introduced so far is some kind of *experience mining*. Many successful applications of CBR have been done in this area. The approach has been extended to more general situations where experiences are recorded. Major examples are the experience factory [2] and the technique *lessons learned* [23]. The approaches differ technically but aim at the same goal.

## 4.2 Question Answering and General Search for Knowledge

The applications of CBR have been generalized extensively. For this, it was necessary to extend the notion of similarity. It had not only to compare old and new problems, but much more general objects. Therefore similarity measures played the role of *"partnership measures"*. The intention of partnership is that both objects cooperate more or less well as partners. Because the possible partners may come from different sets the similarity measure has to compare quite different objects. In the extended view, the measure compares objects like the ones seen in Table 1. This view is presently dominating and the term "case base" from CBR is often replaced by expressions like product base, document base, etc.

**Table 1.** General partners

| Info-needs | Info-Sources |
|---|---|
| Knowledge needed | Documents |
| Questions | Answers |
| Functionalities | Machines |
| Desired products | Available products |

The similarity measure is a way to measure the distance between the objects of interest numerically. The nearest neighbour search then bridges the gap between these objects, for instance, between info-needs and info-sources. The main difficulty is to perform the search context oriented.

A crucial point is also, that, despite the widening of the applications, the essentials of the CBR technology could still be used. Moreover, even the same tools could be applied. An example is CBR-Works [8] from empolis and its extension orange [13].

An example on the group level context is the Simatic *Knowledge Manager,* a comprehensive industrial application developed by empolis. It provides online support and self-service for the group of customers and technicians of Siemens Company. The system is integrated in the call center of the company. The queries can be formulated in natural language

## 4.3 Case Based Reasoning and Its Knowledge Containers

A convenient way to describe Case-Based Reasoning is to introduce the concept of *knowledge containers* [15, 17]. Knowledge containers are not sub modules of a system, because they do not solve any sub problem. They rather are description elements that can be filled with knowledge units. In CBR we identify four major knowledge containers as shown in Figure 4.

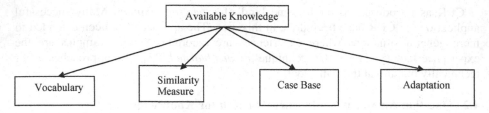

There is an interaction between the containers:

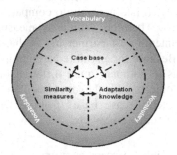

**Fig. 4.** Knowledge Containers

The containers are not simply empty barrels to be filled. The opposite is the case; they are equipped with a partially complex structure.

The importance of the vocabulary container is the same as in any knowledge based system: What has no name cannot be discussed. In order to be convenient for the user each term can be enriched by an explanatory record, the term record (see [14]). The term record can contain synonyms, quasi-synonyms, advises when and how to use, sources etc.

The case base is, mainly for retrieval purposes, usually equipped with additional structures. Structured case bases run also under the name *case memory*.

The similarity container and the adaptation container are discussed below in section 5.

All the containers are strongly related to each other and the knowledge can be shifted between the containers. This gives CBR systems a large degree of flexibility. It allows to employ learning methods and to keep up with context changes.

The containers play a role when a CBR system is maintained or constructed; then the containers have to be filled. We distinguish two phases:

a) The planning (or compilation) phase: That contains everything that happens before an actual problem is presented;
b) The run time phase.

For ordinary programs and knowledge based systems, one has to understand all knowledge that enters the system. In a CBR system, the cases need not to be understood at compile time, they are just filled into the case base container. Understanding the cases is only necessary at run time when they are actually used. This has the advantage that one can start with a system that works somehow, but not necessarily very well. At a later time the system can be improved.

The construction of the measure is called similarity assessment; the measure has to be understood at compile time. This is obvious because it has to reflect the goals and the context. But here also we make use of the flexibility: One can start with a very general context and later on make it more specific.

When going down the hierarchy of context levels all knowledge containers have to be adapted. For instance, individuals have a special vocabulary; terms not of interest should be removed. Adaptation needs are personal and rules should be corrected.

# 5 Similarity Measures and Adaptation Rules

Both, adaptation rules and similarity measures are of particular interest. Similarity is by far the most important concept in CBR; adaptation rules provide a number of difficulties.

## 5.1 Similarity Measures

We introduce some notation for standard concepts. Similarity measures sim are defined on ordered pairs:

$$\text{sim: } U \times U \rightarrow [0, 1] \text{ or sim: } U \times V \rightarrow [0, 1]$$

for sets U and V. For simplicity we assume that all objects from U and V are represented as attribute-value vectors.

The role of $a$ and $b$ in sim($a$, $b$) is not symmetric; usually $a$ is a given object (called the *query object*) and $b$ is a possible *answer object*.

In a sales situation the customer sends a demand to the shop and the query objects are the customer demanded products and the answer objects are the available products. Hence we have $V \subseteq U$. In information retrieval U and V are different. In more general situations like document search U and V may be disjoint.

We denote the nearest *neighbour relation* by NN (a, b), stating that b is a nearest neighbour of a. A CBR system performs two types of computations:

- Computing the similarity value between objects a and b.
- Searching for the nearest neighbour(s).

During the search the nearest neighbour is approximated and in each search step a similarity computation is done.

## 5.2 Adaptation Rules

The rules in the adaptation container take care of changing the retrieved objects for proper use. The situation is that despite the similarity of the answer and the query object, both are different. A serious problem arises if there are very many rules that can be applied. This occurs, for instance, when one searches in catalogues. Often only less than one percent of the available products are listed explicitly; all others are obtained from them by modifications or additions. This excludes in the first place a simple nearest neighbor search because the measure is not informed about the adaptation rules. On the other hand, the adaptation rules do not k now anything about the intended utility and similarity. What one would like to have is a measure that takes the utility of a product after adaptation into account.

An approach to obtain such a measure is described in [22]. It uses genetic algorithms for learning the measure from user feedback. It extends the technique in [22] to learn local similarity measures. This is a non-trivial example of shifting knowledge from the adaptation container to the similarity container.

### 5.3 Retrieval and Communication

Retrieval is in the first place just search. This view is in so far insufficient as the query may initially not be formulated completely and precisely. Both, the user and the knowledge provider are cooperating in this respect. They are both trying to dig out the aspects relevant for the user and the context; this requires a communication. Such *personalization* efforts play presently a big role in recommender systems. They are, among others, intended to present some choice of a set of alternatives of decisions to the user.

As an example for communication problems in the form of a dialog we consider a sales process. In electronic commerce the seller is presented as a web site and this seller gets an initial query from the buyer that needs to be completed. There are a number of conditions for a successful sales talk. The main ones are that it is understandable to the user and it is short. The danger for the web site is that the buyer may become annoyed and will quite before a sale took place. Hence, the dialog has to focus on two aspects simultaneously: To obtain more insight into the context of the user and to come closer to the optimal product to sell.

Several CBR approaches to automated sales dialogs have been suggested so far [20]. The approaches have in common that there is a list of possible questions to ask the user that are presented in the form of attributes where the user has to fill in some value. One goal is to ask a minimal number of questions, i.e., to reduce the dialog length. Fort this purpose, questions will be selected according to their relevance for the customer's utility function. Initially, this is only partially known and has to be completed during the dialog. It is guided by some selection mechanism that selects the next question. This choice is dominated by getting the most information for the intended product. One way is, to make use of ordinary entropy. This, however, neglects the fact that some aspects of the utility of the user are already known. A refined view says that a question leads to a new dialog situation $s$ in which all products that do not exactly match the current attribute value are excluded. This view leads to the information content shown in (1), where A is the selected attribute.

$$extgain(s, A) := - \sum_{v \in \{v_1, ..., v_m\}} p_v \cdot \log_2 \left( \frac{\sum_{c \in C} sim(A(c), v)}{|C|} \right) \quad (1)$$

In orenge 3.1, a new attribute selection method was introduced [13]; it is essentially a slight extension to *extgain*. A further refinement is using the variance of similarities. Higher similarity variance in the set of candidate cases implies better discrimination between possible target cases (products) and unsatisfactory. The *simVar* measure is calculated as shown by (2), where $v$ is a value of attribute A.

$$simVar(q,A,v,C) := \frac{1}{|C|} \cdot \sum_{c \in C} \left( sim(q_{A \leftarrow v}, c) - \mu \right)^2 \quad (2)$$

Here we consider the transition of a dialog situation $s$ to the new situation $s'$ by assigning the value $v$ to the query attribute $A$ of query $q$ (denoted $q_{A \leftarrow v}$); $\mu$ is the average value of all similarities, and $C$ again the case base.

Statistical evaluations suggest that among these (and some other) methods there is no single best method for all scenarios. In most experiments *simVar* has outperformed *extgain,* although there is yet no theoretical foundation for that.

### 5.4 Example

CBR-Works provides a user friendly dialog box as shown in Figure 5. The user gets a question (in natural language for providing the wanted value of some attribute that is chosen as described in 5.3. For this, the user is offered the possible alternatives, for instance, by providing a list or a numerical interval. The attributes are weighted and the weights can be changed by the user. If needed, adaptation can take place. The adaptation rules are invisible by the user. The screen shot shows the two nearest neighbors but more alternatives can be offered on demand. There is also the possibility to show details if wanted so.

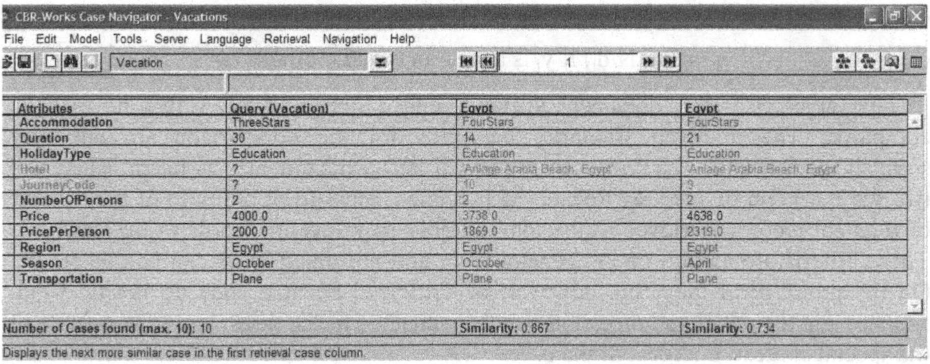
CBR-Works Case Navigator - Vacations
File Edit Model Tools Server Language Retrieval Navigation Help
Vacation
1
Attributes | Query (Vacation) | Egypt | Egypt
Accommodation | ThreeStars | FourStars | FourStars
Duration | 30 | 14 | 21
HolidayType | Education | Education | Education
Hotel | ? | 'Anlage Arabia Beach, Egypt' | 'Anlage Arabia Beach, Egypt'
JourneyCode | ? | 10 | 3
NumberOfPersons | 2 | 2 | 2
Price | 4000.0 | 3738.0 | 4638.0
PricePerPerson | 2000.0 | 1869.0 | 2319.0
Region | Egypt | Egypt | Egypt
Season | October | October | April
Transportation | Plane | Plane | Plane
Number of Cases found (max. 10): 10
Similarity: 0.867
Similarity: 0.734
Displays the next more similar case in the first retrieval case column.

**Fig. 5.** CBR-Works User Interface

The dialog box deals with selling vacations. The user can see where the demands are matched exactly and where not. On the bottom one can see the computed similarities between the query and the offer.

## 6 CBR, Information Retrieval, and Knowledge Extraction

Both, information retrieval and knowledge extraction from texts are concerned with documents. Information retrieval is mostly searching for documents as a whole, while feature extraction searches in one or several documents for useful information.

## 6.1  Information Retrieval and Case Based Reasoning

In this section we compare the traditional vector space model of Information Retrieval (IR) with similarity retrieval in the sense of CBR. Both approaches use similarity measures for describing the usefulness of a document.

In Information Retrieval, the access to a document is done by looking at terms that have been already extracted from the document. The extracted terms form the bridge between the query and the document. Both use the same vocabulary, namely some terms of interest. Which terms are chosen can be based on some knowledge about the domain and the intended user. These terms are compared with the terms in the query.

Each selected term is associated with a term weight that is supposed to reflect the importance of the term. This gives rise to an m-dimensional weight vector that is responsible for the document retrieval. The advantage is that this does not require any additional knowledge. On the other hand, group specific knowledge cannot be entered. A standard approach uses weights on the basis of the term frequency, $f_{ij}$ (the number of occurrence of term $y_j$ in document $x_i$; and the inverse document frequency, $g_j = \log(N/d_j)$, where N is the total number of documents in the collection and $d_j$ is the number of documents containing term $y_i$.

The documents weights $w_{ij}$ and the query weights $v_j$ are

$$w_{kj} = f_{kj} \cdot \log(N/d_j)$$

and

$$v_{ki} = \log(N/d_j) \text{ if } y_j \text{ is a term in q and 0 otherwise.}$$

This gives rise to a document vector d and a query vector v that have to be compared. The involved similarity measures for the comparison are not very sophisticated; usually the *cosine* of a query q and a document d is taken. There are two main criteria of success: Recall and precision, measuring the ratio of the number of relevant records retrieved to the total number of relevant records in the database. These criteria are natural on the general level and not much more can be done there. On the group level they can, however, be criticized because they do not take into account that the recall and precision may be restricted to the documents and queries of the special context and goal of the user.

There are some differences between the vector space approach and the attribute-value representation in CBR. In CBR, the attributes have a domain from which the values are taken. In IR, the vector coordinates are simply numbers; there are no variables that could be instantiated and each coordinate is labelled by a fixed term. In CBR, the weights are parts of the measure; in IR, they are parts of the object representation. It is, however, not difficult to unify the approaches. For this purpose, we introduce for each term an attribute Frequency_t(.) and take the weights as in a weighted Euclidean measure. This measure is equivalent to the measure in the vector space model. Although the principle equivalence, IR is more suitable on the general level while CBR aims at more specific levels.

If the retrieval process is not convincing then both, CBR and IR apply adaptation. The difference is that in CBR the solution is adapted while in IR rather the query is rewritten (because one cannot rewrite a document). A widely used method is query expansion. Here the original query is supplemented with additional terms. The idea is to add such terms to the query that are similar the given ones. This means that the newly introduced terms are close to the old ones with respect to some similarity measure. Automated query expansion uses a frequency measure on pairs of words; i.e., counting how often the words occur together in texts.

This can be based on user feedback, inspection of past optimal queries, or others. In addition, the term weights can be improved; for example; by using statistical information. To some extend query expansion takes care of the user's needs, but only in a very limited way. More refined ways like employing a thesaurus is rarely used.

## 6.2 Information Extraction from Text

Often texts contain useful but hidden information. This happens, for instance, in domains like law, science, medicine etc. For retrieval, IR methods are helpful but rather restricted, like extracting terms. On the other hands, CBR methods are also not directly applicable because the cases are recorded as text. To use them directly, considerable case engineering effort is needed. To overcome this difficulty, natural language processing methods (NLP) seem to be necessary.

An example where this was carried out is the system SMILE, see [7]. This system uses the standard NLP based information extraction system Autoslog [18]. It extracts various kinds of information from the text like certain facts and syntax related information for formulating queries. The cases were legal cases.

A related system on the basis of CBR is jCOLIBRI, [5,11], where a generalizations and learning was applied.

# 7 Conclusion

We described Case Based Reasoning as a knowledge search technology. From this point of view CBR is competing with many other such technologies and the question arises, which one to choose in which situation. There is no general solution to the problem finding an optimal method. One can formulate, however, some directions. For this purpose we introduced levels for contexts. On the general level, existing search machines are superior. The group level occurs often in companies, and there much more expert knowledge is needed. Typical examples of the individual level are provided by e-commerce. Here we can observe a mixture of general search machines and personalization.

# References

1. Aamodt, A., Plaza, E.: Case-Based Reasoning: Foundational Issues, Methodological Variations, and System Approaches. AI Communications 7, 39–59 (1994)
2. Althoff, K.-D., Althoff, B., Althoff, B.A., von Wangenheim, C. G., Tautz, C.: CBR for Experimental Software Engineering. Case-Based Reasoning Technology, 235–254 (1998)
3. Althoff, K.-D., Weber, R.O.: Knowledge Management in Case-Based Reasoning. Knowledge Engineering Review 20(3), 305–310 (2005)
4. Ardito, R., Bara, B.G., Blanzieri, E.: A cognitive Account of Situated Communication COGSCI 2002 (2002)

5. Bello-Tomás, J.J., González-Calero, P.A., Díaz-Agudo, B.: JColibri: an Object-Oriented Framework for Building CBR Systems. In: Funk, P., González Calero, P.A. (eds.) ECCBR 2004. LNCS (LNAI), vol. 3155, Springer, Heidelberg (2004)
6. Bergmann, R., Richter, M.M., Schmitt, S., Stahl, A., Vollrath, I.: Utility-Oriented Matching: A New Research Direction for Case-Based Reasoning. In: Vollrath, I., Schmitt, S., Reimer, U. (eds.) Proc. of the 9th German Workshop on Case-Based Reasoning, GWCBR'01, Baden-Baden, Germany, Baden-Baden, Germany. In: Schnurr, H.-P., Staab, S., Studer, R., Stumme, G., Sure, Y (Hrsg.): Professionelles Wissensmanagement. Shaker Verlag (2001)
7. Brüninghaus, S., Ashley, K.: The Role of Information Extraction in Textual CBR. In: Aha, D.W., Watson, I. (eds.) ICCBR 2001. LNCS (LNAI) (SNLAI), vol. 2080, pp. 74–80. Springer, Heidelberg (2001)
8. CBR-Works    (2003),    sern.ucalgary.ca/courses/SENG/609.13/W2004/06.%20CBR-Works.pdf
9. Holz, H.: Process-Based Knowledge Management Support for Software Engineering, Doctoral Dissertation University of Kaiserslautern, disserertations.de Online-Press (2002)
10. Jacobson, A., Prusak, L.: The Cost of Knowledge. Harvard Business Review (2007)
11. jcolibri (2002) http://gaia.fdi.ucm.es/projects/jcolibri
12. von Neumann, J., Morgenstern, O.: Theory of Games and Behavior, 1953th edn. Princeton University Press, Princeton, NJ (1944)
13. orenge:dialog. In: orenge: Open Retrieval Engine 3.2 Manual. empolis – knowledge management, http://www.km.empolis.com/
14. Richter, M.M.: Terminology in Complex Domains. In: Bock, H., Polasek, W. (eds.) Proc. Of the 19th Annual Conference of the Gesellschaft für Klassifikation. Studies in Classification, Data Analysis and Knowledge Organization, pp. 416–426. Springer, Heidelberg (1995)
15. Richter, M.M.: Introduction. In: Lenz, M., Bartsch-Spörl, B., Burkhard, H.-D., Wess, S. (eds.) Case-Based Reasoning Technology. LNCS (LNAI) (SNLAI), vol. 1400, Springer, Heidelberg (1998)
16. Richter, M.M.: Foundations of Similarity and Utility. In: Proc. FLAIRS07, AAAI Press, Stanford, California (2007)
17. Richter, M.M.: Similarity. In: Perner, P. (ed.) Case-Based Reasoning on Signals and Images, Springer, Heidelberg
18. Riloff, E.: Automatically Extraction Information Patterns from Untagged Text. In: Proc.of the 13th National Conference on Artificial Intelligence, AAAI Press, Stanford, California (1996)
19. Savage, J.L.: 1954 Foundations of Statistics, 2nd Rev. edn. Dover Publications, Mineola (Reprint) (1972)
20. Schmitt, S., Bergmann, F.R.: A formal approach to dialogs with online customers. In: 14th Bled Electronic Commerce Conference (2001)
21. Schmitt, S., Dopichaj, P., Domínguez-Marín, P.: Entropy-based vs. Similarity-influenced: Attribute Selection Methods for Dialogs Tested on Different Electronic Commerce Domains. In: Craw, S., Preece, A.D. (eds.) ECCBR 2002. LNCS (LNAI), vol. 2416, Springer, Heidelberg (2002)
22. Stahl, A.: Learning of Knowledge-Intensive Similarity Measures in Case-Based Reasoning. Kaiserslautern (2003)
23. Weber, R., Aha, D.W., Becerra-Fernandez, I.: Intelligent Lessons Learned Systems. Expert Systems with Applications 20(1), 17–34 (2001)

# Subsets More Representative Than Random Ones

Ilia Nouretdinov

Department of Computer Science
Royal Holloway, University of London
Egham, Surrey TW20 0EX, England
ilia@cs.rhul.ac.uk

**Abstract.** Suppose we have a database that describes a set of objects, and our aim is to find its representative subset of a smaller size. Representativeness here means the measure of quality of prediction when the subset is used instead of the whole set in a typical machine learning procedure. We research how to find a subset that is more representative than a random selection of the same size.

## 1 Introduction

Let us have a training set $Z = \{z_1, \ldots, z_n\}$ and a testing set $Z_T = \{z_{n+1}, \ldots, z_{n+k}\}$, $z_i = (x_i, y_i) \in X \times Y$ where $X = \mathbb{R}^m$ and $Y = \mathbb{R}$.

Suppose $n' < n$ and our aim is to choose a subset $Z' \subset Z$ consisting of $n'$ elements. We call this operation *compression*. We like the most essential information about data $Z$ to be saved in $Z'$.

Suppose we are studying a data set, which is too large to process it directly. To make some conclusion about it, one may take random selection. Such subset is expected to have similar distribution and properties. We can ask the following question. Such selection is preferred to be random, because non-random selection is usually less representative. But a random selection has only random level of represenativeness, not high one! If there are non-random selections, which are less representative than random, then we can expect some other non-random selections to be more representative than random.

So, theoretical point is looking for subsets which are more representative than random. The practical motivation is potential time economy in the empirical comparison procedure.

This work is based mainly on experimental results, but there is some theoretical intuition behind them. To exclude a small amount of typical elements leads to smaller loss of information than to exclude a small amount of marginal elements; but this is not as clear for a larger exclusion.

The idea of our approach is following. We start with a large family of tests for randomness. Other applications of such test for machine learning problems are discussed in [1-4].

Based on this, so-called total randomness deficiency is defined as a function of a set and its element, which is a measure of how this element is informative in comparison to others.

P. Perner (Ed.): ICDM 2007, LNAI 4597, pp. 15–20, 2007.
© Springer-Verlag Berlin Heidelberg 2007

First, we define a method of compression a set of size $q$ into its subset of size $(q - [\log(q)])$, by excluding less informative elements. Next, we compress a set of size $q^2$ into its subset of size $q$, using $q \to (q - [\log(q)])$ compression for different subsets, and some voting procedure.

Experimental check was done on the Boston Housing Dataset. It shows that a selection of subset done by our method performs better than 95% random selections of same size. Additionally, it is almost as good as the whole dataset.

Practically, this method could be useful for the economy of time for comparison different machine learning methods on a training set before applying them to a test set.

In the experimental model of this work, comparison of different machine learning methods is similar to the well-known problem of feature selection (or dimension decrease). We use a nave method of such selection itself, but a specific step is added to this. The samples can be understood (by duality) as features of features, so feature selection can be naturally preceded by feature of feature selection, that is equivalent to our compression of a set into its representative subset.

To sum, this work consists of two parts. First, we describe our method of set compression. It is mainly based on the notion of test for randomness.

The second part is an experimental check. We formulate a practical criterion of representativeness, and then ensure on a real database that $Z'$ fits this criterion better than a random selection of the same size.

## 2    Randomness Theory Background

### 2.1    Tests for Randomness

**Definition 1.** *Suppose $U$ is a linear space, $A \subset U$ is finite, $z \in A$, $I \in \{1, \ldots, N\}$. Then, a function*

$$f : (I, A, z) \to [0, 1]$$

*is called a family of tests for randomness if*

$$\frac{|\{z \in A : f(I, A, z) < \gamma\}|}{|A|} < \gamma$$

*for any fixed $I, A$ and $0 < \gamma < 1$.*

**Definition 2.** *If $f$ is a family of tests for randomness, corresponding total randomness deficiency for an element $z \in A$ is:*

$$\mu_f(z|A) = \sum_I (-\log f(I, A, z)).$$

## 2.2   Example: Test Based on a Method of Prediction

In the papers [2,3] the concept of test for randomness is used as a way of transformation of a method of bare prediction into a method of confident multi-prediction via a test for randomness based on a bare prediction method.

For the current work, we do need all the information for the approaches described in these papers, except the correspondence between methods of prediction and tests for randomness.

So, we need to construct a test for randomness based on a method of bare prediction. Details may be different according to a specific method, but in any case we need to define a measure of strangeness that is a measure of disagreement between a set and its element. For Nearest Neighbour method, disagreement between $z_i$ and $\{z_1, \ldots, z_n)$ is

$$\alpha_i = \frac{\min_{j:j \neq i, y_j = y_i} d(x_i, x_j)}{\min_{j:j \neq i, y_j \neq y_i} d(x_i, x_j)} \tag{1}$$

where $d$ is a metric on $X$.

Let us have a family of different distances $d^1, \ldots, d^N$ For nearest method, the test for randomness is

$$f(I, A, z_i) = \frac{|\{j \mid \alpha_j^I \geq \alpha_i^I\}|}{|A|}. \tag{2}$$

where

$$\alpha_i = |y_i - (y_j \mid j \neq i, dist^I(x_i, x_j) \to \min)| \tag{3}$$

For a method another than Nearest Neighbours, the same idea may work: $\alpha_i$ should be larger if the sample $z_i = (x_i, y_i)$ somehow contradicts the method applied to the whole set $\{z_1, \ldots, z_n\}$, e.g. leave-one-out prediction for it is another than its label.

It can be checked (see e.g. [2]) that this function satisfies the definition of a family of tests for randomness.

## 3   Compression

We base on two ideas: (1) there is a natural correspondence between methods of predictions and tests for randomness; (2) if an example is untypical according to most tests then it is more informative for comparison of corresponding methods of prediction.

### 3.1   Basic Operation

Recall the formula of total randomness deficiency:

$$\mu_f(z|A) = \sum_I \left( -\log f(I, A, z) \right). \tag{4}$$

The family $f$ is variable. We will detail it when describing our experiments.

Now we define the operation $F_r : A \to B$ deleting $r$ the most typical elements $z \in A$ for which $\mu_f(z \mid A)$ is minimal. It is desirable the quantity of such deleted elements be small, otherwise it can affect the distribution too much. This is why we use $r = [\log |A|]$ and do not use basic operation $F_r$ in original form to compress large data sets into little ones.

## 3.2   Next Step of Compression

Let $q$ be a prime number and $|A| = q^2$. Our aim is compression $|A|$ into the set of size $q$.

Fix a numeration of its elements with two indices:

$$A = \{a_{i,j} \mid i, j \in GF_q\} \tag{5}$$

where $GF_q$ is a finite field of the size $q$.

Choose $q^2 + q$ $q$-element subsets of $A$ as follows:

$$A_u = \{a_{i,j} | i = u\} \tag{6}$$

$$A_{u,v} = \{a_{i,j} | j = u + iv\} \tag{7}$$

for $u \in GF_q$, $v \in GF_q$. Such sets hold the following simple properties:

- each $a \in A$ belongs to exactly $q + 1$ different $A_{u,v}$;
- each pair $\{a, b\} \subseteq A$ is a subset of exactly one $A_{u,v}$.

These properties allow running of a voting procedure. Recall that each $F_r(A_{u,v})$ is a subset of $A_{u,v}$ of the size $q - [\log q]$. For each element $z \in A$ let $w(z)$ be the number of different pairs $(u, v)$ such that $z \in F_r(A_{u,v})$. Let $B = F(A)$ consist of $q$ elements with largest $w(z)$. This is called $F : A \to B$ operation with $|A| = q^2$ and $|B| = q$.

## 4   Experimental Check

### 4.1   Data Set

Experiments are done on the Boston Housing Dataset. It contains $n = 401$ training and $k = 105$ test examples, $m = 13$ scalar attributes, and the price (scalar) as a label.

After a linear transformation (extraction of mean value and division by mean square deviation), each attribute has mean value 0 and deviation 1 on the training set. Linear transformation with same coefficients is also applied to the testing set.

### 4.2   Family of Tests

Let

$$f(I, A, z_i) = \frac{|\{j \mid \alpha_j^I \geq \alpha_i^I\}|}{|A|}. \tag{8}$$

with alpha function:

$$\alpha_i = |y_i - (y_j \mid j \neq i, dist^I(x_i, x_j) \to \min)|. \tag{9}$$

It can be checked that this function satisfies the definition of family of tests for randomness.

We suppose $I = 1, \ldots, N = 2^m - 1$ is a numeration of all subsets of the set of 13 attributes and $dist^I$ is the Euclidean distance calculated when only to the attributes from $I$-th set are used (feature selection problem). The total randomness deficiency is

$$\mu_f(z|A) = \sum_I \log f(I, A, x). \tag{10}$$

## 4.3 Step of Compression

As mentioned before, we model only one step of compression $F$ which selects $q$ elements from $q^2$ (see section 3.2). We set $q = 19$ and use only $q^2 = 361$ first training examples during the compression in the set $A$. Compression is done by method from section3.2 with family of tests described in the section4.2.

## 4.4 Empirical Measure of Representativeness

Suppose $U = \{z_1, \ldots, z_q\}$ is a subset of the training set $Z$ and $I$ is a number of a subset of attributes. Let $M_I$ be leave-one-out 1-nearest-neighbour regression restricted to the attributes from $I$-th set, i.e.,

$$\alpha_i = |y_i - (y_j \mid j \neq i, dist^I(x_i, x_j) \to \min)|. \tag{11}$$

The *mean absolute error* of $M_I$ on $U$ is the mean value of $\alpha_1, \ldots, \alpha_q$. Let us denote it as $Q(I, U)$. Let us choose the minimal one:

$$I_U = \arg\min_I \{Q(I, U)\}. \tag{12}$$

(If the minimum is reached several times, the minimal $I$ is preferred.)

So $I_U$ is a number of a set of features such that leave-one-out prediction on $U$ is the best when the attributes are restricted to $I_U$-th set. Check now how $I_U$ fits the whole dataset.

Suppose $Z = \{z_1, \ldots, z_n\}$ is the whole training set and $Z_T = \{z_{n+1}, \ldots, z_{n+k}\}$ is the testing set. For each of the testing examples, consider

$$\alpha_{n+j} = \min_{i=1}^n dist^I(z_i, z_{n+j}). \tag{13}$$

Let $Q(I, Z, Z_T)$ be the mean value of $\alpha_{n+1}, \ldots, \alpha_{n+k}$.

The overall quality corresponding to $U$ is defined as

$$Q(U) = Q(I(U), Z, Z_T). \tag{14}$$

If $Q(U)$ is small then $U$ is better as a representative subset of $Z$.

### 4.5    Experimental Results

Let us use $q^2 + q$ subsets defined in the section 4.2:

$$A_1, \ldots, A_q; A_{1,1}, \ldots, A_{q,q} \tag{15}$$

as a 'control group' for the selection $B = F(Z)$ obtained by our method.

We compare $Q_0 = Q(B)$ with $Q_1 = Q(A_1), \ldots, Q_{q^2+q} = Q(A_{q,q})$. The measure of success is the percentage of $Q_i$ less than $Q_0$.

In the described experiment it is 95%, or 361 of 380. More concretely, $Q(B) = 2.46$, while the whole range of $Q_i$ is from 2.25 to 7.52. The median value of $Q_i$ is 3.08. If the whole training data is used for selection of attributes, $Q(Z) = 2.54 > Q(B)$.

What does this mean? The size of $B$ is the same as the size of $A_i$. Subsets $A_i$ are practically random selections of the size $q$ from $z_1, \ldots, z_{q^2}$. They have about 'normal' (i.e. uniformly distributed) level of representativeness with mean 'success' 50% (in the sense mentioned above). As success of $S$ is close to 100%, this means that $S$ is much more representative than a random selection.

## 5    Conclusion

Practically, basic step $F_r$ is being performed $q^2 + q$ times. Calculating $Q(Z)$ with $|Z| \approx q^2$ once takes approximately same amount of time as calculating $Q(A_i)$ with $|A_i| = q$ for $q^2$ times.

On the other hand, the total randomness deficiency

$$\mu_f(z|A) = \sum_{I=1}^{N} (-\log f(I, A, z)) \tag{16}$$

could be replaced by approximation, if we only sum $N' < N$ randomly chosen tests $I = i_1, \ldots, i'_N$ instead of the whole family $I = 1, \ldots, N$.

For this database it $Q(B) = 2.44$ instead of 2.46 when $N' = \lceil N/10 \rceil$ is used. This is the main source of time economy.

## References

1. Gammerman, A., Vapnik, V., Vovk, V.: Learning by transduction. In: Proceedings of the Fourteenth Conference on Uncertainty in Artificial Intelligence, pp. 148–156. Morgan Kaufmann, San Francisco (1998)
2. Nouretdinov, I., Melluish, T., Vovk, V.: Ridge Regression Confidence Machine. In: Proceedings of the 18th International Conference on Machine Learning (2001)
3. Saunders, C., Gammerman, A., Vovk, V.: Transduction with confidence and credibility. In: Proceedings of the 16th International Joint Conference on Artificial Intelligence, pp. 722–726 (1999)
4. Vovk, V., Gammerman, A., Saunders, C.: Machine-learning applications of algorithmic randomness. In: Bousquet, O., von Luxburg, U., Rätsch, G. (eds.) Advanced Lectures on Machine Learning. LNCS (LNAI), vol. 3176, pp. 444–453. Springer, Heidelberg (2004)

# Concepts for Novelty Detection and Handling Based on a Case-Based Reasoning Process Scheme

Petra Perner

Institute of Computer Vision and applied Computer Sciences,
IBaI Arno-Nitzsche-Str. 43, 04277 Leipzig
pperner@ibai-institut.de
www.ibai-research.de

**Abstract.** Novelty detection, the ability to identify new or unknown situations that were never experienced before, is useful for intelligent systems aspiring to operate in environments where data are acquired incrementally. This characteristic is common to numerous problems in medical diagnosis and visual perception. We propose to see novelty detection as a case-based reasoning process. Our novelty-detection method is able to detect the novel situation, as well as to use the novel events for immediate reasoning. To ensure this capacity we combine statistical and similarity inference and learning. This view of CBR takes into account the properties of data, such as the uncertainty, and the underlying concepts, such as storage, learning, retrieval and indexing can be formalized and performed efficiently.

## 1 Introduction

Novelty detection, recognizing that an input differs in some respect from previous inputs, can be a useful ability for learning systems.

Novelty detection is particularly useful where an important class is under-represented in the data, so that a classifier cannot be trained to reliably recognize that class. This characteristic is common to numerous problems, such as information management [1], medical diagnosis [2], fault monitoring and detection [ 3], and visual perception [4].

In medical image diagnosis, there may be digital images of different modalities showing visual patterns that are referring to a particular disease or, in a simpler case, the interpretation result of such an image just gives a symptom for further medical reasoning.

A prominent application is cell-image analysis. Cell-based assays are used for different purposes: either for diagnostic purposes or for drug development. Hep-2 cell image interpretation is one example for diagnostic purposes. HEp-2 cells are used for the identification of antinuclear autoantibodies (ANA). ANA testing for the assessment of systemic and organ-specific autoimmune diseases has increased progressively since immunofluorescence techniques have first been used to demonstrate antinuclear antibodies in 1957. Hep-2 cells allow for recognition of over 30 different nuclear and cytoplasmic patterns, which are given by upwards of 100 different autoantibodies [5].

P. Perner (Ed.): ICDM 2007, LNAI 4597, pp. 21–33, 2007.
© Springer-Verlag Berlin Heidelberg 2007

Treatment changes, the aging of the population and other medical factors, may change the visual appearance of a pattern, or even a new pattern may appear. The first issue relates to concept drift, whereas the second issue is a novelty-detection problem. An automatic image-diagnosis system should be able to detect the new pattern as a novel event and should also allow to include this novel pattern into the system for further reasoning. Therefore, the system has to analyze the images for the objects-of-interest, then to calculate image features from the discovered objects and, finally, the new pattern must be checked against the existing pattern, based on the calculated image features. When the pattern does not belong to one of the existing classes, the pattern is recognized as a novel event. The novel pattern is introduced into the system by calculating the right attributes and their relevance and by updating the detector based on information about the novel event.

Our novelty-detection approach we describe in this paper is strongly linked to the Case-Based Reasoning (CBR) methodology. That means that we have to treat our novelty detection as a CBR problem. The CBR-based novelty detection consists in successively evolving the previously obtained solutions, taking the data properties, the user's needs and any other prior knowledge into account.

In this paper we propose a general framework for novelty detection based on the CBR methodology [6]. We have developed different concept for novelty detection based on CBR[13]. We studied on a conceptual level how they can be applied to medical problems. One of these concepts is described in this paper. It uses a combination of statistical and similarity-based methods as a solution to the problems underlying the CBR methodology. Our scheme is different form existing work [7]-[10] on novelty detection in that respect that it can perform novelty detection and handling, and it considers the incremental nature of the data.

In Section 2, we describe our proposal for novelty detection and handling. The decision criterion for novelty detection is described in Section 3. Novelty event handling based on similarity inference and case-base management is described in Section 4. The statistical learning method for up-dating existing models and the learning of new models is described in Section 5. In Section 6 we discuss the evaluation issues of the proposed approach. In Section 7 we give a summary and conclusions are given in Section 8.

## 2   New Proposal for Novelty Detection and Handling

We propose novelty detection to be seen as a case-based reasoning problem [6]. According to our understanding of the novelty detection problem, the case-based reasoning process, with its different tasks, has all the functions necessary for handling novelty detection in an efficient way and it satisfies the incremental nature that it is up to many real-world problems. CBR solves problems using the already stored knowledge, and captures new knowledge, making it immediately available for solving the next problem. Therefore, case-based reasoning can be seen as a method for problem solving, and also as a method to capture new experience and make it immediately available for problem solving. It can be seen as a learning and knowledge-discovery approach, since it can capture from new experience some general knowledge, such as case classes, prototypes and some higher-level concept. We take case-based reasoning as the framework to solve our novelty detection problem under which we can run the different theoretical methods that should be used to detect the novel events and handle them.

We chose a scenario for our study for which an attribute-value based representation is suitable. Nonetheless, the general framework we propose for novelty detection can be based on any representation. However, the theoretical methods used to solve the different tasks might then be different to the ones we propose here. Thus the representation used to describe our events is an n-dimensional feature vector. This n-dimensional vector should contain as many features as possible for the description of the events collected so far. That makes our problem to a high-dimensional problem. To ensure sufficient performance of our reasoning process, we have to reduce the dimensionality of our problem. Therefore, the feature-selection unit selects from the whole set of features those features that are relevant to describe the known events. Feature selection is based on the conceptual merit algorithm [24].

The heart of our novelty detector (see Fig. 1) is a set of statistical models that have been learnt in an off-line phase from a set of observations. Each model represents a case-class. The probability-density function implicitly represents the data and prevents us from storing all the cases of a known case-class. This unit acts as a novelty-event detector by using the Bayesian decision-criterion with the mixture model. Since this set of observations might be limited, we consider our model as far from optimal, and update the model based on new observed examples. This is done based on the MML-learning principle. Since updating the model based on single events might badly influence the learnt model [11], and is computationally expensive, we collect a sufficiently large set of samples in a data base before starting to update the model.

Therefore, samples that have been detected as a known event are stored under their class label in a data base. After a certain number of samples have been collected for the particular class, the model will be updated based on the MML-learning principle.

In case our model bank cannot classify an actual event into one of the case-classes, this event is recognized as a novel event. Before this event is given to the similarity-based reasoning unit, it is prescreened for outlier. Therefore, the similarity to the representative of the case-class is determined locally on the attribute values, and globally over all attributes. If there is a big deviation in one attribute value, but the overall similarity gives evidence that the sample might belong to one of the case classes, it is displayed to the user. Based on this information and his domain knowledge, the user will decide to label this event as outlier or novel event. Alternatively, this pre-screening step can be skipped and each novel event will be inserted into the similarity-based reasoning unit. This would make the process automatic, but on the other hand the case base might store too many single events that are not useful. Then a special "forgetting strategy" [12] has to be incorporated into the case-base maintenance process.

The novel event is given to the similarity-based reasoning unit. This unit incorporates this sample into their case base according to a case-selective registration-procedure that allows learning case-classes as well as the similarity between the cases and case-classes. We propose to use a fuzzy similarity measure to model the uncertainty in the image data. By doing so, the unit organizes the novel events in such a fashion that is suitable for learning a new statistical model. In contrast to the statistical model, where the probability-density function summarizes the events belonging to one case-class, the cases in the case base represent explicit knowledge and sufficient storage capacity is needed to keep them.

The case base maintenance unit interacts with the statistical learning unit and gives an advice when a new model has to be learnt. The advice is based on the observation that a case-class is represented by a sufficiently large number of samples that are most dissimilar to other classes in the case-base.

The statistical learning unit takes this case class and proves, based on the MML-criterion, if it is suitable to learn a new model. In case the statistical component recommends not to learn a new model, the case-class is still hosted by the case-base maintenance unit and further up-dated, based on new observed events that might change the inner-class structure, as long as there is new evidence to learn a statistical model.

The similarity-based reasoning unit and the statistical models also act together on the reasoning level. A new observation is first given to the statistical models. If they cannot recognize the new event as belonging to one of their classes, the similarity-based unit finds out if there is a similar event in their case base. In case a similar event is found, the solution associated with the closest case is given as output, and the event is stored in the case base, based on the case-selective case-registration procedure. This procedure ensures that the off-line learnt classes can be handled for reasoning, as well as the new observed novel-events. In this respect the system is not only a novelty-detector, it is also able to handle the novel events and make them immediately available for further reasoning.

In summary, our case-based reasoning process for novelty detection fulfills the following requirements:

1. learning of a (statistical) model for the normal events, as well as
2. updating the model according to new observations, in order to obtain a better model,
3. learning the importance of features for the model according to the observations,
4. recognizing a new event and make it immediately available for further reasoning, and
5. collecting of as much data for the novel event in a structured and incremental fashion as necessary, in order to change from a weak reasoning approach to a strong (statistical) model approach for the recognition of the new event class.

The use of a combination of statistical reasoning and similarity-based reasoning allows implicit and explicit storage of the samples. It allows further to handle well-represented events, as well as rare events.

The above described process can in addition be extended to the specific needs of a classification process [13]. This should be briefly mentioned here, although it is out of the scope of this paper. We can also imagine that the feature description used so far might not be sufficient after having seen more observations. Therefore, our novelty detector should also have a method that can learn new case descriptions. Since new features and observation might change the relevance of the features, we also consider an incremental feature-selection procedure and prototype updating. This goes along with the life-time of a CBR system, and proper procedures for these two tasks will be developed during our study. Since new features and new feature importance change the case structure and the model, we also have to take into account the architectural aspects of the system. The system needs to have sufficient storing capacity, as well as a function that allows changing the description of a data base.

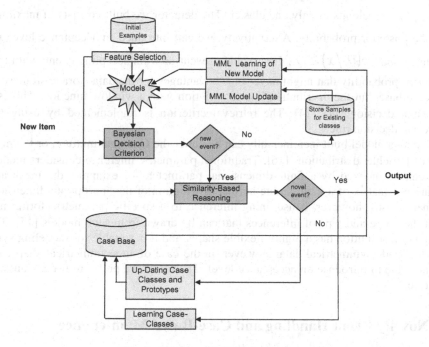

**Fig. 1.** Our Novelty Detection Schema

## 3 Bayesian Decision Making for Novelty Detection

When an event occurs, the first step consists of building a detector that allows recognizing if this event is similar to previously occurring events or if it is new. This detector accepts as input the occurring event and the data model and provides as output the decision and the best case class to which the event belongs. In other words, the detector completes the missing data by providing the cluster label. Let us consider $x$ to be an occurring event, $D$ the available data. The event is similar to existing events when the predictive probability-density function is high:

$$p(x/D) = \int p(\theta/D)p(x/\theta)d\theta \qquad (1)$$

This Bayesian framework for making predictions can be used for all possible data models. Generally speaking, the integral in this equation is intractable. Several approximation methods exist, such as the Bayesian variational method [14], maximum a posteriori (MAP) method [15]. Following the MAP approximation, we use a single-mind model $\hat{\theta}$ that can maximize the posterior $p(\theta/D)$. By setting the approximate predictive probability distribution:

$$p(x/D) = p(\hat{\theta}/D)p(x/\hat{\theta}) \tag{2}$$

By setting the posterior to unity, assuming that $p(x/D) = \sum_k \alpha_k p(x/\hat{\theta}_k)$ and any x $\max_k p(\theta_k / x)$ belongs to only one cluster. The detector we built consists in maximizing the posterior probability. Alternatively, we can introduce an acceptance level $Q$ requiring that $p(\theta_i / x) \geq Q$. That would prevent us from accepting events with low posterior probability that might have some advantages for the data-storage strategy of the case base, but the distribution is a convolution with a window function. This is a Bayesian decision rule [14]. The retrieval criterion is implemented by using the Bayesian decision rule.

The data model built incrementally can be either the Gaussian mixture, or the mixture of Dirichlet distributions [16]. Traditional parametric inference considers models that can be indexed by a finite-dimensional parameter, for example, the mean and covariance matrix of a multivariate normal distribution of the appropriate dimension. In many cases, however, constraining inference to a specific parametric form, may limit the scope and type of inferences that can be drawn from such models [17]. The Dirichlet distribution has a highly flexible shape, and it is suitable for modeling symmetrical and asymmetrical data. However, in the case of an asymmetrical shape, we are not able to introduce an acceptance level. Therefore, we prefer to use a Gaussian mixture.

## 4   Novelty Event Handling and Case-Based Maintenance

Once a new event has been inserted into the case base, it should be made immediately available for reasoning. The novel events might be rare, or it might take some time to collect a sufficiently large set of samples for one case class, in order to be able to learn the pdf for the statistical model. Therefore, the choice is to use similarity-based reasoning and to collect the new events in a hierarchical fashion, based on a similarity relation, into the case base. Similar cases representing one new event should be grouped together in a case class, and new events making up a new case class should be inserted into the case base by taking into account the similarity relation to other case classes.

Therefore, the similarity-based reasoning unit is comprised of two functions: 1. reasoning over novel events and 2. collecting new events.

### 4.1   Similarity-Based Reasoning

For the similarity-based reasoning approach we need an evaluation function that gives us a measure for the similarity between two cases. The chosen similarity-based approach should satisfy the needs for the MML-based learning of the statistical models. The cases should cover the solution space in such a way that it is possible to approximate the final distribution for the statistical models. Therefore we allow the case classes to overlap. The case classes are learnt on a fuzzy conceptual clustering approach. For the similarity-based reasoning we use a fuzzy similarity measure [18].

Let $x_t$ be the new case and $m_k$ ($k = 1,...,M$) be $kth$ case class. The distance between the new case $x_t$ and the $kth$ case class should be the minimum value of the fuzzy objective function

$$d(x_t, m) = \min_u \sum_{k=1}^{M} u_{kt}^n d(x_t, m_k) \qquad (3)$$

where $n > 1$ is the degree of fuzziness, $u_{kt}$ is the fuzzy membership function with the case $x_t$ for the $kth$ case classes and satisfies

$$0 \le u_{kt} \le 1 \qquad \sum_{k=1}^{M} u_{kt} = 1 \qquad (4)$$

The Fuzzy objective function is minimized when

$$u_{kt} = \left[ \sum_{l=1}^{M} [d(x_t, m_k) / d(x_t, m_l)]^{\frac{1}{n-1}} \right]^{-1} \qquad (5)$$

Replacing (5) in (3) gives the minimum of the fuzzy objective function

$$d(x_t, m_k) = \left[ \sum_{k=1}^{M} [d(x_t, m_k)]^{\frac{1}{1-n}} \right]^{1-n} \qquad (6)$$

The selection criteria would be

$$\text{Select Case } x_t \text{ IF } u_j(x_t) > u_i(x_t) \text{ for all } j \ne i \qquad (7)$$

If we have a hierarchy of case classes, this comparison is then done on each level, until we reach a final node.

## 4.2  Learning the Organization of the Case Base

The aim of CBR learning is to group cases together into groups of similar cases in the case base. The case base should be organized in a hierarchical fashion. More general case groups are located at the top of the hierarchy and more specific case groups can be found when tracing down the hierarchy. That allows efficiently retrieving cases for similarity-based reasoning and gives us a scheme for the collection of a sufficiently large number of similar cases for learning new statistical models. The algorithm is of incremental fashion. That satisfies our incremental collection of cases.

The algorithm [19][20] incrementally incorporates cases into the classification tree, where each node is a prototypical concept that represents a case class. During the construction of the classification tree the new item gets tentatively classified through the existing classification tree. Thereby different possibilities are tried for placing an observation function into the hierarchy:

1. The object is placed into an existing case class,
2. A new case class is created,
3. Two existing case classes are combined into a single case class and
4. an existing node is split into two new case classes.

Depending on the value of the utility function for each of the four possibilities, the observation function gets finally placed into one of these four possible places.

The scoring function for learning this hierarchy is based on the fuzzy intra-class and inter-class variance:

$$Score = \frac{1}{M}\left(\frac{1}{M}\sum_{k=1}^{M}d^2(m_k,\bar{x}) - \left(\sum_{k=1}^{M}\frac{1}{\pi_k}\sum_{t=1}^{N}u_{kt}^n d^2(x_{kt},m_k)\right)\right) \quad with \quad \pi_k = \sum_{t=1}^{N}u_{kt} \qquad (8)$$

The normalization to $M$ allows comparing possible different cluster numbers.

The organization of the case base also allows us to take care of rare events. As long as case groups do not give a sufficiently large enough case class, they are represented by higher case groups. If case classes are not used within a certain time period, they can be deleted from the case base.

To our knowledge there exists no algorithm for Fuzzy conceptual clustering yet.

## 5   MML-Based Learning of the Statistical Models

The Minimum Message Length Principle (MML) [21] can be used as a learning approach for updating the existing statistical model, as well as for learning new statistical models, when enough data are available within the temporary collection. From an information-theory point of view, the minimum message length approach is based on evaluating statistical models according to their ability to compress a message containing the data. High compression is obtained by forming good models of the data to be coded. For each model in the model space, the message includes two parts. The first part encodes the model, using only prior information about the model and no information about the data. The second part encodes only the data, in a way that makes use of the model encoded in the first part [22]. According to information theory [22], the optimal number of clusters of the mixture is that which requires a minimum amount of information to transmit the data efficiently from a sender to a receiver. The message length is defined as minus the logarithm of the posterior probability [22].

It has been shown that when this Bayesian information theory criterion is used with the Gausian mixture of pdfs, it performs several established criteria of model selection. To the best of our knowledge the MML has not been used before for novelty detection. Let us consider a set of available data $X = (X_1, \cdots, X_N)$ controlled by a mixture of $M$ distributions with the parameters $\theta = (\theta_1, \cdots, \theta_M)$, and where $\theta_k$ is a vector which contains the parameters of the kth distribution. The new data to be added to the existing model is $Y = (Y_1, \cdots, Y_L)$. The whole amount of data is $D = (X, Y_L)$. Let us consider that the updating consists in adding a subset of new $L_e$ samples to existing classes, and that the remaining subset with $L_n$ samples allows to create a new class; $L = L_e + L_n$. $L_e = 0$ means that all samples are added to a new class and any change in the data model of existing classes is a consequence of adding this new class. When $L_n = 0$, it means that there is no class creation, and the change in? the model data is due to adding new samples in the existing classes. More roughly speaking, after updating, if $L_n = 0$, then the number of classes is $M_n = M$. The new data model $\tilde{\Theta}$ is obtained by updating the previous model $\Theta$, when new data is added to existing classes. In other words, $\Theta$ is equal to $\theta$ obtained during the previous update. However, if $L_n \neq 0$, then the number of classes is $M_n = M + 1$. The new data model $\tilde{\Theta}$ is obtained by updating the previous model $\Theta$, when new data is added to a new class and eventually to existing ones. $\Theta = (\theta, \theta_{M+1})$, where $\theta$ is the data model obtained during the previous update and modified to fulfill any additional constraints due to the adding of a new cluster. For example, in the case of a mixture model, adding a new cluster implies that the summation of mixing parameters must be normalized such that it is equal to one. $\theta_{M+1}$ is the data model of the new class, computed by using a moment method or any other available method.

In the following we will focus on the MML. The MML can be used to check if the new data Y is new or not. For instance, if the MML of the data model, when adding a new cluster, is less than the MML, when these data are added to an existing cluster, then we can decide that the cluster is new ; if MML(M + 1) < MML(M), then a new cluster is created. The naive computation of this decision rule requires taking all the data $D = (X, Y_L)$ into account, which is time-consuming and therefore limits the usefulness of this decision rule. To overcome this drawback, we propose to write the MML in recursion form; that is the $MML_b$ of the whole data is the $MML_a$ of the data available, plus additional terms related to the new data. The formula is given at the end of the paper.

Suppose now that a new data $\vec{X}_{N+1}$ is inserted in a case. The problem now is how to update the different mixture model parameters. For this goal, we use the stochastic ascent gradient parameter updating proposed in [26]:

$$\Theta^{N+1} = \Theta^N + \gamma_N \left( \frac{\partial(p(\vec{X}_{N+1}, \vec{Z}_{N+1} / \Theta^N))}{\partial \Theta} \right) \tag{9}$$

where $\vec{Z}_{N+1}$ is the missed data vector, $\gamma_N$ is a sequence of positive numbers.

## 6 Evaluation Issues for the Proposed Method

A typical medical-image application for novelty detection is the application described in [23]. The image data set is obtained from HEp-2 cell images, comprised of a high number of features, and the class label. These data sets are coming from different manufacturers. The variation among the data is very high since every company uses different imaging and cell lines. Nonetheless, the expected output, the class label, should be the same. That means that the class number in the table represents for each class the same class label. Some classes have a sufficiently large number of samples, while others are under- represented. The sample distribution is shown in table 2.

Only database DB_1 can be used for the learning of a statistical model, since the four classes have a sufficiently large number of samples. Class 1 to 4 in database DB2-DB4 can be used to update the statistical model. All the other classes in the databases should be considered as novel events that occur in sequence.

The evaluation of our method is not easy because of the underlying different aspects. These aspects are:

1. up-dating existing concepts to achieve a better performance of the model or to handle the concept drift,
2. the recognition of novel events,
3. reasoning over novel events and
4. the learning of new concepts.

At the recent status we can only give an outline of the evaluation procedure and the concept behind.

These four tasks might be influenced by different factors:

1. Up-dating existing Concepts
2. There must be some influence of the sample distribution.
3. How many samples are necessary for evaluating the recent performance of the model? According to the literature approximately 100 samples [26] are needed.
4. Recognition of novel events and outliers
5. This has something to do with false/positive recognition
6. Learning New Concepts
7. How many samples are necessary to learn novel concepts? According to the literature [25] approximately 100 samples are needed.
8. How can the case base organization control the learning of the models?

**Table 1.** Name of Database and Number of Classes and Samples per Class

| Name | 1 | 2 | 3 | 4 | 5 | 6 | 7 | 8 | 9 | 10 | 11 | 12 | 13 | 14 | 15 | 16 | 17 | 18 | 19 | 20 | 21 | 22 | 23 | 24 | 25 | 26 | Number of Classes | Number of Cases |
|---|---|---|---|---|---|---|---|---|---|---|---|---|---|---|---|---|---|---|---|---|---|---|---|---|---|---|---|---|
| DB_1 | 105 | 96 | 63 | 83 | | | | | | | | | | | | | | | | | | | | | | | 4 | 347 |
| DB_2 | 8 | 2 | 2 | 14 | 7 | 5 | 15 | 9 | 5 | 4 | 14 | 9 | 8 | 10 | 48 | 23 | 17 | 31 | 3 | 3 | 3 | 7 | 5 | 2 | 13 | 5 | 26 | 298 |
| DB_3 | 7 | 30 | 29 | 28 | 11 | 7 | 13 | 5 | 13 | 13 | | | | | | | | | | | | | | | | | 10 | 156 |
| DB_4 | 25 | 12 | 18 | 21 | 5 | 16 | 22 | 24 | 21 | 20 | 5 | 14 | | | | | | | | | | | | | | | 12 | 203 |

The evaluation of the statistical model can only be done by test-and-train based on a large enough test data set (500 samples according to [25]) which is not available in the proposed kind of application. We rather have to do with a sparse-data set problem. Therefore, we can only evaluate the generalization error of the model, that is the error rate we obtain when presenting the data set to the system that has also been used for learning. Besides that we can calculate the error rate we obtain when presenting the samples belonging to the same class 1 to 4 in the data base DB_2, DB_ 3, and DB_4 to the models.

## 7 Discussion

The idea to combine statistical reasoning and similarity-based reasoning is based on the fact that statistical reasoning has a long history in handling uncertain and imprecise data and implicitly represents the data. That prevents us from having a large data-storing capacity for the system. However, statistical reasoning is not good in handling single events and improving reasoning over time when new data arrive. Therefore, we have introduced the MML-based learning approach to update the model. This up-dating step can be seen as an adaptation of the solution to the current case.

Similarity-based reasoning can handle the single event, for reasoning as well as for organizing it into such a fashion that it can be used for up-dating the model. It can also help to detect outliers. However, the similarity-based reasoning unit explicitly represents the data and therefore enough storage capacity has to be provided for the system.

The hierarchical organization of the case base can also control this MML-based learning process by advising the learning unit to learn a coarse model first and to learn a specialized model when enough data is available in the respective subnode of the hierarchical case base.

In general we have to say that the proposed approach is only applicable if we have enough data samples. The kind of medical applications we usually have to deal with do not fulfill this requirement. Only after the system is in use we can collect enough data for statistical modeling. The idea can be to start with a pure similarity-based approach and create initial statistical models off-line after enough data are available for one class.

# 8  Conclusion

We have outlined in this paper our new approach to novelty detection, which is based on the idea to see novelty detection as a CBR process. Our novelty-detection method is able to detect the novel situation, as well as to handle the novel events for immediate reasoning. We combine statistical and similarity inference and learning. This view of CBR takes into account the properties of data such as the uncertainty, and the underlying concepts such as adaptation, storage, learning, retrieval and indexing can be formalized and performed efficiently.

Known classes are described by statistical models. The performance of the models is improved by the incremental up-dating of the models based on new available events. Since up-dating the model based on single events is not appropriate, a sufficiently large number of cases is collected into a temporary case collection. This case collection is emptied after the model is up-dated. The information about the cases is now implicitly represented by the model, and storage capacity is preserved. New events, not belonging to one of the known case classes, are recognized as novel events. These events are stored by a similarity-based registration procedure in a second case base. The similarity-based learning procedure ensures that similar cases are grouped into case classes, a representative for the case class is learnt and generalization over case classes can be performed. This allows one to efficiently collect novel events and group them in such a way that retrieval over the case base is efficient. The similarity-based unit is also responsible for making novel events immediately available for reasoning.

When a sufficiently large number of cases for a case class is available in the second case base, the case class is given to the statistical learning unit for learning a new statistical model. The statistical learning strategy for up-dating a model and learning new models is based on the MML principle. Now the new case class is handled further by the statistical model and entry in the second case base can be deleted.

**Acknowledgement.** This work has been supported by the German Ministry of Science and Technology BMBF under the grant-No. CAN 06/A07. The author would like to thank Michael Richter and Ron Kenett for their advice and helpful comments.

# References

[1] Schiffmann, B., McKeown, K.R.: Context and Learning in Novelty Detection. In: Proc. HLT-EMNLP 2005, Vancouver, BC (October 2005)

[2] Spinosa, E.J.: André Carlos Ponce Leon Ferreira de Carvalho: SVMs for novel class detection in Bioinformatics. WOB 2004, 81–88 (2004)

[3] Liang, B., Austin, J.: Mining Large Engineering Data Sets on the Grid Using AURA. In: Yang, Z.R., Yin, H., Everson, R.M. (eds.) IDEAL 2004. LNCS, vol. 3177, pp. 430–436. Springer, Heidelberg (2004)

[4] Singh, S., Markou, M.: An approach to novelty detection applied to the classification of image regions. IEEE Transactions on Knowledge and Data Engineering 16(4), 396–407 (2004)

[5] Bradwell, A.R., Stokes, R.P., Johnson, G.D.: Atlas of HEp-2 Patterns. AR Bradwell (1995)

[6] Althoff, K.D.: Case-Based Reasoning. In: Chang, S.K. (ed.) Handbook on Software Engineering and Knowledge Engineering (2001)

[7] Markow, M., Singh, S.: Novelty Detection: A Review-Part 1: Statistical Approaches. Signal Processing 83(12), 2481–2497 (2003)

[8] Markow, M., Singh, S.: Novelty Detection: A Review-Part 2: Neural Network Based Approaches. Signal Processing 83(12), 2499–2521 (2003)

[9] Zhang, Y., Callan, J., Minka, T.: Novelty and Redundancy Detection in Adaptive Filtering. In: Proceedings of the 25th annual international ACM SIGIR conference on Research and development in information retrieval, pp. 81–88. ACM Press, New York (2002)

[10] Tax, D.M.J., Jusycyak, P.: Kernel Whitening for One-Class Classification International Journal of Pattern Recognition and Artificial Intelligence (2003)

[11] Bishop, Ch.M.: Pattern Recognitin and Machine Learning. LNCS. Springer, Heidelberg (2006)

[12] Leake, D.B., Wilson, D.C.: Remembering why to remember: per-formance-guided case-base maintenance. In: Blanzieri, E., Portinale, L. (eds.) Advances in Case-Based Reasoning, pp. 161–172. Springer, Heidelberg (2000)

[13] Perner, P.: Concepts for Novelty Detection and Handling based on Case-Based Reasoning, IBaI-Report (October 2006)

[14] Berger, J.: Statistical Decision Theory and Bayesian Analysis. LNCS. Springer, Heidelberg (1985)

[15] MacKay, D.J.C.: Information Theory, Inference and Learning Algorithm. Cambridge University Press, Cambridge (2003)

[16] Kotz, S., Ng, K.W., Fankg, K.: Symmetric Multivariate and Related Distributions. Chapman and Hall, London / New York (1990)

[17] Sjolandery, K., Karplus, K., Brown, M., Hughey, R., Krogh, A., Saira Mian, I., Haussler, D.: Dirichlet Mixtures: A Method for Improved Detection of Weak but Signicant Protein Sequence Homology. Computer Applications in the Biosciences (1996)

[18] Bezdek, J.C.: Pattern Recognition with Fuzzy Objective Function Algorithms. Kluwer Academic Publishers, Norwell, MA (1981)

[19] Jaenichen, S., Perner, P.: Conceptual Clustering and Case Generalization of two dimensional Forms. Computational Intelligence 22(3/4), 177–193 (2006)

[20] Perner, P.: Case-base maintenance by conceptual clustering of graphs. Engineering Applications of Artificial Intelligence 19(4), 295–381 (2006)

[21] Wallace, C.S.: Statistical and Inductive Inference by Minimum Message Length. Information Science and Statistics. Springer, Heidelberg (2005)

[22] MacKay, D.J.C.: Information Theory, Inference and Learning Algorithm. Cambridge University Press, Cambridge (2003)

[23] Perner, P.: Prototype-Based Classification, Applied Intelligence (to appear)

[24] Hong, S.J.: Use of contextual information for feature ranking and discretization. IEEE Trans. on Knowledge Discovery and Data Engineering, 55–65

[25] Figueiredo, M.A.T., Jain, A.K.: Unsupervised learning of Finite-Mixture Models. IEEE Trans. on PAMI 24(3), 381–396

[26] Gill, P.E., Murray, W., Wright, M.H.: Practical Optimization. Academic Press, San Diego (1981)

# An Efficient Algorithm for Instance-Based Learning on Data Streams

Jürgen Beringer[1] and Eyke Hüllermeier[2]

[1] Fakultät für Informatik
Otto-von-Guericke-Universität Magdeburg
beringer@iti.cs.uni-magdeburg.de
[2] Fachbereich Mathematik und Informatik
Philipps-Universität Marburg
eyke@mathematik.uni-marburg.de

**Abstract.** The processing of data streams in general and the mining of such streams in particular have recently attracted considerable attention in various research fields. A key problem in stream mining is to extend existing machine learning and data mining methods so as to meet the increased requirements imposed by the data stream scenario, including the ability to analyze incoming data in an online, incremental manner, to observe tight time and memory constraints, and to appropriately respond to changes of the data characteristics and underlying distributions, amongst others. This paper considers the problem of classification on data streams and develops an instance-based learning algorithm for that purpose. The experimental studies presented in the paper suggest that this algorithm has a number of desirable properties that are not, at least not as a whole, shared by currently existing alternatives. Notably, our method is very flexible and thus able to adapt to an evolving environment quickly, a point of utmost importance in the data stream context. At the same time, the algorithm is relatively robust and thus applicable to streams with different characteristics.

## 1 Introduction

In recent years, so-called *data streams* have attracted considerable attention in different fields of computer science. As the notion suggests, a data stream can roughly be thought of as an ordered sequence of data items, where the input arrives more or less continuously as time progresses [16]. There are various applications in which streams of this type are produced, such as network monitoring or telecommunication systems.

Apart from other issues such as data processing and querying, the problem of mining data streams has been studied in a number of recent publications (see e.g. [13] for an up-to-date overview). In this connection, different data mining problems have already been considered, such as clustering [1], classification [17], and frequent pattern mining [8]. In this paper, we are concerned with the classification problem. More specifically, we investigate the potential of the instance-based

P. Perner (Ed.): ICDM 2007, LNAI 4597, pp. 34–48, 2007.
© Springer-Verlag Berlin Heidelberg 2007

approach to supervised learning within the context of data streams and propose an efficient instance-based learning algorithm.

The remainder of the paper is organized as follows: Section 2 provides some background information, both on data streams and on instance-based learning, and briefly reviews related work. Our approach to instance-based learning on data streams is introduced in section 3 and empirically evaluated in section 4. The paper concludes with a brief summary in section 5.

## 2   Background

### 2.1   Data Streams and Concept Change

The *data stream model* assumes that input data are not available for random access from disk or memory, such as relations in standard relational databases, but rather arrive in the form of one or more continuous data streams. The stream model differs from the standard relational model in various ways [4]: (i) The elements of a stream arrive incrementally in an "online" manner. That is, the stream is "active" in the sense that the incoming items trigger operations on the data rather than being sent on request. (ii) The order in which elements of a stream arrive are not under the control of the system. (iii) Data streams are potentially of unbounded size. (iv) Data stream elements that have been processed are either discarded or archived. They cannot be retrieved easily unless being stored in memory, which is typically small relative to the size of the stream (stored/condensed information about past data is often referred to as a *synopsis*). (v) Due to limited (memory) resources and strict time constraints, the computation of exact results will often not be possible. Therefore, the processing of stream data does commonly produce *approximate* results.

For the problem of mining data streams, the aforementioned characteristics have a number of important implications. First of all, in order to guarantee that results are always up-to-date, it is necessary to analyze the incoming data in an online manner, tolerating not more than a constant time delay. Since learning from scratch every time is generally excluded due to limited time and memory resources, corresponding learning algorithms must be *incremental*. Moreover, algorithms for learning on data streams must also be *adaptive*, i.e., they must be able to adapt to an evolving environment in which the data (stream) generating process may change over time. Thus, the handling of changing concepts is of utmost importance in mining data streams [5]. It has not only been considered in this context, however. In general, the literature distinguishes between different types of concept change over time [27]. The first type refers to a sudden, abrupt change of the underlying concept to be learned and is often called *concept shift*. Roughly speaking, in case of a concept shift, any knowledge about the old concept will typically become obsolete and the new concept has to be learned from scratch. The second type refers to a gradual evolution of the concept over time. In this scenario, old data might still be relevant, at least to some extent. Finally, one often speaks about *virtual* concept drift if not the concept itself changes but the distribution of the underlying data generating process [29]. Note that in practice virtual and real concept drift can occur simultaneously.

Concept change can be handled in a direct or indirect way. In the indirect approach, the learning algorithm does not explicitly attempt to detect a concept drift. Instead, the use of outdated or irrelevant data is avoided from the outset. This is typically accomplished by considering only the most recent data while ignoring older observations, e.g., by sliding a window of fixed size over a data stream or by weighing the nearest neighbors of new observations, not only according to their distance but also according to their age. More generally, such strategies belong to the class of *instance selection* or *instance weighing* methods. To handle concept change in a more direct way, appropriate techniques for discovering the drift or shift are first of all required. Such techniques are typically based on statistical tests. Roughly speaking, the idea is to compare a certain statistic that refers to recently observed data with a corresponding statistic for older data, and to decide whether the difference between them is significant in a statistical sense. (A corresponding technique will be discussed in section 3 below.)

## 2.2   Instance-Based Learning

As opposed to model-based machine learning methods which induce a general model (theory) from the data and use that model for further reasoning, instance-based learning (IBL) algorithms simply store the data itself. They defer the processing of the data until a prediction (or some other type of query) is actually requested, a property which qualifies them as a *lazy* learning method [3,2]. Predictions are then derived by combining the information provided by the stored examples.

Such a combination is typically accomplished by means of the *nearest neighbor* (NN) estimation principle [9]. Consider the following setting: Let $\mathcal{X}$ denote the instance space, where an instance corresponds to the description $x$ of an object (usually though not necessarily in attribute–value form). $\mathcal{X}$ is endowed with a distance measure $\Delta(\cdot)$, i.e., $\Delta(x, x')$ is the distance between instances $x, x' \in \mathcal{X}$. $\mathcal{L}$ is a set of class labels, and $\langle x, \lambda_x \rangle \in \mathcal{X} \times \mathcal{L}$ is called a labeled instance, a case, or an example. In classification, which is the focus of this paper, $\mathcal{L}$ is a finite (usually small) set comprised of $m$ classes $\{\lambda_1 \ldots \lambda_m\}$.

The current experience of the learning system is represented in terms of a set $\mathcal{D}$ of examples $\langle x_i, \lambda_{x_i} \rangle$, $1 \leq i \leq n = |\mathcal{D}|$. From a machine learning point of view, $\mathcal{D}$ plays the role of the *training set* of the learner. More precisely, since not all examples will necessarily be stored by an instance-based learner, $\mathcal{D}$ is only a subset of the training set. In case-based reasoning, it is also referred to as the *case base*; besides, in the context of data streams, $\mathcal{D}$ corresponds to the aforementioned *synopsis*.

Finally, suppose a novel instance $x_0 \in \mathcal{X}$ (a query) to be given, the class label $\lambda_{x_0}$ of which is to be estimated. The NN principle prescribes to estimate this label by the label of the nearest (most similar) sample instance. The *k-nearest neighbor* (*k*-NN) approach is a slight generalization, which takes the

$k \geq 1$ nearest neighbors of $x_0$ into account. That is, an estimation $\lambda_{x_0}^{est}$ of $\lambda_{x_0}$ is derived from the set $\mathcal{N}_k(x_0)$ of the $k$ nearest neighbors of $x_0$, usually by means of a *majority vote*:

$$\lambda_{x_0}^{est} = \arg\max_{\lambda \in \mathcal{L}} \mathrm{card}\{x \in \mathcal{N}_k(x_0) \mid \lambda_x = \lambda\}. \tag{1}$$

Regarding the suitability of IBL in the context of data streams, note that IBL algorithms are inherently incremental, since adaptation basically comes down to adding or removing observed cases. On the other hand, this training efficiency comes at the cost of high complexity at classification time, which involves retrieving the query's nearest neighbors. Consequently, IBL might be preferable (to model-based methods) in a data stream application if the number of incoming data is large compared with the number of queries to be answered, i.e., if model updating is the dominant factor.

## 2.3 Related Work

Data mining on streams is a topic of active research, and several adaptations of standard statistical and data analysis methods to data streams or related models have been developed recently [12]. Likewise, several online data mining methods have been devised (e.g. [10]), with a particular focus on unsupervised techniques like clustering. Supervised learning on streams, including classification, has received less attention so far, even though some approaches have already been developed.

A very early approach is the FLORA (Floating Rough Approximation) system [30]. The corresponding algorithm learns rule-based binary classifiers on a sliding window of fixed size. The FRANN (Floating Rough Approximation in Neural Networks) algorithm trains RBF networks on a sliding window of adaptive size [22]. The LWF (Locally Weighted Forgetting) algorithm of Salganicoff [25] is among the best adaptive learning algorithms. It is an instance-based learner that reduces the weights of the $k$ nearest neighbors $x_1 \ldots x_k$ (in increasing order according to distance) of a new instance $x_0$ by the factor $\tau + (1 - \tau)\Delta(x_i, x_0)^2/\Delta(x_k, x_0)^2$. An instance is completely removed if its weight falls below a threshold $\theta$. To fix the size of the case base, the parameter $k$ is adaptively defined by $k = \lceil \beta|\mathcal{D}| \rceil$ where $|\mathcal{D}|$ is the size of the current case base. As an obvious alternative to LWF, Salganicoff considers the TWF (Time Weighted Forgetting) algorithm that weights instances according to their age: at time point $t$, the example observed at time $t - k$ is weighted by $w^k$, where $w \in (0, 1)$ is a constant. The Prediction Error Context Switching algorithm (PECS), also proposed in [25], does not delete but only deactivates instances. That is, removed instances are still stored in memory and might be reactivated later on. This strategy can avoid some disadvantages of LWF but entails storage requirements that disqualify PECS for the data stream context.

In the above approaches, the strategies for adapting the size of a sliding window, if any, are mostly of a heuristic nature. In [19], the authors propose to adapt the window size in such a way as to minimize the estimated generalization error

of the learner trained on that window. In [20], this approach is further generalized by allowing for the selection of arbitrary subsets of batches instead of only
uninterrupted sequences. Despite the appealing idea of this approach to window
(training set) adjustment, the successive testing of different window lengths is
computationally expensive and therefore not immediately applicable in a data
stream scenario with tight time constraints.

Recently, some efforts have been made to extend decision tree induction to
the streaming scenario. In their CVFDT (Continuous Very Fast Decision Trees)
algorithm, Hulton and Domingos learn and maintain decision trees on a sliding
window of fixed size [17]. Another approach to adaptive learning is the use
of ensemble techniques [21]. Here, the idea is to train multiple classifiers, often
decision trees, on different blocks of data. To achieve adaptivity, the classifiers are
weighted according to their (recent) performance or, even simpler, only the best
classifier is selected to classify new instances. If concept drift occurs, outdated
or poorly performing classifiers are replaced by new ones.

So-called *editing strategies* for nearest neighbor classification or, more generally, lazy learning have been studied for quite a while [24]. Even though these
strategies are of course related to the problem of adaptive learning and handling
concept change, they are not suitable for data stream applications, mainly for the
following reasons: Firstly, they solely focus on the goal to maximize classification
accuracy while disregarding other aspects like space complexity. Secondly, they
are not flexible and efficient enough for online classification. In this connection,
let us also mention the well-known IB3 algorithm [3], which is built upon IB1
and includes means to delete noisy and old instances that do no longer comply
with the current concept. Even though IB3 is thus principally able to handle
gradual concept drift, the adaptation is relatively slow [30,25].

Finally, we note that there is also a bunch of work on time series data mining
(e.g. [18]). However, even though time series data mining is of course related to
stream data mining, one should not overlook important differences between these
fields. Particularly, time series are still static objects that can be analyzed offline,
whereas the focus in the context of data streams is on dynamic adaptation and
online data mining.

## 3    Instance-Based Learning on Data Streams

This section introduces our approach to instance-based learning on data streams,
referred to as IBL-DS. The learning scenario consists of a data stream that
permanently produces examples, potentially with a very high arrival rate, and
a second stream producing query instances to be classified. The key problem for
our learning system is to maintain an implicit concept description in the form of
a case base (memory). Before presenting details of IBL-DS in section 3.2, some
general aspects and requirements of concept adaptation (case base maintenance)
in a streaming context will be discussed in section 3.1.

## 3.1   Concept Adaptation

The simplest adaptive learners are those using sliding windows of fixed size. Unfortunately, by fixing the number of examples in advance, it is impossible to optimally adapt the size of the case base to the complexity of the concept to be learned, and to react to changes of this concept appropriately. Moreover, being restricted to selecting a subset of successive observations in the form of a window, it is impossible to disregard a portion of observations in the middle (e.g. outliers) while retaining preceding and succeeding blocks of data. To avoid both of the aforementioned drawbacks, non-window-based approaches are needed that do not only adapt the size of the training data but also have the liberty to select an arbitrary *subset* of examples from the data seen so far. Needless to say, such flexibility does not come for free. Apart from higher computational costs, additional problems such as avoiding an unlimited growth of the training set and, more generally, trading off accuracy against efficiency have to be solved.

Instance-based learning seems to be attractive in light of the above requirements, mainly because of its inherently incremental nature and the simplicity of model adaptation. In particular, since in IBL an example has only local influence, the update triggered by a new example can be restricted to a local region around that observation.

Regarding the updating (editing) of the case base in IBL, an example should in principle be retained if it improves the predictive performance (classification accuracy) of the classifier; otherwise, it should better be removed. Unfortunately, this criterion cannot be used directly, since the (future) usefulness of an example in this sense is simply not known. Instead, existing approaches fall back on suitable indicators of usefulness:

- Temporal relevance: According to this indicator, recent observations are considered as potentially more useful and, hence, are preferred to older examples.
- Spatial relevance: The relevance of an example can also depend on its position in the instance space. In IBL, examples can be redundant in the sense that they don't change the nearest neighbor classification of any query. More generally (and less stringently), one might consider a set of examples redundant if they are closely neighbored in the instance space and, hence, have a similar region of influence.
- Consistency: An example might be removed if it seems to be inconsistent with the current concept, e.g., if its own class label differs from those labels in its neighborhood.

Many algorithms use only one indicator, either temporal relevance (e.g. window-based approaches), spatial relevance (e.g. LWF), or consistency (e.g. IB3). A few methods also use a second indicator, e.g. the approach of Klinkenberg (temporal relevance and consistency), but only the window-based system FLORA4 uses all three aspects.

## 3.2    IBL-DS

In this section, we describe the main ideas of IBL-DS, our approach to IBL on data streams, that not only takes all of the aforementioned three indicators into account but also meets the efficiency requirements of the data stream setting.

IBL-DS optimizes the composition and size of the case base autonomously. On arrival of a new example $\langle x_0, \lambda_{x_0} \rangle$, this example is first added to the case base. Moreover, it is checked whether other examples might be removed, either since they have become redundant or since they are outliers (noisy data). To this end, a set $C$ of examples within a neighborhood of $x_0$ are considered as candidates. This neighborhood is given by the $k_{cand}$ nearest neighbors of $x_0$, and the candidate set $C$ consists of the 50% oldest examples within that neighborhood. The 50% most recent examples are excluded from removal due to the difficulty to distinguish potentially noisy data from the beginning of a concept change. Even though unexpected observations will be made in both cases, noise and concept change, these observations should be removed only in the former but not in the latter case.

If the current class $\lambda_{x_0}$ is the most frequent one within a larger test environment of size[1] $k_{test} = (k_{cand})^2 + k_{cand}$, those candidates in $C$ are removed that have a different class label. Furthermore, to guarantee an upper bound on the size of the case base, the oldest element of the similarity environment is deleted, regardless of its class, whenever the upper bound would be exceeded by adding the new example.

Using this strategy, the algorithm is able to adapt to concept drift but will also have a high accuracy for non-drifting data streams. Still, these two situations – drifting and stable concept – are to some extent conflicting with regard to the size of the case base: If the concept to be learned is stable, classification accuracy will increase with the size of the case base. On the other hand, a large case base turns out to be disadvantageous in situations where concept drift occurs, and even more in the case of concept shift. In fact, the larger the case base is, the more outdated examples will have to be removed and, hence, the more sluggish the adaptation process will be.

For this reason, we try to detect an abrupt change of the concept using a statistical test as in [14,15]. If a corresponding change has been detected, a large number of examples will be removed instantaneously from the case base. The test is performed as follows: We maintain the prediction error $p$ and standard deviation $s = \sqrt{\frac{p(1-p)}{100}}$ for the last 100 training instances. Let $p_{min}$ denote the smallest among these errors and $s_{min}$ the associated standard deviation. A change is detected if the current value of $p$ is significantly higher than $p_{min}$. Here, statistical significance is tested using a standard (one-sided) z-test, i.e., the condition to be tested is $p + s > p_{min} + z_\alpha s_{min}$, where $\alpha$ is the level of confidence (we use $\alpha = 0.999$).

---

[1] This choice of $k_{test}$ aims at including in the test environment the similarity environments of all examples in the similarity environment of $x_0$; of course, it does not guarantee to do so.

Finally, in case a change has been detected, we try to estimate its extent in order to determine the number of examples that need to be removed. More specifically, we delete $p_{dif}$ percent of the current examples, where $p_{dif}$ is the difference between $p_{min}$ and the classification error for the last 20 instances. Examples to be removed are chosen at random according to a distribution which is spatially uniform but temporally skewed (see below).

IBL-DS is implemented under the data mining library WEKA [31]. The data is stored in the M-tree data structure of XXL, a query processing library developed and maintained at the Informatics Institute of Marburg University [6]. Below, we describe the distance function employed by IBL-DS and the M-Tree [7] which allows for processing streams with both continuous and categorical attributes and, moreover, to perform nearest neighbor queries in an efficient way even for very large case memories.

As a distance function we use an updateable variant of SVDM which is a simplified version of the VDM distance measure [26] and was successfully used in the classification algorithm RISE [11]. Let an instance $x$ be specified in terms of $\ell$ features $F_1 \ldots F_\ell$, i.e., as a vector $x = (f_1 \ldots f_\ell) \in D_1 \times \ldots \times D_\ell$. Numerical features $F_i$ with domain $D_i = \mathbb{R}$ are first normalized by the mapping $f_i \mapsto f_i/(max - min)$, where $max$ and $min$ denote, respectively, the largest and smallest value for $F_i$ observed so far; these values are permanently updated. Then, $\delta_i(f_i, f'_i)$ is defined by the distance between the normalized values of $f_i$ and $f'_i$. For a discrete attribute $F_j$, the distance between two values $f_j$ and $f'_j$ is defined by the following measure:

$$\delta_i(f_j, f'_j) = \sum_{k=1}^{m} \left\| P(\lambda_k \mid F_j = f_j) - P(\lambda_k \mid F_j = f'_j) \right\|,$$

where $m$ is the number of classes and $P(\lambda \mid F = f)$ is the probability of the class $\lambda$ given the value $f$ for attribute $F$. Finally, the distance between two instances $x$ and $x'$ is given by the mean squared distance

$$\Delta(x, x') = \frac{1}{\ell} \sum_{i=1}^{\ell} \delta_i(f_i, f'_i)^2$$

To delete instances in a spatially uniform but temporally skewed way, we exploit the properties of the M-Tree index structure [7]. In this tree, the leaves store instances that belong to a small sphere within the instance space. The inner nodes combine subnodes to bigger spheres and the root node represents the sphere that corresponds to the whole data set. Each node $n$ consists of a center instance $c_n$ and an associated radius $r_n$. Moreover, each node maintains a list of successors (subnodes) $l_n$. The number of instances or subnodes of a node is restricted to an interval $[minCapacity, maxCapacity]$. Our experience has shown that the interval $[6, 15]$ yields good performances. The stored examples correspond to the instance nodes of the tree (located directly under the leaf nodes), the radius of which is 0.

To delete data with preference to older instances, the number of items to be removed in a node is uniformly spread among the subnodes. In a leaf, only the oldest instances are removed. This way, we ensure that the spatial distribution of the deleted instances is uniform in the instance space. Regarding the temporal distribution, however, old instances are more likely to be removed than more recent examples.

Finally, in order to classify a new query instance $x_0$, we employ a simple majority voting procedure among the $k$ nearest neighbors. As in standard IBL, the computationally most expensive step consists of finding the query's neighbors. In our implementation, this step is again supported by the aforementioned M-tree (more specifically, the nearest neighbors are computed in an iterative way using a (min-)heap $H$ of nodes which is initialized with the root of the M-tree).

# 4    Empirical Evaluation

A convincing experimental validation of online learning algorithms is an intricate problem for several reasons. Firstly, the evaluation of algorithms in a streaming context is obviously more difficult than the evaluation for static data sets, mainly because simple, one-dimensional performance measures such as classification accuracy will now vary over time and, hence, turn into functions (of time) which are not immediately comparable. Besides, additional criteria become relevant, such as the handling of concept drift, many of which are rather vague and hard to quantify. Secondly, real-world and benchmark streaming data is currently not available in a form that is suitable for conducting systematic experiments.

Due to these reasons, we mainly used synthetic data for our experiments, which allows for conducting experiments in a *controlled* way. Besides, a further experimental study using real-world data is presented in section 4.3.

We compared IBL-DS with the following instance-based approaches: The simple sliding window approach with fixed window-sizes of 200, 400, 800, respectively (Win200, Win400, Win800); Local Weighed Forgetting with $\beta = 0.04$ and $\beta = 0.02$ (LWF04, LWF02); Time Weighed Forgetting with $w = 0.996$ and $w = 0.998$ (TWF996, TWF998).

For IBL-DS we used the parameters $k_{cand} = 5$ and a maximal size of 5,000 examples for the case memory. For nearest neighbor classification, the neighborhood size was set to $k = 5$ for all algorithms.[2] In order to show the flexibility of IBL-DS, we employed synthetic data with quite different characteristics (see below).

## 4.1    Performance Measures and Data Sets

The learning scenario we considered is a straightforward extension of supervised learning to the data stream setting: At each point of time a new instance $x_0$ arrives (from the query stream) and its class label $\lambda_{x_0}$ is predicted. After the prediction has been made, the correct label is provided by a teacher, the

---

[2] Note that the primary purpose of our studies is to compare the algorithms under equal conditions. This is why we used a fixed neighborhood size instead of optimizing this parameter.

prediction is evaluated, and the case base is updated (i.e., the new example is submitted to the example stream).

All data streams were tested with 50,000 elements, using an initial training set of 100 examples and adding 5% random noise. We derived two types of classification rate: (i) The *streaming* classification rate measures the accuracy on the last 100 instances of the stream. Thus, it is a kind of real accuracy that refers to a certain section of the stream. (ii) The *absolute* classification rate aims at estimating the accuracy at a particular moment of time. To this end, 1,000 extra test instances are generated at random according to a uniform distribution, and the classification accuracy for this test set is derived by using the current case base; this is done for every 10 time points.

We conducted experiments with 8 different data streams (see table 1), some of which have already been used in the literature before: The streams GAUSS, SINE2, STAGGER and MIXED were used in [14], and the HYPERPLANE data (that we generated for the dimensions $d = 2$ and $d = 5$) was used in multiple experiments for data streams in [28]. Besides, we used the following data streams:

DISTRIB: Instances are uniformly distributed in the unit square $[0, 1] \times [0, 1]$. An instance $(x, y)$ belongs to class 1 if $(x, y) \in [0, 0.5] \times [0, 0.5]$ or $(x, y) \in ]0.5, 1] \times ]0.5, 1]$, otherwise to class 0. Even though the concept remains fixed, the underlying distribution does change: the data is only generated in one quarter of the instance space, changing the quarter clockwise every 2,000 instances.

RANDOM: Instances are uniformly distributed in the unit square $[0, 1] \times [0, 1]$. An instance $(x, y)$ belongs to class 1 with probability $p$, independently of $x$ and $y$. Within an interval of 2,000 examples, the probability $p$ increases linearly from 0 to 1, then decreases linearly from 1 to 0 during the next interval of the same length, and so on.

MEANS: The $n$ classes are defined by $n$ center points in $[0, 1]^d$. An instance belongs to the class of the nearest center. Each center moves with a fixed drift for each dimension. If it leaves the unit interval in one dimension, the drift for this dimension is inverted. We have made experiments with $n = 5$ and $d \in \{2, 5\}$. For each dimension, the drift is initialized by a random value in $[-(1/8)^{-3}, (1/8)^{-3}]$.

**Table 1.** Properties of data streams

|         | attributes        | classes | drift/shift    |
|---------|-------------------|---------|----------------|
| GAUSS   | 2 num             | 2       | shift          |
| SINE2   | 2 num             | 2       | shift          |
| DISTRIB | 2 num             | 2       | virtual shift  |
| RANDOM  | 2 num             | 2       | drift (distr.) |
| STAGGER | 3 discr           | 2       | shift          |
| MIXED   | 2 num + 2 discr   | 2       | shift          |
| HYPER   | 2/5 num           | 2       | drift          |
| MEANS   | 2/5 num           | 5       | drift          |

## 4.2   Results

The absolute and streaming classification rates are shown, respectively, in tables 2 and 3. For the data streams GAUSS, SINE2, RANDOM and MIXED, our method IBL-DS shows the best performance regardless of the type of measure; for DISTRIB it performs best in terms of the absolute classification rate. Even if IBL-DS is not the best method for the remaining streams (STAGGER, HYPER, and MEAN), its results are always competitive and close to optimal.

Apparently, IBL-DS performs comparatively well especially for the data streams with concept shift. Thus, our strategy for handling such situations, including a flexible size of the case base, seems to work in practice. In fact, some other methods do obviously have difficulties with abrupt changes of the concept, as suggested by their relatively poor classification rates. Note that concept shift does also occur in STAGGER. Here, however, only 12 different instances exist, so a small case base is always sufficient. In fact, it is not useful to store all examples that support the current concept; this only makes the model less flexible with regard to the next concept shift but does not lead to a higher accuracy.

**Table 2.** Absolute classification rates

|         | IBL-DS | LWF02 | LWF04 | Win200 | Win400 | Win800 | TWF996 | TWF998 |
|---------|--------|-------|-------|--------|--------|--------|--------|--------|
| GAUSS   | **.843** | .805 | .837 | .834 | .804 | .734 | .750 | .693 |
| SINE2   | **.919** | .863 | .898 | .896 | .868 | .788 | .838 | .762 |
| DISTRIB | **.948** | .913 | .888 | .504 | .508 | .514 | .500 | .505 |
| RANDOM  | **.723** | .706 | .718 | .712 | .704 | .674 | .655 | .625 |
| STAGGER | .956 | .806 | .806 | **.978** | .962 | .917 | .916 | .908 |
| MIXED   | **.906** | .713 | .707 | .898 | .870 | .790 | .840 | .765 |
| HYPER2  | .969 | **.970** | .965 | .959 | .965 | .963 | .923 | .919 |
| HYPER5  | **.904** | .892 | .896 | .876 | .886 | .880 | .839 | .834 |
| MEANS2  | .944 | **.950** | .935 | .918 | .939 | .946 | .913 | .914 |
| MEANS5  | .809 | **.828** | .796 | .736 | .778 | .810 | .735 | .763 |

For the DISTRIB data, the extreme differences between absolute and streaming classification rate call for explanation. To understand these differences recall the special distribution of the training data: After a shift of this distribution, it takes 6,000 time steps (instances) until the next instance for the previous quarter will arrive. All window-based approaches will soon forget all the data of this quarter. Only the LWF algorithm stores all the data the whole time. IBL-DS will have the highest accuracies after training instances have been seen in all quarters (viz. after 6,000 instances). Before, LWF performs slightly better, since this algorithm does not delete as many of the 100 examples used for initialization.

The simple window-based algorithm shows a very good performance for the HYPERPLANE and the MEANS data. Again, there is a simple explanation for this result: These two data streams have a small concept drift rate which does hardly change over time. Therefore, the optimal size of the case base will remain more or less constant as well. Since training data is furthermore uniformly distributed,

**Table 3.** Streaming classification rates

|          | IBL-DS | LWF02 | LWF04 | Win200 | Win400 | Win800 | TWF996 | TWF998 |
|----------|--------|-------|-------|--------|--------|--------|--------|--------|
| GAUSS    | **.807** | .772 | .801 | .798 | .771 | .707 | .724 | .668 |
| SINE2    | **.878** | .827 | .858 | .857 | .833 | .758 | .804 | .738 |
| DISTRIB  | .939 | .943 | **.945** | .943 | .940 | .937 | .900 | .899 |
| RANDOM   | **.724** | .706 | .721 | .714 | .706 | .673 | .654 | .621 |
| STAGGER  | .909 | .770 | .770 | **.929** | .914 | .875 | .872 | .866 |
| MIXED    | **.865** | .691 | .685 | .856 | .831 | .758 | .804 | .738 |
| HYPER2   | .921 | **.922** | .918 | .913 | .918 | .916 | .879 | .875 |
| HYPER5   | **.865** | .855 | .858 | .839 | .849 | .844 | .807 | .804 |
| MEANS2   | .908 | **.914** | .899 | .885 | .903 | .910 | .881 | .881 |
| MEANS5   | .780 | **.800** | .770 | .714 | .751 | .783 | .710 | .740 |

using a window of fixed size is indeed a suitable strategy. Again, however, note that the classification rate of IBL-DS is not much worse.

## 4.3   Real World Data

So far, only synthetic data sets have been used. Even though synthetic data allows one to model special effects and, hence, is advantageous from this point of view, conducting experiments with real-word data is of course also desirable. As already mentioned above, however, real-world data streams are hard to obtain. To overcome this problem, at least to some extent, we decided to use (static) benchmark data sets from the UCI repository and to prepare them as data streams.

In this regard, note that any data set, provided it is not too small, can be considered as a stream, simply by imposing an arbitrary ordering of the data items. More specifically, however, since a data stream is by definition an open-ended sequence, an ordered data set can at best be considered as a *section* of a stream. Besides, concept drift will usually not be present in streams of that kind. To simulate concept drift we did the following, inspired by [23]: First, the data set is put into a random order. Then, the most relevant input feature is identified using the "Correlation-based Feature Subset Selection" method implemented in WEKA, and the data is sorted according to the value of that attribute. Finally, the attribute itself is deleted from the data, thereby becoming a "hidden factor". This way, a kind of concept shift is obtained in the case of discrete attributes, whereas numerical attributes will produce gradual concept drift.

To qualify as a (pseudo-)stream, a data set should first of all not be too small. Moreover, a useful data set will have a reasonable number of classes and more-over, should not contain features that are highly correlated with the attribute used to simulate concept drift. These requirements are satisfied by only a few UCI data sets. For our studies, we selected the Balance, Car and Nursery data. Table 4 summarizes the main properties of these data sets.

**Table 4.** UCI data sets prepared as (pseudo-)streams

| data set | #instances | #classes | #attributes | selected attribute |
|---|---|---|---|---|
| Balance | 625 | 3 | 4 | right-distance (numeric) |
| Car | 1728 | 4 | 6 | safety(nominal) |
| Nursery | 11025 | 5 | 8 | health (nominal) |

IBL-DS was employed in its default parameter setting. For LWF the parameters $\beta = .04$ and $\beta = .1$ are used, TWF is run with $weight = .99$ and $weight = .995$, and the fixed sliding window approach (Win) with $size = 50, 100, 200$. To show that concept drift does really occur, the standard instance based algorithm (IBL) that simply stores all instances is additionally applied.

The results are presented in table 5. As can be seen, IBL-DS again performs very well, even for these different types of data streams, without the need to change its parameters (apart from the case base size). Moreover, the standard instance-based algorithm clearly drops off and cannot compete, probably due to the simulated drift of the concept.

**Table 5.** Streaming classification rates for UCI data

|  | Balance | Car | Nursery |
|---|---|---|---|
| IBL-DS | .805 | .889 | .900 |
| LWF04 | .782 | .700 | .899 |
| LWF10 | .846 | .700 | .842 |
| Win50 | .813 | .819 | .827 |
| Win100 | .815 | .862 | .856 |
| Win200 | .785 | .888 | .878 |
| TWF99 | .795 | .889 | .877 |
| TWF995 | .787 | .887 | .900 |
| IBL | .693 | .745 | .839 |

## 5   Summary and Conclusions

We have presented an instance-based adaptive classification algorithm for learning on data streams. This algorithm, called IBL-DS, has a number of desirable properties that are not, at least not as a whole, shared by existing alternative methods. Our experiments suggest that IBL-DS is very flexible and thus able to adapt to an evolving environment quickly, a point of utmost importance in the data stream context. In particular, two specially designed editing strategies are used in combination in order to successfully deal with both gradual concept drift and abrupt concept shift. Besides, IBL-DS is relatively robust and produces good results when being used in a default setting for its parameters.

The JAVA implementation of IBL-DS is available for experimental purposes and can be downloaded, along with a documentation, under the following address: wwwiti.cs.uni-magdeburg.de/iti_dke.

There are various directions for further research. For example, techniques for model (case base) maintenance and adaptation like the one proposed in [19] are quite interesting, since they are less heuristic than those currently employed in IBL-DS. Even though it is not immediately clear how such techniques can be used in a streaming application with tight time and resource constraints, investigating such approaches in more detail and trying to adapt them correspondingly seems worthwhile.

# References

1. Aggarwal, C., Han, J., Wang, J., Yu, P.: A framework for clustering evolving data streams. In: Aberer, K., Koubarakis, M., Kalogeraki, V. (eds.) Databases, Information Systems, and Peer-to-Peer Computing. LNCS, vol. 2944, Springer, Heidelberg (2004)
2. Aha, D.W. (ed.): Lazy Learning. Kluwer Academic Publishers, Dordrecht (1997)
3. Aha, D.W., Kibler, D., Albert, M.K.: Instance-based learning algorithms. Machine Learning 6(1), 37–66 (1991)
4. Babcock, B., Babu, S., Datar, M., Motwani, R., Widom, J.: Models and issues in data stream systems. In: Proc. 21st ACM SIGACT-SIGMOD-SIGART Symp. on Principles of Database Systems, Madison, Wisconsin, pp. 1–16. ACM Press, New York (2002)
5. Ben-David, S., Gehrke, J., Kifer, D.: Detecting change in data streams. In: Proc. VLDB–04 (2004)
6. Bercken, J., Blohsfeld, B., Dittrich, J., Krämer, J., Schäfer, T., Schneider, M., Seeger, B.: XXL - a library approach to supporting effcient implementations of advanced database queries. In: Proceedings of the VLDB, pp. 39–48 (2001)
7. Ciaccia, P., Patella, M., Rabitti, F., Zezula, P.: Indexing metric spaces with M-tree. In: Proc. SEBD'97, Verona, Italy, June 1997, pp. 67–86 (1997)
8. Cormode, G., Muthukrishnan, S.: What's hot and what's not: tracking most frequent items dynamically. In: Proc. 22nd ACM SIGMOD-SIGACT-SIGART Symp. on Principles of Database Systems, pp. 296–306. ACM Press, New York (2003)
9. Dasarathy, B.V. (ed.): Nearest Neighbor (NN) Norms: NN Pattern Classification Techniques. IEEE Computer Society Press, Los Alamitos (1991)
10. Datar, M., Muthukrishnan, S.: Estimating rarity and similarity over data stream windows. In: Möhring, R.H., Raman, R. (eds.) ESA 2002. LNCS, vol. 2461, pp. 323–334. Springer, Heidelberg (2002)
11. Domingos, P.: Unifying instance-based and rule-based induction. Machine Learning 24, 141–168 (1996)
12. Domingos, P., Hulten, G.: A general framework for mining massive data streams. Journal of Computational and Graphical Statistics, 12 (2003)
13. Gaber, M.M., Zaslavsky, A., Krishnaswamy, S.: Mining data streams: A review. ACM SIGMOD Record 34(1) (2005)
14. Gama, J., Medas, P., Castillo, G., Rodrigues, P.: Learning with drift detection. In: Bazzan, A.L.C., Labidi, S. (eds.) SBIA 2004. LNCS (LNAI), vol. 3171, pp. 286–295. Springer, Heidelberg (2004)
15. Gama, J., Medas, P., Rodrigues, P.: Learning decision trees from dynamic data streams. In: Preneel, B., Tavares, S. (eds.) SAC 2005, pp. 573–577. ACM Press, New York (2005)

48      J. Beringer and E. Hüllermeier

16. Golab, L., Tamer, M.: Issues in data stream management. SIGMOD Rec. 32(2), 5–14 (2003)
17. Hulten, G., Spencer, L., Domingos, P.: Mining time-changing data streams. In: Proceedings of the seventh ACM SIGKDD international conference on Knowledge discovery and data mining, pp. 97–106. ACM Press, New York (2001)
18. Keogh, E., Kasetty, S.: On the need for time series data mining benchmarks: A survey and empirical demonstration. In: 8th ACM SIGKDD International Conference on Knowledge Discovery and Data Mining, Edmonton, Alberta, Canada, July 2002, pp. 102–111. ACM Press, New York (2002)
19. Klinkenberg, R., Joachims, T.: Detecting concept drift with support vector machines. In: Proc. ICML, 17th Int. Conf. on Machine Learning, San Francisco, CA, pp. 487–494 (2000)
20. Klinkenberg, R.: Learning drifting concepts: Example selection vs. example weighting. Intelligent Data Analysis (IDA), Special Issue on Incremental Learning Systems Capable of Dealing with Concept Drift 8(3), 281–300 (2004)
21. Kolter, J.Z., Maloof, M.A.: Dynamic weighted majority: A new ensemble method for tracking concept drift. Technical Report CSTR-20030610-3, Department of Computer Science, Georgetown University, Washington, DC (June 2003)
22. Kubat, M., Widmer, G.: Adapting to drift in continuous domains. In: Lavrač, N., Wrobel, S. (eds.) Machine Learning: ECML-95. LNCS, vol. 912, p. 307. Springer, Heidelberg (1995)
23. Law, Y.N., Zaniolo, C.: An adaptive nearest neighbor classification algorithm for data streams. In: Jorge, A.M., Torgo, L., Brazdil, P.B., Camacho, R., Gama, J. (eds.) PKDD 2005. LNCS (LNAI), vol. 3721, Springer, Heidelberg (2005)
24. McKenna, E., Smyth, B.: Competence-guided editing methods for lazy learning. In: ECAI, pp. 60–64 (2000)
25. Salganicoff, M.: Tolerating concept and sampling shift in lazy learning using prediction error context switching. Artif. Intell. Rev. 11(1-5), 133–155 (1997)
26. Stanfil, C., Waltz, D.: Toward memory-based reasoning. Communications of the ACM 29, 1213–1228 (1986)
27. Tsymbal, A.: The problem of concept drift: definitions and related work. Technical Report TCD-CS-2004-15, Department of Computer Science, Trinity College Dublin, Ireland (2004)
28. Wang, H., Fan, W., Yu, P.S., Han, J.: Mining concept-drifting data streams using ensemble classifiers. In: KDD '03. Proceedings of the ninth ACM SIGKDD international conference on Knowledge discovery and data mining, pp. 226–235. ACM Press, New York (2003)
29. Widmer, G., Kubat, M.: Effective learning in dynamic environments by explicit context tracking. In: Brazdil, P.B. (ed.) Machine Learning: ECML-93. LNCS, vol. 667, pp. 227–243. Springer, Heidelberg (1993)
30. Widmer, G., Kubat, M.: Learning in the presence of concept drift and hidden contexts. Mach. Learn. 23(1), 69–101 (1996)
31. Witten, I., Frank, E.: Data Mining: Practical machine learning tools and techniques, 2nd edn. Morgan Kaufmann, San Francisco (2005)

# Softening the Margin in Discrete SVM

Carlotta Orsenigo[1] and Carlo Vercellis[2]

[1] Dip. di Scienze Economiche, Aziendali e Statistiche, Università di Milano, Italy
carlotta.orsenigo@unimi.it
[2] Dip. di Ingegneria Gestionale, Politecnico di Milano, Italy
carlo.vercellis@polimi.it

**Abstract.** Discrete support vector machines are models for classification recently introduced in the context of statistical learning theory. Their distinctive feature is the formulation of mixed integer programming problems aimed at deriving optimal separating hyperplanes with minimum empirical error and maximum generalization capability. A new family of discrete SVM is proposed in this paper, for which the hyperplane establishes a variable softening of the margin to improve the separation among distinct classes. Theoretical bounds are derived to finely tune the parameters of the optimization problem. Computational tests on benchmark datasets in the biolife science application domain indicate the effectiveness of the proposed approach, that appears dominating against traditional SVM in terms of accuracy and percentage of support vectors.

**Keywords:** discrete support vector machines; statistical learning theory; classification; biolife sciences; data mining.

## 1  Introduction

Statistical learning theory (Vapnik, 1995; 1998) has germinated accurate and practical methods for classification, among which the well known family of *support vector machines* (SVM) (Burges, 1998; Cristianini and Shawe-Taylor, 2000; Schölkopf and Smola, 2002). The structural risk minimization (SRM) principle, which plays a central role in statistical learning theory, establishes that a good classifier trained on a given dataset should simultaneously minimize the empirical classification error and the generalization error, in order to achieve a high discrimination capability on unseen data. To attain this goal, SVM approximate the misclassification error with the sum of the slacks of the training points from the discriminant function, and the generalization error with the reciprocal of the margin of separation.

*Discrete support vector machines*, originally introduced in (Orsenigo and Vercellis, 2003; 2004), are a successful alternative to SVM that is based on the idea of accurately evaluating the number of misclassified examples instead of measuring their distance from the separating hyperplane. Hence, discrete SVM rely on the SRM principle, and their common distinguishing feature is the evaluation of the empirical error by a discrete function which counts the number of misclassified instances. This leads to the formulation of mixed integer programming models that are hard to solve to optimality, but for which good sub-optimal solutions can be obtained by devising

P. Perner (Ed.): ICDM 2007, LNAI 4597, pp. 49–62, 2007.

fast heuristic algorithms. Starting from the original formulation, discrete SVM have been effectively extended in several directions, to deal with multi-class problems (Orsenigo and Vercellis, 2007a) or to learn from a small number of training examples (Orsenigo and Vercellis, 2007b).

In this paper we propose a new variant of discrete SVM for which the optimal discriminating hyperplane establishes a variable softening of the margin of separation by including a new term into the objective function and modifying some of the constraints of the optimization problem. The explicit inclusion of the margin as a variable allows to regulate more effectively the trade-off between the misclassification error on the training data and the generalization capability, by means of the corresponding cost coefficient. When this latter is large, there is an advantage in taking a large margin as well, and the misclassification error increases; by converse, small values of the coefficient induce the margin to decrease, reducing the empirical error at the expense of generalization. In this respect, the proposed model has relations with the line of reasoning behind $\nu$ -SVM (Schölkopf and Smola, 2002). As for previous discrete SVM, a set of binary variables regulate the complexity of the separation rule to further improve the generalization capability of the classifier.

The description of the proposed model in section 3 highlights also a new perspective on previous discrete SVM models, by expressing the objective function as a weighted sum of 1-norms and 0-norms. To avoid numerical difficulties due to ill-conditioning, some theoretical bounds are derived which allow to finely tune the parameters of the optimization model.

Finally, in order to validate the proposed approach, computational tests on benchmark datasets taken from biolife classification problems have been systematically conducted. These problems, described in section 4, represent well-known challenging binary and multicategory classification tasks. The computational results seem to suggest that the proposed classifier dominates in terms of accuracy traditional SVM and $\nu$ -SVM with different kernels, and also improves previous versions of discrete SVM. Furthermore, the new model is characterized by a percentage of support vectors significantly smaller than for the other SVM methods considered.

The chapter is organized as follows. In section 2 we provide a definition of classification problems and a description of traditional SVM. Discrete SVM are introduced in section 3, where the new model for softening the margin is proposed. Finally, computational tests are illustrated in section 4.

## 2  Classification and Support Vector Machines

Classification problems require to discriminate between distinct pattern sets. Formally, $m$ points $(\mathbf{x}_i, y_i), i \in M = \{1, 2, \ldots, m\}$, in the $(n+1)$ -dimensional real space $\Re^{n+1}$ are given, where $\mathbf{x}_i$ is a $n$-dimensional vector of *attributes* or *features* and $y_i$ a scalar representing the *label* or *class* of instance $i$. Let $\mathcal{D} = \{1, 2, \ldots, D\}$ be the set of distinct class values that can be assumed by $y_i$ and $\mathcal{D}^* = \mathcal{D} \cup \{*\}$, where the symbol $\{*\}$ stands for an undefined predicted value. We are then required to determine a *discriminant function* $f_a : \Re^n \to \mathcal{D}^*$ such that a suitable measure of discrepancy between $f_a(\mathbf{x}_i)$ and $y_i$ is minimized over $i \in M$. Here $\boldsymbol{\alpha}$ is a vector of adjustable parameters by which the discriminant function is indexed. It is further assumed that the $m$ points are independently drawn from some common unknown probability distribution $P(\mathbf{x}, y)$.

To assess the accuracy of $f_a(\mathbf{x})$, the whole set of instances is partitioned into two disjoint subsets, denoted respectively as *training* and *test* set. For a given classifier, the discriminant function is learned using only instances from the training set and then applied to predict the class of points in the test set in order to evaluate the accuracy. The attention will be restricted in what follows to binary classification problems arising when $D = 2$, i.e. the class attribute $y_i$ takes only two different values, which may be labeled as $\{-1, +1\}$ without loss of generality.

It has been noticed that most binary classifiers actually generate as output a function $g_a : \Re^n \to \Re$, termed *score function* or *margin*, whose sign discriminates between the two classes, so that $f_a(\mathbf{x}) = \text{sgn}(g_a(\mathbf{x}))$. Moreover, for these binary margin classifiers, the magnitude of the score $g_a(\mathbf{x})$ can be viewed as a measure of confidence in the class assignment.

Let also $\mathcal{A}$ and $\mathcal{B}$ denote the two sets of points represented by the vectors $\mathbf{x}_i$ in the space $\Re^n$ and corresponding respectively to the two classes $y_i = -1$ and $y_i = +1$. If the two point sets $\mathcal{A}$ and $\mathcal{B}$ are linearly separable, that is when their convex hulls do not intersect, at least a separating hyperplane $g_a(\mathbf{x}) = \mathbf{w}'\mathbf{x} - b$ exists which discriminates the points in $\mathcal{A}$ from those in $\mathcal{B}$, i.e. such that

$$\begin{aligned} \mathbf{w}'\mathbf{x}_i - b > 0 \quad \text{if} \quad \mathbf{x}_i \in \mathcal{A} \\ \mathbf{w}'\mathbf{x}_i - b < 0 \quad \text{if} \quad \mathbf{x}_i \in \mathcal{B} \end{aligned} \quad i \in M. \tag{1}$$

In this case $f_a(\mathbf{x}_i) = \text{sgn}(g_a(\mathbf{x}_i)) = y_i$ for every $i \in M$, and $\boldsymbol{\alpha} = (\mathbf{w}, b)$. In order to determine the coefficients $\mathbf{w} \in \Re^n$ and $b \in \Re$ a linear programming problem can be solved, as in (Mangasarian, 1965). Conversely, when the point sets $\mathcal{A}$ and $\mathcal{B}$ are not linearly separable, inequalities (1) cannot be satisfied for all the instances of the dataset and more complex schemes of classification should be devised to minimize a reasonable measure of violation of (1). In this perspective, a successful approach is represented by the theory of support vector machines (SVM) (Vapnik, 1995; 1998). SVM are based on the structural risk minimization (SRM) principle, that establishes the concept of reducing the empirical classification error as well as the generalization error in order to achieve a higher accuracy on unseen data. This leads to the minimization of the expression

$$\frac{\|\mathbf{w}\|_2^2}{2} + \frac{1}{2m} \sum_{i=1}^m | y_i - f_a(\mathbf{x}_i) |, \quad \text{where} \quad \|\mathbf{w}\|_2 = \sqrt{\sum_{j \in N} w_j^2}, \tag{2}$$

assuming conventionally that $|y_i - f_a(\mathbf{x}_i)| = 2$ whenever $f_a(\mathbf{x}_i) = *$, that is when the predicted class of $\mathbf{x}_i$ is left undefined. The first term in (2) is the reciprocal of the *margin of separation*, defined as the distance between the pair of parallel *canonical supporting hyperplanes* $\mathbf{w}'\mathbf{x} - b - 1 = 0$ and $\mathbf{w}'\mathbf{x} - b + 1 = 0$. The geometrical interpretation of the canonical hyperplanes and the margin is given in figure 1. The maximization of this margin increases the generalization capability of the classifier. The second term in (2) is called *empirical risk* and expresses the accuracy of the classifier on the training set through the percentage of misclassified instances. The examples $\mathbf{x}_i, i \in M$, that are positioned precisely on the two canonical supporting hyperplanes are termed *support vectors*, and are in some sense more relevant in the training set than other examples, since they contribute more directly to determining the separating hyperplane. For example, in figure 1 we have three support vectors, two of them of class "white" and the third of class "black".

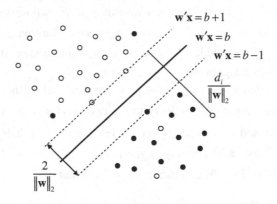

**Fig. 1.** Margin maximization for linearly non separable sets

Define a nonnegative continuous slack variable $d_i, i \in M$, for each instance of the dataset, such that the following linear constraints are satisfied:

$$y_i(\mathbf{w}'\mathbf{x}_i - b) \geq 1 - d_i, \quad i \in M . \tag{3}$$

Then, as noticed in (Vapnik,1995), for sufficiently small $\sigma > 0$ the function

$$F_\sigma(\mathbf{d}) = \sum_{i \in M} d_i^\sigma \tag{4}$$

evaluates the empirical risk by counting the number of misclassification errors on the training set, provided the discriminant function is defined as follows:

$$f_a(\mathbf{x}) = \begin{cases} +1 & \text{if } \mathbf{w}'\mathbf{x} - b \geq 1 \\ -1 & \text{if } \mathbf{w}'\mathbf{x} - b \leq -1 . \\ * & \text{otherwise} \end{cases} \tag{5}$$

Hence, the optimal separating hyperplane can be determined by solving the optimization problem

$$\min \quad \frac{\lambda}{2}\|\mathbf{w}\|_2^2 + \frac{1}{m}\sum_{i\in M} d_i^\sigma \tag{6}$$

$$\text{s. to} \quad y_i(\mathbf{w}'\mathbf{x}_i - b) \geq 1 - d_i, \quad i \in M \tag{7}$$

$$d_i \geq 0, i \in M; \mathbf{w}, b \text{ free},$$

for sufficiently small $\sigma > 0$, where $\lambda$ is a parameter available to control the trade-off between the generalization capability of the classifier and the misclassification error. To avoid computational difficulties, in the classical theory of SVM the empirical risk is regularized and approximated by solving problem (6) only for the value $\sigma = 1$. This leads to a quadratic programming problem, whose solution is obtained via Lagrangean duality which, beside the computational benefits, also provides the interpretation of the support vectors. Taking advantage of the dual formulation and of suitable kernel functions (Cristianini and Shawe-Taylor, 2000; Schölkopf and Smola, 2002), SVM proceed by projecting the original examples into a higher dimensional feature space, in which the linear separation is derived, allowing to efficiently obtain nonlinear discriminations in the original space.

## 3  Softening the Margin in Discrete Support Vector Machines

A different family of classification models, termed *discrete support vector machines*, has been introduced in (Orsenigo and Vercellis, 2003; 2004) and is motivated by a more strict adherence to the SRM principle, by counting the number of misclassified examples instead of measuring their distance from the separating hyperplane. The distinctive trait of discrete SVM is the accurate representation of the empirical error, by using the total misclassification error in the objective function, in place of the sum of the slacks considered in (6) by traditional SVM. Hence, the rational behind discrete SVM is that a precise evaluation of the empirical error could possibly lead to a more accurate classifier.

In this section we extend previous discrete SVM models by proposing a different mathematical programming formulation for determining the optimal separating hyperplane. To derive the objective function we modify the expression given in (2). First, the 2-norm of $\mathbf{w}$ is replaced by the 1-norm

$$\|w\|_1 = \sum_{j\in N} |w_j|. \tag{8}$$

Beside computational advantages, this choice also removes asymmetries between the two terms in (2), as the margin is squared whereas the misclassification error is not. As the second term we utilize the total misclassification rate. Finally, a third term is added to (2) in order to minimize the number of nonzero components of the coefficients vector $\mathbf{w}$, that is the number of features utilized for discrimination. This choice has two main motivations: by reducing the number of used features, it is likely to increase the generalization capability of a model learned on the training set. Furthermore, the induced rules become simpler and more suitable to the interpretation of domain experts; see also (Orsenigo and Vercellis, 2006). The third term we introduce in (2) is given by the following zero-norm

$$\|\mathbf{w}\|_0^0 = \text{card}(i : w_i \neq 0) , \tag{9}$$

where $\text{card}(E)$ is the cardinality of a set $E$. The zero-norm can be seen as the limit of the $p$-th power of the $\ell_p$-norm

$$\|\mathbf{w}\|_p^p = \left( \sum_{j \in N} w_j^p \right)^{1/p} , \tag{10}$$

as in (Weston et al., 2003). The resulting objective function is a weighted combination of three components, with weights $(\beta_1, \beta_2, \beta_3)$ regulating their trade-off:

$$\frac{\beta_1}{2} \|\mathbf{w}\|_1 + \frac{\beta_2}{2m} \sum_{i=1}^{m} | y_i - f_\alpha(\mathbf{x}_i) | + \beta_3 \|\mathbf{w}\|_0^0 . \tag{11}$$

If we let $\theta_i = \theta(\mathbf{x}_i)$ be an indicator function defined as

$$\theta_i = \begin{cases} 0 & \text{if } f_\alpha(\mathbf{x}_i) = y_i \\ 1 & \text{if } f_\alpha(\mathbf{x}_i) \neq y_i \end{cases} \quad i \in M , \tag{12}$$

then (11) can be expressed as a weighted sum of norms

$$\frac{\beta_1}{2} \|\mathbf{w}\|_1 + \frac{\beta_2}{m} \|\boldsymbol{\theta}\|_0^0 + \beta_3 \|\mathbf{w}\|_0^0 . \tag{13}$$

By assuming the discriminant function given in (5), the following discrete support vector machine optimization problem can be formulated to determine the optimal separating hyperplane

$$\min_{\mathbf{w}, b, L \subseteq M} \frac{\beta_1}{2} \|\mathbf{w}\|_1 + \frac{\beta_2}{m} \|\boldsymbol{\theta}\|_0^0 + \beta_3 \|\mathbf{w}\|_0^0 \tag{14}$$

$$\text{s. to} \quad y_i(\mathbf{w}'\mathbf{x}_i - b) \geq 1, \quad i \in L .$$

In problem (14) one is required to simultaneously determine a subset $L \subseteq M$ of points to be left misclassified and the hyperplane coefficients $\mathbf{w}, b$ in a way to minimize the weighted sum of the reciprocal of the margin, the empirical error and the number of active features. Model (14) is a complex combinatorial optimization problem defined over an exponentially high number of subsets. However, it can be transformed into a mixed integer programming model by properly defining binary variables. Indeed, the number of misclassified points is already counted by the binary indicator variables $\theta_i, i \in M$, whereas the following binary variables account for the nonzero components of the vector $\mathbf{w}$

$$\tau_j = \begin{cases} 0 & \text{if } w_j = 0 \\ 1 & \text{if } w_j \neq 0 \end{cases} \quad j \in N. \tag{15}$$

Let $c_i, i \in M$, denote the misclassification cost associated to instance $i$, and $p_j, j \in N$, the penalty cost for using attribute $j$. Let also $Q$ and $P$ be sufficiently large constant values. By linearizing the 1-norm in (13) with nonnegative bounding variables $u_j, j \in N$, problem (14) can thus be formulated as the following mixed binary linear programming problem (DSVM):

$$\min \quad \frac{\beta_1}{2} \sum_{j \in N} u_j + \frac{\beta_2}{m} \sum_{i \in M} c_i \theta_i + \beta_3 \sum_{j \in N} p_j \tau_j \tag{DSVM}$$

$$\text{s. to} \quad y_i(\mathbf{w'x}_i - b) \geq 1 - Q\theta_i, \quad i \in M \tag{16}$$

$$-u_j \leq w_j \leq u_j, \quad j \in N \tag{17}$$

$$u_j \leq P\tau_j, \quad j \in N \tag{18}$$

$$\theta_i \in \{0,1\}, i \in M; u_j \geq 0, \tau_j \in \{0,1\}, j \in N; \mathbf{w}, b \text{ free}.$$

Model (DSVM) is a mixed binary linear optimization problem, notoriously more difficult to solve to optimality than continuous linear optimization. However, it can be solved by means of an efficient heuristic procedure, based on a sequence of linear optimization problems, for obtaining suboptimal solutions. Model (DSVM) can be used as a linear perceptron; alternatively, it can be framed within a recursive procedure for the generation of oblique classification trees, to derive an optimal separating hyperplane at each node of the tree, as in (Orsenigo and Vercellis, 2003; 2004). In the quoted references, it was shown by means of extensive testing that the increase in model complexity is justified by a more accurate discrimination and a higher generalization capability, due to the correct estimation of the empirical misclassification error and the minimization of the number of attributes defining the separating hyperplane.

Here we wish to go one step further in the evaluation of the misclassification error. Observe first that the formulation of the discriminant function $f_a(\mathbf{x})$ implies that all points falling between the pair of canonical supporting hyperplanes are considered unclassified. Correspondingly, constraints (7) in the SVM formulation stick on the same assumption, since they determine a strictly positive slack variable $d_i$, and therefore determine a misclassification error. The same remains true also in the (DSVM) formulation, as constraints (16) imply $\theta_i = 1$ whenever point $\mathbf{x}_i$ lies between the two canonical hyperplanes. In light of this assumption, these models are termed *soft margin* classifiers, because the region between the canonical hyperplanes is left unclassified. The width of the margin between the two canonical hyperplanes is driven by the first term in (DSVM), expressing the norm of $\mathbf{w}$. In this paper we want to exploit the effect of a different classification model, for which the margin is determined by means of the explicit inclusion of a new variable $\varepsilon$. To do this we consider the following discriminant function

$$f_a(\mathbf{x}) = \begin{cases} +1 & \text{if } \mathbf{w}'\mathbf{x} - b \geq \varepsilon \\ -1 & \text{if } \mathbf{w}'\mathbf{x} - b \leq -\varepsilon \end{cases}, \tag{19}$$

where $\varepsilon > 0$ is a variable to be determined. Consequently, the empirical error appearing as the second term in the bound (2) should account only for those points which are actually misclassified by the discriminant separating function. We therefore formulate the $\varepsilon$ -*discrete support vector machine* ( $\varepsilon$-DSVM ) model:

$$\min \quad \frac{1}{2}\sum_{j \in N} u_j + \frac{1}{m}\sum_{i \in M} c_i \theta_i + \mu \sum_{j \in N} p_j \tau_j - v\varepsilon \qquad (\varepsilon\text{-DSVM})$$

$$\text{s. to} \qquad y_i(\mathbf{w}'\mathbf{x}_i - b) \geq \varepsilon - Q\theta_i, \quad i \in M \tag{20}$$

$$-u_j \leq w_j \leq u_j, \quad j \in N \tag{21}$$

$$u_j \leq P\tau_j, \quad j \in N \tag{22}$$

$$\theta_i \in \{0,1\}, i \in M; u_j \geq 0, \tau_j \in \{0,1\}, j \in N; \varepsilon \geq \rho; \mathbf{w}, b \text{ free},$$

where $\rho > 0$ is a lower threshold to prevent the case $\varepsilon = 0$. The variable $\varepsilon$ can be interpreted as a way of progressively softening or hardening the separation between the two classes determined by the optimal hyperplane: when $\varepsilon$ decreases and approaches 0 the soft margin around the separating hyperplane reduces and tend to vanish, whereas the opposite is true when $\varepsilon$ increases.

Notice that the objective function of model ( $\varepsilon$-DSVM ) still incorporates the first term related to margin maximization and the third term for minimizing the number of active features, so that the generalization capability on new data should be preserved. However, the explicit inclusion of the variable $\varepsilon$ allows to fix to the value $\beta_1 = \beta_2 = 1$ of the weight parameters for the first two terms. The trade-off between the misclassification error on the training data and the generalization capability is indeed regulated in model ( $\varepsilon$-DSVM ) by the parameter $v$ : when $v$ is large, there is an advantage in taking $\varepsilon$ large as well, and the misclassification error increases. By converse, small values of $v$ induce $\varepsilon$ to decrease, reducing the empirical error at the expense of generalization. In this respect, model ( $\varepsilon$-DSVM ) has relations with the line of reasoning behind $v$ -SVM (Schölkopf and Smola, 2002). As for (DSVM), the parameter $\mu$ in ( $\varepsilon$-DSVM ) weighs the complexity of the separation rule.

One might be tempted to solve problem ( $\varepsilon$-DSVM ) also for $\varepsilon = 0$. Notice however that in this case constraints (20) might lead to optimal solutions for which $\mathbf{w} = \mathbf{0}$. Efforts have been devoted by some authors to prevent the risk of incurring in such degenerate separating hyperplanes; a survey is given in (Koehler and Erenguc,

1990). Formulation (DSVM) does not disallow trivial solutions in principle; however degenerate solutions may occur solely if $\mathbf{w} = \mathbf{0}$ actually represents the optimal solution to the classification concept, due to the presence of the binary variables $\theta_i$ with their misclassification costs $c_i$. Indeed, a degenerate hyperplane with $\mathbf{w} = \mathbf{0}$ corresponds to labeling all instances with the same class, and arises therefore when any separating hyperplane (with $\mathbf{w} \neq \mathbf{0}$) causes the objective function in (DSVM) to increase. Constraints (20), combined with the inclusion into the objective function of the variable $\varepsilon$, prevent trivial solutions for problem ($\varepsilon$-DSVM).

Models (DSVM) and ($\varepsilon$-DSVM) include two big constants $Q$ and $P$ required to force binary variables to 1. When such feature occurs in a mixed integer programming model, it is well known that the constants should be chosen as smallest as possible in order to prevent numerical difficulties during the solution phase, due to ill-conditioning in the coefficients matrix. Hence, in the sequel we will provide tight bounds on the values that parameters $Q$ and $P$ should assume in order to ensure proper forcing of the binary variables. We start by limiting parameter $Q$. Let $R$ denote the smallest radius of a sphere enclosing all the points of the training dataset. We have

$$2R = \max_{\mathbf{x}_i, \mathbf{x}_j} \sqrt{\sum_{k=1}^{m} (x_{ik} - x_{jk})^2} . \tag{23}$$

Let also

$$s_i = \mathbf{w}'\mathbf{x}_i - b, \quad i \in M , \tag{24}$$

be the slack of point $\mathbf{x}_i$ with respect to the separating hyperplane. Without loss of generality we can assume that the slack of each point $\mathbf{x}_i, i \in M$, with respect to an optimal hyperplane in model ($\varepsilon$-DSVM) is bounded above in modulus by the maximum distance between pairs of points in the training set, that is $|s_i| \leq 2R$. This maximum corresponds to classifying all points in the training set as belonging to the same class. Furthermore, due to constraints (20), parameter $Q$ must be large enough that

$$\varepsilon - y_i(\mathbf{w}'\mathbf{x}_i - b) \leq Q, \quad i \in M . \tag{25}$$

We then want to show that the choice $Q = 2R + 1$ is sufficient to guarantee that conditions (25) are met. Indeed

$$\varepsilon - y_i(\mathbf{w}'\mathbf{x}_i - b) \leq 1 + |y_i(\mathbf{w}'\mathbf{x}_i - b)| \leq 1 + |\mathbf{w}'\mathbf{x}_i - b| = 1 + |s_i| \leq 1 + 2R . \tag{26}$$

The limitation of parameter $P$ follows a different line of reasoning. It is known (Vapnik, 1995) that imposing the condition $\|\mathbf{w}\|_2 \leq A$ implies that the separating hyperplane cannot be closer than $1/A$ to any of the training points $\mathbf{x}_i$. We therefore impose that $P = A/\sqrt{n}$, where $n$ is the number of features of the classification problem, and $A$ is selected as a satisfactory level of closeness between the separating hyperplane and the training points. In light of constraints (17) this choice leads to the required limitation:

$$\left\| \mathbf{w} \right\|_2 = \sqrt{\sum_{j \in N} w_j^2} \leq \sqrt{\sum_{j \in N} u_j^2} \leq A .$$

(27)

Here is a short description of the heuristic procedure for determining a feasible suboptimal solution to model ($\varepsilon$-DSVM), based on a sequence of linear programming (LP) problems. The heuristic starts by considering the LP relaxation of problem ($\varepsilon$-DSVM). Each LP problem ($\varepsilon$-DSVM)$_{t+1}$ in the sequence is obtained by fixing to zero the relaxed binary variable with the smallest fractional value in the optimal solution of the predecessor ($\varepsilon$-DSVM)$_t$. Notice that, if problem ($\varepsilon$-DSVM)$_t$ is feasible and its optimal solution is integer feasible, the procedure is stopped, and the solution generated at iteration $t$ is retained as an approximation to the optimal solution of problem ($\varepsilon$-DSVM). Otherwise, if problem ($\varepsilon$-DSVM)$_{t+1}$ is unfeasible, the procedure modifies the previous LP problem ($\varepsilon$-DSVM)$_t$ by fixing to 1 all of its fractional variables. Problem ($\varepsilon$-DSVM)$_{t+1}$ defined in this way is feasible and any of its optimal solutions is integer. Thus, the procedure is stopped and the solution found for ($\varepsilon$-DSVM)$_t$ is retained as an approximation to the optimal solution of ($\varepsilon$-DSVM).

## 4   Computational Tests

To validate the effectiveness of model ($\varepsilon$-DSVM) some computational tests were performed on three benchmark datasets, each referring to a different biolife application domain. Two of these datasets, "promoter gene sequences" (*Promoter*) and "splice junction gene sequences" (*Splice*), are available from the UCI Machine Learning Repository (Hettich et al., 1998). The third dataset, indicated as *Structure* in the sequel, is obtained by collecting the samples proposed in (Ding and Dubchak, 2001). In particular, the *Promoter* dataset consists of 106 examples each represented by 57 sequential nucleotide positions, which may take one of the values in the set {a, c, g, t}. Each example is labeled with the class {+} if it represents a promoter, that is a gene sequence with a biological promoter activity, and with the class {-} if it is given by a non-promoter sequence. The problem is to discriminate between promoters, which initiate the process of gene expression, and non-promoter gene sequences. The *Splice* dataset contains 3175 examples each represented by 60 sequential nucleotide positions which, as for the *Promoter* dataset, take their values in the set {a, c, g, t}. In this case, each sequence may belong to one of three different classes, according to the inclusion of a splicing site. More specifically, the generic example may be an "acceptor site" (IE), a "donor site" (EI) or neither of them, and the problem is to discriminate between acceptors and donors in the presence of imperfect domain theory. Finally, the *Structure* dataset is composed by 698 protein sequences which derive by the union of two samples. The first one, collected by (Dubchak et al., 1999) and generally used for the training process, consists of 313 proteins having no more than 35% identity with each other. The second dataset, utilized as an independent test sample, is the PDB-40D set developed by the authors of the SCOP database (Andreeva et al., 2004; Murzin et al., 1995). It contains 385 proteins possessing less than 40% of the sequence identity and having less than 35% identity with the proteins contained in the first dataset. The proteins in these two samples are associated to their secondary structural class, which takes one of the following values: $\alpha$ ($\alpha$-helix secondary structure), $\beta$ ($\beta$-sheet secondary structure), $\alpha/\beta$ (mixed or alternating $\alpha$-helix and $\beta$-sheet segments) and $\alpha+\beta$ ($\alpha$-helix and $\beta$-sheet segments not mixed). Here the problem is to predict the secondary structure of a protein. The number of classes, attributes and examples for each dataset is given in table 1.

**Table 1.** Description of the datasets

| Dataset | Description | | | | |
| | classes | examples | attributes | (training,tuning) | prediction |
|---|---|---|---|---|---|
| Promoter | 2<br>(+, -) | 106 | 57<br>numerical<br>attributes | (60, 14)<br>50% class +<br>50% class - | 32<br>50% class +<br>50% class - |
| Splice | 3<br>(IE, EI, N) | 3175 | 60<br>numerical<br>attributes | (600, 100)<br>24% class IE<br>24% class EI<br>52% class N | 1000<br>24% class IE<br>24% class EI<br>52% class N |
| Structure | 4<br>($\alpha$, $\beta$, $\alpha/\beta$,<br>$\alpha+\beta$) | 698 | 83<br>numerical<br>attributes | (214, 99)<br>18% class $\alpha$<br>34% class $\beta$<br>37% class $\alpha/\beta$<br>11% class $\alpha+\beta$ | 385<br>16% class $\alpha$<br>30% class $\beta$<br>37% class $\alpha/\beta$<br>17% class $\alpha+\beta$ |

Eight alternative classification approaches were selected for comparison to model ($\varepsilon$-DSVM): discrete SVM (DSVM), ($\varepsilon$-LSVM), which is obtained by replacing in the ($\varepsilon$-DSVM) model the misclassification rate with the sum of the slacks of the misclassified examples, and six methods derived by combining SVM and $\nu$-SVM with linear (SVM$_{LIN}$), Gaussian (SVM$_{GAUSS}$) and radial basis function (SVM$_{RBF}$) as kernels. The results for classifiers ($\varepsilon$-DSVM), (DSVM) and ($\varepsilon$-LSVM) were obtained using the sequential LP-based heuristic described in section 3, whereas the computations for SVM methods were achieved by means of LIBSVM library (Chang and Lin, 2001). In order to perform the multicategory classification of *Splice* and *Structure*, all the methods were framed within the *round robin* scheme (Allwein et al., 2000; Orsenigo and Vercellis, 2007a). Moreover, in applying all the classifiers the attributes describing each dataset were converted into numerical explanatory variables. In particular, for the *Promoter* dataset the generic nucleotide position $s_i \in \{a,c,g,t\}$ was replaced by the conditional probability of observing the symbol $s_i$ given the positive promoter status of a gene sequence. Notice that the same could be done for the non-promoter class value. For the *Splice* dataset, which leads to a multicategory classification task, each nucleotide position $s_i \in \{a,c,g,t\}$ was replaced by the corresponding numeric value in the set $\{1,2,3,4\}$. Finally, for the *Structure* dataset four sets of numerical attributes were used for representing the amino acids sequences: these are amino acids composition (20 attributes), predicted secondary structure (21 attributes), hydrophobicity (21 attributes) and polarity (21 attributes). This choice was motivated by the fact that on the same dataset these attributes exhibited a notable explanatory power (Ding and Dubchak, 2001; Orsenigo and Vercellis, 2007c).

For evaluating the performance of the competing methods we proceeded in the following way. Each dataset was divided into three subsets, representing respectively the training, the tuning and the prediction set. For *Promoter* and *Splice* this last sample was extracted from the original dataset, whereas for *Structure* we used the out-of-sample dataset described above. Table 1 indicates for each dataset the size of the samples which share the same composition of the corresponding original datasets in terms of class values representatives. Then we applied *holdout estimation* (Kohavi, 1995) using the training and the tuning sets, in order to properly regulate the parameters of each classification models and assess their accuracy on the past examples. The accuracy values as well as the average computational time required for the training process are indicated in tables 2 and 3.

**Table 2.** Comparison among $\varepsilon$-DSVM, SVM and discrete SVM: holdout accuracy (%), prediction accuracy (%) on the out-of-sample datasets, computational time for training (sec)

| Dataset | Method | | | | |
|---|---|---|---|---|---|
| | $\varepsilon$-DSVM | DSVM | $SVM_{LIN}$ | $SVM_{RBF}$ | $SVM_{GAUSS}$ |
| Promoter | **100** | 92.9 | 92.9 | 92.9 | 92.9 |
| | **100** | 96.9 | **100** | **100** | **100** |
| | 0.5 | 0.5 | 0.3 | 0.3 | 0.3 |
| Splice | **86.0** | 83.0 | 65.0 | 74.0 | 66.0 |
| | **83.9** | 83.1 | 74.7 | 77.7 | 76.3 |
| | 12 | 7 | 1 | 1 | 1 |
| Structure | **88.9** | 86.9 | 85.9 | 83.8 | **88.9** |
| | **76.9** | 75.3 | 75.1 | 74.5 | 75.8 |
| | 3 | 3 | 0.3 | 0.3 | 0.3 |

**Table 3.** Comparison among $\varepsilon$-DSVM, $\varepsilon$-LSVM and $v$-SVM: holdout accuracy (%), prediction accuracy (%) on the out-of-sample datasets, computational time for training (sec)

| Dataset | Method | | | | |
|---|---|---|---|---|---|
| | $\varepsilon$-DSVM | $\varepsilon$-LSVM | $v$-$SVM_{LIN}$ | $v$-$SVM_{RBF}$ | $v$-$SVM_{GAUSS}$ |
| Promoter | **100** | **100** | **100** | **100** | **100** |
| | **100** | **100** | **100** | **100** | **100** |
| | 0.5 | 0.2 | 0.3 | 0.3 | 0.3 |
| Splice | **86.0** | 75.0 | 67.0 | 70.0 | 64.0 |
| | **83.9** | 80.7 | 75.6 | 79.2 | 77.5 |
| | 12 | 0.5 | 1 | 0.8 | 0.5 |
| Structure | **88.9** | 85.9 | 85.9 | 85.9 | 83.8 |
| | **76.9** | 75.1 | 75.1 | 75.1 | 76.6 |
| | 3 | 1 | 0.3 | 0.3 | 0.3 |

Finally, we applied the optimal classification function obtained by holdout estimation on the prediction datasets, to the end of investigating the discriminatory ability of each classifier on future unseen examples. The prediction accuracy achieved on the out-of-sample datasets is shown in tables 2 and 3.

From the results presented in tables 2 and 3 we can draw the empirical conclusion that model ($\varepsilon$-DSVM) represents an effective classification method, since it is able to achieve the highest accuracy for all the datasets considered in our tests. This remark holds true for the holdout estimation as well as for the out-of-sample datasets classification. Notice that the higher accuracy achieved in the training process, which might lead to overfitting, allows model ($\varepsilon$-DSVM) to reach a higher precision in predicting the class value of future examples, therefore achieving also a high generalization capability. Moreover, it is worth to observe that the optimal value of the variable $\varepsilon$ controlling the softening of the margin in model ($\varepsilon$-DSVM) is far from 1, since it ranges in the interval [0.1,0.4] for the three datasets considered in our tests.

To further explore the usefulness of model ($\varepsilon$-DSVM) we counted the number of support vectors (SVs) corresponding to the optimal separating hyperplane of each competing method. Tables 4 and 5, which contain the percentage of examples that each classifier used as support vectors for performing the discrimination, show that the optimal separating function obtained by means of ($\varepsilon$-DSVM) is consistently based on a smaller number of SVs. This means that the classification rules generated by the proposed method are more robust and capable of a higher generalization capability.

**Table 4.** Support vectors (%) for $\varepsilon$-DSVM , SVM and discrete SVM

| Dataset | Method | | | | |
| --- | --- | --- | --- | --- | --- |
| | $\varepsilon$-DSVM | DSVM | $SVM_{LIN}$ | $SVM_{RBF}$ | $SVM_{GAUSS}$ |
| Promoter | **8.3** | 26.7 | 100 | 100 | 100 |
| Splice | **7.8** | 13.3 | 36.0 | 56.2 | 40.5 |
| Structure | **44.4** | 44.9 | 44.9 | 73.8 | 51.9 |

**Table 5.** Support vectors (%) for $\varepsilon$-DSVM , $\varepsilon$-LSVM and $v$-SVM

| Dataset | Method | | | | |
| --- | --- | --- | --- | --- | --- |
| | $\varepsilon$-DSVM | $\varepsilon$-LSVM | $v$-$SVM_{LIN}$ | $v$-$SVM_{RBF}$ | $v$-$SVM_{GAUSS}$ |
| Promoter | **8.3** | 43.3 | 35.0 | 35.0 | 31.6 |
| Splice | **7.8** | 18 | 37.3 | 69.0 | 46.0 |
| Structure | **44.4** | 62 | 44.9 | 59.3 | 47.7 |

# References

Allwein, E., Schapire, R., Singer, Y.: Reducing multiclass to binary: a unifying approach for margin classifiers. Journal of Machine Learning Research 1, 113–141 (2000)

Andreeva, A., Howorth, D., Brenner, S.E., Hubbard, T.J., Chothia, C., Murzin, A.G.: SCOP database in 2004: refinements integrate structure and sequence family data. Nucleic Acids Res. 32, D226–D229 (2004)

Burges, C.J.C.: A Tutorial on Support Vector Machines for Pattern Recognition. Data Mining and Knowledge Discovery 2, 121–167 (1998)

Chang, C.C., Lin, C.J.: LIBSVM: A library for support vector machines (2001)

Cristianini, N., Shawe-Taylor, J.: An introduction to support vector machines and other kernel-based learning methods. Cambridge University Press, Cambridge (2000)

Ding, C.H., Dubchak, I.: Multi-class protein fold recognition using support vector machines and neural networks. Bioinformatics 17, 349–358 (2001)

Dubchak, I., Muchnik, I., Mayor, C., Dralyuk, I., Kim, S.H.: Recognition of a protein fold in the context of the Structural Classification of Proteins (SCOP) classification. Proteins 35, 401–407 (1999)

Hettich, S., Blake, C., Merz, C.: UCI repository of machine learning databases. (1998), http://www.ics.uci.edu/ mlearn/MLRepository.html

Koehler, G.J., Erenguc, S.: Minimizing misclassifications in linear discriminant analysis. Decision Sciences 21, 63–85 (1990)

Kohavi, R.: A study of cross-validation and bootstrapping for accuracy estimation and model selection. In: Proc. of the 14th International Joint Conference on Artificial Intelligence, pp. 338–345. Morgan Kaufmann, San Francisco (1995)

Mangasarian, O.L.: Linear and nonlinear separation of patterns by linear programming. Operations Research 13, 444–452 (1965)

Murzin, A.G., Brenner, S.E., Hubbard, T., Chothia, C.: SCOP: a structural classification of protein database for the investigation of sequence and structures. J. Mol. Biol. 247, 536–540 (1995)

Orsenigo, C., Vercellis, C.: Multivariate classification trees based on minimum features discrete support vector machines. IMA Journal of Management Mathematics 14, 221–234 (2003)

Orsenigo, C., Vercellis, C.: Discrete support vector decision trees via tabu-search. Journal of Computational Statistics and Data Analysis 47, 311–322 (2004)

Orsenigo, C., Vercellis, C.: Rule induction through discrete support vector decision trees. In: Triantaphyllou, E., Felici, G. (eds.) Data Mining and Knowledge Discovery Approaches Based on Rule Induction Techniques, pp. 305–325. Springer, Heidelberg (2006)

Orsenigo, C., Vercellis, C.: Multicategory classification via discrete support vector machines. Computational Management Science (in press) (2007a)

Orsenigo, C., Vercellis, C.: Accurately learning from few examples with a polyhedral classifier. Computational Optimization and Applications (in press) (2007b)

Orsenigo, C., Vercellis, C.: Protein folding classification through multicategory discrete SVM. In: Felici, G., Vercellis, C. (eds.) Mathematical Methods for Knowledge Discovery and Data Mining, Idea Group, USA (in press) (2007c)

Schölkopf, B., Smola, A.J.: Learning with kernels. Support vector machines, regularization, optimization and beyond. MIT Press, Cambridge (2002)

Vapnik, V.: The nature of statistical learning theory. Springer, Heidelberg (1995)

Vapnik, V.: Statistical Learning Theory. Wiley, Chichester (1998)

Weston, J., Elisseeff, A., Schölkopf, B., Tipping, M.: Use of the Zero-Norm with Linear Models and Kernel Methods. Journal of Machine Learning Research 3, 1439–1461 (2003)

# Feature Selection Using Ant Colony Optimization (ACO): A New Method and Comparative Study in the Application of Face Recognition System

Hamidreza Rashidy Kanan, Karim Faez, and Sayyed Mostafa Taheri

Image Processing and Pattern Recognition Lab, Electrical Engineering Department,
Amirkabir University of Technology (Tehran Polytechnic), Hafez Avenue, Tehran, Iran, 15914
{rashidykanan, kfaez, mostafa_taheri}@aut.ac.ir

**Abstract.** Feature Selection (FS) and reduction of pattern dimensionality is a most important step in pattern recognition systems. One approach in the feature selection area is employing population-based optimization algorithms such as Genetic Algorithm (GA)-based method and Ant Colony Optimization (ACO)-based method. This paper presents a novel feature selection method that is based on Ant Colony Optimization (ACO). ACO algorithm is inspired of ant's social behavior in their search for the shortest paths to food sources. Most common techniques for ACO-Based feature selection use the priori information of features. However, in the proposed algorithm, classifier performance and the length of selected feature vector are adopted as heuristic information for ACO. So, we can select the optimal feature subset without the priori information of features. This approach is easily implemented and because of using one simple classifier in it, its computational complexity is very low. Simulation results on face recognition system and ORL database show the superiority of the proposed algorithm.

**Keywords:** Feature Selection, Ant Colony Optimization (ACO), Genetic Algorithm, Face Recognition.

## 1 Introduction

Several parameters can affect the performance of pattern recognition system. Among them, feature extraction and representation of patterns can be considered as a most important. Reduction of pattern dimensionality via feature extraction and selection belongs to the most fundamental step in data processing [1].

Feature Selection (FS) is extensive and spread across many fields, including document classification, data mining, object recognition, biometrics, remote sensing and computer vision [2]. Given a feature set of size n, the FS problem is to find a minimal feature subset of size m (m<n) while retaining a suitably high accuracy in representing the original features. In real word problems FS is a must due to the abundance of noisy, irrelevant or misleading features [3].

As a simplest way, the best subset of features can be found by evaluating all the possible subsets, which is known as exhaustive search. This procedure is quite

P. Perner (Ed.): ICDM 2007, LNAI 4597, pp. 63–76, 2007.
© Springer-Verlag Berlin Heidelberg 2007

impractical even for a moderate size feature set. Because the number of feature subset combinations with m features from a collection of n (m<n, $m \neq 0$) feature is $n!/[m!(n-m)!]$ and the total number of theses combinations is $(2^n - 2)$.

For most practical problems, an optimal solution can only be guaranteed if a monotonic criterion for evaluating features can be found, but this assumption rarely holds in the real-world [4]. As a result, we must find solutions which would be computationally feasible and represent a trade-off between solution quality and time.

Usually FS algorithms involve heuristic or random search strategies in an attempt to avoid this prohibitive complexity. However, the degree of optimally of the final feature subset is often reduced [3].

Among too many methods which are proposed for FS, population-based optimization algorithms such as Genetic Algorithm (GA)-based method and Ant Colony Optimization (ACO)-based method have attracted a lot of attention. These methods attempt to achieve better solutions by using knowledge from previous iterations.

Genetic algorithms (GA's) are optimization techniques based on the mechanics of natural selection. They used operations found in natural genetics to guide itself through the paths in the search space [5]. Because of their advantages, recently, GA's have been widely used as a tool for feature selection in pattern recognition.

Metaheuristic optimization algorithm based on ant's behavior (ACO) was represented in the early 1990s by M. Dorigo and colleagues [6]. ACO is a branch of newly developed form of artificial intelligence called Swarm Intelligence. Swarm intelligence is a field which studies "the emergent collective intelligence of groups of simple agents" [7]. In groups of insects which live in colonies, such as ants and bees, an individual can only do simple task on its own, while the colony's cooperative work is the main reason determining the intelligent behavior it shows [8].

ACO algorithm is inspired of ant's social behavior. Ants have no sight and are capable of finding the shortest route between a food source and their nest by chemical materials called pheromone that they leave when moving.

ACO algorithm was firstly used in solving Traveling Salesman Problem (TSP) [9]. Then has been successfully applied to a large number of difficult problems like the Quadratic Assignment Problem (QAP) [10], routing in telecommunication networks, graph coloring problems, scheduling and etc. This method is particularly attractive for feature selection as there seems to be no heuristic that can guide search to the optimal minimal subset every time [3]. In the other hand, if features are represented as a graph, ant will discover best feature combinations as they traverse the graph.

In this paper a new modified ACO-Based feature selection algorithm has been introduced. The classifier performance and the length of selected feature vector are adopted as heuristic information for ACO. So proposed algorithm needs no priori knowledge of features. Proposed algorithm is applied to two different feature subsets that are Pseudo Zernike Moment Invariant (PZMI) and Discrete Wavelet Transform (DWT) Coefficients in the application of face recognition system and finally the classifier performance and the length of selected feature vector are considered for performance evaluation.

The rest of this paper is organized as follows. Section 2 presents a brief overview of feature selection methods. Ant Colony Optimization (ACO) and Genetic Algorithm (GA) are described in Sections 3 and 4 respectively. Section 5 explains the proposed feature selection algorithm and finally, Sections 6 and 7 attain the experimental results and conclusion.

## 2 An Overview of Feature Selection (FS) Approaches

Feature selection algorithms can be classified into two categories based on their evaluation procedure [11]. If an algorithm performs FS independently of any learning algorithm (i.e. it is a completely separate preprocessor), then it is a filter approach (open-loop approach). This approach is based mostly on selecting features using between-class separability criterion [11]. If the evaluation procedure is tied to the task (e.g. classification) of the learning algorithm, the FS algorithm employs the wrapper approach (closed-loop approach). This method searches through the feature subset space using the estimated accuracy from an induction algorithm as a measure of subset suitability.

The two mentioned approaches are also classified into five main methods which they are Forward Selection, Backward elimination Forward/Backward Combination, Random Choice and Instance based method.

FS methods may start with no features, all features, a selected feature set or some random feature subset. Those methods that start with an initial subset usually select these features heuristically beforehand. Features are added (Forward Selection) or removed (Backward Elimination) iteratively and in the Forward/Backward Combination method features are either iteratively added or removed or produced randomly thereafter.

The disadvantage of Forward Selection and Backward Elimination methods is that the features that were once selected/eliminated cannot be later discarded/re-selected. To overcome this problem, Pudil et al. [12] proposed a method to flexibly add and remove features. This method has been called floating search method.

In the wrapper approach the evaluation function calculates the suitability of a feature subset produced by the generation procedure and compares this with the previous best candidate, replacing it if found to be better. A Stopping criterion is tested every iteration to determine whether the FS process should continue or not.

Other famous FS approaches are based on the Genetic Algorithm (GA) [13], Simulated Annealing [3] and Ant Colony Optimization (ACO) [3, 8, 14, 15, 16].

[14] has proposed a hybrid approach for speech classification problem. This method has used combination of mutual information and ACO. [15] has used the hybrid of ACO and mutual information for selection of features in the forecaster. [16] has utilized the Fisher Discrimination Rate (FDR) as a heuristic information in the ACO-Based feature selection method which is used for selection of network intrusion features. [3] has used a ACO for finding rough set reducts. [8] has introduced a Ant-Miner which is used a difficult pheromone updating strategy and sate transition rule.

Also, some surveys of feature selection algorithms are given in [1, 17, 18].

## 3 Ant Colony Optimization (ACO)

In the early 1990s, ant colony optimization (ACO) was introduced by M. Dorigo and colleagues as a novel nature-inspired metaheuristic for the solution of hard combinatorial optimization (CO) problems [19]. ACO belongs to the class of metaheuristics, which are approximate algorithms used to obtain good enough solutions to hard CO problems in a reasonable amount of computation time [19].

The ability of real ants to find shortest routes is mainly due to their depositing of pheromone as they travel; each ant probabilistically prefers to follow a direction rich in this chemical. The pheromone decays over time, resulting in much less pheromone on less popular paths. Given that over time the shortest route will have the higher rate of ant traversal, this path will be reinforced and the others diminished until all ants follow the same, shortest path (the "system" has converged to a single solution) [3].

In general, an ACO algorithm can be applied to any combinatorial problem as far as it is possible to define:

* ❖ Appropriate problem representation. The problem must be described as a graph with a set of nodes and edges between nodes.
* ❖ Heuristic desirability ($\eta$) of edges. A suitable heuristic measure of the "goodness" of paths from one node to every other connected node in the graph.
* ❖ Construction of feasible solutions. A mechanism must be in place whereby possible solutions are efficiently created.
* ❖ Pheromone updating rule. A suitable method of updating the pheromone levels on edges is required with a corresponding evaporation rule. Typical methods involve selecting the n best ants and updating the paths they chose.
* ❖ Probabilistic transition rule. The rule that determines the probability of an ant traversing from one node in the graph to the next.

### 3.1  ACO for Feature Selection

The feature selection task may be reformulated into an ACO-suitable problem. ACO requires a problem to be represented as a graph. Here nodes represent features, with the edges between them denoting the choice of the next feature. The search for the optimal feature subset is then an ant traversal through the graph where a minimum number of nodes are visited that satisfies the traversal stopping criterion. Figure 1 illustrates this setup. The ant is currently at node *a* and has a choice of which feature to add next to its path (dotted lines). It chooses feature *b* next based on the transition rule, then *c* and then *d*. Upon arrival at *d*, the current subset *{a; b; c; d}* is determined to satisfy the traversal stopping criterion (e.g. a suitably high classification accuracy has been achieved with this subset). The ant terminates its traversal and outputs this feature subset as a candidate for data reduction.

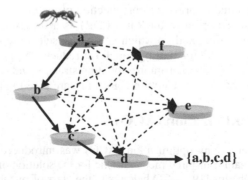

**Fig. 1.** ACO problem representation for FS

A suitable heuristic desirability of traversing between features could be any subset evaluation function - for example, an entropy-based measure [19], rough set dependency measure [20] or the Fisher Discrimination Rate (FDR)[16]. The heuristic desirability of traversal and edge pheromone levels are combined to form the so-called probabilistic transition rule, denoting the probability of an ant at feature i choosing to travel to feature j at time t:

$$
p_{ij}^{k}(t) = \begin{cases} \dfrac{[\tau_{ij}(t)]^{\alpha}.[\eta_{ij}]^{\beta}}{\sum_{l \in J_{i}^{k}} [\tau_{il}(t)]^{\alpha}.[\eta_{il}]^{\beta}} & \text{if } j \in J_{i}^{k} \\ 0 & otherwise \end{cases}
\tag{1}
$$

Where $k$ is the number of ants, $\eta_{ij}$ is the heuristic desirability of choosing feature **j** when at feature **i** ( $\eta_{ij}$ is optional but often needed for achieving a high algorithm performance [21]), $J_{i}^{k}$ is the set of neighbor nodes of node **i** which have not yet been visited by the ant **k**. $\alpha \succ 0$, $\beta \succ 0$ are two parameters that determine the relative importance of the pheromone value and heuristic information (the choice of $\alpha, \beta$ is determined experimentally) and $\tau_{ij}(t)$ is the amount of virtual pheromone on edge (i,j).

The overall process of ACO feature selection can be seen in figure 2. The process begins by generating a number of ants, k, which are then placed randomly on the graph (i.e. each ant starts with one random feature). Alternatively, the number of ants to place on the graph may be set equal to the number of features within the data; each ant starts path construction at a different feature. From these initial positions, they traverse edges probabilistically until a traversal stopping criterion is satisfied. The resulting subsets are gathered and then evaluated. If an optimal subset has been found or the algorithm has executed a certain number of times, then the process halts and outputs the best feature subset encountered. If neither condition holds, then the pheromone is updated, a new set of ants are created and the process iterates once more.

The pheromone on each edge is updated according to the following formula:

$$
\tau_{ij}(t+1) = (1 - \rho).\tau_{ij}(t) + \rho.\Delta\tau_{ij}(t)
\tag{2}
$$

Where:

$$
\Delta\tau_{ij}(t) = \sum_{k=1}^{n} (\gamma(S^{k})/|S^{k}|)
\tag{3}
$$

This is the case if the edge (i;j) has been traversed; $\Delta\tau_{ij}(t)$ is 0 otherwise. The value $0 \le \rho \le 1$ is decay constant used to simulate the evaporation of the pheromone, $S^{k}$ is the feature subset found by ant **k**. The pheromone is updated

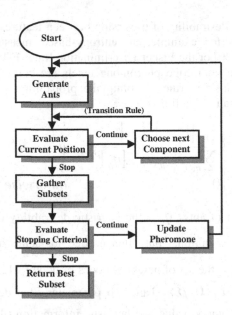

**Fig. 2.** ACO-based feature selection overview

according to both the measure of the "goodness" of the ant's feature subset $\gamma'$ and the size of the subset itself. By this definition, all ants update the pheromone.

## 4   Genetic Algorithm (GA)

The GA's is a stochastic global search method that mimics the metaphor of natural biological evolution [5]. These algorithms are general purpose optimization algorithms with a probabilistic component that provide a means to search poorly understood, irregular spaces.

GA's work with a population of points rather than a single point. Each "point" is a vector in hyperspace representing one potential (or candidate) solution to the optimization problem. A population is, thus, just an ensemble or set of hyperspace vectors. Each vector is called a chromosome in the population. The number of elements in each vector (chromosome) depends on the number of parameters in the optimization problem and the way to represent the problem. How to represent the problem as a string of elements is one of the critical factors in successfully applying a GA (or other evolutionary algorithm) to a problem.

A typical series of operations carried out when implementing a GA paradigm is:

 ❖ Initialize the population;
 ❖ Calculate fitness for each chromosome in population;
 ❖ Reproduce selected chromosomes to form a new population;
 ❖ Perform crossover and mutation on the population;
 ❖ Loop to second step until some condition is met.

Initialization of the population is commonly done by seeding the population with random values. The fitness value is proportional to the performance measurement of the function being optimized. The calculation of fitness values is conceptually simple. It can, however, be quite complex to implement in a way that optimizes the efficiency of the GA's search of the problem space. It is this fitness that guides the search of the problem space.

After fitness calculation, the next step is reproduction. Reproduction comprises forming a new population, usually with the same total number of chromosomes, by selecting from members of the current population using a stochastic process that is weighted by each of their fitness values. The higher the fitness, the more likely it is that the chromosome will be selected for the new generation. One commonly used way is a "roulette wheel" procedure that assigns a portion of a roulette wheel to each population member where the size of the portion is proportional to the fitness value. This procedure is often combined with the elitist strategy, which ensures that the chromosome with the highest fitness is always copied into the next generation.

The next operation is called crossover. To many evolutionary computation practitioners, crossover is what distinguishes a GA from other evolutionary computation paradigms. Crossover is the process of exchanging portions of the strings of two "parent" chromosomes. An overall probability is assigned to the crossover process, which is the probability that given two parents, the crossover process will occur. This probability is often in the range of 0.65–0.80. The final operation in the typical GA procedure is mutation. Mutation consists of changing an element's value at random, often with a constant probability for each element in the population. The probability of mutation can vary widely according to the application and the preference of the person exercising the GA. However, values of between 0.001 and 0.01 are not unusual for mutation probability.

### 4.1  GA for Feature Selection

Several approaches exist for using GAs for feature subset selection. The two main methods that have been widely used in the past are as follow. First is due to [13], of finding an optimal binary vector in which each bit corresponds to a feature (Binary Vector Optimization method (BVO)). A '1' or '0' suggests that the feature is selected or dropped, respectively. The aim is to find the binary vector with the smallest number of 1's such that the classifier performance is maximized. This criterion is often modified to reduce the dimensionality of the feature vector at the same time [21]. The second and more refined technique [22]) uses an m-ary vector to assign weights to features instead of abruptly dropping or including them as in the binary case. This gives a better search resolution in the multidimensional space [23].

## 5  Proposed Feature Selection Algorithm

The main steps of proposed algorithm are as follows:

1) Initialization
   - Determine the population of ants (p).
   - Set the intensity of pheromone trial associated with any feature.
   - Determine the maximum of allowed iterations (k)

2) Generation ants and evaluation of each ants

- Any ant ($A_i$, i=1:p) randomly is assigned to one feature and it should visit all features and build solutions completely. In this step, the evaluation criterion is Mean Square Error (MSE) of the classifier. If any ant could not decrease the MSE of the classifier in three successive steps, it finished its work and exit.

3) Evaluation of the selected subset of each ant

- In this step the importance of the selected subset of each ant is evaluated through classifier performance. Then the subsets according to their MSE are sorted and some of them are selected according to ACS and $AS_{rank}$ algorithms.

4) Check the stop criterion

- If the number of iterations is more than the maximum allowed iteration exit, otherwise continue.

5) Pheromone updating

- For features which are selected in the step 3 pheromone intensity are updated.

6) Go to 2 and continue

## 6   Experimental Results

To show the utility of proposed feature selection algorithm and to compare with GA-Based approach two sets of experiments were carried out. For experimental studies we have considered ORL gray scale face image database. This database contains 400 facial images from 40 individuals in different states. So, the number of classes in our experiments is 40. The total number of images in each class is 10.

Figure 3 shows some samples images of this database.

**Fig. 3.** Some samples of ORL database

Two different sets of features were extracted from each face image which they are Pseudo Zernike Moment Invariant (PZMI) and Discrete Wavelet Transform (DWT)

Coefficient. Then proposed ACO-based and GA-based feature selection methods are applied to each feature set and finally, the length of selected feature vector and classifier performance are considered for evaluating the proposed algorithm.

The details of experiments are as follows:

## 6.1  Feature Extraction

After preprocessing (histogram equalization) of facial images, we extract the PZMI and DWT coefficients as a feature vector.

In the PZMI feature extraction step, the PZMI of orders 1 to 20 and their repetitions are extracted from any face image. I.e. for any **n** (order of PZMI), we extract one feature vector of order **n** and all repetitions **m** $(m \leq n)$. For example if we choose $n = n_0$, we have one feature vector which has $(n_0 + 1)$ elements [24, 25].

In the DWT feature extraction step, Discrete Wavelet Transform is applied to any face images. Since the face images are not continuous, we used Haar wavelet which is also discrete. We applied pyramid algorithm to each preprocessed image for decomposing it into 3 resolution levels. Then we used the approximation of images at level 3 and converted them into vectors by concatenating the columns. Dimensions of ORL database images is $92 \times 112$, so after decomposing them, the length of wavelet feature for each image is 168 [26].

For scale invariancy of extracted features (PZMI and DWT Coefficients), we normalized them.

## 6.2  Feature Selection

After the extraction of PZMI and DWT Coefficients, ACO and GA are used to select the optimal feature sets.

We consider our system as a block diagram that is shown in Figure 4.

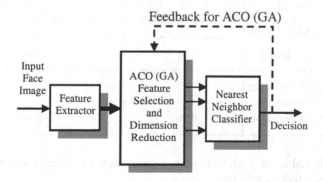

**Fig. 4.** Block Diagram of proposed feature selection scheme

For GA-based feature selector, we set the length of chromosomes to **L** which L=20 for PZMI features and L=168 for DWT Coefficients features. Each gene

$g_i (i = 1,2,...,L)$ corresponds to a specific order of PZMI or specific DWT Coefficient feature component.

If $g_i = 1$, this means we select this order (this feature component) as one of optimal orders (optimal components). Otherwise, $g_i = 0$ means discard it. Because most of orders (feature components) may be selected, the probability of every bit being equal to 1 is set to 0.8 when the initial population of chromosomes is creating. Its purpose is to speed up the convergence.

Given a chromosome q the fitness function F(q) is defined as:

$$F(q) = \frac{1}{\sum_{x \in \Omega} \delta(x,q)} \tag{4}$$

Here $\Omega$ is the training image set for GAs and $\delta(x,q)$ is defined as:

$$\delta(x,q) = \begin{cases} 1, & \text{if } x \text{ is classified correctly} \\ 0, & \text{if } x \text{ is misclassified} \end{cases} \tag{5}$$

For simplicity, we have used the nearest neighbor classifier and the aim is to find a binary vector with the smallest number of 1's such that the classifier performance is maximized. In order to select the individuals for the next generation, GA's roulette wheel selection method was used.

Further Genetic Algorithms parameters are summarized in Table 1.

**Table 1.** GA-Based Feature Selection Parameters

|  | PZMI Features | DWT Coefficients Features |
|---|---|---|
| Population size | 50 | 50 |
| Number Of Generation | 25 | 25 |
| Chromosome length | 20 | 168 |
| Probability of crossover | 0.7 | 0.7 |
| Probability of mutation | 0.003 | 0.003 |

For ACO-Based feature selector, we use same primary features which are utilized in the GA-Based feature selector.

In this step, we have applied proposed algorithm to the extracted features in the formats of ACS and $AS_{rank}$ with the same parameters.

Various parameters for leading to better convergence are tested and the best parameters that are obtained by simulations are as follows:

$\alpha=1$, $\beta=0.1$, $\rho=0.2$, the initial pheromone intensity of each feature is equal to 1, the number of Ant in every iteration p=50 and the maximum number of iterations k=25. These values are chosen to justify the comparison with GA. Selected features of each method are classified using nearest neighbor classifier and the obtained MSE is considered for performance evaluation.

## 6.2.1  Comparison of ACO-Based and GA-Based Methods

The results of this step are summarized in Tables 2 and 3.

Table 2 gives, for each method, the best MSE and the average of execution time.

**Table 2.** MSE and execution time of Three Different Methods

| Method | MSE | | Time (s) | |
|---|---|---|---|---|
| | PZMI | DWT | PZMI | DWT |
| GA | 3.5% | 2% | 1080 | 1560 |
| ACO (ACS) | 3% | 1% | 780 | 1320 |
| ACO ($AS_{rank}$) | 1.5% | 0.25% | 300 | 960 |

Both ACO-Based methods (ACS and $AS_{rank}$) produce much lower classification errors and execution times than GA-Based method. ACS and $AS_{rank}$ algorithms have comparable performance. The ACS method is faster than $AS_{rank}$ method however it has lower performance. Also, Table 3 gives the optimal selected features for each method. Both ACO-Based and GA-Based methods significantly reduce the number of original features. But ACO-Based method (ACS and $AS_{rank}$) chooses fewer features.

**Table 3.** Selected Features of Three Different Methods

| Method | Selected Features | | Number of Selected Features | |
|---|---|---|---|---|
| | PZMI (Order) | DWT (Component) | PZMI | DWT |
| GA | 2, 4, 8, 10, 12, 13 | 1, 4, 5, 6, 12, 14, 15, 17, 21, 26, 29, 32, 35, 37, 40, 44, 47, 49, 52, 53, 57, 58, 62, 64, 69, 72, 74, 79, 84, 88, 91, 93, 98, 100, 107, 111, 117, 125, 136, 137, 139, 145, 149, 155, 161, 167, 168 | 55 | 47 |
| ACO (ACS) | 4, 6, 9, 12, 13 | 4, 5, 20, 25, 29, 30, 37, 42, 44, 49, 58, 62, 68, 70, 73, 93, 94, 95, 96, 100, 102, 109, 112, 113, 114, 118, 120, 121, 125, 132, 138, 139, 141, 147, 149, 152, 156, 157, 158, 159, 163, 168 | 49 | 42 |
| ACO ($AS_{rank}$) | 6, 8, 10, 14 | 2, 6, 18, 21, 22, 42, 49, 57, 58, 73, 75, 83, 93, 95, 96, 100, 116, 118, 122, 125, 136, 138, 144, 147, 149, 153, 157, 158, 160, 167 | 42 | 30 |

Tables 2 and 3 show that using proposed method, we can achieve 99.75% and 98.5% recognition rate only with 30 and 42 selected features for DWT coefficients and PZMI features respectively.

Since feature selection is typically done in an off-line manner, the execution time of a specific algorithm is of much less importance than its ultimate classification performance. So, we can say that the $AS_{rank}$ method gives better results. Finally, selected features of each method are classified and the obtained recognition rates are shown in Figures 5 and 6.

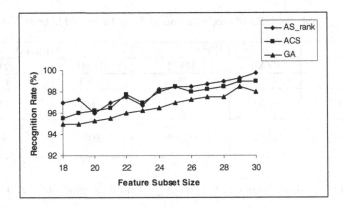

**Fig. 5.** Recognition Rate of DWT Feature Subsets Obtained Using $AS_{rank}$, ACS and GA

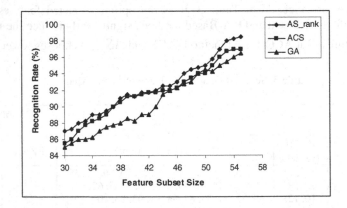

**Fig. 6.** Recognition Rate of PZMI Feature Subsets Obtained Using $AS_{rank}$, ACS and GA

It can be seen that the performance of both ACS and $AS_{rank}$ was found to be much better than that of GA-Based method and proposed ACO-Based algorithm was able to achieve better performance than GA-Based algorithm in most of the cases.

# 7  Conclusion

In this paper a novel ACO-Based feature selection algorithm is presented. In the proposed algorithm, the classifier performance and the length of selected feature vector are adopted as heuristic information for ACO. So, we can select the optimal feature subset without the priori knowledge of features. Proposed approach is simulated in the ACS and $AS_{rank}$ algorithm formats. To show the utility of proposed algorithm and to compare with GA-Based approach two sets of experiments were carried out on two different sets of features that they are PZMI and DWT coefficients. Simulation results on face recognition system and ORL database show that the proposed ACO-Based method outperforms GA-Based method since, it achieved better performance with the lower number of features and execution time.

## Acknowledgment

This research was supported by the Iran Telecommunication Research Center (ITRC).

## References

1. kml, L., Kittler, J.: Feature set search algorithms. In: Chen, C.H. (ed.) Pattern Recognition and Signal Processing, Sijhoff and Noordhoff, the Netherlands (1978)
2. Ani, A.A.: An Ant Colony Optimization Based Approach for Feature Selection. In: Proceeding of AIML Conference (2005)
3. Jensen, R.: Combining rough and fuzzy sets for feature selection. Ph.D. Thesis, University of Edinburgh (2005)
4. Kohavi, R.: Feature Subset Selection as search with Probabilistic Estimates. AAAI Fall Symposium On Relevance (1994)
5. Srinivas, M., Patnik, L.M.: Genetic Algorithms: A Survey. IEEE Computer Society Press, Los Alamitos (1994)
6. Dorigo, M., Caro, G.D.: Ant Colony Optimization: A New Meta-heuristic. In: Proceeding of the Congress on Evolutionary Computing (1999)
7. Bonabeau, E., Dorigo, M., Theraulaz, G.: Swarm Intelligence: From Natural to Artificial Systems. Oxford University Press, New York (1999)
8. Liu, B., Abbass, H.A., McKay, B.: Classification Rule Discovery with Ant Colony Optimization. IEEE Computational Intelligence 3(1) (2004)
9. Dorigo, M., Maniezzo, V., Colorni, A.: The Ant System: Optimization by a Colony of Cooperating Agents. IEEE Transactions on Systems, Man, and Cybernetics, Part B 26(1), 29–41 (1996)
10. Maniezzo, V., Colorni, A.: The Ant System Applied to the Quadratic Assignment Problem. Knowledge and Data Engineering 11(5), 769–778 (1999)
11. Duda, R.O., Hart, P.E.: Pattern Recognition and Scene Analysis. Wiley, Chichester (1973)
12. Pudil, P., Novovicova, J., Kittler, J.: Floating search methods in feature selection. Pattern Recognition Letters 15, 1119–1125 (1994)
13. Siedlecki, W., Sklansky, J.: A note on genetic algorithms for large-scale feature selection. Pattern Recognition Letters 10(5), 335–347 (1989)

14. Ani, A.A.: Ant Colony Optimization for Feature Subset Selection. Transactions On Engineering, Computing And Technology 4 (2005)
15. Zhang, C.K., Hu, H.: Feature Selection Using The Hybrid Of Ant Colony Optimization and Mutual Information For The Forecaster. In: Proceedings of the Fourth International Conference on Machine Learning and Cybernetics (2005)
16. Gao, H.H., Yang, H.H., And Wang, X.Y.: Ant Colony Optimization Based Network Intrusion Feature Selection And Detection. In: Proceedings of the Fourth International Conference on Machine Learning and Cybernetics (2005)
17. Bins, J.: Feature Selection of Huge Feature Sets in the Context of Computer Vision. Ph.D. Dissertation, Computer Science Department, Colorado State University (2000)
18. Siedlecki, W., Sklansky, J.: On Automatic Feature Selection. International Journal of Pattern Recognition and Artificial Intelligence 2(2), 197–220 (1988)
19. Dorigo, M., Blum, C.: Ant colony optimization theory: A survey. Theoretical Computer Science 344, 243–278 (2005)
20. Pawlak, Z.: Rough Sets: Theoretical Aspects of Reasoning About Data. Kluwer Academic Publishing, Dordrecht (1991)
21. Yang, J., Honavar, V.: Feature Subset Selection Using a Genetic Algorithm. IEEE Intelligent Systems 13, 44–49 (1998)
22. Punch, W.F., Goodman, E.D., Pei, L.C.S.M., Hovland, P., Enbody, R.: Further research on Feature Selection and Classification using Genetic Algorithms. In: Proc. Int. Conf. Genetic Algorithms, pp. 557–564 (1993)
23. Raymer, M., Punch, W., Goodman, E., Kuhn, L., Jain, A.K.: Dimensionality Reduction Using Genetic Algorithms. IEEE Transactions on Evolutionary Computing 4, 164–171 (2000)
24. Rashidy Kanan, H., Faez, K., Ezoji, M.: Face Recognition: An Optimized Localization Approach and Selected PZMI Feature Vector Using SVM Classifier. In: Huang, D.-S., Li, K., Irwin, G.W. (eds.) ICIC 2006. LNCS, vol. 4113, pp. 690–696. Springer, Heidelberg (2006)
25. Rashidy Kanan, H., Faez, K., Ezoji, M.: An Efficient Face Recognition System Using a New Optimized Localization Method. In: ICPR'2006. Proceeding of the 18th International Conference on Pattern Recognition (2006)
26. Rashidy Kanan, H., Faez, K.: ZMI and Wavelet Transform Features and SVM Classifier in the Optimized Face Recognition system. In: ISSPIT 2005. Proceeding of the 5th IEEE International Symposium on Signal Processing and Information Technology, pp. 295–300. IEEE Computer Society Press, Los Alamitos (2005)

# Outlier Detection with Streaming Dyadic Decomposition

Chetan Gupta[1] and Robert Grossman[2]

[1]Dept. Of Mathematics, Statistics and Computer Science, University Of Illinois, Chicago and Hewlett Packard Labs
[2]Open Data Partners

**Abstract.** In this work we introduce a new algorithm for detecting outliers on streaming data in $\mathbf{R}^n$. The basic idea is to compute a dyadic decomposition into cubes in $\mathbf{R}^n$ of the streaming data. Dyadic decomposition can be obtained by recursively bisecting the cube the data lies in. Dyadic decomposition obtained under streaming setting is understood as streaming dyadic decomposition. If we view the streaming dyadic decomposition as a tree with a fixed maximum (and sufficient) size (depth), then outliers are naturally defined by cubes that contain a small number of points in the cube itself or the cube itself and its neighboring cubes. We discuss some properties of detecting outliers with streaming dyadic decomposition and we present experimental results over real and artificial data sets.

## 1   Introduction

Detecting outliers is an important data mining task. In this paper, we are concerned with outlier detection using a streaming data model in which we examine each point once and must detect outliers independent of the stream length.

As streaming data has become more ubiquitous, the problem of detecting outliers on streams has become more important. To give two examples: For example in case of network data, we need to be able to predict the attack patterns in real time over streaming data. In our experimental section we present results over such a data set. Other examples include highway data. If the data is being collected through sensors we need to be able to detect the traffic disruptions in real time as the data streams in.

There are several different definitions of outliers, and quite a few different approaches to detecting them. Some of these are described in the next section.

Roughly speaking, a dyadic decomposition divides $\mathbf{R}^n$ into cubes. A cube may be further divided into sub-cubes, by splitting the edge in each dimension in half. This decomposition produces a collection of dyadic cubes at different scales. It also a produces a tree, which we call a dyadic tree. Each node $u$ of the dyadic tree is associated with a dyadic cube $C_u$, and a node $u$ is child of another node $v$ in case the corresponding cube $C_u$ arises by dividing each edge of the cube $C_v$ in half, as described above. A formal definition is given in Section 3.

P. Perner (Ed.): ICDM 2007, LNAI 4597, pp. 77–91, 2007.

One natural definition of an outlier is to say a point $p$ in a data set $D$ is an outlier if it is in the cube $C_u$ of a leaf node $u$. In this case we say that the point $p$ is an *outlier defined by a dyadic decomposition* or ODD. More generally, we can define $k$-outliers if the cube contains $k$ points or less.

This generalization is useful in identifying members of a minority class.

As a simple example consider a set of points in a 2-D plane. Enclose all the points in a square, divide the square into four smaller squares, such that you could think of them as four quadrants. If all but but one point lie in in Quadrants 1, 2, 3 and only one point lies in Quadrant 4, it is considered an outlier. To present a more trivial example with ordinal variables, consider a set of all tennis players till 1986, with two variables, Wimbledon winners or not and age less than 18 or not. There are lot of players who are less than 18, a lot of players who have won the Wimbledon, but only Boris Becker won it under 18. If the data is plotted in the above manner in a square with four smaller squares, there will be a box with only Boris Becker in it and he is an outlier.

Wherever a large amount of data is streaming in and there is a need to detect anomalous patterns, our approach can prove useful. The other advantage of our approach is that it can handle both the scenarios in a streaming setting: individual outliers or identifying members of a minority class. Our approach is simple, intuitive and works well with both continuous and categorical variables. We have experimented with various data sets and some of the results are presented in the paper. This approach can be extended to identify cluster centers in a streaming setting but due to lack of space we do not present those results here.

The organization of this work is as follows: In Section 2 we give an overview of the existing related work. In Section 3 we define dyadic decompositions. Section 4 we present the algorithm for computing ODDs. Section 5 contains some discussion and Section 6 is experimental studies. Section 6 contains the conclusion.

## 2   Related Work

Outlier detection is a problem considered in statistics and data mining. In Knorr's [1] work, a point $p$ is defined as an outlier with respect to parameter $k$ and $\lambda$, if no more than $k$ points are a distance $\lambda$ or less from $p$. In Ramaswamy's [2] work, an outlier is defined as: Given a $k$ and a $n$, a point $p$ is an outlier if the distance to its $k - th$ nearest neighbor is smaller than the corresponding value for no more than $n - 1$ other points. Breunig [3] gives every point a LOF (Local Outlier Factor), which measures how isolated an object is from its surrounding. They assign a degree to every point of being an outlier. They give an example to illustrate the importance of looking at the local rather than the global neighborhood. Since our approach is multiscale in nature, the "global" and "local" change with scale and our approach like [3] takes care of local and global outliers. The above techniques are not presented for streaming data and ours is a streaming data algorithm.

A dynamic programming approach to finding deviants (outliers in a sense) is presented by Jagdish [4]. Muthu [5] uses this idea to construct a near optimal algorithm in a streaming setting for univariate streams. They extend this as a heuristic for a multivariate setting. Another method in streaming clustering/outlier detection is TECNO-STREAMS [6].

Our approach could be understood as a multi-resolution approach. Wavelets are popular in multi-resolution approaches. WaveCluster [7] is a grid-based clustering method that uses wavelet transform to filter the data. Scale-based clustering has been presented before. One idea is scale space clustering. Chakravarty, in [8] uses Radial Basis Function Network(RBFN) for scale-based clustering. In Wong's [9] work a statistical mechanic-based approach is used where the temperature is the scaling parameter. Another interesting work along similar lines is that of Leung [10] which attempts to provide a unified framework for various scale space approaches. Roberts [11] uses a scale-based smoothing function to estimate probability density function. Our algorithm shows similar properties to these scale-based algorithms. Our way of scaling is different since it is based on dyadic decomposition. Another work is using fractal dimensions is that of Barbara [12].

We can also look at this as a grid based approach. An early grid-based clustering algorithm is that of Warnekar [13]. They address the issue of "neighbors" in a grid setting. Two more grid based techniques are Bang [14] and GRIDCLUST [15] which also create hierarchical clustering using grids. GRIDCLUST is also in a scale-based grid clustering algorithm. Their grid structure is based on a k-d tree. In GRIDCLUST first the cells are arranged in order of their density and merged in that order. Clusters at different scale can be merged also. It is a bottom up approach. Our grid structure is different and we use a top down approach where the idea is to study each scale and see if certain parts of data should be studied at that or a finer scale. DBSCAN [16] is also a similar approach, but it is primarily a clustering algorithm and is not a multiscale dyadic cube approach. We have used data sets from Cure [17] and Chameleon [18]. Again none of these approaches have been presented in context of streaming data.

Recently, clustering algorithms for large data sets and streaming data sets have been developed. BIRCH (Balanced Iterative Reducing and Clustering) [19] clusters large data sets by using specialized tree structures to work with out-of-memory data. CLARANS (Clustering Large Applications based on RANdom Search) [20] identifies candidate cluster centroids through analysis of repeated random samples of the original data. The k-mediod problem is a variation of k-means. Guha, et al. [21] have presented streaming algorithms using local clustering to solve the k-mediod problem. Additional work was done by Bradley, et al. [22] and some of the improvements were made by Farnstrom [23]. Aggarwal [24] presents a method for clustering high dimension data using projections. Outlier detection could be treated as a byproduct of these clustering approaches.

## 3    Dyadic Decompositions

In this section we provide formal definitions of dyadic decompositions and outliers defined by dyadic decompositions (ODDs). We begin by collecting and restating some standard definitions involving cubes and dyadic decompositions [25].

**Definition 1.** Dyadic decompositions *are defined recursively as follows. Let the data set be $D \subseteq \mathbf{R}^n$. Let $|D| = N$ denote the number of points in D. First, we enclose the n-dimensional data set D in a cube. The scale of this initial cube is defined to be one. We define additional cubes in our decomposition recursively as follows. For an integer $k > 1$, we divide a cube whose scale is k, into 2 or more cubes whose scale we define to be $k + 1$, by bisecting one or more edges of the larger cube. This produces $2^c$ new cubes, where the number of bisections c satisfies: $1 \leq c \leq n$. We continue this process until a stopping criterion is reached, such as a cube contains fewer than a specified number of points, say, $\epsilon$, which may be scale dependent in the sense that $\epsilon = \epsilon(k)$. We define this to be* dyadic decomposition.

**Definition 2.** *The cubes obtained during dyadic decomposition are called* dyadic cubes.

**Definition 3.** *The dyadic decomposition produces a* dyadic tree, *where each node u is associated with cube $C_u$, and a node u in the tree is child of another node v when the corresponding cube $C_u$ arises by dividing one or more edges of the cube $C_v$ in half.*

We close this section with a remark:

*Remark 1.* Note that a cube in 2-dimensions (a square) has 8 possible adjacent cubes, and a cube in 3-dimensions has 26 possible neighboring cubes. In general, there are $3^d - 1$ adjacent cubes for a cube in $d$-dimensions.

# 4    Computing the Streaming Dyadic Tree Associated with a Data Set

In a streaming setting since we can look at each point only once and since we have fixed space the tree that we built can only be of a fixed depth. Building a dyadic decomposition as described above requires us to know the whole data set, i.e., before we can divide the cube containing the data set we need to know the dimensions of the cube the data set lies in. This means that we cannot have a top down construction as discussed above. This motivates the construction of streaming dyadic trees.

Let the data stream $D$ be a sequence of points $p_1$, $p_2$, ... in $\mathbf{R}^n$. Fix the maximum depth of a tree, an integer, $r_{max} \geq 0$. Let $u_0$ denote the root of a dyadic tree $T$ and with a slight abuse of notation, let $C_{u_0}$ denote the corresponding dyadic cube. If $u$ is a node in $T$, and $C_u$ is the corresponding dyadic cube, let $Count_u$ denote the number of points in the cube $C_u$.

The idea behind constructing a streaming dyadic tree is simple. Roughly speaking, take the first two points in the stream and build a cube that contains both points. If a new point comes in and it is outside the current cube keep doubling the cube (doubling will result in new cubes) while maintaining the depth of the tree till the new point is in a region covered by the new cubes.

This is Step 4. If a new point lies in a region already covered by cubes the point travels to the smallest cube that could contain the point. This is Step 3, Case 1. If the leave is maximum depth increment the count of the leaf and discard the point, this is Step 3, Case 2, otherwise spit the node making a new leaf for the point. This is Step 3, Case3. The precise formulation is presented below.

For given a data stream, the decomposition obtained by the following algorithm is called a *streaming dyadic decomposition*. Associate a tree $T$ with this decomposition.

## Algorithm 1. Computing a Streaming Dyadic Tree

1. Let $C_0$ denote a cube that contains the point $p_1$. Set $C = C_0$.
2. For $i \geq 2$, score the point $p_i$ using $T$ as follows. Let $C_{u_0}$ denote the cube associated with the root node $u_0$. Set $C = C_{u_0}$ and proceed to the next step.
3. If $p_i$ is in the cube $C = C_u$ associated with the node $u$ of $T$, then check each of the following three cases in order:
   - Case 1. In this case, we are at an interior node and will continue processing the point $p_i$. More precisely, (1) The node $u$ has children, which divide the cube $C_u$ into sub-cubes $C_{u_1}$, $C_{u_2}$, ..., with corresponding nodes $u_1$, $u_2$, ... and (2) the nodes $u_i$ *are not* at the maximum depth $r_{\max}$. In this case, $p_i$ is in one of the sub-cubes, say $C_{u_j}$. Set $C = C_{u_j}$, increment the count of the cube $C_{u_j}$ and goto Step 3.
   - Case 2. In this case, we have reached the maximum depth of the tree and we will discard the point $p_i$. More precisely, (1)The node $u$ has children, which divide the cube $C_u$ into sub-cubes $C_{u_1}$, $C_{u_2}$, ..., with corresponding nodes $u_1$, $u_2$, ... and (2) the nodes $u_i$ *are* at the maximum depth $r_{\max}$. In this case, $p_i$ is in one of the sub-cubes, say $C_{u_j}$. Increment the counter associated with the node $u_j$ and discard the point $p_i$. Goto Step 2.
   - Case 3. In this case, we add a new leaf to the tree containing the point $p_i$. More precisely, if the cube $C$ has no children (i.e., is a leaf) and the node $u$ *is not* at the maximum depth $r_{\max}$, then split the node $u$ to produce sub-cubes $C_{u_1}$, $C_{u_2}$, .... Note that in this case, by the construction, the node $C_u$ contains a least one point prior to the arrival of the point $p_i$. Also note, as mentioned, that the new leaf contains the point $p_i$. Goto Step 2.
4. Else, if $p_i$ is not in the $C_{u_0}$, double the cube $C_{u_0}$ until the point $p_i$ is contained in it. Each time, the root is doubled, maintain the maximum depth of $T$ by merging all the leaves with their parents as required. Process the point $p_i$, by letting $C = C_{u_0}$ and going to Step 3.

The tree obtained in the above algorithm is called a *streaming dyadic tree* associated with a data set $D$.

### 4.1   Outliers Associated with Streaming Dyadic Decompositions

Using the dyadic tree associated with a stream, we can now define outliers.
Let $D$ be a data stream and $T_{sD}$ the associate streaming dyadic tree.

**Definition 4.** *A* outlier associated with a streaming dyadic decomposition or ODD *is a point that i) is contained in cube $C_u$ associated with a leaf node $u$ of the tree $T_{sD}$; and ii) the cube $C_u$ contains precisely one point. We say the ODD is of depth $d$ in case the leaf $C_u$ is at depth $d$ from the root.*

The above definition can be extended to a *k-outlier associated with a dyadic decomposition or k-ODD* by stipulating that the cube $C_u$ contain at-most k points.

  This concept can prove useful in certain practical problems where two or more points are close to each other and away from rest of the points.

  Our approach has two key ideas:

1. In our approach we do a streaming division of space into dyadic cubes. If a point lies outside the currently bounded space we can keep doubling the space (while maintaining the depth of the tree) along all the dimensions till the point is inside the bounds. If it lies inside the bounds we either find a path to a leaf or we can keep subdividing the cubes till either the point lies in its own cube or the maximum depth is reached and further subdivision is not permissible.

2. Since a streaming setting means a restriction of space we save space by storing just those points that are possible ODDs. That is why only leaves of the streaming dyadic tree, $T_{sD}$, can store points. All points which are stored in the leaves are candidate ODDs. At the end of the stream we just need to look at the leaves containing point(s)to obtain our list of ODDs.

We close this section with few remarks:

*Remark 2.* We can relate this definition of an outlier to Knorr's definition of an outlier. A point $p$ is an defined as an *Knorr outlier* with respect to parameters $k$ and $\lambda$, if no more than $k$ points are a distance $\lambda$ or less from $p$. We see that ODDs at depth $d$ are similar in spirt to Knorr outliers but have a natural scale associated with them and use (empty or sparse) dyadic decompositions at scale $d$ instead of a distance $\lambda$.

*Remark 3.* We can put restrictions on the space in which a point can exist inside a dyadic cube. This can result in more restrictive definition of an ODD.

*Remark 4.* The depth of the tree needs to be fixed in advance. It is easy to see that more the depth more nodes are available in the tree, increasing the number of candidate ODDs.

## 4.2   Complexity

The algorithm to building a streaming dyadic tree is designed to work for streaming data. Hence the space and time requirements are severe. Let the tree contain a total $N_t$ nodes and leaves at any time $t$. $N_t$ is bounded by fixing the maximum depth of the tree. The worst case scenario for any operation is traversing the complete tree for a worst case complexity of $O(N_t)$.

The space required is to store these nodes, $O(N_t)$ and the candidate ODDs.

*Pruning* is an effective solution for saving time and space. The tree can be pruned without losing any information. Once all the children of a particular node contain more than one element that node can be considered full. If a point falls within the bounds of that node it cannot be an outlier and it is discarded. This obviously saves the computation involved in further travelling down that branch of the tree. This does not affect the accuracy of the results.

In our experiments, even with a data sets of two million points in eight dimensions space was never an issue since typically, the data clusters naturally to a few branches of the tree.

## 5   Experimental Results

We have completed some experimental studies on artificial and real data sets using the algorithm described above.

The only variable the user needs to input is the maximum depth of the tree. We want to see how many outliers we are able to identify as ODDs.

To test the algorithm we did four series of experiments.

1. 2-D data sets: The first series of experiments used synthetic 2-D data sets.
2. The second series of experiments used large synthetic 2-D data sets.
3. The third series used data set containing computer network alerts.
4. The fourth series used data sets of NASA shuttle data.

For some experiments we have computed two measures, *Sensitivity* and *Specificity* and their sum *Goodness*.

$$Sensitivity = \frac{True\ Positives}{Total\ Positives} \tag{1}$$

$$Specificity = 1 - \frac{False\ Positives}{Data\ Set\ Size} \tag{2}$$

$$Goodness = Sensitivity + Specificity \tag{3}$$

Note that declaring all the points as outliers gives *sensitivity* as one but *specificity* is almost zero making the total *goodness* almost one. Not declaring any point as an outlier makes *specificity* one but the *sensitivity* is zero, making the *goodness* again one. Randomly declaring any point as an outlier with probability half also leads to a *goodness* of one. Therefore, any improvement over one is an improvement in terms of outlier detection. If an algorithm is indiscriminate in labelling points as outliers, and in the process wrongly labels a lot of points as outliers, the *sensitivity* might be high but the *specificity* goes down. On the other hand if an algorithm declares too few points as outliers, false positives would decrease and *specificity* will be high but the *sensitivity* will go down. In our experiments, as the maximum value for the depth of the tree $r_{max}$ is increased the *sensitivity* goes up but the *specificity* goes down.

The algorithm is designed for a streaming setting. To simulate a streaming setting we read one record at a time from a file stored on a drive and discarded the point after that. Some of the real data sets that we have used contain categorical variables. We converted them to a set of binary variables using the simple technique of converting each category as yes/no value and adding it as an attribute.

## 5.1   2-D Data Sets

These are the Cure [17] and Chameleon [18] data sets which have non-spherical clusters and some outlier points distributed through the plane. In Figure 5.1 (Please see the last page) for the three individual figures, we have colored points identified as ODDs with the color blue. It is easy to see from the figures that in general what would appear as an outlier to the naked eye is also identified as an ODD by our algorithm. The first three data sets have 8000 points and the last one has 10000 points.

## 5.2   Large Data Sets

We created 30 large synthetic data sets. They were of three types, consisting of ten sets each:

1. The first type was in four dimensions and had $100,000$ points. The data was distributed in four clusters and $1,\ldots,10$ percent of the points (meaning 1000 to 10,000) were distributed randomly to create ten data sets respectively. The random points are expected to be the outliers our algorithm identifies as ODDs.
2. The second type was in four dimensions and had $1,000,000$ points. The data was distributed as with the previous experiment.
3. The third type was in eight dimensions and had $2,000,000$ points. The data was distributed as previously but with five clusters.

**Results.** In Table 1 we have tabulated these results. True positives indicate the number of correct labels, i.e., the number of outliers that were identified as ODDs by our algorithm and the false negatives indicate the number of outliers that the algorithm failed to identify as ODDs.

For the majority of the experiments, the sensitivity was greater than 0.99. In other words, the algorithm identifies almost all outliers as ODDs. For the majority of the experiments, the specificity was greater than 0.99 and the picks included very few false negatives, i.e., those outliers that the algorithm failed to identify as ODDs.

## 5.3   KDD Data: Network Alert Data

We did experiments using a KDD-99 data set [http://kdnuggets.org/] to create several data sets to test our algorithm. Since it can be tricky to identify a point a-priori as an outlier in a data set, we used the KDD labels. The data set had a total

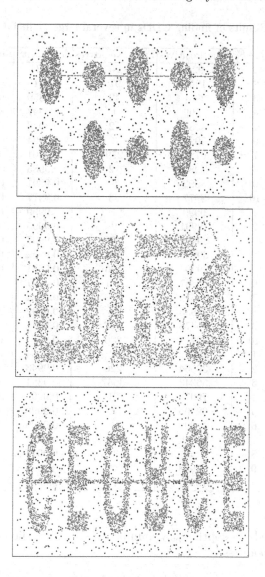

**Fig. 1.** Visual description of results of outlier detection for a data set drawn from Cure/Chameleon data sets

311,029 records with 37 different types of network attack patterns and records labelled "normal". We picked one record each at random from every attack type and randomly picked either $\{1000, 5000, 10000, 25000, 50000\}$ of the normal patterns for a total of $\{1037, 5037, 10037, 25037, 50037\}$ points respectively.

We ran our algorithm on five data sets for each size (for a total of 25 data sets) and for a maximum depth, $r_{max}$ of six to ten. We tabulate the results in Table 2. Due to lack of space, for each data set we have chosen one sample run.

**Table 1.** Results of finding ODDs in several large artificial data sets

| Number Points | Noise % | True Positives | False Negatives | Sensitivity | Specificity | Goodness |
|---|---|---|---|---|---|---|
| $0.1 * 10^6$ | 1 | 924 | 76 | 0.924 | 0.99995 | 1.92395 |
| $0.1 * 10^6$ | 2 | 1903 | 97 | 0.9515 | 0.99994 | 1.95144 |
| $0.1 * 10^6$ | 3 | 2957 | 42 | 0.9859 | 0.99979 | 1.98569 |
| $0.1 * 10^6$ | 4 | 3999 | 1 | 0.9997 | 0.99881 | 1.99851 |
| $0.1 * 10^6$ | 5 | 4988 | 12 | 0.9976 | 0.99976 | 1.99736 |
| $0.1 * 10^6$ | 6 | 5996 | 3 | 0.9994 | 0.99866 | 1.99806 |
| $0.1 * 10^6$ | 7 | 6721 | 279 | 0.9601 | 0.9999 | 1.96 |
| $0.1 * 10^6$ | 8 | 7988 | 12 | 0.9985 | 0.99949 | 1.99799 |
| $0.1 * 10^6$ | 9 | 8992 | 8 | 0.9991 | 0.99867 | 1.99777 |
| $0.1 * 10^6$ | 10 | 9977 | 23 | 0.9977 | 0.99981 | 1.99751 |
| $1.0 * 10^6$ | 1 | 9999 | 1 | 0.9999 | 0.99952 | 1.99942 |
| $1.0 * 10^6$ | 2 | 19991 | 9 | 0.9995 | 0.99763 | 1.99713 |
| $1.0 * 10^6$ | 3 | 29991 | 9 | 0.9997 | 0.99737 | 1.99707 |
| $1.0 * 10^6$ | 4 | 39930 | 69 | 0.9982 | 0.99988 | 1.99808 |
| $1.0 * 10^6$ | 5 | 49404 | 596 | 0.9881 | 0.99998 | 1.98808 |
| $1.0 * 10^6$ | 6 | 59887 | 111 | 0.9981 | 0.9999 | 1.998 |
| $1.0 * 10^6$ | 7 | 69678 | 320 | 0.9954 | 0.99997 | 1.99537 |
| $1.0 * 10^6$ | 8 | 79935 | 65 | 0.9992 | 0.99985 | 1.99905 |
| $1.0 * 10^6$ | 9 | 89473 | 527 | 0.9941 | 0.99992 | 1.99402 |
| $1.0 * 10^6$ | 10 | 99711 | 286 | 0.9971 | 0.99984 | 1.99694 |
| $2.0 * 10^6$ | 1 | 19827 | 91 | 0.9954 | 0.9999 | 1.9953 |
| $2.0 * 10^6$ | 2 | 39564 | 226 | 0.9943 | 0.9998 | 1.9941 |
| $2.0 * 10^6$ | 3 | 56343 | 3657 | 0.9391 | 0.9999 | 1.939 |
| $2.0 * 10^6$ | 4 | 79979 | 21 | 0.9997 | 0.9999 | 1.9996 |
| $2.0 * 10^6$ | 5 | 99999 | 1 | 0.9999 | 0.9971 | 1.997 |
| $2.0 * 10^6$ | 6 | 11999 | 1 | 0.9999 | 0.9993 | 1.9992 |
| $2.0 * 10^6$ | 7 | 139044 | 956 | 0.9931 | 0.9999 | 1.993 |
| $2.0 * 10^6$ | 8 | 158687 | 1313 | 0.9917 | 0.9999 | 1.9916 |
| $2.0 * 10^6$ | 9 | 17998 | 2 | 0.9999 | 0.8731 | 1.873 |
| $2.0 * 10^6$ | 10 | 19981 | 19 | 0.9999 | 0.9995 | 1.9994 |

We have tabulated the depth, $r_{max}$, number of correct outlier labels, sensitivity, specificity and goodness.

**Results.** In all our runs more than half the attack patterns were flagged as ODDs by our algorithm. Notice that except for one, all of the goodness values are above 1.5 and most of them are greater than 1.6.

Typically, as $r_{max}$ is increased the number of points flagged as ODDs increases. This would mean that sensitivity, which measures true positives, goes up but false positives go up too, reducing the specificity. In Table 2, for all experiments more true outliers could have been flagged as ODDs than the number indicated, but it would have resulted in a loss of goodness. Moreover, the attack types that the algorithm failed to identify were invariably almost the same over all the different experiments.

**Table 2.** Results of finding ODDs in network alert data

| Number Points | Depth | True Positive | Sensitivity | Specificity | Goodness |
|---|---|---|---|---|---|
| 1000 | 6 | 24 | 0.648648649 | 0.94021215 | 1.588860799 |
| 1000 | 9 | 33 | 0.891891892 | 0.753134041 | 1.645025932 |
| 1000 | 6 | 22 | 0.594594595 | 0.941176471 | 1.535771065 |
| 1000 | 7 | 30 | 0.810810811 | 0.849566056 | 1.660376867 |
| 1000 | 6 | 22 | 0.594594595 | 0.947926712 | 1.542521306 |
| 5000 | 8 | 27 | 0.72972973 | 0.900933095 | 1.630662825 |
| 5000 | 9 | 28 | 0.756756757 | 0.848520945 | 1.605277702 |
| 5000 | 10 | 33 | 0.891891892 | 0.786182251 | 1.678074143 |
| 5000 | 7 | 30 | 0.810810811 | 0.922771491 | 1.733582302 |
| 5000 | 9 | 33 | 0.891891892 | 0.805042684 | 1.696934576 |
| 10000 | 8 | 25 | 0.675675676 | 0.926472053 | 1.602147729 |
| 10000 | 9 | 28 | 0.756756757 | 0.870279964 | 1.627036721 |
| 10000 | 9 | 27 | 0.72972973 | 0.89628375 | 1.62601348 |
| 10000 | 10 | 31 | 0.837837838 | 0.786191093 | 1.624028931 |
| 10000 | 10 | 28 | 0.756756757 | 0.861313141 | 1.618069898 |
| 25000 | 9 | 27 | 0.72972973 | 0.880257219 | 1.609986949 |
| 25000 | 8 | 29 | 0.783783784 | 0.90142589 | 1.685209673 |
| 25000 | 10 | 26 | 0.702702703 | 0.89603387 | 1.598736573 |
| 25000 | 10 | 27 | 0.72972973 | 0.885809003 | 1.615538732 |
| 25000 | 10 | 29 | 0.783783784 | 0.86995247 | 1.653736254 |
| 50000 | 10 | 23 | 0.621621622 | 0.87401323 | 1.495634852 |
| 50000 | 9 | 30 | 0.810810811 | 0.937706097 | 1.748516908 |
| 50000 | 10 | 23 | 0.621621622 | 0.916841537 | 1.538463159 |
| 50000 | 9 | 26 | 0.702702703 | 0.921737914 | 1.624440617 |
| 50000 | 10 | 27 | 0.72972973 | 0.893478826 | 1.623208555 |

## 5.4   Identifying a Minority Class

In the experiments just described, streaming ODDs were defined by using leaves in the trees that contain a single point. In the next series of experiments, we relaxed this restriction and let the leaves contain $k$ or fewer points. This time we also picked $k$ attack patterns for every attack type.

**Experiment 1.** The results are summarized in Table 3, where $k$ is called the threshold. This time all of the goodness values are above 1.5 and again most of them are greater than 1.6.

**Experiment 2.** In another experiment with the network data set, we picked all the examples of those attack types that had less than 25 examples. In total there were 166 attack patterns. There were 20 such attack types. We also randomly picked 5000 points. We tried various threshold cardinalities.

The best result (in terms of goodness) was for $k = 7$ of a k-ODD, which gave goodness of 1.59 and 121 of 166 attack patterns were identified. For $k = 9$ we were able to capture 146 of 156 attack patterns, but the specificity was low.

**Table 3.** Results of finding those outliers in network alert data that might not occur as singletons

| Points | Threshold | ODDs | True Positive | Sensitivity | Specificity | Goodness |
|--------|-----------|------|---------------|-------------|-------------|----------|
| 5000 | 2 | 73 | 54 | 0.739726027 | 0.8928 | 1.632526027 |
| 5000 | 3 | 103 | 69 | 0.669902913 | 0.9084 | 1.578302913 |
| 5000 | 4 | 132 | 105 | 0.795454545 | 0.8156 | 1.611054545 |
| 5000 | 5 | 160 | 114 | 0.7125 | 0.909 | 1.6215 |
| 10000 | 2 | 73 | 53 | 0.726027397 | 0.8954 | 1.621427397 |
| 10000 | 3 | 103 | 77 | 0.747572816 | 0.9022 | 1.649772816 |
| 10000 | 4 | 132 | 92 | 0.696969697 | 0.903 | 1.599969697 |
| 10000 | 5 | 160 | 119 | 0.74375 | 0.8818 | 1.62555 |
| 25000 | 2 | 73 | 51 | 0.698630137 | 0.90832 | 1.606950137 |
| 25000 | 3 | 103 | 83 | 0.805825243 | 0.84108 | 1.646905243 |
| 25000 | 4 | 132 | 98 | 0.742424242 | 0.9188 | 1.661224242 |
| 25000 | 5 | 160 | 104 | 0.65 | 0.94492 | 1.59492 |

The higher cardinality works because (1) Some patterns of the same attack types are very similar. (2) Different attack types sometimes also have similar patterns. (3) Some normal patterns occur with the attack types.

### 5.5 NASA Shuttle Data

This data has seven classes and 14,500 trained examples in nine dimensions [http://kdnuggets.org/]. There are 11,478 examples of class one, 12 examples of class two, 38 examples of class three, 2155 examples of class four, 807 examples of class five, 4 examples of class six and 2 of class seven.

Our algorithm identifies all 6 points belonging to class six and seven as ODDs in a list of 36 ODDs.

### 5.6 Building Forests

Instead of using single trees to find streaming ODDs trees we can also use forests of trees to compute streaming CDDs . In Table 4 we have presented some results with one technique for creating forests. The data set consisted of 2 million points with outliers varying from 1-10%.

**Results.** We have tabulated the depth at which both specificity and sensitivity is greater that 0.99 for the first time (with noise of 9%, the forest approach could not reach the level of 0.99 sensitivity). It can be seen though that for most experiments the depth of a forest is less than that of a single tree.

A number of approaches can be used to create a forest. Our idea is simple:

1. Insert a new point in the tree within whose root's bounds the point falls.
2. If no such tree exists:
   (a) If a tree has less than maximum depth, insert the point in that tree.
   (b) Else create a new tree.

**Table 4.** Maximum depth needed to achieve greater that 0.99 specificity and sensitivity for streaming ODDs for a data set with $2 \times 10^6$ points and outlier varying form $1 - 10\%$ using single tree and forest

| Outlier Percent | Single Tree | Forest |
|---|---|---|
| 1 | 9 | 7 |
| 3 | 10 | 9 |
| 4 | 9 | 7 |
| 5 | 7 | 7 |
| 6 | 8 | 8 |
| 7 | 10 | 10 |
| 8 | 11 | 9 |
| 9 | 7 | - |
| 10 | 9 | 7 |

(c) Once the number of trees is equal to maximum number of allowable trees in the forest, insert the new point in a tree that will require the least doubling to accommodate the point within its bounds.

## 5.7  Discussion

We have conducted experiments with two artificial and and two real life data sets.

The only variable we need to fix to run the algorithm is to fix the maximum depth of the dyadic tree.

The maximum depth of the tree determines the number of points that are identified as ODDs. More the depth, greater the number of points identified as ODDs. In our experiments a depth of 6-10 seems to have worked well. The same holds true for identifying member of a minority class.

One possible drawback of our approach is sparse data, in which it is difficult to define what an outlier is.

## 6  Conclusions

In this work, we have introduced a streaming algorithm for detecting outliers that is simple, effective and naturally exploits the multiscale nature of many common data sets. It is based upon a natural modification of a dyadic decomposition of a data set when the data is presented in the form of a stream and only a finite amount of space is available to construct the dyadic tree.

Once we have constructed a dyadic tree under a streaming setting we use it to find outliers in a streaming setting. We have described a few modifications to our approach, e.g., forests, k-ODDs. Finally, we have conducted experiments on artificial and real data sets to demonstrate the use of our algorithm.

# References

1. Knorr, E., Ng, R.: Algorithms for mining distance based outliers in large datasets. In: VLDB '98. Proceedings of International Conference on Very Large Databases, pp. 392–402 (1998)
2. Ramaswamy, S., Rastogi, R., Shim, K.: Effcient algorithms for mining outliers from large data sets. In: SIGMOD '00. Proceedings of the ACM International Conference Management Of Data, pp. 427–438. ACM Press, New York (2000)
3. Breunig, M.M., Kriegel, H., Ng, R.T., Sander, J.: Lof: Identifying density based local outliers. In: Proceedings of the ACM International Conference Management Of Data, pp. 93–104. ACM Press, New York (2000)
4. Jagdish, H.V., Koudas, N., Muthukrishnan, S.: Mining deviants in a time series data base. In: VLDB '99. Proceedings of International Conference on Very Large Databases (1999)
5. Muthukrishnan, S., Shah, R., Vitter, J.S.: Mining deviants in time series data streams. Technical Report DIMACS TR 2003-43, DIMACS (2003)
6. Nasraoui, O., Uribe, C.C., Coronel, C.R., Gonzalez, F.: Tecno-streams: Tracking evolving clusters in noisy data streams with a scalable immune system learning model. In: ICDM'03. Third IEEE International Conference on Data Mining, IEEE Computer Society Press, Los Alamitos (2003)
7. Sheikholeslami, G., Chatterjee, S., Zhang, A.: Wavecluster: A multi-resolution clustering approach to very large databases. In: VLDB '98. Proceedings of the 24th VLDB Conference (1998)
8. Chakravarty, S.V., Ghosh, J.: Scale based clustering using the radial basis function network. IEEE Transactions on Neural Networks (1996)
9. Wong, Y.F.: Clustering data by melting. Neural Computation 5(1), 89–104 (1993)
10. Leung, Y., Zhang, J.S., Xu, Z.B.: Clustering by scale-space filtering. IEEE Transactions on Pattern Analysis And Machine Intelligence 22(12) (2000)
11. Roberts, J.S.: Parametric and non-parametric unsupervised cluster analysis. Pattern Recognition 30(2), 261–272 (1997)
12. Barbara, D., Chef, P.: Using fractal dimension to cluster data sets. In: Proceedings of the 6th ACM SIGKDD, pp. 260–264. ACM Press, New York (1999)
13. Warnekar, C.S., Krishna, G.: A heuristic clustering algorithm using union of overlapping pattern cells. Pattern Recognition 11, 85–93 (1979)
14. Schikuta, E., Erhart, M.: The bang clustering system: A grid based data analysis. In: Proceedings Advances in Intelligent Data Analysis, Reasoning About Data 2nd International Symposium, pp. 513–524 (1997)
15. Schikuta, E.: Grid clustering: A fast hierarchical clustering method for very large data sets. In: Proceedings 13th International Conference on Pattern Recognition, vol. 2, pp. 101–105 (1996)
16. Ester, M., Kriegel, H.P., Sander, J., Xu, X.: A density-based algorithm for discovering clusters in large spatial databases with noise. In: Proceedings of the Second Intl Conference on Knowledge Discovery and Data Mining (1996)
17. Guha, S., Rastogi, R., Shim, K.: Cure: An effcient clustering algorithm for large databases. In: Proceedings of 1998 ACM-SIGMOD International Conference on Management of Data, ACM Press, New York (1998)
18. Karypis, G., Han, E.H., Kumar, V.: Chameleon: Hierarchical clustering using dynamic modelling. IEEE Computer 32(8), 68–75 (1999)
19. Zhang, T., Ramkrishnan, R., Linvy, M.: Birch: An effcient data clustering method for very large databases. SIGMOD 25(2), 103–114 (1996)

20. Ng, R., Han, J.: Very large data bases. In: VLDB '94. Proceedings of the 20th International Conference on Very Large Data Bases, pp. 144–155 (1994)
21. Guha, S., Mishra, N., Motwani, R., O'Callaghan, L.: Clustering data streams. In: The Annual Symposium on Foundations of Computer Science, IEEE, Los Alamitos (2000)
22. Bradley, P.S., Fayyad, U.M., Reina, C.A.: Scaling clustering algorithms to large databases. In: Terano, T., Chen, A.L.P. (eds.) PAKDD 2000. LNCS, vol. 1805, pp. 9–15. Springer, Heidelberg (2000)
23. Farnstrom, F., Lewis, J., Elkan, C.: True scalability of clustering algorithms. SIGKDD Explorations (2000)
24. Aggarwal, C.C., Han, J., Yu, P.S.: A framework for projected clustering of high dimensional data streams. In: Proceedings of the 30th VLDB Conference (2004)
25. Stein, E.M.: Singular Integrals and Differentiability Properties of Functions. Princeton University Press, Princeton (1970)

# VISRED –Numerical Data Mining with Linear and Nonlinear Techniques

Antonio Dourado, Edgar Ferreira, and Paulo Barbeiro

Centro de Informática e Sistemas
Department of Informatics Engineering, University of Coimbra, 3030-290 Coimbra Portugal
{dourado, edgar, pbarbeiro}@dei.uc.pt

**Abstract.** Numerical data mining is a task for which several techniques have been developed that can provide a quick insight into a practical problem, if an easy to use common software platform is available. **VISRED**- Data **Vis**ualisation by Space **Red**uction presented here, aims to be such a tool for data classification and clustering. It allows the quick application of Principal Component Analysis, Nonlinear Principal Component Analysis, Multi-dimensional Scaling (classical and non classical). For clustering several techniques have been included: hierarchical, k-means, subtractive, fuzzy k-means, SOM- Self Organizing Map (batch and recursive versions). It reads from and writes to Excel sheets. Its utility is shown with two applications: the visbreaker process part of an oil refinery and the UCI benchmark problem of breast cancer diagnosis.

**Keywords:** multidimensional scaling; numerical data mining; principal component analysis; applications.

## 1 Introduction

Monitoring of large scale industrial processes, diagnosis in medical problems, decision support in finance and services, are tasks that can profit from data-mining of the numerical data available in today's' information system. In industry every day a huge amount of data, from thousands of sensors, is available and should be used for supporting mill's managers and operators. Medical doctors have databases with thousands of patients that can be precious in supporting diagnosis. An application to ease that operation is being developed. It is based on the concept of reduction of the dimension of the original space to a three or two dimensional space, where information is easily represented and interpreted by humans [1]. Multidimensional scaling [2] has been adopted for that purpose. It is a technique that has been used in social sciences for long-time, rooted in the pioneer works of psychologists Young and Householder [3]. Its application to industrial problems has been recently identified as an important development in industrial data mining activities [4][5][6]. Presently there are some efforts to use it in process control as the present work does. In medical diagnosis, when a large amount of quantitative data from a population of patients is available, multidimensional scaling may give a quick and important support to diagnosis.

P. Perner (Ed.): ICDM 2007, LNAI 4597, pp. 92–106, 2007.

VISRED- Data Visualization by Space Reduction is an application developed in the Matlab environment[22] to adapt and integrate a set of techniques for quantitative (numerical) data mining. It integrates the following techniques:

- Linear Principal Component Analysis
- Non Linear Principal Component Analysis
- Classical Multidimensional Scaling
- Multidimensional Scaling

After reduction of the dimension, data is clustered (in the reduced space) by one of several clustering techniques available (hierarchical, k-means, fuzzy k-means, subtractive, dignet, SOM, RSOM).

Several measures can be chosen in the original high dimensional space and in the target low dimensional space for the dissimilarities and to optimize the results.

In the following paragraphs the application will be presented. In paragraph 2 a brief presentation of the techniques intends to support the understanding of the user-interface presented in paragraph 3 (for dimension reduction) and 4 (for clustering). Its application to two representative cases will be shown in paragraph 5, followed by the conclusions.

## 2 A Brief Description of the Techniques for Dimension Reduction

### 2.1 Linear Principal Component Analysis

Principal Components Analysis (PCA) [7] is a technique for simplifying a high-dimensional data set by reducing it to a lower dimension. PCA transforms the data, using an orthogonal linear transformation, to a new coordinate system, such that the greatest variance, by any projection of the data, lies on the first coordinate (called the first principal component), the second greatest variance on the second coordinate, and so on. PCA can be used for dimensionality reduction in a data set while retaining those characteristics of the data that contribute most to its variance, by keeping lower-order principal components and ignoring higher-order ones. The low-order components must contain the main features of the data to preserve information. However this is not always possible, and is not whenever the data is produced by a nonlinear system.

### 2.2 Nonlinear Principal Component Analysis

Nonlinear Principal Component Analysis allows extending to nonlinear relations the concept of principal component, which is the decisive concept for data representation in a reduced space. The technique implemented in VISRED is the one of Hsieh [8] and based on the pioneer developments of Kramer [9] with the contributions of Daszykowski [10].

Nonlinear PCA is implemented by using a bottleneck neural network (BNN), a neural network which has few neurons (normally one to three) in the central layer, surrounded by a symmetric architecture of hidden, input and output neurons (see[9]).

The number of inputs is the same of the outputs, and the goal of training is to achieve as output the same values that were provided as inputs. The hidden neurons are nonlinear. The bottleneck layer will contain a representation of data with fewer dimensions, nonlinearly related to the inputs. There are two distinct ways to obtain several nonlinear (principal) components. If $n$ nonlinear components are desired, one of the approaches would be to use $n$ neurons in the bottleneck layer, to obtain $n$ nonlinear components.

A second approach consists in using only one neuron in the bottleneck layer to extract the first nonlinear principal component. Then, the residual error is used as input (and target output) for a second BNN that computes the second nonlinear principal component, and so on for higher order components. This approach, implemented in VISRED, assures that the nonlinear principal components are orthogonal to each other, contrarily to the first approach [9]. The implementation is based on the software NeuMATSA from Hsieh [8].

## 2.3 Classical Multidimensional Scaling and Multidimensional Scaling

Given a set of $p$ points in an original $n$ dimensional space, some measure of dissimilarity between each pair of them can be defined. A dissimilarity matrix is then constructed with these dissimilarities. Using Euclidean distances as the dissimilarity measure, construct the dissimilarity matrix $\Delta_n$ in the original $n$-dimensional space. Now classical multidimensional scaling will find a distribution of points into an $m$-dimensional space, $m<<n$, such that the Euclidian distances between the dissimilarity matrix $\Delta_n$ and the dissimilarity matrix $\Delta_m$ in the $m$-dimensional space is minimized in the least squares sense (1). The matrix distance (1) is defined as the sum of the Euclidian distances between every point in one and the corresponding point in the other. For more details see [6].

$$J = \left\| \Delta_n - \Delta_m \right\|^2 = \sum_{i=1}^{p} \sum_{j=1}^{p} \left\| (\Delta_n)_{ij} - (\Delta_m)_{ij} \right\|^2 \tag{1}$$

If the distance used to quantify dissimilarity is not Euclidian, but for example, City block, Mahalanobis, etc., then one must apply multidimensional scaling. Multidimensional scaling is an optimization process aiming at minimizing a distance between the two dissimilarity matrices. If the final distance would be zero then the points in the reduced space would be a perfect view of the points in the original high dimensional space. In this situation all the information content expressed by the positions of the points is perfectly preserved when the dimension reduction is performed. This may be said a topology preserving method. However in practical problems that distance J is never zero and its minimization is the goal. The minimization is performed by some optimization technique. The optimization must be initialized at some matrix. Usually one chooses to initialize by classical multidimensional scaling that can be computed by matrix calculus and produces the best lower ($m$)-rank approximation in the least-squares sense (1). This means that classical scaling is equivalent to multidimensional scaling with Euclidian distance.

## 3  The User Interface of VISRED

Figure 1 shows the main interface of VISRED. It is composed by three main panels: The Raw Data panel, the Dimension Reduction panel, and the Clustering panel. It has been conceived to ease the task of defining the needed parameters for the several methods.

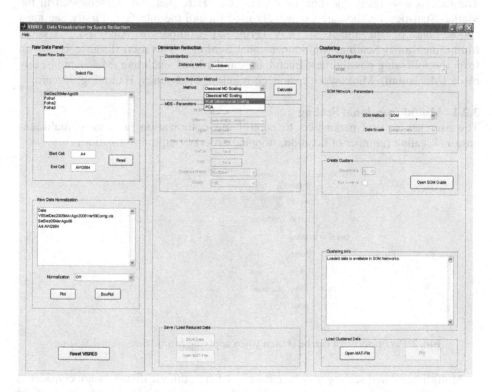

**Fig. 1.** The main user interface of VISRED. It is divided in three main parts: Raw Data Panel, Dimension Reduction, and Clustering.

### 3.1  The Raw Data Panel: Reading, Normalizing, Plotting

The user selects an excel file and a sheet in the file where the data is collected. The first columns of the sheet can have non-numerical data for labeling of the points. The remaining columns contain the coordinates of the first dimension and the following columns the following dimensions. There is no limit, except memory and computational times, for the number of dimensions. The user must specify the first and the last cells to be read. The first cell is A4 by default. It is the one that contains the names of the labels of the points (it can be empty). The last one is the last data to be used.

After reading the data, normalization is applied or not. Data can be normalized by mean value only, by standard deviation only (if it is greater than one), or by both simultaneously.

Data can then be plotted in a new window and analyzed (before or after normalization) and outliers can be observed. User can decide to eliminate some outliers in the excel sheet and restart the analysis.

## 3.2  Dimension Reduction

The data is now ready for dimension reduction. Here methods implemented in the Matlab Statistics Toolbox are extensively used though the interface. Firstly one must choose one of the methods: PCA (Principal Component Analysis), Classical Multidimensional Scaling, Multidimensional Scaling. The used distance is chosen from the following possibilities: Euclidian, standardized Euclidian, Mahalanobis, city block (Manhattan), Minkowski, cosine, correlation, Chebychev, Hamming, Jaccard.

### 3.2.1  Multidimensional Scaling

The user has several parameters to control the optimization process of multidimensional scaling (number of iteration, stopping criteria, output information)

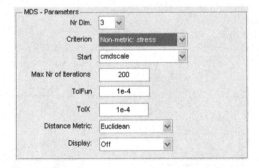

**Fig. 2.** Parameters that can be chosen when applying Multi Dimensional Scaling

Multidimensional scaling may be numeric, where numeric distances are considered for the objective function to be minimized, or non-numeric where only ordinal relations must be preserved. In VISRED, a slightly improved version of Matlab mdscale m-function is used: one can choose which distance will be used to calculate the dissimilarity matrix, instead of being restricted to the standard metric (Euclidean). The used distance is selected in the user interface.

After applying Classical Multidimensional Scaling or Principal Component Analysis, it is possible to analyze the data based on the eigenvalues. The pareto analysis (Fig.3) allows the user to compute the number of dimensions needed for a certain percentage of explained variation. The user can also compute and graph in a separate window the distances between the elements of the dissimilarity matrices and analyze the dispersion around the average (Fig. 4 ) or to count the outliers for a certain percentage. Outliers influence can be studied here and identified. Fixed a percentage of outliers, VISRED identifies in a separate window the data points that result. The user may chose to eliminate them in the data sheet and restart the study.

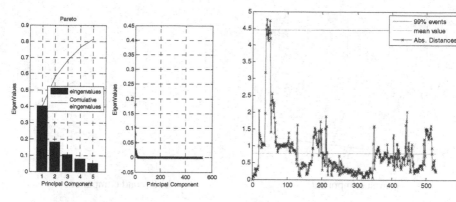

**Fig. 3.** Pareto Analysis                    **Fig. 4.** Absolute Distance Analysis

### 3.2.2 Nonlinear PCA

In order to simplify user's manipulation of values and training of the BNN network, a user-friendly interface was built (Fig.5), where one can easily adjust the needed parameters of the BNN method. Up to three nonlinear principal components can be successively calculated and saved. Points and labels can also be saved for later clustering on VISRED interface.

The nonlinear principal components define a nonlinear base where the data can be represented. Fig. 6 shows, for an example, three components and the resulting data representation in the 3-dimensional space, to which the clustering operation will then be applied.

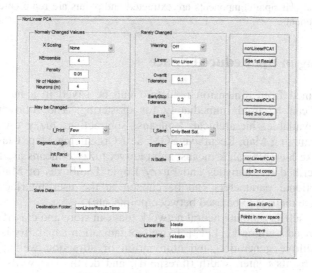

**Fig. 5.** Nonlinear PCA interface

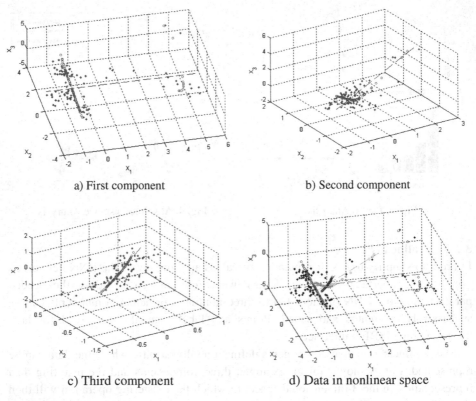

a) First component                    b) Second component

c) Third component                    d) Data in nonlinear space

**Fig. 6.** The nonlinear principal components extraction process. The process starts on input data until all nonlinear principal components are extracted and points are represented in 3D space with these components.

## 4   Clustering in the Reduced Space

The data obtained from dimension reduction can be saved in a mat file for later processing or can be used immediately for clustering. The following clustering methods are available: hierarchical, k-means, subtractive, fuzzy c-means, dignet, SOM-Self Organizing Map, Recursive SOM-Self Organizing Map. Classical clustering methods like hierarchical, k-means, subtractive, fuzzy c-means are fully implemented and described by Statistics and Fuzzy Logic Toolboxes of Matlab. For each method its optional parameters can be chosen in the user interface (number of clusters, distance metrics to be used between points, etc).

Dignet is a self-organizing neural network that can store and classify noisy inputs without supervised training [11] [12]. Its self-organization capability is based on the idea of competitive generation and elimination of attraction wells. Each well is char-acterized by its center, width (threshold), and depth. The wells are generated around presented patterns which are clustered according to their distance from the center of wells. The center of a well is moved dynamically towards the highest

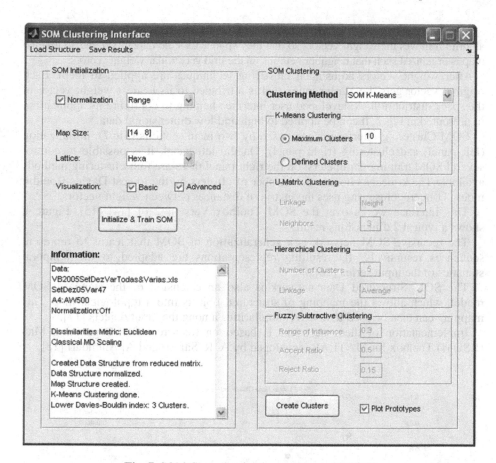

**Fig. 7.** SOM Clustering implementation in VISRED

concentration of clustered points in the pattern constellation. The depth of a well indicates the strength of learning, and influences the inertia of the center of the well when new data falls within its region of attraction; the deeper the well is, the less its center moves towards a new data point[12].

The similarity between patterns in Dignet is measured using a distance which could be Euclidean, angular (cosine) or hyper-cubic (Chebychev). For angular metric it is assumed that all patterns are normalized [11], so that the magnitude of a pattern does not affect the classification capability of the network.

Self-Organizing Map (SOM), proposed by Kohonen [13], is an unsupervised neural network method which has properties of both vector quantization and vector projection algorithms. The prototype vectors are positioned on a regular low-dimensional grid in an ordered fashion, making the SOM a powerful visualization tool [14]. Each neuron is a $n$-dimensional weight vector where $n$ is equal to the dimension of the input vectors. The neurons are connected to adjacent neurons by a neighborhood relation, which dictates the topology, or structure, of the map [15]. In the approach, topology is defined by local lattice structure (hexagonal or rectangular).

The SOM can be thought of as a net which is spread to the data cloud. The SOM training algorithm moves the weight vectors so that they span across the data cloud and so that the map is organized such that neighbor neurons on the grid get similar weight vectors.

After weight vectors adjustment clustering techniques are applied to them. Each original vector gets the cluster index that is attributed to its nearest weight vector in the space distribution. A developed user interface helping to configure its application, in presented in Fig.7. It can be applied to high and low dimensional data.

SOM Clustering Interface is composed by two main sections (Fig.7): initialization (left panel) and clustering (right panel). On the left panel, it is possible to control several SOM training parameters; on the right panel there are four clustering methods available. The k-means chooses the number of clusters by the lowest Davies-Bouldin index; U-matrix clustering uses the matrix of distances between weight vectors.

This interface works over the SOM Toolbox Version 2 of [14] [15]. Figure 8 shows a typical 2 dimensions result.

The recursive SOM network is a generalization of SOM that learns to represent sequences recursively. Its resulting representations are adapted to the temporal statistics of the input series [16].

The SOM Structured Data network is also an extension of the standard SOM model, which allows the mapping of structured objects into a topological map. This mapping can then be used to discover similarities among the input objects [17].

Implementation of these networks is based on Recurrent Self-Organizing Map (RSOM) Toolbox for MATLAB, developed by A. R. Saffari and A. Alamdari [18].

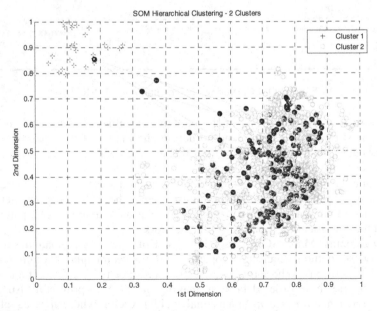

**Fig. 8.** SOM Hierarchical Clustering. Data has two isolated clouds of points; the linked weight vectors are the result of SOM training and are positioned in order to represent distribution and density of data. Hierarchical clustering applied to weight vectors perfectly separates the point clouds of original data.

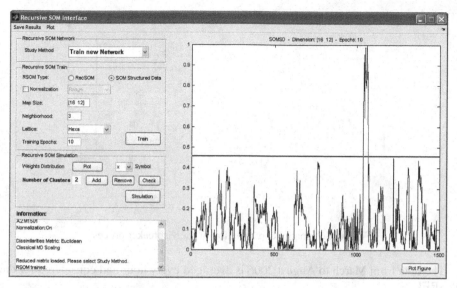

**Fig. 9.** Recursive SOM Clustering implementation in VISRED. This method can be applied to both high and low dimensional data.

Recursive SOM Interface allows training of recursive SOM with defined parameters, like network type (recursive or structured data); the other parameters are similar to those used in SOM training. Graphic area shows network output for training data; this graphics can be divided into clusters by using mouse movable lines that represent cluster thresholds.

Results of recursive SOM train and clustering can be saved and applied to unknown data that represents a similar dimensional space (dimensions of train and simulation must match).

# 5 Applications

## 5.1 The Visbreaker Process

The Visbreaker Unit, an important process in an oil refinery, is intended to reduce the viscosity of some intermediate products (the residual coming from the vacuum column) in the refining chain. With this objective a thermal cracking process is used with a relatively low temperature, and a long residence time. As a result of the thermal process a low viscosity visbreaker residual is obtained, as well as lighter products, such as hydrocarbonets (gas oil diesel, gasoline and gases).The great economical advantage of the visbreaker process lies in fact that it produces a residual with a lower viscosity than the load feed. By this way, it is possible to use a lower quantity of "cutterstocks" (some of them of high benefit) for the production of fuel oil.

Figure 10 [19] presents its flow sheet. It is composed of several sub-processes, and its main part is a kiln operating at about 310 ºC. Actually, data from 160 tags is available. From these, after correlation analysis and process expertise, 59 were selected as sufficiently representative of the process. Multidimensional scaling is then applied to those 59 dimensions.

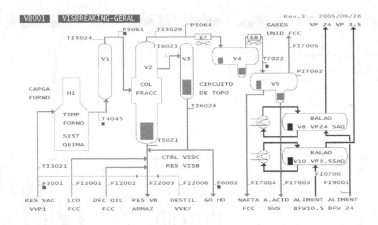

**Fig. 10.** Schematic representation of the visbreaker process

The data from March to August 2006 is averaged every hour and considered for the VISRED.

Fig. 11 shows the results with Classical Multidimensional Scaling (CMDS). Two regions and some outliers are identified. These regions correspond to different operational conditions.

Applying Multidimensional Scaling, with City block distance, Figure 15 is obtained. The dispersion of the points is very similar to CMDS (see however the difference in axes scales).

There are some points in Figures 11 and 12 that could be considered outliers (although they are an average of one hour). Proceeding by this way, applying again CMDS with Euclidian distance, followed by hierarchical clustering with Euclidian averaged distance, with 5 clusters, one obtains Fig. 13. Now two main clouds are identified and grouped in one cluster for each. With Matlab graphical capabilities one can see the dates corresponding to each of the clusters, which can help the plant managers to evaluate the performance of the mill.

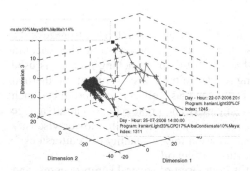

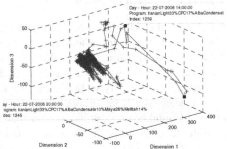

**Fig 11.** Classical scaling with Euclidian distance

**Fig. 12.** Multidimensional scaling with cityblock distance

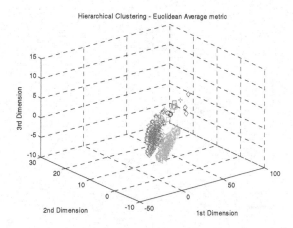

**Fig. 13.** Hierarchical clustering of CMDS results after elimination of some outliers of Fig. 12. The changement of axes is due to the graphication part.

## 5.2  Breast Cancer Diagnosis

Breast cancer diagnosis  (1- malign or 2-beningn) is performed using 30 continuous variables measured in 567 patients , (UCI Repository of Machine Learning Databases and Domain Theories [20]) from the University of Wisconsin Hospitals, Madison [21]. Using VISRED the data has been reduced to three dimensions. Table 1 synthesizes the results for several methods implemented in VISRED.

**Table 1.** Breast cancer diagnosis using several combinations of reduction and clustering in VISRED. Best predicting combinations are marked.

| Normali-zation | Red. Method (Criterium /Start) | Distance Metric | Clustering Method | Dim. | Clustering Metric | Err ors | Predicting % |
|---|---|---|---|---|---|---|---|
| Off | CMD | Euclidean | Hierarchical | 3 | Euclidean | 375 | 33,86 |
| Standard | CMD | Euclidean | Hierarchical | 3 | Euclidean | 106 | 81,31 |
| On | CMD | Euclidean | Dignet | 3 | Euclidean | 38 | 93,30 |
| Range(SOM) | | | SOM / K-Means | 30 | | 25 | 95,59 |
| Range (SOM) | | | SOM / Subtract | 30 | | 33 | 94,18 |
| On | CMD | Chebychev | Dignet | 3 | Euclidean | 66 | 88,36 |
| On | CMD | Cityblock | Dignet | 3 | Euclidean | 37 | 93,47 |
| On | MDS /NM stress | Cityblock | Dignet | 3 | Euclidean | 36 | 93,65 |
| On | NL-PCA | Euclidean | C-Means | 3 | | 78 | 86,24 |
| On | NL-PCA | Euclidean | Subtractive | 3 | | 75 | 86,77 |
| On | NL-PCA | Euclidean | SOM/ K-Means | 3 | | 82 | 85,54 |
| Range | RecSOM | | | 30 | | 72 | 87,30 |
| Range | SOM-SD | | | 30 | | 67 | 88,18 |

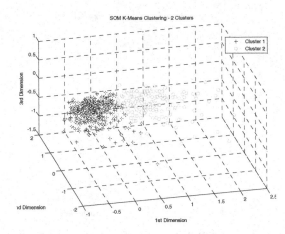

**Fig. 14.** Space distribution by PCA projection and clustering plot of the best breast cancer predicting combination using SOM and k-means

As can be seen in Table 1, several combinations of methods achieve a good match ratio on predicting breast cancer diagnosis. The best combination uses k-means clustering after SOM training with no dimensional reduction; the second best performance is achieved by dignet clustering with Euclidean metric, after dimensional reduction by MDS cityblock.

Both predicting rates (95,59% and 93,65%) show that good combinations of data-mining methods can be applied to real data. VISRED has a high flexibility in choosing the methods to be applied.


## 6  Conclusion

VISRED is an application to ease the activity of researchers and practitioners of numeric data mining. It is public, under GNU principles, and the main effort is being put into the design of friendly and useful user interfaces, in Matlab environment [22]. It is a work in progress, but its present form allows already the quick study of any application with data in standard excel sheets. Comparison of several techniques, linear or non linear, for data analysis based on dimensional reduction can readily be done and the extensive graphical tools present allow the user to gain an insight into the problem under study.

The authors hope that this platform will be useful for all the data mining community.

The software is public GNU licensed and is available at http://eden.dei.uc.pt/~dourado/Visred/VisRed.zip

Further work to improve the VISRED platform is being developed to enhance the multidimensional scaling performance. The optimization task should avoid local minima and find the global optimal dissimilarity matrix in the reduced space. Meta heuristics like genetic algorithms and simulated annealing are being investigated with this aim.

The authors would appreciate any comments, suggestions, and contributions of the data mining community in order to build up a powerful free software for data mining.

## Ackowledgments

This work was supported by Portuguese Foundation for Science and Technology (Project CLASSE, POSC/EIA/58162/2004) and Feder. Edgar Ferreira and Paulo Barbeiro were supported by a BIC grant from CLASSE project. The Sines refinery data was supplied by Eng. Dora Nogueira and Eng. Luís Amaral. The authors would like to thank the authors of GNU software that have been adapted to be used in VISRED (W.W. Hsieh, J. Vesanto, A. R. Saffari).

## References

1. de Oliveira, M.C.F., Levkowitz, H.: From visual data exploration to visual data mining: A survey. IEEE Trans on Visualization and Computer Graphics 9(3), 378–394 (2003)
2. Borg, I., Groenen, P.: Modern Multidimensional Scaling, Theory and Applications, 2nd edn. Springer, Heidelberg (2005)
3. Young, G., Householder, A.S.: A note on multidimensional psycho-physical analysis. Psychometrika 6, 331–333 (1941)
4. Cox, T.F.: Multidimensional Scaling in Process Control. In: Khattree, R. (ed.) Handbook of Statistics 22. Statistics in Industry North Holland (2003)
5. Cox, F.T.: Multidimensional Scaling, 2nd edn. Chapman and Hall CRC Press, New York (2001)
6. Matheus, J., Dourado, A., Henriques, J.: Iterative Multidimensional Scaling for Industrial Process Monitoring. In: Trans. IEEE SMC Int. Conf., Seoul, Taiwan, October 8-7,11, 2006 (2006)
7. Jolliffe, I.T.: Principal Component Analysis, 2nd edn. Springer, Heidelberg (October 2002)
8. Hsieh, W.W.: Neuralnets for Multivariable and Time Series Analysis (NeuMATSA): A User Manual, www.ocgy.ubc.ca/ william/Pubs/NN.manual.pdf
9. Kramer, M.A.: Nonlinear Principal Component Analysis Using Autoassociative Neural Networks. AIChE Journal 37(2), 233–243 (1991)
10. Daszykowski, B., Walczak, 1, Massart, D.L.: A journey into low-dimensional spaces with autoassociative neural networks. In: Talanta, vol. 59, pp. 1095–1105. Elsevier, Amsterdam (2003)
11. Thomopoulos, S.C.A., Bougoulias, D.K, Wann, C.-D.: Dignet an Unsupervised-Learning Clustering Algorithm for Clustering and Data Fusion. IEEE Trans On Aerospace and Electronic Systems 31(1) (1995)
12. Wann, C.-D., Thomopoulos, S.C.A: A comparative study of self-organizing clustering algorithms Dignet and ART2. Neural Networks 10(4), 737 (1997)
13. Kohonen, T.: Self-Organizing Maps, 3rd Extended edn. Springer Series in Information Sciences, vol. 30. Springer, Heidelberg (2001)
14. Vesanto, J., Himberg, J., Alhoniemi, E., Parhankangas, J.: SOM Toolbox for Matlab 5. Helsinki University of Technology (2000)
15. Vesanto, J., Himberg, J., Alhoniemi, E., Parhankangas, J.: Self-organizing map in Matlab: the SOM Toolbox. In: Proceedings of the Matlab DSP Conference, Espoo, Finland, November 16-17, 1999, pp. 35–40 (1999)

16. Voegtlin, T.: Recursive self-organizing maps. Neural Networks 15, 979–991 (2002)
17. Hagenbuchner, M., Sperduti, A., Tsoi, A.C.: A self-organizing map for adaptive processing of structured data. IEEE Transactions on Neural Networks 14(3), 491–505 (2003)
18. Saffari, A.R., Alamdari, A.: Recurrent Self-Organizing Map (RSOM) Toolbox for MATLAB (July 2005), http://www.ymer.org/amir/software/recurrent-self-organizing-maps
19. Galp data, Sines Refinery (2006)
20. Murphy, P.M.: UCI Repository of Machine Learning Databases and Domain Theories (online), Avaiable at http://www.ics.uci.edu/ mlearn/MLRepository.html
21. Wolberg, W.H., Street, W.N., Mangasarian, O.L.: Machine learning techniques to diagnose breast cancer from fine-needle aspirates. Cancer Letters 77, 163–171 (1994)
22. Matlab is a trademark of Mathworks, Inc

# Clustering by Random Projections

Thierry Urruty[1], Chabane Djeraba[1], and Dan A. Simovici[2]

[1] LIFL-UMR CNRS 8022, Laboratoire d'Informatique Fondamentale de Lille,
Université de Lille 1, France
urruty,djeraba@lifl.fr
[2] University of Massachusetts Boston, Department of Computer Science, Boston,
Massachusetts 02125, USA
dsim@cs.umb.edu

**Abstract.** Clustering algorithms for multidimensional numerical data must overcome special difficulties due to the irregularities of data distribution. We present a clustering algorithm for numerical data that combines ideas from random projection techniques and density-based clustering. The algorithm consists of two phases: the first phase that entails the use of random projections to detect clusters, and the second phase that consists of certain post-processing techniques of clusters obtained by several random projections. Experiments were performed on synthetic data consisting of randomly-generated points in $\mathbb{R}^n$, synthetic images containing colored regions randomly distributed, and, finally, real images. Our results suggest the potential of our algorithm for image segmentation.

## 1 Introduction

Clustering is a central preoccupation in data mining and clustering algorithms impact a multitude of data mining applications ([5,19,7]), including multimedia data mining. The problem has been studied by several research communities ranging from statistics to machine learning and the state of the art is exposed in surveys that appeared with some regularity over the years (see [12,9]). Clustering in spaces with low dimensionality is relatively easy. For example, in a unidimensional space it is easy to identify the regions of high density of points by a simple linear scan. With increased dimensionality the problem grows in complexity. The notion of projected clustering was introduced by Agrawal et al. in [1], who made the crucial observations that points may cluster better in subspaces of lower dimensionality than in the entire space $\mathbb{R}^n$. They developed the CLIQUE algorithm that works starting with low dimensional subspaces towards higher dimensional subspaces. In [3] Aggarwal et al. focus on a technique to discover clusters in small dimensional subspaces, which is the focus of their PROCLUS algorithm. The theoretical support of these techniques can be found in Johnson-Lindenstrauss Lemma [11] which asserts that a set of points in a high-dimensional Euclidean space can be projected into a low-dimensional Euclidean space such that the distance between any two points changes by only a factor of $1 \pm \epsilon$ for $\epsilon \in (0, 1)$. Simplifications of the proof of this result have been obtained by Frankl and Maehara [8] and by Dasgupta and Gupta [6]. An especially useful source is the monograph [17].

The number of clusters is a given parameter in PROCLUS and the algorithm identifies these clusters and a set of dimensions associated with each cluster such that the

P. Perner (Ed.): ICDM 2007, LNAI 4597, pp. 107–119, 2007.

points of the cluster are correlated with these dimensions. Another contribution to projective clustering is [2], where an objective function is introduced that takes into account a tradeoff between the dimension of a subspace and the clustering error; an extension of $k$-means to projective clustering in arbitrary subspaces is introduced. Our approach is similar to the approach adopted in [1] in that we construct clusters in low dimensional spaces and then select those dimensions that can best help to identify clusters in the original data set. Our main contribution consists in choosing a random frame of reference for the data set and execute the projections on the subspaces that correspond to this randomly chosen axes. We show that this process has a certain advantage over using the natural system of coordinates in that it diminishes the chance of the occultation phenomenon, which occurs when the projections of two distinct clusters of the data on a subspace are not disjoint. Static segmentation of images regarded as partitioning an image into a number of regions that represent a meaningful part of the image can be helped, as we show, by applying clustering techniques (see [10]). Our clustering algorithm combines ideas from random projection techniques and density-based clustering. The distance between points in $\mathbb{R}^n$ is the Euclidean distance. The proposed algorithm is applicable to numeric data, that is, to data in $\mathbb{R}^n$ and involves projecting the data on a randomly chosen base. Then, histograms of the uni-dimensional projections are combined to yield the locations of clusters in $\mathbb{R}^n$.

The paper begins with a probabilistic evaluation of the projection technique. Namely, in Section 2 we evaluate the probability that the distance between random projections on subspaces reproduces to a certain extent the distance between the original points in $\mathbb{R}^n$ and the probabilities that random projections of separate clusters may have non-empty intersection and, therefore, reduce the usefulness of certain projections. In Section 3 we discuss the clustering algorithm including two important post-processing techniques and we show that the time complexity is of the order of $O(N \log N)$ when the size of the data set is large compared to the number of dimensions, comparable with density-based clustering [15]. Section 4 presents our experimental work performed on three types of data: synthetic data, data obtained from synthetic images, and data obtained from real images. Experiments with groupings of pixels extracted from images, particularly from real images show the potential of the algorithm as a segmentation technique and provide a good criterion for validation of clusterings.

## 2    Clusters and Random Projections

Let $S$ be a finite subset of $\mathbb{R}^n$ and let $\delta$ be a positive real number. Consider a measure $m : \mathcal{P}(\mathbb{R}^n) \longrightarrow \mathbb{R}_{\geq 0}$. The value $m(C)$ is, in general, the volume of the projection of $C$ on a subspace of $\mathbb{R}^n$.

A $\delta$-clustering of $S$ is a family $\kappa = \{C_1, \dots, C_p\}$ of non-empty subsets of $\mathbb{R}^n$ (referred to as the constituents of the clustering) that satisfy the following conditions:

1. the sets of $\kappa$ that are pairwise disjoint;
2. for every $i$, $1 \leq i \leq p$ density of the points of $S$ in any of the sets $C_i$ exceeds $\delta$, that is, we have:

$$\frac{|S \cap C_i|}{m(C_i)} \geq \delta.$$

The *clusters* of the clustering $\kappa$ are the sets $S \cap C_i$ for $1 \leq i \leq p$.

The set of points located outside the sets $C_i$, $\mathsf{UNC}(\kappa) = S - \bigcup_{i=1}^{p} C_i$ is the *set of unclassified points of S*.

A *clustering of S* is a family $\kappa = \{C_1, \ldots, C_p\}$ that is a $\delta$-clustering of $S$ for some $\delta > 0$.

The second condition of the above definition insures that the density of the points in each of the sets $C_i$ is sufficiently high.

Projections on the subspace of $\mathbb{R}^n$ determined by the coordinates $i_1, \ldots, i_t$ are denoted by $\mathsf{proj}_{i_1 \ldots i_t} : \mathbb{R}^n \longrightarrow \mathbb{R}^t$.

Let $\mathbf{H}$ be a random $n \times n$-matrix that is orthogonal. Such a matrix can be obtained, for example, by randomly choosing the components on an $n \times n$-matrix using an uniform distribution on an interval and, then, applying the Gram-Schmidt technique to produce an orthogonal matrix.

A random projection of $\mathbb{R}^n$ is a linear transformation $\Phi_{\mathbf{H}} : \mathbb{R}^n \longrightarrow \mathbb{R}^n$ defined by $\Phi_{\mathbf{H}}(\mathbf{x}) = \mathbf{H}\mathbf{x}$ for $\mathbf{x} \in \mathbb{R}^n$. The set of rows $\mathbf{u}_1, \ldots, \mathbf{u}_n$ of $\mathbf{H}$ is referred to an $n$-dimensional *random frame*.

Identifying clusters in one dimension is a relatively straightforward process using an algorithm (described in Section 3) that builds histograms of the line coordinates of the projections of the points. The inverse statement does not hold; if the projection of a subset $K$ of $\mathbb{R}^n$ on a lower dimension subspace is a cluster we cannot conclude that the set $K$ itself is a cluster. Another difficulty is that disjoint clusters in the $n$-dimensional space may have non-disjoint projections on lower-dimensional subspaces of $\mathbb{R}^n$, a phenomenon that we refer to as *occultation*.

Let $C, D$ be two clusters in $\mathbb{R}^n$ and let $\mathbf{u}$ be a unit vector in the same space. To simplify the presentation assume that $C$ and $D$ are approximated by spheres of radius $r_1$ and $r_2$, centered in the points $\mathbf{c}$ and $\mathbf{d}$, respectively. The orthogonal projection of a set $K$ on a vector $\mathbf{u}$ is the set:

$$\mathsf{proj}_u(K) = \{\mathbf{u} \cdot \mathbf{x} | \mathbf{x} \in K\}.$$

An *$u$-occultation* of the clusters $C, D$ occurs if

$$\mathsf{proj}_u(C) \cap \mathsf{proj}_u(D) \neq \emptyset,$$

a situation which is represented in Figure 1.

This is an inconvenient situation from our point of view since it fuses the two projections of $C$ and $D$ on the vector $\mathbf{u}$.

We need to evaluate the probability that an $\mathbf{u}$-occultation may occur for clusters since we will use cluster uni-dimensional projections for the identification of these clusters in $\mathbb{R}^n$. As before, we assume that $\mathbf{u}$ is a unit random vector. The angle $\alpha$ between $\mathbf{u}$ and the vector $\mathbf{d} - \mathbf{c}$ is uniformly distributed in the interval $[0, 2\pi]$. The discussion is essentially the same for projections on subspaces having an arbitrary dimensionality. Under the previous assumptions, an $\mathbf{u}$-occultation of the clusters $C, D$ occurs when the length of the projection of the segment that joins $\mathbf{c}$ to $\mathbf{d}$ is inferior to $r_1 + r_2$; in other words if $|\mathbf{u} \cdot (\mathbf{d} - \mathbf{c})| = \| \mathbf{d} - \mathbf{c} \| | \cos \alpha | \leq r_1 + r_2$.

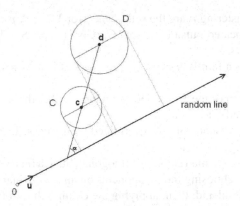

**Fig. 1.** Cluster Occultation

Consequently, the probability of an **u**-occultation of the clusters is the number:

$$P\left(-\frac{r_1 + r_2}{\parallel \mathbf{d} - \mathbf{c} \parallel} \le \cos\alpha \le \frac{r_1 + r_2}{\parallel \mathbf{d} - \mathbf{c} \parallel}\right),$$

which is easily seen to equal to

$$1 - \frac{2}{\pi}\arccos\left(\frac{r_1 + r_2}{\parallel \mathbf{d} - \mathbf{c} \parallel}\right),$$

whenever $\parallel \mathbf{d} - \mathbf{c} \parallel \ge r_1 + r_2$, which happens when the clusters are sufficiently tight. Using the MacLaurin series expansion of $\arccos z$,

$$\arccos z = \frac{\pi}{2} - \left(z + \frac{z^3}{6} + \frac{3}{40}\frac{z^5}{5} + \cdots\right),$$

we can approximate this value by $z = \frac{2(r_1+r_2)}{\pi\|\mathbf{d}-\mathbf{c}\|}$.

Let $O_i$ be the event that takes place when an occultation occurs on the $i$-th projection of the random frame, for $1 \le i \le n$. We need to evaluate the probability that there is at least one projection that avoids the occultation, that is, $P(\overline{O_1} \cup \cdots \cup \overline{O_n}) = 1 - P(O_1 \cap \cdots \cap O_n)$. Assuming that the events $O_1, \ldots, O_n$ are independent we have

$$P(\overline{O_1} \cup \cdots \cup \overline{O_n}) = 1 - \left(\frac{2(r_1 + r_2)}{\pi \parallel \mathbf{d} - \mathbf{c} \parallel}\right)^n.$$

Of course, the independence supposition does not hold in reality. We adopt it here to obtain an estimate that is plausible and is verified by experimental work.

Thus, the probability that there is a dimension that avoids occultation is increasing quite rapidly with the number of dimensions and with the inter-cluster separation. This shows the usefulness of the randomly chosen frame in separating, at least partially, and with a degree of uncertainty, clusters that may not be differentiated through their projections on the initial system of coordinates.

## 3   The Clustering Algorithm

Our algorithm has a heuristic nature. The input consists of a numerical $n$-dimensional data set $D$ and entails two phases: in the first phase we apply random projections to the data set and we obtain the primary clusters; in the second phase we refine the clustering by using two processes: bimodulation and cluster expansion.

The projection phase begins with a randomly chosen orthogonal $n \times n$-matrix $\mathbf{H}$ of real numbers whose rows are the $\mathbf{u}_1, \ldots, \mathbf{u}_n$. Then, the data set $D$ is projected onto each of the $n$ dimensions of the newly chosen randomly chosen base, resulting in $n$ histograms. We begin by clustering the points of each of the selected uni-dimensional projections.

Each $i$-th histogram contains a number of $k$ bins of width $\ell_i$ and the choice of $k$ depends on the size of $D$. For example, for $|D| = 10^4$ we used $k = 50$. On each histogram we identify the peaks and the valleys. The peaks $h_1^i, \ldots, h_{m_i}^i$ of this histogram may correspond to $n$-dimensional clusters.

Suppose that the peak $h_j^i$ of the $i$-th projection is located between the lows $l_j^i$ and $l_{j+1}^i$. Then, the set $C_j^i$ consists of the points that belong to the $p$ bins located at the left of $h_j^i$ whose heights vary between $\beta h_j^i + (1 - \beta)l_j^i$ and $h_j^i$ and the $q$ bins located at the right of $h_j^i$ whose heights vary between $\beta h_j^i + (1 - \beta)l_{j'}^i$ and $h_j^i$ (see Figure 2). Here $\beta$ is a parameter chosen by the user that allows us to guarantee a certain cluster density.

Note that the density of the cluster $\mathsf{proj}_i(S) \cap C_j^i$ is at least

$$\frac{h_j^i + p[\beta h_j^i + (1 - \beta)l_j] + q[\beta h_j^i + (1 - \beta)l_{j+1}]}{(p + q + 1)\ell_i},$$

which is easily seen to be at least $\frac{h_j^i \beta}{\ell_i}$. So, if we choose

$$\beta \geq \max\{\frac{\delta_1 \ell_i}{\min h_j^i} | 1 \leq i \leq n\},$$

we guarantee that the uni-dimensional clusters have the minimal density $\delta_1$. The choice of $\delta_1$ is determined, as we shall see by the parameter $\delta$.

The quality of a projection is evaluated using the product between the average height of peaks and the logarithm of the number of peaks of the histogram. Only a percentage of the dimensions that correspond to these top histograms are retained for the next phase. Initially we seek to obtain a clustering that corresponds to these projections. In our experiments we used the top 10% of the histograms, a choice that is supported by our experiments (see Section 4.2).

Suppose that the peaks of the $i$-th random projection correspond to the intervals $C_1^i, \ldots, C_{p_i}^i$. Let $t$ be the number of top projections. We use a file $\mathcal{F}$ that contains records having $1 + n + t$ components, whose structure is shown in Table 1. Each record represents one of the points $\mathbf{x} = (x_1, \ldots, x_n)$ to be clustered and contains a point

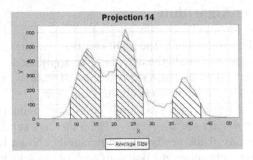

**Fig. 2.** Intervals around peaks in a projection

**Table 1.** The Structure of the file $\mathcal{F}$

| $\mathcal{F}$ | | | | | | |
|---|---|---|---|---|---|---|
| Point id. | $x_1$ | $\cdots$ | $x_n$ | $B(1, \mathbf{x})$ | $\cdots$ | $B(t, \mathbf{x})$ |
| $\vdots$ | $\vdots$ | $\vdots$ | $\vdots$ | $\vdots$ | $\vdots$ | $\vdots$ |
| $h$ | $a_1$ | $\cdots$ | $a_n$ | $b_1$ | $\cdots$ | $b_t$ |
| $\vdots$ | $\vdots$ | $\vdots$ | $\vdots$ | $\vdots$ | $\vdots$ | $\vdots$ |

identifier, the original $n$ coordinates $x_1, \ldots, x_n$, and, for each projection $i$, a number $B(\mathbf{x}, i)$ defined by:

$$B(\mathbf{x}, i) = \begin{cases} j & \text{if the } i^{th} \text{ projection of} \\ & \mathbf{x} \text{ belongs to } C_j^i, \\ 0 & \text{otherwise.} \end{cases}$$

Records containing at least one 0 are discarded since they contain points that at this stage of the algorithm are not yet affiliated with any cluster. Then, the file $\mathcal{F}$ is sorted on the fields $B(1, \mathbf{x}), \cdots, B(t, \mathbf{x})$. Each set of points that correspond to a vector $(b_1, \ldots, b_t)$ corresponds to a set

$$C_{b_1 \cdots b_t}^{i_1 \cdots i_t} = C_{b_1}^{i_1} \times \cdots \times C_{b_t}^{i_t}$$

which we regard as a constituent of the clustering. The condition

$$\frac{|\mathsf{proj}_{i_1 \cdots i_t}(S) \cap C_{b_1 \cdots b_t}^{i_1 \cdots i_t}|}{m(C_{b_1 \cdots b_t}^{i_1 \cdots i_t})} \geq \delta$$

insures that the clusters

$$\mathsf{proj}_{i_1 \cdots i_t}(S) \cap C_{b_1 \cdots b_t}^{i_1 \cdots i_t},$$

where $\mathsf{proj}_{i_1 \cdots i_t}(S)$ is the projection of $S$ on the dimensions $i_1 \cdots i_t$ of the random frame of coordinates will have the minimum density $\delta$ provided by the user. In our experiments we used $\delta = 0.01$ which reflects our decision of regarding clusters that contain less that 1% as consisting of outliers.

Note that

$$|\text{proj}_{i_1 \cdots i_t}(S) \cap C_{b_1 \cdots b_t}^{i_1 \cdots i_t}| \leq \min_r |\text{proj}_{i_r}(S) \cap C_{b_r}^{i_r}|.$$

Therefore, the minima density condition imposed on the clusters implies that the unidimensional density $\delta_1$ must be at least $\delta \ell^{t-1}$, where $\ell$ is the width of the bins defined above.

The time required to compute the histograms is $O(n^2 N)$, where $n$ is the number of dimensions and $N$ is the number of points to be clustered. The cost of sorting the file $\mathcal{F}$ is $O(N \log N)$, which brings the total cost of the algorithm to $O(n^2 N + N \log N)$. Thus, the asymptotic cost of the algorithm is $O(N \log N)$; however, when the number of dimensions is important relative to the logarithm of the number of points the $O(n^2 N)$ component is not negligible.

The post-processing of the clusters described below does not alter this asymptotic evaluation.

Assigning points left outside the clusters, to the extent that this is possible, is achieved using multiple random projections. Suppose that two random projections yield two clusterings:

$$\kappa = \{C_1, \ldots, C_p\} \text{ and } \mu = \{D_1, \ldots, D_q\}$$

and let $U_i = \text{UNC}(\mu) \cap C_i$ for $1 \leq i \leq p$ and $V_j = \text{UNC}(\kappa) \cap D_j$ for $1 \leq j \leq q$. Clusterings obtained by distinct random projections may be used to produce better clusterings by a process that will be referred here as *bimodulation*.

Let $\text{PART}(S)$ be the set of partitions of a set $S$ and let $\text{CL}(S)$ be the set of clusterings of same set $S$. Every clustering $\kappa = \{C_1, \ldots, C_p\}$, defines a partition $\pi_\kappa = \{C_1, \ldots, C_p, \text{UNC}(\kappa)\}$ of the set $S$.

Let $d : \text{PART}(S) \times \text{PART}(S) \longrightarrow \mathbb{R}$ be a distance defined on the set of partitions of the set $S$. A *d-bimodulation* is a mapping: $\Psi : \text{CL}(S) \times \text{CL}(S) \longrightarrow \text{CL}(S) \times \text{CL}(S)$ such that if $\Psi(\kappa, \mu) = (\kappa', \mu')$, then $d(\kappa', \mu') \leq d(\kappa, \mu)$. In other words, an application of a bimodulation to a pair of clusterings results in a new pair of clusterings whose partitions are closer to each other than the partitions associated to the initial pair of clusterings. We can use as a distance between partitions the Barthélemy-Montjardet distance introduced in [4]. If $\pi, \sigma$ are two partitions in $\text{PART}(S)$ given by:

$$\pi = \{K_1, \ldots, K_m\} \text{ and } \sigma = \{H_1, \ldots, H_n\},$$

then the distance between $\pi$ and $\sigma$ is given by:

$$d(\pi, \sigma) = \sum_{i=1}^m |K_i|^2 + \sum_{j=1}^n |H_j|^2 - 2 \sum_{i=1}^m \sum_{j=1}^n |K_i \cup H_j|^2.$$

It is possible to show that for any two clusterings $\kappa = \{C_1, \ldots, C_p\}$ and $\mu = \{D_1, \ldots, D_q\}$ a d-bimodulation can be defined by adding to each cluster $C_i$ the set of objects located in the cluster $D_j$ that has the largest intersection with $C_i$ and applying a similar expansion to the clusters $D_j$.

The second method applied for cluster post-processing is using the minimum bounding hyper-rectangle $\text{MBH}(C)$ of a cluster $C$. Suppose that:

$$\text{MBH}(C) = [a_1, b_1] \times \cdots \times [a_r, b_r].$$

The *density of* $C$ is defined as the number:

$$\text{dens}(C) = \frac{|C|}{\text{vol}(\text{MBH}(C))}.$$

An $\epsilon$-*expansion of* $C$ is the set $C^\epsilon = C \cup L^\epsilon$, where

$$L^\epsilon = \text{UNC}(\kappa) \cap ([a_1 - |a_1|\epsilon, b_1 + |b_1|\epsilon] \times \cdots$$
$$\cdots \times [a_r - |a_r|\epsilon, b_r + |b_r|\epsilon]).$$

If $C_i^\epsilon \cap C_j^\epsilon \neq \emptyset$, then we assign the points of $K_\epsilon$ to the cluster that has the larger density among the clusters $C_i^\epsilon$ or to $C_j^\epsilon$.

Experimental results show that these post-processing techniques improve significantly the quality of the clustering; this is clearly visualized by the improvement of the quality of the image segmentation that we discuss in Section 4.3.

## 4    Experimental Results

We performed experimental work on three types of data: synthetic data consisting of randomly-generated points in $\mathbb{R}^n$, synthetic images containing colored regions randomly distributed, and, finally, real images. The implementations of $k$-means [13] and DBSCAN [15] provided by the open-source WEKA package [18] were used for performance comparisons.

To evaluate the extent to which the algorithm retrieves the original clusters we computed several classification-oriented measure of cluster validity (see [16], p. 549). We assume that we start with $r$ clusters $K_1, \ldots, K_r$ and the clusters retrieved by the algorithm are $C_j$, where $1 \leq j \leq q$. Also, the probability that an object of the cluster $C_j$ belongs to $K_\ell$ is the number $p_{j\ell} = \frac{|C_j \cap K_\ell|}{|D_j|}$, which is also known as the *precision* of $C_j$ relative to $K_\ell$.

### 4.1    Experiments on Synthetic Data

We tested our technique on a data set containing 10000 points in $\mathbb{R}^{30}$ distributed in four clusters: $K_1, K_2, K_3, K_4$. We recaptured a major part of the data set, as shown in Table 2.

Table 2 represents the intersections between the original clusters $K_1, \ldots, K_4$ (which correspond to the columns of the table) with the clusters $C_1, \ldots, C_4$ obtained by our algorithm. The last row represents the points that the algorithm left outside the clusters. Before the postprocessing phase a substantial fraction of the points of the initial clusters are placed into clusters (almost 50%); however, many points are left unaffiliated with any of the clusters. These points are classified using the second phase of the algorithm.

After bimodulation and a 5% expansion the data distribution looks as shown in Table 3.

We further tested our algorithm using a similar data set (10000 points in $\mathbb{R}^{30}$) and added 10% of noisy data. The results are shown in Table 4, which shows that the noise has little effect on the clusters.

**Table 2.** Intersections between initial clusters and retrieved clusters before postprocessing

| $C_i$ identified | $K_1$ | $K_2$ | $K_3$ | $K_4$ |
|---|---|---|---|---|
| $C_1$ | 0 | 54 | 0 | 0 |
| $C_2$ | 0 | 305 | 0 | 0 |
| $C_3$ | 0 | 272 | 0 | 0 |
| $C_4$ | 0 | 0 | 0 | 274 |
| $C_5$ | 0 | 0 | 0 | 1170 |
| $C_6$ | 2 | 0 | 74 | 0 |
| $C_7$ | 1103 | 0 | 0 | 0 |
| $C_8$ | 138 | 0 | 0 | 0 |
| UNC($data$) | 2094 | 1083 | 712 | 2146 |

**Table 3.** Intersections between initial clusters and retrieved clusters after postprocessing

| $C_i$ identified | $K_1$ | $K_2$ | $K_3$ | $K_4$ |
|---|---|---|---|---|
| $C_1$ | 0 | 514 | 2 | 0 |
| $C_2$ | 0 | 312 | 0 | 0 |
| $C_3$ | 0 | 801 | 9 | 0 |
| $C_4$ | 0 | 0 | 0 | 1189 |
| $C_5$ | 0 | 0 | 0 | 2930 |
| $C_6$ | 30 | 85 | 770 | 41 |
| $C_7$ | 1761 | 0 | 0 | 0 |
| $C_8$ | 1543 | 0 | 0 | 0 |
| UNC($data$) | 3 | 2 | 5 | 5 |

**Table 4.** Intersections between initial clusters and retrieved clusters after introduction of noise

| Clusters identified | $K_1$ | $K_2$ | $K_3$ | $K_4$ | Noise |
|---|---|---|---|---|---|
| $C_1$ | 0 | 2885 | 3 | 0 | 8 |
| $C_2$ | 0 | 2 | 803 | 0 | 3 |
| $C_3$ | 0 | 0 | 0 | 1929 | 10 |
| $C_4$ | 1056 | 0 | 0 | 0 | 14 |
| Data outside clusters | 328 | 1472 | 591 | 931 | 965 |

We applied the $k$-means and the DBSCAN algorithms to the same data sets and obtained similar results for synthetic data without noise containing four clusters. Then, we tested these algorithms on a data set containing four clusters to which 10% noise was added. Several runs using the $k$-means algorithm with $k = 4$ result sometimes in having the noise distributed among each of the four clusters and, on occasions, producing 1 to 3 clusters with the remaining classes containing noise. The results of DBSCAN are similar to those of $k$-means; however, the misclassifications are much less frequent and the noise is well detected.

The application of the three algorithms to a database containing 11,000 objects in with 30 dimensions results in computation times of 750s, 1700 s, and 9s for our algorithm, the $k$-means algorithm and the DBSCAN algorithm, respectively. Our time is less than half of the DBSCAN. The $k$-means algorithm is much faster, but, as we shall see, has a rather bad precision and recall in experiments on synthetic images.

## 4.2  Experiments on Synthetic Images

In a second series of experiments we tested the algorithm on Mondrian-like images [14] containing randomly distributed and randomly colored rectangles. The typical images used in these experiments contained between 10 and 40 such regions and we show an example of an image in Figure 3.

The objectives of this series of experiments were to demonstrate that the algorithm can retrieve the original clusters and also, to test the behavior of the algorithm on data with a larger number of dimensions. Starting from an image containing $240 \times 320 = 76,800$ pixels represented as a set of points in $\mathbb{R}^5$ we grouped the pixels into $4 \times 4$

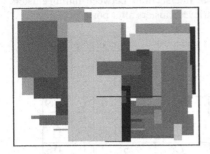

| True positive TP | Colored points retrieved as colored | 63.29% |
|---|---|---|
| False positive FP | White points retrieved as colored | 0.09% |
| True negative TN | White points retrieved as white | 28.9% |
| False negative FN | Colored points retrieved as white | 7.79% |

**Fig. 3.** Example of an image    **Fig. 4.** Terms used in algorithm evaluation

squares containing 16 pixels. Each square was represented as a vector in $\mathbb{R}^{80}$ and we worked with sets of 9600 points in $\mathbb{R}^{80}$.

In a first phase we examined the capability of our algorithm to differentiate between the colored regions which we treat as clusters) and the white pixels. We are using the top five projections with an expansion factor of 5%. The terms used for this evaluation are shown in Figure 4. The precision and recall for this type of evaluations are given by

$$\text{Precision} = \frac{\text{TP}}{\text{TP} + \text{FP}} = 0.99 \text{ and Recall} = \frac{\text{TP}}{\text{TP} + \text{FN}} = 0.89,$$

respectively. The $F_1$ measure that is the harmonic average of precision and recall is 0.94. These numbers indicate a high capability of our algorithm in identifying points that belong to clusters.

The dependency of the precision, recall and $F_1$ measures are shown in Figures 5-7, respectively.

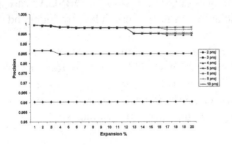

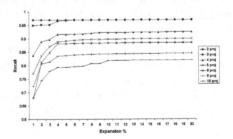

**Fig. 5.** Dependency of precision on $\epsilon$    **Fig. 6.** Dependency of recall on $\epsilon$

By contemplating these figures it becomes apparent that there is no substantial improvement of the recall or of the $F_1$ factor when expansion is greater than 6% and the number of projections considered is greater than 6 (see Figures 7 and 6). This observation informs the experiments described in the next section.

The time requirements of the algorithm were validated in experiments including data in $\mathbb{R}^{20}$ and in $\mathbb{R}^{80}$ (see Figure 8). The results shown represent averages over 4-fold

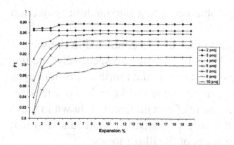 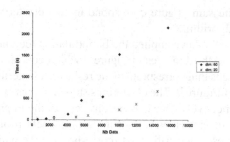

**Fig. 7.** Dependency of $F_1$ on $\epsilon$          **Fig. 8.** Dependency of time (sec.) on the number of objects

complete applications of the algorithm including post-processing with different random projection frames. They are consistent with our previous asymptotic estimate of $O(N \log N)$.

In Table 5 we compare the precision, recall and $F_1$ measure for $k$-means, DBSCAN, and for our algorithm.

**Table 5.** Time measures

|  | Algorithm | | |
|---|---|---|---|
|  | $k$-means | DBSCAN | Our algorithm |
| TP (%) | 62 | 58 | 63.3 |
| FP (%) | 28 | 3 | 0.1 |
| TN (%) | 10 | 34 | 28.9 |
| FN (%) | 1 | 5 | 7.8 |
| Precision | 0.69 | 0.95 | 0.99 |
| Recall | 0.98 | 0.92 | 0.89 |
| $F_1$ | 0.81 | 0.94 | 0.94 |

For synthetic images the precision of the $k$-means algorithm is rather low even if $k$ is chosen to obtain the best results. On the other hand, the results of DBSCAN and of our algorithm are comparable; we obtain a better precision but a lower recall which results in similar values for the $F_1$ measures.

The advantage of our algorithm over DBSCAN is a better time performance, which is more evident with the increase in the size of the data set.

### 4.3   Experiments on Real Images

To contemplate possible applications of our algorithm to multimedia data set we used the data set underlying the left picture shown in Figure 9. This data set contains 32,000 points in $\mathbb{R}^5$. The dimensions correspond to the two spatial coordinates and the three color components of each pixel (red, green and blue). The two following images of the same figure correspond to two clusterings obtained using our random projection algorithm.

We have applied the bimodulation technique to the clusters contained in the second and third images of Figure 9 which consist of 10 and 12 clusters, respectively; the images that correspond to the resulting clusterings are shown in the fourth and fifth images of Figure 9. The clusterings shown in these two images consist of 11 and 13 clusters, respectively. One can visually remark the improvement of certain features shown in these clusters. However, an important fraction of the data points still remain unclassified; these unclassified data correspond to the white spots of the illustrations.

Finally, we used the $\epsilon$-expansion of the minimally bounding rectangles of the clusters. The new clusters obtained by applying a 10% expansion are presented in the last two images shown in Figure 9.

**Fig. 9.** Images obtained at different phases of our algorithm

The quality of the last two images is clearly improved over the others images. This observation suggests that our clustering techniques have the potential of being helpful in image segmentation .

## 5    Conclusions

We proposed a new method of clustering using random projections. The algorithm consists in two phases: a projection phase (which creates uni-dimensional histograms and aggregates these histograms to produce the initial clusters) and a post-processing phase that improves the clusterings using two supplementary techniques: bimodulation and $\epsilon$-expansion. The time requirement of the algorithm is $O(N \log N)$, where $N$ is the number of objects subjected to clustering. The algorithm has a potential for being useful for multimedia applications, which will be the focus of our future investigations.

We will investigate future directions of cluster post-processing as well as more refined ways of combining projection histograms. Finding optimal values for the parameters chosen in the execution of the algorithm based on the statistical distribution of the set of objects remains an open problem.

# References

1. Agrawal, R., Gehrke, J., Gunopulos, D., Raghavan, P.: Automatic subspace clustering of high dimensional data for data mining applications. In: Proceedings of the ACM-SIGMOD Int. Conf. Management of Data, pp. 94–105. ACM Press, New York (1998)
2. Agarwal, P., Mustafa, N.H.: k-means projective clustering. In: Proceedings of PODS, pp. 155–165 (2004)
3. Aggarwal, C.C., Procopiuc, C., Wolf, J.L., Yu, P.S., Park, J.S.: Fast algorithms for projected clustering. In: Proceedings of ACM-SIGMOD Conference on Management of Data, pp. 61–72. ACM Press, New York (1999)
4. Barthélemy, J.P., Leclerc, B.: The median procedure for partitions. In: Partitioning Data Sets. American Mathematical Society, pp. 3–14. Providence, RI (1995)
5. Chaudhri, A.B., Unland, R., Djeraba, C., Lindner, W. (eds.): EDBT 2002. LNCS, vol. 2490. Springer, Heidelberg (2002)
6. Dasgupta, S., Gupta, A.: An elementary proof of the johnson-lindenstrauss lemma. Technical Report TR-99-006, International Computer Science Institute (1999)
7. Djeraba, C. (ed.): Multimedia Mining - A Highway to Intelligent Multimedia Documents. Kluwer, Dordrecht (2003)
8. Frankl, P., Maehara, H.: The johnson-lindenstrauss lemma and the sphericity of some graphs. J. Comb. Theory B 44, 355–362 (1988)
9. Jain, A.K., Dubes, R.: Algorithms for Clustering Data. Prentice-Hall, Englewood Cliffs (1988)
10. Jain, A.K., Flynn, P.J.: Image segmentation using clustering. In: Advances in Image Understanding: A Festschrift for Azriel Rosenfeld, Piscataway, NJ, pp. 65–83. IEEE Press, Los Alamitos (1996)
11. Johnson, W.B., Lindenstrauss, J.: Extensions of lipshitz mappings into hilbert spaces. Contemporary Mathematics 26, 189–206 (1984)
12. Jain, A.K., Murty, M.N., Flynn, P.J.: Data clustering: A review. ACM Computing Surveys 31, 264–323 (1999)
13. MacQueen, J.B.: Some methods for classification and analysis of multivariate observations. In: Proceedings of 5-th Berkeley Symposium on Mathematical Statistics and Probability, Berkeley, pp. 281–297. University of California Press, California (1967)
14. Mondrian, P.: http://artchive.com/artchive/M/mondrian.html
15. Sander, J., Ester, M., Kriegel, H.P., Xu, X.: Density-based clustering in spatial databases: The algorithm gdbscan and its applications. Data Mining and Knowledge Discovery, an International Journal 2, 169–194 (1998)
16. Tan, P.N, Steinbach, M., Kumar, V.: Introduction to Data Mining. Pearson/Addison-Wesley, Boston (2006)
17. Vempala, S.S.: The Random Projection Method. American Mathematical Society. Providence, Rhode Island (2004)
18. Witten, I.H., Frank, E.: Data Mining - Practical Machine Learning Tools and Techniques, 2nd edn. Morgan Kaufmann, San Francisco (2005)
19. Zaïane, O.R., Simoff, S.J., Djeraba, C. (eds.): MDM/KDD 2002 and KDMCD 2002. LNCS (LNAI), vol. 2797. Springer, Heidelberg (2002)

# Lightweight Clustering Technique for Distributed Data Mining Applications*

Lamine M. Aouad, Nhien-An Le-Khac, and Tahar M. Kechadi

School of Computer Science and Informatics
University College Dublin - Ireland
{lamine.aouad,an.le-khac,tahar.kechadi}@ucd.ie

**Abstract.** Many parallel and distributed clustering algorithms have already been proposed. Most of them are based on the aggregation of local models according to some collected local statistics. In this paper, we propose a lightweight distributed clustering algorithm based on minimum variance increases criterion which requires a very limited communication overhead. We also introduce the notion of distributed perturbation to improve the globally generated clustering. We show that this algorithm improves the quality of the overall clustering and manage to find the real structure and number of clusters of the global dataset.

## 1 Introduction

Clustering is one of the fundamental technique in data mining. It groups data objects based on information found in the data that describes the objects and their relationships. The goal is to optimize similarity within a cluster and the dissimilarities between clusters in order to identify interesting structures in the underlying data. This is a difficult task in unsupervised knowledge discovery and there is already a large amount of literature in the field ranging from models, algorithms, validity and performances studies, etc. However, there is still several open questions in the clustering process including the optimal number of clusters, how to assess the validity of a given clustering, how to allow different shapes and sizes rather than forcing them into balls and shapes related to the distance functions, how to prevent the algorithms initialization and the order in which the features vectors are read in from affecting the clustering output, and how to find which clustering structure in a given dataset, i.e why would a user choose an algorithm instead of another. Most of these issues come from the fact that there is no general definition of what is a cluster. In fact, algorithms have been developed to find several kinds of clusters; spherical, linear, dense, drawnout, etc.

In distributed environments, clustering algorithms have to deal with the problem of distributed data, computing nodes and domains, plural ownership and users, and scalability. Actually, moving the entire data to a single location for

---

* This study is part of ADMIRE [15], a distributed data mining framework designed and developed at University College Dublin, Ireland.

P. Perner (Ed.): ICDM 2007, LNAI 4597, pp. 120–134, 2007.
© Springer-Verlag Berlin Heidelberg 2007

performing a global clustering is not always possible due to different reasons related to policies or technical choices. In addition, the communication efficiency of an algorithm is often more important than the accuracy of its results. In fact, communication issues are the key factors in the implementation of any distributed algorithm. It is obvious that a suitable algorithm for high speed network can be of little use in WAN-based platforms. Generally, it is considered that an efficient distributed algorithm needs to exchange a few data and avoids synchronization as much as possible.

In this paper, we propose a lightweight distributed clustering technique based on a merging of independent local subclusters according to an increasing variance constraint. This improves the overall clustering quality and finds the number of clusters and the global inherent clustering structure in the whole dataset. However, a proper maximum increasing value has to be selected. This can be deduced from the problem domain or found out using various methods. The rest of the paper is organized as follows, the next section surveys some previous parallelization and distribution efforts in the clustering area. Then, section 3 presents our distributed algorithm. Section 4 shows some experimental results and evaluations, and highlights directions for future work and versions. Finally, section 5 concludes the paper.

## 2 Related Work

This section survey some works in parallel and distributed clustering, and discusses the latest projects and proposals especially regarding grid-based approaches.

Clustering algorithms can be divided into two main categories, namely partitioning and hierarchical. Different elaborated taxonomies of existing clustering algorithms are given in the literature. Details about these algorithms is out of the purpose of this paper, we refer the reader to [8] and [19]. Many parallel clustering versions based on these algorithms have been proposed [3][4][5][6][13][20], etc. In [3] and [13], message-passing versions of the widely used k-means algorithm were proposed. In [4] and [20], the authors dealt with the parallelization of the DBSCAN density based clustering algorithm. In [5] a parallel message passing version of the BIRCH algorithm was presented. In [6], the authors introduced a parallel version of a hierarchical clustering algorithm, called MPC for Message Passing Clustering, which is especially dedicated to Microarray data. Most of the parallel approaches need either multiple synchronization constraints between processes or a global view of the dataset, or both.

The distributed approaches are different, even many of the proposed distributed algorithms are based on algorithms which were developed for parallel systems. Actually, most of them typically act by producing local models followed by the generation of a global model by aggregating the local results. The processes participating to the computation are independent and usually have the same computation level. After this phase, the global clustering is obtained based on only local models, without a global view of the whole dataset. All these algorithms are then based on the global reduction of so-called sufficient statistics, probably followed by a broadcast of the results. Some works are presented in [9][10][11][12][21], mostly related to the k-means algorithm or variants and the DBSCAN density based algorithm.

On the other hand, grid and peer-to-peer systems have emerged as an important area in distributed and parallel computing[1]. In the data mining domain, where massive datasets are collected and need to be stored and performed, the grid can be seen as a new computational and large-scale support, and even as a high performance support in some cases. Some grid or peer-to-peer based projects and frameworks already exist or are being proposed in this area; Knowledge Grid [2], Discovery Net [7], Grid Miner [14], ADMIRE [15], etc. Beyond the architecture design of these systems, the data analysis, integration or placement approaches, the underlying middleware and tools, etc. the grid-based approach needs efficient and well-adapted algorithms. This is the motivation of this work.

## 3   Algorithm Description

This section describes the distributed algorithm and gives some formal definitions. The key idea of this algorithm is to choose a relatively high number of clusters locally (which will be called subclusters in the rest of the paper), or an optimal local number using an approximation technique, and to merge them at the global level according to an increasing variance criterion which require a very limited communication overhead. All local clustering are independent from each other and the global aggregation can be done independently, from and at any initial local process.

### 3.1   Algorithm Foundations

At the local level, the clustering can be done by different clustering algorithms depending on the characteristics of the data. This includes k-means, k-harmonic-means, k-medoids, or their variants, or using the statistical interpretation with the expectation-maximization algorithm which finds clusters by determining a mixture of Gaussian distributions. The merging process of the local subclusters at the global level exploits locality in the feature space, i.e. the most promising candidates to form a global cluster are subclusters that are the closest in the feature space, including subclusters from the same site. Each participating process can perform the merging and subtract the global clusters formation, i.e. which subclusters are subject to form together a global cluster.

Before describing the algorithm itself, we first give developments on some used notions. A global cluster border represents local subclusters at its border. These are susceptible to be isolated and added to another global cluster in order to

---

[1] The designation 'parallel' is used here to highlight the fact that the computing tasks are interdependent, which is not necessarily the case in distributed computing.

contribute to an improvement of the clustering output. These subclusters are referred to as perturbation candidates. Actually, the initial merging order may affect the clustering output, as well as the presence of non well-separated global clusters, this action is intended to reduce the input order impact. The global clusters are then updated. The border is collected by computing the common Euclidean distance measure. The $b$ farthest subclusters are then the perturbation candidates, where $b$ is a user predefined number which depends on the chosen local number of clusters. Furthermore, multi-attributed subclusters are naturally concerned by this process.

The aggregation part of the algorithm starts with $\sum_{i \in s} k_i$ subclusters, where $s$ is the number of sites involved and $k_i$, for $i = 1, ..., s$, are the local numbers of clusters in each site. Each process has the possibility to generate a global merging. An important point here is that the merging is logical, i.e each local process can generate correspondences, i.e. labeling, between local subclusters, without necessarily constructing the overall clustering output. That is because the only bookkeeping needed from the other sites are centers, sizes and variances. The aggregation is then defined as a labeling process between local subclusters in each participating site. On the other hand, the perturbation process is activated if the merging action is no longer applied. $b$ candidates are collected for each global cluster from its border, which is proportional to the overall size composition as quoted before. Then, this process moves these candidates by trying the closest ones and with respect to the gain in the variance criterion when moving them from the neighboring global clusters. In the next section we will formally define the problem, notions and criterions.

### 3.2   Definitions and Notations

This section formalizes the clustering problem and the notions described in the previous section. Let $X = \{x_1, x_2, ..., x_N\}$ be a dataset of $N$ elements in the $p$-dimensional metric space. The problem is to find a clustering of $X$ in a set of clusters, denoted by $C = \{C_1, C_2, ..., C_M\}$. The most used criterion to quantify the homogeneity inside a cluster is the variance criterion, or sum-of-squared-error criterion:

$$S = \sum_{i=1}^{M} E(C_i)$$

where

$$E(C) = \sum_{x \in C} \| x - u(C) \|^2$$

and

$$u(C) = \frac{1}{|C|} \sum_{x \in C} x$$

is the cluster mean.

Traditional constraint used to minimize the given criterion is to fix the number of clusters $M$ to an a priori known number, as in the widely used k-means, k-harmonicmeans, k-medoids or its variants like CLARA, CLARANS, etc. [16][19][22]. This constraint is very restrictive since this number is most likely not known in most cases. However, many approximation techniques exist such as the gap statistic which compares the change within cluster dispersion to that expected under an appropriate reference null distribution [17], or the index due to Calinski & Harabasz [1], etc. This can be used locally as quoted before. The imposed constraint here states that the increasing variance of the merging, or union, of two subclusters is below a dynamic limit $\sigma_{i,j}^{max}$. This parameter is defined to be twice the highest individual variance from subclusters $C_i$ and $C_j$ [18].

The border $B_i$ of the global cluster $C_i$ is the set of the $b$ farthest subclusters from the generated global cluster center. Let $SC_i = \{scc_1, scc_2, ..., scc_{n_i}\}$ be the set of the $n_i$ subclusters centers merged into $C_i$. $B_i$ is defined as:

$$B_i(b) = F(u(C_i), b, C_i, SC_i)$$

where

$$F(u(C_i), b, C_i, SC_i) =$$

$$\begin{cases} fsc(u(C_i), b, C_i, SC_i) \cup F(u(C_i), b-1, C_i, SC_i - fsc(u(C_i), b, C_i, SC_i)), & b > 0 \\ \emptyset, & b = 0 \end{cases}$$

$fsc(u(C_i), b, C_i, SC_i)$ are the $b$ farthest subclusters centers from $u(C_i)$:

$$fsc(u(C_i), b, C_i, SC_i) = arg \max_{x \in SC_i} Euclidean(x, u(C_i))$$

These sets are then performed once the merging is no longer applied, and as quoted before, the multi-attributed subclusters will belong to it.

### 3.3 Summarized Algorithm

According to the previous definitions and formalism, the Algorithm 1 summarize the proposed approach. In the first step, local clustering are performed on each local dataset, the local number of clusters can be different in each site. Then, each local clustering in a site $i$ gives as output $k_i$ subclusters identified by a unique identifier, $cluster_{\{i, number\}}$ for $number = 0, ..., k_i - 1$, and their sizes, centers and variances. At the end of local processes, local statistics are sent (5 - 9) to the chosen merging process $j$ at step (4). Then, the subclusters aggregation is done in two phases; merging (10 - 12) and perturbation (13 - 24). In the latter phase, the border $B_i(b)$ is found (14 - 15), with $i \in k_g$, and $b$ is a user defined parameter. For each $x \in B_i(b)$, the closet global cluster $j$ is found and the new variance is computed. The actual perturbation, which still a labeling at the global level, is done if the new global variance is smaller (16 - 23). At the step (11), the new global statistics, namely the size, center and variance, are:

$$N_{new} = N_i + N_j$$

$$c_{new} = \frac{N_i}{N_{new}} c_i + \frac{N_j}{N_{new}} c_j$$

---

**Algorithm 1.** Variance-based distributed clustering

---

**Input:** $X_i$ $(i = 1, \ldots, s)$ datasets, and $k_i$ the number of subclusters in each site $S_i$
**Output:** $k_g$ global clusters, i.e the global subclusters distribution labeling
 1: **for** $i = 1$ to $s$ **do**
 2:     $LS_i = cluster(X_i, k_i)$
 3: **end for**
 4: $j = select\_aggr\_site()$
 5: **for** $i = 1$ to $s$ **do**
 6:     **if** $i \neq j$ **then**
 7:         $send(sizes_i, centers_i, variances_i, j)$
 8:     **end if**
 9: **end for**
     at site the aggregation site $j$:
10: **while** $var(C_i, C_j) < \sigma_{i,j}^{max}$ **do**
11:     $merge(C_i, C_j)$
12: **end while**
13: **for** $i = 1$ to $k_g$ **do**
14:     $find\_border(b, i)$
15:     $add\_multi\_attributed(i)$
16:     **for** $x = 1$ to $b$ **do**
17:         $j = closer\_global(x)$
18:         $var_{new} = var(C_i - C_x, C_j + C_x)$
19:         **if** $var_{new} < var$ **then**
20:             $label(x, j)$
21:             $var = var_{new}$
22:         **end if**
23:     **end for**
24: **end for**

---

$$var_{new} = var_i + var_j + inc(i, j), \quad \forall C_i, C_j, i \neq j$$

where

$$inc(i, j) = \frac{N_i \times N_j}{N_i + N_j} \times Euclidean(C_i, C_j)$$

represents the increasing in the variance while merging $C_i$ and $C_j$.

As in all clustering algorithms, the expected large variability in clusters shapes and densities is an issue. However, as we will show in the experiments section, the algorithm is efficient to detect well separated clusters and distribution with their effective distribution number. Otherwise, a clear definition of a cluster does not exist anymore. This is also an efficient way to improve the output for the k-means clustering and derivatives for example, without an a priori knowledge about the data or an estimation process for the number of clusters.

### 3.4 Performance Analysis

The computational complexity of this distributed algorithm depends on the algorithm used locally, the communication time, which is a gather operation and the merging computing time:

$$T = T_{comp} + T_{comm} + T_{merge}$$

If the local clustering is a k-means, the complexity $T_{comp}$ is of order $O(N_i k_i d)$, where $d$ is the dimension of the dataset. The communication time is the reduction of $3d \sum_{i \in s} k_i$ elements. Actually, the aggregation process gathers local information in order to perform the merging. If $t^i_{comm}$ is the communication cost for one element from site $i$ to the aggregation process $j$ then

$$T_{comm} = 3d \sum_{i \in s, i \neq j} t^i_{comm} k_i$$

Since $k_i$ is much less large than $N_i$, the generated communication overhead is very small.

The merging process is executed a number of times, say $u$. This is the number of iterations until the condition $var(C_i, C_j) < \sigma^{max}_{i,j}$ is no longer applied. This cost is then equal to $u \times t_{newStatistcs}$, which corresponds to $O(d)$. This is followed by a perturbation process, which the cost is of order $O(bk_g k_i)$. Actually, since this process computes for each of the $b$ chosen subcluster at the border of $C_i$, $k_i$ distances for each of the $k_g$ global clusters. The total cost is then:

$$T = O(N_i k_i d) + O(d) + O(bk_g k_i) + T_{comm}, \quad T_{comm} \ll O(N_i k_i d)$$

## 4   Experiments

In this section, we show the effectiveness of the proposed algorithm with some artificial and real datasets. We give a description of the data, the experimentation details and a discussion. As quoted before, the constraint parameter, i.e the maximum merging variance, is set up as twice the highest individual subcluster variance.

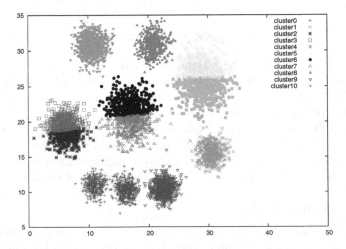

**Fig. 1.** Global k-harmonicmeans clustering using the gap statistic to find the optimal $k$ of the dataset, $k = 11$

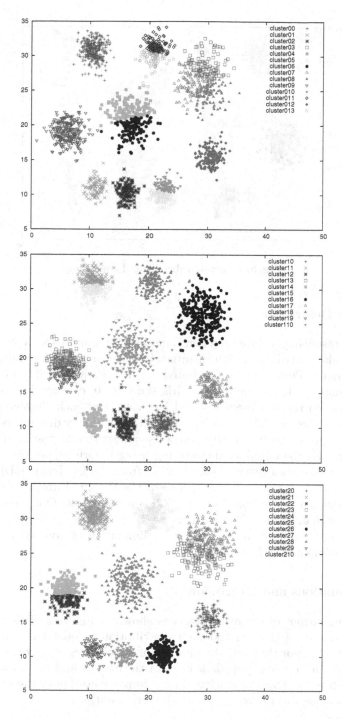

**Fig. 2.** Local k-harmonicmeans clustering in each process using the gap statistic to find the optimal number of clusters, $k_1 = 14$, $k_2 = 11$, $and$ $k_3 = 11$

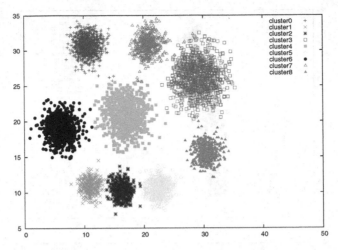

**Fig. 3.** Generated distributed clustering

## 4.1    Data Description

The first dataset is a generated random Gaussian distributions with 6000 samples. Figure 1 displays this dataset with an initial clustering using k-harmonicmeans and the gap statistic. The data was distributed in three sets as shown in Figure 2.

The second set is the well-known Iris dataset. It consists in three classes of irises (Iris setosa, Iris versicolor and Iris virginica) each characterized by 8 attributes and there is 150 instances. The set was randomly distributed as shown in Figure 4 (presented by the attributes "sepal area" and "petal area"). This figure shows also the initial local clustering using k-harmonicmeans with $k = 5$.

The last dataset is a census data available from the UC Irvine KDD Archive. It is derived from the one percent sample of the PUMS (Public Use Microdata Samples) person records from the full 1990 census sample. Our tests use a discretized version of this set. There are 68 attributes[2]. The set originally contains 2458285 records reduced to 1998492 after elimination of doubled records. The data is distributed over 7 processes.

## 4.2    Evaluations and Discussion

The merging output of the first dataset is shown in Figure 3. This result finds the right number of clusters and their distribution independently of the local used clustering algorithm and the number of subclusters. The local number of clusters found using the gap statistic is 14 for the first set and 11 for the two other sets (cf. Figure 2). The gap statistic based implementation of the expectation-maximization algorithm give the same clustering output.

---

[2] The caseid is ignored during analysis. The list of attributes and the coding for the values can be found at http://kdd.ics.uci.edu/

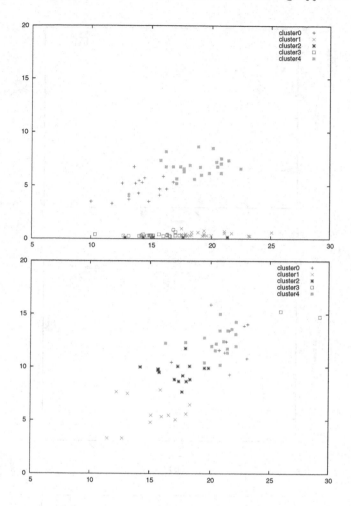

**Fig. 4.** Iris sub-sets and local clustering using k-harmonicmeans, $k_i = 5$,   $i = 0, 1$

The resulting global clustering for the Iris dataset, and a global k-harmonicmeans clustering using the entire dataset, are given is Figure 5. The algorithm manages to find the class distribution of the Iris dataset, leading to 3 classes based on 5 or 7 local subclusters. However, because the k-harmonicmeans does not impose a variance constraint it could find a lower sum-of-squared-error which is the case here. These two examples show the independence from the nature and size of the initial clustering. Actually, if there is a real structure in the dataset then true clusters are found and joined together.

For the census dataset, the algorithm leads to 3 clusters based on 20 subclusters locally on 7 processes, and using all the attributes. The local clustering uses the k-means algorithm. This version is based on multiple k-means (user defined parameter) and keep the best output. Firstly, the Figure 6 shows the rank of the values of 9 attributes among the 68 for the whole dataset. The values

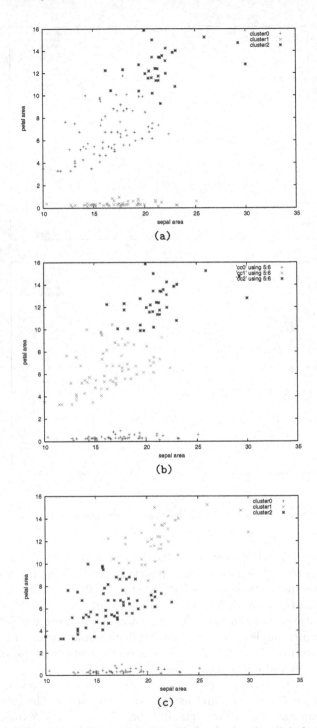

**Fig. 5.** The output using 5 (a) and 7 (b) subclusters, and a global clustering using k-harmonicmeans in (c)

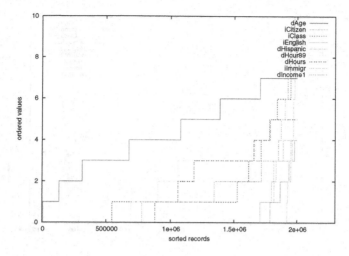

**Fig. 6.** Rank of the values of 9 attributes of the census database

distribution of two generated global clusters is given in Figure 7. Note that a global sequential clustering is not possible due to the memory restriction related to the fact that the whole data must fit in main memory. Most of the widely used clustering algorithms are concerned with this scalability issue. Beyond the signification of such clustering especially for this dataset and using the entire set of the categorical variables, this experiment shows the scalability of the proposed algorithm. Indeed, specific measurements on the dataset will take into account a specific set of variables. However, the Figure 7 shows, by the selected sorted attributes, different characteristics of these two global clusters concerning age or income for example. Still, the visualization mode does not allow to show the real measurement related to these attributes since they are sorted, which means that there is no true initial observations thereon.

In contrast to many other distributed algorithms, the presented one uses a simple global constraint, a very limited communication overhead, and does not need to know the data structure a priori. This algorithm is effective in finding proper clustering. However, future versions will take into account some other facts as considering the perturbation process during the merging operations and inside subclusters, or of whether or not multi-attributed clusters are present to consider a different approach at this level. Also, varying the constraint criterion could be considered as well as adding other similarity functions.

In fact, the merging process could perform a distance between the distributed subclusters. Each one could be described by additional objects and metrics, as the covariance matrices for example. A general definition of such a distance measure can be $d(x_i, x_j) = (c_j - c_i)^T A (c_j - c_i)$, where the inclusion of $A$ results in weighting according to statistical properties of the features. Other distances or similarity measures include; Euclidean, Manhattan, Canberra, Cosine, etc. The general form of some of these distances is $d_{i,j} = [\sum_K |x_{ki} - x_{kj}|^N]^{\frac{1}{N}}$, and depending on $N$, the enclosed region takes different shapes. That is to say

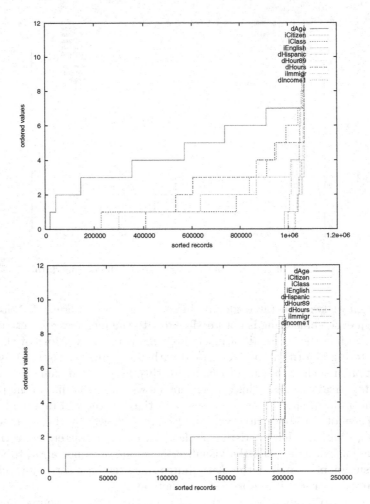

**Fig. 7.** Values distribution of two generated global clusters

that the merging process could take into account one or different proximity (i.e similarity or dissimilarity) function to improve the quality of the resulting clustering. This will be considered in future versions. However, the key issue is the selection of an appropriate function, especially, *which kind of measures for which kind of data?* Actually, general observations recommend some distances for some type of data, Euclidean-based for example for dense, continuous data. Still, no true rules exist and the user needs to be familiar and expertise his data.

## 5    Conclusion

In this paper, we evoked the need of efficient distributed and grid-based clustering algorithms. Actually, a huge effort has been made in sequential clustering but there is only few algorithms which tackle the distribution problem especially in loosely coupled environments such as the grid. We proposed a lightweight distributed algorithm based on an increasing variance constraint. It clusters the data locally and independently from each other and only limited statistics about the local clustering are transmitted to the aggregation process which carries out the global clustering, defined as labeling between subclusters. This is done by means of a merging and a perturbation processes. The global model can then be broadcasted to all participating processes if needed, which will use it to label their subclusters.

The algorithm gives good performances at identifying well separated clusters and the real structure of the dataset. In fact, when data are not well separated, the notion of cluster is very confused and does not even exist in the literature. The number of clusters is also automatically found, this resolves the problem of estimating the number of clusters a priori. Furthermore, in addition to classical constraints in distributed clustering, related to the usually infeasible data centralization due to technical, security reasons or local policies, this algorithm can also tackle large and high dimensional datasets that cannot fit in memory since most of the clustering algorithms in literature require the whole data in the main memory and also tend to scale poorly as the size and dimension grow. Nevertheless, open issues could be considered as in the merging process or the choice of the possible better local models and algorithms, in addition to those described in the previous section.

# References

1. Calinski, R.B., Harabasz, J.: A dendrite method for cluster analysis. Communication in statistics 3 (1974)
2. Cannataro, M., Congiusta, A., Pugliese, A., Talia, D., Trunfio, P.: Distributed Data Mining on Grids: Services, Tools, and Applications. IEEE Transaction on System, Man, and Cybernetics 34(6) (2004)
3. Dhillon, I.S., Modha, D.: A Data-Clustering Algorithm on Distributed Memory Multiprocessors. In: Large-Scale Parallel Data Mining, Workshop on Large-Scale Parallel KDD Systems. SIGKDD (1999)
4. Ester, M., Kriegel, H.-P, Sander, J., Xu, X.: A Density-Based Algorithm for Discovering Clusters in Large Spatial Databases with Noise. In: 2nd Int. Conf. on Knowledge Discovery and Data Mining (KDD) (1996)
5. Garg, A., Mangla, A., Bhatnagar, V., Gupta, N.: PBIRCH: A Scalable Parallel Clustering algorithm for Incremental Data. In: IDEAS'06. 10th International Database Engineering and Applications Symposium (2006)
6. Geng, H., Deng, X., Ali, H.: A New Clustering Algorithm Using Message Passing and its Applications in Analyzing Microarray Data. In: ICMLA'05. Proceedings of the Fourth International Conference on Machine Learning and Applications, pp. 145–150. IEEE Computer Society Press, Los Alamitos (2005)
7. Ghanem, V.M., Kohler, Y.M., Sayed, A.J., Wendel, P.: Discovery Net: Towards a Grid of Knowledge Discovery. In: Eight Int. Conf. on Knowledge Discovery and Data Mining (2002)
8. Jain, A.K., Murty, M.N., Flynn, P.J.: Data Clustering: A Review. ACM Computing Surveys (1999)

9. Januzaj, E., Kriegel, H-P., Pfeifle, M.: Towards Effective and Efficient Distributed Clustering. In: Int. Workshop on Clustering Large Data Sets. 3rd Int. Conf. on Data Mining, ICDM (2003)
10. Januzaj, E., Kriegel, H-P., Pfeifle, M.: DBDC: Density-Based Distributed Clustering. In: Bertino, E., Christodoulakis, S., Plexousakis, D., Christophides, V., Koubarakis, M., Böhm, K., Ferrari, E. (eds.) EDBT 2004. LNCS, vol. 2992, Springer, Heidelberg (2004)
11. Januzaj, E., Kriegel, H-P., Pfeifle, M.: Scalable Density-Based Distributed Clustering. In: Boulicaut, J.-F., Esposito, F., Giannotti, F., Pedreschi, D. (eds.) PKDD 2004. LNCS (LNAI), vol. 3202, Springer, Heidelberg (2004)
12. Jin, R., Goswani, A., Agrawal, G.: Fast and Exact Out-of-Core and Distributed K-Means Clustering. Knowledge and Information Systems 10 (2006)
13. Joshi, M.N.: Parallel K-Means Algorithm on Distributed Memory Multiprocessors. Technical report, University of Minnesota (2003)
14. Kickinger, G., Hofer, J., Brezany, P., Tjoa, A.M.: Grid Knowledge Discovery Processes and an Architecture for their Composition. Parallel and Distributed Computing and Networks (2004)
15. Le-Khac, N-A., Kechadi, M.T., Carthy, J.: ADMIRE framework: Distributed Data Mining on Data Grid platforms. In: ICSOFT 2006. first Int. Conf. on Software and Data Technologies (2006)
16. Ng, R.T., Han, J.: Efficient and Effective Clustering Methods for Spatial Data Mining. In: VLDB 1994. Proceedings of 20th International Conference on Very Large Data Bases, Santiago de Chile (1994)
17. Tibshirani, R., Walther, G., Hastie, T.: Estimating the number of clusters in a dataset via the Gap statistic. Technical report, Stanford University (March 2000)
18. Veenman, C.J., Reinders, M.J., Backer, E.: A Maximum Variance Cluster Algorithm. IEEE Transactions on pattern analysis and machine intelligence 24(9) (2002)
19. Xu, R., Wunsch, D.: Survey of Clustering Algorithms. IEEE Transactions on Neural Networks 16 (2005)
20. Xu, X., Jager, J., Kriegel, H.-P.: A Fast Parallel Clustering Algorithm for Large Spatial Databases. Journal of Data Mining and Knowledge Discovery 3 (1999)
21. Zhang, B., Forman, G.: Distributed Data Clustering Can be Efficient and Exact. Technical report, HP Labs (2000)
22. Zhang, B., Hsu, M., Dayal, U.: K-Harmonic Means - A Data Clustering Algorithm. Technical report, HP Labs (1999)

# Predicting Page Occurrence in a Click-Stream Data: Statistical and Rule-Based Approach

Petr Berka and Martin Labský

Department of Information and Knowledge Engineering,
University of Economics, W. Churchill Sq. 4, 130 67 Prague, Czech Republic
{berka,labsky}@vse.cz

**Abstract.** We present an analysis of the click-stream data with the aim
to predict the next page that will be visited by an user based on a history
of visited pages. We present one statistical method (based on Markov
models) and two rule induction methods (first based on well known set
covering approach, the other base on our compositional algorithm KEX).
We compare the achieved results and discuss interesting patterns that
appear in the data.

## 1 Introduction

Our work described in the paper fits into the area of web usage mining. Web
usage mining mines the data derived from interactions of users while browsing
the web. Web usage data includes the data from web server access logs, proxy
server logs, browser logs, user profiles, registration data, cookies, user queries
etc. A web server log is an important source for performing web usage mining
because it explicitly records the browsing behavior of site visitors. The typical
problem (solved in the data preprocessing step) is thus distinguishing among
unique users, server sessions episodes etc.

Web usage mining focuses on techniques that could predict user behavior while
the user interacts with the web. The applications of web usage mining could be
classified into two main categories: (1) learning user profile or user modeling,
and (2) learning user navigation patterns [10]. The methods used for web usage
mining are (descriptive) statistical analysis, association rules (to relate pages
that are often referenced together), clustering (to build usage clusters or page
clusters), classification (to create user profiles), sequential pattern discovery (to
find inter-session patterns such that the presence of a set of page views is followed
by another set of page views in a time-ordered set of episodes), or dependency
modeling (to capture significant dependencies among various variables in the
web domain) [13]. Some systems already exist in this area: WebSIFT (uses clustering, statistical analysis and association rules) [4], WUM (looks for association
rules using an extended version of SQL) [12], or WebLogMiner (combines OLAP
and KDD) [17]. An overview of web page recommendation systems is presented
in [7].

P. Perner (Ed.): ICDM 2007, LNAI 4597, pp. 135–147, 2007.
© Springer-Verlag Berlin Heidelberg 2007

The algorithms described in this paper are motivated by two goals – (1) to predict user's behavior (i.e. to recommend the next page of interest given previously visited pages), and (2) to find interesting patterns in the visited page sequences. In the following we describe predictors of the next page type visited (e.g. product detail, FAQ, advice) and of the next product type of interest (e.g. digital cameras or zoom lenses). Both predictors can be used by web servers to recommend to users where they could go next. For practical purposes, such predictors might produce several recommendations so that the user spots an interesting page with greater probability. On the other hand, interesting patterns identified in page sequences provide important information both to webmasters and marketing specialists – e.g. about two products often bought together, or about a product detail page often being followed by a visit to a FAQ page. We present two types of algorithms – one statistical, which is appropriate for the next page prediction task, and two rule-based, which are suitable for both page prediction and pattern discovery.

In section 2 we list basic statistics of the data. Section 3 presents results of a statistical Markov N-gram page predictor. Section 4 describes two rule-based approaches, based on a set covering algorithm and a compositional algorithm. Section 5 compares the above and sections 6 and 7 conclude with directions for future research.

## 2    Click-Stream Data

The analyzed data comes from a Czech company that operates several e-shops. The log file (about 3 millions of records – the traffic of 24 days) contained the usual information: time, IP address, page request URL and referer. In addition to this, the log data contained also a generated session ID so the identification of users was relatively easy (see Fig. 1)– we treated each sequence of pages with the same ID as one session.

```
unix time;  IP address;          session ID;              page request; referee;
1074589200; 193.179.144.2; 1993441e8a0a4d7a4407ed9554b64ed1; /dp/?id=124; www.google.cz;
1074589201; 194.213.35.234; 3995b2c0599f1782e2b40582823b1c94; /dp/?id=182;
1074589202; 194.138.39.56; 2fd3213f2edaf82b27562d28a2a747aa; /; http://www.seznam.cz;
1074589233; 193.179.144.2; 1993441e8a0a4d7a4407ed9554b64ed1; /dp/?id=148; /dp/?id=124;
1074589245; 193.179.144.2; 1993441e8a0a4d7a4407ed9554b64ed1; /sb/; /dp/?id=148;
1074589248; 194.138.39.56; 2fd3213f2edaf82b27562d28a2a747aa; /contacts/; /;
1074589290; 193.179.144.2; 1993441e8a0a4d7a4407ed9554b64ed1; /sb/; /sb/;
```

**Fig. 1.** Part of the web log

The whole dataset consists of $522,410$ sessions, of which $318,523$ only contain a single page visit. In the following, we will reduce our dataset to the $203,887$ sessions that contain at least two page visits. The average length of these sessions was 16; the median was 8 and modus 2. A session length histogram is shown in Fig. 2. For evaluation purposes, we split the $203,887$ sessions into three sets: a

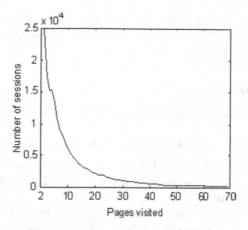

**Fig. 2.** Session length histogram

training set (the first $100,000$ sessions[1]), a test set (the second $60,000$ sessions) and a held-out set (the remaining $43,887$ sessions).

In addition to the log data, we had the following information: table `shop` listed all e-shops (7 entries), table `category` listed general product categories (65 entries), table `product` contained product subcategories (157 entries) and table `brand` listed all sold brands (197 entries).

Each page request had the same structure: `page_type/content_ID`. This allowed us to identify two interesting types of information in the click-streams: sequences of page types (e.g. detail of a product, shopping cart, product comparison), and sequences of product categories (both the `product` and `category` tables combined). For page types, we appended an extra 'end' page to the end of each page sequence, since it seemed important to model which page sequences lead to leaving the web. There were 22 distinct page types including the 'end' page. The majority class was the listing of products (37.7%) followed by a detail view of a product (31.3%). For product categories, no 'end' pages were appended. Based on the `product` and `category` tables, we defined 32 new product categories that grouped similar entries from both tables and used these to define the product sequences. The majority class were cameras (13.1%) followed by video & DVD (10.3%). All pages that did not contain product category information were removed from product sequences. Subsequent occurrences of the same product category were replaced by a single occurrence. The average length of the resulting product sequences was 2.

## 3   Markov N-Gram Predictor

Statistical approaches to modeling sequences are widely used in areas such as speech recognition, natural language processing or bio-informatics. As our first approach, we trained various *Markov N-gram models* (N-gram models for short)

---

[1] Sessions were sorted by session start time.

from click-stream sequences. Using these models, we predicted the most likely page following after each history in test data. A model similar to our implementation is described in [6].

## 3.1  N-Gram Model

An N-gram model models the probability of an observed page sequence $A_1 A_2 \ldots A_n$ as:

$$P(A_1 A_2 \ldots A_n) = \Pi_{i=1}^{n} P(A_i | A_{i-k} \ldots A_{i-1}) \tag{1}$$

where $k$ is the length of history taken into account. A model with $k$-token histories is called a $(k+1)$-gram model and obeys the Markov property of limited memory and stationarity [8].

An important decision is how to model the probability $P(A_i | A_{i-k} \ldots A_{i-1})$. Based on counts observed in training data, a $k$-gram probability $P_k$ only conditioned on $(k-1)$-length histories can be estimated as

$$P_k(A_i = c | A_{i-k+1} = a \ldots A_{i-1} = b) = \frac{n(a \ldots bc)}{n(a \ldots b)} \tag{2}$$

where $n(xy)$ is the count of page sequence $xy$ observed in training data. However, choosing just one fixed history length is problematic since long histories suffer from data sparsity and short histories may not contain sufficient information about the next page. It is therefore a common approach to interpolate $P_k$ with lower-order probabilities (i.e. those conditioned on shorter histories). The interpolated (smoothed) $k$-gram distribution is thus given as a weighted sum of the fixed history length distributions:

$$P(A_i | A_{i-k+1} \ldots A_{i-1}) = \lambda_0 P_0(A_i) + \lambda_1 P_1(A_i) + \lambda_2 P_2(A_i | A_{i-1}) + \\ + \cdots + \lambda_k P_k(A_i | A_{i-k+1} \ldots A_{i-1}) \tag{3}$$

where

$$\sum_{i=0}^{k} \lambda_i = 1, \forall_{i=0}^{k} \lambda_i \geq 0, \lambda_i \leq 1 \tag{4}$$

In Eq. 3, $P_0$ is a uniform distribution over all existing pages, $P_1$ is the unigram distribution only based on page frequencies without taking history into account, and the remaining $P_i$ distributions are conditioned on histories of length $i - 1$.

The weights $\lambda_i$ are best determined by an unsupervised EM algorithm [8], which iteratively re-estimates weights using held-out data until convergence. First, all the components $P_i$ ($i = 1 \ldots k$) are computed from counts observed in the *training dataset* according to Eq 2. Second, weights are set to some initial non-zero (we chose uniform) values. Third, the probability of a *held-out dataset* is computed using the interpolated distribution in Eq. 3 with the working weights. For each addend in Eq. 3, its share on the total held-out data probability is collected. After running through all held-out data, the new weights are obtained by normalizing the shares of each addend. Step three is repeated until none of the $\lambda_i$ weights changes significantly.

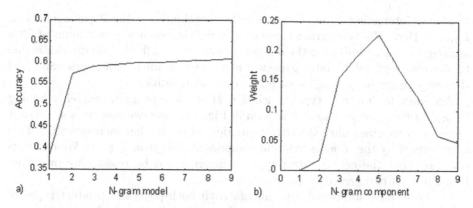

**Fig. 3. a.** N-gram accuracy for page types **b.** Weights of 9-gram components

## 3.2   N-Gram Results

We trained N-gram models to predict the next page type, and the next product category a user might be interested in.

All N-gram models are only trained using the training data set, and smoothed using the held-out data set. We evaluate the N-gram predictors by comparing the real item in test data with the most likely item that would follow the observed history according to the model. Prediction accuracy is given as the number of correct predictions over all predictions. The best results are compared to rule-based methods in Table 1. The table also includes results achieved on training data; in these cases, N-gram model weights were estimated on training data as well, which caused the highest-order component to always have a weight of 1.

Accuracy for page types reached 0.61 and is reported in detail in Fig. 3a for N-gram models with N ranging from 1 (a unigram model only smoothed with uniform distribution) to 9 (a 9-gram model smoothed with 9 lower order distributions). We observe that accuracy climbs significantly until the trigram model, thus the chosen page type depends mostly on the two preceding pages.

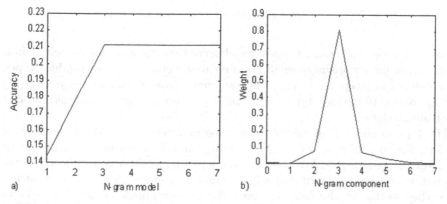

**Fig. 4. a.** N-gram accuracy for product types **b.** Weights of 7-gram components

It is also interesting to note the smoothing weights for the 9-gram model in Fig. 3b. Here, the pentagram component's weight reaches a maximum of 23% although its contribution to the overall accuracy is small. We assume this is due to abundance of data – data sparseness is not significant yet for pentagrams and thus we can get large weights for high-order probabilities.

Accuracy for product types reached 0.21 for a heptagram model; climbing from 0.14 for a unigram model, as seen in Fig. 4a. Here, we observe a significant increase in accuracy until the trigram model, where further increases stop. This is confirmed by the superior trigram component weight in Fig. 4b. We can thus conclude that the next product type of interest can be reasonably predicted based just on two preceding products.

We performed additional experiments with both page and product types to find out how the prediction accuracy varies with the amount of available training data. For this purpose we trained 5-gram models from training sets of the following sizes (in sessions): 20, 50, 100, 200, 500, 1k, 2k, 5k, 10k, 20k, 50k and the full 100k training sessions. All data sets were constructed by taking the first $K$ sessions from the full training set. For each model, its N-gram component weights were re-estimated on the held-out set. Accuracies of these models were measured on the test set and are shown in Fig. 5.

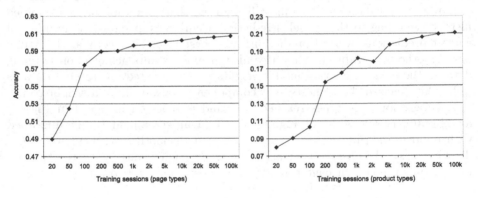

**Fig. 5.** 5-gram model accuracies for reduced training data sizes

For both page and product types, we observe that the model accuracies climb steeply even for surprisingly small training data sets. In case of product types the climb is less steep since the product sequences are shorter (average length is 2 compared to 16 for page types) and thus the same amount of sessions contains less training data.

The 5-gram component weights were also monitored for each of the trained models. Fig. 6 confirms that larger training data leads to better estimates of the N-gram components. We observe that when trained on larger data, the re-estimation procedure distributes more weight to the higher order components since they better fit the held-out data. The graph shows cumulative weights starting from the uniform component (0), unigram (1), up to the 5-gram.

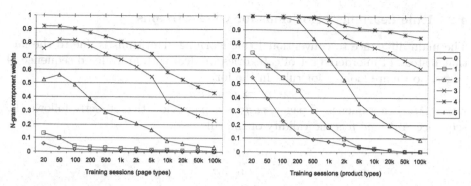

**Fig. 6.** Development of 5-gram component weights for reduced training data sizes

# 4 Rule-Based Predictors

## 4.1 Classical Rule Learning Algorithms

Decision rules in the form

$$Ant \Rightarrow Class$$

where *Ant* (antecedent, condition) is a conjunction of values of input attributes (called categories or selectors) and *Class* is a category of class attribute $C$, are one of most popular formalisms how to express classification models learned from data. The commonly used approach to learning decision rules is the *set covering approach* also called "separate and conquer". The basic idea of this approach is to create a rule that covers some examples of a given class and remove these examples form the training set. This is repeated for all examples not covered so far. There are two basic ways how to create a single rule:

1. by rule generalization, i.e. by removing categories from antecedent of a potential rule (starting from a rule with categories of all input attributes in the antecedent) - this method is used in the AQ algorithms by Michalski (see e.g. [11]).
2. by rule specialization, i.e. by adding categories to the antecedent of a potential rule (starting from a rule with empty antecedent) – this method is used e.g. in CN2 [5] or CN4 [3].

The other way how to create decision rules is the *compositional approach*. In this approach the covered examples are not removed during learning, so an example can be covered with more rules. Thus more rules can be used during classification. In compositional approach, all applicable rules are used and their particular contributions to classification are combined into the final decision. To do this, some numerical value is usually added to the rule, the simplest one is the rule confidence (also called validity) defined as $n(Ant \wedge Class)/n(Ant)$, where $n(Ant \wedge Class)$ is the number of examples that match both *Ant* and *Class* and $n(Ant)$ is the number of examples that match *Ant* in the data.

## 4.2   Rule Learning Algorithms for Click-Streams

The main difference to conventional rule learning algorithms is due to the fact that instead of unordered set of categories we deal with an ordered sequence of pages. So we are looking for rules in the form

$$Ant \Rightarrow page(p)$$

where $Ant$ is a sequence of pages, $page$ is a page view that directly follows the sequence $Ant$, and $p$ is the validity of the rule

$$p = \frac{n(Ant//page)}{n(Ant)}.$$

In the formula above we denote the number of occurrences of a sequence in the data by $n(sequence)$ and a concatenation of two sequences $s1$ and $s2$ by $s1//s2$.

We propose two rule learning algorithms for click-streams: a set covering and a compositional one [2]. We follow the rule learning approach based on rule specialization in our algorithms as well. As we assume that most relevant for prediction of occurrence of a page are pages that are closest to this page, the specialization of the rule $Ant \Rightarrow page$ is done by adding a new page to the beginning of the sequence $Ant$. Analogously, a generalization of the rule $Ant \Rightarrow page$ is done by removing a page from the beginning of the sequence $Ant$.

The main idea of our *set covering* algorithm is to add (for a particular page to be predicted) rules of growing length of $Ant$. We check each rule against its *generalization* created so far. Adding a new rule $Ant \Rightarrow page$ to the model is determined by $\chi^2$ test that compares the validity of these two rules. If the rule in question is added to the model, its *generalization is updated* by re-computing the validity by ignoring (removing) sequences that are covered by the newly added rule (Fig. 7).

The main idea of our *compositional* algorithm (Fig. 8) is again to add (for a particular page to be predicted) rules of growing length of $Ant$. We check each rule against the *results of classification* done by all rules created so far. Adding a new rule $Ant \Rightarrow page$ to the model is determined by $\chi^2$ test that compares its validity $p$ with the weight of predicted page inferred during classification for the sequence $Ant$. The weight $\mathrm{w}^{\oplus}(Ant)$ of predicted page is computed according to the formula

$$w_1 \oplus w_2 = \frac{w_1 \times w_2}{w_1 \times w_2 + (1 - w_1) \times (1 - w_2)}, \tag{5}$$

$w_1$ and $w_2$ in this formula denote weights of rules that are applicable to the sequence $Ant$.

## 4.3   Rule Learning Algorithm Results

In the first set of experiments we were looking for rules that can be interpreted as interesting by the data providers. We identified as interesting e.g. the rules

---

**Initialization**
for each page occurring in the data
1. compute its relative frequency in the data as $P = $ (no. of occurrences of *page* in the input episodes)/(no. of all input episodes)
2. if $P \geq n_{min}$
   2.1 add *default* $\Rightarrow$ *page* into the list of rules *Rules*
   2.2 add *page* into list of pages *Pages*
   2.3 add *default* $\Rightarrow$ *page* into list of implications *Impl*

**Main loop**
while Impl not empty do
1. take first rule $Ant \Rightarrow page$ from *Impl*
2. if length of $Ant < l_{max}$ then
   2.1 for each page *pp* from *Pages*
      2.1.1 find the most specific generalization of the rule $pp//Ant \Rightarrow page$ in *Rules* (denote it $AntX \Rightarrow page$)
      2.1.2 compare (using chi2 test) the validity of rules $pp//Ant \Rightarrow page$ and $AntX \Rightarrow page$
   2.2 from all created rules $pp//Ant \Rightarrow page$ select the one with the most significant difference in validity (denote this rule $pp_{best}//Ant \Rightarrow page$)
   2.3 if $pp_{best}//Ant \Rightarrow page$ significantly at a given significance level differs from $AntX \Rightarrow page$ then
      2.3.1 add rule $pp_{best}//Ant \Rightarrow page$ to *Rules* and *Impl*
      2.3.2 re-compute the validity of rule $AntX \Rightarrow page$ by taking into account only episodes containing $AntX$ and not containing $Ant$
      2.3.3 recursively update Rules (i.e. find the most specific generalization of $AntX \Rightarrow page$, compare this generalization with $AntX \Rightarrow page$, remove $AntX \Rightarrow page$ from *Rules* if the difference is not significant etc.)
3. remove $Ant \Rightarrow page$ from *Impl*

---

**Fig. 7.** The set covering rule learning algorithm for click-stream analysis

```
dp, sb -> sb (Ant: 5174; AntPage: 4801; P: 0.93)
   ct -> end (Ant: 5502; AntPage: 1759; P: 0.32)
 faq -> help (Ant: 594; AntPage: 127; P: 0.21).
```

for the sequences concerning page types. In the listing above, ct stands for "contact", Ant stands for $n(Ant)$ and AntPage stands for $n(Ant//Page)$. Among rules concerning product categories we found e.g.

```
loud-speakers -> video + DVD (Ant: 14840, AntPage: 3785, P: 0.26)
   data cables -> telephones (Ant: 2560, AntPage: 565, P: 0.22)
PC peripheries -> telephones (Ant: 8671, AntPage: 1823, P: 0.21)
```

The obtained rule sets can directly be used to predict the behavior of a user. So e.g. for a sequence of pages dp, sb the system will predict sb as the next page, and for the sequence loud-speakers the system will predict video + DVD.

---

**Initialization**
for each page occurring in the data
  1. compute its relative frequency in the data as $P = $ (no. of occurrences
     of *page* in the input episodes)/(no. of all input episodes)
  2. if $P \geq n_{min}$
     2.1 add $default \Rightarrow page$ into the list of rules *Rules*
     2.2 add *page* into list of pages *Pages*
     2.3 add $default \Rightarrow page$ into list of implications *Impl*

**Main loop**
while Impl not empty do
  1. take first rule $Ant \Rightarrow page$ from *Impl*
  2. if length of $Ant < l_{max}$ then
     2.1 for each page *pp* from *Pages*
         2.1.1 create the rule $pp//Ant \Rightarrow page$ and compute its validity $p$
         2.1.2 from all rules in *Rules* that cover the sequence $pp//Ant$ com-
               pute the resulting weight for page as $w^{\oplus}(pp//Ant)$
         2.1.3 compare (using chi2 test) $p$ and $w^{\oplus}(pp//Ant)$
         2.1.4 if $p$ significantly differs from $w^{\oplus}(pp//Ant)$ then
             2.1.4.1 compute $w$ from the formula $w \oplus w^{\oplus}(pp//Ant) = p$
             2.1.4.2 add rule $pp//Ant \Rightarrow page(w)$ to *Rules* and *Impl*
         2.1.5 add $pp//Ant \Rightarrow page(w)$ to *Impl*
     2.2 remove $Ant \Rightarrow page$ from *Impl*

---

**Fig. 8.** The compositional rule learning algorithm for click-stream analysis

In the second set of experiments we were interested in classification accuracy of our rule sets. We have run our algorithms repeatedly for both page sequences (first set of experiments) and product sequences (second set of experiments). When looking at the differences between the set covering and compositional algorithms, we can observe different trade offs between comprehensibility and accuracy: the set covering algorithm offers higher accuracy but lower comprehensibility (larger number of rules) than the compositional algorithm (see Tab. 1). The default accuracy refers to the accuracy of the "zero rule" model, that always predicts the most frequent page. In all experiments we exceeded this "base line". Since both rule-based methods make no use of held-out data, this data was appended to the training data in all cases.

## 5    A Comparison of N-Gram and Rule-Based Models

In Table 1, accuracy is computed as the number of correct guesses according to the model and to the observed history, divided by the total number of guesses (all pages from the evaluated data). For the N-gram model, the predicted page is the one with the highest conditional probability given an observed history of pages. For both rule based methods, the predicted page is the page for which the combined weight of all applicable rules (given history) is maximal.

**Table 1.** Empirical comparison of algorithms

| page sequences | default[a] accuracy | N-gram accuracy | set covering no.rules accuracy | | compositional no.rules accuracy | |
|---|---|---|---|---|---|---|
| test data | 0.40 | **0.61** | 1088 | 0.59 | 371 | 0.49 |
| training data | 0.40 | **0.67** | 1088 | 0.60 | 371 | 0.50 |
| product sequences | | | | | | |
| test data | 0.14 | 0.21 | 2176 | **0.24** | 903 | 0.19 |
| training data | 0.14 | **0.24** | 2176 | 0.23 | 903 | 0.18 |

[a] Default accuracy corresponds to a model that will always predict the most frequent page, i.e. it is the relative frequency of the majority page.

We observe that for both page and product types, the accuracy of the N-gram models on test data is comparable to the set covering algorithm. For page types, the best prediction accuracy of 0.61 was reached by a 9-gram model, while the set covering algorithm achieved the highest accuracy of 0.24 for product types. When applied as a page recommendation system, both predictors should yield more than one recommendation about the next page to let the user choose from several relevant pages. In terms of performance on training data, the 9-gram model achieves 0.67 accuracy, which is however caused by over-fitting the training data. On the other hand, both rule-based algorithms seem to be resistant to over-fitting, surprisingly for product sequences they achieve slightly better results on test data than on the training set.

To compare N-gram and both rule based methods, we may view N-gram models as exhaustive sets of weighted rules. Each non-zero probability $P_i(c|a \ldots b)$ from Eq. 2, weighted by the corresponding weight $\lambda_i$, can be treated as confidence of a corresponding rule $a \ldots b \Rightarrow c$. For a particular history $a \ldots b$, the weighted confidences of relevant rules are summed to produce a probability for each possible predicted class. This similarity in learnt models seems to be the reason why the set-covering algorithm with large amounts of rules performed comparably to the N-gram models.

Viewing N-gram models as sets of rules, there are however several major distinctions from the rule-based algorithms. First, the number of N-gram "rules" is exhaustive, although we could e.g. remove all "rules" conditioned on histories having count less than a chosen threshold. Second, the contributions of N-gram "rules" are based on confidence (as for the set covering algorithm), however they are further weighted by a constant factor that expresses the reliability of all rules with a certain length of antecedent. To relax this constraint, N-gram weights could be alternatively specified for intervals of history frequencies (referred to as bucketed smoothing) instead of history lengths; in this case frequent histories would receive higher weights as they are more reliable. Yet another difference lies in the method how contributions of multiple rules are combined. In the compositional approach, Eq. 5 is used, whereas a weighted sum in Eq. 3 is used for the N-gram model to yield probability. Last of all, unlike the set covering algorithm, in the N-gram case multiple rules are used during a single classification, as in the compositional approach.

When the analysis goal is user's understanding of learnt models (rather than prediction), a method which learns few comprehensive rules is generally preferable. In our case, this is the compositional approach. The learnt weights of N-gram model components also seem to contain useful information on how long histories still influence user's behavior.

## 6    Future Work

For the N-gram predictor, we plan to implement other smoothing methods, starting with bucketed smoothing based on history frequencies. For the rule-based models, we will analyze how rule learning parameters impact accuracy and compare our algorithms with state-of-the-art methods. Another experiment we would like to perform on the described dataset is predicting the next page based on a richer set of features observed in history. These features would include page types, visited product types, product makes, session length, and the time spent on these pages. A suitable prediction algorithm that would benefit from a large feature set could be a Maximum Entropy Model, which was successfully applied in a web recommendation system described in [9].

## 7    Conclusion

We presented and compared two approaches for clickstream data analysis – one statistical and two rule-based algorithms. Using these algorithms, we predicted the next page type visited and the next product type of interest. The statistical N-gram algorithm and the set-covering rule-based algorithm achieved comparable prediction accuracies for both page and product types. On the other hand, the compositional rule-based algorithm, which was inferior in terms of prediction accuracy, proved to be suitable for discovering interesting patterns in page sequences. The described algorithms can be applied by web servers to recommend relevant pages to their users, and to identify interesting patterns in their log files.

## Acknowledgements

The research is supported by the grant no.MSM138439910 of the Ministry of Education of the Czech Republic and the grant no.201/05/0325 of the Czech Science Foundation.

## References

1. Berka, P., Ivánek, J.: Automated knowledge acquisition for PROSPECTOR-like expert systems. In: Bergadano, F., De Raedt, L. (eds.) Machine Learning: ECML-94. LNCS, vol. 784, pp. 339–342. Springer, Heidelberg (1994)
2. Berka, P., Laš, V., Kočka, T.: Rule induction for click-stream analysis: set covering and compositional approach. In: IIPMW 2005. LNCS, pp. 13–22. Springer, Heidelberg (2005)

3. Bruha, I., Kočková, S.: A support for decision making: Cost-sensitive learning system. Artificial Intelligence in Medicine 6, 67–82 (1994)
4. Cooley, R., Tan, P.N., Srivastava, J.: Discovery of interesting usage patterns from web data. Tech. Rep. TR 99-022, Univ. of Minnesota (1999)
5. Clark, P., Niblett, T.: The CN2 induction algorithm. Machine Learning 3, 261–283 (1989)
6. Deshpande, M., Karypis, G.: Selective Markov Models for Predicting Web-Page Accesses. Technical Report 56, University of Minnesota (2000)
7. Gündüz, S., Özsu, M.T.: Recommendation Models for User Accesses to Web Pages. In: Kaynak, O., Alpaydın, E., Oja, E., Xu, L. (eds.) ICANN 2003 and ICONIP 2003. LNCS, vol. 2714, Springer, Heidelberg (2003)
8. Jelinek, F.: Statistical Methods for Speech Recognition. MIT Press, Cambridge (1998)
9. Jin, X., Mobasher, B., Zhou, Y.: A Web Recommendation System Based on Maximum Entropy. In: Proc. IEEE International Conference on Information Technology Coding and Computing, Las Vegas (2005)
10. Kosala, R., Blockeel, H.: Web Mining Research: A Survey. In: SIGKDD Explorations, vol. 2(1) (2000)
11. Michalski, R.S.: On the Quasi-minimal solution of the general covering problem. In: Proc. 5th Int. Symposium on Information Processing FCIP'69, Bled, pp. 125–128 (1969)
12. Spiliopoulou, M., Faulstich, L.: WUM: A tool for web utilization analysis. In: Atzeni, P., Mendelzon, A.O., Mecca, G. (eds.) The World Wide Web and Databases. LNCS, vol. 1590, Springer, Heidelberg (1999)
13. Srivastava, J., Cooley, R., Deshpande, M., Tan, P.N.: Web Usage Mining: Discovery and Applications of Usage Patterns from Web Data. SIGKDD Explorations 1(2) (2000)
14. Witten, I.H., Frank, E.: Generating Accurate Rule Sets Without Global Optimization. In: Proc. of the 15th Int. Conference on Machine Learning, Morgan Kaufmann, San Francisco (1998)
15. Witten, I.H., Frank, E.: Data Mining: Practical Machine Learning Tools and Techniques with Java Implementations. Morgan Kaufmann, San Francisco (1999)
16. Zaiane, O., Han, J.: WebML: Querying the World-Wide Web for resources and knowledge. In: Workshop on Web Information and Data Management WIDM'98, Bethesda, pp. 9–12 (1998)
17. Zaiane, O., Xin, M., Han, J.: Discovering web access patterns and trends by applying OLAP and data mining technology on web logs. In: Advances in Digital Libraries (1998)

# Improved IR in Cohesion Model for Link Detection System

K. Lakshmi and Saswati Mukherjee

Anna University, India
Lakshmi_tamil@hotmail.com, msaswati@yahoo.com

**Abstract.** Given two stories, Story Link Detection System identifies whether they are discussing the same event. Standard approach in link detection system is to use cosine similarity measure to find whether the two documents are linked. Many researchers applied query expansion technique successfully in link detection system, where models are built from the relevant documents retrieved from the collection using query expansion. In this approach, success depends on the quality of the information retrieval system. In the current research, we propose a new information retrieval system for query expansion that uses intra-cluster similarity of the retrieved documents in addition to the similarity with respect to the query document. Our technique enhances the quality of the retrieval system thus improving the performance of the Link Detection System. Combining this improved IR with our Cohesion Model provides excellent result in link detection. Experimental results confirm the effect of the improved retrieval system in query expansion technique.

**Keywords:** Topic Detection and Tracking, Story Link Detection System, Information Retrieval System, Cohesion Model.

## 1 Introduction

Topic Detection and Tracking System is receiving an increased attention in recent days for its application in many areas like information retrieval, question answering system and summarization. In information retrieval systems, users are interested in extracting information about a specific topic. In question answering system, it is necessary to organize the document according to particular topic and search for answer within the topic set. Users may be interested in viewing summarized information about certain topic. Therefore organizing information on the basis of topic is important in many applications [1] [2].

TDT consists of five sub tasks: Story Segmentation - Segmenting a stream of data into distinct stories, First Story Detection - Identifying those news stories that are the first to discuss a new event occurring in the news, Cluster Detection - Given a small number of sample news stories about an event, finding all following stories in the stream, Tracking - Monitoring the news stream for finding additional incoming stories that can be added to the existing topics, and Link Detection – Deciding whether any two randomly selected stories discuss the same topic [3].

P. Perner (Ed.): ICDM 2007, LNAI 4597, pp. 148–162, 2007.
© Springer-Verlag Berlin Heidelberg 2007.

Out of the five subtasks, Link detection system is considered to be the core component of TDT, as it can be used for performing all the other tasks as well. This paper deals with the link detection system. Task in hand is to identify whether the two given stories talks about the same event, where an event is something that happens at a specific place and time and involves specific participants, be they human or otherwise [4].

## 1.1 Proposed Model

Encouraged by the good performance of the query expansion technique in link detection system, we propose to use an improved query expansion model. Performance of such systems depends on the quality of the retrieved documents. Given two documents D1and D2 as input to the link detection system, each document is considered as query and documents that are relevant to the query are retrieved from the collection. The given documents D1 and D2 are named as query documents and will be referred as such in the following discussion. From the relevant documents of each query document $D_k$, corresponding model $M_k$ is built. Information retrieval systems retrieve not only relevant documents but also non-relevant documents. Worse is, many a time, negative documents are classified as relevant documents. When a model $M_k$ is built out of relevant as well as non-relevant documents, many terms that are not relevant to the original query document $D_k$ will be placed in the model $M_k$. Under such circumstances, $M_k$ is not the true representative of $D_k$. To avoid this problem, we propose an improved information retrieval system that filters the retrieved documents through one additional level, so that only relevant documents are obtained. This additional level of filtering is performed based on the intra similarity, thereby improving the quality of the overall information retrieval system and reducing the chances of retrieving non-relevant documents. This, therefore, improves the quality of the model generated from the retrieved relevant set.

Reference [14] has used cohesion model in story link detection system, where query expansion has been employed using the concepts of cohesion technique. In this approach, mechanism of model building exploits the terms' individual contribution and its distribution in the relevant documents. To achieve this, four factors, *viz*, Sense of belonging, Feelings of morale, Goal consensus, and Network cohesion have been used. This approach has produced improved result over the basic model. Our proposed model combines the improved IR along with cohesion model.

Once the models are built for each of the query documents, they are compared using Modified Fraction similarity [10]. Modified Fractional Similarity measure gives credit for the overlapping term and reduces the similarity score for having non-overlapping terms. Hence the similarity score in this method depends on both similar as well as non-similar terms. With the encouraging performance in text classification, we use Modified Fractional Similarity to compare the models in our link detection system. Query documents D1 and D2 are declared as linked if the similarity measure between the models is greater than a predefined threshold.

We have organized this paper with section 2 discussing about the related work, section 3 elaborates the proposed system, section 4 about the experiment results and the next section discusses further possible enhancements.

## 2  Related Works

A number of research groups have developed story link detection systems. The basic model of link detection system proposed by [7] used vector space model to represent the given documents D1 and D2. Then D1 and D2 are compared using cosine similarity. This method is a well-established method that produces consistent result in various tasks and data set.

Reference [5] proposed a model that uses source-pair information and various similarity measures of document pairs for training the support vector machine. As the documents come from different sources like broadcast and newswire, each has different characteristics. Similarity measure between broadcast-broadcast, newswire-newswire and broadcast-newswire are different. They have captured this information and shown that inclusion of source-pair information helps to improve the link detection.

Reference [11] has used the concept of query expansion, a well-established technique in IR. Here document given for link detection is considered as query and the documents that are relevant are retrieved from the collection. By using local context analysis technique, terms in the relevant documents are added to the query document. Thus each document is expanded and then compared. This technique showed slight improvement over the link detection system that does not use any query expansion. However success of the model depends on how successfully relevant documents alone are fetched and how the terms are assigned weights. In their paper they have indicated that expanding document using non-relevant document set would move the model in the wrong direction and would severely affects the performance of the link detection system.

Reference [6] has used probability method for obtaining the relevant documents, *i.e.,* probability of a document to be retrieved, for the given query $P(D|Q)$, is calculated and then topic model is built for each given story (query). Each term in the relevant documents are assigned weight according to the term's probability in the document $P(w|D)$ and the probability of the document to be retrieved for the given query $P(D|Q)$. The two topic models thus obtained are compared by using Clarity adjusted Kullback-Leibler divergence method.

In the language models terms in a document are considered to be independent of each other, which is not true in the real case. Reference [9] has exploited term dependency to capture the underlying semantics in the document. They proposed modeling sentences, rather than words or phrases as individual entities.

Using "soundex" in comparing documents of different sources (broadcast and newswire) is proposed by [13]. When broadcast news is converted to text, most of the nouns are given different spelling. So when a broadcast news and newswire news are compared, some of the terms do not match and this may lead to low similarity value. System proposed by [13] addressed this problem. However, they were not able to produce better result due to poor named-entity recognizer for ASR documents.

## 3  Cohesion Model with Improved IR

Documents relevant to the query documents are retrieved using the proposed improved IR. Document $D_k$ is expanded using the terms in the relevant documents.

Then each term is assigned weight according to social cohesion concept. The expanded models are compared to decide whether the given two documents are linked.

For comparing the documents, we have used Modified Fractional Similarity measure proposed in [10]. Modified Fractional Similarity is given in equation (1). In this phase of link detection, it is employed to compare the query document with each of the documents in the collection. The choice of this similarity measure here has stemmed from the fact that this similarity technique provides better precision and reduces false positives in the overall retrieved set.

First step of the process is to get the relevant documents considering the given document as query and the second step is to assign weight to the terms of relevant documents.

### 3.1  Relevant Documents

For expanding the query documents, terms in the retrieved relevant document set are used. In this context, it is important that we consider only the relevant documents, since false positives may move the model into a wrong direction. Thus improved IR technique having very high accuracy is the need of the hour. To obtain this high precision, we propose to obtain the set of relevant documents in two steps. First the relevant documents are obtained using IR and then this set is filtered further to take out any noncontributing documents that may have been retrieved.

$$\text{Mfraction}(d1,d2) = 2*\alpha /( \beta+ \gamma) \qquad \text{if } \{d1\} - \{d2\} \neq \varphi$$
$$= \alpha \qquad \text{if } \{d1\} - \{d2\} = \varphi$$

$$\alpha = \sum_{i=1}^{p} w_i * v_i \qquad \text{if } term_i \in d1 \text{ and } \in d2$$

$$\beta = \sum_{i=1}^{m} w_i \qquad \text{if } term_i \in d1 \text{ and } \notin d2 \tag{1}$$

$$\gamma = \sum_{i=1}^{n} v_i \qquad \text{if } term_i \in d2 \text{ and } \notin d1$$

$w_i$ – weight of $term_i$ in d1
$v_i$ – weight of $term_i$ in document d2
m – number of terms in the d1
n – number of terms in the document d2
p – number of terms in both d1 and d2

As the first step, modified fractional similarity (equation 1) is used to retrieve documents those are relevant to the query document $D_k$. For this purpose, we use, as collection, documents that are temporally closer to the query document. This reduces the search time. We propose to use $n$ previous days documents as our background collection for our first level IR. This period of n days is known as the deferral period.

Our observation is that the consideration of only those documents within the deferral period is sufficient since the events are time specific.

We set a threshold experimentally. Documents that are greater than this predefined threshold are considered as relevant documents.

As shown in Fig. 1, documents $R_1$-$R_n$ are relevant documents obtained.

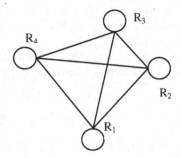

**Fig. 1.** R1-R4 are the relevant documents. Edges shows connectivity between documents in the relevant document set.

Fig. 1 shows the ideal case of connectivity among the retrieved documents, *i.e.*, all the retrieved documents are connected to each other. In other words all the relevant documents that are obtained in step 1 are similar to each other. But this may not be always true. To ensure minimum connectivity among the retrieved documents, step 2 is implemented as the next filtering step. For this purpose, we use intra-cluster similarity. In this step, similarity of each retrieved document is further measured with respect to other retrieved documents using equation 2 and the relevance is judged on the basis of this measure.

$$c(R_i) = \sum_{R_j \in \{RL\}} s(R_i, R_j) / [(n-1)] \qquad (2)$$

Where
$c(R_i)$ – cluster similarity
$\{RL\}$ – Relevant documents set
$s(R_i, R_j)$ – Cosine similarity between $R_i$ and $R_j$
$n$ – no of relevant documents $|RL|$

Equation 2 uses cosine similarity given by equation 3. Cosine similarity value for two completely relevant documents is 1. Thus the assumption in equation (2) is that, if the document is a true relevant document, its intra similarity (connectivity to other documents) should be equal to (n-1), *i.e.*, equal to the total number of possible edges from this node as shown in the Fig.1. Thus the maximum value for cluster similarity for a document is 1. Document with high connectivity is considered to be more relevant to the given query. For each relevant document, connectivity is measured as the ratio of sum of all similarity measures with respect to other relevant documents and the maximum possible connections (*i.e.*, the number of edges).

$$Cos(d1,d2) = \Sigma \ d1.d2/|d1||d2| \qquad (3)$$

The final similarity measure $FS(D_k,R_i)$ between query document $D_k$ and the relevant document $R_i$ is calculated using equation 4. If the final similarity is greater than a threshold $t$ specified apriory, $R_i$ is considered to be relevant to the given query.

$$FS(\ D_k,R_i)\ = \alpha * s(D_k,R_i) + (1-\alpha) * c\ (R_i) \qquad (4)$$

Where
$FS(D_k,R_i)$ – Final Similarity between two documents $D_k$ and $R_i$,
$D_k$ is the query document and $R_i$ is the relevant document, $R_i \in RL$
$\alpha$ - Control parameter
$s(D_k,R_i)$ – similarity between $D_k$ and $R_i$
$c\ (R_i)$ – cluster similarity

Equation 4 is a weighted sum of $s(D_k,R_i)$ and $c\ (R_i)$, where $s(D_k,R_i)$ is calculated by equation 1 and $c\ (R_i)$ is calculated using equation 2. Control parameter $\alpha$ is the used to decide the importance between the two values.

Next step in the process is to assign weight to the terms. Following sub-section explains how the terms are assigned weight according to cohesion-model.

### 3.2  Building Cohesion-Model

Reference [12] describes an iterative process where "community dialogue" and "collective action" work together to produce social change in a community that improves the health and welfare of all of its members. It discusses Social Cohesion to be one of the factors affecting the Social Change. Social cohesion is an important antecedent and consequence of successful collective action. In [14], this has been used as the base and the corresponding mechanism of building a query expansion model using cohesion factors has been employed.

Since social cohesion consists of the forces that act on members of a group or community to remain in, and actively contribute to the group, a direct mapping of the terms of the relevant documents has been established in [14] to the members in the society. In the current research, we use the term's contribution and the relationship among them in the relevant documents. Terms in model $M_k$ are assigned weights according to different social cohesion factors.

There are four factors that has been used in the cohesion model for the purpose of Link Detection System. These are:

- Sense of belonging
- Feelings of morale,
- Goal consensus,
- Network cohesion.

**Sense of belonging -** is the extent to which individual members feel as if they are an important part of the group or community. This can be directly mapped with the term's frequency in the relevant documents.

$$tf(t) = [1/N]^* \sum_{d \in rl} tf(t,d) \tag{5}$$

Where
tf (t)  = term frequency of terms in relevant documents
rl – relevant documents
tf(t,d) = term frequency of term t in document d
N – Total no of relevant documents

**Feelings of morale** – This refers to the extent to which members of a group or community are happy and proud of being a member. We can map this to the *inverse document frequency (idf)* factor of the term. Presence of a term in all or most of the documents across the boundaries of groups in the collection can be viewed as lack of confidence and lack of enthusiasm to identify itself with the group.

**Goal consensus** – It is the degree to which members of the community agree on the objectives to be achieved by the group. Here we translate it as how many times each term in the relevant document set is repeated in relevant documents. We calculate the *document frequency* (df) of the term in the relevant document set using equation 6. More number of times the term is repeated more overlap is expected among the relevant document set.

$$Df(t) = [1/N]^* docfreq(t) \tag{6}$$

Where
df (t)  =document frequency of terms t
docfreq –no.of documents term t appears in relevant documents
N – Total no of relevant documents

**Network cohesion** - This can be viewed as the term's co-occurrence in the relevant documents. By adding co-occurrence weight in calculating the terms weight is expected to eliminate the problem described in [11]. Even though the quality of the retrieval is poor *i.e.,* the retrieved document set contains negative documents, terms of the negative documents may not co-occur with the positive document terms. Equation 7 is used to calculate the co-occurrence weight.

$$Cnet(t_i) = \sum_{ti,tj \in \{T\}} [n(t_i \cap t_j)/n(t_i)] * [tf(t_i) / p] \tag{7}$$

Where
T – All terms in the relevant documents
Cnet ($t_i$) - Cohesion value of term $t_i$
$n(t_i \cap t_j)$ – no of times terms $t_i$ & $t_j$ co-occurred in relevant documents
$n(t_i)$ - document frequency of term $t_i$ in relevant documents
p - no.of terms in the relevant documents
tf ($t_i$) – term frequency of term $t_i$

With all the parameter final weight of the term is calculated as given in equation 8.

$$w(t_i)=c1*tf(t_i)+c2*idf(t_i)+c3*df(t_i)+c4*Cnet(t_i) \qquad (8)$$

Where
w $(t_i)$ - weight of term $t_i$
tf $(t_i)$ = term frequency of terms in relevant documents
idf $(t_i)$ = inverse document frequency of term $t_i$ in relevant documents
df$(t_i)$ = document frequency of term $t_i$ in relevant documents
Cnet $(t_i)$ - Cohesion value of term $t_i$
c1-c4 - constants

Each term is given weight as the weighted sum of the tf, idf, df and Cnet. Equation 8 shows how the term weight of each term is calculated. Constants c1-c4 are selected empirically.

Thus a combined work using improved IR and cohesion model is established in this work.

### 3.3 Comparing Models

For each query document $D_k$ relevant documents are retrieved. Model $M_k$, which is a representative of $D_k$, is built from the terms of the relevant documents. In $M_k$ terms are assigned weights according to cohesion mechanism. Two models $M_1$ and $M_2$ built for the two query documents are compared using MF Similarity to establish link.

## 4  Experimental Results

In this section we evaluate performance of Cohesion Model with improved IR on the Link detection task of TDT. First, we describe the experimental setup and the evaluation methodology

### 4.1  Experimental Set Up

We have used TDT4 data for evaluating our proposed system. We have considered 16 topics' data for the experiment. Test data contains 377 positive links and 1277 negative links. The news stories were collected from different sources; newswire sources (Associated Press and New York Times) and broadcast sources (Voice of America and Public Radio International). We consider only English stories for our experiments. Though the corpus contains other language documents, those are not considered for these experiments. Text version of the broadcast news is used for this evaluation.

### 4.2  Evaluation Method

The system is evaluated in terms of its ability to detect the pairs of stories that discuss the same topic. During evaluation, the Link Detection System emits a YES or NO decision for each story pair. If our system emits a YES for an off-target pair, we get a False Alarm error; if the system emits a NO for on-target pair, we get a Miss error. Otherwise the system is correct.

Link Detection is generally evaluated in terms of F1-Measure as in classification system or Cost Function given by equation 9, which is the weighted sum of probabilities of getting a Miss and False Alarm [8].

$$Cost = P(Miss)CMiss + P(FA)CFA \qquad (9)$$

In the present work, we have considered F1-measure as the main factor for the evaluation of the performance of the various systems that we have used for our experimentation. F1-measure has been chosen because we want to use the system as a basic component of TDT. In [8], Chen *et al.* has shown that optimized story link detection is not equivalent to optimized new event detection. An optimal link detection system tries to reduce the false alarm (as the weight of the false alarm is high). But false alarm of Link Detection system is equivalent to miss in New Event Detection System (NED). Thus an optimized Link Detection System does lead to optimized NED. So we have used F1-measure to indicate the performance of the Link Detection System, as F1-measure is a harmonic mean of precision and recall.

We have considered 14 different Story Link Detection systems for evaluation as given in table 1.

**Table 1.** Various Link Detection Systems considered for testing

| S.No | SLD Systems |
|------|-------------|
| 1 | Tf |
| 2 | tf+idf |
| 3 | tf+Cnet |
| 4 | tf+50*Cnet |
| 5 | tf+df |
| 6 | tf+idf+50*Cnet |
| 7 | tf+idf+Cnet |
| 8 | tf+idf+df |
| 9 | tf+df+50*Cnet |
| 10 | tf+df+Cnet |
| 11 | tf+idf+df+50*Cnet |
| 12 | tf+idf+df+Cnet |
| 13 | tf*idf |
| 14 | tf*idf*df |

Various factors of social cohesion are considered in addition to the base factor sense of belonging, which is represented using *term frequency (tf)*. Then one by one, other factors are added with different weights to evaluate their contribution in the system performance. Systems 1-12 consider linear combination of these factors. Of these, systems 1, 2, 3, 5, 7, 8, 10 and 12 belong to one group in the sense that in these systems all the factors considered have contributed equally, if they are present. On the other hand, in systems 4,6,9 and 11 cnet factor has been assigned a weightage of 50 to increase the importance of this factor. The rest of the two systems, system 13 and 14 assign weight to the terms according to generative values.

System1 is the simple system with query expansion model. We have retrieved the relevant document from the collection using improved IR. To create the model, terms in the relevant documents are assigned weight according to the equation 5. In system2 (tf+idf), idf is included for sense of moral, with term frequency (tf). Here tf and idf are considered without any weighting factor. System 3 (tf+Cnet) includes Cnet for network cohesion with term frequency (tf). Here tf and Cnet are considered without any weighting factor. In System 5 (tf+df), document frequency (df) for goal consensus is added with term frequency (tf). In System 7 (tf+idf+Cnet), apart from network cohesion cnet, we have idf, which is included for sense of moral. System 8 (tf+idf+df) considers tf, idf and df, to verify the effect of inclusion of idf with tf and df. System 10 (tf+df+Cnet) considers tf, df and cnet, to verify the effect of inclusion of cnet with tf and df. In System 12 (tf+idf +df+Cnet) considers tf, df, idf and cnet, to verify the effect of inclusion of cnet and idf with tf and df.

Systems 4,6,9 and 11 show the effect of weighted Cnet. As Cnet value is very small compared to the term frequency, we increase this value by multiplying a constant $c$. Here we have empirically fixed the value of c to be 50. Systems 3,7,10 and 12 consider Cnet without weight value.

In System 13 (tf*idf) assigns weight according to generative value of tf and idf. This system is constructed to evaluate the generative effect of tf and idf. In System 14 (tf*idf*df) assigns weight according to generative value of tf, idf and df.

Table 2 shows the F1-measure, Accuracy and Cost of the various systems discussed above. Fig. 2, 3 and 4 show comparison of the various systems with respect to F1-measure, Accuracy and Cost.

**Table 2.** F1-Measure of Various Link Detection Systems

| Systems | Cost | Improv-ement | F1-Measure | Improv-ement | Accuracy | Improv-ement |
|---|---|---|---|---|---|---|
| ltfdf | 0.116747 | -0.02 | 0.751696 | 2.42% | 0.889359 | 1.57% |
| ltfdfnw | 0.116747 | -0.02 | 0.751696 | 2.42% | 0.889359 | 1.57% |
| tfdf50nw | 0.117447 | -0.02 | 0.740638 | 1.31% | 0.886941 | 1.33% |
| tfidfdf | 0.124241 | -0.013 | 0.737838 | 1.03% | 0.882709 | 0.91% |
| ltfidfdf50nw | 0.130504 | -0.007 | 0.736842 | 0.93% | 0.879081 | 0.54% |
| ltfidfdf | 0.136056 | -0.001 | 0.73385 | 0.63% | 0.875453 | 0.18% |
| ltfidfdfnw | 0.136056 | -0.001 | 0.73385 | 0.63% | 0.875453 | 0.18% |
| ltf50nw | 0.131328 | -0.006 | 0.732804 | 0.53% | 0.877872 | 0.42% |
| ltfnw | 0.136406 | -8E-04 | 0.72846 | 0.09% | 0.874244 | 0.06% |
| tf | 0.137173 | 4E-07 | 0.72751 | 0.00% | 0.87364 | 0.00% |
| tfidf | 0.141721 | 0.0045 | 0.724936 | -0.26% | 0.870617 | -0.30% |
| ltfidf50nw | 0.12098 | -0.016 | 0.724187 | -0.33% | 0.882104 | 0.85% |
| ltfidfnw | 0.122278 | -0.015 | 0.721358 | -0.62% | 0.880895 | 0.73% |
| ltfidf | 0.123046 | -0.014 | 0.720339 | -0.72% | 0.88029 | 0.67% |

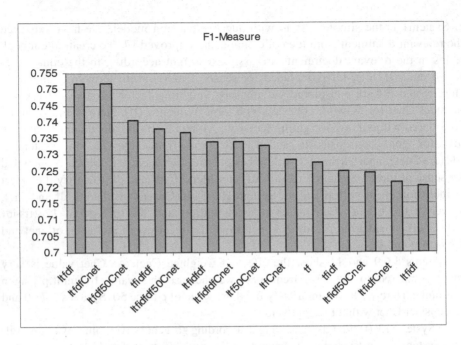

**Fig. 2.** F1-Measure of various Link Detection Systems

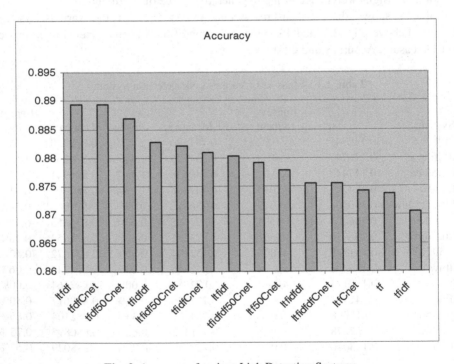

**Fig. 3.** Accuracy of various Link Detection Systems

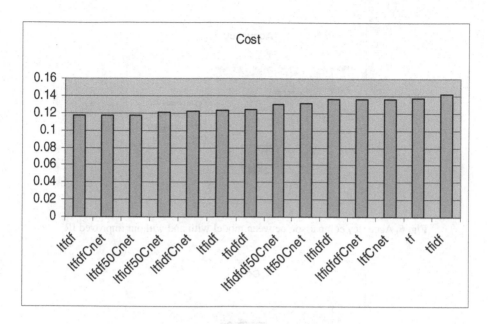

**Fig. 4.** Cost of various Link Detection Systems

As is evident from Fig. 2-4, System5 is a linear combination of tf-df and shows the best performance compared to all the other systems. System 5 shows 6% increase in F1-measure, 3% increase in accuracy and 0.03724 reductions in cost, when compared to the base system that uses cosine similarity for comparing the two documents without any query expansion technique. This system is able to achieve good true positive at the same time maintaining less false positive and this leads to excellent system performance. System 9 (Tf+df+Cnet), shows same performance as system 5. As the Cnet value is very less, it didn't contribute to the performance of the system.

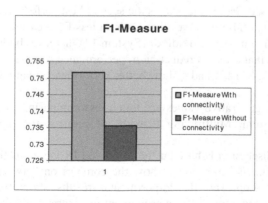

**Fig. 5.** F1-Measure comparison between model with and without improved IR

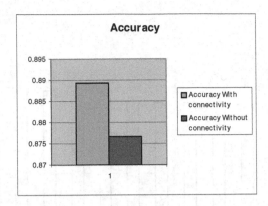

**Fig. 6.** Accuracy comparison between model with and without improved IR

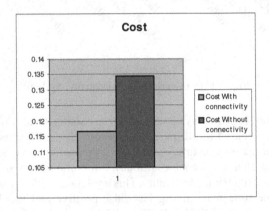

**Fig. 7.** Cost comparison between model with and without improved IR

System 10 with raised Cnet value, shows the second best performance. It reduces both the true positives and false positives that leads to less F1-measure when compared to System 5. Generative model of tf*idf*df (System 14) increases both the true positives and false positives that causes a reduction in performance when compared to system 9 and 10. Systems 11, 8, 12, 3 and 4 show better performance than the base system that uses only tf.

Performance of generative values are much less comparing to most of the given link detection system. Multiplying tf with idf reduces the performance of the system.

Next point of discussion is how far the improved IR increases the performance of the cohesion model. Fig. 5, 6 and 7 show the comparison between cohesion model with and without improved IR. Experimental results show that there is 1.5% improvement in F1-measure, 1.2% improvement in accuracy and the cost has reduced from 0.135 to 0.115 by using improved information retrieval system.

# 5 Conclusions and Enhancements

Systems with query expansion technique use improved retrieval system for retrieving relevant documents by using the intra cluster similarity. As the relevant documents are the basis for preparing model for the given input documents, it is important to select high quality relevant documents and reduce the number of irrelevant documents. Social cohesion is used as the basis for assigning weight in Cohesion-Model. We have taken four factors of social cohesion and constructed number of link detection system with various combinations of the basic factors sense of belonging (tf), sense of moral, goal consensus (df) and network cohesion (cnet). Most of the models constructed with various combination of social cohesion factor performed better than base cosine similarity method.

Best performance is achieved by linear combination of tf-df. It shows 6% increase in F1-measure, 3% increase in accuracy and 0.034 reductions in cost, when compared with the base system that use cosine similarity to compare the document pairs. Inclusion of df with tf work better than linear combination of tf-cnet. Inclusion of Cnet with tf, works better than simple tf by reducing the false positives. However the combined effect of tf-df-cnet does not produce the best performance, as its true positives are less. Inclusion of idf increases the false positive, which degrades the system performance compared to system without idf. Experimental results show that the weight given to Cnet affected adversely the performance of link detection system in the current set up. Performance of the link detection system with different weights has to be explored to verify the ultimate effect of Cnet on such systems.

We strongly feel the cohesion model can further be improved by modifying the ways the various factors are measured. As shown in this research work, improvement in IR system will definitely improve the over all link detection.

# References

1. Allan, J.: Introduction to Topic Detection and Tracking, Topic Detection and Tracking: Event-based Information Organization, pp. 1–16. Kluwer Academic Publishers, Dordrecht (2002)
2. Allan, J., Carbonell, J., Doddington, G., Yamron, J., Yang, Y.: Topic detection and tracking pilot study: Final report. In: Proceedings of the DARPA Broadcast News Transcription and Understanding Workshop, pp. 194–218. Morgan Kaufmann publishers, San Francisco (1998)
3. Topic Detection and Tracking (TDT) Project.homepage: http://www.nist.gov/ speech/ tests/tdt/
4. Lavrenko, V.: A Generative Theory of Relevance, PhD Thesis, University Of Massachusetts Amherst (September 2004)
5. Chen, F., Farahat, A., Brants, T.: Multiple Similarity Measures and Source-Pair Information in Story Link Detection. In: Proceedings of HLT-NAACL, pp. 313–320 (2004)
6. Lavrenko, V., Allan, J., DeGuzman, E., LaFlamme, D., Pollard, V., Thomas, S.: Relevance models for topic detection and tracking. In: Proceedings of Human Language Technologies Conference, HLT, pp. 104–110 (2002)

7. Yang, Y., Ault, T., Pierce, T., Lattimer, C.W.: Improving text categorization methods for event tracking. In: SIGIR'00. Proceedings of the 23rd Annual international ACM SIGIR Conference on Research and Development in information Retrieval, Athens, Greece, July 24-28, 2000, pp. 65–72. ACM Press, New York (2000)
8. Farahat, A., Chen, F., Brants, T.: Optimizing Story Link Detection is not Equivalent to Optimizing New Event Detection. In: Dignum, F.P.M. (ed.) ACL 2003. LNCS (LNAI), vol. 2922, pp. 232–239. Springer, Heidelberg (2004)
9. Nallapati, R., Allan, J.: Capturing Term Dependencies using a Language Model based on Sentence Trees. In: CIKM'02, McLean, Virginia (November 4-9, 2002)
10. Lakshmi, K., Mukherjee, S.: An Improved Feature Selection using Maximized Signal to Noise Ratio Technique for TC. In: ITNG 2006. Proceedings of Information Technology: New Generations, pp. 541–546 (April 2006)
11. Allan, J., Lavrenko, V., Frey, D., Khandelwal, V.: UMass at TDT 2000. In: Proceedings of the Topic Detection and Tracking Workshop (2000)
12. Figueroa, M., Lawrence Kincaid, D., Rani, M., Lewis, G. (eds.): Communication for Social Change: An Integrated Model for Measuring the Process and Its Outcomes. The Rockefeller Foundation New York (2002)
13. Raghavan, H., Allan, J.: Using soundex codes for indexing names in ASR documents. In: Proceedings of the HLT NAACL Workshop on Interdisciplinary Approaches to Speech Indexing and Retrieval (2004)
14. Lakshmi, K., Mukherjee, S.: Using Cohesion-Model for Story Link Detection System. IJCSNS International Journal of Computer Science and Network Security 7(3), 59–66 (2007)

# Improving a State-of-the-Art Named Entity Recognition System Using the World Wide Web

Richárd Farkas [1], György Szarvas [1,2], and Róbert Ormándi [2]

[1] University of Szeged, Department of Informatics
6721 Szeged, Hungary
[2] Research Group on Artificial Intelligence
of the Hungarian Academy of Sciences and University of Szeged
6721 Szeged, Hungary
rfarkas,szarvas@inf.u-szeged.hu
ormandi.robert@stud.u-szeged.hu

**Abstract.** The development of highly accurate Named Entity Recognition (NER) systems can be beneficial to a wide range of Human Language Technology applications. In this paper we introduce three heuristics that exploit a variety of knowledge sources (the World Wide Web, Wikipedia and WordNet) and are capable of improving further a state-of-the-art multilingual and domain independent NER system. Moreover we describe our investigations on entity recognition in simulated speech-to-text output. Our web-based heuristics attained a slight improvement over the best results published on a standard NER task, and proved to be particularly effective in the speech-to-text scenario.

**Keywords:** World Wide Web, web based techniques, named entity recognition, machine learning.

## 1  Introduction

The identification and classification of Named Entities (NE) in plain text is of key importance in numerous natural language processing applications. In Information Extraction systems NEs generally carry important information about the text itself, and thus are targets for extraction. In machine translation, Named Entities and other sorts of words have to be handled in a different way due to the specific translation rules that apply to them.

We applied the NE Recognition and Classification (NER) system described in [10] which was designed for English language, and also worked with minor changes for Hungarian and domains different from newswire texts (medical records) [11]. To our best knowledge, this system gives the best results on the standard CoNLL-2003 task.

In this paper we investigate three heuristics that utilize online information (the World Wide Web and the Wikipedia online encyclopedia) to improve the performance of this state-of-the-art Named Entity Classification system.

As we plan to integrate our entity recognizer and classifier module into a multi-modal Information Extraction system, we tested the NER system in an artificial

P. Perner (Ed.): ICDM 2007, LNAI 4597, pp. 163–172, 2007.
© Springer-Verlag Berlin Heidelberg 2007

scenario simulating speech-to-text output. As regards the problem of NER on the output of a general purpose speech-to-text application, it assumes that neither capitalization nor punctuation marks are available in the text. These restrictions make entity recognition a more challenging task. Experiments showed that the NER problem can be handled in such circumstances, without a serious loss of classification performance, while our web-based heuristics are particularly useful here.

In this paper we performed experiments for the English newswire NER task only but our heuristics should be portable across languages as long as the appropriate knowledge sources are available for the target language, with sufficient coverage[1].

## 1.1 Related Work

The NER task was introduced during the nineties as a part of the shared tasks in the Message Understanding Conferences (MUC) [4]. The goal of these conferences was the recognition of proper nouns (*person*, *organization*, *location* names), and other phrases denoting dates, time intervals, and measures in texts from English newspaper articles. The best systems [1] following the MUC task definition achieved outstanding accuracies (nearly 95% F measure).

Later, as a part of the Computational Natural Language Learning (CoNLL) conferences [12], a shared task dealt with the development of systems like this that work for multiple languages and were able to correctly identify *person*, *organization* and *location* names, along with other proper nouns treated as *miscellaneous* entities.

There are some important differences between the CoNLL style task definition and the MUC approach that made NER a much harder problem. The most important is that CoNNL considers only whole phrases classified correctly (which is more suitable for real world applications). The F measure of the best performing systems [7] dropped below 89% for English.

There are several papers in the literature that investigate the usability of online resources for various NE-related tasks. The available systems seek to collect lists of Named Entities belonging to pre-specified classes from the WWW [5][6] or use online information for Named Entity Disambiguation [2], which differ from the problem addressed in this paper. We found no articles on using Web-searches to improve a NER system.

## 1.2 Structure of the Paper

In the following section we will introduce the NER problem in general, along with the details of the CONLL-2003 English task and the evaluation methodology. We also discuss the learning methods and other main characteristics of the NER system we applied. In section 3 we describe our web-based heuristics designed to improve the classification performance of a state-of-the-art NER system, followed by the description of our experiments on artificial speech-to-text data (Section 4). Experimental results are summarized in the last section along with some concluding remarks.

---

[1] German, the language with the second largest Wiki encyclopedia has one third entries compared to English.

## 2 Description of the NER System Applied

In this section we introduce the domain- and language independent NER system we used for our experiments. An NER system in English was trained and tested on a sub-corpus of the Reuters Corpus[2] (the CoNLL 2003 shared task database), consisting of newswire articles from 1996 provided by Reuters Inc. The data is available free of charge for research purposes and contains texts from diverse domains ranging from sports news to politics and the economy. The best result published in the CoNLL 2003 conference was an F measure of 88.76% obtained from the best individual model [7].

### 2.1 Evaluation Methodology

To make our results easier to compare with those given in the literature, we employed the same evaluation script that was used during the CoNLL conference shared tasks for entity recognition. This script calculates Precision, Recall and $F_{\beta=1}$[3] value scores by analyzing the text at the phrase level. This way evaluation is very strict as it can penalize single mistakes in longer entity phrases doubly.

It is worth mentioning that this kind of evaluation places a burden on the learning algorithms as they usually optimize their models based on a different accuracy measure. Fitting this evaluation into the learning phase is not straightforward because of some undesired properties of the formula that can adversely affect the optimization process.

### 2.2 Complex NER Model

The NER system we use here treats the NER problem as the classification of separate tokens. Following Szarvas et al. [10], we apply decision tree classifiers (with boosting). This way our model is fast to train and evaluate, and incorporates a very

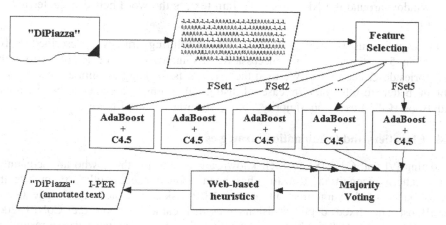

**Fig. 1.** The structure of our NER system

---

[2] http://www.reuters.com/researchandstandards/
[3] In this paper we always mean $F_{\beta=1}$ under F measure.

rich feature set (described in detail in [10]). The model also takes into account the relationship between consecutive words as well through a window with appropriate window size. The rich feature set enables to split the set, build models on each subset and then recombine their results. Figure 1 sketches the structure of the complex model.

## 2.3 Feature Set

**Initial features.** We employed a very rich feature set for our word-level classification model, describing the characteristics of the word itself along with its actual context (a moving window of size four). Our features fell into the following major categories:

- gazetteers of *unambiguous NEs* from the train data: we used the NE phrases which occur more than five in the train texts and got the same label more than 90 percent of the cases,
- *dictionaries* of first names, company types, sport teams, denominators of locations (mountains, city) and so on: we collected 12 English specific lists from the Internet,
- *orthographical features*: capitalization, word length, common bit information about the word form (contains a digit or not, has uppercase character inside the word, regular expressions and so on). We collected the most characteristic character level bi/trigrams from the train texts assigned to each NE class,
- *frequency information*: frequency of the token, the ratio of the token's capitalized and lowercase occurrences, the ratio of capitalized and sentence beginning frequencies of the token,
- *phrasal information*: chunk codes and forecasted class of few preceding words (we used online evaluation),
- *contextual information*: POS codes, sentence position, document zone (title or body), topic code, trigger words (the most frequent and unambiguous tokens in a window around the NEs) from the train text, is the word between quotes and so on.

In our experiments we used a similar feature set splitting strategy as described in [10] to obtain 5 different (but not necessarily disjunctive) sets of features from the categories described above. We used these five sets for bagging similar classifiers to obtain better results than in case of using all features together. The 5 similar AdaBoost+C4.5 boxes and Majority Voting illustrates this in Figure 1.

## 2.4 Classifiers and Combination Strategies

Boosting [9] and C4.5 [8] are well known algorithms for those who are acquainted with pattern recognition. Boosting has been applied successfully to improve the performance of decision trees in several NLP tasks. A system that made use of AdaBoost and fixed depth decision trees [3] came first on the CoNLL-2002 conference shared task for Dutch and Spanish, but gave somewhat worse results for English and German (it was ranked fifth, and had an F measure of 85.0% for English) in 2003.

As the results of [10] show, the combination of AdaBoost and C4.5 can bring some improvement in classification accuracy and preserves the superiority of decision tree learning in term of CPU time used for training and evaluating a model. In our experiments we used the implementations available in the WEKA [13] library, an open-source data mining software written in Java.

**Combination of classifiers.** There are several well known meta-learning algorithms in the literature that can lead to a 'better' model (in terms of classification accuracy) than those serving as a basis for it, or can significantly decrease the CPU time of the learning phase without loss of accuracy. The decision function used to integrate the five hypotheses (learnt on different subsets of features) was the following: *if any three of the five learners' outputs coincided we accepted it as a joint prediction, with a forecasted 'O' label referring to a non-named entity class otherwise.* This cautious voting scheme is beneficial to system performance as a high rate of disagreement often means a poor prediction rate. For a CoNLL type evaluation it is better to make such mistakes that classifies an NE as non-named entity than to place an NE in a wrong entity class (the latter detrimentally affects precision and recall, while the former only affects the recall of the system).

Here we used the same voting strategy for the baseline system, and tested other alternative voting schemes that exploit online information to assign NE labels in case of disagreement of the learnt models. This will be discussed in detail in the next section.

# 3   WWW Based Improvement of the NER System

Using online knowledge sources in Human Language Technology (HLT) and Data Mining problems has been an emerging field of research in the past few years. This trend is boosted by several special and interesting characteristics of the World Wide Web. First of all, it provides a practically limitless source of (unlabeled) data to exploit, and, more important it can bring some dynamism to applications. As online data changes and rapidly expands with time, a system can remain up-to-date and extending its knowledge without the need of fine tuning, or any human intervention (like retraining on up-to-date data for example). These features make the Web a very useful source of knowledge for HLT applications as well. On the other hand, the usage of WWW is a new challenge to overcome for language processing applications as data cannot be accessed directly (only via a search engine) and might prove to be time consuming as task-specific pre-processing and collection of data is not feasible.

## 3.1   Fine-Tuning Phrase Boundaries

A significant part of system errors in NER taggers is caused by the erroneous identification of the beginning (or end) of a longer phrase. Token-level classifiers (like the one we applied here) are especially prone to this as they classify each token of a phrase separately.

We considered a tagged entity as a candidate long-phrase NE if it was followed or preceded by a non-tagged uppercase word, or one/two stop words and an uppercase word. The underlying hypothesis of this heuristic is that if the boundaries were marked correctly and the surrounding words are not part of the entity, then the number of web-search results for the longer query should be significantly lower (the NE is followed by the particular word in just certain contexts). But in the case of a dislocated phrase boundary, the number of search results for the extended form must be comparable to the results for the shorter phrase (over 0.1%[4] of it). This means that every time when we found a tagged phrase that received more than 0.1% web query hits in an extended form, we extended the phrase with its neighboring word (or words). This decision function was fine tuned and found to be optimal on the training and development sets of the CoNLL task; the following evaluations have been performed on the CoNLL evaluation set.

This web-based post-processing heuristic improved the performance of the applied NER model from 89.02% to 89.15% F measure. The relatively small improvement is due to the classification error of some extended phrases (this heuristic extended the phrase boundaries precisely in several cases where the class label was assigned incorrectly by the classifier, and those left the system performance unchanged).

### 3.2 Using the Most Frequent Role in Uncertain Cases

Some examples are easier to classify for a given model than others. In our applied NER system, the final decision was obtained by applying the majority voting procedure of 5 classifiers (which were all trained on different sets of features). A simple way of interpreting the uncertainty of a decision is to measure the level of disagreement among the individual models. We considered a token as a difficult or uncertain example if no more than 2 models gave coinciding decisions (we should mention here that each models chose the most probable of 5 different possible answers, so this indeed meant a high level of uncertainty).

Our hypothesis here was that the most frequent role of a named entity can be statistically useful information. Thus we did the following: if the system was unable to decide the class label of a phrase (it could not find evidence in the context of the certain phrase) then we mined the most frequent usage of the corresponding NE using the WWW and took that as prediction.

The most frequent role searching method we applied here was inspired by the category extraction methods of Etzioni et al. [6]. This approach works by invoking several special Google queries in order to find such noun phrases following or preceding the pattern that is a category name for a particular class. The following queries were used to obtain category names from web search results:

| |
|---|
| NP such as NE |
| NP including NE |
| NP especially NE |
| NE is a NP |
| NE is the NP |
| NE and other NP |
| NE or other NP |

---

[4] We sought to keep the evaluation set blind. All the heuristics were fine-tuned on CoNLL-2003 developement set.

**Category names from the training data.** We used the lists of unambiguous NEs collected from the training data to acquire common NE category names. We sent Google queries for NEs in the training data and all the patterns shown above. The heads of the corresponding NPs were extracted from the snippets of the best ten Google responses.

We found 173 reliable category names by performing a limited number of Google queries. Using these category lists as a disambiguator (we assigned the class sharing the most words in common with those extracted for the given NE) when the NER system was unable to give a reliable prediction was beneficial to overall system performance. The system F Measure improved from 89.15% to 89.28%. We should mention here that the baseline NER system labeled these examples as non-entities, whose prediction was incorrect in the majority of the cases.

**Enriching category lists using WordNet.** We enlisted the help of a linguist expert to determine the WordNet synset corresponding to each category name we found and give its most common substituting synset (the one highest in hypo/hypernym hierarchy) that was still usable as a category name for the particular NE class. Using these WordNet synsets we extended our category lists (to a size of 19537) with all literals that appear in their hyponym subtree (with sense #1). This additional knowledge further improved the F measure of the NER system to 89.35%.

## 4   Experiments on Speech-to-Text Data

Named Entity Recognition on the output of a speech-to-text system has to handle the problem of several missing features (like capitalization) that are particularly useful for entity recognition.

We used the same data as for the experiments described above, but modified the text so it looked as if it had been obtained from a speech-to-text system. First we converted all tokens to lowercase, thus the feature that is undoubtedly the most important for NER became unavailable. Second, we removed all punctuation marks from the original corpus (they do not appear explicitly in the audio stream, only in the accent hence it is doubtful that any punctuation can be retrieved efficiently). This means we assumed that all word forms were recognized correctly.

In the majority of cases, consecutive Named Entities either follow each other with a separating punctuation mark (enumerations), or belong to different classes. In the first case, a non-labeled token separates the two phrases, while in the second case the different class labels identify the boundaries. Rarely do two or more NEs of the same type appear consecutively in a sentence. In such cases the phrasal boundaries must be marked with a tag ('B-' instead of the common 'I-' prefix). We changed 'I-' tags to 'B-' where it was necessary in the simulated speech-to-text data to retain the correct phrase boundaries. This conversion resulted in over ten times more consecutive NEs (those separated with 'B-' tag), and hence the separation of such phrases became no longer negligible.[5]

We should add here that this simulation of the output of a speech-to-text system seemed obvious for two reasons. First, we wanted to test how a NER system behaves in significantly different circumstances, not a speech-to-text system itself. Second, by doing this we could avoid the need for a NE-labeled real speech database and also have better grounds for comparison between written text and speech-to-text output as we used a standard database. The performance of the baseline NER system on this converted text decreased to 81.1% $F_{\beta=1}$. Even though this simplification does not take into account that real speech-to-text data would certainly contain word errors, it fits to our purposes well (it is capable of demonstrating the usability of online knowledge sources to improve NER in speech-to-text data).

## 4.1 Identifying Consecutive NEs

As we stated above 'B-' tags are even more common in texts obtained from a speech-to-text system due to the absence of punctuation marks. We exploited the encyclopedic knowledge of Wikipedia to enable our system to distinguish between long phrases and consecutive entities.

**The B-tag heuristic.** We queried the Wikipedia site for all entities that had two or more tokens. If we found an article sharing the same title as the whole query, or the majority of the occurrences of the phrase in the Google snippets occurred without punctuation marks inside, we treated the query phrase as a single entity. If a punctuation mark was inside the phrase in the majority of the cases, we separated the phrase at the position of the punctuation mark. This method allowed us to separate phrases like 'Golan Heights | Israel'. If there was no hit for the query in the Wikipedia, but we were able to find a specific article for two or more parts of the query, we put phrase boundaries following the Wiki entries. This way we identified successfully phrases like 'Taleban | MiG-19' and many enumerations that lacked the separating commas due to the removal of punctuation marks from the data. We made use of a first names list here containing 3217 first names which allowed us to avoid the erroneous separation of full names (First name, Last name pairs). Of course a more comprehensive first names list would be beneficial. Our system suffered from the lack of Romanian or Arabic First names. This heuristic improved the overall performance of the NER tagger on speech-to-text data by a significant 1.42% (8,1% error reduction). The heuristic itself managed to recognize the 'B-' tags with an $F_{\beta=1}$-measure of 75.19% (precision 71.7%; recall 79.03%).

We should also mention here that some of the 'B-' phrases in the CoNLL database are arguably consecutive NEs, but are actually single entities (e.g. 'English Moslems' or 'City State' phrases like 'Rochester NY'). Our heuristic does not divide up such cases as they usually seem to be single NEs for the online encyclopedia – and they

---

[5] Most of the best performing NER systems deliberately ignore the separation of consecutive phrases as they are too sparse to handle efficiently in written text data. This problem has no significant effect on performance either (there are only 20 'B-' tokens out of 50,000 in the CoNLL-2003 test dataset).

can be treated as single entities as well in an Information Extraction system. Without these cases the recall of our system would have been even higher.

## 5  Summary of the Results

A brief summary of the heuristic improvements achieved on the various systems can be seen in Table 1. Here we show the system described in Section 2 (and in [10] in more details), **Base NER**; its voting with the 2 best CoNLL systems, **Voting**; the system described in Section 2 on the speech-to-text data, **Speech-to-text**. The boundary heuristic is not applicable in the speech-to-text task, because it is dependant on the capitalization of the context. The **Voting** column adds a further voting level to the system (not showed in Figure 1.), it is obtained by the majority voting the best performing CoNLL systems and **Base NER**. This hybrid method was also discussed in [10]; we show here that the improvement of our web based heuristics carries over to this hybrid model also.

**Table 1.** Results of the three heuristics, $F_{\beta=1}$

|                 | Base NER | Voting  | Speech-to-text |
|-----------------|----------|---------|----------------|
| Baseline        | 89.02%   | 91.40%  | 81.10%         |
| B-tag           | 89.02%   | 91.40%  | 82.52%         |
| Boundary id.    | 89.15%   | 91.51%  | n/a            |
| Most freq. role | 89.35%   | 91.67%  | 82.64%         |

## 6  Conclusion

The aim of this paper was to show the potentials of the WWW in HLT problems like named entity recognition. Our heuristics are based on the assumption that, even though the World Wide Web contains much useless and incorrect information, regarding our simple features the correct usage of language dominates over misspellings and other sorts of noise. Our experiments confirmed this hypothesis. We showed experimentally that these heuristics could further improve a state-of-the-art NER system on the standard text processing task and they proved to be particularly useful on a more challenging simulated speech-to-text task. We believe that our results are valuable due to two main reasons: first, we managed to give improvements on a top performing model for the task of NER that is of great importance even if the improvement is slight. Second, we showed that the WWW can be exploited with significant success to overcome the drawback caused by the lack of certain information that is extremely important and characteristic for certain HLT applications (like the absence of punctuation or capitalization is NER).

**Acknowledgments.** We would like to thank the anonymous reviewers for their valuable comments.

# References

1. Bikel, D.M., Schwartz, R.L., Weischedel, R.M.: An algorithm that learns what's in a name. Machine Learning 34(1-3), 211–231 (1999)
2. Bunescu, R., Paşca, M.: Using Encyclopedic Knowledge for Named Entity Disambiguation. In: Proceedings of 11th Conference of the European Chapter of the Association for Computational Linguistics (2006)
3. Carreras, X., Márques, L., Padró, L.: Named Entity Extraction using AdaBoost Proceedings of CoNLL-2002, Taipei, Taiwan, pp. 167–170 (2002)
4. Chinchor, N.: MUC-7 Named Entity Task Definition. In: Proceedings of Seventh MUC (1998)
5. Cimiano, P., Handschuh, S., Staab, S.: Towards the self-annotating web. In: Proceedings of the 13th WWW Conference (2004)
6. Etzioni, O., Cafarella, M., Downey, D., Popescu, A.-M., Shaked, T., Soderland, S., Weld, D.S., Yates, A.: Unsupervised named-entity extraction from the web: an experimental study. Artificial Intelligence 165(1), 91–134 (2005)
7. Florian, R., Ittycheriah, A., Jing, H., Zhang, T.: Named Entity Recognition through Classifier Combination. In: Proceedings of CoNLL-2003 (2003)
8. Quinlan, R.: C4.5: Programs for machine learning. Morgan Kaufmann, San Francisco (1993)
9. Shapire, R.E.: The Strength of Weak Learnability. Machine Learnings 5, 197–227 (1990)
10. Szarvas, Gy., Farkas, R., Kocsor, A.: A multilingual named entity recognition system using boosting and c4.5 decision tree learning algorithms. In: Todorovski, L., Lavrač, N., Jantke, K.P. (eds.) DS 2006. LNCS (LNAI), vol. 4265, pp. 267–278. Springer, Heidelberg (2006)
11. Szarvas, G., Farkas, R., Iván, S., Kocsor, A., Busa-Fekete, R.: An iterative method for the de-identification of structured medical text. Workshop on Challenges in Natural Language Processing for Clinical Data (2006)
12. Tjong Kim Sang, E.F., De Meulder, F.: Introduction to the CoNLL-2003 Shared Task: Language-Independent Named Entity Recognition. In: Proceedings of CoNLL-2003 (2003)
13. Witten, I.H., Frank, E.: Data Mining: Practical Machine Learning Tools and Techniques, 2nd edn. Morgan Kaufmann Series in Data Management Systems. Morgan Kaufmann, San Francisco (2005)

# ISOR-2: A Case-Based Reasoning System to Explain Exceptional Dialysis Patients

Olga Vorobieva[1], Alexander Rumyantsev[2], and Rainer Schmidt[1]

[1] Institute for Medical Informatics and Biometry, University of Rostock, Germany
rainer.schmidt@medizin.uni-rostock.de
[2] Pavlov State Medical University, St.Petersburg, Russia

**Abstract.** In medicine many exceptions occur. In medical practice and in knowledge-based systems too, it is necessary to consider them and to deal with them appropriately. In medical studies and in research, exceptions shall be explained. We present a system that helps to explain cases that do not fit into a theoretical hypothesis. Our starting points are situations where neither a well-developed theory nor reliable knowledge nor a priori a proper case base is available. So, instead of reliable theoretical knowledge and intelligent experience, we have just some theoretical hypothesis and a set of measurements.

In this paper, we propose to combine CBR with a statistical model. We use CBR to explain those cases that do not fit the model. The case base has to be set up incrementally, it contains the exceptional cases, and their explanations are the solutions, which can be used to help to explain further exceptional cases.

## 1 Introduction

In medicine many exceptions occur. In medical practice and in knowledge-based systems too, these exceptions have to be considered and have to be dealt with appropriately. In ISOR-1, we demonstrated advantages of case-based reasoning (CBR) in situations where a theoretically approved medical decision does not produce the desired and usually expected results [1, 2].

In medical studies and in research, exceptions shall be explained. The present research is a logical continuation of our previous work. It is still the same system and the same structure of dialogues, but now ISOR-2 deals with situations where neither a well-developed theory nor reliable knowledge nor a proper case base is available. So, instead of reliable theoretical knowledge and intelligent experience, we now have just some theoretical hypothesis and a set of measurements. In such situations the usual question is, how do measured data fit to theoretical hypotheses. To statistically confirm a hypothesis it is necessary, that the majority of cases fit the hypothesis. Mathematical statistics determines the exact quantity of necessary confirmation [3]. However, usually a few cases do not satisfy the hypothesis. We examine these cases to find out why they do not satisfy the hypothesis. ISOR-2 offers a dialogue to guide the search for possible reasons in all components of the data system. The exceptional cases belong to the case base. This approach is justified by a certain mistrust of

P. Perner (Ed.): ICDM 2007, LNAI 4597, pp. 173–183, 2007.

statistical models by doctors, because modelling results are usually unspecific and "average oriented" [4], which means a lack of attention to individual "imperceptible" features of concrete patients.

The usual CBR assumption is that a case-base with complete solutions is available. Our approach starts in a situation where such a case-base is not available but has to be set up incrementally (figure 1). So, we must

1. Construct a model,
2. Point out the exceptions,
3. Find causes why the exceptional cases do not fit the model, and
4. Develop a case-base.

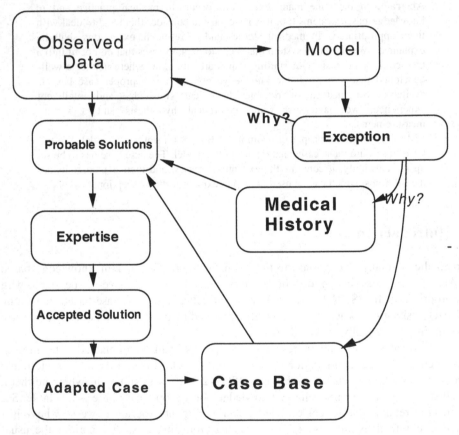

**Fig. 1.** ISOR-2's general program flow

So, we combine case-based reasoning (CBR) with a model, in this specific situation with a statistical one. The idea to combine CBR with other methods is not new. For example Care-Partner resorts to a multi-modal reasoning framework for the co-operation of CBR and Rule-based Reasoning (RBR) [5]. Another way of combining hybrid rule bases with CBR is discussed by Prentzas and Hatzilgeroudis

[6]. The combination of CBR and model-based reasoning is discussed in [7]. Statistical methods are used within CBR mainly for retrieval and retention (e.g. [8, 9]). Arshadi proposes a method that combines CBR with statistical methods like clustering and logistic regression [10].

## 1.1 Dialysis and Fitness

Hemodialysis means stress for a patient's organism and has significant adverse effects. Fitness is the most available and a relative cheap way of support. It is meant to improve a physiological condition of a patient and to compensate negative dialysis effects. One of the intended goals of this research is to convince the patients of the positive effects of fitness and to encourage them to make efforts and to go in for sports actively. This is important because dialysis patients usually feel sick, they are physically weak, and they do not want any additional physical load [11].

At our University clinic in St. Petersburg, a specially developed complex of physiotherapy exercises including simulators, walking, swimming etc. was offered to all dialysis patients but only some of them actively participated, whereas some others participated but were not really active. The purpose of this fitness offer was to improve the physical conditions of the patients and to increase the quality of their lives.

## 2   Incremental Development of an Explanation Model for Exceptional Dialysis Patients

For each patient a set of physiological parameters is measured. These parameters contain information about burned calories, maximal power achieved by the patient, his oxygen uptake, his oxygen pulse (volume of oxygen consumption per heart beat), lung ventilation and others. There are also biochemical parameters like haemoglobin and other laboratory measurements. More than 100 parameters were planned for every patient. But not all of them were really measured.

Parameters are supposed to be measured four times during the first year of participating in the fitness program. There is an initial measurement followed by a next one after three months, then after six months and finally after a year. Unfortunately, since some measurements did not happen, many data are missing. Therefore the records of the patients often contain different sets of measured parameters.

It is necessary to note that parameter values of dialysis patients essentially differ from those of non-dialysis patients, especially of healthy people, because dialysis interferes with the natural, physiological processes in an organism. In fact, for dialysis patients all physiological processes behave abnormally. Therefore, the correlation between parameters differs too.

For statistics, this means difficulties in applying statistical methods based on correlation and it limits the usage of a knowledge base developed for normal people. Non-homogeneity of observed data, many missing values, many parameters for a relatively small sample size, all this makes our data set practically impossible for usual statistical analysis.

Our data set is incomplete therefore we must find additional or substitutional information in other available data sources. They are data bases – the already existent Individual Base and the sequentially created Case Base and the medical expert as a special source of information.

## 2.1 Setting Up a Model

We start with a medical problem that has to be solved based on given data. In our example it is: "Does special fitness improve the physiological condition of dialysis patients?" More formally, we have to compare physical conditions of active and non-active patients. Patients are divided into two groups, depending on their activity, active patients and non-active ones.

According to our assumption, active patients should feel better after some months of fitness, whereas non-active ones should feel rather worse. We have to define the meaning of "feeling better" and "feeling worse" in our context. A medical expert selects appropriate factors from ISOR's menu. It contains the list of field names from the observed data base.

The expert selects the following main factors

- F1: O2PT - Oxygen pulse by training
- F2: MUO2T - Maximal Uptake of Oxygen by training
- F3: WorkJ – performed Work (Joules) during control training

Subsequently the "research time period" has to be determined. Initially, this period was planned to be twelve months, but after a while the patients tend to give up the fitness program. This means, the longer the time period, the more data are missing. Therefore, we had to make a compromise between time period and sample size. A period of six months was chosen.

The next question is whether the model shall be quantitative or qualitative? The observed data are mostly quantitative measurements. The selected factors are of quantitative nature too. On the other side, the goal of our research is to find out whether physical training improves or worsens the physical condition of the dialysis patients.

We do not have to compare one patient with another patient. Instead, we compare every patient with his own situation some months ago, namely just before the start of the fitness program. The success shall not be measured in absolute values, because the health statuses of patients are very different. Thus, even a modest improvement for one patient may be as important as a great improvement of another. Therefore, we simply classify the development in two categories: "better" and "worse". Since the usual tendency for dialysis patients is to worsen in time, we added those few patients where no changes could be observed to the category" better".

The three main factors are supposed to describe the changes of the physical conditions of the patients. The changes are assessed depending on the number of improved factors:

- Weak version of the model: at least one factor has improved
- Medium version of the model: at least two factors have improved
- Strong version of the model: all three factors have improved

The final step means to define the type of model. Popular statistical programs offer a large variety of statistical models. Some of them deal with categorical data. The easiest model is a 2x2 frequency table. Our "Better/ Worse" concept fits this simple model very well. So the 2x2 frequency table is accepted. The results are presented in table 1.

**Table 1.** Results of Fisher's Exact Test, performed with an interactive Web-program: http://www.matforsk.noIola/fisher.htm

| Improve-ment mode | Patient's physical condition | Active | Non-active | Fisher Exact p |
|---|---|---|---|---|
| Strong | Better | 28 | 2 | < 0.0001 |
| | Worse | 22 | 21 | |
| Medium | Better | 40 | 10 | < 0.005 |
| | Worse | 10 | 12 | |
| Weak | Better | 47 | 16 | < 0.02 |
| | Worse | 3 | 6 | |

According to our assumption after six months of active fitness the conditions of the patients should be better.

Statistical analysis shows a significant dependence between the patient's activity and improvement of their physical condition. Unfortunately, the most popular Pearson Chi-square test is not applicable here because of the small values "2" and "3" in table 1. But Fisher's exact test [3] can be used. In the three versions shown in table 1 a very strong significance can be observed. The smaller the value of p is, the more significant the dependency.

**Exceptions.** So, the performed Fisher test confirms the hypothesis that patients doing active fitness achieve better physical conditions than non-active ones. However, there are exceptions, namely active patients whose health conditions did not improve.

Exceptions should be explained. Explained exceptions build the case base. According to table 1, the stronger the model, the more exceptions can be observed and have to be explained. Every exception is associated with at least two problems. The first one is "Why did the patient's condition get worse?" Of course, "worse" is meant in terms of the chosen model. Since there may be some factors that are not included in the model but have changed positively, the second problem is "What has improved in the patient's condition?" To solve this problem we look for significant factors where the values improved.

In the following section we explain the set-up of a case base on the strongest model version.

## 2.2 Setting Up a Case Base

We intend to solve both problems (mentioned above) by means of CBR. So we begin to set up the case-base up sequentially. That means, as soon as an exception is explained, it is incorporated into the case-base and can be used to help explaining further exceptional cases. We chose a random order for the exceptional cases. In fact, we took them in alphabetical order.

The retrieval of already explained cases is performed by keywords. The main keywords are the usual ISOR ones, namely "problem code", "diagnosis", and "therapy".   In the situation of explaining exceptions for dialysis patients the instantiations of these keywords are "adverse effects of dialysis" (diagnosis), "fitness" (therapy), and two specific problem codes. Besides the main ISOR keywords additional problem specific ones are used. Here the additional key is the number of worsened factors. Further keywords are optional. They are just used when the case-base becomes bigger and retrieval is not simple any longer.

However, ISOR-2 does not only use the case-base as knowledge source but further sources are involved, namely the patient's individual base (his medical history) and observed data (partly gained by dialogue with medical experts). Since in the domain of kidney disease and dialysis the medical knowledge is very detailed and much investigated but still incomplete, it is unreasonable to attempt to create an adequate knowledge base. Therefore, a medical expert, observed data, and just a few rules serve as medical knowledge sources.

### 2.2.1  Expert Knowledge and Artificial Cases

Expert's knowledge can be used in many different ways. First we use it to acquire rules, second it can be used to select appropriate items from the list of retrieved solutions, to propose new solutions and last but not least – to create artificial cases.

Initially artificial cases are created by an expert, afterwards they can be used in the same way as real cases. They are created in the following situation. An expert points out a factor F as a possible solution for a query patient. Since many values are missing, it can happen that just for the query patient values of factor F are missing. The doctor's knowledge in this case can not be applied, but it is sensible to save it anyway. Principally there are two different ways to do this. The first one means to generate a correspondent rule and to insert it into ISOR-2's algorithms. Unfortunately, this is very complicated, especially to find an appropriate way for inserting such a rule. The alternative is to create an artificial case. Instead of a patient's name an artificial case number is generated. The other attributes are either inherited from the query case or declared as missing. The retrieval attributes are inherited. This can be done by a short dialogue (figure2) and ISOR-2's algorithms remain intact. Artificial cases can be treated in the same way as real cases, they can be revised, deleted, generalised etc.

### 2.2.2  Solving the Problem "Why Did Some Patients Conditions Became Worse?"

As results we obtain a set of solutions of different origin and different nature. There are three categories of solution: additional factor, model failure, and wrong data.

**Additional factor.** The most important and most frequent solution is the influence of an additional factor. Only three main factors are obviously not enough to describe all medical cases. Unfortunately, for different patients different additional factors are important. When ISOR-2 has discovered an additional factor as explanation for an exceptional case, the factor has to be confirmed by a medical expert before it can be accepted as a solution. One of these factors is Parathyroid Hormone (PTH). An increased PTH level sometimes can explain a worsened condition of a patient [11]. PTH is a significant factor, but unfortunately it was measured only for some patients.

Some exceptions can be explained by indirect indications. One of them is a very long time of dialysis (more than 60 months) before a patient began with the training program.

Another solution was a phosphorus blood level. We used the principle of artificial cases to introduce the factor phosphorus as a new solution. One patient's record contained many missing data. The retrieved solution meant high PTH, but PTH data in the current patient's record was missing too. The expert proposed an increased phosphorus level as a possible solution. Since data about phosphorus data was missing too, an artificial case was created, who inherited all retrieval attributes of the query case while the other attributes were recorded as missing. According to the expert high phosphorus can explain the solution. Therefore it is accepted as an artificial solution or a solution of an artificial case.

**Model failure.** We regard two types of model failures. One of them is deliberately neglected data. Some data had been neglected. As a compromise we just considered data of six months and further data of a patient might be important. In fact, three of the patients did not show an improvement in the considered six month but in the following six months. So, they were wrongly classified and should really belong to the "better" category. The second type of model failure is based on the fact that the two-category model was not precise enough. Some exceptions could be explained by a tiny and not really significant change in one of the main factors. Wrong data are usually due to a technical mistake or to not really proved data. For example, one patient was reported as actively participating in the fitness program but really was not.

### 2.2.3 Solving the Problem "What in the Patient's Condition Became Better?"
There are at least two criteria to select factors for the model. Firstly, a factor has to be significant, and secondly there must be enough patients for which this factor was measured at least for six months. So, some principally important factors were initially not taken into account because of missing data. The list of solutions includes these factors (figure 2): haemoglobin, maximal power (watt) achieved during control training. Oxygen pulse and oxygen uptake were measured in two different situations, namely during the training under loading and before training in a rest state. Therefore we have two pairs of factors: oxygen pulse in state of relax (O2PR) and during training (O2PT); maximal oxygen uptake in state of relax (MUO2R) and during training (MUO2T). Measurements made in a state of relax are more indicative and significant than those made during training. Unfortunately, most measurements were made during training. Only for some patients correspondent measurements in relax state exist. Therefore O2PT and MUO2T were accepted as main factors and were taken into the model. On the other side, O2PR and MUO2R serve as solutions for the current problem.

In the case base every patient is represented by a set of cases, every case represents a specific problem. This means that a patient is described from different points of view and accordingly different problem keywords are used for retrieval.

## 2.3 Illustration of ISOR-2's Program Flow

Figure 2 shows the main dialogue of ISOR-2 where the user at first sets up a model (steps one to four), subsequently gets the result and an analysis of the model (steps five to eight), and then attempts to find explanations for the exceptions (steps nine and ten). Finally the case base is updated (steps eleven and twelve). On the menu (figure 2) we have numbered the steps and explain them in detail.

At first the user has to set up a model. To do this he has to select a grouping variable. In this example CODACT was chosen. It stands for "activity code" and means that active and none active patients are to be compared. Provided alternatives are the sex and the beginning of the fitness program (within the first year of dialysis or later). In another menu the user can define further alternatives. Furthermore, the user has to select a model type (alternatives are "strong", "medium", and "weak"), the length of time that should be considered (3, 6 or 12 months), and main factors have to be selected. The list contains the factors from the observed database. In the example three factors are chosen: O2PT (oxygen pulse by training), MUO2T (maximal oxygen uptake by training), and WorkJ (work in joules during the test training). In the menu list, the first two factors have alternatives: "R" instead of "T", where "R" stands for state of rest.

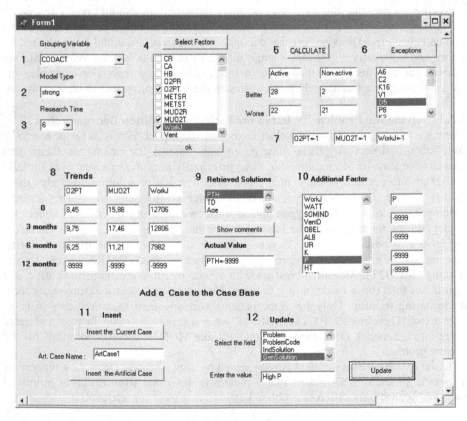

**Fig. 2.** ISOR-2's main menu

When the user has selected these items, the program calculated the table. "Better" and "worse" are meant in the sense of the chosen model, in the example of the strong model. ISOR-2 does not only calculate the table but additionally extracts the exceptional patients from the observed database. In the menu, the list of exceptions shows the code names of the patients. In the example patient "D5" is selected" and all further data belong to this patient. The goal is to find an explanation for the exceptional case "D5". In point seven of the menu it is shown that all selected factors worsened (-1), and in point eight the factor values according to different time intervals are depicted. All data for twelve months are missing (-9999).

The next step means creating an explanation for the selected patient "D5". From the case base ISOR-2 retrieves general solutions. The first retrieved one in this example, the PTH factor, denotes that the increased Parathyroid hormone blood level may explain the failure. Further theoretical information (e.g. normal values) about a selected item can be received by pressing the button "show comments". The PTH value of patient "D5" is missing (-9999). From menu point ten the expert user can select further probable solutions. In the example an increased phosphorus level (P) is suggested. Unfortunately, phosphorus data are missing too. However, the idea of an increased phosphorus level as a possible solution shall not be lost. So, an artificial case has to be generated.

The final step means inserting new cases into the case base. There are two sorts of cases, query cases and artificial cases. Query cases are stored records of real patients from the observed database. These records contain a lot of data but they are not structured. The problem and its solution transform them into cases and they get a place in the case base.

Artificial cases inherit the key attributes from the query cases (point seven in the menu). Other data may be declared as missing, by the update function data can be inserted. In the example of the menu, the generalised solution "High P" is inherited, it may be retrieved as a possible solution (point 9 of the menu) for future cases.

## 2.4  Example: A New Problem

Above we described just one of many problems that can arise based on the observed data set and that can be solved and analysed by the dialogue of figure 2. The question to be discussed is "Does it make sense to begin with the fitness program during the first year of dialysis?" The question arises, because the conditions of the patients are considered to be unstable during their first year of dialysis. So, the question is expressed in this way "When shall patients begin with the fitness program, earlier or later?" The term "Earlier" is defined as "during the first year of dialysis". The term "Later" means that they begin with their program after at least one year of dialysis. To answer this question we consider two groups of active patients, those who began their training within the first year of dialysis and those who began it later (table 2).

**Table 2.** Changed conditions for active patients

|        | Earlier | Later |
|--------|---------|-------|
| Better | 18      | 10    |
| Worse  | 6       | 16    |

According to Fisher's Exact Test dependence can be observed, with p < 0,05. However, it is not as it was initially expected. Since patients are considered as unstable during their first year of dialysis, the assumption was that an earlier beginning might worsen conditions of the patients. But the test revealed that the conditions of active patients who began with their fitness program within the first year of dialysis improved more than those of patients starting later.

However, there are 6 exceptions, namely active patients starting early and their conditions worsened. The explanations of them are high PTH or high phosphorus level.

## 3  Conclusion

In this paper, we have proposed to use CBR in ISOR-2 to explain cases that do not fit a statistical model. Here we presented one of the simplest statistical models. However, it is relatively effective, because it demonstrates statistically significant dependencies, in our example between fitness activity and health improvement of dialysis patients, where the model covers about two thirds of the patients, whereas the other third can be explained by applying CBR. Since we have chosen qualitative assessments (better or worse), very small changes appear to be the same as very large ones. We intend to define these concepts more precisely, especially to introduce more assessments. The presented method makes use of different sources of knowledge and information, including medical experts. It seems to be a very promising method to deal with a poorly structured database, with many missing data, and with situations where cases contain different sets of attributes.

## Acknowledgement

We thank Professor Aleksey Smirnov, director of the Institute for Nephrology of St-Petersburg Medical University and Natalia Korosteleva, researcher at the same Institute for collecting and managing the data.

## References

1. Schmidt, R., Vorobieva, O.: Case-Based Reasoning Investigation of Therapy Inefficacy. Knowledge-Based Systems 19(5), 333–340 (2006)
2. Schmidt, R., Vorobieva, O.: Adaptation and Medical Case-Based Reasoning Focusing on Endocrine Therapy Support. In: Miksch, S., Hunter, J., Keravnou, E.T. (eds.) AIME 2005. LNCS (LNAI), vol. 3581, pp. 308–317. Springer, Heidelberg (2005)
3. Kendall, M.G., Stuart, A.: The advanced theory of statistics, 4th edn. Macmillan publishing, New York (1979)
4. Hai, G.A.: Logic of diagnostic and decision making in clinical medicine. Politheknica publishing, St. Petersburg (2002)
5. Bichindaritz, I., Kansu, E., Sullivan, K.M.: Case-based Reasoning in Care-Partner. In: Smyth, B., Cunningham, P. (eds.) EWCBR 1998. LNCS (LNAI), vol. 1488, pp. 334–345. Springer, Heidelberg (1998)

6. Prentzas, J., Hatzilgeroudis, I.: Integrating Hybrid Rule-Based with Case-Based Reasoning. In: Craw, S., Preece, A.D. (eds.) ECCBR 2002. LNCS (LNAI), vol. 2416, pp. 336–349. Springer, Heidelberg (2002)
7. Shuguang, L., Qing, J., George, C.: Combining case-based and model-based reasoning: a formal specification. In: Proc APSEC'00, p. 416 (2000)
8. Corchado, J.M., Corchado, E.S., Aiken, J., et al.: Maximum likelihood Hebbian learning based retrieval method for CBR systems. In: Ashley, K.D., Bridge, D.G. (eds.) ICCBR 2003. LNCS, vol. 2689, pp. 107–121. Springer, Heidelberg (2003)
9. Rezvani, S., Prasad, G.: A hybrid system with multivariate data validation and Case-based Reasoning for an efficient and realistic product formulation. In: Ashley, K.D., Bridge, D.G. (eds.) ICCBR 2003. LNCS, vol. 2689, pp. 465–478. Springer, Heidelberg (2003)
10. Arshadi, N., Jurisica, I.: Data Mining for Case-based Reasoning in high-dimensional biological domains. IEEE Transactions on Knowledge and Data Engineering 17(8), 1127–1137 (2005)
11. Davidson, A.M., Cameron, J.S., Grünfeld, J.-P., et al. (eds.): Oxford Textbook of Nephrology, vol. 3. Oxford University Press, Oxford (2005)

# The Role of Prototypical Cases in Biomedical Case-Based Reasoning

Isabelle Bichindaritz

University of Washington, 1900 Commerce Street, Box 358426,
Tacoma, WA 98402, USA
ibichind@u.washington.edu

**Abstract.** Representing biomedical knowledge is an essential task in biomedical informatics intelligent systems. Case-based reasoning (CBR) holds the promise of representing contextual knowledge in a way that was not possible before with traditional knowledge representation and knowledge-based methods. A main issue in biomedical CBR has been dealing with maintenance of the case base, and particularly in medical domains, with the rate of generation of new knowledge, which often makes the content of a case base partially obsolete. This article proposes to make use of the concept of prototypical case to ensure that a CBR system would keep up-to-date with current research advances in the biomedical field. It proposes to illustrate and discuss the different roles that prototypical cases can serve in biomedical CBR systems, among which to organize and structure the memory, to guide the retrieval as well as the reuse of cases, and to serve as bootstrapping a CBR system memory when real cases are not available in sufficient quantity and/or quality. This paper presents knowledge maintenance as another role that these prototypical cases can play in biomedical CBR systems.

## 1 Introduction

Case-based reasoning is a valued knowledge management methodology in biomedical domains because it founds its recommendations on contextual knowledge. This type of knowledge is much more detailed and to the point for solving clinical problems, and allows to account for some of the complexity inherent to working in clinical domains. If the value of contextual, instance-based knowledge, is not in question, main issues for CBR methodology are how to keep up with the rate of generation of new biomedical knowledge, and how to maintain the recency of the knowledge represented as cases in a case base [21]. The system presented here proposes to automate the process of maintaining the recency of the knowledge represented in cases through maintenance prototypical cases, which can be mined from current biomedical literature. In the system presented in this article, prototypical cases serve as a structuring mechanism for the case-based reasoning, the case base being organized around them. They also guide the different steps of the reasoning process, for example the retrieval and the reuse. During reuse, current medical recommendations, represented in these prototypical cases mined from biomedical literature, guide the reuse of past cases and automatically revise obsolete recommendations from past cases.

P. Perner (Ed.): ICDM 2007, LNAI 4597, pp. 184–198, 2007.
© Springer-Verlag Berlin Heidelberg 2007

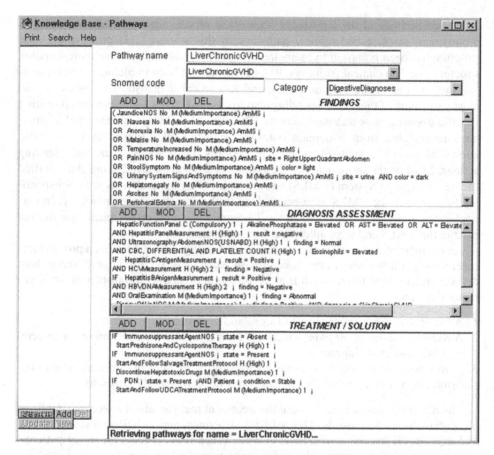

**Fig. 1.** A prototypical case, called here a clinical pathway, for liver chronic graft versus host disease (CGVHD)

The prototypical case structure adopted here is the one chosen for the Mémoire project, which is presented in the next section. The third section explains the role of case-based knowledge to represent contextual knowledge in biomedicine. The fourth section summarizes how prototypical cases can capture latest advances in biomedical literature, through a text mining mechanism. The fifth section presents how prototypical cases can serve as preserving the currency of a case base. A detailed example is presented in the sixth section. It is followed by an evaluation, a discussion, and a conclusion.

## 2 Mémoire Project

The goal of the Mémoire project [7] at the University of Washington is to provide a framework for the creation and interchange of cases, concepts, and CBR systems in biology and medicine.

The cornerstone of the knowledge acquisition process has been the conception of prototypical cases, called clinical pathways in this system. This prototypical case structure has been proposed in Mémoire as a generic prototypical case representation structure [7]. The clinical pathways, 91 of them having been implemented in a previous test version of the system, correspond to clinical diagnostic categories for the most part, some of them corresponding also to essential signs and symptoms requiring specific assessment or treatment actions. The clinical pathways are knowledge structures represented from a domain ontology, namely: all diseases, functions (also known as signs and symptoms), labs, procedures, medications, sites, and planning actions. Most of the terms naming these objects are standardized using the Unified Medical Language System (UMLS) terminology [15]. Only the terms not corresponding to objects in the UMLS have been added to the domain specific ontology. In particular, the planning actions used in the Treatment part of a prototypical case did not exist in the UMLS and were all created for the system.

An example of a prototypical case is provided in Fig. 1. It shows that a prototypical case, mostly a diagnostic category or disease, such as here chronic graft versus host disease affecting the liver, which is a complication of stem-cell transplantation, comprises three parts:

1. A list of *findings*, corresponding to signs and symptoms.
2. A *diagnosis assessment plan*, which is a plan to follow for confirming (or informing) the suspected diagnosis.
3. A *treatment plan*, which is a plan to follow for treating this disease when confirmed, or a solution when the pathway does not correspond to a disease.

The diagnosis assessment part and the treatment part can also be seen as simplified algorithms, since they use IF-THEN-ELSE structures, and LOOP structures, as well as SEQUENCE structures of actions in time. When instantiated with actual patients' data, this knowledge structure allows for sophisticated adaptation.

## 3    Cases as Contextual Knowledge

The gold standard for evaluating the quality of biomedical knowledge relies on the concept of evidence. Pantazi et al. propose an extension of the definition of *biomedical evidence* to include knowledge in individual cases, suggesting that the mere collection of individual case facts should be regarded as evidence gathering [16] (see Fig. 2). To support their proposal, they argue that the traditional, highly abstracted, hypothesis centric type of evidence that removes factual evidence present in individual cases, implies a strong *ontological commitment* to methodological and theoretical approaches, which is the source of the never-ending need for *current* and *best* evidence, while, at the same time, offering little provisions for the reuse of knowledge disposed of as obsolete. By contrast, the incremental factual evidence about individuals creates, once appropriately collected, a growing body of context-dependent evidence that can be reinterpreted and reused as many times as possible.

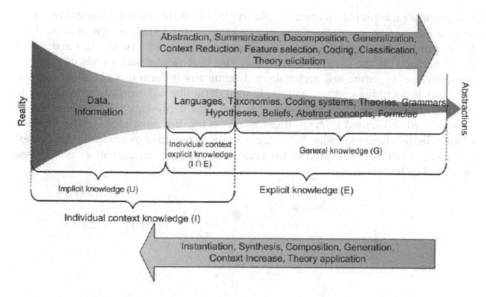

**Fig. 2.** The knowledge spectrum in biomedical informatics [16]

Currently, the concept of evidence most often refers to an abstract proposition derived from multiple, typically thousands of cases, in the context of what is known as a *randomized control trial*. Hypothesis forming is the cornerstone of this kind of biomedical research. Hypotheses that pass an appropriately selected statistical test become evidence. However, the process of hypothesis forming also implies a commitment to certain purposes (e.g., research, teaching, etc.), and inherently postulates ontological and conceptual reductions, orderings and relationships. All these are direct results of the particular conceptualizations of a researcher that is influenced by experience, native language, background, etc. This reduction process will always be prone to errors as long as uncertainties are present in our reality. In addition, even though a hypothesis may be successfully verified statistically and may become evidence subsequently, its applicability will always be hindered by our inability to fully construe its complete meaning. This meaning is fully defined by the complete context where the hypothesis was formed and which include the data sources as well as the context of the researcher that formed the hypothesis.

The discussion about commitment to research designs, methodological choices, and research hypotheses led Pantazi et al. to the proposal to extend the definition and the understanding of the concept of evidence in biomedicine and align it with an intuitively appealing and an important direction of research: *Case-Based Reasoning* (CBR) [17]. From this perspective, the concept of evidence, traditionally construed on the basis of knowledge applicable to populations, is evolved to a more complete, albeit more complex construct which emerges naturally from the attempt to understand, explain and manage unique, individual cases. This new perspective of the concept of evidence is surprisingly congruent with the current acceptation of the notion of evidence in forensic science for instance. Here, by evidence, one also means, besides general patterns and trends that apply generally to populations, the recognition of any spatio-temporal form (i.e., pattern, regularity) in the spatio-temporal context of a case (e.g., a hair, a fibre, a piece of clothing, a smell, a fluid spot, a sign of struggle, a finger print on a certain object, the reoccurrence of a certain event, etc.) and which may be relevant to the solution to that case. This new view where a body of evidence is incremental in nature and accumulates dynamically in form of facts about individual cases is a striking contrast with traditional definitions of biomedical evidence. In addition, case evidence, once appropriately collected, represents a history that can be reinterpreted and reused as many times as necessary. But most importantly, the kind of knowledge where the "what is", i.e., case data, is regarded as evidence can be easily proven to be less sensitive to the issues of *recency* (i.e., current evidence) and *validity* (i.e., best evidence).

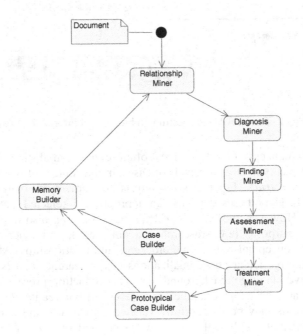

**Fig. 3.** ProConceptMiner architecture

If the question of up-to-date or current knowledge is not as critical for cases as for general knowledge, it is nevertheless an interesting research question to study how to keep the content of a case base current. Biomedical procedures, tests, and practices change, while recorded cases do not. This article proposes prototypical cases as a media for merging current and alternate medical practice with the highly context specific content of a case base.

## 4  Prototypical Case Mining

ProCaseMiner system (see Fig. 3) mines for cases and prototypical cases from biomedical literature [8]. A selection of documents for a given medical domain is the input to this system. Pertinent documents may be literature articles, but also textual clinical practice guidelines, and medical case studies. It is important that such documents should all be related to a given domain, such as in our example stem-cell transplantation.

ProConceptMiner core component is the RelationshipMiner, which mines for triples *<concept1-1, relationship-1,2, concept-2>* from a document. It also attaches a condition to a triple when it finds it to represent the information that IF a condition occurs, then an action or test is undertaken. This can be represented as *<concept-1, relationship-1,2, concept-2>* IF *<concept-3, relationship-3,4, concept-4>*. An example can be *<Patient, startTreatment, PrednisoneAndCyclosporineTherapy>* IF *<absent, property_of, ImmunosuppressantAgentNOS>*. This structure is called a triple pair.

ProConceptMiner interprets the results from RelationshipMiner by successively mining for diagnoses in DiagnosisMiner, findings in FindingMiner, assessments in AssessmentMiner, and treatments in TreatmentMiner. Following, it builds cases from these results in CaseBuilder or PrototypicalCaseBuilder. The order between these two components can be altered since in some cases, learnt relationships will be associated with conditions, which signals a prototypical case, and in others there will not be any of these conditions, which signals a practice case. Generally, from medical articles and clinical practice guidelines, the learnt artifact will be a prototypical case. From clinical case studies, the learnt artifact will be a practice case. The previous steps deal with prototypical cases and practice cases built from scratch from a single document. A next step is to consolidate learning results across documents. This step is called MemoryBuilder [8].

## 5  Prototypical Cases for Knowledge Maintenance

Mémoire system relies on a generic prototypical case representation to perform its case-based reasoning and to maintain the recency of its knowledge.

### 5.1  Case Representation

The elements of the representation language are those of semantic networks:

- *A domain ontology*, which is the set of *class symbols* (also called concepts in the UMLS [15]) C, where $C_i$ and $C_j$ denote elements of C. Specific subdomains are for example findings (signs and symptoms, noted $F_i$ ), tests and procedures ($A_i$), and planning actions ($P_i$).
- *A set of individual symbols* (also called instances) I, where i and j denote elements of I. Among these, some refer to instances of classes, others to numbers, dates, and other values. Instances of a class $C_i$ are noted $aC$..
- *A set of operator symbols* O, permits to form logical expressions composed of classes, instances and other values, and relationships. Prototypical cases and clinical cases are expressed this way, and such a composition permits to represent complex entities in a structured format. The set of operators comprises the following:

$$\land \text{(AND)}$$
$$\lor \text{(OR)}$$
$$\text{ATLEAST } n$$
$$\text{ATMOST } n$$
$$\text{EXACTLY } n$$
$$\text{IF}$$

Prototypical cases are expressed as *<problem situation, solution>*, where *problem situation* is expressed in the object-oriented knowledge representation language above as a composition of instances with operators and where *solution* also has the same representation, but adds other operators to express conditional expressions (*IF*):

$$\textit{problem situation} = \quad \Theta \ aF_i \{ \ <att_i, val_i> \ \}$$
$$\textit{solution} \ = \quad \Theta \ aA_i \{ \ <att_i, val_i> \ \}$$
$$\Theta \ aP_i \{ \ <att_i, val_i> \ \}$$

with for prototypical cases: $\Theta \in O$, the default value being $\lor$ for prototypical cases, and for clinical cases: $\Theta \in \{ \land \}$, the default value being $\land$ for clinical cases.

The default representation for clinical cases is the same as for prototypical cases, except that the only connector available here is the connector $\land$ both for problem situation and for solution. Since a case is not abstracted, cases are expressed using only $\land$.

## 5.2 Memory Organization

The memory of the system is organized in several layers, where the prototypical cases index the clinical cases (see Fig. 4). Several kinds of prototypical cases may be available:

- The *expert prototypical cases*, which were provided by the experts when the system was built. The roles of these cases are to provide a structure to the memory, and to organize the clinical/experiential cases so as to facilitate the search through the memory.
- The *maintenance prototypical cases*, which provide the updates coming from the literature. These may be reviewed by humans as well – regular staff or experts. The role of these cases is to maintain the knowledge represented in the case base.
- The *learnt prototypical cases*, which are learnt through conceptual clustering from the cases that enrich the memory over time [6]. These prototypical cases have for main role to facilitate the search through the memory, as well as a role of suggesting research questions [5].

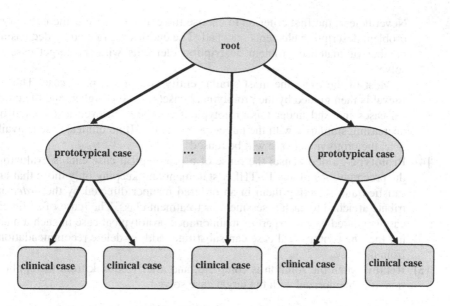

**Fig. 4.** Memory organization

## 5.3 Reasoning Process

The reasoning process starts with the presentation to the system of a new problem to solve. This system is capable of handling the wide variety of problems that physicians can face when they take care of patients, and the first task of the system is to determine the nature of the problem to solve. Classically, the reasoning of the system proceeds through the following steps [1]:

[1] **Interpretation:** given the description of a patient problem, the system constructs, by interpretation, the initial situation expressed in the knowledge representation language of the system. Abstraction is the main reasoning type used here, and in particular temporal abstraction to create trends from time-stamped data. Numerical values are abstracted into qualitative values. Let $c_c$ be the target patient case to solve, represented as a conjunction of findings:

$$c_c = \Theta \ aF_i \{ <att_i, val_i> \}$$

[2] **Prototype-guided retrieval:** the case-base is searched for prototypical cases and cases matching this new problem to solve through case-based retrieval. The result is a set containing both cases and prototypical cases. Let $CS$ be this conflict set: $CS = \{ c_i, p_j \}$ where the $c_i$ are cases and the $p_j$ are prototypical cases. Cases are only retrieved directly if they are not indexed under a prototypical case – which is rare.

[3] **Conflict resolution ($R_r$):** the following hierarchy of reuse is followed:
  I.   reuse expert prototypical cases
  II.  reuse maintenance prototypical cases
  III. reuse learnt prototypical cases
  IV.  reuse cases

Nevertheless, the first criterion to choose the entity to reuse is the number of problem description elements matched. The entities are ranked by decreasing number of matched problem description elements with the target case to solve.

Most of the time, the most similar entity is a prototypical case. The retrieval is then guided by the prototypical case(s) ranked higher, and the clinical cases indexed under this prototypical case are retrieved and ranked by decreasing similarity with the target case to solve. If no clinical case is available, the prototypical case will be reused.

[4] **Prototype-guided reuse:** the reuse of a prototypical case entails evaluating the preconditions of any IF-THEN statement and keeping only those that are satisfied and selecting them in an ordered manner directed by the *order* attribute attached to each assessment or treatment class. The reuse of a clinical case is guided by the expert or maintenance prototypical case in such a manner that the prototypical case can substitute, add, or delete recommendations from the case.

[5] **Retain:** when the solution is complete, and after feedback from the application, it is memorized with the target case solved.

The system provides a list of recommendations represented as instances of assessment and/or planning actions.


# 6   Example

This section presents an example of prototypical case guided retrieval and reuse. A patient consults his doctor about new symptoms occurring after his transplant. The patient's symptoms are: *Nausea, Malaise*, and *PainNOS* localized in the upper right portion of the abdomen. The physician records the main complaint of the patient, which is the unusual abdominal pain.

The physician reviews the drugs the patient is taking, as well his chart with the latest labs and physical exams. The patient is not taking any immunosuppressant drug, nor any hepato-toxic drug.

## 6.1   Prototype Guided Retrieval

The three symptoms of the patient each trigger several prototypical cases:

- *Nausea* triggers 18 prototypical cases: *LiverChronicGVHD, HepatitisAcute-NOS, LiverDrugToxicity, GastricChronicGVHD, GastricHemorraghe, Colon-ChronicGVHD, DrugInducedNauseaAndVomiting, DuodenalChronicGVHD, EsophagealChronicGVHD, EsophagealInfection, IntestinalDrugToxicity, AdrenalInsufficiency, UrethralInfection, BladderInfection, RecurrentNonHodgkin'sLymphoma, NonInfectiousPericarditisNOS, AcuteCholecystitis*, and *Hypomagnesemia*.
- *Malaise* triggers 4 prototypical cases: *LiverChronicGVHD, HepatitisAcuteNOS, LiverDrugToxicity*, and *InfectiousMononucleosis*.

- *PainNOS* in *RightUpperQuadrant* triggers 4 prototypical cases: *Liver-ChronicGVHD, LiverDrugToxicity, HepatitisAcuteNOS*, and *AcuteCholecystitis*.

The similarity measure ranks highest *LiverChronicGVHD* and *HepatitisAcuteNOS*, because *LiverDrugToxicity* is ruled out by the fact that the patient is not taking any hepato-toxic drug. Therefore the cases chosen to base the reuse are: Liver-ChronicGVHD (see Fig. 5 and Fig. 6 for this prototypical case) and *HepatitisAcuteNOS*.

In this particular example, the system does not retrieve the cases indexed under these prototypical cases because all the features describing the case to solve are accounted for in the prototypical cases. Most of the time though the actual clinical cases would be retrieved, since they would often match some of the features not present in a prototypical case.

## 6.2  Prototype Guided Reuse

The reuse in this case combines the diagnosis assessment and eventually the treatment plan of two prototypical cases: *LiverChronicGVHD* and *HepatitisAcuteNOS*.

The diagnosis assessment proceeds in four stages, as indicated by the range of *order* in the *LiverChronicGVHD* prototypical case (from 1 to 4, rightmost column in Fig, 5 and Fig. 6).

- First, request a *HepaticFunctionPanel*, a *HepatitisPanel*, an *Ultrasonography-AbdomenNOS*, and a *CBC*. The first steps of diagnosis assessment for both *LiverChronicGVHD* and *HepatitisAcuteNOS* being the same, the system does not propose any additional procedures to be performed at first.
- Second, after the results have come in, and if they have the values indicated in the case, proceed with *HCVRNAMeasurement* if *HepatitisCAntigenMeasurement* was positive, and with *HBVDNAMeasurement* if *HepatitisBAntigenMeasurement* was positive. The patient tested negative to hepatitis, therefore these procedures are not requested.
- Third, request an *OralExamination*, a *BiopsyOfLipNOS*, a *BiopsyOfSkinNOS*, and a *SchirmerTearTest*. The patient undertook all of these, and tested positive for *SkinChronicGVHD* in his lip biopsy.
- Fourth, because the patient tested positive for *SkinChro*nicGVHD, he will not have to undergo *BiopsyOfLiver*, and his diagnosis of *LiverChronicGVHD* is established.

The treatment plan starts in this prototypical case only after the diagnosis is established because of the order of 1 indicated in the rightmost column of the treatment plan (see Fig. 6). If the order had been 0, some treatment would have started just by triggering this case. Since the patient is not taking any immunosuppressant drug, he will be placed on prednisone and cyclosporine therapy (*StartPDNCSPTherapy*). The other actions are eliminated because their preconditions are not met (for the second one), and not yet met (for the third one). After some time, if the patient is considered as stable, the third statement will be considered: *ConsiderUDCARxProtocol*.

**GastrointestinalDiagnoses : LiverChronic GVHD (-----------------)**

<u>Findings</u>

Importance:    N (NecessaryAndSufficient) C (Compulsory), H (High Importance), M (MediumImportance),
               L (LowImportance), S (SecondaryImportance)    [default = 'M'].
Level:         A (Absent), m (Mild), M (Moderate), S (Severe)    [default = 'AmMS'].

| Connector | Finding Name | Snomed code | (Properties, Values) | Importance | Level |
|---|---|---|---|---|---|
|  | (JaundiceNOS | M-57610 |  | H |  |
| OR | Nausea | F-52760 |  | M |  |
| OR | Anorexia | F-50015 |  | M |  |
| OR | Malaise | F-01220 |  | M |  |
| OR | Fever | F-03003 |  | M |  |
| OR | PainNOS | F-A2600 | site=RightUpperQuadrantAbdomen | M |  |
| OR | Stool | T-59666 | color=light | M |  |
| OR | Urine | T-70060 | color=dark | M |  |
| OR | Hepatomegaly | D5-81220 |  | M |  |
| OR | Ascites | D5-70400 |  | M |  |
| OR | PeripheralEdema) | M-36330 |  | M |  |
| AND | HepatoToxicDrug |  |  | H | A |

<u>Diagnosis Assessment</u>

| Connector | Procedure Name | Snomed code | (Properties, Values) | Importance | Order |
|---|---|---|---|---|---|
|  | HepaticFunctionPanel | P3-09100 | finding=AlkalinePhosphataseMeasurement(ALKP)( P3-71350) result=elevated OR finding=ASTMeasurement(AST)(P3-72000) result=elevated OR finding=ALTMeasurement(ALT)(P3-71220) result=elevated OR finding=LDHMeasurement(LDH)(P3-73380)result=elevated | C | 1 |
| AND | HepatitisPanel | P3-09110 | finding=HepatitisPanelMeasurement(P3-64000) result=negative | H | 1 |
| AND | UltrasonographyAbdomenNOS(USNABD) | P5-BB200 | finding=Normal | H | 1 |
| AND | CBC | P3-30100 | Finding = Eosinophils result = elevated | H | 1 |
| IF HepatitisC AntigenMeasurement( P3-64054) .result = Positive | HCVRNAMeasurement | P3-64050 | finding=negative AND synonym=HCVMeasurement | H | 2 |
| IF HepatitisB Antigen Measurement(P3-64021) result=Positive | HBVDNAMeasurement |  | finding=negative | H | 2 |

**Fig. 5.** Liver ChronicGVHD (part I) prototypical case representation with its list of findings (corresponding to diagnoses), and its list of diagnosis assessment steps

# 7 Evaluation

A formal evaluation of the approach followed by Memoire can be found in CARE-PARTNER decision-support performance [7]. On 163 different clinical situations or cases, corresponding to contacts between the system and a clinician about three patients, the system was rated 82.2% as *Meets all standards*, and 12.3% as *Adequate*, for a total of 94.5% of results judged clinically acceptable by the medical experts. The advice provided by the system covers most of the clinicians' tasks: labs and procedure results interpretation, diagnosis assessment plan, treatment plan, and pathways information retrieval. Pathways represent prototypical cases retrieved by the system, and correspond to diagnostic categories (see Fig. 1 for an example). Important in this system is the evolution of the competency of the system over time, reaching 98.6% *Meets all standards/Adequate* for patient 3 for all his 54 contacts.

# 8 Discussion

Some may object to the need of maintenance prototypical cases from the literature, stating that a case base will naturally evolve into a more current one by adding newly solved cases over time. Actually this is an important advantage of case-based reasoning to constantly learn and improve its case-based knowledge over time in an incremental manner. Nevertheless, from the experience of Carepartner system [7], the availability of clinical guidelines is considered as a required standard of care in a medical domain. They represent the level of care to which clinicians are legally required to abide. It is therefore essential for CBR in biomedicine to provide a mechanism to infuse clinical guideline based knowledge within case-based recommendations.

In CBR research, generalized cases are named in varied ways, such as prototypical cases, abstract cases, prototypes, stereotypes, templates, classes, categories, concepts, and scripts – to name the main ones [13]. Although all these terms refer to slightly different concepts, they represent structures that have been abstracted or generalized from real cases either by the CBR system, or by an expert. When these prototypical cases are provided by a domain expert, this is a knowledge acquisition task [3]. More frequently, they are learnt from actual cases. In CBR, prototypical cases are often learnt to structure the memory.

Many authors mine for *prototypes*, and simply refer to *induction* for learning these. CHROMA [2] uses induction to learn prototypes corresponding to general cases, which each contain a pair *<situation, plan>*, where the situation is an object whose slots have several values possible – values are elements of a set. Bellazzi et al. organize their memory around prototypes [4]. The prototypes can either have been acquired from an expert, or induced from a large case base. Schmidt and Gierl point that prototypes are an essential knowledge structure to fill the gap between general knowledge and cases in medical domains [14]. The main purpose of this prototype learning step is to guide the retrieval process and to decrease the amount of storage by erasing redundant cases. A generalization step becomes necessary to learn the knowledge contained in stored cases. They use several threshold parameters to adjust their prototypes, such as the number of cases the prototype is filled with, and the minimum frequency of each contraindication for the antibiotic therapy domain [20].

Others specifically refer to *generalization*, so that their prototypes correspond to generalized cases. An example of system inducing prototypes by generalization is a computer aided medical diagnosis system interpreting electromyography for neuropathy diagnosis [12]. The first prototypes are learnt from the expert by supervised learning, then the prototypes are automatically updated by the system by generalizing from cases. Prototypes can fusion if one is more general than the other ones, or new prototypes can be added to the memory. Portinale and Torasso in ADAPTER organize their memory through E-MOPs learnt by generalization from cases for diagnostic problem-solving [19]. E-MOPs carry the common characteristics of the cases they index, in a discrimination network of features used as indices to retrieve cases. Mougouie and Bergmann present a method for learning generalized cases [14]. This method, called the Topkis-Veinott method, provides a solution to the computation of similarity for generalized cases over an n-dimensional Real values vector. Maximini et al. have studied the different structures induced from cases in CBR systems [13]. They point out that several different terms exist, such as generalized case, prototype, schema, script, and abstract case. The same terms do not always correspond to the same type of entity. They define three types of cases. A point case is what we refer to as a real case. The values of all its attributes are known. A generalized case is an arbitrary subspace of the attribute space. There are two forms: the attribute independent generalized case, in which some attributes have been generalized (interval of values) or are unknown, and the attribute dependent generalized case, which cannot be defined from independent subsets of their attributes.

Yet other authors refer to *abstraction* for learning abstract cases. Branting proposes case abstractions for its memory of route maps [9]. The abstract cases, which also contain abstract solutions, provide an accurate index to less abstract cases and solutions. [18] learns prototypes by abstracting cases as well.

Finally, many authors learn *concepts* through *conceptual clustering*. MNAOMIA [5, 6] learns concepts and trends from cases through *conceptual clustering* similar to GBM [11]. Perner learns a hierarchy of classes by *hierarchical conceptual clustering*, where the concepts represent clusters of prototypes [18].

Dìaz-Agudo and Gonzàlez-Calero use *formal concept analysis* (FCA) – a mathematical method from data analysis - as another induction method for extracting knowledge from case bases, in the form of *concepts* [10].

The system presented here also uses prototypical cases to organize its memory, direct its retrieval and its adaptation. Its originality lies in reusing both clinical cases and prototypical cases, judiciously combining their recommendations to build more up-to-date recommendations. The prospect of using prototypical cases for case base maintenance is also novel, even in comparison with Schmidt and Gierl [14] whose maintenance is directed toward summarizing several cases, and not toward providing more current knowledge. In addition, the mining process for mining prototypical cases from the literature is also novel in CBR, and is explained in [8].

## 9 Conclusion

This system proposes to keep a case base up-to-date by automatically learning prototypical cases from biomedical literature. These prototypical cases are an important memory structure which the systems relies upon for guiding its retrieval and reuse steps. These prototypical cases, called maintenance prototypical cases, provide a method for enabling a case base to naturally evolve and follow the otherwise overwhelming flow of biomedical advances. Coupled with the concept of mining prototypical cases from biomedical literature, this methodology moves a step forward in the direction of automatically building and maintaining case bases in biomedical domains. Future areas of research are to study how prototypical cases learnt from clinical cases, from the experts, and from the literature can complement one another, and how the reasoner can take advantage of the knowledge provided by each in a harmonious and advantageous way.

## References

[1] Aamodt, A., Plaza, E.: Case-Based Reasoning: Foundational Issues, Methodologies Variations, and Systems Approaches. AI Communications, IOS Press 7(1), 39–59 (1994)

[2] Armengo, E., Plaza, E.: Integrating induction in a case-based reasoner. In: Haton, J.-P., Manago, M., Keane, M.A. (eds.) Advances in Case-Based Reasoning. LNCS, vol. 984, pp. 243–251. Springer, Heidelberg (1995)

[3] Bareiss, R.: Exemplar-Based Knowledge Acquisition. Academic Press, San Diego (1989)

[4] Bellazzi, R., Montani, S., Portinale, L.: Retrieval in a Prototype-Based Case Library: A Case Study in Diabetes Therapy Revision. In: Smyth, B., Cunningham, P. (eds.) EWCBR 1998. LNCS (LNAI), vol. 1488, pp. 64–75. Springer, Heidelberg (1998)

[5] Bichindaritz, I.: A case based reasoner adaptive to several cognitive tasks. In: Aamodt, A., Veloso, M.M. (eds.) Case-Based Reasoning Research and Development. LNCS, vol. 1010, pp. 391–400. Springer, Heidelberg (1995)

[6] Bichindaritz, I.: Case-Based Reasoning and Conceptual Clustering: For a Co-operative Approach. In: Watson, I.D. (ed.) Progress in Case-Based Reasoning. LNCS, vol. 1020, pp. 91–106. Springer, Heidelberg (1995)

[7] Bichindaritz, I.: Mémoire: Case-based Reasoning Meets the Semantic Web in Biology and Medicine. In: Funk, P., González Calero, P.A. (eds.) ECCBR 2004. LNCS (LNAI), vol. 3155, pp. 47–61. Springer, Heidelberg (2004)

[8] Bichindaritz, I.: Prototypical Case Mining from Biomedical Literature. Applied Intelligence (in press) (2007)

[9] Branting, K.L.: Stratified Case-Based Reasoning in Non-Refinable Abstraction Hierachies. In: Leake, D.B., Plaza, E. (eds.) ICCBR 97. LNCS, vol. 1266, pp. 519–530. Springer, Heidelberg (1997)

[10] Dìaz-Agudo, B., Gonzàlez-Calero, P.: Classification Based Retrieval Using Formal Concept Analysis. In: Aha, D.W., Watson, I. (eds.) ICCBR 2001. LNCS (LNAI), vol. 2080, pp. 173–188. Springer, Heidelberg (2001)

[11] Lebowitz, M.: Concept Learning in a Rich Input Domain: Generalization-Based Memory. In: Michalski, R.S., Carbonell, J.G., Mitchell, T.M. (eds.) Machine Learning: An Artificial Intelligence Approach, vol. 2, pp. 193–214. Morgan Kaufmann, San Francisco (1986)

[12] Malek, M., Rialle, V.: A Case-Based Reasoning System Applied to Neuropathy Diagnosis. In: Haton, J.-P., Manago, M., Keane, M.A. (eds.) Advances in Case-Based Reasoning. LNCS, vol. 984, pp. 329–336. Springer, Heidelberg (1995)

[13] Maximini, K., Maximini, R., Bergmann, R.: An Investigation of Generalized Cases. In: Ashley, K.D., Bridge, D.G. (eds.) ICCBR 2003. LNCS, vol. 2689, pp. 261–275. Springer, Heidelberg (2003)

[14] Mougouie, B., Bergmann, R.: Similarity Assessment for Generalized Cases by Optimization Methods. In: Craw, S., Preece, A.D. (eds.) ECCBR 2002. LNCS (LNAI), vol. 2416, pp. 249–263. Springer, Heidelberg (2002)

[15] National Library of Medicine: The Unified Medical Language System. [Last access: 2005-04-01] (1995) http://umls.nlm.nih.gov

[16] Pantazi, S.V., Arocha, J.F.: Case-based Medical Informatics. BMC Journal of Medical Informatics and Decision Making 4(1), 19–39 (2004)

[17] Pantazi, S.V., Bichindaritz, I., Moehr, J.R.: The Case for Context-Dependent Dynamic Hierarchical Representations of Knowledge in Medical Informatics. In: Proceedings of ITCH '07 (in press) (2007)

[18] Perner, P.: Different Learning Strategies in a Case-Based Reasoning System for Image Interpretation. In: Smyth, B., Cunningham, P. (eds.) EWCBR 1998. LNCS (LNAI), vol. 1488, pp. 251–261. Springer, Heidelberg (1998)

[19] Portinale, L., Torasso, P.: ADAPTER: An Integrated Diagnostic System Combining Case-Based and Abductive Reasoning. In: Aamodt, A., Veloso, M.M. (eds.) Case-Based Reasoning Research and Development. LNCS, vol. 1010, pp. 277–288. Springer, Heidelberg (1995)

[20] Schmidt, R., Gierl, L.: Experiences with Prototype Designs and Retrieval Methods in Medical Case-Based Reasoning Systems. In: Smyth, B., Cunningham, P. (eds.) EWCBR 1998. LNCS (LNAI), vol. 1488, pp. 370–381. Springer, Heidelberg (1998)

[21] Wilson, D., Leake, D.B.: Mainting Case Based Reasoners: Dimensions and Directions. Computational Intelligence Journal 17(2), 196–213 (2001)

# A Search Space Reduction Methodology for Large Databases: A Case Study

Angel Kuri-Morales[1] and Fátima Rodríguez[2]

[1] Departamento de Computación. Instituto Tecnológico Autónomo de México
[2] Posgrado en Ciencias e Ingeniería de la Computacion, Universidad Nacional
Autónoma de México, Mexico
akuri@itam.mx, frodrigueze@uxmcc2.iimas.unam.mx

**Abstract.** Given the present need for Customer Relationship and the increased growth of the size of databases, many new approaches to large database clustering and processing have been attempted. In this work we propose a methodology based on the idea that statistically proven search space reduction is possible in practice. Two clustering models are generated: one corresponding to the full data set and another pertaining to the sampled data set. The resulting empirical distributions were mathematically tested to verify a tight non-linear significant approximation.

**Keywords:** Large databases, Sampling, Space reduction, Preprocessing, Clustering.

## 1 Introduction

Nowadays, commercial enterprises are importantly oriented to continuously improving customer-business relationship. With the increasing influence of CRM[1] Systems, such companies dedicate more time and effort to maintain better customer-business relationships. The effort implied in getting to better know the customer involves the accumulation of enormous data bases where the largest possible quantity of data regarding the customer is stored.

Data warehouses offer a way to access detailed information about the customer's history, business facts and other aspects of the customer's behavior. The databases constitute the information backbone for any well established company. However, from each step and every new attempted link of the company to its customers the need to store increasing volumes of data arises. Hence databases and data warehouses are always growing up in terms of number of registers and tables which will allow the company to improve the general vision of the customer.

Data warehouses are difficult to characterize when trying to analyze the customers from company's standpoint. This problem is generally approached through the use of data mining techniques [1]. However, to attempt direct clustering over a data base of several terabytes with millions of registers results in a costly and not always fruitful effort. There have been many attempts to solve this problem. For instance, with the

---

[1] Customer Relationship Management.

P. Perner (Ed.): ICDM 2007, LNAI 4597, pp. 199–213, 2007.
© Springer-Verlag Berlin Heidelberg 2007

use of parallel computation, the optimization of clustering algorithms, via alternative distributed and grid computing and so on. But still the more efficient methods are unwieldy when attacking the clustering problem for databases as considered above.

In this article we present a methodology derived from the practical solution of an automated clustering process over large database from a real large sized (over 20 million customers) company. We emphasize the way we used statistical methods to reduce the search space of the problem as well as the treatment given to the customer's information stored in multiple tables of multiple databases.

Because of confidentiality issues the name of the company and the actual final results of the customer characterization are withheld.

**Paper Outline**

The outline of the paper is as follows. First, we give an overview of the analysis of large databases in section 2; next we give a clustering, sampling, and feature selection overview. In section 3 we briefly discuss the case study treated with the proposed methodology. Explanation of the methodology follows in Section 4. Finally, we concluded In Section 5.

# 2   Analysis of Large Databases

To extract the best information of a database it is convenient to use a set of strategies or techniques which will allow us to analyze large volumes of data. These tools are generically known as data mining (DM) which targets on new, valuable, and nontrivial information in large volumes of data. It includes techniques such as clustering (which corresponds to non-supervised learning) and statistical analysis (which includes, for instance, sampling and multivariate analysis).

## 2.1   Clustering in Large Databases

Clustering is a popular data mining task  which consist of processing a large volume of data to obtain groups where the elements of each group exhibit quantifiably (under some measure) small differences between them and, contrariwise, large dissimilarities between elements of different groups. Given its importance as a very important data mining task, clustering has been the subject of multiple research efforts and has proven to be useful for many purposes [2].

Many techniques and algorithms for clustering have been developed, improved and applied [3], [4]. Some of them try to ease the process on a large database as in [5], [6] and [7]. On the other hand, the so-called "Divide and Merge" [8] or "Snakes and Sandwiches" [9] methods refer to clustering attending to the physical storage of the records comprising data warehouses. Another strategy to work with a large database is based upon the idea of working with statistical sampling optimization [10].

## 2.2   Sampling and Feature Selection

Sampling is a statistical method to select a certain number of elements from a population to be included in a sample. There exist two sampling types: probabilistic and nonprobabilistic. For each of these categories there exists a variety of sub methods. The probabilistic better known ones include: a) Random sampling, b) Systematic sampling, and c) Stratified sampling. On the other hand the nonprobabilistic ones include methods such as convenience sampling, judgment sampling, and quota sampling. There are many ways to select the elements from a data set and some of them are discussed in [11]. This field of research, however, continues to be an open one [12], [13].

The use of sampling for data mining has received some criticism since there is always a possibility that such sampling may hamper a clustering algorithm's capability to find small clusters appearing in the original data [10]. However, small clusters are not always significant; such is the case of costumer clusters. Since the main objective of the company is to find significant and, therefore, large customer clusters, a small cluster that may not be included in a sample is not significant for CRM.

Apart from the sampling theory needed to properly reduce the search space, we need to perform feature selection to achieve desirable smaller dimensionality. In this regard we point out that feature selection has been the main object of many researches [14], [15], and these had resulted in a large number of methods and algorithms [16]. One such method is "multivariate analysis". This is a scheme (as treated here) which allows us to synthesize a functional relation between a dependent and two or more independent variables. There are many techniques to perform a multivariate analysis. For instance, multivariate regression analysis, principal component analysis, variance and covariance analysis, canonical correlation analysis, etc., [17]. Here we focus on the explicit determination of a functional which maximizes the resulting correlation coefficient while minimizing its standard error. Clearly, this approach requires a sufficiently large number of models to consider, as will be discussed in the sequel.

## 3  Case Study

A data mining project was conducted for a very large multi-national Latin American company (one of the largest in Latin America) hereinafter referred to as the "Company". The Company has several databases with information about its different customers, including data about services contracted, services' billing (registered over a period of several years) and other pertinent characterization data. The Company offers a large variety of services to millions of users in several countries. Its databases are stored on IBM Universal Database version 7.0. In our study we applied a specific data mining tool (which we will refer to as "the miner") which works directly on the database. We also developed a set of auxiliary programs intended to help in data pre-processing.

The actual customer information that was necessary for the clustering process was extracted from multiple databases in the Company. Prior to the data mining process, the Company's experts conducted an analysis of the different existent databases and selected the more important variables and associated data related to the project's purpose: to identify those customers amenable to become *ad hoc* clients for new products under development and others to be developed specifically from the results of the study. Due to the variety of platforms and databases, such process of selection and collection of relevant information took several months and several hundred man-hours.

The resulting database displayed a table structure that contains information about the characteristics of the customers, products or services contracted for the customer and monthly billing data over a one year period.

To test the working methodology the project teamed worked with a subset of 400,000 customers registers, consisting of a total of 415 variables divided in 9 data tables. Table 1 displays the characteristics of the data sources treated in this study.

**Table 1.** Data sources

| Table | Columns | Rows | Description |
|-------|---------|------|-------------|
| TFB | 25 | 400,000 | Customer billing |
| TINT | 121 | 400,000 | Internet services |
| TPK | 49 | 400,000 | Data package services |
| TGRL | 11 | 400,000 | Customer's general data |
| TAC | 2 | 73 | Supply areas |
| TCC | 2 | 4 | Customer's credit rank code |
| TPA | 3 | 183 | Customer's permanence |
| TLPC | 121 | 400,000 | Local services |
| TSD | 85 | 400,000 | Digital services |

**Main Objective**

As stated above, the main objective of the data mining project was to characterize the customers of the Company allowing in the near future - in accordance to customer characteristics - to offer new services and/or increase sales to existent or new customers.

## 4  Methodology

In order to apply a methodology whereupon the search space is efficiently and effectively reduced it is necessary to comply with several steps leading to the adequate representation and/or behavior of the data regardless of its primary origin. These steps are discussed in what follows.

- Data preprocessing
- Search space reduction
- Clustering

### 4.1  Data Preprocessing

This step included data cleaning by exhaustively searching for incomplete, inconsistent or missing data [18]. Additionally, we also had to transform non-numeric to numeric data. Resulting from this process unrecoverable registers were deleted. The number of such deleted records, however, was not significant.

From the original multiple-tables structure we defined a single-table view structure for which a process of denormalization was performed. This followed from an analysis of the key-structure. In this view tables with the same key were merged and tables with different keys were included in the referenced tables as additional columns. The transformation resulted in a view with a structure with 415 attributes.

## 4.2 Search Space Reduction

To reduce the search space we work with the original data to obtain a sample which is not only a subspace but, rather, one that properly represents the original (full) set of data. We reduce the set both horizontally (reducing the number of tuples) and vertically (reducing the number of attributes) to obtain the "minable view". Simultaneous reduction - horizontal and vertical - yields the smallest representation of the original data set. Vertical reduction is possible from traditional statistical methods, while horizontal reduction, basically, consists of finding the best possible sample. The following subsections discuss how we performed both reductions.

### Vertical Reduction
To perform vertical reduction, multivariate analysis is required. There exist many methods to reduce the original number of variables. Here we simply used Pearson's correlation coefficients. An exploration for correlated variables was performed over the original data. We calculate a correlation matrix for the 415 variables. We considered (after consulting with the experts) that those variables exhibiting a correlation factor equal or larger than 0.75 were redundant. Hence, from the original 415 variables only 129 remained as informationally interesting. In principle, out of a set of correlated variables only one is needed for clustering purposes. Which of these is to be retained is irrelevant; in fact, we wrote a program which simply performed a sequential binary search to select the (uncorrelated) variables to be retained.

### Horizontal Reduction
This step is based on the hypothesis that a sample will adequately represent the full set of data. The size of the sample was determined at the offset by the Company's experts; hence, 20% of the original data (after vertical reduction) was sampled. The elements of such sample were randomly (uniformly) selected. From the sample we validated the representation adequacy of this subset. A central issue to our work was the way the sample is validated. The process consists of the following steps:

1. Select several n equally sized samples. In our case n = 5.
2. Select sets of m variables to perform a goodness-of-fit test. We selected couples (m=2) of variables to prove that, within each sample, the behavior of the selected variables is statistically equivalent.
3. Perform a search for the best regressive function. To this effect we programmatically analyzed, in every case, 34 models (listed in table 2). From these we selected the one which displayed the highest Pearson correlation factor.
4. Perform steps 2 and 3 as long as there are more variables to evaluate.

**Table 2.** Evaluated regressive models

| Family | Model | Equation |
|---|---|---|
| | Linear | $y = a + bx$ |
| | Quadratic | $y = a + bx + cx^2$ |
| | nth Order Polynomial | $y = a + bx + cx^2 + dx^3 + ...$ |
| Exponential Family | Exponential | $y = ae^{bx}$ |
| | Modified Exponential | $y = ae^{b/x}$ |
| | Logarithm | $y = a + b \ln x$ |
| | Reciprocal Log | $y = \dfrac{1}{a + b \ln x}$ |
| | Vapor Pressure Model | $y = e^{a + b/x + c \ln x}$ |
| Power Law Family | Power | $y = ax^b$ |
| | Modified Power | $y = ab^x$ |
| | Shifted Power | $y = a(x - b)^c$ |
| | Geometric | $y = ax^{bx}$ |
| | Modified Geometric | $y = ax^{b/x}$ |
| | Root | $y = ab^{1/x}$ |
| | Hoerl Model | $y = ab^x x^c$ |
| | Modified Hoerl Model | $y = ab^{1/x} x^c$ |
| Yield-Density Models | Reciprocal | $y = \dfrac{1}{ax + b}$ |
| | Reciprocal Quadratic | $y = \dfrac{1}{a + bx + cx^2}$ |
| | Bleasdale Model | $y = (a + bx)^{-1/c}$ |
| | Harris Model | $y = \dfrac{1}{(a + bx^c)}$ |
| Growth Models | Saturation-Growth Rate | $y = \dfrac{ax}{b + x}$ |
| | Exponential Association 2 | $y = a(1 - e^{-bx})$ |
| | Exponential Association 3 | $y = a(b - e^{-cx})$ |

**Table 2.** (*continued*)

| Family | Model | Equation |
|---|---|---|
| Sigmoidal Models | Gompertz Relation | $y = ae^{-e^{b-cx}}$ |
| | Logistic Model | $y = \dfrac{a}{1 + be^{-cx}}$ |
| | Richards Model | $y = \dfrac{a}{(1 + e^{b-cx})^{1/d}}$ |
| | MMF Model | $y = \dfrac{ab + cx^d}{b + x^d}$ |
| | Weibul Model | $y = a - be^{-cx^d}$ |
| Miscellaneous | Hiperbolic | $y = a + \dfrac{b}{x}$ |
| | Sinusoidal | $y = a + b\cos(cx + d)$ |
| | Heat Capacity | $y = a + bx + \dfrac{c}{x^2}$ |
| | Gaussian Model | $y = ae^{\frac{-(x-b)^2}{2c^2}}$ |
| | Rational Function | $y = \dfrac{a + bx}{1 + cx + dx^2}$ |

The following graphs illustrate the fact that several functions resulting from paired variables yield similar regressive fits. The data displayed in graphs 1a and 1b are closely adjusted with an MMF model; those of graphs 2a and 2b are, analogously, adjusted by a $4^{th}$ degree polynomial; finally, the data displayed in graphs 3a and 3b are tightly fit by a rational function. Interestingly, the correlation coefficient in all three couples is better than 0.93 indicating the very high quality of the fit. Hence, we rest assured that all samples display statistically significant equivalence. (We note that, because of space limitations, we are unable to show the entire set; however, very similar remarks do apply in all cases). On the other hand, for different couples we obtain best fit with *different* models: MMF $[(ab+cx^d)/(b+x^d)]$ for couple 1; $4^{th}$ degree polynomial $(a+bx+cx^2+dx^3+ex^4)$ for couple 2 and a rational function $[(a+bx)/(1+cx+dx^2)]$ for couple 3. This fact reinforces our expectation that different variables distribute differently even though the samples behave equivalently. A hypothetical possibility which is ruled out from this behavior is that all variables were similarly distributed. If this were the case, then ALL models would behave similarly and no significant conclusion could be derived from our observations.

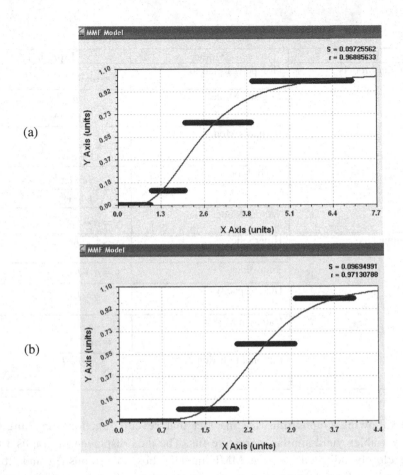

**Fig. 1.** Regressive fits. (a) MMF model for sample 1. (b) MMF model for sample 2.

It may be argued, upon first analysis, that the high correlation coefficients contradict the fact that our variables derive from the elimination of such correlation. Notice, however, that even if the variables with which we worked are not correlated (as discussed above) this non-correlation is *linear* (as pertaining to a Pearson coefficient) whereas the models considered here are basically highly non-linear, which resolves the apparent contradiction.

The probability of displaying results as shown by chance alone is less than $10^{-12}$. We must stress the fact that this analysis is only possible because we were able to numerically characterize each of the subsets in 34 different forms and, thus, to select the most appropriate ones. Furthermore, not only characterization was proven; we also showed that, in every case, the said characterization was similar when required and dissimilar in other cases.

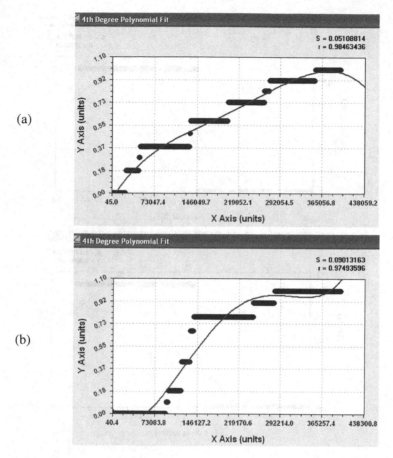

**Fig. 2.** Regressive fits. (a) 4th degree polynomial model for sample 1. (b) 4th degree polynomial model for sample 2.

## 4.3  Clustering Phase

Once the search space is reduced the clustering phase is reached. Before attempting the clustering proper, we impose certain a priori assumptions, as follows.

- The number of clusters is to be determined automatically (without applying any aprioristic rules).
- The "best" number (N) of clusters is derived from information theoretical arguments.
- The theoretical N is to be validated empirically from the expert analysis of the characteristics of such clusters.

In order to comply with our assumptions we follow the next steps:

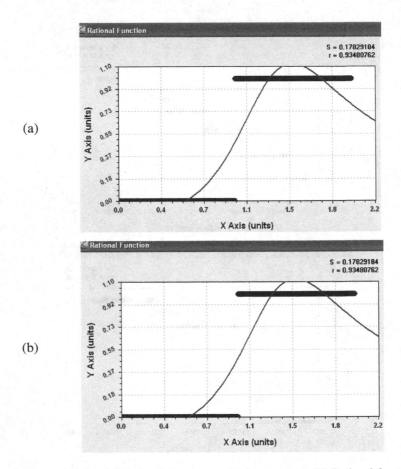

**Fig. 3.** Regressive fits. (a) Rational function model for sample 1. (b) Rational function model for sample 2.

1. Consecutively obtaining the clusters (via a Fuzzy C Means algorithm) assuming n clusters for n=2, 3, ...., k; where "k" represents the largest acceptable number of clusters.
2. Determine the "optimal" number of clusters according to "elbow" criterion [10].
3. Clustering with a self organizing map algorithm to find the optimal segmentation.

The minable view with the 129 variables was processed. The Fuzzy C Means (FCM) algorithm was used on the uncorrelated data and the elbow criterion was applied [19]. It is important to stress the fact that the use of fuzzy logic allows us to determine the content of information (the entropy) in every one of the N clusters into which the data set is divided. Other clustering algorithms based on crisp logic do not provide such alternative. Since the elements of a fuzzy cluster belong to all clusters it is possible to establish an analogy between the membership degree of an element in the set and the probability of its appearance. In this sense, the "entropy" is calculated as the expected value of the membership for a given cluster. Therefore we are able to calculate the partition's entropy PE (see below). Intuitively, as the number of clusters is increased the value of PE increases since the structure within a cluster is disrupted. In the limit, where there is a cluster for every member in the set, PE is maximal. On the other hand, we are always able to calculate the partition coefficient: a measure of how compact a set is. In this case, such measure of compactness decreases with N. The elbow criterion stipulates that the "best" N corresponds to the point where the corresponding *tendencies* of PE to increase and PC to decrease *simultaneously* change. That is, when the curvature of the graph of tendencies changes we are faced with an optimal number of clusters. Table 3 displays part of the numeric data values of PC and PE. These coefficients were calculated with formulas 1 and 2.

$$PC = \sum_{k=1}^{K} \sum_{i=1}^{c} \frac{(\mu_{ik})^2}{K} \tag{1}$$

$$PE = -\frac{1}{K} \sum_{k=1}^{K} \sum_{i=1}^{c} \mu_{ik} \ln(\mu_{ik}) \tag{2}$$

**Table 3.** Numeric data for the elbow criterion

| Clusters | 2 | 3 | 4 | 5 | 6 | 7 | 8 | 9 | 10 | 11 | 12 |
|---|---|---|---|---|---|---|---|---|---|---|---|
| PC | 0.879 | 0.770 | 0.642 | 0.560 | 0.498 | 0.489 | 0.413 | 0.414 | 0.400 | 0.359 | 0.349 |
| PE | 0.204 | 0.436 | 0.639 | 0.812 | 0.982 | 1.036 | 1.220 | 1.224 | 1.272 | 1.403 | 1.433 |

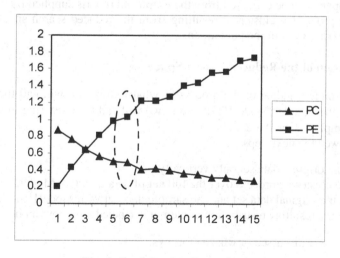

**Fig. 4.** Graph for the elbow criterion

Figure 4 shows the graph for the numeric data of table 3. In the graph the "elbow" point is located between the cluster 6 and 7, indicating that there is a high probability that the optimal number of clusters is in that point, i.e. N=6.

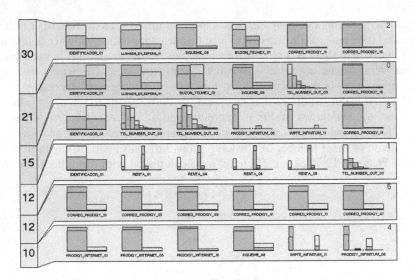

**Fig. 5.** Graph view of the clustering result supplied by the Miner

The last phase of our analysis implied the use of the miner and the theoretically determined best number of clusters, as shown in figure 5.

The graph shows at the left side the percentage of elements grouped in each cluster. On the right the neuron number which represents the cluster. Each cluster shows the more important variables for the results, ordered by Chi-squared characterization of the variable's behavior in the cluster and in the whole sample. The cluster information for the Company can be extracted from the graph and reports supplied by the tool. We should now prove that clustering resulting from the reduced search space reflects a correct clustering view of the population.

### 4.4   Validation of the Reduced Search Space

To ease the understanding of the process in what follows we will call the clustering model from the sample "Model1"; likewise, we will call the clustering model derived from the complete data "Model2".

We followed the next steps:

1. Reduce the original data set only vertically.
2. Execute a clustering process over the full set of data to obtain Model2.
3. Label all the original data set and the sample data set with Model1 and Model2.
4. Compare the resulting distribution of elements labeled with both models.

The results are discussed in what as follows.

### Comparison of Model1 and Model2

Table 4 shows the percentages for the two models. The names of the clusters were replaced by letters to avoid possible confusions with the neuron numbers shown in the Miner's results. As table 4 shows, the result clusters are very similar.

**Table 4.** Clusters' comparison for Model1 and Model2

| Clusters | Model1 (%) | Model2 (%) | Difference (%) |
|:---:|:---:|:---:|:---:|
| A | 30 | 27 | 3 |
| B | 21 | 20 | 1 |
| C | 15 | 18 | 3 |
| D | 12 | 15 | 3 |
| E | 12 | 12 | 0 |
| F | 10 | 8 | 2 |

## Clustering from Sampling (Model1)

Having the clustering Model1, we labeled the sample data and the full data sets. The resulting distribution of elements into the different 6 clusters was expressed in percentages for comparison effects. As the table 5 shows the resulting distribution for the sample and for the full data are almost equal. This proves that the sample represents the full data set adequately.

**Table 5.** Labeling from the Model1 applied to the sampled and full data sets

| Cluster | Sample (%) | Full Data (%) | Difference (%) |
|:---:|:---:|:---:|:---:|
| A | 30.06 | 30.24 | 0.18 |
| B | 21.01 | 20.91 | 0.10 |
| C | 15.45 | 15.37 | 0.08 |
| D | 12.27 | 12.25 | 0.02 |
| E | 11.54 | 11.55 | 0.01 |
| F | 9.67 | 9.68 | 0.01 |

## Cross Validation

Finally, we labeled the sample and the entire data with both algorithms. The results are shown in table 6.

**Table 6.** Comparison of Full and Sampled Data Clusters

| Cl | Labeling derived from sampled Data | | | | Labeling derived from Complete Data | | | |
|:---:|:---:|:---:|:---:|:---:|:---:|:---:|:---:|:---:|
| | Model1 | Model2 | Differ. | %Popu. | Model1 | Model2 | Differ. | %Popu. |
| A | 23906 | 21503 | 2403 | 3% | 120961 | 108084 | 12877 | 3% |
| B | 16712 | 16155 | 557 | 1% | 83655 | 81420 | 2235 | 1% |
| C | 12285 | 14327 | 2042 | 3% | 61471 | 72367 | 10896 | 3% |
| D | 9760 | 11828 | 2068 | 3% | 49013 | 59313 | 10300 | 3% |
| E | 9179 | 9580 | 401 | 1% | 46195 | 48356 | 2161 | 1% |
| F | 7687 | 6136 | 1551 | 2% | 38705 | 30460 | 8245 | 2% |

As table 6 shows the differences between the distributions of elements into the clusters are similar between the two clustering models. Analog clusters share the same cardinality with a difference of less than 3%.

## 5  Conclusions

As we pointed out in the introduction, data mining may be an important strategic tool for commercial enterprises. But the management of large volumes of data (both physically and logically) may become a practical problem of large proportions and difficult to solve. Applying the methodology advanced herein it is possible to drastically reduce the size of the data base to be processed. In this case we were able to reduce the size in close to 93.78%. Originally we had to deal with 166 million elements (i.e 400,000 registers with 415 attributes each); instead we used a simple with only 10.32 million such elements (80,000 records with 129 attributes). The reduced sample, however, performed in a way that made it statistically indistinguishable from the original data. Apart from the benefit resulting from having quicker access to strategic information the use of this methodology yields economic benefits derived from the ability to process a smaller sample (increased speed and capacity for data processing; decreased amount of primary and secondary storage, costs of software and hardware, among others). Considering that the company had important improvements with the application of the results of this investigation, we consider that continuing research is needed and justified, since much work remains to be done if we wish to set a bound on the characteristics of the data which will allow us to generalize the results reported here.

## Acknowledgments

Although the determination of the experimental probability distributions was achieved from the application of software designed by the authors, we wish to acknowledge that the graphs shown were obtained with CurveExpert v.1.3 (http://curveexpert.webhop.biz/) and clustering was performed with IBM® Intelligent Miner v.6.1

## References

1. Palpanas, T.: Knowledge Discovery in Data Warehouses. ACM SIGMOD record. 29(3), 88–100 (2000)
2. Jain, K., Murty, M.N., Flynn, P.J.: Data Clustering: A Review. ACM Computing Surveys 31(3), 264–323 (1999)
3. Berkhin, P.: Survey of Clustering Data Mining Techniques. Accrue Software (2002)
4. Kleinberg, J., Papadimitriou, C., Raghavan, P.: Segmentation Problems. Journal of the ACM 51(2), 263–280 (2004)
5. Guha, S., Rastogi, R., Shim, K.: CURE: An efficient clustering algorithm for Large Databases. In: ACM SIGMOD Proceedings, pp. 73–84. ACM Press, New York (1998)

6. Peter, W., Chiochetti, J., Giardina, C.: New unsupervised clustering algorithm for large datasets. In: ACM SIGKDD Proceedings, pp. 643–648. ACM Press, New York (2003)
7. Raymong, T.N., Jiawei, H.: Efficient and Effective Clustering Methods for Spatial Data Mining. 20th International Conference on Very Large Data Bases, pp. 144–155 (1994)
8. Cheng, D., Kannan, R., Vempala, S., Wang, G.: A Divide-and-Merge Methodology for Clustering. In: ACM SIGMOD Proceedings, pp. 196–205. ACM Press, New York (2005)
9. Jagadish, H.V., Lakshmanan, L.V., Srivastava, D.: Snakes and Sandwiches: Optimal Clustering Strategies for a Data Warehouse. In: ACM SIGMOD Proceedings, pp. 37–48. ACM Press, New York (1999)
10. Palmer, C.R., Faloutsos, C.: Density Biased Sampling: An Improved Method for Data Mining and Clustering. In: ACM SIGMOD Record, pp. 82–92. ACM Press, New York (2000)
11. Liu, H., Motoda, H.: On Issues of Instance Selection. Data Mining and Knowledge Discovery, vol. 6(2), pp. 115–130. Springer, Heidelberg (2002)
12. Zhu, X., Wu, X.: Scalable Representative Instance Selection and Ranking. In: Proceedings of the 18th IEEE international conference on pattern recognition, pp. 352–355. IEEE Computer Society Press, Los Alamitos (2006)
13. Brighton, H., Mellish, C.: Advances in Instance Selection for Instance-Based Learning Algorithms. Data Mining and Knowledge Discovery 6, 153–172 (2002)
14. Vu, K., Hua, K.A., Cheng, H., Lang, S.: A Non-Linear Dimensionality-Reduction Technique for Fast Similarity Search in Large Databases. In: ACM SIGMOD Proceedings, pp. 527–538. ACM Press, New York (2006)
15. Zhang, D., Zhou, Z., Chen, S.: Semi-Supervised Dimensionality Reduction. In: Proceedings of the SIAM International Conference on Data Mining (2007)
16. Fodor, I.K.: A survey of dimension reduction techniques. U.S. Department of Energy, Lawrence Livermore National Laboratory (2002)
17. Hair, J.F., Anderson, R.E., Tatham, R.L., Black, W.C.: Análisis Multivariante, 5th edn., pp. 11–15. Pearson Prentice Hall, Madrid (1999)
18. Delmater, R., Hancock, M.: Data Mining Explained: A Manager's Guide to Customer-Centric Business Intelligence (Chapter 6). Digital press (2001)
19. Bezdek, J.C.: Cluster Validity with Fuzzy Sets. Journal of Cybernetics (3), 58–72 (1974)

# Combining Traditional and Neural-Based Techniques for Ink Feed Control in a Newspaper Printing Press

Cristofer Englund[1] and Antanas Verikas[1,2]

[1] Intelligent Systems Laboratory, Halmstad University, Box 823,
S-301 18 Halmstad, Sweden
cristofer.englund@ide.hh.se
[2] Department of Applied Electronics, Kaunas University of Technology, Studentu 50,
LT-3031, Kaunas, Lithuania
antanas.verikas@ide.hh.se

**Abstract.** To achieve robust ink feed control an integrating controller and a multiple models-based controller are combined. Experimentally we have shown that the multiple models-based controller operating in the training region is superior to the integrating controller. However, for data originating from outside the multiple models training region, the integrating controller has the advantage. It is, therefore, suggested to combine the two techniques in order to improve robustness of the control system.

## 1 Introduction

Colour images, as such appearing on a camera display or a computer monitor are composed of a mixture of three primary colours; red (R), green (G) and blue (B). The *RGB* primaries correspond to the three types of colour sensing elements—*cones*—found in the human eye [1]. *RGB* is an additive colour system meaning that the spectra of the light coming from the three primary sources are added to reproduce the spectrum of a certain colour. When the three primaries are mixed in equal portions a grey shade is conceived. The lower the intensity the darker does the colour appear.

A white substrate, for example paper, is usually used in printing. White paper possesses approximately the same reflection coefficient for all wavelengths in the visible spectrum. When the white paper is illuminated, the colour perceived by the observer approximately matches that of the light source. To attain colours during printing, in contrast to the additive system, a subtractive colour system is used where portions of the light are absorbed by the printed ink. The type of ink determines in what part of the spectrum the absorption takes place. The primary colours usually used in four-colour printing are cyan (C), magenta (M), yellow (Y), and black (K), *CMYK*. A *CMY* overprint creates black colour. However, black ink (K) is also used in printing. Due to economical reasons, black ink often replaces the *CMY* overprints. Moreover, black ink is often used to improve the

P. Perner (Ed.): ICDM 2007, LNAI 4597, pp. 214–227, 2007.

quality of colour pictures. Since colour images are usually obtained in the $RGB$ colour space, while printed using the $CMYK$ primaries, printing involves the so called colour separation process, where $RGB$ images are transformed into the $CMYK$ colour space [2,3].

Usually the printing press operator samples the print manually throughout the job run. The sample is compared to the approved sample print and an effort is made to compensate for colour deviations detected in the print. Each operator performs the adjustments based on the experience gained from working at the press. Typically, the perception of the printed result is very subjective and consequently great variations may appear in the printed result. By using an automatic control system one can eliminate the inconsistent sampling and subjective colour compensations made by the operator and one can expect a number of favourable affects on the printed result, i.e. more uniform print quality through the production. Amongst the advantages of using an automatic control system are the continuous sampling, its swiftness, the consistency in control actions and that it is indefatigable. Operator's time is also set free for the benefit of service and maintenance of the printing press equipment.

There are few successful attempts to automatically control the ink feed in an offset newspaper printing press. In [4], a decision support system is discussed. The print is measured and a knowledge base, build up from observing an experienced operator, is used to help a novice operator to adjust the printing press to compensate for ink density deviations in the print. The decision support system developed in [5] is used in a wall-covering rotogravure printing industry. The system measures a number of characteristics of the print, including colour. If drift is detected in any of the parameters, the system instructs the operator to make adequate adjustments to the process variables. The system developed in [6] for online ink feed control is able to drive the ink density of the print, to the desired target density level. The decision support system developed in [7] has been developed for defect recognition and misprint diagnosis in offset printing. The system is able to recognize defects based on an image sensor, classify the defects into one of 47 categories including color drift and suggests what action the operator should take to eliminate the cause of defect.

In all the aforementioned works, the ink feed control is based on controlling the ink density measured on a solid print area, as that shown on the left of Fig. 1. However, printed pictures are made of dots, see the image on the right of Fig. 1. Since not only the ink density, but also the size of the dots may vary in the printing process, ink density does not provide enough information for controlling the printing process. The amount of ink integrating information on both the ink density and the dot size should be used instead. Therefore, the printed amount of ink estimated in the double grey bar, shown in the image on the right of Fig. 1, is the control variable used in this work. The double grey bar consists of two parts, one part is printed using the black ink and the other part using the cyan, magenta and yellow inks.

We use the technique proposed in [8] to estimate the amount of ink in the double grey bar. To estimate the amount of ink, the $RGB$ image recorded from

**Fig. 1.** *Left*: Solid print areas. *Right*: The double grey bar.

the double grey bar by a colour $CCD$ camera is transformed into the $L^*$ $a^*$ $b^*$ counterpart and the average $L^*$ $a^*$ $b^*$ values are calculated for both parts of the double grey bar. The neural networks-based technique [8] then transforms the pair of $L^*$ $a^*$ $b^*$ values into the amount of inks. The neural network is trained using colour patches printed with constant ink density and varying tonal value (the percentage of area covered by the ink). If the ink density used to print a test patch is equal to that kept when printing patches for training the neural network, the printed amount of ink may vary between 0 and 100. If the ink density exceeds the one used to print the training patch, the measured amount of ink may exceed 100 (for an area with 100% ink coverage). In this work, the given amount of ink is the target signal the controller has to maintain.

An approach to automatic data mining and printing press modelling has recently been proposed [9]. Based on this approach we have developed a multiple models-based technique for ink feed control, which has shown good performance in controlling the ink flow in an offset printing press [10]. There are a number of models of different complexity, specialised and general ones, engaged in controlling the printing process. The specialised models are trained on specialised data sets, while the general models are trained on the union of the data sets used to train the specialised models. A committee of specialised models is also incorporated into the set of multiple models. By using the adaptive data mining and modelling approach we provide the multiple models-based controller with up to date models.

Multiple models-based controllers have shown to be efficient in many industrial control applications due to their ability to improve stability and increase the modelling performance [11,12,13]. However, neural networks-based models run into generalisation problems when data outside the training region need to be processed. Such situations are encountered in printing industry, since new unknown jobs may always appear. To cope with the problems we suggest building a hybrid control system consisting of an integrating controller and a multiple models-based controller. In industry applications, integrating controllers are commonly used due to their simplicity and efficiency.

## 2    Description of Process Variables

The printing press operator samples the print throughout the job run. As colour deviation from the approved sample print is detected the ink flow is changed, increased or decreased, by adjusting the ink keys. The ink keys are situated at

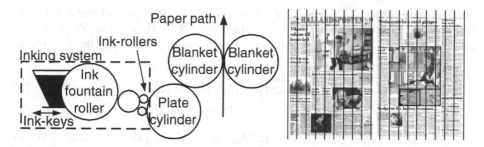

**Fig. 2.** *Left*: A schematic illustration of the inking system. *Right*: An illustration of how the ink zones subdivide the paper fold.

the bottom of the ink tray, Fig. 2 (left). At the press at hand there are 36 ink keys for each colour and side of the web. The ink key adjusts the ink feed in an approximately 4 cm wide zone (ink zone), see Fig. 2 (right).

In the present work, to create a multiple models-based controller for adjusting the ink key opening, we utilise models of the printing process, build from historical process data. The data collected in one ink zone are called specialised data and hence, used to train the specialised models. The union of all the speicalised data is used to train the general models. Both inverse models, where the ink key opening value constitutes the model output and direct models, where the printed amount of ink constitutes the output, are built. The process parameters used to model one ink $(C, M, Y,$ or $K)$ are given below. Depending on the modelling task, inverse or direct, different combinations of these parameters are utilised.

$x_1$ — printing speed in copies per hour.

$x_2$ — ink fountain roller speed.

$x_3$ — ink temperature. The temperature of the ink in the ink tray. The temperature affects the viscosity of the ink. The higher the temperature the lower the viscosity—the easier does the ink flow through the inking system.

$x_{4,5,6}$ — estimated ink demand for the current, adjacent to the left, and to the right ink zone, respectively. The ink demand equals to the percentage of area covered by ink in the corresponding ink zone.

$x_{7,8,9}$ — ink key opening for the current, adjacent to the left, and to the right ink zone, respectively —is the signal controlling the amount of ink dispersed on the paper.

$x_{10}$ — amount of ink of a specific colour estimated from the double grey bar.

In the direct modelling, $x_{10}(t + 1)$ is the model output. However, for inverse modelling, where the modelling task is to predict the ink key opening, the $x_{10}(t + 1)$ value is used as an input parameter, while the parameter $x_7(t+1)$ constitutes the model output. The variables $x_7$ and $x_{10}$ are used from both the current time step $(t)$ and the next $(t + 1)$. Experimental studies have shown that no further performance gain is achieved by exploiting more previous time steps e.g. $(t - 1)$ or $(t - 2)$. The variables $x_{4,5,6}$, describe the ink demand in the current zone $(x_4)$

and the two adjacent zones $(x_5, x_6)$. Since ink flows between adjacent zones in the printing press, the variables $x_{4,5,6}$ are replaced by their mean $\overline{x_{4,5,6}}$, in the models. For simplicity we denote the variables incorporated in the direct and inverse model as:

$$\mathbf{v}^d = [x_1(t), x_2(t), x_3(t), \overline{x_{4,5,6}(t)}, x_7(t+1), x_7(t), x_8(t), x_9(t), x_{10}(t)] \quad (1)$$

$$\mathbf{v}^i = [x_1(t), x_2(t), x_3(t), \overline{x_{4,5,6}(t)}, x_7(t), x_8(t), x_9(t), x_{10}(t+1), x_{10}(t)] \quad (2)$$

It should be noted that these variables are used to train the models. When the models are used for control the variable $x_7(t+1)$ is replaced by the output of the inverse model $u(t+1)$ and $x_{10}(t+1)$ is replaced by the desired amount of ink $y^{des}$. Note also that the ink key opening value varies in the range [0,100]. To obtain data necessary for the modelling, a web offset newspaper printing press was equipped with an online press monitoring system. A detailed description of the monitoring system can be found in [10].

## 3   Methods

### 3.1   Printing Process Modelling

Due to wear of the printing press, the process can be classified as slowly time-varying. In addition, depending on a printing job, the time the process stays in a predefined part of the input variable space may vary significantly, from minutes to several days. If the process starts to operate in a new region of the input variable space, different from the training region, the model performance may deteriorate significantly. To handle such situations, we have recently proposed an adaptive data mining and modelling approach [9]. The data mining tool monitors the process data and keeps an up to date data set of a reasonable size characterising the process. The adaptive modelling is aiming at building models of optimal complexity. Starting with a linear model, a number of nonlinear models of increasing complexity (MLP with an increasing number of hidden units) are built. Then a model with the lowest generalisation error is selected for modelling the process. During the process run, the need to update the models is automatically detected and the models are retrained. In this work, we use this technique to create and update the process models.

Four types of models are used in this work for modelling the printing process.

- A model specific for each ink key/zone. These models are called specialised, since they have specific knowledge about a certain ink key/zone. Each specialised model is trained using data from a specific ink zone.
- A committee of specialised models. Specialised models implementing similar functions are aggregated into a committee. In [14] we developed an approach for building committees of models where both the number of members and the aggregation weights of the members are data dependent. We use this approach to create committees of models.

- A nonlinear general model that is built using the data from all the ink-zones. The general model is built using more data than the specialised one and therefore it generalises better than the specialised models.
- A linear general model built using data from all the ink zones.

The specialised models and committees of the models provide the highest modelling accuracy. However, due to the limited training data set used, the models may run into generalisation problems. In such situations, general models are used instead, which are built using much more data points than the specialised ones. Since the complexity of the models is determined automatically the general model may be linear or nonlinear. If a nonlinear general model is automatically selected, a linear general model is also built. The linear general model exhibits the lowest modelling accuracy, however the best generalisation ability.

## 4    Ink Key Control

The data acquisition system is not only capable of reading the status of the printing press control system but also sending control signals to the press. The process controller was implemented in a closed loop control system where the signals to and from the controller are sent via the data acquisition system. The sampling time is approximately 100 seconds i.e. the time needed for the monitoring system to traverse the camera once over the paper web to take an image of each of the 36 double grey bars and return to the initial position.

Model-based control systems are common in industry because process models have the ability to mimic both the direct and inverse behavior of the process. Multiple models-based controllers have shown to be efficient in different industrial control applications due to their ability to improve stability and increase the modelling performance [11,12,13]. A detailed description of the multiple models-based design we have developed for ink feed control can be found in [10]. Here we provide only a brief summary of the technique.

### 4.1    Multiple Models-Based Controller Design

Fig. 3 illustrates the multiple models-based configuration, where the denotation IM stands for inverse model and DM means direct model. Models incorporated in the control configuration are:

*Sing*—a single specialised model.
*Com*—a committee of specialised models.
*NLGen*—a single general nonlinear model.
*LGen*—a single general linear model.

The control configuration functions as follows. The control signal $u(t+1)$ is given by the output of one of the inverse models. We assume that the inverse model output is normally distributed with the mean given by the model output and the standard deviation $\sigma$. A large standard deviation of the predicted control

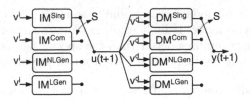

**Fig. 3.** The multiple models-based control configuration

signal indicates model uncertainty. By sampling from the distribution of the inverse model output, as suggested in [15], we produce a set of control samples $U(t+1) = [u_1(t+1), u_2(t+1), ..., u_D(t+1)]$ that are evaluated using the direct model, see Fig. 3. The number of samples $D$ is determined by the model standard deviation $\sigma$. The larger the $\sigma$ the more samples are generated.

The output of the inverse model $u(t+1)$ and the direct model $y(t+1)$ are given by

$$u(t+1) = f^i(\mathbf{v}^i; \boldsymbol{\theta}^i) \tag{3}$$
$$y(t+1) = f^d(\mathbf{v}^d; \boldsymbol{\theta}^d) \tag{4}$$

where $\boldsymbol{\theta}$ is the model parameter vector and the functions $f$ are either linear or nonlinear.

The control signals $u_{i1}(t+1), u_{i2}(t+1), ..., u_{iD}(t+1)$ generated by each of the inverse models $(i = 1, ..., 4)$ are used to calculate the outputs $y_{11}(t+1), y_{21}(t+1), ..., y_{41}(t+1), ..., y_{4D}(t+1)$ of the direct models. The output $y_{ij}(t+1)$ is given by

$$y_{ij}(t+1) = f^d(\mathbf{v}_{ij}^d; \boldsymbol{\theta}^d) \tag{5}$$

where, $i = 1, ..., 4$ refers to a model. The model selected is that minimising the error $e_{ij}$, the difference between the output of the direct model $y_{ij}(t+1)$ and the target (the desired amount of ink) $y^{des}$: $e_{ij} = ||y_{ij}(t+1) - y^{des}||$. Having all $e_{ij}$s, the indices $p, q$ of the control signal $u_{pq}(t+1)$ sent to the press are found as follows:

$$p, q = \arg\min_{i,j} e_{ij} \tag{6}$$

The control signal selected is denoted $u^{mm}(t+1)$. If for a given $\mathbf{v}$, $e_{pq} > \beta$ and $p \neq 3$, the linear general model is used to avoid using the nonlinear model with a large prediction error.

## 4.2   Robust Ink Feed Control

Fig. 4 illustrates the case, where the neural networks-based controller runs into generalisation problems. The left graph shows the ink key control signal (above) and the measured amount of ink along with the target amount of ink indicated by the solid line (below). Initially the multiple models-based controller runs the process. At sample no. 7 and 9 the target amount of ink is changed. Accordingly, the multiple models-based controller is adjusting the ink key opening to obtain the desired amount of ink. As it can be seen, the ink key adjustments do not bring the process output to the desired level. At sample no. 21 and 22 the control action from the multiple models-based controller is manually overridden and the desired target level is reached. Fig. 4 (right) explains the origin of the problem. The right graph of Fig. 4 shows the training data (∗) and the data from the current job (△ and □) projected onto the first two principal components of the training data. We clearly see that the data indicated by the squares are well separated from the training data. It is obvious that to successfully use the multiple models-based controller the models need to be retrained. However, to retrain the models, training data are to be collected. We suggest using an integrating controller during this period of time. Though with lower accuracy, the integrating controller can handle the process temporary.

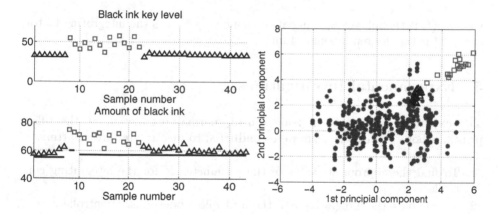

**Fig. 4.** *Left* (*top*): Ink key opening and (*bottom*): the measured and the target (solid line) amount of ink. *Right*: The data projected onto the space spanned by the first two principal components.

We use the difference between the predicted amount of ink $y(t-1)$ and the measured amount of ink at time $t$, $y^{mes}(t)$ to detect the situations. The schematic illustration of the robust ink feed controller is shown in Fig. 5. The control signal $u(t+1)$ is given by:

$$u(t+1) = \begin{cases} u^{ic}(t+1) & if\left(y^{mes}(t) - y(t)\right) > \xi \\ u^{mm}(t+1) & otherwise \end{cases} \tag{7}$$

where $u^{mm}(t+1)$ is the ink key opening predicted by the multiple models, $u^{ic}(t+1)$ is the ink key opening predicted by the integrating controller, $y(t)$ is the amount of ink predicted by the multiple models at $t-1$, and $y^{mes}(t)$ is the measured amount of ink at the current time step $t$. By using this approach

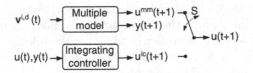

**Fig. 5.** The proposed control configuration

the process is controlled, either by the integrating or multiple models-based controller.

### 4.3 Integrating Controller Design

The control signal generated by the integrating controller is estimated as

$$u^{ic}(t+1) = u(t) + K\left(y^{des} - y^{mes}(t)\right) \tag{8}$$

where $u(t)$ is the ink key opening at the time step $t$, $K$ is the integrating factor, and $y^{des}$ is the desired amount of ink.

## 5    Experimental Investigations

The experiments have been made during normal production at the offset printing-shop. The experiments were conducted to investigate three matters:

1. To find the appropriate value of the parameter $K$ for the integrating controller.
2. To compare the integrating and the multiple models-based controllers.
3. To demonstrate the benefit of the proposed control configuration.

### 5.1    Selecting the Parameter K

To find the appropriate $K$ value, the parameter was varied between 0.2 and 2.5. In Fig. 6, we present three examples of control and output signals for different $K$ parameter values. The top graph shows the control signal, the lower graph shows the measured and the desired (the solid line) amount of ink. The desired amount of ink is constant during the experiment. The controller starts running the process at sample 4. As it can be seen, the larger the $K$, the larger is control action.

It was found that $K=0.7$ is a good choice since at this value, on average, the controller was reasonably fast and not too sensitive to noise. As it can be seen in Fig. 6, at $K = 0.2$ the rise time is very long. At $K=1.4$ both the control signal and the output signal are rather noisy. The standard deviation of the output signal (noise level) is 3.3, 2.5 and 2.3 for $K=0.2$, 0.7 and 1.4, respectively.

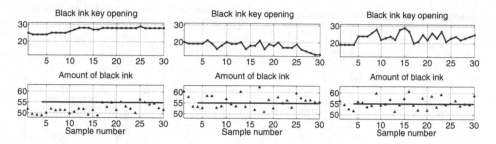

**Fig. 6.** The control signal (top) and the measured along with the desired (solid line) amount of ink for different $K$ values (bottom). $K = 0.2, 0.7$ and $1.4$ for the left, middle, and the right graph, respectively.

## 5.2  Comparison of the Controllers

To make the comparison feasible, we use the controllers in the same ink zone for the same printing job. We begin by saving the initial settings for the press and start the experiment using one of the controllers. Then, we restore the settings of the printing press and continue the same experiment using the other controller. Two issues are studied, the rise time and the sensitivity to noise.

**Rise Time.** A short rise time is desirable to reduce the paper waste. In Fig. 7, we present the response of the controllers operating on the same ink key for two different colours. For each colour, the left graphs show the results from the integrating controller, whereas the right graphs present the results from the multiple models-based controller. The top graphs show the ink key control signal and the bottom graphs present the measured and the target (solid line) amount of inks. The controller is used from sample 3 (where the solid line appears). In the figures, ID stands for ink demand.

As it can be seen, the integrating controller requires more samples to drive the output to the desired target level. The multiple models-based controller exhibits a shorter rise time than the integrating controller.

Fig. 8 presents two more control examples. The results presented are for the case where the target amount of ink is less than the initial printed amount of ink. Again, for both examples, the multiple models-based controller drives the amount of ink to the desired level faster than the integrating controller.

**Noise in the Control and Output Signals.** Our previous studies have shown that, on average, the noise level in the measured amount of ink is approximately equal to 2 units [9]. The examples presented show that the integrating controller does not produce as stable output as the multiple models-based controller does. On average, the noise level for the integrating controller was larger than for the multiple models-based controller. Table 1 summarises the standard deviation $\sqrt{\frac{1}{N-1} \sum (y^{mes} - y^{des})^2}$, of the output signal, for the examples presented in Fig. 7 and Fig. 8 and for the long time experiments carried out during normal

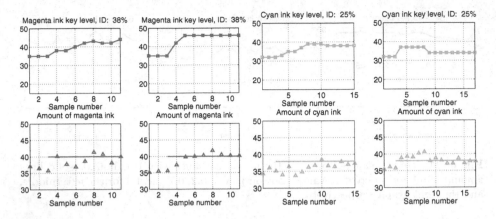

**Fig. 7.** Results from the integrating controller (first and third columns) and the multiple models-based controller

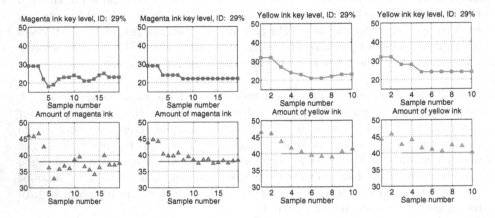

**Fig. 8.** Results from the integrating controller (first and third columns) and the multiple models-based controller

production. Observe that the target amount of ink was constant. The long time experiments lasted for 3 hours.

## 5.3   Robust Ink Feed Control

The printing process may start to operate in a new region of the input variable space, different from the training region, as it was discussed earlier and illustrated in Fig. 4. Fig. 9 presents an example illustrating the benefit of the approach proposed in such situations. The top left graph in Fig. 9 shows the ink key control signal. The target (solid line) and the measured amount of inks are shown in the middle left graph. The prediction error and the threshold of the error are presented in the bottom left graph. We distinguish three regions in the control sequence. At the beginning, the multiple models-based controller runs

**Table 1.** The standard deviation of the measured amount of ink for the experiments illustrated in Fig. 7, Fig. 8, and for the long time measurements (LT). IC stands for integrating controller, MM for multiple models-based controller, and $C, M, Y, K$ for cyan, magenta, yellow, and black.

| Controller | Fig. 7(M) | Fig. 7(C) | Fig. 8(M) | Fig. 8(Y) | LT(C) | LT(M) | LT(Y) | LT(K) |
|---|---|---|---|---|---|---|---|---|
| IC | 1.68 | 3.79 | 3.70 | 2.91 | 5.8 | 4.5 | 4.3 | 5.7 |
| MM | 1.12 | 1.97 | 1.65 | 1.94 | 2.5 | 2.7 | 2.4 | 3.4 |

the process. At the point where the difference between the predicted and the measured amount of ink exceeds the threshold, $\xi = 6$, the integrating controller takes over the control, samples indicated by diamonds (◇). The integrating controller brings the process to the target amount of ink and the prediction error of the model is low again. The right graph in Fig. 9 shows the input data projected onto the first two principal components. As it can be seen the data resulting in high prediction error appear at the edge of the main bulk of the training data (shown as stars *). This explains why the multiple models-based controller has problems with these data points.

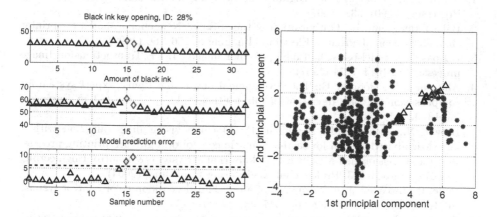

**Fig. 9.** *Left above*: The ink key opening. *Left middle*: The measured and the target (solid line) amount of ink. *Left below*: The error of the predicted amount of ink and the threshold of the error (dashed line). *Right:* The data projected onto the first two principal components.

# 6   Conclusions

A technique for robust ink feed control in an offset lithographic printing press has been presented in this paper. The technique combines a traditional integrating controller and a neural networks-based (multiple modes-based) controller. We have shown that the multiple models-based controller is superior to the integrating controller by both lower rise time and lower noise in the output signal. However, as the process starts operating in a new region of the input space, the multiple models may run into generalisation problems. Such situations are automatically detected and the integrating controller temporary takes over the process control. We have shown experimentally that the proposed technique is able to automatically control the ink feed in the newspaper printing press according to the target amount of ink.

In future work long term experiments will be carried out for a wide variety of printing jobs where the performance of the system under the influence of disturbances such as reel changes, temperature and printing speed changes, etc will be investigated.

## Acknowledgements

We gratefully acknowledge the financial support from the Knowledge Foundation Sweden and Holmen Paper, StoraEnso, and VTAB groups Sweden.

## References

1. Sharma, G., Trussell, H.J.: Digital color imaging. IEEE Transactions on Image Processing 6, 901–932 (1997)
2. Balasubramanian, R.: Optimization of the spectral Neugebauer model for printer characterization. Journal of Electronic Imaging 8, 156–166 (1999)
3. Pappas, T.: Model-based halftoning of color images. IEEE Transactions on Image processing 6, 1014–1024 (1997)
4. Almutawa, S., Moon, Y.B.: The development of a connectionist expert system for compensation of color deviation in offset lithographic printing. AI in Engineering 13, 427–434 (1999)
5. Brown, N., Jackson, M., Bamforth, P.: Machine vision in conjunction with a knowledge-based system for semi-automatic control of a gravure printing process. In: Proceedings of the I MECH E Part I Journal of Systems & Control Engineering, vol. 218, pp. 583–593. Professional Engineering Publishing (2004)
6. Pope, B., Sweeney, J.: Performance of an on-line closed-loop color control system. In: TAGA 2000 Proceedings, pp. 417–431 (2000)
7. Perner, P.: Knowledge-based image inspection system for automatic defect recognition, classification and process diagnosis. Mashine Vision and Applications 7, 135–147 (1994)
8. Verikas, A., Malmqvist, K., Bergman, L.: Neural networks based colour measuring for process monitoring and control in multicoloured newspaper printing. Neural Computing & Applications 9, 227–242 (2000)
9. Englund, C., Verikas, A.: A SOM based data mining strategy for adaptive modelling of an offset lithographic printing process. Engineering Applications of Artificial Intelligence 20, 391–400 (2007)
10. Englund, C., Verikas, A.: Ink flow control by multiple models in an offset lithographic printing process. Computers & Industrial Engineering (in review) (2006)
11. Chen, L., Narendra, K.S.: Nonlinear adaptive control using neural networks and multiple models. Automatica 37, 1245–1255 (2001)
12. Ravindranathan, M., Leitch, R.: Model switching in intelligent control systems. AI in Engineering 13, 175–187 (1999)

13. Yu, W.: Multiple recurrent neural networks for stable adaptive control. Neurocomputing 70, 430–444 (2006)
14. Englund, C., Verikas, A.: A SOM based model combination strategy. In: Wang, J., Liao, X.-F., Yi, Z. (eds.) ISNN 2005. LNCS, vol. 3496(Part 1), pp. 461–466. Springer, Heidelberg (2005)
15. Herzallah, R., Lowe, D.: A mixture density network approach to modelling and exploiting uncertainty in nonlinear control problems. Engineering Applications of Artificial Intelligence 17, 145–158 (2004)

# Active Learning Strategies: A Case Study for Detection of Emotions in Speech

Alexis Bondu, Vincent Lemaire, and Barbara Poulain

R&D France Telecom,
TECH/EASY/TSI
2 avenue Pierre Marzin 22300 Lannion

**Abstract.** Machine learning indicates methods and algorithms which allow a model to learn a behavior thanks to examples. Active learning gathers methods which select examples used to build a training set for the predictive model. All the strategies aim to use the less examples as possible and to select the most informative examples. After having formalized the active learning problem and after having located it in the literature, this article synthesizes in the first part the main approaches of active learning. Taking into account emotions in Human-machine interactions can be helpful for intelligent systems designing. The main difficulty, for the conception of calls center's automatic shunting system, is the cost of data labeling. The last section of this paper propose to reduce this cost thanks to two active learning strategies. The study is based on real data resulting from the use of a vocal stock exchange server.

## 1 Introduction

Active learning methods come from a parallel between active educational methods and learning theory. The learner is from now a statistical model and not a student. The interactions between the student and the teacher correspond to the opportunity (possibility) to the model to interact with a human expert. The examples are situations used by the model to generate knowledge on the problem.

Active learning methods allow the model to interact with its environment by selecting the more "informative" situations. The purpose is to train a model which uses as litle as possible examples. The elaboration of the training set is done in interaction with a human expert to maximize progress of the model. The model must be able to detect the more informative examples for its learning and to ask to the expert: "what should be done in these situations".

The purpose of this paper is to present two main active learning approaches found in the state of the art. These approaches are presented in a generic way without considered a kind of model (the one which learns using examples delivered by the expert after every of its requests). Others approaches exist but they are not presented in this paper although references are given for the reader who would be interested in.

P. Perner (Ed.): ICDM 2007, LNAI 4597, pp. 228–241, 2007.

The next section of this paper introduce the topic, formalize active learning in a generic way and establish mathematical notations used. The aim of this section is to place active learning among others statistical learning methods (supervised, unsupervised...). The fourth section presents in details two main active learning approaches. These two strategies are then used in the fifth section on a real problem. Finally the last section is a discussion on question open in this paper.

# 2  Active Learning

## 2.1  General Remarks

The objective of statistical learning (unsupervised, semi-supervised, supervised[1]) is to "inculcate" a behavior to a model using observations (examples) and a learning algorithm. The observations are points of view on the problem to be resolved and constitute the learning data. At the end of the training stage the model has to generalize its learning to unseen situations in a "reasonable" way.

For example let's imagine a model which try to detect "happy" and "unhappy" people from passport photo. If the model realizes good predictions for unseen people during its training stage then the model correctly generalize.

Characteristics of used data change depending on the learning mode. Unsupervised learning is a method of machine learning where a model is fit to observations. It is distinguished from supervised learning by the fact that there are no a priori outputs on data. The learner has to discover itself correlations between examples which are shown to it. In case of the example above ("happy" / "unhappy" people), the model is trained using passport photos deprive of label and has no indication on what we try to make it learn. Among unsupervised learning methods one finds clustering methods [2] and association rules methods [3].

Semi-supervised learning [4] is a class of techniques that makes use of both labeled and unlabeled data for training; typically a small amount of labeled data and a large amount of unlabeled data. Among possible utilization of this learning mode, we could distinguish (i) semi-supervised clustering which tries to group similar instances but using information given by the small amount of labeled data [5] and (ii) semi-supervised classification [6] which is based first on labeled data to elaborate a first model and then unlabeled data to improve the model.

Supervised learning is a machine learning technique for creating a function from training data. The training data consist of pairs of input objects (typically vectors), and desired outputs. The output of the function can be a continuous value (called regression), or can predict a class label of the input object (called classification). The task of the supervised learner is to predict the value of the function for any valid input object after having seen a number of training examples (i.e. pairs of input and target output). In case of the illustrative example above, examples would be passport photos associated to labels "happy" or "unhappy".

---

[1] Reinforcement learning is not presented here, reader interested could read [1].

At last, active learning, as the name suggests, is a type of learner which is less passive than the others described above. This strategy allows the model to construct its own training set in interaction with a human expert. The learning starts with few desired outputs (class labels for classification or continuous value for regression). Then, the model selects examples (without desired outputs) that it considers the more informative and asks to the human expert their desired outputs. In case of the illustrative example, the model asks class labels of passport photos presented to the human expert. In this paper, we restrict active learning to classification but it is obvious that our presentation of active learning strategies can be transpose for regression.

Active learning is different from all others learning methods because it interacts with its environment; the examples are not randomly chosen. Active learning strategies allow the model to learn faster (the learner rich the best performances using less data) considering first the more informative examples. This approach is more specifically attractive when data are expensive to obtain or to label.

### 2.2   Two Possible Scenarios

The distinction between raw data and data descriptors (which are associated) is important. In the illustrative example above, the raw data are passport photos and the data descriptors are attributes describing the photos (pixel, luminosity, contrasts, etc.). The model makes the prediction of the class "happy" or "unhappy" to every vector of descriptors. The elaboration of descriptors from raw data is not always bijective; sometimes it is impossible to compose raw data using list of descriptors. Adaptive sampling and selective sampling, which are the two main scenarios to set active learning [7], use respectively "data descriptors" and "raw data".

In the case of **adaptive sampling** [8] the model requires of expert labels corresponding to vectors of descriptors. The model is not restricted and can explore all the space of variations of the descriptors, searching area to be sampled more finely. Adaptive sampling can pose problem in its implementation when it is difficult to know if the vectors of descriptors (generated by the model) have a meaning with respect to the initial problem. Let us suppose that the model requires the label associated with the vector $[10, 4, 5..., 12]$. Does this vector correspond to a set of descriptors which represent a passport photo, a human face photo, a flower or something else?

In the case of **selective sampling** [9], the model observes only one restricted part of the universe materialized by training examples stripped of label. Consequently, the input vectors selected by the model always correspond to a raw data. The image of a *"bag'"* of instances for which the model can ask labels associated (to the examples in the bag) is usually used. The model requires the label associated with the vector $[10, 4, 5..., 12]$ which corresponds to a passport photo.

Emotion detection is a problem where it is easy to obtain a great number of unlabeled examples and for which labeling is expensive. Therefore, from now the point of view of selective sampling is only considered. In practice, the choice of selective or adaptive sampling depends primarily on the applicability where the model is authorized, or not, "to generate" new examples.

## 2.3   Notations

$\mathcal{M} \in \mathbb{M}$ is the predictive model which is trained thanks to an algorithm $\mathcal{L}$. $\mathbb{X} \subseteq \mathbb{R}^n$ represents all the possible input examples of the model and $x \in \mathbb{X}$ is a particular examples. $\mathbb{Y}$ is the set of the possible outputs (answers) of the model; $y \in \mathbb{Y}$ a class label[2] related (associated) to $x \in \mathbb{X}$.

During its training, the model observes (see Figure 1) only one part $\Phi \subseteq \mathbb{X}$ of the universe. The set of examples is limited and the labels associated to these examples are not necessarily known. The set of examples where the labels are known (at a step of the training algorithm) is called $L_x$ and the set of examples where the labels are unknown is called $U_x$ with $\Phi \equiv U_x \cup L_x$ and $U_x \cap L_x \equiv \emptyset$.

The concept which is learned can be seen as a function, $f : \mathbb{X} \to \mathbb{Y}$, with $f(x_1)$ is the desired answer of the model for the example $x_1$ and $\widehat{f} : \mathbb{X} \to \mathbb{Y}$ the obtained answer of the model; an estimation of the concept. The elements of $L_x$ and the associated labels constitute a training set $T$. The training examples are pairs of input vectors and desired labels such as $(x, f(x)) : \forall x \in L_x, \exists!(x, f(x)) \in T$.

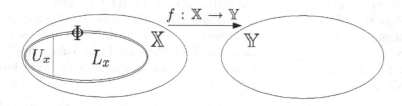

**Fig. 1.** Notations

# 3   Active Learning Methods

## 3.1   Introduction

The problem of selective sampling was posed formally by Muslea [10] (see Algorithm 1). It uses an utility function, $Utility(u, \mathcal{M})$, which estimates the utility of an example $u$ for the training of the model $\mathcal{M}$. Thanks to this function, the model presents to the expert examples for which it hopes the greatest improvement of its performances.

The Algorithm 1 is generic insofar as only the function $Utility(u, \mathcal{M})$ must be modified to express a particular active learning strategy. How to measure the interest of an example will be discuss now.

---

[2] The word "label" is used here for a discrete value in classification problems or a continuous value in regression problems.

Considering:

- $\mathcal{M}$ a predictive model provided with a training algorithm $\mathcal{L}$
- $U_x$ et $L_x$ the sets of examples respectively not labeled and labeled
- $n$ the desired number of training examples
- $T$ the training set with $\|T\| < n$
- $\mathcal{U} : \mathbb{X} \times \mathbb{M} \rightarrow \Re$ the function which estimates the utility of an example for the training of the model

**Repeat**
  (A) Train the model $\mathcal{M}$ thanks to $\mathcal{L}$ and $T$ (and possibly $U_x$).
  (B) Look the example such as $q = argmax_{u \in U_x} \mathcal{U}(u, \mathcal{M})$
  (C) Withdraw $q$ of $U_x$ and ask the label $f(q)$ to the expert.
  (D) Add $q$ to $L_x$ and add $(q, f(q))$ to $T$
**until** $\|T\| < n$

**Algorithm 1.** Selective sampling, Muslea 2002

## 3.2   Uncertainty Sampling

Uncertainty sampling is an active learning strategy [11,12] which is based on confidence that the model has in its predictions. The model used must be able to estimate the reliability of its answers, to provide the probabilities, $y_j$, to observe each class ($j$) for an examples $u$. Thus the model can make a prediction choosing the most probable class for $u$. The choice of new examples to be labeled proceeds in two steps:

- the model available at the iteration $t$ is used to predict the labels of the unlabeled examples;
- examples with the more uncertain prediction are selected.

The uncertainty of a prediction can also be defined using a threshold of decision. For example (see Figure 2) if the model gives answers between 0 and 1 a threshold is defined to take a decision and say which examples will be classified 0 and those which will be classified 1. The closer an answer of the model is to the threshold of decision, the more uncertain is the decision.

This first approach has the advantage to be intuitive, easy to implement and fast. The uncertainty sampling shows its limits however when the problem to be solved is not separable by the model. Indeed, this strategy will tend to select the examples to be labeled in mixture zones, where there is nothing any more to learn.

## 3.3   Risk Reduction

The purpose of this approach is to reduce the generalization error, $E(\mathcal{M})$, of the model [13]. It chooses examples to be labeled so as to minimize this error. In

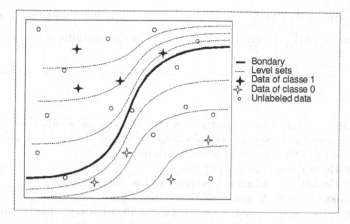

**Fig. 2.** A binary classification problem: the boundary plotted represents the threshold of decision. Level sets are plotted too and their distances from the boundary lines indicate the uncertainty. Unlabeled data close to the boundary line are the more uncertain and will be selected to be labeled by the expert.

practice this error cannot be calculated because the distribution of the examples, $\mathbb{X}$, is unknown. However it can be write, at an iteration $t$, using a loss function $(\mathcal{L}oss(\mathcal{M}^t, x))$ which evaluates the error of the model for a given example $x \in \mathbb{X}$ such as:

$$E(\mathcal{M}^t) = \int_{\mathbb{X}} \mathcal{L}oss(\mathcal{M}^t, x) P(x) dx$$

The same model at the next iteration $t + 1$ is defined as: $\mathcal{M}^{t+1}_{(x^\diamond, y^\diamond)}$. This model takes into account a new training example: $(x^\diamond, y^\diamond)$. For real problems, the output of the model $y^\diamond$ is unknown since $x^\diamond$ is a not labeled data. To estimate the generalization error at $t+1$, all the possibilities of the $\mathbb{Y}$ set have to be considered and to be balanced using their probability to be observed. The generalization error expected is therefore:

$$E(\mathcal{M}^{t+1}_{x^\diamond}) = \int_{\mathbb{X}} \int_{\mathbb{Y}} P(y|x^\diamond) \mathcal{L}oss(\mathcal{M}^{t+1}_{(x^\diamond, y)}, x) P(x) dx dy$$

This strategies selects the example $q$ which minimizes $E(\mathcal{M}^{t+1}_{x^\diamond})$. Once labeled, this example is incorporated to the training set. Step by step this procedure tries to elaborate an optimal training set.

Nicholas Roy [9] shows how to bring this strategy into play since all the elements of $\mathbb{X}$ are not known. He uses an uniform prior for $P(x)$ which gives :

$$\widehat{E}(\mathcal{M}^t) = \frac{1}{\|L_x\|} \sum_{i=1}^{\|L_x\|} \mathcal{L}oss(\mathcal{M}^t, x_i)$$

This strategy, where different loss functions can be used, is summarized in the algorithm 2. The model is, for all examples $i$, trained several times ($\|\mathbb{Y}\|$

times), to estimate $\widehat{E}(\mathcal{M}_{(x_i,y_j)}^{t+1})$. The example $i$ which minimizes the expected loss function $(\widehat{E}(\mathcal{M}_{(x_i)}^{t+1}))$ will be incorporated in the training set.

---

Considering:

- $\mathcal{M}$ a predictive model provided with a training algorithm $\mathcal{L}$
- $U_x$ and $L_x$ the sets of examples respectively not labeled and labeled
- $n$ the desired number of training examples
- $T$ the training set with $\|T\| < n$
- $\mathbb{Y}$ the label set which can be given to the examples of $U_x$
- $\mathcal{L}oss : \mathrm{M} \to \Re$ the generalization error
- $\mathcal{E}rr : U_x \times \mathrm{M} \to \Re$ the expected generalization error for the model $\mathcal{M}$ trained with an additional example, $T \cup (x_i, f(x_i))$

**Repeat**
  (A) Train the model $\mathcal{M}$ thanks to $\mathcal{L}$ and $T$
**For** all examples $x_i \in U_x$ **do**
  **For** all label $y_j \in \mathbb{Y}$ **do**
    i) Train the model $\mathcal{M}_{i,j}$ thanks to $\mathcal{L}$ and $(T \cup (x_i, y_j))$
    ii) Compute the generalization error $\widehat{E}(\mathcal{M}_{(x_i,y_j)}^{t+1})$
  **end For**
  Compute the generalization error
  $\left| \widehat{E}(\mathcal{M}_{x_i}^{t+1}) = \sum_{y_j \in \mathbb{Y}} \widehat{E}(\mathcal{M}_{(x_i,y_j*)}^{t+1}).P(y_j|x_i) \right.$
**end For**
(B) Look for the example $q = argmin_{u \in U_x} \widehat{E}(\mathcal{M}_{x_i}^{t+1})$
(C) Withdraw $q$ of $U_x$ ans ask the label $f(q)$ to the expert.
(D) Add $q$ to $L_x$ and add $(q, f(q))$ to $T$
**until** $\|T\| < n$

---

**Algorithm 2.** Apprentissage actif *"optimal"*, de Nicholas Roy 2000

A example of use of this strategy is presented in [14] where X. Zhu estimates the generalization error $(E(\mathcal{M}))$ using the empirical risk:

$$\widehat{E}(\mathcal{M}) = R(\mathcal{M}) = \sum_{n=1}^{N} \sum_{y_j \in \mathbb{Y}} {}_{\{f(l_n) \neq y_j\}} P(y_j|l_n)P(l_n) \text{ with } l_n \in L_x$$

where $f$ is the model which estimates the probability that an example belong to a class (a Parzen window [15] in [14]), $P(y_i|l_n)$ the real probability to observe the class $y_i$ for the example $l_n \in L_x$, the indicating function equal to 1 if $f(l_n >) \neq y_i$ and equal to 0 if not. Therefor $R(\mathcal{M})$ is the sum of the probabilities that the model makes a bad decision on the training set $(L_x)$.

Using an uniform prior to estimate $P(l_n)$:

$$\hat{R}(\mathcal{M}) = \frac{1}{N} \sum_{n=1}^{N} \sum_{y_j \in \mathbb{Y}} \{f(l_n) \neq y_j\} \hat{P}(y_j | l_n)$$

The expected cost for any single example $u$ ($u \in U_x$) added to the training set (for binary classification problem) is then:

$$\hat{R}(\mathcal{M}^{+u}) = \sum_{y_j \in \mathbb{Y}} \hat{P}(y_j | u) \hat{R}(\mathcal{M}^{+(u,y_j)}) \text{ with } u \in U_x$$

### 3.4  Discussion

Both strategies described above are not the only ones which exist. The reader can see a third main strategy which is based on Query by Committee [16,17] and a fourth one where authors focus on a model approach to active learning in a version-space of concepts [18,19,20].

## 4  Application of Active Learning to Detection of Emotion in Speech

### 4.1  Introduction

Thanks to recent techniques of speech processing, many automatic phone call centers appear. These vocal servers are used by customers to carry out various tasks conversing with a machine. Companies aim to improve their customer's satisfaction by redirecting them towards a human operator, in the event of difficulty. The shunting of unsatisfied users amounts detecting the negative emotions in their dialogues with the machine, under the assumption that a problem of dialogue generates a particular emotional state in the subject.

The detection of expressed emotions in speech is generally considered as a supervised learning problem. The detection of emotions is limited to a binary classification since taking into account more classes rises problem of the objectivity of labeling task [21]. The acquisition and the labeling of data are expensive in this framework. Active learning can reduce this cost by labeling only the examples considered to be informative for the model.

### 4.2  Characterization of Data

This study is based on a previous work [22] which characterizes vocal exchanges, in optimal way, for the classification of expressed emotions in speech. The objective is to control the dialogue between users and a vocal server. More precisely, this study deals the relevance of variables describing data, according to the detection of emotions.

The used data result from an experiment involving 32 users who test a stock exchange service implemented on a vocal server. According to the users point of view, the test consists in managing a virtual wallet of stock options, the goal is to realize the strongest profit. The obtained vocal traces constitute the corpus of this study: 5496 "speech turns" exchanged with the machine. Speech turns are characterized by 200 acoustic variables, describing variations of the sound intensity, variations of voice height, frequency of elocution... etc. Data are also characterized by 8 dialogical variables describing the rank of a speech turn in a given dialogue (a dialogue contains several speech turn), the duration of the dialogue... Each speech turn is manually labeled as carrying positive or negative emotions.

The subset of the most informative variables with respect to the detection of expressed emotions in speech is given thanks to a naive Bayesian selector [23]. At the beginning of this process (the selection of the most informative variables), the set of attributes is empty. The attribute which most improves the predictive quality of the model is then added at each iteration. The algorithm stops when the addition of attributes does not improve any more the quality of the model. Finally, 20 variables were selected to characterize vocal exchanges. In this article, used data result from the same corpus and from this previous study. So, every speech turnis characterized by 20 variables.

## 4.3   The Choice of the Model

The large range of models able to solve classification problems (and sometimes the great number of parameters useful to use them) may represent difficulties to measure the contribution of a learning strategy. A Parzen window, with a Gaussian kernel [15], is used in experiments below since this predictive model uses a single parameter and is able to work with few examples. The "output" of this model is an estimate of the probability to observe the label $y_j$ conditionally to the instance $u$:

$$\hat{P}(y_j|u) = \frac{\sum_{n=1}^{N} \{f(l_n)=y_j\} K(u, l_n)}{\sum_{n=1}^{N} K(u, l_n)} \qquad avec\ l_n, \in L_x\ et\ u \in U_x \cup L_x \qquad (1)$$

where

$$K(u, l_n) = e^{\frac{||u - l_n||^2}{2\sigma^2}}$$

The optimal value ($\sigma^2 = 0.24$) of the kernel parameter was found thanks to a cross-validation on the average quadratic error, using the whole of available training data [24]. Thereafter, this value is used to fix the Parzen window parameter. The results obtained by this model (using the whole of training data) are similar with the previous results obtained by a naive Bayesian classifier [22]. Consequently, Parzen windows are considered satisfying and valid for the following active learning procedures. Kernel methods and closer neighbors methods are usually used in classification of expressed emotions in speech [25].

The model must be able to assign a label $\hat{f}(u)$ to an input data $u$, so a decision threshold noted $Th(L_x)$ is calculated at each iteration. This threshold minimizes the error of the model[3] on the available training set. The label attributed is $\hat{f}(u_n) = 1$ if $\{\hat{P}(y_1|u_n) > Th(L_x)\}$, else $\hat{f}(u_n) = 0$. Since the single parameter of the Parzen window is fixed, the training stage is reduced to count instances (within the meaning of the Gaussian kernel). The strategies of examples selection, without being influenced by the training of the model, are thus comparable.

## 4.4  Used Active Learning Strategies

Two Active learning strategies are considered in this paper; the active learning strategy which tries to reduce the generalization error of the model and the strategy consists in selecting the instance for which the prediction of the model is most uncertain have been tested.

For the first strategy the Parzen window estimates $P(y_i|l_n)$. The empirical risk is approximated adopting a uniform a priori on the $P(l_n)$. The purpose is to select the unlabeled instance $u_i \in U_x$ which will minimize the risk of the next iteration. $R(\mathcal{M}^{+u_n})$ the *"expected"* risk resulting from the labeling of the instance $u_n$ (iteration $t + 1$) is estimated. Available labeled data are used to do this estimation when the assumption $f(u_n) = y_1$ *[resp $f(u_n) = y_0$]* to estimate $\hat{R}(\mathcal{M}^{+(u_n,y_1)})$ *[resp $\hat{R}(\mathcal{M}^{+(u_n,y_0)})$ ]* is done.

For the second strategy the *uncertainty* of a prediction is maximum when the output probability of the model approaches the decision threshold.

Apart from these two active strategies, a "stochastic" approach which uniformly selects the examples according to their probability distribution is considered. This last approach play a role of reference used to measure the contribution of the active strategies.

## 4.5  Results

The presented results come from several experiments on previous learning strategies. Each experiment has been done five times[4]. At the beginning of the experiments, the training set is only constituted by two examples (one positive and one negative) selected randomly. At each iteration, ten examples are selected to be labeled and added to the training set. The considered classification problem, here, is unbalanced: there are 92% of "positive or neutral" emotions and 8% of "negative" emotions. To observe correctly the classification profits (when adding labeled examples), the model evaluation is done using the area under ROC curve (AUC) on the test set[5] A ROC curve is calculated from the detection rate of

---

[3] The used error measurement is the *"Balanced Error Rate"*, for more details see section 4.5.

[4] the natches on the curves of the figure 3 correspond to 4 times the variance of the results ($\pm 2\sigma$).

[5] The test set include 1613 examples and the training set 3783 examples.

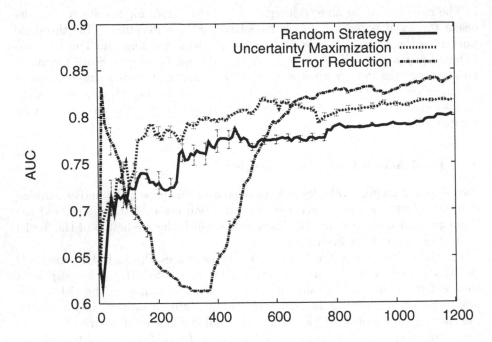

**Fig. 3.** Focus of the results on the test using [0:1200] training examples

a single class. Consecently, we use the sum of the AUCs weighted by reference class's prevalence in the data.

The "risk reduction" is the strategy which maximizes the quality of the model for a number of training examples in the range [2:100]. Between 100 and 700 the strategy based on uncertainty wins. After 600 training examples the three strategies converge to the optimal AUC (Area Under Roc Curve).

The two active strategies allow obtaining faster than the random strategy the optimal result (the optimal AUC is 0.84 using the whole training set). The use of active learning is positive in this real problem. However the results obtained raise questions which will detailed in the next section.

## 5    Discussion and Conclusion

This paper shows the interest of active learning for a field where acquisition and labeling of data are particularly expensive. Obtained results show that active learning is relevant for the detection of expressed emotions in speech. But whatever the strategy considered (even the two strategies evoked in section 3.4 but not derailed in this paper) several question exist and can be raised:

– **evaluation** - The quality of an active strategy is usually represented by a curve assessing the performance of the model versus the number of training examples labeled (see Figure 3). The performance criterion used can take several different ways according to the problem. This type of curve allows only comparisons between strategies in a punctual way, i.e. for a point on the curve (a given number of training examples). If two curves pass each other (as in the Figure 3, it is impossible to determine if a strategy is better than another (on the total set of training examples). The elaboration of a criterion which measures the contribution of a strategy compared to the random strategy on the whole data set should be interesting. This point will be discussed in a future paper.

- **test set** - Active learning strategies are, often, used when data acquisition is expensive. Therefore, in practice, a test set is not available (otherwise it can be used to the training) and the evaluation of the model during a strategy is difficult to implement.

- **stopping criterion** - The maximal number of examples to labeled, or an estimation of the progress of the model, can be used to stop the algorithm. This is very link to the use of a test set or the model employed. For example in the Figure 3 the strategy based on the risk gives the same results when 15 examples have been labeled than results using all the available data. In this case the cost using 15 examples and 600 will be not the same... A good criterion should be independent of the model and of a test set. Actual experiments (not yet published) will allow us to propose a criterion of this type at the end of 2007.

- **number of examples to be labeled** - the state of the art seems to incorporate an only one example at each step of the strategy. But in real case the expert is a human and when the model needs time to learn at each iteration of the strategy this could be not efficient. Sometimes more than one example must be incorporated. This aspect has been a litle bit studied in [26] but it has to be more analyse in the future.

- **uncertain environment** - If an answer could be given to the points above then active strategies could be used for on-line learning in an uncertain environment. For example to tag part of graph (graph here is social network). When writing this paper we hope that this point will accepted and incorporated in a proposition sent to a French Project (and financed by the French National Agency of Research (ANR)) grouping industrial and universities.

Generally, active learning strategies estimate the utility of training examples. These criteria could be used for on-line training. The training set would be consisted of the N examples the more "useful" seen until now (with N fixed). This approach would be able to consider non stationary problems and it is able to train a model which adapts itself to the variations of the observed system.

For the detection of expressed emotions in speech could be treated by a double strategy reducing the cost linked to the data : (i) a variables selection allowing to preserve only the necessary and sufficient characteristics for classification; (ii) an examples selection allowing to preserve only useful instances for training. This will be explored in future work.

# References

1. Harmon, M.: Reinforcement learning: a tutorial (1996)
   http://eureka1.aa.wpafb.af.mil/rltutorial/
2. Jain, A.K., Murty, M.N., Flynn, P.J.: Data clustering: a review. ACM Computing Surveys 31(3), 264–323 (1999)
3. Jamy, I., Jen, T.-Y., Laurent, D., Loizou, G., Sy, O.: Extraction de règles d'association pour la prédiction de valeurs manquantes. Revue Africaine de la Recherche en Informatique et Mathématique Appliquée ARIMA Spécial CARI04, 103–124 (2005)
4. Chapelle, O., Schölkopf, B., Zien, A.: Semi-Supervised Learning. MIT Press, Cambridge, MA (in press) (2006),http://www.kyb.tuebingen.mpg.de/ssl-book/ssl_toc.pdf
5. Cohn, D., Caruana, R., McCallum, A.: Semi-supervised clustering with user feedback. Technical Report 1892, Cornell University (2003)
6. Chapelle, O., Zien, A.: Semi-supervised classification by low density separation. In: Proceedings of the Tenth International Workshop on Artificial Intelligence and Statistics (2005)
7. Castro, R., Willett, R., Nowak, R.: Faster rate in regression via active learning. In: NIPS (Neural Information Processing Systems), Vancouver (2005)
8. Singh, A., Nowak, R., Ramanathan, P.: Active learning for adaptive mobile sensing networks. In: IPSN '06. Proceedings of the fifth international conference on Information processing in sensor networks, pp. 60–68. ACM Press, New York (2006)
9. Roy, N., McCallum, A.: Toward optimal active learning through sampling estimation of error reduction. In: Proc. 18th International Conf. on Machine Learning, pp. 441–448. Morgan Kaufmann, San Francisco (2001)
10. Muslea, I.: Active Learning With Multiple View. Phd thesis, University of southern california (2002)
11. Lewis, D., Gale, A.: A sequential algorithm for training text classifiers. In: Croft, W.B., van Rijsbergen, C.J. (eds.) Proceedings of SIGIR-94. 17th ACM International Conference on Research and Development in Information Retrieval, Dublin. LNCS, pp. 3–12. Springer, Heidelberg (1994)
12. Thrun, S.B., Möller, K.: Active exploration in dynamic environments. In: Moody, J.E., Hanson, S.J., Lippmann, R.P. (eds.) Advances in Neural Information Processing Systems, vol. 4, pp. 531–538. Morgan Kaufmann Publishers, San Francisco (1992)
13. Cohn, D.A., Ghahramani, Z., Jordan, M.I.: Active learning with statistical models. In: Tesauro, G., Touretzky, D., Leen, T. (eds.) Advances in Neural Information Processing Systems, vol. 7, pp. 705–712. The MIT Press, Cambridge (1995)
14. Zhu, X., Lafferty, J., Ghahramani, Z.: Combining active learning and semi-supervised learning using gaussian fields and harmonic functions. In: ICML (International Conference on Machine Learning), Washington (2003)
15. Parzen, E.: On estimation of a probability density function and mode. Annals of Mathematical Statistics 33, 1065–1076 (1962)
16. Freund, Y., Seung, H.S., Shamir, E., Tishby, N.: Selective sampling using the query by committee algorithm. Machine Learning 28(2-3), 133–168 (1997)
17. Seung, H.S., Opper, M., Sompolinsky, H.: Query by committee. In: Computational Learning Theory, pp. 287–294 (1992)
18. Dasgupta, S.: Analysis of greedy active learning strategy. In: NIPS (Neural Information Processing Systems), San Diego (2005)

19. Cohn, D.A., Atlas, L., Ladner, R.E.: Improving generalization with active learning. Machine Learning 15(2), 201–221 (1994)
20. Tong, S., Koller, D.: Support vector machine active learning with applications to text classification. In: Langley, P. (ed.) Proceedings of ICML-00. 17th International Conference on Machine Learning, Stanford, US, pp. 999–1006. Morgan Kaufmann Publishers, San Francisco (2000)
21. Liscombe, J., Riccardi, G., Hakkani-Tür, D.: Using context to improve emotion detection in spoken dialog systems. In: InterSpeech, Lisbon (2005)
22. Poulain, B.: Sélection de variables et modélisation d'expressions d'émotions dans des dialogues hommes-machine (in french). In: EGC (Extraction et Gestion de Connaissance) (2006), Lille. + Technical Report avalaible here: http://perso.rd.francetelecom.fr/lemaire
23. Boullé, M.: An enhanced selective naive bayes method with optimal discretization. In: Guyon, I., Gunn, S., Nikravesh, M., Zadeh, L. (eds.) Feature extraction, foundations and Application, August 2006. LNCS, pp. 499–507. Springer, Heidelberg (2006)
24. Chappelle, O.: Active learning for parzen windows classifier. In: AI & Statistics, Barbados, pp. 49–56 (2005)
25. Guide, V., Rakotomamonjy, C.S.: Méthode à noyaux pour l'identification d'émotion. In: RFIA (Reconnaissance des Formes et Intelligence Artificielle) (2003)
26. Bondu, A., Lemaire, V.: Etude de l'influence du nombre d'exemples à étiqueter dans une procédure d'apprentissage actif. In: CAP 2006 (Conference francophone sur l'apprentissage automatique) (submitted to, 2006)

# Neural Business Control System

M. Lourdes Borrajo[1], Juan M. Corchado[2], E.S. Corchado[3], and M.A. Pellicer[3]

[1] Dept. Informática, University of Vigo,
Esc. Superior de Ingeniería Informática, Edificio Politécnico,
Campus Universitario As Lagoas s/n, 32004, Ourense, Spain
[2] Departamento de Informática y Automática, University of Salamanca,
Plaza de la Merced s/n, 37008 Salamanca, Spain
[3] Dept. de Ingeniería Civil, University of Burgos,
Esc. Politécnica Superior, Edificio C, C/ Francisco de Vitoria, Burgos, Spain

**Abstract.** The firms have need of a control mechanism in order to analyse whether they are achieving their goals. A tool that automates the business control process has been developed based on a case-based reasoning system. The objective of the system is to facilitate the process of internal auditing. The system analyses the data that characterises each one of the activities carried out by the firm, then determines the state of each activity and calculates the associated risk. This system uses a different problem solving method in each of the steps of the reasoning cycle. A Maximum Likelihood Hebbian Learning-based method that automates the organization of cases and the retrieval stage of case-based reasoning systems is presented in this paper. The proposed methodology has been derived as an extension of the Principal Component Analysis, and groups similar cases, identifying clusters automatically in a data set in an unsupervised mode. The system has been tested in 10 small and medium companies in the textile sector, located in the northwest of Spain and the results obtained have been very encouraging.

## 1 Introduction

The firms need a control mechanism in order to analyse whether they are achieving their goals, being based on a series of organizational policies and specific procedures. This group of policies and procedures are named "controls", and they all conform to the structure of business control of the company. Therefore, periodic internal audits are necessary. Nevertheless the firms are characterized by their great dynamism. It is necessary to construct models that facilitate the analysis of work carried out in changing environments, such as finance.

The processes carried out inside a firm are grouped in functional areas [5] denominated "Functions". A Function is a group of coordinated and related activities, which are necessary to reach the objectives of the firm and are carried out in a systematic and iterative way [22]. The functions that are usually carried out within a firm are: Purchases, Cash Management, Sales, Information Technology, Fixed Assets Management, Compliance to Legal Norms and Human Resources. In turn, each one of these functions is broken down into a series of activities. Each activity is composed

P. Perner (Ed.): ICDM 2007, LNAI 4597, pp. 242–254, 2007.

of a number of tasks. Control procedures have also to be established in the tasks to ensure that the established objectives are achieved.

The objective of the developed system is to identify the state or situation of each one of activities of the company and to calculate the risk associated with this state. The system is implemented using a case-based reasoning (CBR) system [1, 19, 27, 21]. The CBR system uses different problem solving techniques [14, 23].

This paper presents a Maximum Likelihood Hebbian Learning (MLHL) based model to automate the process of case indexing and retrieval, which may be used in problems in which the cases are characterised predominantly by numerical information.

Maximum Likelihood Hebbian Learning (MLHL) based models were first developed as an extension of Principal Component Analysis [24, 25]. Maximum Likelihood Hebbian Learning Based Method attempts to identify a small number of data points, which are necessary to solve a particular problem to the required accuracy. These methods have been successfully used in the unsupervised investigation of structure in data sets [3, 4]. We have previously investigated the use of Artificial Neural Networks [8] and Kernel Principal Component Analysis (KPCA) [11, 13] to identify cases, which will be used in a case based reasoning system. In this paper, we present a novel hybrid technique. The ability of the Maximum Likelihood Hebbian Learning-based methods presented in this paper to cluster cases/instances and to associate cases to clusters can be used to successfully prune the case-base without losing valuable information.

This paper first presents the Maximum Likelihood Hebbian Learning Based Method and its theoretical background. We review Principal Component Analysis (PCA) which has been the most frequently reported linear operation involving unsupervised learning for data compression, which aims to find that orthogonal basis which maximises the data's variance for a given dimensionality of basis. Then, the Exploratory Projection Pursuit (EPP) theory is outlined. It is shown how Maximum Likelihood Hebbian Learning Based Method may be derived from PCA and it could be viewed as a method of performing EPP. Then, the proposed CBR based model is presented. The system results are evaluated and, finally, the conclusions are presented.

## 2  Maximum Likelihood Hebbian Learning Based Method

The use of Maximum Likelihood Hebbian Learning Based Method has been derived from the work of [4, 11, 12, 13], etc. in the field of pattern recognition as an extension of Principal Component Analysis (PCA) [24, 25].

### 2.1  Principal Component Analysis (PCA)

Principal Component Analysis (PCA) is a standard statistical technique for compressing data; it can be shown to give the best linear compression of the data in terms of least mean square error. There are several artificial neural networks which have been shown to perform PCA e.g. [24, 25]. We will apply a negative feedback implementation [10].

The basic PCA network is described by equations (1)-(3). Let us have an N-dimensional input vector at time $t$, $\boldsymbol{x}(t)$, and an M-dimensional output vector, $\boldsymbol{y}$, with $W_{ij}$ being the weight linking input $j$ to output $i$. $\eta$ is a learning rate. Then the activation passing and learning is described by

$$\text{Feedforward: } y_i = \sum_{j=1}^{N} W_{ij} x_j , \forall i \tag{1}$$

$$\text{Feedback: } e_j = x_j - \sum_{i=1}^{M} W_{ij} y_i \tag{2}$$

$$\text{Change weights: } \Delta W_{ij} = \eta e_j y_i \tag{3}$$

We can readily show that this algorithm is equivalent to Oja's Subspace Algorithm [24]:

$$\Delta W_{ij} = \eta e_j y_i = \eta (x_j - \sum_k W_{kj} y_k) y_i \tag{4}$$

and so this network not only causes convergence of the weights but causes the weights to converge to span the subspace of the Principal Components of the input data. We might ask then why we should be interested in the negative feedback formulation rather than the formulation (4) in which the weight change directly uses negative feedback. The answer is that the explicit formation of residuals (2) allows us to consider probability density functions of the residuals in a way which would not be brought to mind if we use (4).

Exploratory Projection Pursuit (EPP) is a more recent statistical method aimed at solving the difficult problem of identifying structure in high dimensional data. It does this by projecting the data onto a low dimensional subspace in which we search for its structure by eye. However not all projections will reveal the data's structure equally well. We therefore define an index that measures how "interesting" a given projection is, and then represent the data in terms of projections that maximise that index.

The first step in our exploratory projection pursuit is to define which indices represent interesting directions. Now "interesting" structure is usually defined with respect to the fact that most projections of high-dimensional data onto arbitrary lines through most multi-dimensional data give almost Gaussian distributions [7]. Therefore if we wish to identify "interesting" features in data, we should look for those directions onto which the data-projections are as far from the Gaussian as possible.

It was shown in [17] that the use of a (non-linear) function creates an algorithm to find those values of W which maximise that function whose derivative is f() under the constraint that W is an orthonormal matrix. This was applied in [10] to the above network in the context of the network performing an Exploratory Projection Pursuit. Thus if we wish to find a direction which maximises the kurtosis of the distribution which is measured by s4, we will use a function f(s) $\approx$ s3 in the algorithm. If we wish to find that direction with maximum skewness, we use a function f(s) $\approx$ s2 in the algorithm.

## 2.2 ε-Insensitive Hebbian Learning

It has been shown [29] that the nonlinear PCA rule

$$\Delta W_{ij} = \eta \left( x_j f(y_i) - f(y_i) \sum_k W_{kj} f(y_k) \right) \tag{5}$$

can be derived as an approximation to the best non-linear compression of the data. Thus we may start with a cost function

$$J(W) = 1^T E\left\{ \left( \mathbf{x} - Wf\left(W^T \mathbf{x}\right) \right)^2 \right\} \tag{6}$$

which we minimise to get the rule (5). [20] used the residual in the linear version of (6) to define a cost function of the residual

$$J = f_1(\mathbf{e}) = f_1(\mathbf{x} - W\mathbf{y}) \tag{7}$$

where $f_1 = \|.\|^2$ is the (squared) Euclidean norm in the standard linear or nonlinear PCA rule. With this choice of $f_1(\ )$, the cost function is minimised with respect to any set of samples from the data set on the assumption that the residuals are chosen independently and identically distributed from a standard Gaussian distribution. We may show that the minimisation of J is equivalent to minimising the negative log probability of the residual, $\mathbf{e}$, if $\mathbf{e}$ is Gaussian.

$$\text{Let } p(\mathbf{e}) = \frac{1}{Z} \exp(-\mathbf{e}^2) \tag{8}$$

Then we can denote a general cost function associated with this network as

$$J = -\log p(\mathbf{e}) = (\mathbf{e})^2 + K \tag{9}$$

where $K$ is a constant. Therefore performing gradient descent on $J$ we have

$$\Delta W \propto -\frac{\partial J}{\partial W} = -\frac{\partial J}{\partial \mathbf{e}} \frac{\partial \mathbf{e}}{\partial W} \approx \mathbf{y}(2\mathbf{e})^T \tag{10}$$

where we have discarded a less important term. See [17] for details.

In general [26], the minimisation of such a cost function may be thought to make the probability of the residuals greater dependent on the probability density function (pdf) of the residuals. Thus if the probability density function of the residuals is known, this knowledge could be used to determine the optimal cost function. [13] investigated this with the (one dimensional) function:

$$p(\mathbf{e}) = \frac{1}{2 + \varepsilon} \exp\left(-|\mathbf{e}|_\varepsilon\right) \tag{11}$$

where $|e|_\varepsilon = \begin{cases} o & \forall |e| < \varepsilon \\ |e| - \varepsilon & otherwise \end{cases}$  (12)

with $\varepsilon$ being a small scalar $\geq 0$.

Fyfe and MacDonald [13] described this in terms of noise in the data set. However, we feel that it is more appropriate to state that, with this model of the pdf of the residual, the optimal $f_1(\ )$ function is the $\varepsilon$-insensitive cost function:

$$f_1(\mathbf{e}) = |\mathbf{e}|_\varepsilon$$  (13)

In the case of the negative feedback network, the learning rule is

$$\Delta W \propto -\frac{\partial J}{\partial W} = -\frac{\partial f_1(\mathbf{e})}{\partial \mathbf{e}} \frac{\partial \mathbf{e}}{\partial W}$$  (14)

which gives:

$$\Delta W_{ij} = \begin{cases} o & if |e_j| < \varepsilon \\ otherwise & \eta y(sign(e)) \end{cases}$$  (15)

The difference with the common Hebb learning rule is that the sign of the residual is used instead the value of the residual. Because this learning rule is insensitive to the magnitude of the input vectors $x$, the rule is less sensitive to outliers than the usual rule based on mean squared error. This change from viewing the difference after feedback as simply a residual rather than an error permits us to consider a family of cost functions each member of which is optimal for a particular probability density function associated with the residual.

## 2.3 Applying Maximum Likelihood Hebbian Learning

The Maximum Likelihood Hebbian Learning algorithm is constructed now on the bases of the previously presented concepts as outlined here. Now the $\varepsilon$-insensitive learning rule is clearly only one of a possible family of learning rules which are suggested by the family of exponential distributions. This family was called an exponential family in [16] though statisticians use this term for a somewhat different family. Let the residual after feedback have probability density function

$$p(\mathbf{e}) = \frac{1}{Z} \exp(-|\mathbf{e}|^p)$$  (16)

Then we can denote a general cost function associated with this network as

$$J = E(-\log p(\mathbf{e})) = E(|\mathbf{e}|^p + K)$$  (17)

where $K$ is a constant independent of $W$ and the expectation is taken over the input data set. Therefore performing gradient descent on $J$ we have

$$\Delta W \propto -\frac{\partial J}{\partial W}\,|_{W(t-1)} = -\frac{\partial J}{\partial e}\frac{\partial e}{\partial W}\,|_{W(t-1)} \approx E\{\mathbf{y}(p\,|\,\mathbf{e}\,|^{p-1}\,sign(\mathbf{e}))^T\,|_{W(t-1)}\} \qquad (18)$$

where T denotes the transpose of a vector and the operation of taking powers of the norm of *e* is on an element wise basis as it is derived from a derivative of a scalar with respect to a vector.

Computing the mean of a function of a data set (or even the sample averages) can be tedious, and we also wish to cater for the situation in which samples keep arriving as we investigate the data set and so we derive an online learning algorithm. If the conditions of stochastic approximation [18] are satisfied, we may approximate this with a difference equation. The function to be approximated is clearly sufficiently smooth and the learning rate can be made to satisfy $\eta_k \geq 0, \sum_k \eta_k = \infty, \sum_k \eta_k^2 < \infty$ and so we have the rule:

$$\Delta W_{ij} = \eta.y_i.sign(e_j)|\,e_j\,|^{p-1} \qquad (19)$$

We would expect that for leptokurtotic residuals (more kurtotic than a Gaussian distribution), values of p<2 would be appropriate, while for platykurtotic residuals (less kurtotic than a Gaussian), values of p>2 would be appropriate. Researchers from the community investigating Independent Component Analysis [15, 16] have shown that it is less important to get exactly the correct distribution when searching for a specific source than it is to get an approximately correct distribution i.e. all supergaussian signals can be retrieved using a generic leptokurtotic distribution and all subgaussian signals can be retrieved using a generic platykutotic distribution. Our experiments will tend to support this to some extent but we often find accuracy and speed of convergence are improved when we are accurate in our choice of p. Therefore the network operation is:

$$\text{Feedforward: } y_i = \sum_{j=1}^{N} W_{ij} x_j, \forall_i \qquad (20)$$

$$\text{Feedback: } e_j = x_j - \sum_{i=1}^{M} W_{ij} y_i \qquad (21)$$

$$\text{Weights change: } \Delta W_{ij} = \eta.y_i.sign(e_j)|\,e_j\,|^{p-1} \qquad (22)$$

Fyfe and MacDonald [13] described their rule as performing a type of PCA, but this is not strictly true since only the original (Oja) ordinary Hebbian rule actually performs PCA. It might be more appropriate to link this family of learning rules to Principal Factor Analysis since PFA makes an assumption about the noise in a data set and then removes the assumed noise from the covariance structure of the data before performing a PCA. We are doing something similar here in that we are basing our PCA-type rule on the assumed distribution of the residual. By maximising the likelihood of the residual with respect to the actual distribution, we are matching the learning rule to the probability density function of the residual.

More importantly, we may also link the method to the standard statistical method of Exploratory Projection Pursuit: now the nature and quantification of the interestingness is in terms of how likely the residuals are under a particular model of the probability density function of the residuals. In the results reported later, we also sphere the data before applying the learning method to the sphered data and show that with this method we may also find interesting structure in the data.

## 2.4 Sphering of the Data g

Because a Gaussian distribution with mean $a$ and variance $x$ is no more or less interesting than a Gaussian distribution with mean $b$ and variance $y$ - indeed this second order structure can obscure higher order and more interesting structure - we remove such information from the data. This is known as "sphering". That is, the raw data is translated till its mean is zero, projected onto the principal component directions and multiplied by the inverse of the square root of its eigenvalue to give data which has mean zero and is of unit variance in all directions. So for input data X we find the covariance matrix.

$$\sum = \left\langle \left(X - \langle X \rangle\right)\left(X - \langle X \rangle\right)^T \right\rangle = UDU^T \tag{23}$$

Where $U$ is the eigenvector matrix, $D$ the diagonal matrix of eigenvalues, $T$ denotes the transpose of the matrix and the angled brackets indicate the ensemble average. New samples, drawn from the distribution are transformed to the principal component axes to give $y$ where

$$y_i = \frac{1}{\sqrt{D_i}} \sum_{j=1}^{n} U_{ij} \left(X_i - \langle X_i \rangle\right), for 1 \le i \le m \tag{24}$$

Where $n$ is the dimensionality of the input space and $m$ is the dimensionality of the sphered data.

## 3 Phases of the Proposed System

This section describes the business control system in detail. Although the aim is to develop a generic model useful in any type of small to medium enterprise, the initial work has focused in the textile sector to facilitate the research and its evaluation. The model here presented may be extended or adapted for other sectors. Twenty two companies from the North-west of Spain have collaborated in this research, working mainly for the Spanish market. The companies have different levels of automation and all of them were very interested in a tool such as the one developed in the framework of this investigation. After analyzing the data relative to the activities developed within a given firm, the constructed system is able to determine the state of each of the activities and calculate the associated risk. The problem solving mechanism developed takes its decision using the help of a CBR system whose memory has been fed with cases constructed with information provided by the firm and with prototypical cases identified by 34 business control experts who have collaborated and supervised the model developed.

The cycle of operations of the developed case based reasoning system is based on the classic life cycle of a CBR system [1, 28]. A case represents the "shape" of a given activity developed in the company. Each case is composed of the following attributes:

- *Case number:* Unique identification: positive integer number.
- *Input vector:* Information about the tasks (n sub-vectors) that constitute an industrial activity: $((IR_1,V_1),(IR_2,V_2),...,(IR_n,V_n))$ for n tasks. Each task sub-vector has the following structure $(IR_i,V_i)$:
    - $IR_i$: importance rate for this task within the activity. It can only take one of the following values: VHI (Very high importance), HI (High Importance), AI (Average Importance), LI (Low Importance), VLI (Very low importance)
    - $V_i$: Value of the realization state of a given task: a positive integer number (between 1 and 10).
- *Function number:* Unique identification number for each function
- *Activity number:* Unique identification number for each activity
- *Reliability:* Percentage of probability of success. It represents the percentage of success obtained using the case as a reference to generate recommendations.
- *Degree of membership:* $((n_1,\mu_1), (n_2, \mu_2), ..., (n_k, \mu_k))$
    - $n_i$: represents the $i^{th}$ cluster
    - $\mu_i$: represents the membership value of the case to the cluster $n_i$
- *Activity State*: degree of perfection of the development of the activity, expressed by percentage.

Every time that it is necessary to obtain a new estimate of the state of an activity, the system evolves through several phases. This evolution allows the system, on the one hand, (i) to identify the latest situations most similar to the current situation, (ii) to adapt the current knowledge to generate an estimate of the risk of the activity being analysed. The following sections describe the different phases of the proposed model.

### 3.1 Evaluation of the State of the Activity

For each activity to analyse, the system uses the data for this activity, introduced by the firm's internal auditor, to construct the problem case. For each task making up the activity analyzed, the problem case is composed of the value of the realization state for that task, and its level of importance within the activity (according to the internal auditor).

In the retrieval step, the system retrieves K cases – the most similar cases to the problem case. This is done with the Maximum Likelihood Hebbian Learning proposed method. Applying equations 20 to 22 to the case-base, the MLHL algorithm groups the cases in clusters automatically. The proposed indexing mechanism classifies the cases/instances automatically, clustering together those of similar structure. One of the great advantages of this technique is that it is an unsupervised method so we do not need to have any information about of the data before hand. When a new case is presented to the CBR system, it is identified as belonging to a particular type by applying also equations 20 to 22 to it. This mechanism may be used as a universal retrieval and indexing mechanism to be applied to any problem similar to the presented here.

Maximum Likelihood Hebbian Learning techniques are used because of the size of the database and the need to group the most similar cases together in order to help retrieve the cases that most resemble the given problem.

Maximum Likelihood Hebbian Learning techniques are especially interesting for non-linear or ill-defined problems, making it possible to treat tasks involved in the processing of massive quantities of redundant or imprecise information. It allows the available data to be grouped into clusters with fuzzy boundaries, expressing uncertain knowledge.

The following step, the re-use phase, aims to obtain an initial estimation of the state of the activity analysed using a RBF networks are used [9, 6, 8]. As in the previous stage, the number of attributes of the problem case depends on the activity analyzed. Therefore it is necessary to establish an RBF network system, one for each of the activities to be analysed.

The retrieved K cases are used by the RBF network as a training group that allows it to adapt its configuration to the new problem encountered before generating the initial estimation.

The RBF network is characterized by its ability to adapt, to learn rapidly, and to generalize (especially in interpolation tasks). Specifically, within this system the network acts as a mechanism capable of absorbing knowledge about a certain number of cases and generalizing from them. During this process, the RBF network, interpolates and carries out predictions without forgetting part of those already carried out. The system's memory acts as a permanent memory capable of maintaining many cases or experiences while the RBF network acts as a short term memory, able to recognize recently learnt patterns and to generalize from them.

The objective of the revision phase is to confirm or refute the initial solution proposed by the RBF network, thereby obtaining a final solution and calculating the control risk. In view of the initial estimation or solution generated by the RBF network, the internal auditor will be responsible for deciding if the solution is accepted. For this it is based on the knowledge he/she retains, specifically, knowledge about the company with which he/she is working. If he/she considers that the estimation given is valid, the system will take the solution as the final solution and in the following phase of the CBR cycle, a new case will be stored in the  case base consisting of the problem case and the final solution. The system will assign the case an initial reliability of 100%. If on the other hand, the internal auditor considers the solution given by the system to be invalid, he will give his own solution which the system will take as the final solution and which together with the problem case will form the new case to be stored in the case base in the following phase. This new case will be given a reliability of 30%. This value has been defined taking into account the opinion of various auditors in terms of the weighting that should be assigned to the personal opinion of the internal auditor.

From the final solution: state of activity, the system calculates the control risk associated with the activity. Every activity developed in the business sector has a risk associated with it that indicates the negative influence that affects the good operation of the firm. In other words, the control risk of an activity measures the impact that the current state of the activity has on the business process as a whole. In this study, the level of risk is valued at three levels: low, medium and high. The calculation of the level of control risk associated with an activity is based on the current state of the activity and its level of importance. This latter value was obtained after analysing data obtained from a series of questionnaires (98 in total) carried out by auditors throughout Spain. In these questionnaires the auditors were asked to rate subjects from 1-10 according to the importance or weighting of each activity in terms of the function that it belonged to. The higher the importance of the activity, the greater its weighting within the business control system. The level of control risk was then calculated from the level of importance given to the activity by the auditors and the final solution obtained after the revision phase. For this purpose, if-then rules are employed.

The last phase of the system is the incorporation of the system's memory of what has been learnt after resolving a new problem. Once the revision phase has been completed, after obtaining the final solution, a new case (*problem + solution*) is constructed, which is stored in the system's memory. Apart from the overall knowledge update involving the insertion of a new case within the system memory, the hybrid system presented carries out a local adaptation of the knowledge structures that it uses.

Maximum Likelihood Hebbian Learning technique contained within the prototypes related to the activity corresponding to the new case is reorganised in order to respond to the appearance of this new case, modifying its internal structure and adapting itself to the new knowledge available.

The RBF network uses the new case to carry out a complete learning cycle, updating the position of its centres and modifying the value of the weightings that connect the hidden layer with the output layer.

## 4 Results and Conclusions

A complete set of tests has been carried out over a total amount of 10 small to medium companies. From the total number of 10, 6 were medium-sized, while 4 were small sized firms, all of them pertaining to the textile sector. Spanish auditors performed 98 surveys in order to obtain the data that would feed the process of generating the prototype cases, needed to build the system's base classes. Another 34 surveys were carried out by different experts of functional areas of firms within this sector.

For a given company, each one of its activities was evaluated by the system, obtaining a level of risk. On the other hand, we request to five external and independent auditors that they analyzed the situation of each company. The mission of the auditors is to estimate the state of each activity, the same as the proposed system makes. Then, we compare the result of the evaluation obtained by the auditors with the result obtained by the system. Figure 1 shows the differences between the results obtained by the system and the external auditors about the function "Information Technology". It can be observed that the results obtained by the system are very similar to those obtained by the external auditors.

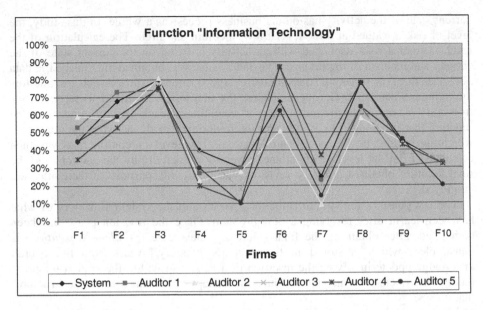

**Fig. 1.** Obtained results

In general, it could be said that these results demonstrate the suitability of the techniques used for their integration in the developed intelligent control system.

This article presents a neuro-symbolic system that use a CBR system employed as a basis for hybridization of a Maximum Likelihood Hebbian Learning technique, and a RBF net.

The used reasoning model can be applied in situations that satisfy the following conditions:

1. Each problem can be represented in the form of a vector of quantified values.
2. The case base should be representative of the total spectrum of the problem.
3. Cases must be updated periodically.
4. Enough cases should exist to train the net.

The prototype cases used for the construction of the case base are artificial and have been created from surveys carried out with auditors and experts in different functional areas. The system is able to estimate or identify the state of the activities of the firm and their associated risk.

Estimation in the environment of firms is difficult due to the complexity and the great dynamism of this environment. However, the developed model is able to estimate the state of the firm with precision. The system will produce better results if it is fed with cases related to the sector in which it will be used. This is due to the dependence that exists between the processes in the firms and the sector where the company is located. Future experiments will help to identify how the constructed prototype will perform in other sectors and how it will have to be modified in order to improve its performance. We have demonstrated a new technique for case indexing and retrieval, which could be used to construct case-based reasoning systems. The basis of the method is a Maximum Likelihood Hebbian Learning algorithm. This method provides us with a very robust model for indexing the data and retrieving instances without any need of information about the structure of the data set.

# References

1. Aamodt, A., Plaza, E.: Case-Based Reasoning: foundational Issues, Methodological Variations, and System Approaches. AICOM 7(1) (1994)
2. Borrajo, L.: Sistema híbrido inteligente aplicado a la auditoría de los sistemas internos. Phd Thesis. Teses de doutoramento da Universidade de Vigo. Universidade de Vigo (Spain). ISBN: 84-8158-274-3 (December 2003)
3. Corchado, E., Fyfe, C.: Maximum and Minimum Likelihood Hebbian Rules as a Exploratory Method. 9th International Conference on Neural Information Processing, November 18-22, 2002, Singapore (2002)
4. Corchado, E., MacDonald, D., Fyfe, C.: Optimal Projections of High Dimensional Data. In: ICDM '02. The 2002 IEEE International Conference on Data Mining, Maebashi TERRSA, Maebashi City, December 9-12, 2002, IEEE Computer Society, Los Alamitos (2002)
5. Corchado, J.M., Borrajo, L., Pellicer, M.A., Yáñez, J.C.: Neuro-symbolic System for Business Internal Control. In: Perner, P. (ed.) ICDM 2004. LNCS (LNAI), vol. 3275, pp. 302–9743. Springer, Heidelberg (2004)
6. Corchado, J.M., Díaz, F., Borrajo, L., Fdez-Riverola, F.: Redes Neuronales Artificiales: Un enfoque práctico. Departamento de publicaciones de la Universidad de Vigo (2000)
7. Diaconis, P., Freedman, D.: Asymptotics of Graphical Projections. The Annals of Statistics 12(3), 793–815 (1984)
8. Fdez-Riverola, F., Corchado, J.M.: FSfRT: Forecasting System for Red Tides. Applied Intelligence. Special Issue on Soft Computing in Case-Based Reasoning 21(3), 251–264 (2004) ISSN 0924-669X
9. Fritzke, B.: Fast Learning with Incremental RBF Networks. Neural Processing Letters 1(1), 2–5 (1994)
10. Fyfe, C., Baddeley, R.: Non-linear data structure extraction using simple Hebbian networks. Biological Cybernetics 72(6), 533–541 (1995)
11. Fyfe, C., Corchado, E.: Maximum Likelihood Hebbian Rules. 10th European Symposium on Artificial Neural Networks, ESANN'2002, Bruges, April 24-25-26 (2002a)
12. Fyfe, C., Corchado, E.: A New Neural Implementation of Exploratory Projection Pursuit. In: Yin, H., Allinson, N.M., Freeman, R., Keane, J.A., Hubbard, S. (eds.) IDEAL 2002. LNCS, vol. 2412, pp. 12–14. Springer, Heidelberg (2002b)
13. Fyfe, C., MacDonald, D.: ε-Insensitive Hebbian learning, Neuro Computing (2001)
14. Hunt, J., Miles, R.: Hybrid case-based reasoning. The Knowledge Engineering Review 9(4), 383–397 (1994)
15. Hyvärinen, A.: Complexity Pursuit: Separating interesting components from time series. Neural Computation 13, 883–898 (2001)
16. Hyvärinen, A., Karhunen, J., Oja, E.: Independent Component Analysis. Wiley, Chichester (2002)
17. Karhunen, J., Joutsensalo, J.: Representation and Separation of Signals Using Non-linear PCA Type Learning. Neural Networks 7, 113–127 (1994)

18. Kashyap, R.L., Blaydon, C.C., Fu, K.S.: Stochastic Approximation. In: Mendel, J.M. (ed.) A Prelude to Neural Networks: Adaptive and Learning Systems, Prentice Hall, Englewood Cliffs (1994) ISBN 0-13-147448-0
19. Kolodner, J.: Case-Based Reasoning. Morgan Kaufmann, San Francisco (1993)
20. Lai, P.L., Charles, D., Fyfe, C.: Seeking Independence using Biologically Inspired Artificial Neural Networks. In: Girolami, M.A. (ed.) Developments in Artificial Neural Network Theory: Independent Component Analysis and Blind Source Separation, Springer, Heidelberg (2000)
21. Lenz, M., Bartsch-Spörl, B., Burkhard, H.-D., Wess, S. (eds.): Case-Based Reasoning Technology. LNCS (LNAI), vol. 1400. Springer, Heidelberg (1998)
22. Mas, J., Ramió, C.: La Auditoría Operativa en la Práctica. Ed. Marcombo, Barcelona (1997)
23. Medsker, L.R.: Hybrid Intelligent Systems. Kluwer Academic Publishers, Dordrecht (1995)
24. Oja, E.: Neural Networks, Principal Components and Subspaces. International Journal of Neural Systems 1, 61–68 (1989)
25. Oja, E., Ogawa, H., Wangviwattana, J.: Principal Components Analysis by Homogeneous Neural Networks, part 1, The Weighted Subspace Criterion. IEICE Transaction on Information and Systems E75D, 366–375 (1992)
26. Smola, A.J., Scholkopf, B.: A Tutorial on Support Vector Regression. Technical Report NC2-TR-1998-030, NeuroCOLT2 Technical Report Series (1998)
27. Watson, I.: Applying Case-Based Reasoning: Techniques for Enterprise Systems. Morgan Kaufmann, San Francisco (1997)
28. Watson, I., Marir, F.: Case-Based Reasoning: A Review. The Knowledge Engineering Review 9(4), 355–381 (1994)
29. Xu, L.: Least Mean Square Error Reconstruction for Self-Organizing Nets. Neural Networks 6, 627–648 (1993)

# A Framework for Discovering and Analyzing Changing Customer Segments

Mirko Böttcher, Martin Spott, and Detlef Nauck

Intelligent Systems Research Centre, BT Group plc
Adastral Park, IP5 3RE Ipswich, United Kingdom
{Mirko.Boettcher, Martin.Spott, Detlef.Nauck}@bt.com

**Abstract.** Identifying customer segments and tracking their change over time is an important application for enterprises who need to understand what their customers expect from them. Customer segmentation is typically done by applying some form of cluster analysis. In this paper we present an alternative approach based on associaton rule mining and a notion of interestingness. Our approach allows us to detect arbitrary segments and analyse their temporal development. Our approach is assumption-free and pro-active and can be run continuously. Newly discovered segments or relevant changes will be reported automatically based on the application of an interestingness measure.

## 1 Introduction

Businesses, especially in the service industry, need to understand their customers in order to serve them best. Understanding customers involves collecting as much data as possible about interactions between customers and the business, analyse this data to turn it into information and finally learn from it and take action. This process is supported by techniques from data warehousing, data quality management, knowledge discovery in databases (or data mining), business intelligence, business process management etc. In this paper we will look at a particular aspect of the analytical process – the discovery of changing customer segments.

When we hear about customer segments we typically think about marketing-driven demographic groups that are defined using a great deal of domain understanding. This approach requires typcially running extensive surveys on a significant part of the customer base to learn about their preferences, views, standard of living, consumer behavior etc. Based on domain understanding a number of segments are then identified and customers are assigned to segments based on some similarity measure. Typically, approaches from cluster analysis are used to initially identify groups in the data which are then interpreted as potential customer segments. The whole process is based on manual analysis and is typically expectation and goal driven. In a nutshell, you would detect the segments you are looking for.

The difficulties of this approach are threefold. Firstly, the employed analytics – clustering – requires and underlying similarity measure which typically reduces the data to numeric features. Cluster analysis that can work with symbolic attributes do exist, but are less well-known and typically not supported by commercially available software.

P. Perner (Ed.): ICDM 2007, LNAI 4597, pp. 255–268, 2007.
© Springer-Verlag Berlin Heidelberg 2007

The existence of a similarity measure is required, otherwise neither cluster analysis can be applied nor can customers be assigned to clusters.

Secondly, assigning customers to segments is a problem, because survey data that was used to form segments is not available for the vast majority of customers. That means customers are assigned into segments by available information about them which at best contains data about the products and services they use but at worst is based only on rather inadequate data like the postcode, for example.

Thirdly, the segmentation approach is to a large extent goal driven and static. That means the data that is used has been collected with the assumption that it is ultimately relevant for segmentation. Data or attributes not considered to be relevant are dropped from the analytical process early on to make cluster analysis feasible and aid the interpretation of detected clusters which is essential to form meaningful segments. The danger of this approach is that potentially relevant features are ignored meaning certain segments may not be detected. The approach is also static, which means that once segments have been established change in those segments is not monitored because of the practical repercussions like regularly running expensive surveys etc. This results in missing important trends, threats and opportunities because segments and change in several ways. New groups can appear, disappear, merge, move, shrink or grow.

A promising approach would be to concentrate on data that is actually relevant in describing the relationship between customers and the business, i.e. data about interactions with customers and their usage profile of products and services. The data would be a mixture of symbolic data, like product types, fault codes, complaint reasons etc and numeric data on different scales like counts, costs, revenues, frequencies etc. If data types have to be consolidate it is typically better to discretise numerical data and loose some information instead of turning symbolic values into numbers and thus introducing spurious information like distances and relations.

In this paper we are looking at using association rule mining for detecting *interesting* segments in data. We define interesting segments as segments that display some temporal change reflected in the data. We relate growing or shrinking segments to threats and opportunities the business must know about. We explain how tracking the temporal changes of support and confidence values can lead to a notion of interestingness. We will illustrate our approach by applying it to two data sets from customer surveys and network usage.

## 2   Related Work

Customer segmentation is the process of dividing customers into homogeneous groups on the basis of common attributes. In most application customer segmentation is accomplished by defining numerical attributes which describe a customer's value based on economical and market considerations. Cluster algorithms are then commonly employed in order to discover groups of customers with similar attribute values. For example, in [1] three different clustering algorithms are compared to segment stock trading customers based on their amount of trade in different trading scenarios. Segmentation methods based on clustering require a user to carefully select the used attributes by hand in a tedious process. Since the number of used attributes is rather low, commonly only two or three, the analysis of segment change can still be done manually. This might be the reason why to our knowledge no automated approach has been published yet.

Several approaches have been proposed to analyse changes in customer behaviour, for instance in retail marketing [2], in an internet shopping mall [3,4] and in an insurance company [5]. These approaches typically compare two sets of rules generated from datasets of two different periods. For rule representation either decision trees [5,4] or association rules [3,2] are used. For example, in a telecommunication retail application, such approaches may detect that customers used to order a certain tariff with a certain special option—now they still order this tariff, but seldom with the special option. The aforementioned approaches only detect *what* has changed rather than *how* something changes. Picking up on the last example this means, they cannot spot the declining trend in the ordered special options. Spotting trends, however, is crucial for many cooperations.

In the area of association rules, the discovery of interesting changes has been studied by several authors. In [6] a query language for shapes of histories is introduced. A fuzzy approach to reveal the regularities in how measures for rules change and to predict future changes was presented by [7]. A framework to monitor the changes in association rule measures based on simple thresholds for support and confidence is described in [8].

## 3  Preliminaries

### 3.1  Frequent Itemsets

We define a customer segment as a set of customers which have common features or attributes. Given a data set which describes customers any attribute value combination of each subset of its attributes therefore qualifies as a candidate customer segment. However, we are only interested in customer segments which are frequent in relation to the overall population. This means, we do not aim for segments which present only a tiny fraction of customers, but for those which are larger than an user defined frequency threshold.

Customer segments defined this way can be represented by *frequent itemsets*. The discovery of frequent itemsets is a broadly used approach to perform a nearly exhaustive search for patterns within a data set [9]. Its goal is to detect all those attribute values which occur together within a data set and whose relative frequency exceeds a given threshold. The advantage of frequent itemset discovery is the completeness of its results: it finds the exhaustive set of all significant patterns. For this reason it provides a rather detailed description of a data set's structure. On the other hand, however, the set of discovered itemsets is typically vast.

Formally, frequent itemset discovery is applied to a set $\mathcal{D}$ of *transactions* $\mathcal{T} \in \mathcal{D}$. Every transaction $\mathcal{T}$ is a subset of a set of items $\mathcal{L}$. A subset $\mathcal{X} \subseteq \mathcal{L}$ is called *itemset*. It is said that a transaction $\mathcal{T}$ *supports* an itemset $\mathcal{X}$ if $\mathcal{X} \subseteq \mathcal{T}$. As usual, the frequency of an itemset $\mathcal{X}$ is measured by its *support* $\mathrm{supp}(\mathcal{X})$ which estimates $P(\mathcal{X}) \subseteq \mathcal{T})$, or short $P(\mathcal{X})$. For example, suppose that we are given a data set, which contains survey results about customer satisfaction, the following frequent itemset could have been discovered from it:

$$\text{AGE} > 50\,,\ \text{SATISFIED} = \text{YES}$$

The support of this itemset is the relative frequency of customers that are over 50 years old and satisfied, i.e., it describes the relative size of the customer segment.

In the following we will use the notions of a customer segment and a frequent itemsets synonymously.

## 3.2  Support Histories

The underlying idea of our framework is to detect interesting changes in a customer segment, represented by an itemset, by analysing the support of the itemset along the time axis. The starting point of such an approach is as follows: a timestamped data set is partitioned into intervals along the time axis. Frequent itemset discovery is then applied to each of these subsets. This yields sequences—or *histories*—of support for each itemset, which can be analysed further. Of particular interest are regularities in the histories which we call *change patterns*. They allow us to make statements about the future development of a customer segment and thus provide a basis for proactive decision making.

Let $\mathcal{D}$ be a time-stamped data set and $[t_0, t_n]$ the minimum time span that covers all its tuples. The interval $[t_0, t_n]$ is divided into $n > 1$ non-overlapping periods $T_i := [t_{i-1}, t_i]$, such that the corresponding subsets $\mathcal{D}(T_i) \subset \mathcal{D}$ each have a size $|\mathcal{D}(T_i)| \gg 1$. Let $\hat{T} := \{T_1, \ldots, T_n\}$ be the set of all periods, then for each $T_i \in \hat{T}$ frequent itemset discovery is applied to the transaction set $\mathcal{D}(T_i)$ to derive item sets $\mathcal{I}(\mathcal{D}(T_i))$.

Because the support of every itemset $\mathcal{X}$ is now related to a specific transaction set $\mathcal{D}(T_i)$ and thus to a certain time period $T_i$ we need to extend its notation. This is done straightforward and yields $\text{supp}(\mathcal{X}, T_i) \approx P(\mathcal{X}| T_i)$. Each itemset $\mathcal{X} \in \hat{\mathcal{I}}(\mathcal{D}) := \bigcap_{i=1}^{n} \mathcal{I}(\mathcal{D}(T_i))$ is therefore described by $n$ values for support. Imposed by the order of time the values form a sequence called *support history* $H(\mathcal{X}) := (\text{supp}(\mathcal{X}, T_1), \ldots \text{supp}(\mathcal{X}, T_n))$ of the itemset $\mathcal{X}$. These histories are then used in subsequent steps to detect interesting change patterns.

To continue our example, suppose that we may discover that the support of the itemset

$$\text{AGE} > 50 \, , \ \text{SATISFIED} = \text{YES}$$

has an downward trend. This, in turn, can be interpreted as that the group of all satisfied customers over 50 steadily gets smaller.

## 4  Architecture of the Framework

As already mentioned above our approach builds upon the idea of deriving frequent itemsets as representations of customer segments at different points in time, which are then analysed for changes. To derive a history, data sets collected during many consecutive periods have to be analysed for frequent itemsets. After each analysis session the discovered itemsets have to be compared to those discovered in previous periods and their histories have to be extended. On the other hand, history values may be discarded if their age exceeds an application dependent threshold. Therefore, itemsets and histories have to be stored on a long term basis. Taking all of the aforesaid into account the first task of our framework is:

1. Frequent itemsets have to be *discovered* and their histories efficiently stored, managed and maintained.

If histories with a sufficient length are available, the next task is straightforward:

2. Histories that exhibit specific change patterns have to be reliably *detected*.

Frequent itemset discovery is generally connected with two problems. In the first place, a vast number of itemsets will be detected. Secondly, frequent itemsets may be obvious, already known or not relevant.

Since a history is derived for each rule, the first problem also affects our framework: it has to deal with a vast number of histories and thus it is likely that many change patterns will be detected. Moreover, as we will briefly discuss in Section 5, methods that were developed to deal with this problem for itemsets cannot be used when it comes to analyzing change. Furthermore, there is also a quality problem: not all of the detected change patterns are equally interesting to a user and the most interesting are hidden among many irrelevant ones. Overall, the third task is:

3. Histories with a change pattern have to be analysed for redundancies and *evaluated* according to their interestingness.

Because the aforementioned tasks build upon each other, they can be seen as layers of a processing framework. According to their task the layers are termed *Segment Detector*, *Change Analyser* and *Interestingness Evaluator*, respectively.

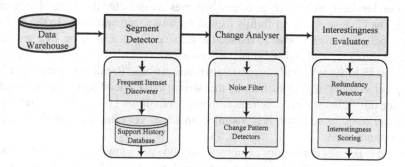

**Fig. 1.** Architecture of our framework

## 5    Segment Detector

Given a timestamped data set collected during a certain period, the task of the Segment Detector is to discover and store the customer segments in it. Since in our application each frequent itemset is a potentially interesting customer segment the first component of this layer is an algorithm for frequent itemset discovery, its second component is a database that stores and manages itemsets and their histories. Both components, but also the choice of the time periods, will be explained in the following.

In order to obtain the data set, the period length has to be chosen. Two aspects have to be considered. Long periods lead to many transactions in the individual data sets for the different periods and thus can enhance the reliability of the calculated support. Short periods allow to measure support more frequently, which may lead to a more reliable and earlier detection of change patterns. The choice of periods length should therefore depend on the available amount of data.

After the data set is available, frequent itemset discovery is applied to it. A typical approach may not only consist of the discovery method itself, but also of methods for pruning and constrained mining. Such methods have been developed to cope with the aforementioned problem of a vast amount of discovered itemsets in each period. This itemset quantity problem directly affects our application. A huge number of histories has to be processed and consequently far too many change patterns will be reported. In order to cope with this problem, pruning methods have been developed in order to constrain the itemsets. From the perspective of our framework such pruning methods treat itemsets generated in different time periods independently from another. However, in our application we process many, temporally ordered itemsets. Thus the itemset property utilized for pruning—in general a measure based on itemset statistics—may vary for some itemsets over time, but still match the pruning criterion in each itemset. Although these variations may render itemsets interesting, they are discarded by existing approaches for itemset pruning. Consequently, we cannot directly use them.

# 6   Change Analyzer

The task of the *Change Analyzer* is to discover change patterns in support histories. In this paper, however, we only discuss how histories are detected that are stable or exhibit a trend. The Change Analyzer fulfills its task by a two step approach. In the first step a filter is applied to the histories to reduce the noise contained in them. In a second step statistical tests for trend and stability are conducted.

Support histories inherently may contain random noise. Random noise may influence subsequent analysis steps in such a way that wrong and misleading results are produced. To reduce this effect we use *double exponential smoothing* [10] in order to reveal more clearly any trend or stability. It is a simple and fast, yet effective method, which can easily be automated.

A trend is present if a history exhibits steady upward growth or a downward decline over its whole length. This definition is rather loose, but in fact there exists no fully satisfactory definition for trend [10]. From a data mining perspective a trend describes the pattern that each value is likely to be larger or smaller than all its predecessors within a sequence, depending on whether the trend is upward or downward. Hence it is a qualitative statement about the current and likely future development of a history. However, taking aspects of interpretability and usefulness into account, such a statement is sufficient in the case of our application. When faced with a vast number of customer segments and their histories, a user often has a basic expectation whether they should exhibit a trend and of what kind. By comparing his expectations with reality he will mostly be able to roughly assess the implications for his business. On the other hand, a user will rarely know in advance how trends should look like quantitatively, for example, their shape or target values. Thus he may be unable to exploit the advantages of more sophisticated trend descriptions, like regression models.

To choose a method for trend detection, it has to be taken into account that the number of histories to examine is huge. Whenever a trend is reported the user is basically forced to rely on the correctness of this statement, because it is infeasible for him to verify each trend manually. In addition to the requirement of reliable detection, the method should incorporate no assumptions about any underlying model, because it is very unlikely that it will hold for all or at least most sequences. Therefore non-parametric statistical tests are the appropriate choice for trend detection.

Within our framework we provide two statistical tests for trend, the *Mann-Kendall test* [11] and the *Cox-Stuart test* [12]. The Cox-Stuart test exploits fewer features of the history, leading to a computational effort that increases linearly with the history length. Although this may render the Cox-Stuart test susceptible to noise, because the influence of artefacts on the test result is stronger, it is considerably faster for long histories. In contrast to this, the Mann-Kendall test is much more robust, but its computational effort increases quadratically with the history length. Therefore it has to be determined which of the two issues—speed or robustness—is more important depending on the actual characteristics of the data used.

Roughly speaking, a history is considered stable if its mean level and variance are constant over time and the variance is reasonably small. Similar to trends, a clear definition of stability is difficult. For example, a history may exhibit a cyclical variation, but may nevertheless be stable on a long term scale. Depending on the actual interest of a user, either the one or the other may have to be emphasised. From a data mining perspective stability describes the pattern that each value is likely to be close to a constant value, estimated by the mean of its predecessors. Thus it is, like a trend, a qualitative statement about the future development of a history. However, in contrast to a trend, it can easily be modeled in an interpretable and useful way, e.g., by the sample mean and variance. Generally, stable customer segments are more reliable and can be trusted—an eminently useful and desirable property for long term business planning.

To test for stability we use a method based on the well-known $\chi^2$ test. However, since the $\chi^2$ test does not take the inherent order of a history's values into account, our method may infrequently also classify histories as stable, which actually exhibit a trend. Therefore, we chose to perform the stability test as the last one in our sequence of tests for change patterns.


# 7    Interestingness Evaluator

Since usually a vast number of change patterns for customer segments will be detected, it is essential to provide methods which reduce their number and identify potentially interesting ones. This is the task of the *Interestingness Evaluator*. To reduce the number of candidate segments the Interestingness Evaluator contains a redundancy detection approach, based on so-called derivative histories [13]. Although this approach proves to be very effective, the number of temporally non-redundant customer segments may still be too large for manual examination. Therefore a component for interestingness evaluation is provided, which contains a set of interestingness measures.

## 7.1   Redundancy Detection

Generally, most changes captured in a segment's history—and consequently also change patterns—are simply the snowball effect of the changes of other segments. Suppose we are looking at customer satisfaction surveys and our framework would discover that the support of the segment

$$\mathcal{X}_1 : \text{AGE} > 50, \text{SATISFIED}=\text{YES}$$

shows an upward trend. That is, the fraction of customers over 50 who are satisfied increases. However, if the fraction of males among all over 50 year old satisfied customers is stable over time, the history of

$$\mathcal{X}_2 : \text{AGE} > 50, \text{GENDER}=\text{MALE}, \text{SATISFIED}=\text{YES}$$

shows qualitatively the same trend. In fact, the history of segment $\mathcal{X}_2$ can be *derived* from the one of $\mathcal{X}_1$ by multiplying it with a gender related constant factor. For this reason, the segment $\mathcal{X}_2$ is *temporally redundant* with respect to its support history.

It is reasonable to assume that a user will generally be interested in customer segments with non-derivative and thus non-redundant histories, because they are likely key drivers for changes. Moreover, derivative segments may lead to wrong business decisions. In the above example a decision based on the change in segment $\mathcal{X}_2$ would account for the gender as one significant factor for the observed trend. In fact, the gender is completely irrelevant. Therefore, the aim is to find segments that are non-redundant in the sense that their history is not a derivative of related segments' histories. In a way, the approach is searching and discarding segments that are not the root cause of a change pattern which, in turn, can be seen as a form of pruning. In order to find derivative segments we have to answer the following questions. First, what is meant by *related* itemsets (segments, respectively), and second, what makes a history a *derivative* of other histories. Regarding the first question, we use the superset relation to define *related itemsets*: an itemset $\mathcal{Y}$ is related to an itemset $\mathcal{X}$ iff $\mathcal{X} \prec \mathcal{Y} := \mathcal{X} \supset \mathcal{Y}$. We also say that $\mathcal{Y}$ is *more general* than $\mathcal{X}$ because its supporting transaction set is larger. In the following we write $\mathcal{X}\mathcal{Y}$ for $\mathcal{X} \cup \mathcal{Y}$. We then define:

**Definition 1.** *Let* $\mathcal{X}$, $\mathcal{X}_1, \mathcal{X}_2 \ldots \mathcal{X}_p$ *be itemsets with* $\mathcal{X} \prec \mathcal{X}_i$ *for all* $i$ *and* $p > 0$. *Let the* $\mathcal{X}_i$ *be pairwise disjoint. Let* supp *the support,* $\text{supp}(T) := \text{supp}(\mathcal{X}, T)$ *and* $\text{supp}_i(T) := \text{supp}(\mathcal{X}_i, T)$ *its functions over time and* $\mathcal{M} := \{g : \mathbb{R} \longrightarrow \mathbb{R}\}$ *be the set of real-valued functions over time. The history* $H(\mathcal{X})$ *is called* derivative *iff a function* $f : \mathcal{M}^p \longrightarrow \mathcal{M}$ *exists such that for all* $T \in \hat{T}$

$$\text{supp}(T) = f(\text{supp}_1, \text{supp}_2, \ldots, \text{supp}_p)(T) \tag{1}$$

For simplicity, we call an itemset *derivative* iff its history is derivative.

The main idea behind the above definition is that the history of an itemset is derivative, if it can be constructed as a mapping of the histories of more general itemsets. To compute the value $\text{supp}(\mathcal{X}, T)$ the values $\text{supp}(\mathcal{X}_i, T)$ are thereby considered. The definition above does not allow for a pointwise definition of $f$ on just the $T \in \hat{T}$, but instead states a general relationship between the support values independent from the point in time. It can therefore be used to predict the value of $\text{supp}(\mathcal{X})$ given future values of the $\text{supp}(\mathcal{X}_i)$. A simple example we will see below is $\text{supp} = f(\text{supp}_1) = c \, \text{supp}_1$, i.e. the support history can be obtained by multiplying the support history of a more general itemset with a constant $c$.

In the following we introduce two criteria for detecting derivative support histories which can be used in combination or independently from another. The functions $f$ are quite simple and we make sure that they are intuitive.

The first criterion checks if the support of an itemset can be explained with the support of exactly one less specific itemset.

**Criterion 1.** *The term* $\text{supp}(\mathcal{X}\mathcal{Y}, T) / \text{supp}(\mathcal{Y}, T)$ *is constant over* $T \in \hat{T}$ *given disjoint itemsets* $\mathcal{X}$ *and* $\mathcal{Y}$.

The meaning of the criterion becomes clear when being rewritten as

$$c = \text{supp}(\mathcal{X}\mathcal{Y}, T) / \text{supp}(\mathcal{Y}, T) = P(\mathcal{X}\mathcal{Y} \mid T) / P(\mathcal{Y} \mid T) = P(\mathcal{X} \mid \mathcal{Y}T)$$

with a constant $c$. The probability of $\mathcal{X}$ is required to be constant over time given $\mathcal{Y}$, so the fraction of transactions containing $\mathcal{X}$ additionally to $\mathcal{Y}$ constantly grows in the same proportion as $\mathcal{Y}$. For this reason the influence of $\mathcal{X}$ in the itemset $\mathcal{X}\mathcal{Y}$ on the support history is not important. Due to

$$\text{supp}(\mathcal{X}\mathcal{Y}, T) = c \cdot \text{supp}(\mathcal{Y}, T) \tag{2}$$

with $c = \text{supp}(\mathcal{X}\mathcal{Y}, T) / \text{supp}(\mathcal{Y}, T)$ for any $T \in \hat{T}$, $\mathcal{X}\mathcal{Y}$ is obviously a derivative of $\mathcal{Y}$ with respect to support history as defined in Definition 1.

Figures 2 and 3 show an example of a derivative support history. Figure 2 shows the support histories of the less specific itemset at the top and the more specific itemset underneath over 20 time periods. The shape of the two curves is obviously very similar and it turns out that the history of the more specific rule can be approximately reconstructed using the less specific one based on (2). As shown in Figure 3, the reconstruction is not exact due to noise. A suitable statistical test was proposed in [13].

Opposed to the criterion above, the following is based on the idea of explaining the support of an itemset with the support values of two subsets.

**Criterion 2.** *The term* $\frac{\text{supp}(\mathcal{X}\mathcal{Y},T)}{\text{supp}(\mathcal{X},T)\,\text{supp}(\mathcal{Y},T)}$ *is constant over* $T \in \hat{T}$ *given disjoint itemsets* $\mathcal{X}$ *and* $\mathcal{Y}$.

$\text{supp}(\mathcal{X}\mathcal{Y}, T)$ measures the probability of the itemset $\mathcal{X}\mathcal{Y}$ in period $T$ which is $P(\mathcal{X}\mathcal{Y} \mid T)$. The term $\frac{\text{supp}(\mathcal{X}\mathcal{Y},T)}{\text{supp}(\mathcal{X},T),\text{supp}(\mathcal{Y},T)} = \frac{P(\mathcal{X}\mathcal{Y} \mid T)}{P(\mathcal{X} \mid T)P(\mathcal{Y} \mid T)}$ is quite extensively used in data mining to measure the degree of dependence of $\mathcal{X}$ and $\mathcal{Y}$ at time $T$. The criterion therefore expresses that the degree of dependence between both itemsets is constant over time.

The support history of $\mathcal{X}\mathcal{Y}$ can then be constructed using

$$\text{supp}(\mathcal{X}\mathcal{Y}, T) = c \cdot \text{supp}(\mathcal{X}, T)\, \text{supp}(\mathcal{Y}, T) \tag{3}$$

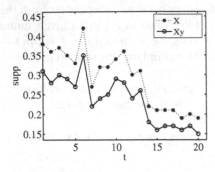

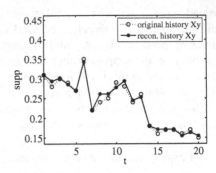

**Fig. 2.** Histories of the segment $\mathcal{X}$ and its derivative segment $\mathcal{X}y$

**Fig. 3.** Reconstructed history of $\mathcal{X}y$ using the history of $\mathcal{X}$

with $c = \mathrm{supp}(\mathcal{X}\mathcal{Y}, T)/(\mathrm{supp}(\mathcal{X}, T) \, \mathrm{supp}(\mathcal{Y}, T))$ for any $T \in \hat{T}$, that is the individual support values of the less specific itemsets are used corrected with the constant degree of dependence on another. According to Definition 1 the support history of $\mathcal{X}\mathcal{Y}$ is therefore derivative.

Overall, an itemset is considered derivative if more general itemsets can be found, such that at least one of the Criteria 1 or 2 holds.

### 7.2 Interestingness Scoring

To assess the interestingness of detected trends and stabilities it has to be considered that each history is linked to a segment which itself has a certain relevance to a user. The detection of a specific change pattern may significantly influence this prior relevance. However, there is no broadly accepted and reliable way of measuring an itemset's interestingness up to now [14]. Therefore we consider any statement about the interestingness of a history also as a statement about the interestingness of its related itemset.

To assess stable histories two things should be considered: in the first place, most data mining methods typically assume that the domain under consideration is stable over time. Secondly, support is an interestingness measure for itemsets themselves. Taking all this into account, a stable history is in some way consistent with the abovementioned assumption of data mining. It is summarised by the mean of its values, which in turn can then be treated as an objective interestingness measure. Here the variance of the history can be neglected, since it is constrained by the stability detection method.

To develop objective interestingness measures for trends is more complex due to their richness of features. For identifying salient features of a given trend, it is essential to provide reference points for comparison. As such we chose the assumptions a user naively makes in the absence of any knowledge about the changes in support histories. From a psychological perspective they can be seen as the anchors relative to which histories with a trend are assessed: a trend becomes more interesting with increasing inconsistency between its features and the user's naive assumptions. We identified three

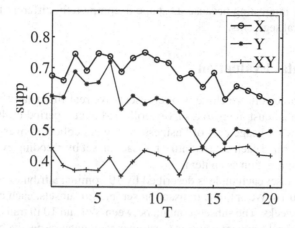

**Fig. 4.** Examples of interesting histories which exhibit a trend

such assumptions and defined heuristic measures for the discrepancy between a history and an assumption:

- **Stability:** Unless other information is provided, a user assumes that histories are stable over time. This assumption does not mean that he expects no trends at all, but expresses his naive expectations in the absence of precise knowledge about a trend. It should be noted that this is consistent with many data mining approaches, which implicitly assumes that the patterns hidden in the data are stable over time. The histories of the segment $\mathcal{XY}$ in Figure 4 would violate the stability assumption because its trend is very clear.
- **Non-rapid Change:** Since a user shapes its business, he will be aware that the domain under consideration changes over time. However, he will assume that any change is continuous in its direction and moderate in its value. For example, if a business starts a new campaign, it will probably assume that the desired effect on the customers evolves moderately, because, for instance, not all people will see a commercial immediately. On the other hand, a rapid change in this context attracts more attention, because it may hint at an overwhelming success or an undesired side effect. For example, the history of the segment $\mathcal{Y}$ in Figure 4 would be very interesting according to the non-rapid change assumption because the depicted trend is very pronounced and steep.
- **Homogeneous Change:** If the support of an itemset changes over time, it is assumed that the rate and direction of changes in the support of all its supersets are the same. This basically means that the observed change in the itemset does not depend on further items. For example, a user may know that the fraction of satisfied customers increases. The homogeneous change assumptions states that the observed change in satisfaction affects all customers and not only selected subpopulations, e.g. customers over fifty. For example, the fraction of satisfied males among all customers may increase. According to the homogeneous change assumption a user would conclude that the fraction of all satisfied married male customers increases at the same rate. For example, the history of the segments $\mathcal{XY}$ in Figure 4

would be very interesting because its shape is completely different from those of its more general segments.

# 8    Experimental Evaluation

To evaluate our framework we chose two representative real-life dataset. One contains answers of residential customers to a survey collected over a period of 40 weeks. The other contains network usage data of business customers collected over a period of 9 months. We transformed each dataset into a transaction set by recoding every (attribute, attribute value) combination as an item.

In the survey dataset each tuple is described by 19 nominal attributes with a domain size between 2 and 10. We split the transaction set into 20 subsets, each corresponding to a period of two weeks. The subsets contain between 829 and 1049 transactions. From each subset we derived frequent itemsets (customer segments, respectively) with a support greater than 0.04 and not more than 5 describing attributes per segment. From the obtained 20 frequent itemsets we created a compound itemset by intersecting them. Its size is 1202.

The network usage dataset is described by 24 nominal attributes with a domain size of 5. We split the transaction set into 9 subsets each covering a period of one month and having a size of 37 transactions. From each subset we derived frequent itemsets (customer segments, respectively) with a support greater than 0.1 and not more than 5 describing attributes per segment. The intersection of these itemset has a size of 8984.

Subsequently we applied the proposed framework using the Mann-Kendall test for trend detection. Thereby two objectives are linked with our evaluation. First, the number of segments exhibiting trends or stabilities has to be determined. Second, the number of derivative rule histories has to be determined. The results of our analysis are shown in Table 1 and Table 2.

**Table 1.** Absolute number of segments which exhibit a trend or are stable differentiated by non-redundancy

| | segments | | downward trend | | upward trend | | stable | |
| --- | --- | --- | --- | --- | --- | --- | --- | --- |
| | all | non-redund. | all | non-redund. | all | non-redund. | all | non-redund. |
| Surveys | 1202 | 457 | 50 | 31 | 147 | 50 | 830 | 307 |
| Network Usage | 8984 | 1909 | 3030 | 294 | 100 | 43 | 5854 | 1572 |

As we can see the number of segments which exhibit a trend or stability strongly depends on the data set. For example, in the survey data set approximately 4.2% of the segments show an upward trend compared to 33.7% for the network usage data. It shows, however, that segments which exhibit some kind of regular change exist and that they can be rather frequent. Looking in the columns for non-redundant changes we can see that only a small fraction of changing segments cannot be explained by the change of more general segments. As we discussed earlier, segments with redundant changes can lead to suboptimal business decisions. As we see in our results they also

**Table 2.** Relative number of segments which exhibit a trend or are stable differentiated by non-redundancy

|  | segments | | downward trend | | upward trend | | stable | |
|---|---|---|---|---|---|---|---|---|
|  | all | non-redund. | all | non-redund. | all | non-redund. | all | non-redund. |
| Surveys | 100.0% | 38.0% | 4.2% | 2.6% | 12.2% | 4.2% | 69.1% | 25.5% |
| Network Usage | 100.0% | 21.2% | 33.7% | 3.3% | 1.1% | 0.5% | 65.2% | 7.5% |

significantly increase the number of changing segments. This, again, underlines the need for redundancy detection in our framework for which we provided a powerful method.

## 9  Conclusions

We have shown how association rule mining, combined with tracking temporal developments of support and confidence and the application of an interestingness notion can be used for detecting and monitoring customer segments. This is a very important challenge for customer-focussed enterprises. Many businesses regularly collect huge volumes of time-stamped data about all kinds of customer interactions. This data reflects changes in customer behavior. It is crucial for the success of most businesses to detect these changes, correctly interpret their causes and finally to adapt or react to them. Hence there is a significant need for data mining approaches that are capable of finding the most relevant and interesting changes in a data set.

We have proposed a framework for our approach that can provide detailed knowledge about how customer behaviour evolves over time. We successfully applied our framework to two problem domains which are very significant for a telecommunications company: customer analytics, to investigate what is likely to drive customer satisfaction in the future, and network usage, to understand the drivers of change in customer behavior when they are using services.

## References

1. Shin, H., Sohn, S.: Segmentation of stock trading customers according to potential value. Expert Systems with Applications 27(1), 27–33 (2004)
2. Chen, M.C., Chiu, A.L., Chang, H.H.: Mining changes in customer behavior in retail marketing. Expert Systems with Applications 28(4), 773–781 (2005)
3. Song, H.S., Kim, J.K.: Mining the change of customer behavior in an internet shopping mall. Expert Systems with Applications 21(3), 157–168 (2001)
4. Kim, J.K., Song, H.S., Kim, T.S., Kim, H.K.: Detecting the change of customer behavior based on decision tree analysis. Expert Systems 22(4), 193–205 (2005)
5. Liu, B., Hsu, W., Han, H.S., Xia, Y.: Mining changes for real-life applications. In: Kambayashi, Y., Mohania, M.K., Tjoa, A.M. (eds.) DaWaK 2000. LNCS, vol. 1874, pp. 337–346. Springer, Heidelberg (2000)
6. Agrawal, R., Psaila, G.: Active data mining. In: Proceedings of the 1st International Conference on Knowledge Discovery and Data Mining, pp. 3–8 (1995)

7. Au, W.H., Chan, K.: Mining changes in association rules: a fuzzy approach. Fuzzy Sets and Systems 149(1), 87–104 (2005)
8. Spiliopoulou, M., Baron, S., Günther, O.: Efficient monitoring of patterns in data mining environments. In: Kalinichenko, L.A., Manthey, R., Thalheim, B., Wloka, U. (eds.) ADBIS 2003. LNCS, vol. 2798, pp. 253–265. Springer, Heidelberg (2003)
9. Agrawal, R., Imielinski, T., Swami, A.: Mining association rules between sets of items in large databases. In: Proceedings of the ACM SIGMOD International Conference on Management of Data, Washington DC, pp. 207–216. ACM Press, New York (1993)
10. Chatfield, C.: Time-Series Forecasting. Chapman and Hall/CRC, New York (2001)
11. Mann, H.: Nonparametric tests against trend. Econometrica 13, 245–259 (1945)
12. Cox, D., Stuart, A.: Some quick sign tests for trend in location and dispersion. Biometrika 42, 80–95 (1955)
13. Böttcher, M., Spott, M., Nauck, D.: Detecting temporally redundant association rules. In: Proceedings of 4th International Conference on Machine Learning and Applications, pp. 397–403. IEEE Computer Society Press, Los Alamitos (2005)
14. Tan, P.N., Kumar, V., Srivastava, J.: Selecting the right objective measure for association analysis. Information Systems 29(4), 293–313 (2004)

# Collaborative Filtering Using Electrical Resistance Network Models

Jérôme Kunegis and Stephan Schmidt

DAI-Labor, Technische Universität Berlin, Franklinstraße 28, 10587 Berlin, Germany
{jerome.kunegis, stephan.schmidt}@dai-labor.de

**Abstract.** In a recommender system where users rate items we predict the rating of items users have not rated. We define a rating graph containing users and items as vertices and ratings as weighted edges. We extend the work of [1] that uses the *resistance distance* on the bipartite rating graph incorporating negative edge weights into the calculation of the resistance distance. This algorithm is then compared to other rating prediction algorithms using data from two rating corpora.

## 1   Introduction

In recommender systems items are recommended to users. Collaborative filtering is a common approach to implementing recommender systems. One way of implementing a recommender system is by collaborative filtering. Instead of calculating an item score based on item features, a collaborative filtering algorithm analyzes existing ratings from users to predict the rating of an item a certain user has not seen.

Items are typically documents, songs, movies or anything that can be recommended to users and that users can rate. Ratings can be given by users explicitly such as with the five star scale used by some websites or can be collected implicitly by monitoring the users' actions such as recording the number of times a user has listened to a song.

The approach presented here models rating databases as bipartite graphs with users and items as the two vertex sets and ratings as weighted edges. [1] describes how this graph can be seen as a network of electrical resistances and how the total equivalent resistance between any two nodes can be used to define a similarity function either between two users, two items or users and items. In the referenced paper edges are not weighted and thus all resistances are modeled as unit resistances.

We extend this work by using the actual ratings as edge weights. Because ratings can be negative, modifications to the previous approach are necessary in order for the similarity function we define to satisfy three basic conditions, which we present in the section defining the rating graph. We use this similarity for predicting ratings and compare the results to common prediction algorithms.

Based on the graph representation of a rating database we can formulate three conditions a good prediction measure should satisfy:

**Parallelity.** Parallel paths of edges between two nodes contribute monotonically to the similarity between the two nodes. If multiple paths exist between two nodes, the overall similarity between the two nodes should be greater than the similarity taken on each path separately.

P. Perner (Ed.): ICDM 2007, LNAI 4597, pp. 269–282, 2007.
© Springer-Verlag Berlin Heidelberg 2007

**Transitivity.** A long path of edges with positive weight results in a lower similarity than a short path with similar weights.

**Negative ratings.** A path consisting of both positive and negative edges leads to a negative similarity exactly if the number of negative edges is odd. This follows from the observation that users that both like or both dislike an item are similar while two users are not similar when one of them like an item the other one dislikes.

We will show later that our method satisfies all three conditions while the original algorithm [1] only satisfies the first two.

*Outline.* In Section 2 we present mathematical definitions and the two basic rating prediction methods: rating normalization and weighted rating sum based on the Pearson correlation between users. Section 3 defines the bipartite rating graph and the meaning of the rating values. Section 4 defines the similarity between two graph nodes based on electrical resistances in the case that no ratings are negative. In Section 5, the usage of negative ratings is explored and a modified formula is presented that satisfies the three conditions presented above. Section 6 discusses algorithms for solving the system of equations. In Section 7 our similarity measure is compared to two standard prediction measures and to the prediction measure defined in [1]. Section 8 finishes with some remarks about the accuracy of our method and with future work.

# 2    Related Work

This section presents the two prediction methods used in our evaluation that are not based on the rating graph. The method of [1] is presented after the definition of the rating graph.

## 2.1    Definitions

Let $\mathcal{U} = \{U_1, U_2, \ldots, U_m\}$ be the set of users and $\mathcal{I} = \{I_1, I_2, \ldots, I_n\}$ the set of items.

The rating by user $U_i$ of item $I_j$ is denoted $r_{ij}$. We keep $r_{ij}$ undefined if user $U_i$ has not rated item $I_j$.

Let $\mathcal{I}_i$ be the set of items rated by user $U_i$ and $\mathcal{U}_j$ the set of users that rated item $I_j$.

## 2.2    Rating Scales

Different rating systems use different rating scales. When user ratings correspond to labels such as *good* or *bad*, they are represented by an integer value ranging for instance from 1 to 5, where 5 represents the highest rating (*very good*), and 1 represents the lowest rating (*very bad*). Users can give neutral ratings when the number of different values is odd. These ratings can be adjusted such that a neutral value is represented by the value 0. They can also be scaled to fit in the $[-1, +1]$ range, but this is not necessary because the data is normalized as described below as a first step in most algorithms. In some cases ratings may be unbounded, for instance if they represent a document view count.

## 2.3 Normalization

Different users have a different idea of what *good* and *bad* ratings mean, so some users give the extremal ratings rarely while others always rate items as either very good or very bad. Assuming that the distribution of item ratings should be similar for all users we can scale each user's ratings around the mean rating such that the standard deviation of each user's ratings is a constant. Using the same argument, we can offset each user's ratings so that his mean rating is zero. This kind of transformation is described in [2].

## 2.4 Mean Rating

As the simplest prediction algorithm, we chose the user's mean rating as a prediction for his rating of any item he has not rated. This is equivalent to always predicting a rating of zero after normalization. For each user $U_i$, we define the mean rating $\bar{r}_i$:

$$\bar{r}_i = \frac{1}{|\mathcal{I}_i|} \sum_{j \in \mathcal{I}_i} r_{ij}$$

This method is very simple as it does not take into account other users' ratings.

## 2.5 Pearson Correlation

To take other users' ratings into account, a simple method to predict the rating for a user $U \in \mathcal{U}$ is to calculate the mean rating other users have given to the item in question. However, other users may have a different taste than user $U$. Therefore we need a similarity function applicable between user $U$ and other users. This similarity value can then be used as weights to get a weighted mean as a rating prediction. The similarity function used can even admit negative values, indicating that users are likely to have opposing tastes.

A similarity function satisfying these conditions is the Pearson correlation between users calculated using normalized ratings as described in [3]. This correlation is normally calculated using only items the two users have both rated. As described in [3], it is also possible to take the correlation over all items rated by at least one user, filling missing ratings with a default value.

Let $\mathcal{I}_{ab} = \mathcal{I}_a \cap \mathcal{I}_b$. The Pearson correlation between the users $U_a$ and $U_b$ is defined as

$$w(a, b) = \frac{\sum_{j \in \mathcal{I}_{ab}} (r_{aj} - \bar{r}_a)(r_{bj} - \bar{r}_b)}{\sqrt{\sum_{j \in \mathcal{I}_{ab}} (r_{aj} - \bar{r}_a)^2 \sum_{j \in \mathcal{I}_{ab}} (r_{bj} - \bar{r}_b)^2}}$$

where $\bar{r}_a$ and $\bar{r}_b$ are taken over $\mathcal{I}_{ab}$. The rating prediction of item $U_j$ for user $U_i$ is now given by

$$r_{ij}^p = \left( \sum_a w(i, a) \right)^{-1} \sum_a w(i, a) r_{aj} \tag{1}$$

where sums are taken over all users that have rated items in common with user $U_i$. This expression is not defined when the sum of correlations is zero.

Alternatively, we can use all items at least one user has rated, and substituting these missing ratings with a neutral value such as the user's mean rating. Throughout this paper only the first option will be used as it is common practice in collaborative filtering recommender systems.

## 3   The Rating Graph

In this section, we define the weighted rating graph. Given sets of users, items and ratings, users and items are represented by vertices, while ratings are modeled as the edges connecting them. Rating values become edge weights.

As observed by [4] and [5], this rating graph is bipartite. We can assume that the graph is connected. If it is not, it can be made connected by only keeping the connected component containing the vertices we want to compare. If the vertices to be compared are not connected, then the graph cannot be used to predict the rating in question since the vertices are not part of the same rating subgraph. In fact, the absence of a path between two nodes means that there is no way to say anything about the relation between the two users or items, and no algorithm or model can give results in this case.

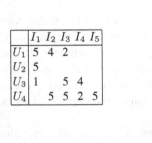
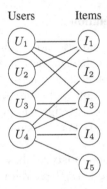

**Fig. 1.** User-item rating table and graph, on a scale from 1 (very bad) to 5 (very good)

In Figure 1 four users ($U_1$–$U_4$) have rated five items ($I_1$–$I_5$). However, not all possible ratings were given. Empty cells in the rating table on the left denote ratings users have not given.

The corresponding bipartite rating graph is shown on the right. It contains one edge for each rating. In this case, the graph is connected.

As explained in the introduction, the purpose of the graph is to find connections between users and items. As an example for the graph given above, we could ask the question: How would user A rate item $I_5$? Since the user has not rated the item, we must use the known ratings to predict a rating for the corresponding vertex pair.

Because users and items are both represented as vertices, our method for calculating a similarity them can also be used for calculating similarities of two users or two items. In this paper, we restrict ourselves to calculating the similarity between a user and an item.

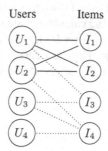

Users        Items

**Fig. 2.** In this example, the edges not taken into account by the Pearson correlation calculation are shown as dotted lines

In the case covered in [1], the graph is not bipartite, but tripartite: Vertices represent users, movies that can be rated, and categories of movies (such as comedies). In the resulting tripartite graph however, the problems given in [1] can all be modeled as the similarity between two vertices. Therefore, we will consider the general case of graphs that need not necessarily be bipartite.

Given a weighted graph and two vertices, a similarity measure between the two vertices can now be defined. As mentioned before, edges are weighted, and their weights are signed. Positive values indicate a positive association between the nodes, negative values indicate a negative association between the nodes. The measure we want to define must satisfy the three conditions presented in the introduction. These conditions translate to the following mathematical properties:

**Long paths.** Paths from one vertex to another can be compared by the number of edges they contain. Long paths must correspond to smaller similarities than short paths. If, for instance, two users have rated the same item, then their similarity must be higher than if they had only rated items in common with a third user. However, long paths must not give a similarity of zero. This condition may be called transitivity.

**Parallel paths.** If a large number of distinct paths exist between two vertices, the similarity value between the two vertices must be higher than for the case where only few paths exist.

**Negative edges.** If the two vertices are connected by exactly one path, then the resulting similarity must be of the same sign as the product of the weights of the path edges. This condition corresponds to the sensible assumption that one will dislike items that are disliked by users with similar taste.

We will now show that the Pearson correlation based rating prediction does not satisfy all three conditions.

In the bipartite rating graph, the Pearson correlation can only be calculated between two user vertices that are connected by a path of length two. If the distance between the two vertices is longer than two edges, the Pearson correlation cannot be calculated because the users have not rated any items in common. Thus, the Pearson correlation does not satisfy the requirement on long paths. However, it does satisfy the requirement on parallel paths and the requirement on negative edges.

In Figure 2, the Pearson correlation between users $U_1$ and $U_2$ is calculated. Edges that are not taken into account during calculation are shown as dotted lines. This example shows that while both user $U_1$ and user $U_2$ have something in common with user $U_3$, these connections are simply ignored by the Pearson correlation. Furthermore, user $U_4$ has no ratings in common with user $U_1$, so the Pearson correlation cannot be calculated between these two users.

## 4    Resistance Distance

This section describes the similarity function based on electrical resistance as described in [1].

We have previously proposed that a sensible similarity measure needs to be smaller as paths get longer and larger when there are parallel paths. A similar behavior can be encountered in electrical engineering regarding electrical resistances: When in series, their values add to each other; when in parallel, the inverse of their values add to each other, and the resulting resistance is lower than individual resistances.

Our function is required to yield the opposite result: A path of edges in the rating graph (corresponds to resistances in series) must result in a lower value. Similarly, parallel paths must lead to a rating value that is the sum of the individual path values. Therefore, we use the inverse of the resistance in our function. The inverse of the electrical resistance is the electrical conductance. In this paper, we use the letter $r$ to denote ratings, which must not be confused with the letter $R$ that usually denotes resistances.

In [1] all ratings are initialized with the unit rating ($r_{\text{unit}} = 1$) to avoid negative ratings, which are problematic as we will see below. Figure 3 shows some examples containing only unit resistances (or, equivalently, unit conductances). The corresponding resulting conductance is given for each graph, illustrating how the length of paths influences the similarity value, and how parallel edges result in higher similarity values. As mentioned in [6], the resistance distance between nodes of a graph is a metric.

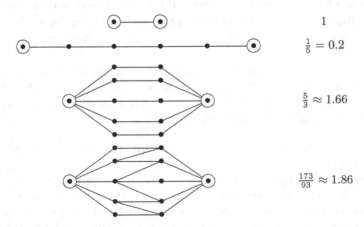

**Fig. 3.** Bipartite rating graphs annotated with resistance distance values between pairs of highlighted nodes. All edges have unit weight.

We will now describe a method for calculating this total conductance between vertices $A$ and $B$. When applying a unit voltage on the two vertices, the current through the network will equal the total conductance. In order to compute the value of the current passing through the network, we first need to calculate the potential on $A$ and on the vertices adjacent to $A$. To this end, we introduce a variable $x_V$ for each vertex $V$. We then simulate the application of a unit voltage between $A$ and $B$ by setting $x_A = 0$ and $x_B = 1$. For each vertex $V$ adjacent to the vertices $V_1 \ldots V_k$, we know that the total current entering $V$ must be zero. Let $I_i$ be the current going from $V_i$ to $V$ and $r_i$ the conductance of the edge $(V, V_i)$. We obtain the following system of equations:

$$\sum_i I_i = 0$$

$$\sum_i r_i(x_V - x_{V_i}) = 0$$

$$\sum_i r_i x_V - r_i x_{V_i} = 0$$

$$\left(\sum_i r_i\right) x_V = \sum_i r_i x_{V_i} \tag{2}$$

At this point, an additional variable is introduced for each vertex in the graph. Solving this system of equations will yield potentials for all vertices of the graph. The current flow from $A$ to $B$ is now given by taking the sum of the current over all edges $(A, V_i)$ incident to $A$:

$$I_{AB} = \sum_i I_{AV_i}$$

$$= \sum_i r_{AV_i}(x_{V_i} - x_A)$$

$$= \sum_i r_{AV_i} x_{V_i}$$

The resistance distance is now given by:

$$r_{eq} = \frac{I_{AB}}{x_B - x_A}$$

$$= I_{AB}$$

$$= \sum_i r_{AV_i} x_{V_i} \tag{3}$$

And inverse resistance distance gives our similarity between two nodes $A$ and $B$:

$$\text{sim}_{unit} = r_{eq}^{-1}$$

We observe that finding the total conductance between $A$ and $B$ is equivalent to solving a linear system of $n$ equations and $n$ variables, where $n$ is the number of vertices in the rating graph.

## 5  Negative Ratings

As we have seen, the inverse resistance distance satisfies the first two conditions we imposed on similarity functions. However, it is easy to see that it does not conform to the third condition; for instance in a path containing an odd number of negative edges, the similarity should be negative, but the inverse resistance distance is always positive.

Instead of just setting all ratings to the value one to avoid negative edge weights, we will try to keep the real values, and try to define a new similarity measure satisfying all three conditions.

We now examine the consequences of inserting the *original*, possibly negative rating values into the equations above. Figure 4 shows a very simple electrical network with negative resistances, and its corresponding inverse resistance distance is calculated using the formula known from physics stating that two resistance in series of magnitude $r_1$ and $r_2$ are equivalent to a single resistance of magnitude $\frac{r_1 r_2}{r_1+r_2}$.

$$\overset{r_1=+1}{\bullet\!-\!-\!-\!-\!-\!\bullet}\overset{r_2=-1}{-\!-\!-\!-\!-\!-\!\bullet}\quad r_{\mathrm{eq}} = \frac{r_1 r_2}{r_1+r_2} = \frac{1\cdot(-1)}{1+(-1)} = \frac{-1}{0}$$

**Fig. 4.** The inverse resistance distance on graph with negative edge weights may not be defined

As can be seen, the formula leads to a division by zero. However, we require the result value to be smaller than 1 in absolute value (from the first condition) and negative (from the third condition). The desired result is obtained in a different way; the absolute value of our result is equal to the value calculated using the formula containing the absolute values of the conductances. The sign of the result then has the sign of the product of the two ratings. Thus we want:

$$r_{\mathrm{eq}} = \mathrm{sgn}(r_1)\mathrm{sgn}(r_2)\frac{|r_1|\cdot|r_2|}{|r_1|+|r_2|} = \frac{r_1\cdot r_2}{|r_1|+|r_2|}$$

Figure 5 displays some examples and their resulting similarities using this formula.

Now, the question arises how the general equations given in Equation 2 are to be adapted to yield the desired result for our simple example cases. If we interpret an edge with rating $-r$ not as a negative resistance of conductance $-r$, but as a resistance with conductance $r$ that "inverts" the potential difference across the resistance, then on the right side of our equation the factor of $x_{V_i}$ remains $r_i$, but in the sum on the left side the absolute value of $r_i$ must be used. This means that for each vertex $V$, we replace the equation

$$\left(\sum_i r_i\right) x_V = \sum_i r_i x_{V_i}$$

with

$$\left(\sum_i |r_i|\right) x_V = \sum_i r_i x_{V_i}$$

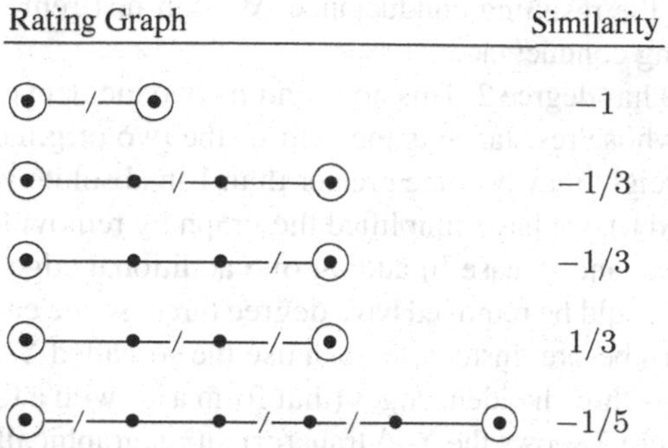

| Rating Graph | Similarity |
|---|---|
| ⊙—/—⊙ | −1 |
| ⊙———•—/—•———⊙ | −1/3 |
| ⊙———•——•—/—⊙ | −1/3 |
| ⊙———•—/—•—/—⊙ | 1/3 |
| ⊙—/———•——•—/—•——/—•———⊙ | −1/5 |

**Fig. 5.** Rating graphs with negative edges and the similarity between the highlighted nodes calculated taking into account the negative values. Edges with a slash have weight −1, other edges have weight +1.

For the examples of Figure 5, these equations yield the desired results. In the next section, methods for solving the resulting system of equations are given.

## 6  Y-Δ Simplification

Calculating the resistance distance between two nodes in a network involves solving a system of $n$ equation of $n$ variables, where $n$ is the number of nodes in the network. Before solving a system of equations however, we can try to simplify the network without changing the resistance distance. The examples in Figure 6 show simple cases where this is possible.

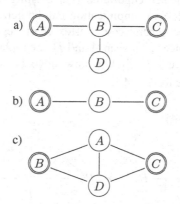

**Fig. 6.** Simple cases of vertex elimination. The similarity is to be calculated between the doubly circled nodes.

In case a), node D has degree 2. No current can enter this node, so nodes D and B always have the same potential. Therefore, the conductance $r_{ab}$ of the edge $(B, D)$

has no influence on the resulting conductance. We can just remove this edge without changing the resulting conductance.

In case b), node B has degree 2. This node and its two incident edges can be replaced with a single edge whose resistance is the sum of the two original edges. In this case, the resulting edge weight may become greater than 1 in absolute value.

In the cases a) and b), we have simplified the graph by removing one vertex, removing its incident edges, and in case b) adding one additional edge. In case c) however, the two vertices that could be removed have degree three, so we cannot apply one of the two simplifications as before. Instead, we can use the so-called Y-$\Delta$ simplification. We replace node B and its three incident edges (that form a Y) with a triangle of three edges (that form a $\Delta$). Figure 7 shows the Y-$\Delta$ transformation graphically. The formulas giving the new resistance values are fundamental to the theory of electrical resistances, as given e.g. in [7].

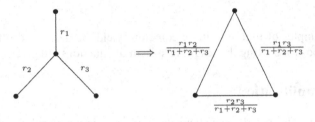

**Fig. 7.** Principle of Y-$\Delta$ simplification

Note that if an edge of the triangle already exists in the graph prior to Y-$\Delta$ transformation, the resulting graph will have parallel edges. As parallel conductances are additive, we can just add the new edge value to an existing edge value if necessary.

As further shown in [7], Y-$\Delta$ simplification can be generalized to removal of vertices of any degree. In the general case, vertex $A$ of degree k adjacent to vertices $\{B_1, \ldots, B_k\}$ with resistance $r_i$ between $A$ and $B_i$ are replaced by $\binom{k}{2}$ new edges. Between each pair of vertices $(B_i, B_j)$, a new edge is added with weight $\frac{r_i r_j}{\sum_k r_k}$. Figure 8 shows an example for $k = 4$.

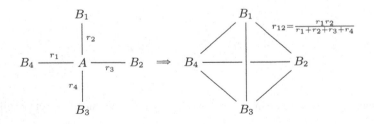

**Fig. 8.** Elimination of a vertex with degree four

While this generalized removal of nodes works in the simple case of only positive conductance values, it does not work with our modified total conductance. Figure 9 gives an example where according to our definition, the conductance between A and B is 1/5, but by using simplification of nodes, we get the result 1/3.

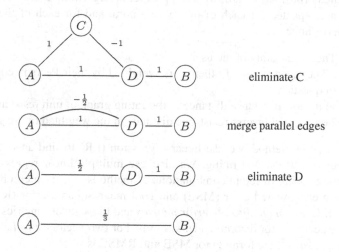

**Fig. 9.** Simple vertex elimination results in different similarity value than defined

This result, however, does not correspond to the system of equations presented above. The following system of equations must be solved to get the value of the total conductance between A and B according to our definition:

$$x_A = 0$$
$$x_B = 1$$
$$2x_C = x_A - x_D$$
$$3x_D = x_A + x_B - x_C$$

Solving this system, we get $r_{eq} = x_C + x_D = 1/5$. This example shows that Y-$\Delta$ elimination can not be applied in the case of modified resistance distance calculation. Therefore, the system of equations defined by Equation 2 must be solved. As shown in [8] and [9], this system of equations is sparse when the rating matrix is sparse, and this is the case in practice because each user will only rate a small number of items compared to the total number of items available.

As mentioned in [9], the minimum degree algorithm has a runtime of $O(n^3)$, where $n$ is the number of users and items. In the typical case, many users have rated only very few items, and many items were only rated by few users. Because the corresponding nodes have small degrees, they are eliminated first, and in this phase of the algorithm, the runtime is linear.

# 7  Evaluation

We use two corpora for evaluation: MovieLens [1] and Jester [2]. Each evaluation test consists of the following steps: First we choose a rating at random, then we remove this rating from the corpus. Afterward, we use a prediction algorithm to predict that rating. These steps are repeated for each of the two corpora, and for each of the following prediction algorithms:

**Mean (M).** The mean rating of the user
**Pearson (P).** The mean rating of other users weighted by their Pearson correlation to the user in question
**Unit (U).** The inverse resistance distance in the rating graph of unit resistances
**Deep (D).** The modified inverse resistance distance in the weighted rating graph

For each prediction method, we use linear regression (LR) to find an optimal affine function predicting the actual rating. We also use multiple linear regression (MLR) to predict ratings using different combinations of methods. For each combination, we calculate the mean squared error (MSE) and root mean squared error (RMSE) [10]. MSE and RMSE are *mean absolute error metrics* and the standard metrics to evaluate the predictive accuracy for recommender systems. For two vectors $x = (x_1, \dots, x_n)^T$ and $y = (y_1, \dots, y_n)^T$, the formula for MSE and RMSE is

$$\text{RMSE}(x, y) = \sqrt{\text{MSE}(x, y)} = \sqrt{\frac{\sum_{i=1}^{n}(x_i - y_i)^2}{n}} \tag{4}$$

The test results are shown in Figure 10.

| Corpus | | | MovieLens | | | Jester |
|--------|-----|------|------------------|-----|------|------------------|
|        | MSE | RMSE | LR/MLR function  | MSE | RMSE | LR/MLR function |
| M      | 0.265 | 0.514 | 0.0023 +0.9928M | 0.240 | 0.490 | 0.01 +0.799M |
| P      | 0.315 | 0.560 | 0.276+0.0005P | 0.280 | 0.537 | 0.0325+0.059P |
| U      | 0.307 | 0.554 | 0.1299+0.0027U | 0.292 | 0.541 | -0.149 +0.0073U |
| D      | 0.285 | 0.534 | 0.236+3.03D | 0.261 | 0.510 | 0.044+1.38D |
| M+D    | 0.239 | 0.489 | -0.024+0.952M+2.81D | 0.204 | 0.452 | 0.024+0.828M+1.478D |
| M+P+D  | 0.239 | 0.489 | -0.024+0.952M+0.004P+2.84D | 0.203 | 0.451 | 0.024+0.828M+0.022P+1.417D |

**Fig. 10.** Evaluation results. Numbers indicate the MSE (mean squared error) and the RMSE (root mean squared error).

We observe that the Pearson correlation has a much smaller predictive accuracy than the other predictions, and that the mean rating is the best single prediction method tested. As users tend to give rating only within a certain range, for example only rating movies they like using exclusively positive ratings.

---

[1] http://movielens.umn.edu/
[2] http://www.ieor.berkeley.edu/ goldberg/jester-data/

The mean rating and deep similarity combined perform better than the mean rating alone, and adding the Pearson based prediction does not lower the error.

## 8    Conclusion and Future Work

In the rating graph given by a rating system, we have defined a measure of similarity between nodes. This measure is based on work from [1] extended by the support for negative ratings.

The modified inverse resistance distance was shown to predict ratings more accurately than a Pearson correlation based algorithm, and using it in combination with other basic prediction methods gives better results than any method for itself.

The following areas of research remain to be explored.

- Formulate a modified Y-$\Delta$ elimination such that the modified resistance distance is preserved. As we have seen, the trivial algorithm does not give the desired results. This line of research would allow an implementation to work on a graph-based representation of the problem.
- Compare and combine the modified inverse resistance distance with other prediction methods. Many other collaborative filtering algorithms exist [3] and could be used in combination with our approach. Since we have seen that a combination of predictions can lead to a better prediction, this line may be promising.
- Analyze the complexity of calculating the modified inverse resistance distance and use methods such as clustering to reduce the rating graph size. As done with other prediction algorithms, the rating graph may first be reduced using methods such as clustering to improve the runtime.
- The modified resistance distance can be calculated between any two nodes in the graph. Calculating it between two users or items leads to a similarity (or distance) measure. This would be useful in recommendation systems and in social software when groups of similar users are to be detected.

## References

1. Fouss, F., Pirotte, A., Saerens, M.: The application of new concepts of dissimilarities between nodes of a graph to collaborative filtering. ACM Trans. Math. Softw. (2003), Also TR-03-010 at www.cise.ufl.edu/tech-reports
2. Billsus, D., Pazzani, M.J.: Learning collaborative information filters. In: Proc. 15th International Conf. on Machine Learning, pp. 46–54. Morgan Kaufmann, San Francisco (1998)
3. Breese, J.S., Heckerman, D., Kadie, C.: Empirical analysis of predictive algorithms for collaborative filtering. In: Proc. of the Fourteenth Annual Conference on Uncertainty in Artificial Intelligence, pp. 43–52 (1998)
4. Mirza, B.J., Keller, B.J., Ramakrishnan, N.: Evaluating recommendation algorithms by graph analysis. CoRR cs.IR/0104009 (2001)
5. Keller, B.J., mi Kim, S., Vemuri, N.S., Ramakrishnan, N., Perugini, S.: The good, bad and the indifferent: Explorations in recommender system health, San Diego, California (2005), http://www.grouplens.org/beyond2005/full/keller.pdf

6. Klein, D.J.: Resistance-distance sum rules. Croatica Chemica Acta 75(2), 633–649 (2002)
7. Qin, Z., Cheng, C.K.: Linear network reduction via Y-$\Delta$-Transformation. technical report 2002-0706, University of California, San Diego, United States (2002)
8. George, A., Liu, W.H.: The evolution of the minimum degree ordering algorithm. SIAM Rev. 31(1), 1–19 (1989)
9. Heggernes, P., Eisenstat, S., Kumfert, G., Pothen, A.: The computational complexity of the minimum degree algorithm (2001)
10. Herlocker, J.L., Konstan, J.A., Terveen, L.G., Riedl, J.T.: Evaluating collaborative filtering recommender systems. ACM Trans. Inf. Syst. 22(1), 5–53 (2004)

# Visual Query and Exploration System for Temporal Relational Database

Shaul Ben Michael and Ronen Feldman

Bar Ilan University, Department of Computer Science
Ramat Gan, Israel
{Shaybm1, Ronenf}@gmail.com

**Abstract.** This research is focused on developing effective visualization tools for query construction and advanced exploration of temporal relational databases. Temporal databases enable the retrieval of each of the states observed in the past and even planned future states. Several query languages for relational databases have been introduced, but only a few of them deal with temporal databases. Moreover, most users are not highly skilled in query formulation and hence are not able to define complex queries. The visual approach introduced here aims at simplifying the query construction process. It gives the user the option to define complex temporal constructs and provides visual tools with which to explore the returned networks intuitively. The exploration process should provide better insight into networks of entities, reveal patterns between the entities, and enable the user to forecast the behavior of entities in the future. A visual query language as an isolated subsystem is not sufficient in itself for a complete data analysis process. A query's output should be further explored to find patterns that are hidden in the output.

**Keywords:** visual query, temporal database, relational database, link analysis, text mining, data mining, social networks, risk management, data exploration, graph matching.

## 1 Introduction

The September 11 attacks brought into focus the malfunctioning of information agencies in the USA. In fact, many terrorist attacks could have been prevented if the available intelligence had been properly utilized. All the raw intelligence materials were available before these attacks were committed; the main problem was to push aside all the material that was not relevant to the investigation, to integrate all the relevant facts, and to construct a clear and complete picture of all the decentralized information available. In order to face these threats, intelligence agencies should adopt new strategies of data collection and data analysis. Text Mining is a new and exciting research area that tries to solve the information overload problem by using techniques from data mining, machine learning, NLP, IR, and knowledge management. Text Mining involves the preprocessing of document collections, information extraction, the storage of the intermediate representations, and techniques to analyze these intermediate representations. Link Analysis is the graphic portrayal

P. Perner (Ed.): ICDM 2007, LNAI 4597, pp. 283–295, 2007.
© Springer-Verlag Berlin Heidelberg 2007

of extracted/derived data, in a manner designed to facilitate the understanding of large amounts of data and particularly to allow analysts to develop possible relationships between entities that otherwise would remain hidden by the mass of data obtained. The purpose of this research is to create a visual environment in which the end user is able to query and explore a temporal relational database. This research brings into focus methods and visual facilities that aid the user to extract relations according to their temporal behavior and to explore the evolution of the relations over time. The major assumption is that the analysis of static networks does not yield satisfactory information. If the time dimension is taken into consideration much more interesting conclusions can be inferred. Tracking relations over time may assist the user to identify special temporal patterns, to classify similar patterns, and to predict the future behavior of a relation. The system developed during this research is called pureVision in line with its designated purpose: to bring into focus uncharted trails hidden by the mass of data.

## 2  Related Work

Only a few research studies have dealt with the development of visual queries for relational data. Most visual query languages primarily deal with the query construction aspects and devote less attention to the results exploration aspects. Moreover, most of them do not support time-oriented properties. Visual query languages are used in various fields and aim to replace the traditional IR systems. These IR systems are designated for the retrieval of individual words or phrases ignoring the possible relationships between pieces of information within the text. Visual queries, however, are designated to identify complex patterns in raw digital information.

Multimedia is a good example where the standard methods of data retrieval are not sufficient. Digitized representation of images and video is usually heterogeneous and their content has semantic meaning, and hence a query based on simple comparisons of text/numerical values is not satisfactory. The user should be able to define complex structures of media components and their semantic relations. Several studies [1], [2], [3] proposed visual query interfaces for multimedia database management systems.

Other visual queries languages [4] take into consideration the structure of documents and enable more precise queries. These languages are not designated to mine the raw text as our language is, but rather only to extend the standard IR system by providing the option to look for textual items regarding structures unique to those items.

Our research deals with part of a group of visual query languages that are designated for knowledge discovery in relational database. Some of these studies treat static relational data [5] while others [6, 7, 8], like this work, try to expand the idea and develop methods to manage temporal relational databases. [6] introduced a Visual Language for Querying Spatial-Temporal Databases. [7] introduced Intelligent Visualization and Exploration of Time-Oriented Clinical Data. [8] addresses the issue of visual query formulation for temporal databases. This research introduces a number of visual constructs that allow the user to build queries in a modular fashion; however it presents only theoretical issues and less effort has been devoted to the construction of a real system. Moreover tools for further data exploration are not used.

## 3  pureVision Architecture

The pureVision architecture enables incremental exploration for temporal relational data. Figure 1 illustrates the flow among the different stages of exploration in pureVision. pureVision analizes temporal relational data as received from the text mining process and stored in a temporal relational DB. The system is divided into two main parts. The first part is dedicated to query management and the second to visual exploration. The analysis process may commence in two different ways. The user may use the visual query editor to construct his/her query or alternatively explore the output of previous queries. When the user has completed the query construction, the visual query engine translates the visual query into textual query. TLAL -Textual Link Analysis Language [9] is used as the textual query language. The textual query is used to search for graph matching in the DB. However, since TLAL does not support temporal patterns, the temporal extension is implemented. This module receives TLAL output and filters TLAL graph matchings according to the temporal constraints specified in the visual query. The exploration engine receives these graph matchings and displays them as networks of entities and relationships. The exploration engine provides visual tools that assist users to carry out advanced exploration and to elicit knowledge hidden inside those networks. All of the components mentioned here will be described in detail in the next chapters.

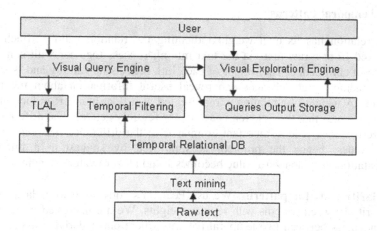

**Fig. 1.** Architecture of the pureVision system

## 4  Visual Query Engine

The visual query engine enables a visual construction of temporal queries. This kind of query enables users who are not highly skilled to define complex queries. The language is capable of representing any type of graph structure, representing many kinds of temporal and non temporal constraints; additionally the language supports the definition of temporal patterns which aim to confine suspicious behavior of relations over time

## 4.1 Visual Query Components

The visual query engine includes several visual components which replace the components in the textual query. Figure 2 displays each of the visual components in the engine. The working window is specifically designed for the construction of visual queries; it functions as a space in which the user can drag visual elements and create the query graph. Ontologies define the hierarchical structure for a group of elements and they aid the user to navigate the query elements. The user can drag each element from a hierarchical structure directly into a working window and thus construct a query graph. The properties window enables the user to define constraints for relations and entities in the query graph. In a temporal database, each property is associated with a temporal field which represents the lifespan of the property. Therefore a temporal field is assigned to each property in the properties window. The temporal designer enables the construction of visual skits that represent a temporal pattern. Through the visual designer, the user may define time intervals in which a relation was active (the strength of a relation is positive) or passive (the strength of a relation is 0). Different rates of similarity can be applied to the temporal patterns constraint. The similarity rate determines the minimal correlation required between the skits and the temporal evolution of a relation as extracted from the database.

## 4.2 Temporal Patterns

Each relation has its own weight indicating the relation validity. Each relation is extracted from a raw text via the text mining process together with some statistical degree of confidence. The weight of each link reflects its validity and is stored in the DB. Tracing weight changes can reveal useful information about the nature of a relation. A weight of a relation is represented as a float number; in fact any non-zero value indicates that this relation is active (or feasibly active). The difference between non-zero values is less important compared to the difference between zero and non zero values; hence the problem is simplified by suggesting a binary weights presentation. Any non-zero value becomes 1 and all zero values remain the same.

**Similarity tests for patterns.** We use Pearson's correlation formula to measure the similarity between patterns with regular weights. We are interested in detecting linear dependencies between two temporal patterns where our underlying assumption is that the distribution of temporal patterns is normal (a temporal relation between entities mostly occurs in a specific period on a time scale where it tends to be rarer in times far from that period). Pearson's correlation formula is appropriate for this purpose. If the aim is to compare binary patterns, the number of occurrences when the two compared relations were active or passive at the same time can simply be counted, and the sum is divided by the total number of time points in the intersections of both patterns. High correlation between two patterns means that patterns are more likely to be similar.

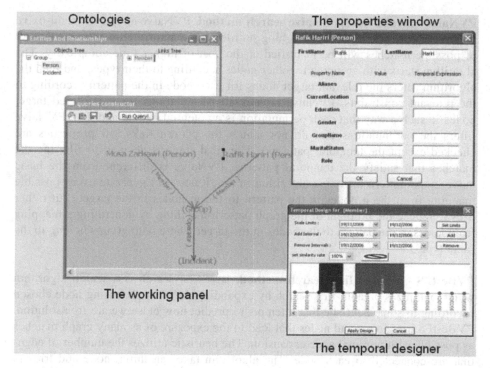

**Fig. 2.** The visual query components

# 5   TLAL API and TLAL Temporal Extension

## 5.1   TLAL API

The visual query engine presented in this thesis is built on the top of TLAL, an external library used in this system. The visual query is translated into TLAL scripts before any manipulation of the database can take effect. TLAL is designated to identify matches between patterns (such as the query graphs created by the visual query engine) and networks stored in a relational DB. TLAL is used rather than SQL because it is more suitable for handling textual data and for defining complex patterns (that are based on constrained networks)

## 5.2   Temporal extension for TLAL

The main and critical disadvantage of TLAL is its inability to manage temporal patterns. An extension for TLAL was therefore developed in order to cope with the deficiency. The aim of the temporal extension is to filter TLAL output according to the temporal patterns defined in the query. The process executed by the temporal extension is similar to the process TLAL carries out in order to find graphs in relational database. The target of this extension is to filter graphs that do not match the corresponding temporal patterns. Two methods are introduced here, developed for efficient graph pattern-matching.

**PVNaive- pureVision semi naïve search method.** PVNaive adopts the semi-naïve method for the graph pattern-matching problem. The algorithm guarantees that all of possible matches will be identified at the cost of higher time complexity. The algorithm starts with grouping together nodes according to their types, and then the algorithm filters the relevant target nodes for each node in the pattern according to the relevant constraints. PVNaive creates all permutations for the filtered target nodes in such a way that each permutation is a potential match, and then PVNaive filters the permutations that do not match the pattern links (all properties are checked except the temporal patterns). The final stage is devoted to filtering the matches that satisfy the temporal patterns. PVNaive is different from the basic naive graph pattern-matching algorithm in that it does not generate every possible mapping from the n nodes in the pattern to the m nodes in the target, but rather tries to reduce the problem of the graph pattern-matching by generating a mapping from nodes in the pattern to the nodes in the target where both groups belong to the same type

**PVBestFS - a based first search method.** Best-first search is a search algorithm which optimizes breadth-first search by expanding the most promising node chosen according to some heuristic that attempts to predict how close we are to a solution. PVBestFS tries to expand nodes that lead to the exposure of as many graph matches as possible with minimal node expansion. The heuristic utilizes the number of edges that are connected to each node. The algorithm takes an initial node and tries to expand it in order to find complete graph matches. In order to choose the initial node the algorithm generates a mapping from nodes in the pattern to the nodes in the target where both groups belong to the same type and target nodes satisfy the pattern constraints. The most promising target group is chosen (according to the heuristic function). The algorithm ignores the direction of the links since the graph matching problem with undirected graphs is simpler. PVBestFS expands each of the nodes in the chosen group as explained in the following pseudo code. The algorithm works in an iterative way in order to identify complete matches for the structure of the pattern.

The pseudo code for the based first search method

```
PVBestFS (v)
1. Q <- insert (v, score=0, ancestors=nil)
2. While Q! = Ø do:
   a. Target Nodes <- pick the best group (Q)
   b. if Target Nodes cannot be expanded using the
   pattern do
      i. add ancestors to final solution
   c. Get links and descendant nodes (Target Nodes)
   d. create all permutations of Links and Descendants
   Nodes against the pattern
   e. for every permutation do:
      i. for all unexplored pNode and pLink in
```

```
permutation do:
     1. If pNode or pLink do not match the pattern
     invalidate the permutation
     ii. Score <- calculate (permutation). Assign the
     successor nodes a score using the evaluation
     function
     iii. If permutation matches the pattern: add to
     solution
     iv. Q <- insert (Descendants Nodes, score,
     ancestors)
  f. POP (Q)
```

# 6  Visual Exploration System

The visual exploration engine enables the user to explore the results of the visual query. The visual exploration engine receives textual input that represents temporal networks; it provides visual tools that assist users to carry out advanced exploration and to elicit knowledge hidden inside those networks. There are two main exploration modes that can be adapted. The first mode deals with static graphs that exist at a given point in time. The second mode takes the temporal aspects of the networks into consideration, and gives a deeper insight into the evolution of temporal networks over time.

## 6.1  Temporal Networks Formalization

The formalization introduced here is inspired by the TEER data model [8]. A temporal network can be represented by a temporal graph G (E, L), where E is a set of entities and L is a set of temporal links between the entities.

Let T be an accountably infinite set of totally ordered discrete points in time. A time interval [ts, te] is defined to be a set of consecutive points in time; that is, the totally ordered set:

$$\{ts, ts+1...te\} \subset T \tag{1}$$

A temporal element, denoted as TE, is a finite union of time intervals, denoted by {I1...In}, where Ii is an interval in T.

A link type L of degree 2 has two participating entity types, E1, E2. Each link instance l in L is a 2-tuple $l = <e1, e2>$ where each ei $\in$ Ei . Each link instance l is associated with a temporal element TE(l) which gives the lifespan of the link instance. TE(l) must be a subset of the intersection of the temporal elements of the entities e1, e2 that participate in l. Formally,

$$TE(l) \subseteq (TE (e1) \cap TE (e2)) \tag{2}$$

This is because, for the link instance to exist at some point t, all the entities participating in that link instance must also exist at t.

## 6.2  Temporal Networks Display and Exploration

The main exploration frame can display networks in two ways: a sliced network of relations defined in a specific time point and a complete network that includes the union of relations in each time point. Formally A link   l = <e1, e2 > exists at a time point t iff t ∈ TE (l). In complete networks only one representative relation is drawn for each pair of entities. The user can navigate between temporal slices using the visual interface. A temporal network may be displayed in two modes: the normal mode and the 'difference' mode. Relations displayed in normal mode are colored by their type, and the color in that mode is not affected by the state of a relation in previous or following points in time. The 'difference' mode, however, aims at highlighting the changes of relations activities in different time slices. Relations that do not appear in the preceding display are painted in a different manner.

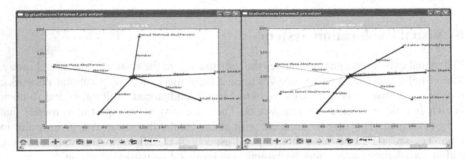

**Fig. 3.** Navigation in temporal network

During the exploration process the user may notice a suspicious entity or relation and may be interested in investigating it. Clicking on any element in a network exhibits a list of properties with their values. Additionally, several optional operations are introduced to the user. The user may investigate an entity in two ways: find the shortest path from the source entity to another target entity specified by the user, and find all paths according to a specified depth. Shorter paths between entities may reveal the significant semantic relations between them. The user may investigate the evolution of a relation over time. A special sub-frame is dedicated to the display of the degree of confidence for each time point when the relation was observed. The exploration of the relation's evolution may expose suspicious patterns. Circular patterns, for example, can highlight the periods when the relation is active and aid the user to predict when the relation is going to be active in the future.

The quality of temporal networks is determined in particular by their reliability. Relations characterized by a lesser degree of confidence are not as interesting as relations with a higher degree of confidence. There are two ways in which the user can easily spot the difference in relations reliability. First, temporal networks are visualized in such a way that more reliable relations are distinguished by broader links. Second, the relations can be ranked by their reliability and shown in a different frame as a ranked list.

The size of explored networks tends to be correlated with the size of the relational database and with the generality of the queries. Special features are introduced in order to manage large networks. The user may focus on a sub-network of special interest by zooming into it or alternatively zooming out to see a more general view of relationships. The pan feature enables the user to move networks from their original position to another position where they do not fit the size of the panel in which they are displayed. Every manipulation carried out on the visual networks is saved, and hence the user can retrieve previous states of the network display.

**Multiple working frames.** A working frame is supposed to handle a temporal network as returned from a single query. However, it is frequently necessary to compare the output of different queries. Here are introduced the intersection and union methods for temporal networks. Let us define source graphs G1, G2 and result graph Gres as a pair (E, L) where E is a set of entities, and L is a set of temporal links between those entities. Gres is the intersection of G1 and G2 if it satisfies the following conditions:

$$\text{Link } l = <e1, e2> \in L \longleftrightarrow l1 = <e1, e2> \text{ and } l2 = <e1, e2> \text{ and } TE\,(l1) \cap TE$$
$$(l2) \neq \varnothing \text{ and Type}\,(l1) = \text{Type}(l2) \; \forall \, l1 \in L1 \; \forall \, l2 \in L2 \tag{3}$$

$$\text{Entity } e \in E \longleftrightarrow <e, x> \in L \text{ or } <x,e> \in L \; \forall \, x \in E. \tag{4}$$

The union graph Guni can be defined as a pair (E,L) where

$$L = L1 \; U \; L2 \text{ and } E = E1 \; U \; E2 \tag{5}$$

$$l1 = <e1, e2> \text{ and } l2 = <e1, e2> \text{ and Type}\,(l1) = \text{Type}\,(l2) \rightarrow TE\,(l) = TE\,(l1)$$
$$U \; TE\,(l2) \; \forall \, l1 \in L1 \; \forall \, l2 \in L2 \tag{6}$$

The user can carry out these operations by dragging one working frame on another and choose the appropriate operation.

## 6.3  Temporal Clustering

In general, a cluster is defined as a set of similar objects. This "similarity" in a given set may vary according to data. We focus here on the temporal clustering problem, our purpose being to group together relations with similar temporal behavior. The identification of relations with a high similarity rate can bring into focus hidden connections between entities that are not explicitly connected within the network structure. The distance between two relations is determined by the correlation function mentioned above. There is an opposite ratio between the distance function and the correlation function, since highly correlated relations should belong to the same cluster.

DBSCAN - density based spatial clustering of applications with noise [10] is used as the clustering algorithm. DBSCAN relies on a density-based notion of clusters which is designed to discover clusters of arbitrary shape. DBSCAN performs good efficiency on large databases. DBSCAN requires only two input parameters, density reachability and density connectivity. These concepts depend on two parameters: eps - the epsilon (radius) neighborhood of a point, and minp - the minimum number of points in the epsilon neighborhood. Density reachability is defined as follows. A point p is density reachable from point q if the two following conditions are satisfied: first the points are close enough to each other - distance(p; q) < eps and second there are enough points in q neighborhood. Density connectivity is defined as follows. A point p is density-connected to a point q if there is a point o such that both, p and q, are density reachable from o.

Clusters are not displayed on a static panel. Like the networks display, the clusters display can be manipulated in order enable the user to explore the clusters. The user can click on any relation and explore its evolution over time; this facility directs the user towards comparing the evolution of different relations from the same cluster as well as from different clusters.

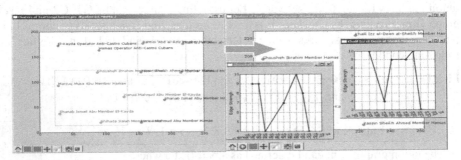

**Fig. 4.** Illustration of zooming into a cluster and the exploration of the clusters relations

### 6.4 The Graph Drawing Problem

There are many ways to visualize the structure of networks. The optimal visualization is the clearest to the user. The graph drawing problem is simpler in our domain because we treat here drawings in which edges are drawn as straight lines and the purpose is to determine the position of the vertices. The implementation of Kamada and Kawai [11] is used in order to solve the graph drawing problem. Kamada and Kawai's is a simple but successful algorithm for drawing undirected weighted graphs. The basic idea of Kamada and Kawai is as follows. The desirable "geometric" (Euclidian) distance between two vertices in the drawing graph is the "graph theoretic" distance between them in the corresponding graph. The algorithm introduces a virtual dynamic system in which every two vertices are connected by a "spring" of such a desirable length. Then the optimal layout of vertices is regarded as the state in which the total spring energy of the system is minimal.

## 7  Evaluation

We are interested in examining the performance of PVNaive and PVBestFS on different kind of inputs. We are primarily interested in examining how these algorithms compare on complex query graphs, and how they compare on different kinds of networks that are processed by them. We designed two experiments to test each of these goals. For the first experiment several queries were constructed which varied in their graph complexity where query1 is the simplest and query5 is the most complex. The more edges in the query graph, the more complex it is considered to be.

pureVision receives temporal networks that are returned by TLAL and uses PVBestFS and PVNaive in order to filter those networks according to the temporal constraints specified in the query. However, we want to isolate the impact of the query graph complexity so that the variable size of the networks will not impact the results. Therefore we used the same simulated output for all queries scripts (instead of the output of TLAL) and no constraints were set in the queries because constraints may prune the search space of the algorithms and we want to isolate the impact of query graph complexity.

Figure 5 shows that PVBestFS achieved better results for all observations. The gap between the results is more remarkable for more complex patterns. There is a correlation between the patterns complexity and the ratio between the time performance of PVBestFS and PVNaive. PVBestFS can cope with complex graphs structures more efficiently, and this advantage is important when the user is interested in constructing complex queries and the networks returned from TLAL are too large to be managed by the naïve method.

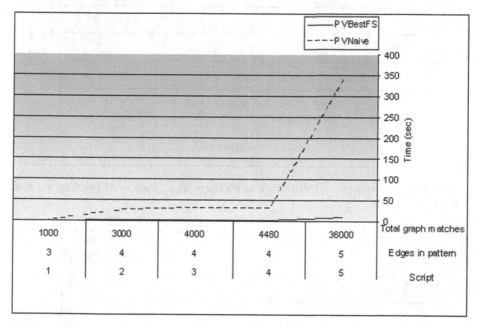

**Fig. 5.** The Time complexity of PVBestFS and PVNaive as a function of query graph complexity

For the second experiment two sets of networks were constructed. The first set of networks is designated to test the impact of temporal links on performance. In this set all of the networks have the same nodes, and the networks are varied in the number of temporal links between each two nodes (each link represents different time). The same query graph is used in all the tests since we want to isolate the impact of temporal factor of the tested networks.

Figure 6 shows that the time complexity is almost linear for both of the algorithms and the form of the graphs is almost identical. The meaning of this finding is that temporal links have no significant impact on the difference between the performances of PVBestFS and PVNaive.

The second set of networks is designated to test the impact of network density on performance. Network density measures the ratio between quantity of links in a given network and a full network (as received from the given network).

It can be seen in Figure 7 that network density has a great impact on the difference between the performances of the algorithms. PVBestFS achieved much better results when tested on low density networks where the results of PVNaive showed minor changes.

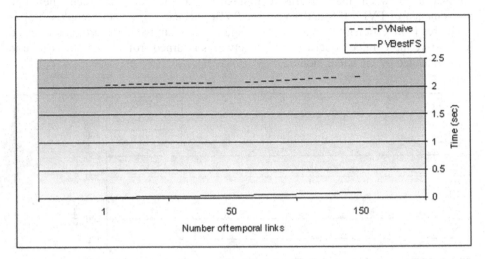

**Fig. 6.** Time performance of PVBestFS and PVNaive as a function of the temporal links number

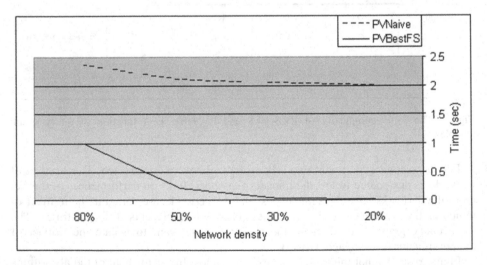

**Fig. 7.** Time performance of PVBestFS and PVNaive as a function of network density

The second experiment shows that PVBestFS can handle networks with medium or lower density much more efficiently than can PVNaive. In practice these kinds of networks are much more frequent and thus this finding is notable; however PVBestFS had no remarkable advantage over PVNaive when the temporal factor was tested. Only the non temporal structure of networks (where temporal links are not taken into consideration and each pair of nodes can be connected by a single link or not) results in an increasing gap between the performances.

# 8 Discussion

In this research study the issue of visual query language and advanced exploration systems for temporal relational data is addressed. One complete system was developed that enables the user to construct complex queries and to identify suspicious patterns in temporal relational data in an incremental fashion. Using pureVision, even naïve users are able to discover suspicious patterns in a significant pool of data. This research is part of the link analysis field and it aims at developing disciplines to explore relational data that are returned from the text mining process. The research was focused on the temporal aspects of relations. pureVision makes it possible to search for relations according to certain temporal patterns defined by the user, to investigate the evolution of relations over the time, to identify suspicious behavior of relations, to cluster relations with similar behavior, and to approximate the behavior of relations in the future. Advanced graph matching algorithm was developed to improve the time performance for complex queries and for medium and low density networks. These algorithms are designated to make pureVision more interactive system.

# References

1. Yoshitaka, A., Ichikawa, T.: A Survey on Content-Based Retrieval for Multimedia Databases. IEEE knowledge and data eng., pp. 81–93. IEEE Computer Society Press, Los Alamitos (1999)
2. El-Medani, G.: A Visual Query Facility for Multimedia Databases, University of Alberta, Technical Report, pp. 18–95 (1995)
3. Oria, V., Xu, B., Cheng, L.I., Iglinski, P.J.: VisualMOQL: the DISIMA Visual Query Language, Multimedia Computing and Systems, pp. 536–542 (1995)
4. Baeza-Yates, R., Navarro, G., Vegas, G., De La Fuente, P.: A model and visual query language for structured text, String Processing and Information Retrieval, pp. 7–13 (1998)
5. Blau, H., Immerman, N., Jensen, D.: A visual query language for relational knowledge discovery, University of Massachusetts Amherst, Technical Report, pp. 1–28 (2001)
6. Bonhomme, C., Trepied, C., Aude-Aufaure, M., Laurini, R.: A Visual Language for Querying Spatio-Temporal databases, pp. 34–39. ACM Press, New York (1999)
7. Shahar, Y., Cheng, C.: Intelligent Visualization and Exploration of Time-Oriented Clinical Data. The 32nd Annual Hawaii International Conference, pp. 15–31 (1999)
8. Kouramajian, V., Gertz, M.: A visual query language for temporal databases, Hannover, pp. 388–399 (1995)
9. Feldman, R., Ozz, R.: Link Analysis in Networks of Entities, Technical Report, Bar-Ilan University (2007)
10. Ester, M., Kriegel, H.-P., Sander, J., Xu, X.: A Density-Based Algorithm for Discovering Clusters in Large Spatial Databases with Noise, KDD'96, pp. 226–231 (1996)
11. Kamada, T., Kawai, S.: An algorithm for drawing general undirected graphs, pp. 7–15. Elsevier, Amsterdam (1989)

# Towards an Online Image-Based Tree Taxonomy

Paul M. de Zeeuw, Elena Ranguelova, and Eric J. Pauwels

CWI, Kruislaan 413, 1098 SJ Amsterdam, The Netherlands
paul.de.zeeuw,elena.ranguelova,eric.pauwels@cwi.nl

**Abstract.** This paper reports on a first implementation of a webservice that supports image-based queries within the domain of tree taxonomy. As such, it serves as an example relevant to many other possible applications within the field of biodiversity and photo-identification. Without any human intervention matching results are produced through a chain of computer vision and image processing techniques, including segmentation and automatic shape matching. A selection of shape features is described and the architecture of the webservice is explained. Classification techniques are presented and preliminary results shown with respect to the success rate. Necessary future enhancements are discussed. Benefits are highlighted that could result from redesigning image-based expert systems as web services, open to the public at large.

## 1 Introduction

The pervasiveness of broadband Internet and mobile telephony has created an unprecedented connectivity between people and computational devices such as computers, mobile phones, digital camera's and GPS units. As a consequence, a growing number of initiatives is harnessing this infrastructure to set up new communities and exploit novel opportunities for large-scale interaction and participation. As Internet access thresholds continue to fall, the public at large is slowly being transformed from passive content consumers into active and avid content producers. Indeed, the likes of Wikipedia, Flickr, and YouTube have demonstrated beyond any doubt the viability of *"crowd sourcing"* development projects (a.k.a *Peer Productions*, e.g. Yahoo Answers) in which a comprehensive, high quality product emerges as the result of modest contributions from literally thousands or even millions of participants. This goes to show that there is a tremendous amount of talent and resources "out there" of people who both have the means and the aspiration to contribute to online communities that have captured their interest.

In this paper we report on our ongoing efforts to set up a (to the best of our knowledge, first!) *web-based tree taxonomy searchable by image query*. More specifically, we have created a webservice[1] that aspires to assist users in identifying trees by uploading a photograph of one of their leaves. This photograph is then processed by the web server and matched against a database of exemplars

---

[1] http://biogrid.project.cwi.nl/projects/leaves_v2/

P. Perner (Ed.): ICDM 2007, LNAI 4597, pp. 296–306, 2007.
© Springer-Verlag Berlin Heidelberg 2007

of known species. As a result, a web page is created showing the, say, ten most similar exemplars along with species information, inviting the user to make the final choice and provide feedback. If the user considers the determination to be successful, the image is retained as a new exemplar for future queries. If the user deems the identification to be unsuccessful, the image is forwarded to an expert-biologist for a second opinion.

We envisage that in the near future it will become possible to point the camera in your mobile phone at a plant or tree, take a snapshot of one of the leaves and send it as an MMS message to a designated phone number, such as 1-800-whichtree, say. Half a minute later you receive an sms serving up both the Latin and common name for the tree, as well as the link to the Wikipedia page where more information can be found. Moreover, it is our explicit intention to open this webservice up to the public at large so that *in addition to querying* everyone can *contribute*o to the exemplar database by uploading information and images of tree species.

## 1.1 Previous and Related Work

Although there are a number of online tree taxonomies available, the proposed web service is, in our opinion, innovative to the extent that it supports image-based queries and therefore contributes to the small but growing collection of applications that try to extend Internet search beyond the classic keyword paradigm. The best-known web-applications that support similar input modalities are focusing primarily on face recognition, such as FaceIt, myheritage.com or Riya.

It is clearly apparent that, given the pervasiveness of digital cameras, biologists are waking up to the possibilities of computer-assisted photo-identification, and a number of stand-alone systems are under development (cf. [1,3,6,7]). However, to the best of our knowledge the proposed website is the first to offer a vision-based taxonomy system as a web service.

## 2   Architecture of the Webservice

Broadly speaking the webservice is designed as a 2-tier system: The front-end allows the user to upload query images which are then shipped to the back-end server for processing and matching. The results are included in a webpage which is then transferred to the front-end for display and feedback. The system therefore comprises the following main components:

- **Database of exemplars on back-end.** Predictably, one starts by creating a database of *exemplars* that encapsulate the domain knowledge — for the taxonomy application we will often refer to them as *exemplars*. This database contains, for each of the target tree species, information such as the common name (e.g. *white oak*), the genus and species as specified in the Linnaeus binomial nomenclature (e.g. *Quercus alba*), a link to Wikipedia (if available), as well as one or more relevant photographs. Associated with

**Fig. 1.** Webpage generated by the taxonomy webservice in response to a submitted query image (top left). The result of the automatic segmentation is shown top right. The most similar images in the cases-database are displayed on the second row, together with relevant metadata such as genus and species. The displayed shortlist of most similar leaves offers the user the possibility to pick – as a final selection – the leaf that best matches his query image.

each photograph is a set of automatically computed numerical features that characterize the shape of the corresponding leaf (for more details on these features, see section 3).

- **Front-end.** The front-end is a straightforward webpage that allows the user to upload an image of the query leaf. To improve performance we request users to adhere to certain standards (e.g. the leaf should be photographed against high contrast background) which greatly increase the reliability of the automatic image segmentation.
- **Processing on back-end.** Uploading a query image triggers a sequence of algorithms that *(i)* segment the leaf from the background and extract the result as a binary mask, and *(ii)* computes ten numerical shape features (for more details, see Section 3). The results are then checked against the pre-computed exemplar features and the most similar ones are shortlisted.

- **Feedback** . Once the similarity-based shortlist is available, a response web-page is compiled displaying images of the $n$ best matches (where $n$ typically ranges between 3 and 10). Each image has a caption detailing the genus, species and common name of the corresponding tree. Showing a ranked short-list of images (see Fig. 1) allows the user to perform a final visual check and discard any obvious mismatches.

## 3   Features for Shape Matching to Exemplars

### 3.1   Image Segmentation: Segregating Foreground from Background

Prior to computing the features detailed below, both exemplar and query im-ages are first segmented into actual leaf (foreground) and a background. In what follows, we will use the term *mask* to refer to the resulting binary image that specifies the foreground pixels. Note that we can think of leaves as flat objects (something everyone who assembled a herbarium book can relate to) which sim-plifies the analysis of the image considerably as we can restrict our attention to measures for 2D shapes.

Automatic leaf segmentation proceeds through a number of steps. First, the colour image is converted to gray scale in several different manners (using the RGB and the HSV values). Then, each gray-level representation is segmented using a gray-level histogram to which a mixture of Gaussian density is fitted. The local minimum of the density is then used as a data-driven threshold for segmentation. In this manner, several initial segmentations are obtained. For each binary segmentation the number of 1 - connected components is computed and the best initial segmentaiton is chosen as the one with minimum number.

The next step of the algorithm uses the initial segmentation to guide a *water-shed transformation* on the best gray-level representation of the original image. The watershed transformation is a powerful and well-established mathematical morphology tool for image segmentation which has been used in many appli-cations [5]. Any grey-level image can be considered as a topographical surface. Flooding this surface from its minimum while preventing the merging of water coming from difference sources, will result in a partitioning of the image into catchment basins associated with each minimum. The boundaries between the catchment basins are the watershed lines. If we apply this transformation to the gradient of an image, we should obtain catchment basins corresponding to ho-mogeneous grey-level regions. It is well-known however, that the transform tends to produce an over-segmentation due to the local variations in the gradient. A *marker-controlled transformation* is a solution to this problem: The gradient im-age is modified via morphological reconstruction [5] in order to keep only the most significant gradient edges in the areas of interest between the markers. The biggest connected component from the chosen initial segmentation is used as the *foreground marker* and the image boundaries as the *background marker*. As a result of this step one gets the leaf boundaries.

The last step is the stem detection and removal. The stem is considered as a significant deviation from the main leaf shape. All such deviations are detected using the *top-hat transform* [5] of the binary segmentation. The detected deviations are the "teeth" of the leaf margin and the stem. The stem is singled out by imposing the additional restriction for large eccentricity and major axis. After the stem removal, the remainder is used as the binary leaf shape mask.

## 3.2    Shape Matching

Shape – even planar shape – is notoriously tricky to characterize accurately in a short sequence of numerical features. In order to cope with the considerable variations encountered in the dataset, we have implemented a number of features, each tailored to capture specific shape aspects. The idea is that combining them will produce a more discerning similarity measure. Below we briefly discuss the selection of features that are currently being used. It is likely that this set will be expanded in future versions of the search engine. All of them are computed on the binary image (a.k.a. mask) that results from the segmentation. This means that all internal structure, such as colour, texture and (most importantly) vein-structure has been discarded. This is an obvious weakness in the current system that we intend to remedy in a subsequent version. We also assume that the stem has been pruned so that only the intrinsic leaf shape remains. For ease of future reference we denote by $L$ the resulting 2-dimensional shape, and by $\partial L$ its contour.

*Solidity (Sol).* To measure the extent to which a leaf is lobed, we compute its *solidity* which is defined by comparing the area of the leaf to the area of its convex hull $(CH(L))$ to obtain a number between 0 and 1:

$$\text{Sol} = \frac{\text{area}(L)}{\text{area}(CH(L))}.$$

*Isoperimetric factor (IF).* This is another measure that roughly captures how winding (oscillatory) the contour is. If the perimeter is defined as $\ell = \text{length}(\partial L)$ and $A = \text{area}(L)$ then $IF$ is defined as

$$IF = \frac{4\pi A}{\ell^2} \leq 1.$$

Equality prevails if and only if the contour is a circle.

*Eccentricity (X).* The third straightforward measure we employ is the eccentricity of ellipse with identical second moment as the leaf shape $L$.

*Moment Invariants for Shape Characterization.* The next set of measures are less straightforward. Hu's invariants [2], based on centralized moments, serve as a classic tool for recognizing geometrical shapes. An image is regarded as a density distribution function $f$. A central moment $\mu_{pq}(f)$ of $f$ is given by

$$\mu_{pq}(f) = \iint_{\mathbb{R}^2} (x - x_c)^p (y - y_c)^q f(x, y) \, dx \, dy, \tag{1}$$

where $p$ and $q$ are non-negative integers and $(x_c, y_c)$ is the center of mass. Such a central moment is said to be of $(p+q)$th order. In our case a binary foreground mask plays the role of the image which $f$ which equals 1 inside the leaf region and 0 outside of it. By their definition it is immediate that central moments are translation invariant. Hu constructed polynomials with variables $\mu_{pq}$ in such a way that the outcome is invariant under rotations and reflections (the latter apart from sign). Two polynomials are built with second-order moments, four polynomials with third-order moments and one combines second-order and third-order moments.

$$I_1 = \mu_{20} + \mu_{02}, \tag{2}$$

$$I_2 = (\mu_{20} - \mu_{02})^2 + 4\mu_{11}^2, \tag{3}$$

$$I_3 = (\mu_{30} - 3\mu_{12})^2 + (3\mu_{21} - \mu_{03})^2, \tag{4}$$

$$I_4 = (\mu_{30} + \mu_{12})^2 + (\mu_{21} + \mu_{03})^2, \tag{5}$$

$$I_5 = (\mu_{30} - 3\mu_{12})(\mu_{30} + \mu_{12})((\mu_{30} + \mu_{12})^2 - 3(\mu_{21} + \mu_{03})^2) +$$
$$(3\mu_{21} - \mu_{03})(\mu_{21} + \mu_{03})(3(\mu_{30} + \mu_{12})^2 - (\mu_{21} + \mu_{03})^2), \tag{6}$$

$$I_6 = (\mu_{20} - \mu_{02})((\mu_{30} + \mu_{12})^2 - (\mu_{21} + \mu_{03})^2) +$$
$$4\mu_{11}(\mu_{30} + \mu_{12})(\mu_{21} + \mu_{03}), \tag{7}$$

$$I_7 = (3\mu_{21} - \mu_{03})(\mu_{30} + \mu_{12})((\mu_{30} + \mu_{12})^2 - 3(\mu_{21} + \mu_{03})^2) -$$
$$(\mu_{30} - 3\mu_{12})(\mu_{21} + \mu_{03})(3(\mu_{30} + \mu_{12})^2 - (\mu_{21} + \mu_{03})^2). \tag{8}$$

We elaborate briefly on the numerical computation of the moments. Using the values of the image pixels we construct an interpolating function based on piecewise constant approximation. The piecewise constant basisfunctions have their support on squares centering around the pixels. Furthermore, the rectangular domain of an image is scaled in the sense that the size of the short side is equal to 1. As the supports of the basisfunctions are square, the size of the longer side of the domain follows at once. Hereby we can now perform the integration in (1) numerically.

So far, the expressions defined by (2)–(8) using (1) are invariant under translation, rotation and reflection (provided we ignore the sign of $I_7$). For shape invariance we still need to enforce similitude invariance, that is, after a mere change in dimensions of an object (leaf) it is identified as the same. Such invariance can be obtained by normalizing the moments $\mu_{pq}$. Dilations (changes in size) by a scalar $\alpha > 0$ of the whole image or of objects in an image against a neutral background result in new central moments given by [2]

$$\mu'_{pq} = \alpha^{p+q+2}\mu_{pq}. \tag{9}$$

It follows in particular that $\mu'_{00} = \alpha^2\mu_{00}$, and also $\mu'_{20} + \mu'_{02} = \alpha^4(\mu_{20} + \mu_{02})$. Combining this result with Eq. (9) yields

$$\frac{\mu'_{pq}}{(\mu'_{00})^{(p+q+2)/2}} \frac{\mu_{pq}}{\mu_{00}^{(p+q+2)/2}}, \qquad \frac{\mu'_{pq}}{(\mu'_{20} + \mu'_{02})^{(p+q+2)/4}} \frac{\mu_{pq}}{(\mu_{20} + \mu_{02})^{(p+q+2)/4}}$$

respectively. As we recall that both $\mu_{00}$ and $\mu_{20} + \mu_{02}$ are invariants with respect to rotation and reflection this demonstrates how to normalize the moments to achieve invariance under dilation. The first choice leads to the following new set of invariant generators [4]

$$I_1' = I_1/\mu_{00}^2, \ I_2' = I_2/\mu_{00}^4, \ I_3' = I_3/\mu_{00}^5, \ I_4' = I_4/\mu_{00}^5,$$
$$I_5' = I_5/\mu_{00}^{10}, \ I_6' = I_6/\mu_{00}^{10}, \ I_7' = I_7/\mu_{00}^7. \tag{10}$$

The second choice leads to a different but similar result. It may be more suitable (as a starting point) in case the density distribution corresponds to wavelet detail coefficients, see [4].

Finally, it is clear that the *shape* of the foreground in the binary image $f$ should be invariant under a change in luminosity; in mathematical parlance: $f \longmapsto \lambda f$ where $\lambda > 0$. As a scalar multiplication of the distribution function $f$ does not affect the center of mass, it follows from (1) that

$$\mu_{pq}(\lambda f) = \lambda \mu_{pq}(f), \text{ for all } \lambda \neq 0. \tag{11}$$

One observes that the feature vector $I'$ defined element by element through (10)

$$(I_1', \ I_2', \ I_3', \ I_4', \ I_5', \ I_6', \ I_7')$$

then changes into

$$(\lambda^{-1}I_1', \ \lambda^{-2}I_2', \ \lambda^{-3}I_3', \ \lambda^{-3}I_4', \ \lambda^{-6}I_5', \ \lambda^{-4}I_6', \ \lambda^{-6}I_7')$$

which is an undesirable result. (The result when moments would not be normalized would be equally undesirable.) To overcome this inhomogeneous change in the feature vector we use the following operator

$$R_p(u) = \text{sign}(u)|u|^{1/p}, \text{ with } p \in \mathbb{N} \text{ and } u \in \mathbb{R}. \tag{12}$$

When applied to an invariant $I_k$ it produces again an invariant. It is a "legal" operation that invariants can be subjected to, i.e., neither their invariance properties nor their discriminative power are lost. We define the homogenized feature vector as

$$\tilde{I}' = (I_1', \ R_2(I_2'), \ R_3(I_3'), \ R_3(I_4'), \ R_6(I_5'), \ R_4(I_6'), \ R_6(I_7')). \tag{13}$$

This feature vector $\tilde{I}'$ now satisfies the *homogeneity condition* [4,8] in that a rescaling of the luminosity now affects all components in a homogeneous fashion:

$$f \longmapsto \lambda f \quad \Longrightarrow \quad \tilde{I}' \longmapsto \lambda^{-1} \tilde{I}'. \tag{14}$$

In addition, it turns out that hereby all elements operate in the same order of magnitude and that Mahalanobis's method is superfluous.

# 4  Results and Discussion

## 4.1  Populating the Exemplar Database Through Webharvesting

For the above outlined system to be successful, it needs to have access to a sufficiently large and comprehensive database of exemplars (cases). In order to create
this with minimal effort we have taken recourse to webharvesting. More precisely,
using Wikipedia we have first compiled a long list of the (Latin) Linnaeus classification (i.e. *genus* and *species*) of the tree species we are interested in. This
list is fed into a programme that submits each combination into Google's *Image
Search* and collects all the images that are returned. Relatively straightforward
image processing software then winnows down this collection by rejecting all pictures that lack a convincing oval-shaped foreground. In most cases this prunes
the collection down to a few percent of the original "harvest". The final selection is done by a human supervisor who reject everything except images where
the well-defined foreground corresponds to a leaf. These images then go in the
exemplar database and the Linnaeus classification (i.e. the *genus* and *species*
that were used as search terms) are inserted as metadata. Once these images
have been added to the exemplar database, the residing feature agents jump
into action and compute the necessary features so that these new exemplars can
be compared to any incoming image queries.

As mentioned earlier we have realised a first implementation of the above
outlined webservice. To date we have compiled a small database of exemplars
which comprises 23 unique genus-species combinations harvested from the web.
For each of these genus-species combinations we have on average 5 to 10 exemplar
images, adding up to 146 images in total. All the images have been segmented
and the above-mentioned 10 shape parameters have been computed (i.e. solidity,
isoperimetric factor, eccentricity and 7 moment invariants). We have then tested
the two classification tools which we describe next.

## 4.2  Classification Trees

Classification trees seemed a first obvious choice for the classification of leaves (no
pun intended!). The full 10-dimensional feature vector of section (3.2) was used
to predict class-membership (running from 1 through 23 as there are 23 unique
genus-species combinations). However, when we tested performance using cross-
validation, the prediction success turned out to be disappointingly low 42%. For
that reason we switched to a nearest neighbour classifier described in the next
section.

## 4.3  Nearest Neighbour Classification

Since the 10-dimensional feature-vector is an amalgamation of qualitatively different characteristics (dimension-wise $10 = 1+1+1+7$), we decided that it was
best to first compute distances in each space separately, and then produce a
resulting distance by computing an (empirically optimized) linear combination

of these partial results. We settled for the straightforward (1-dimensional) Euclidean distance for the solidity, eccentricity and isoperimetric features (denoted by $d_{Sol}, d_X$ and $d_{IF}$ respectively). Further, because of (14) we opted for the (normalized) cosine distance in the 7-dimensional space of homogenized moment invariants:

$$d_{HM}(\overrightarrow{x}, \overrightarrow{y}) = \frac{2}{\pi} \arccos \left( \frac{| < \overrightarrow{x}, \overrightarrow{y} > |}{\|\overrightarrow{x}\|.\|\overrightarrow{y}\|} \right).$$

All distances are within the $0-1$ range, simplifying comparison and combination.

We proceed by making the assumption that the comprehensive distance is a straightforward linear combination of the above:

$$d_{LC} = d_{HM} + \alpha d_{Sol} + \beta d_X + \gamma d_{IF}.$$

The values for the weight parameters are determined by systematically searching for the combination that produces the best results on the exemplar database, i.e. each exemplar is used as a test-image and assigned to the same class as its nearest neighbour (in the $d_{LC}$-metric). The discriminative power of $d_{HM}$ turns out to be predominant but even though $\alpha, \beta, \gamma \ll 1$ the other distances cannot be dispensed with.

We have estimated the classification accuracy by simulating the results that would be displayed on the webpage. More precisely, for each exemplar we have computed the 10 nearest $d_{LC}$-neighbours as these would be displayed on the webpage if the selected exemplar was submitted as a query. The results are shown in Fig. 2. If we insist that classification is only successful if the most

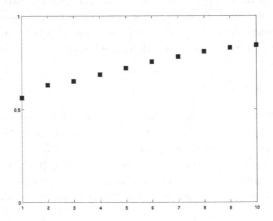

**Fig. 2.** Query success rate in terms of the number ($k$) of retrieved nearest neighbours. If we allow the user to inspect the ten most similar images, then the success rate is slightly higher than 85%. See main text for more details.

similar has the correct genus and species, then the success rate is about 53%. However, this is unduly pessimistic as not one but ten nearest neighbours are shown on the webpage, and the user is invited to manually pick the best match. This means that the query will be successful if the correct genus and species are found among the 10 nearest neighbours (i.e. $k = 10$ in Fig. 2). It turns out that for this less stringent success-criterion, the success rate is approximately 85%. The complete distance matrix is shown in Fig. 3.

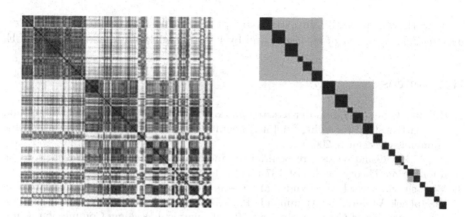

**Fig. 3.** *Left:* Schematic representation of the $(146 \times 146)$ $d_{LC}$-distance matrix for the database of exemplars. Bright points represent large distances while dark shades indicate similarity. *Right:* The corresponding class delineation: black blocks corresponds to leaves that have identical genus and species, while gray shades indicate identical genus but different species within that genus. Ideally, the $d_{LC}$ matrix on the left should look very similar to the classification groundtruth depicted on the right.

## 5   Conclusions and Future Directions

In this paper we have reported on a first implementation of a webservice that supports image-based queries within the domain of tree taxonomy. We have argued that thanks to computer vision and image processing it is now feasible to gain good segmentation and recognition results with little or no input from a human supervisor. This opens the door to efficient searches through large databases of photographic material and therefore allows us to tackle classification problems for which the domain knowledge is primarily encoded in visual form. These developments are effectively extending the scope of image-based search task where traditionally, most efforts have been focused on face recognition. Clearly, photo-identification of plant and animal species (individual animals even) opens up a vast and exciting new application domain, the relevance of which is beyond dispute given the current concerns about the conservation and biodiversity.

The preliminary results that are obtained seem acceptable but clearly leave considerable scope for improvement. Apart from employing a much larger dataset, we see at least two directions that remain to be explored. First, we could add more sophisticated shapes measure to fine-tune the global distance $d_{LC}$. It is obvious from Fig. 3 that the current version of that distance is far from optimal. Secondly, and more importantly, classification of leaves also depends on their vein-structure, something which we completely neglected. These issues will be addressed in a forthcoming follow-up paper.

## Acknowledgments

This work was partially supported by project NWO 613.002.056 *Computer-assisted identification of cetaceans* and by FP6 Network of Excellence MUSCLE.

## References

1. Hillman, G., et al.: Computer-assisted photo-identification of flukes using blotch and scar patters. In: Proceedings of 15th Biennial Conference on the Biology of Marine Mammals (December 2003)
2. Hu, M.K.: Visual pattern recognition by moment invariants. IRE Transactions on Information Theory IT-8, 179–187 (1962)
3. Mizroch, S., Beard, J., Lynde, M.: Computer Assisted Photo- Identification of Humpback Whales. In: Hammond, P., Mizroch, S., Donovan, G. (eds.) Individual Recognition of Cetaceans, pp. 63–70. International Whaling Commission, Cambridge (1990)
4. Oonincx, P.J., de Zeeuw, P.M.: Adaptive lifting for shape-based image retrieval. Pattern Recognition 36, 2663–2672 (2003)
5. Soille, P.: Morphological Image Analysis. Springer, Heidelberg (2003)
6. Ranguelova, E., Pauwels, E.J.: Saliency Detection and Matching Strategy for Photo-Identification of Humpback Whales. In: GVIP05. International Conference on Graphics, Vision and Image Processing, Cairo, Egypt, pp. 81–88 (December 2005)
7. Van Tienhoven, A., den Hartog, J., Reijns, R., Peddemors, V.: A computer-aided program for pattern-matching of natural marks on the spotted raggedtooth shark carcharias taurus. Journal of Applied Ecology 44(2), 273–280 (2007)
8. de Zeeuw, P.M.: A toolbox for the lifting scheme on quincunx grids (lisq). CWI Report PNA-R0224, Centrum voor Wiskunde en Informatica, Amsterdam (2002)

# Distributed Generative Data Mining

Ruy Ramos and Rui Camacho

LIACC, Rua de Ceuta 118 - 6° 4050-190 Porto, Portugal
FEUP, Rua Dr Roberto Frias, 4200-465 Porto, Portugal

**Abstract.** A process of Knowledge Discovery in Databases (KDD) involving large amounts of data requires a considerable amount of computational power. The process may be done on a dedicated and expensive machinery or, for some tasks, one can use distributed computing techniques on a network of affordable machines. In either approach it is usual the user to specify the *workflow* of the sub-tasks composing the whole KDD process before execution starts.

In this paper we propose a technique that we call *Distributed Generative Data Mining*. The *generative* feature of the technique is due to its capability of generating new sub-tasks of the Data Mining analysis process at execution time. The *workflow* of sub-tasks of the DM is, therefore, dynamic.

To deploy the proposed technique we extended the Distributed Data Mining system HARVARD and adapted an Inductive Logic Programming system (IndLog) used in a Relational Data Ming task.

As a proof-of-concept, the extended system was used to analyse an artificial dataset of a credit scoring problem with eighty million records.

**Keywords:** Data Mining, Parallel and Distributed Computing, Inductive Logic Programming.

# 1 Introduction

As a result of more complex and efficient data acquisition tools and processes there is, in almost all, organisations huge amounts of data stored. Large amounts of money are invested in designing efficient data warehouses to store the collected data. This is happening not only in Science but mainly in industry. Analysis of such amounts of data has to be done using (semi-)automatic data analysis tolls. Existing OLAP techniques are adequate for relatively simple analysis but completely inadequate for in-depth analysis of data. The discipline of Knowledge Discovery is Databases (KDD) is a valuable set of techniques to extract valuable information from large amounts of data (data ware houses). However, KDD [1] is facing nowadays two major problems. The amounts of data are so large that it is impractical or too costly to download the data into a single machine to analyse it. Also, due to the amounts of data or to its distributed nature in large corporations, it is the case that the data is spread across several physically

P. Perner (Ed.): ICDM 2007, LNAI 4597, pp. 307–317, 2007.
© Springer-Verlag Berlin Heidelberg 2007

separated databases. These two problems prompted for a new area of research called Distributed and Parallel Data Mining[2]. This new area addresses the problem of analysing distributed databases and/or making the analysis in a distributed computing setting.

There are parallel versions of Decision Trees algorithms [3], parallel Association Rules Algorithms [4] and parallel Inductive Logic Programming (ILP) |algorithms [5,6] that may be used in the (Relational) Data Mining step of KDD. To handle the large amounts of data these algorithms these use a data partition approach and distribute the analysis work over a cluster of machines. One weakness of these systems is that if one of the machines fails the whole process has to be restarted, which is a serious drawback for long task's execution time. The implementation of such parallel DM algorithms are not designed with fault-tolerant features.

In this paper we propose a solution to make parallel DM algorithms such as Decision Trees, Association Rules or Inductive Logic Programming to be fault-tolerant and able to run on conventional PCs without disturbing the normal workings of an organisation. For that purpose we have extended the HARVARD [7] system to accommodate such desirable features for the parallel DM algorithms. The HARVARD system (**HARV**esting **A**rchitecture of idle machines fo**R D**ata mining) has been developed as a computational distributed system capable of extracting knowledge from (very) large amounts of data using techniques of Data Mining (DM) namely Machine Learning (ML) algorithms. We take advantage of its following features. In a Condor [20] fashion, the system only assigns tasks to idle resources in the organisation. The system may access data distributed among several physically separated databases. The system is *independent* of the data analysis (ML) tool. It has very good facilities to recover from both slave and master nodes failure.

To integrate a parallel algorithm such as parallel Decision Trees, parallel Association Rules or parallel ILP we included in the HARVARD system the possibility of creating new tasks at run time at the HARVARD's task description level. This is the new *generative* feature of the distributed computing characteristic of HARVARD. The parallel DM algorithm on the other hand has to be adapted to be able to suggest new tasks in the HARVARD task description language. We present in this paper an example for the Inductive Logic Programming IndLog [9].

With this proposal we may include fault-tolerant features in some of the most popular distributed DM algorithms.

The rest of the paper is organised as follows. In the Section 2 we present the HARVARD system. In Section 3 we present basic notions of Inductive Logic Programming enough for the reader to understand the coupling of the analysis tool with the HARVARD system. We explain the generative technique for Data Mining in Section 4. The deployment of the HARVARD system extension is described in Section 5. Section 6 compares other projects with features close to HARVARD capabilities. We conclude in Section 7.

## 2   The HARVARD System

### 2.1   The Architecture

The KDD process is composed of a set of tasks that are executed according to a workflow plan. Both the tasks description and the workflow plan are provided by the user in two files. One file contains the tasks description and the second one contains the workflow. The workflow is specified using a control description language. Each task specification is made using XML. The information concerning each individual task include the name and location of the tool used in the task, the location of the data being processed in the task and the computational resources required (platform type, memory and disc requirements).

The distributed architecture of the HARVARD system is composed of a Master node and a set of computing nodes called Client (or Slave) nodes. The Master node is responsible for the control and scheduling the sub-tasks of the whole KDD process. Each Slave node executes application (sub-)tasks assigned by the Master node. Each node is composed by four modules that execute specific tasks to make the overall system working.

In what follows we refer to Figure 1 for the modular structure of both the Master and the Slave nodes. We now describe in detail the each node type.

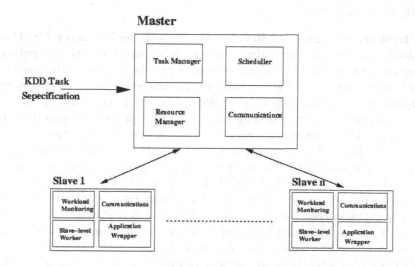

**Fig. 1.** The Harvard basic system architecture

**The Master Node.** The Master node is responsible for reading the KDD process specification and executing it. Each task is of the KDD process is handle by the system as a **Working Unit (WU)**. Each WU will be assigned to a one or more machines. The assignment of a WU to more than one machine makes the the system more tolerant to faults. It occurs when there are idle machines available and the task is expected to have long running times. There are other fault tolerant features that we will refer bellow. When a WU finishes the results is associated with that WU and the status of the workflow graph updated. When the graph is completely traversed, meaning that the KDD process has finished, the result is returned to the user.

The Master node is composed by four modules: the Task manager; the Scheduler; the Resource Manager and; the Communications module.

**The Task Manager Module.** The basic function of the **Task Manager** (TM) module is to store and maintain and provide information concerning the tasks of the KDD process. The TM module constructs a graph structure representing the workflow of tasks.

It first reads and stores the specifications of all tasks composing the KDD process and then reads the workflow plan of the tasks and constructs a workflow graph structure. This module updates the status of the tasks in the graph and associates the results of each one when finished. At the end informs the user of the results of the KDD process. It may also be used to monitor the whole KDD process providing the user with information about the task finished, running and waiting computational resources to run.

The TM interacts with the Scheduler module. Looking at the workflow graph this module informs the Scheduler of ready to process tasks, provides a complete specification of each task and receives information concerning the terminations and results of each task.

**The Resources Manager Module.** The **Resources Manager (RM)** module stores and periodically updates information concerning the computational resources usable by the HARVARD system. When the system starts this module loads from a database the static information concerning all the computational resources usable by the system. That information is dynamically updated during the system execution. The information of each resource includes the type of platform and CPU, the amount of memory and disc space and a time-table with the periods the machine may be used. The workload of each machine is communicated periodically to this module to update so the system has a updated view of the resources. The RM module has a method (a match maker) to compute the "best" computational resource for a given request from the Scheduler. Each computation resources has a time-table of availability of the resource and the policy of use. This information state when the machine is available and in what conditions. The usage conditions may indicate that the system may use the machine only when there are no users logged in or by specifying a workload threshold that must be respected at all times.

The Task Manager module receives, from the Scheduler, requests for available machines satisfying a set of resources requirements and returns a best match at the moment. This module alerts the Scheduler that a task must be reassigned in two situations: if a machine is severely delayed to notify the TM module of its workload and; if the pre-established period of use of the machine is expired[1]. The TM module receives periodically the workload of all running machines.

---

[1] In this case the task running on the machine is terminated.

**The Communications Module.** The **Communications (COM)** module is the only channel to access the world outside a node. All messages or requests concerning components or resources outside the node are processed by the COM module. This module exists in both Master and Slave nodes. To accomplish that task it implements several communication protocols that includes: RMI, socket, HTTP and JDBC. All these allows a client to download the task required software (HTTP), download the data (JDBC), send messages to the Master (sockets or RMI) and allows the Master to send messages to the Slaves (socket or RMI). It also allows the Master to keep a DB backup of its status and activities (JDBC) to allow a full recover in case of fault.

This Master COM module interacts via RMI or sockets with the COM module of the Slave to send messages. In a Master node the messages to be sent are received from the Scheduler module or the Resources Manager module. The former sends messages concerning task assignments and control directives whereas the later sends tasks status updated to be stored in a DB (fault tolerant purposes). The COM module receives and redirects the workload messages for the RM module. Received messages concerning tasks results are redirected to the Scheduler module.

**The Scheduler Module.** The **Scheduler** module controls the execution of the tasks composing the KDD process, launching, rescheduling or stopping the Work Units. The scheduler may also decide to assign a WU[2] to more than one Slave node. The scheduler inspects the workflow graph where the tasks interconnections and status are represented to decide what tasks to activate and when.

The Scheduler asks the Resource Manager module for the best match machine satisfying a given Work Unit requirements. With the results of such request the Scheduler assigns that WU to the given Slave and notifies the Slave via the Communications module. Whenever there is a change in the status of a WU the Scheduler is informed by the Task Manager of that event and triggers the (re)scheduling a new task.

**A Slave Node.** A Slave node does the actual data analysis work by running the Data Ming tool. In order to have a distributed system that is independent of the Data Mining tool the DM tool is involved in a wrapper that directly controls the DM tool. Each Slave also reports periodically its workload to the Resource Manager module of the Master. It is through the Slave's Communications module that the Slave downloads the DM tool and the data to be processed, and stores the results of the local analysis.

Each Slave has four modules: the Workload Monitoring (WM); the Worker (SW); the Application Wrapper (AW) and; the Communications (COM) module.

**The Worker Module.** The WU message is interpreted in this module. A WU usually results in several steps to be performed. A typical WU for analysing

---
[2] The ones considered more critical for some reason like training longer execution times.

data involves the downloading of the analysis tool, the download of the data, the processing and the return of the results. The Worker module controls all these steps by asking the Communications module to access the software and data and triggering the Application Wrapper module to execute the analysis. Finally it sends (via Communications module) the results to the Master.

The Worker nodes interacts with the Communication modules by sending it request to download the software and data and to return the final result. It also asks the Application Wrapper to start the analysis task and collects the results from it.

**The Application Wrapper Module.** The AW module completely controls the DM tool. It supplies the DM tool input stream and collects whatever appears at the DM output stream. Through the input stream the module provides the commands for the DM tool. The commands are provided in a file specified in the Working Unit specification. The output stream is stored in a file as the results file. The results file is uploaded to a database entry as specified in the WU specification. For the time being all the analysis of the results files are done in other follow up WU where special scripts written by the user do the necessary analysis. This permits the system to be independent of the DM tool.

**The Workload Monitoring Module.** This module monitors periodically the workload of the machine it is running and reports that information to the Resources Manager module of the Master. It also detects in a user has login into the machine. In that later case the Master is informed that the task running will be terminated. The Slaves enters a idle state where it just waits for the machine to be idle again.

**Communications Module.** The slave Communicating module is the only channel to the outside world. It has capabilities to download software using HTTP or ftp protocol, it may download data from a DB using JDBC and it can send and receive messages to and from the Master using RMI or sockets.

The Communications module interacts with all modules of the Slave node delivering and receiving messages.

## 2.2   Sub-tasks Workflow Description Language

The HARVARD system accepts as input a file describing the workflow of the sub-tasks composing the KDD process. The workflow is a graph with two kinds of nodes: sequential nodes and; parallel nodes. Each node stores a set of tasks to be executed or edges to other nodes. In a sequential node the set has an order and that order represents the sequential execution of the sub-tasks that must be respected. In a parallel node the tasks in the set may start all at the same time. In a parallel node there may be a *barrier* specifying the tasks that must terminate before the "execution" of the node is considered terminated. The graph has a root node where the tasks of the KDD process start executing.

Some of the steps in a KDD process are done quite frequent and most often are the same for a vast number of domains. For example feature subset selection or the DM tool parameter tuning are quite frequent pre-processing tasks in the KDD process. For these frequent tasks the task description language provides a set of macros for these complex operations. For example: to do a top-down feature selection up to two attributes or tune the "p" parameter using the values p1, p2 and p3. The system will then "unfold" those macros into the corresponding graph structure.

## 3    ILP in a *Tiny Nutshell*

Inductive Logic Programming (ILP)[10,11] is a discipline in the intersection of Machine Learning and Logic Programming. ILP studies techniques to (automatically) induce models for data. In ILP both the given data and the induced models are represented using First Order Logic. The data provided to an ILP system are of two kinds: i) examples and; ii) background knowledge. Examples are instances of the concept whose definition the system will induce. The background knowledge is any information the user thinks is relevant to construct the model. In the most popular ILP systems the induction process is mapped into a search on the space of all possible hypotheses (the hypothesis space). The system then uses any if well-know search algorithms to search the hypothesis space and return *the best* hypothesis according some specified criterion.

Some advantages of using ILP in DM tasks are the following. It has a very powerful description language to encode the constructed models. The user may give the system easily any information he considers relevant to produce the model. The background knowledge may include not only relation's definitions but also numerical computations like regression models, geometric or statistical models etc. that are nicely combined in the final model. Most often ILP induced models are comprehensible to the user.

A major shortcoming of ILP systems is its efficiency. One possible approach the overcome ILP's lack of efficiency is through the use of parallelism.

As described in [6] there are several approaches to parallelise an ILP system. One of the most simple but providing good results (see [5] for a comparison of several methods) consists in establishing a partition of the data and apply an ILP system to each subset of the data. The models induced by each ILP system on each subset are sent to a master node that combines the models. If the assembled model "explains" all the examples then the process stops and the model is the final model. Otherwise there are a next round of the same procedure where the examples not "explained" are subject a learning process equal to the first step. We have implemented in IndLog this approach to parallel ILP. It is a similar approach to the one described in [2] where classifiers are constructed for each set of the data partition and then sent to a central node where they are combined. In the ILP case this process is repeated until all examples are "explained".

# 4    Distributed Generative Data Mining

The main cycle of a DM algorithm, such as Decision Trees, Association Rules or ILP is run a number of times that depend, among other things, on the input data. The number of nodes in a Decision Tree is not fixed before the algorithm hat constructs the tree is run. The number of clauses in that and ILP algorithm induces is also not fixed before the algorithm processes the data. When developing parallel versions of these algorithm the number of tasks on each run will depend on the dataset being processed. On the other hand in a KDD process the number of tasks and their workflow is established by the user, using a tool like YALE[12] for example, and stays unchanged during the execution of the KDD process. To be able to integrate a parallel version of a DM algorithm in a automatic KDD setting one as to allow the tool to have a dynamic workflow of the tasks. For example new tasks are generated whenever a parallel Decision Tree constructed splits a new node. To accommodate such situation we extended the HARVARD system to be able to dynamically accept new tasks during run time. New tasks are encoded as new nodes in the graph that represents the task's workflow.

In the data parallel version of IndLog a master node decides the split of the examples and assigns each slave node a subset. Instead of assigning directly the "sub-tasks" to the slaves via MPI interface, the IndLog translates the sub-tasks requests to a format that the Master node (Task Manager module) of the HARVARD understands. The HARVARD scheduler then assigns each task to existing idle machines. If there are too many idle machines then the same task my be run (redundantly) in more than one machine. In case of failure of one of the machine the analysis completes without delay.

The main advantages of the generative technique proposed in this paper is to increase the fault-tolerance of the analysis tool and to take full advantages of the HARVARD system. Using the HARVARD system the analysis does not disturb the normal workings of the organisation, does not require dedicated machines and has tolerance to failure of both the Master node and any of the Slave nodes.

# 5    Deployment of the HARVARD System

Just to test the feasibility of our approach and not to compare the systems performance on a specific problem we produced a large artificial data set with realistic information. The data set is on the domain of credit scoring. We characterised each instance with 55 attributes that correspond to the 55 fields of an actual form used by a real bank. The information used to generate the records was based on census information publicly available at the Brazilian national statistics office. We used a bank expert to provide the rules that assign the class value to the generated registers. The data set has 80 million registers. The data was stored in three MySQL databases in different machines. We used a laboratory with 15 PCs where Master students have classes and use for developing their practical works. The machines have dual boot so sometimes they start with Linux and sometimes with Windows. It takes several hours to analyse the data set on the reported computational environment using the HARVARD system with IndLog.

To analyse the data using IndLog [13,9] we had to provide scripts for the Application Wrapper of the Client node (see Figure 1) to control the IndLog system. The IndLog system was run in a data parallel fashion allowing a maximum of 50000 examples at each node.

To evaluate the fault-tolerant features we deliberately generated failures in some machines during the analysis process and under two circumstances. First we disconnect a machine running a task that was also assigned to other machine and notice no increase in the analysis time. Secondly we disconnected a machine were a task was running that was not assigned to any other machine. With a small overhead that task was reassigned to another machine an the analysis continued then normally.

# 6   Related Work

Our system is designed to take advantage of idle computers in an organisation and adequate for problems that may be decomposed into coarse grain sub-tasks. We present some related projects that can reach this objective but of differentiated form our architecture.

The Globus Alliance [14] is an international collaboration that does research in grid computing that seeks to enable "the construction of computational grids providing pervasive, dependable, and consistent access to high-performance computational resources, despite geographical distribution of both resources and users". One of the results of this research is "The Globus Toolkit"that is a "bag of services"like: resource allocation manager that provides creation, monitoring and management services; security infrastructure; monitoring and discovery services. For each of their services there is a programming interface in programming language C.These core services are used by other organisations and Globus to make high level components and systems [15,14,16].

The Boinc (Berkeley Open Infrastructure for Network Computing)[3] is a platform that makes it easy for scientists to create and operate public-resource computing projects. Workstations connected to the Internet by phone or DSL line can be participate some project and share its own power computer to solve scientific problem when device is idle. The process is very sample, people interested to participate just installing a software client that connect a project master server. So, when workstation is idle some tasks may be executing. Some projects like SETI@home, Folding@home using the Boinc platform [17].

The Knowledge Grid is a specialised architecture in data mining tools that uses basic global services from Globus architecture [18]. The architecture design for Knowledge Grid following some principles: data heterogeneity and large data sets handling; algorithm integration and independence; compatibility with grid infrastructure and grid awareness; openness, scalability, security and data privacy [19].

Condor operates in workstation environment. The system aims to maximise the utilisation of workstation with as little interference as possible between

---

[3] **University of California - Berkeley-** http://boinc.berkeley.edu/

the jobs is schedules and the activities of the people who own workstations.
"Condor is specialised job and resource management system for compute intensive jobs. Like other full-featured systems, Condor provides a job management
mechanism, scheduling policy, priority scheme, resource monitoring and resource
management. Users submit theirs jobs to Condor when and where to run the
based upon policy, monitors their progress, and ultimately informs the user upon
completion"[20]. Condor allows almost any application that can run without user
interaction to be managed. This is different from systems like Set@home and Protein Folding@home. These programs are custom written. Source code does not
have to be modified in anyway to take advantage of these benefits. Code that
can be re-linked with the Condor libraries gain two further abilities: the jobs can
produce check-points and they can perform remote system calls [20].

Like the project Boinc, our architecture intends to use of idle workstations
and also the system considers the heterogeneous environment with different operational systems (Linux, Windows, OS-X) but instead of it has a light client
installed in each workstation it uses the Java Virtual Machine. A new approach
will be present that to use old applications for data mining without re-build or
re-compile with a new libraries like Condor or another approaches.

Besides, our proposal implements two-level language. A specific semantics for
the administration of the data mining process, and other for specification of
tasks of distributed processing. While a language is destined to the user for the
definition of the process of the knowledge discovery, the other language is used
by the system to manage the distributed processing.

# 7    Conclusions

We have made a proposal to run parallel Data Mining algorithms, such as parallel
decision Trees, parallel Association Rules and parallel Inductive Logic Programming systems in a fault-tolerant setting. To achieve the desired fault-tolerant features we have extended the HARVARD system and have adapted the IndLog ILP
system. The HARVARD system was extended with the possibility of including at
run-time new tasks to schedule. In the ILP system a new module was encoded to
communicate with the HARVARD Master node to suggest new tasks in the format
of the task description language the the HARVARD system recognises.

The extended HARVARD system and the Inductive Logic Programming system IndLog were used to analyse an eighty million credit scoring dataset. The
fault-tolerant features proved useful when simulating several failures on the machines during the analysis process.

# References

1. Han, J., Kamber, M.: Data Mining: Concepts and Techniques. Morgan-Kaufmann
   Publishers, San Francisco (2001)
2. Kargupta, H., Chan, P.: Advances in Distributed and Parallel Knowledge Discovery. AAAI/MIT Press, Cambridge (2000)

3. Amado, N., Gama, J., Silva, F.M.A.: Parallel Implementation of Decision Tree Learning Algorithms. In: Brazdil, P.B., Jorge, A.M. (eds.) EPIA 2001. LNCS (LNAI), vol. 2258, pp. 6–13. Springer, Heidelberg (2001)
4. Agrawal, R., Shafer, J.C.: Parallel mining of association rules. IEEE Trans. On Knowledge And Data Engineering 8, 962–969 (1996)
5. Fonseca, N.A., Silva, F., Camacho, R.: Strategies to Parallelize ILP Systems. In: Kramer, S., Pfahringer, B. (eds.) ILP 2005. LNCS (LNAI), vol. 3625, Springer, Heidelberg (2005)
6. Fonseca, N.A.: Parallelism in Inductive Logic Programming Systems. University of Porto, Porto (2006)
7. Ramos, R., Camacho, R., Souto, P.: A commodity platform for Distributed Data Mining – the HARVARD System. In: Perner, P. (ed.) ICDM 2006. Springer, Heidelberg (2006)
8. Litzkow, M.J., Livny, M., Mutka, M.W.: Condor–A Hunter of Idle Workstations. In: Proceedings of the 8th International Conference on Distributed Computing Systems, San Jose, California, pp. 104–111 (1988)
9. Camacho, R.: IndLog - Induction in Logic. In: Alferes, J.J., Leite, J.A. (eds.) JELIA 2004. LNCS (LNAI), vol. 3229, pp. 718–721. Springer, Heidelberg (2004)
10. Muggleton, S.: Inductive Logic Programming. New Generation Computing 8, 295–318 (1991)
11. Muggleton, S., De Raedt, L.: Inductive Logic Programming: Theory and Methods. Journal of Logic Programming 19/20, 629–679 (1994)
12. Mierswa, I., Wurst, M., Klinkenberg, R., Scholz, M., Euler, T.: YALE: rapid prototyping for complex data mining tasks. In: KDD '06: Proceedings of the 12th ACM SIGKDD International Conference on Knowledge Discovery and Data Mining, pp. 935–940 (2006)
13. Camacho, R.: Inducing Models of Human Control Skills using Machine Learning Algorithms. PhD thesis, Faculty of Engineering, University of Porto, Porto - Portugal (2000)
14. Foster, I., Kesselman, C.: The Grid: Blueprint for a New Computing Infrastructure, pp. 259–278. Morgan-Kaufmann Publishers, San Francisco (1999)
15. Foster, I., Kesselman, C.: Globus: A Metacomputing Infrastructure Toolkit. International Journal of Supercomputer Applications 11(2), 115–128 (1997)
16. Foster, I.T., Kesselman, C., Tuecke, S.: The Anatomy of the Grid - Enabling Scalable Virtual Organizations. CoRR, vol. cs.AR/0103025 (2001)
17. Anderson, D.P.: BOINC: A System for Public-Resource Computing and Storage. In: David, P. (ed.) Proceedings on Fifth IEEE/ACM International Workshop on Grid Computing, pp. 4–10 (2004)
18. Foster, I., Kesselman, C.: The Grid: Blueprint for a New Computing Infrastructure, pp. 259–278. Morgan-Kaufmann Publishers, San Francisco (1999)
19. Cannataro, M., Talia, D.: The Knowledge Grid. Communications of the ACM 46(1), 89–93 (2003)
20. Litzkow, M.J., Livny, M., Mutka, M.W.: Condor–A Hunter of Idle Workstations. In: Proceedings of the 8th International Conference on Distributed Computing Systems, San Jose, California, pp. 104–111 (1988)

# Privacy-Preserving Discovery of Frequent Patterns in Time Series

Josenildo Costa da Silva and Matthias Klusch

German Research Center for Artificial Intelligence
Deduction and Multiagent Systems
Stuhlsatzenhausweg 3, 66123 Saarbruecken, Germany
{jcsilva,klusch}dfki.de

**Abstract.** We present DPD-HE, a privacy preserving algorithm for mining time series data. We assume data is split among several sites. The problem is to find all frequent subsequences of time series without revealing local data to any site. Our solution exploit density estimate and secure multiparty computation techniques to provide privacy to a given extent.

## 1 Introduction

Frequent patterns discovery is an important step in many data mining algorithms, such as classification and clustering. Informally, a time series pattern is a subsequence that presents a given property and that occurs at different locations in the time series. In this paper we address the problem of finding *frequent, unknown* patterns given time series data split among different sites.

An important aspect we consider in this work is privacy of ownership and local data values. We assume that the sites are not willing to disclose exact values of original time series. Moreover, sites do not want other sites tracking any information to a specific site.

To solve this problem we introduce a density-based algorithm, which identify the most frequent subsequences occurring in the data set, considering the union of the data sets. The main idea is to represent subsequences of time series as points in a multidimensional space and compute the data density in this space. Using the additive property of density estimates, we produce a global density out of local ones. The pattern discovery problem is reduced to identifying local maxima in the density space. We show that our approach does protect the privacy of: (i) exact value of time series data; and (ii) identity of sites owning the data.

In the following we discuss related work (section 2) and show how we approach this problem (section 3). After that we present results and discussion of our experiments (section 4). Finally, we conclude and discuss future work (section 5).

## 2 Related Work

Pattern discovery problem has been extensively studied in bio-informatics, where the goal is to find frequent patterns in sequences of symbols, e.g. microarray data

P. Perner (Ed.): ICDM 2007, LNAI 4597, pp. 318–328, 2007.
© Springer-Verlag Berlin Heidelberg 2007

analysis [1]. Recently this problem was extended to handle real-valued data [2]. More formally the problem is to identify the k-most frequent pattern occurring in the time series. Many approaches to PDTS problem have been proposed. Mörchen and Ultsch [3], for example, proposes using a grammar-based approach and Kadous [4] suggests clustering subsequences of the original time series to find prototypical shapes. These approaches, however, have some disadvantages. The grammar-based approach is too dependent on the knowledge of the possible patterns to be discovered and the clustering-based approach has been shown to be very problematic [5]. Liu et al. [6] proposed effective heuristics to solve PDTS problem defining patterns size $m$ as multidimensional points in $\mathbb{R}^m$. Our work extends the original setting by adding distribution and privacy issues.

A related problem is sequence mining [7,8] where the time points are not equally spaced. The goal is to find temporal rules like "if event A happens then event B will happen after $t$ units of time with $c\%$ confidence". In our work we focus on equally spaced time points.

Works on privacy preserving data mining follow three main approaches. *Sanitation*, aims to modify the dataset such that sensitive patterns cannot be inferred. It was developed primarily to association rule mining (cf. [9,10]). The second approach is *data distortion*, in which the true value of any individual record is modified while keeping "global" properties of the data (cf. [11,12] among others). Finally, *SMC-based* approaches apply techniques from secure multi-party computation (SMC), which offers an assortment of basic tools for allowing multiple parties to jointly compute a function on their inputs while learning nothing except the result of the function (cf. [13,14]). In a SMC problem we are given a distributed network with each party holding secret inputs. The objective is to compute a function with the secret inputs ensuring that no party learns anything but the output. The general SMC problem was investigated by Goldreich et. al [15]. Latter, Lindell and Pinkas showed that privacy-preserving data mining problems could be solved using techniques of SMC [16]. Many applications of SMC to data mining have been proposed so far (cf. [17], [18], to name a few).

## 3 Density-Based Pattern Discovery in Time Series

In this section we present our approach to pattern discovery. First we describe our solution assuming centralized dataset. After that, we extend the ideas to the distributed case.

The following notation is used throughout this paper. Let $f : \mathbb{N} \to \mathbb{R}$ be a function from time stamps to reals. We define a time series $T = \{x_t = f(t) | 1 \leq t < m\}$ as ordered sequence of real numbers $x$ coming from the measurement function $f$. The ordering is with respect to the time stamp $t$. A subsequence of $T$ is denoted $\langle x_t, \ldots, x_{t+v} \rangle$, for given integers $1 \leq t < m$ and $1 \leq v < m - t$. A frequent pattern in time series is a subsequence of the time series that reoccurs at different points of $T$.

## 3.1   Centralized Case

The pattern discovery problem we are addressing is defined as follows. Given a real-valued time series $T$, an integer $k$, to find the $k$-most frequent patterns occurring in $T$.

A brute force algorithm to solve this problem needs $O(|T|^2)$ comparisons, where $|T|$ represents the size of $T$. A more interesting approach follows a three-step scheme (cf. [19,2]):

1. Dimension reduction of the original time series $T$;
2. Discretization of the reduced time series $T$ into a sequence of symbols $S$ over a given finite alphabet $\Sigma$;
3. Pattern discovery algorithm using the symbol sequence $S$ from the previous step.

This general scheme has the advantage of handling the high dimensionality of data, do not assume any knowledge on the structure of patterns and finally, provides a clear separation on the tree different tasks at hand. Our contribution here is a new strategy to perform the last step.

*Dimension Reduction.* Given a time series $T$ and an integer $n$, reduce the dimensionality of $T$ by averaging subsequences size $n$. Actually, this operation (proposed elsewhere [20]) is known as piecewise aggregate approximation (PAA):

$$\bar{x}_j = \frac{1}{n} \sum_{t=n(j-1)+1}^{nj} x_t \tag{1}$$

*Discretization.* Given a reduced time series from the previous step, compute the string $S$ by substituting an element $\bar{x}_j$ by a correspondent symbol $\sigma$ in a given finite alphabet $\Sigma$. This is achieved by choosing break points $\{\beta_a\}$, $1 \leq a < |\Sigma| + 1$, such that each occurrence of a given value $\bar{x}_j$ has the same probability [2]. Finally, the substitution rule is applied:

$$s_j = \begin{cases} \sigma_a & \text{iff } \beta_{a-1} \leq \bar{x}_j < \beta_a, 1 \leq a \leq |\Sigma| \\ \sigma_{|\Sigma|} & \text{otherwise} \end{cases} \tag{2}$$

To make sure this equation works we additionally requires that $\beta_1 = -\infty$ and $\beta_{|\Sigma|+1} = +\infty$

*Discovery.* The final part of the algorithm consists of estimating the density of subsequences $\sigma$ of $S$ and searching for those subsequences $\sigma$ which have high density. The idea is to reduce the search for frequent subsequences to the search for dense regions in the pattern space. If we take subsequences of S of fixed size $w$, the pattern space is $\Sigma^w$.

A general approach to compute data density function is kernel-based density estimation. For a given kernel function $\mathcal{K}$ such that $\int_{\infty}^{+\infty} \mathcal{K} dx = 1$, an estimate of the true density is given by:

$$\hat{\varphi}(x) = \frac{1}{Nh} \sum_{x_i \in Neigh(x)} \mathcal{K} \left( \frac{D(x, x_i)}{h} \right) \qquad (3)$$

where $N$ is the total number of points, $D()$ is a distance function, $h$ is a bandwidth parameter and $Neigh(x)$ is the neighborhood of point $x$ (including the point $x$). We use the triangle kernel $\mathcal{K} = (1 - (\frac{x - x_i}{h})) I (\frac{x - x_i}{h} \leq 1)$, where $I$ is the indicator function. We choose this kernel for its simplicity, but any other kernel can be used instead. The radius $r$ is the bandwidth parameter. $D$ is the Euclidean distance assuming the alphabet has a total order. An arbitrary points is denoted $\sigma$. Moreover, for a given string $S$, there are $\frac{S}{w}$ subsequences to consider. Finally, the estimate of the density of subsequences is:

$$\hat{\varphi}(\sigma) = \frac{w}{|S|r} \sum_{\sigma_i \in Neigh(\sigma)} \left( 1 - \left( \frac{D(\sigma, \sigma_i)}{r} \right) \right) I \left( \frac{D(\sigma, \sigma_i)}{r} \leq 1 \right) \qquad (4)$$

Local maxima in pattern space correspond to strings that reoccur more frequently than others. The set of frequent patterns $\mathcal{P}$ is a set of reoccurring strings, each of them representing a local maxima.

$$\mathcal{P} = \{\sigma \in \Sigma^w : \forall \sigma' \in \Sigma^w \ (|\sigma - \sigma'| \leq r \rightarrow \varphi(\sigma) > \varphi(\sigma'))\} \qquad (5)$$

The parameter $r$ works as a radius assuring that the center of density region is a good descriptor of frequent subsequences inside the ball radius $r$. This constraint reduces the number of pattern taking only the most representatives ones.

To find local maxima quickly we store a representation of each point in the pattern space together with its density estimates. This structure is ordered by density. When a set of candidates is chosen we just weed out the pattern which are to similar according to the radius $r$, as already explained

The space complexity can be very high for large values of $w$. In practice, however, only a few variations of all possible patterns appear. Consequently, we can exploit this scarcity to improve the density estimate storage costs.

Now we extend the pattern discovery problem to the distributed case.

## 3.2   Distributed Case

The problem of discovering pattern in distributed time series can be described as follows. Given an integer k, and a set of sites $\mathcal{L} = \{L_i\}_{1 \leq i \leq P}$, each of them with a local time series $T_i$, the problem is to find the set $\mathcal{P}$ of the $k$-most frequent patterns occurring in $T = \bigcup_{i=1}^{P} T_i$, such that:

1. The total communication cost is minimized
2. The result using the distributed data $T_i$ is the same if the algorithm runs using $T = \bigcup_{i=1}^{P} T_i$

The key observation here is that the density estimate is additive. Therefore we can compute local density and sum them up to produce the global estimates. With the global density estimate we can perform the discovery step locally using the ideas discussed in centralized case.

We assume that the time series data collected at different sites refers to the same variable and has the same time spacing. We also assume that the sites negotiate on the parameters $k$, $n$, $w$, $\Sigma$, $r$. If the negotiation fails the protocol stops. If an agreement is found, then they can proceed.

### 3.3  Addressing Privacy

In a distributed environment, there is always the threat that an eavesdropper is listening in on the conversation among the sites. To avoid this threat we use a secure multiparty computation technique: homomorphic encryption.

Homomorphic Encryption (HE) scheme allows for parties to perform arithmetical operation directly without decryption. Here we are using Paillier scheme [21] which is an additive homomorphic. So, given two messages $m_1$ and $m_2$ the following holds: $E(m_1) \cdot E(m_2) = E(m_1 + m_2)$ . Paillier scheme consists of the following steps:

**Key Generation.** Let $N = pq$ be a RSA modulus and $g$ be an integer of order $\alpha N \mod N^2$, for some integer $\alpha$. The public key is $(N, g)$ and the private key is $\lambda(N) = lcm((p - 1), (q - 1))$.

**Encryption.** The encryption of message $m \in \mathbb{Z}_N$ is $E(m) = g^m r^N \mod N^2$, with r randomly selected from $\mathbb{Z}_N$

**Decryption.** Given a cipher text $c$ the message is computed as follows:

$$m = \frac{L(c^{\lambda(N)} \mod N^2)}{L(g^{\lambda(N)} \mod N^2)}$$

where $L(u) = \frac{u-1}{N}$.

Now, we show how we put all together in the DPD-HE algorithm.

### 3.4  DPD-HE Algorithm

DPD-HE is our algorithm based on the ideas discussed in the previous sections. Its main phases are:

*Phase 1: preparation.* The mining group $\mathcal{L}$ agrees on the parameters and each party computes the local density of the words generated from the local time series data. The initiator, which is the peer that proposes and coordinates the mining session, create a key pair and publicize its public key.

*Phase 2: computing global estimates.* Each party encrypts its local density estimate using the public key from the initiator. Then after it receives the encrypted partial sum from its neighbor, sums its local encrypted density estimate, and then sends it to the next neighbor.

*Phase 3: termination.* When all parties added its local encrypted density estimate the last party sent the encrypted sum to the initiator. The initiator decrypts it, adds its own local density estimates, and finally, searches the local maxima in the global density estimate. The result is sent back to the mining group encrypted with the public key of each party.

---

**Algorithm 1.** Initiator

---

**Input:** $k$, $T_i$, $n$, $w$, $\Sigma$, $\mathcal{L}$, $r$;
**Output:** $\mathcal{P}$;
    At the initiator do:
1: $(n, w, \Sigma) \leftarrow$ negotiateParameters($\mathcal{L}$);
2: $\mathcal{H}_1 \leftarrow$ createsHashTable($T_1, n, w, \Sigma$);
3: $LDE_1 \leftarrow \mathcal{H}_1$.density($\theta, T_1$);
4: $(PK, SK) \leftarrow$ generateKeyPairs();
5: broadcast($\mathcal{L}$, $PK$);
6: $EGDE_{|\mathcal{L}|-1} \leftarrow$ receive($L_{|\mathcal{L}|-1}$, $Encr(PK, \sum_{j=1}^{|\mathcal{L}|-1} LDE_j)$);
7: $GDE \leftarrow$ Decr($SK, EGDE_{|\mathcal{L}|-1}$) + $LDE_1$;
8: $\mathcal{P} \leftarrow GDE$.findDensityCenters($k, r$);
9: **for** $i = 1$ to $|\mathcal{L}|$ **do**
10:     broadcast($\mathcal{L}$, $Encr(PK_i, \mathcal{P})$);
11: **end for**

---

---

**Algorithm 2.** Arbitrary Party

---

**Input:** $k$, $T_i$, $n$, $w$, $\Sigma$, $\mathcal{L}$, $r$;
**Output:** $\mathcal{P}$;
    At an arbitrary party j do:
1: $(n, w, \Sigma) \leftarrow$ negotiateParameters($\mathcal{L}$);
2: $\mathcal{H}_j \leftarrow$ createsHashTable($T_j, n, w, \Sigma$);
3: $LDE_j \leftarrow \mathcal{H}_j$.density($\theta, T_j$);
4: $PK \leftarrow$ receive($L_1$);
5: $EGDE_{j-1} \leftarrow$ receive($L_{j-1}$);
6: send($L_{j+1}$, $Encr(PK, LDE_j)$ + $EGDE_{j-1}$);
7: $\mathcal{P} \leftarrow$ Decr($SK_j$, receive($L_1$));

---

DPD-HE takes $O(|T|)$ steps, where $|T|$ means the size of the original time series, mainly due the reduction and discretization steps, which requires a pass through the entire dataset. On the other hand it requires $O(|\Sigma|^w)$ space, which can be controlled by the value of $w$. There are only 2 rounds of messages, one of which informs the mining results. Each message has size $O(|\Sigma|^w)$, for given globals $w$ and $\Sigma$. The communication costs may be controlled by choosing the value of $w$.

Let us now discuss the privacy properties of the proposed approach. In general there are two main attack scenarios in a distributed data mining application. The first scenario is an attack from an insider, who may acts like a normal member of the mining group. The second scenario is an attack from an outsider. In this case the attacker listens into the conversation and tries to learn information from the eavesdropped messages.

In this paper we focus on the first scenario. By using the homomorphic encryption we can expect that an outside attack won't be successful with high probability. The critical situation is when the outsider has a partner inside the group. But this reduces the problem to an inside scenario. Therefore, we concentrate here on how much privacy is provided against an insider attack.

We assume that the attacker know all parameters, for it is an insider. Now, let us define the privacy of a time series as the accuracy of reconstructed data an attacker may produce. This is along with the information-theoretical definition of privacy proposed elsewhere [22]. The privacy of a given random variable is proportional to its uncertainty, which translates to entropy in the information theory.

**Definition 1.** *Given a random variable $Y$ with domain $\Omega_Y$ and probability density function $p(y)$ its privacy* **PR** *is given by*

$$\mathbf{PR}(Y) = 2^{h(Y)} \tag{6}$$

*where $h(Y)$ is the differential entropy of $Y$ with $h(Y) = -\int_{\Omega_Y} p(y)\log_2 p(y)dy$.*

One interpretation of this definition is that the privacy of a given variable $A$ is the length of the interval where the attacker knows it is located with probability 1, which is $2^{h(A)}$. The larger the interval from the point of view of the attacker, the more privacy we have. The idea is that the discretization step in DPD-HE provides a given amount of uncertainty. We want to use the information on the discretization transform to compute the uncertainty and consequently the privacy of each point in the original time series $X$. The following theorem captures this idea.

**Theorem 1.** *Let $\Sigma$ be an alphabet of symbols used by the DPD-HE protocol. Let $T$ be a time series and $S \in \Sigma^w$ be its transform according to the discretization step. Let $\{\beta_j \in \mathbb{R}\}_{j=1}^{|\Sigma+1|}$ be a set of breakpoints which divides the domain of the time series $T$ in $|\Sigma|$ equiprobable regions. For a given point $x_t$ if its transformed counterpart $s_j = \sigma_a$ is known, than its privacy level is given by:*

$$\mathbf{PR}(x_t) = |\beta_{a+1} - \beta_a| \tag{7}$$

*Proof.* This is a consequence of the discretization step. Since we know that the symbol $\sigma_a$ comes from the substitution rule in the discretization step, we know that average $\bar{x}_j$ of the points in the subsequence $\langle x_t, \ldots, x_{t+n} \rangle$ lies in the interval $(\beta_a, \beta_{a+1})$. In the absence of further information, the only suitable option is to model $\bar{x}_j$ as a random variable uniformly distributed in the given interval, i.e. $\bar{x}_j \sim U(\beta_a, \beta_{a+1})$. Now, using the privacy metric in Eq. (7) we have:

$$\mathbf{PR}(x_t) = 2^{h(x_t)} = 2^{\int_{\beta_a}^{\beta_{a+1}} p(x)log_2 p(x)dx}$$
$$= 2^{log_2(\beta_{a+1}-\beta_a)} = |\beta_{a+1} - \beta_a|$$

As a consequence, the more symbols in the alphabet, the less privacy we get, which is according to the intuition, as the discretized version tends to get the "shape" of the original data.

**Theorem 2.** *Assuming no collusion among attackers, DPD-HE keeps the privacy about ownership of a given the local density estimate.*

*Proof.* (Sketch) The overall security is a consequence of the security of the Paillier encryption scheme, which was shown to be semantically secure elsewhere [21]. Since no local density is decrypted at any site but the initiator, assuming that the initiator do not collude, we have that an attacker cannot assign any of information a specific site.

## 4   Experiments

In the following we present some results of our experiments. We implemented our approach in GNU Octave, which is a high-level language for numerical computation.

In the experiments reported here we used the *power data* records the electricity consumption from Netherlands Energy Research Foundation (ECN) for one year, recorded every 15 minutes. There are 35 040 data points corresponding to the year of 1997. Figure 1 shows an excerpt of the power data. This data set has a pattern structure that can be observed visually.

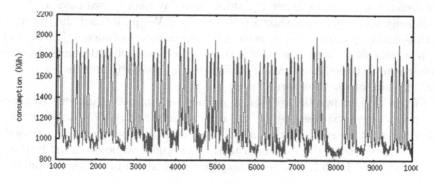

**Fig. 1.** Excerpt of power data

We set the parameter as follows. Subsequence size $n = 96$, which corresponds to one day (with one measurement every 15 minutes). We choose pattern size $w = 7$ for it represents a week. The alphabet $\Sigma$ was set to { a, b, c, d}. Symbol 'a' represents lowest values and 'd' represents highest value of consumption. The radius was set to $r = 1$. Larger values of $r$ produces larger neighborhoods. The density landscape becomes smoother which may reduce the number of local maxima and consequently the number of patterns. Choosing smaller values of $r$ produces a more spiky density with more local maxima and more patterns. Therefore, $r$ help us to control the number of patterns. With these parameters values we found 2 frequent patterns. The first pattern is "cccccaa" which corresponds to a normal week. The second pattern is "acccaa" which correspond to weeks having a holiday on the first day. Figure 2 shows one instance of each pattern.

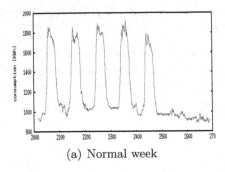

(a) Normal week

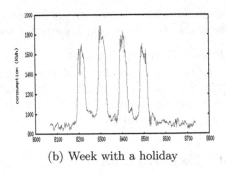

(b) Week with a holiday

**Fig. 2.** (a) An instance of a *normal week*, the most frequent subsequence in the power data, showing high consumption on work days and low consumption at weekends. (b) An instance of a *week with holiday* pattern in the power data. In this example, the Monday was a holiday.

Results with different alphabet sizes, with all other parameters set as above, found an increasing number of patterns. This is mainly because larger alphabets produce more accurate discretization, what allows for a more detailed differentiation among the patterns. These additional patterns basically presented refinements of the more general pattern "five day high + two days low".

Results of performance shown in figure 3(a). We performed the experiments with the same parameters values as in the previous experiments. For the performance tests we created a synthetic time series with 300 000 points, by cloning power data 10 times. As shown in the figure 3(a), the CPU time increases linearly with the size of the time series.

Figure 3(b) shows the results of privacy vs. size of alphabet. To measure the privacy we used the interval size corresponding to each alphabet symbol in the discretization step. In the initial case, with just one symbol, we used the size of interval from the minimum to the maximum value observed in the time series, which is 1 056 KWh. Assuming that max and min values are public, the

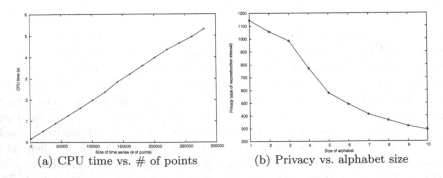

(a) CPU time vs. # of points

(b) Privacy vs. alphabet size

**Fig. 3.** (a) Time performance with increasing size of time series; (b) Privacy level with increasing size of alphabet

attacker can compute the entropy of a random variable $X$ over this interval, and consequently the privacy level $2^h(X)$. That is the privacy we get when the sequence consists of symbols from a singleton alphabet. In the figure we see the decrease of privacy by using more symbols to discretize the time series. With 10 symbols we get a privacy level of 300 KWh, which means that an attacker cannot reconstruct a data point within an interval smaller than 300 KWh. It is up to the user, however, to decide whether or not a given privacy level is enough.

## 5  Conclusion

We presented the DPD-HE, an algorithm for pattern discovery in distributed time series. It is time efficient (linear in the size of time series) and provides privacy of ownership and data values. The main idea is to use density estimation to identify the most frequent subsequences. The additive of density estimates allow us to extend the basic idea to the distributed case. By using a cryptographic protocol, it is possible to compute the global density without disclosing local data. Experiments on real and synthetic data sets showed that most of frequent patterns can be found, and no false negative is produced.

Future work includes an application to distributed time series clustering. We also have plans to improve the privacy level in scenarios where the attackers form collusion. In this case we may use permutation on the secure sum protocol. Another interesting extension is to work with multivariate data, which calls for a more efficient space usage and investigation on possible data leakage through correlation, which is typically very high in time series data.

## Acknowledgments

The authors are very grateful to the "UCR Time Series Data Mining Archive" [23] for providing us the with time series data. The authors also thank German Ministry of Education and Research for support through grant BMBF 01-IW-D02-SCALLOPS and the Brazilian Ministry for Education for support through grant CAPES 0791/024.

## References

1. Jensen, K.L., Styczynski, M.P., Rigoutsos, I., Stephanopoulos, G.N.: A generic motif discovery algorithm for sequential data. Bioinformatics 22, 21–28 (2006)
2. Lin, J., Keogh, E., Lonardi, S., Patel, P.: Finding motifs in time series. In: Proc. of the Second Workshop on Temporal Data Mining, Edmonton, Alberta, Canada (July 2002)
3. Moerchen, F., Ultsch, A.: Discovering temporal knowledge in multivariate time series. In: Proc. GfKl 04, Dortmund, Germany (2004)
4. Kadous, M.W.: Learning comprehensible descriptions of multivariate time series. In: Proc. 16th International Conf. on Machine Learning, pp. 454–463. Morgan Kaufmann, San Francisco (1999)
5. Lin, J., Keogh, E., Truppel, W.: Clustering of streaming time series is meaningless. In: Proc. of the 8th ACM DMKD, San Diego, California, pp. 56–65. ACM Press, New York (2003)

6. Liu, Z., Yu, J.X., Lin, X., Lu, H., Wang, W.: Locating motifs in time-series datas. In: Ho, T.-B., Cheung, D., Liu, H. (eds.) PAKDD 2005. LNCS (LNAI), vol. 3518, pp. 343–353. Springer, Heidelberg (2005)
7. Agrawal, R., Srikant, R.: Mining sequential patterns. In: Yu, P.S., Chen, A.S.P. (eds.) Eleventh International Conference on Data Engineering, Taipei, Taiwan, pp. 3–14. IEEE Computer Society Press, Los Alamitos (1995)
8. Srikant, R., Agrawal, R.: Mining sequential patterns: Generalizations and performance improvements. In: Apers, P.M.G., Bouzeghoub, M., Gardarin, G. (eds.) EDBT. Proc. 5th Int. Conf. Extending Database Technology, 25–29    1996, vol. 1057, pp. 3–17. Springer, Heidelberg (1996)
9. Atallah, M., Bertino, E., Elmagarmid, A., Ibrahim, M., Verykios, V.: Disclosure limitation of sensitive rules. In: KDEX'99. Proceedings of 1999 IEEE Knowledge and Data Engineering Exchange Workshop, Chicago,IL, November 1999, pp. 45–52. IEEE Computer Society Press, Los Alamitos (1999)
10. Saygin, Y., Verykios, V.S., Elmagarmid, A.K.: Privacy preserving association rule mining. In: Reseach Issues in Data Engineering (RIDE) (2002)
11. Evfimievski, A., Srikant, R., Agrawal, R., Gehrke, J.: Privacy preserving mining of association rules. In: Proceedings of 8th ACM SIGKDD Intl. Conf. on Knowledge Discovery and Data Mining (KDD), Edmonton, Alberta, Canada, ACM Press, New York (2002)
12. Agrawal, R., Srikant, R.: Privacy-preserving data mining. In: Proc. of the ACM SIGMOD Conference on Management of Data, Dallas, Texas, May 2000, pp. 439–450. ACM Press, New York (2000)
13. Pinkas, B.: Cryptographic techniques for privacy-preserving data mining. ACM SIGKDD Explorations Newsletter 4(2), 12–19 (2002)
14. Vaidya, J., Clifton, C.: Secure set intesection cardinality with application to association rule mining, Submited to ACM Transactions on Information and Systems Security (March 2003)
15. Goldreich, O., Micali, S., Wigderson, A.: How to play any mental game. In: In Proc. of the 19th annual ACM conference on Theory of computing, pp. 218–229. ACM Press, New York (1987)
16. Lindell, Y., Pinkas, B.: Privacy preserving data mining. In: Bellare, M. (ed.) CRYPTO 2000. LNCS, vol. 1880, pp. 36–54. Springer, Heidelberg (2000)
17. Du, W., Zhan, Z.: Building Decision Tree Classifier on Private Data. In: IEEE ICDM Workshop on Privacy, Security and Data Mining, Maebashi City, Japan. CRPIT, vol. 14, pp. 1–8. IEEE Computer Society Press, Los Alamitos (2002)
18. Kantarcioglu, M., Vaidya, J.: Privacy preserving naive bayes classifier for horizontally pertitioned data. In: IEEE ICDM Workshop on Privacy Preserving Data Mining, November 2003, pp. 3–9. IEEE Computer Society Press, Los Alamitos (2003)
19. Tanaka, Y., Iwamoto, K., Uehara, K.: Discovery of time-series motif from multidimensional data based on mdl principle. Machine Learning 58, 269–300 (2005)
20. Keogh, E.J., Chakrabarti, K., Pazzani, M.J., Mehrotra, S.: Dimensionality reduction for fast similarity search in large time series databases. Knowledge and Information Systems 3(3), 263–286 (2000)
21. Paillier, P.: Public-key cryptosystems based on composite degree residuosity classes. In: Stern, J. (ed.) EUROCRYPT 1999. LNCS, vol. 1592, p. 223. Springer, Heidelberg (1999)
22. Agrawal, D., Aggarwal, C.C.: On the design and quantification of privacy preserving data mining algorithms. In: 20th ACM PODS, Santa Barbara, Califonia, May 2001, pp. 247–255. ACM Press, New York (2001)
23. Keogh, E., Folias, T.: The ucr time series data mining archive (2002), http://www.cs.ucr.edu/~eamonn/TSDMA/index.html

# Efficient Non Linear Time Series Prediction Using Non Linear Signal Analysis and Neural Networks in Chaotic Diode Resonator Circuits

M.P. Hanias and D.A. Karras

Chalkis Institute of Technology, Greece, Automation Dept., Psachna, Evoia,
Hellas (Greece) P.C. 34400
dakarras@teihal.gr, dakarras@ieee.org, mhanias@teihal.gr

**Abstract.** A novel non linear signal prediction method is presented using non linear signal analysis and deterministic chaos techniques in combination with neural networks for a diode resonator chaotic circuit. Multisim is used to simulate the circuit and show the presence of chaos. The Time series analysis is performed by the method proposed by Grasberger and Procaccia, involving estimation of the correlation and minimum embedding dimension as well as of the corresponding Kolmogorov entropy. These parameters are used to construct the first stage of a one step / multistep predictor while a back-propagation Artificial Neural Network (ANN) is involved in the second stage to enhance prediction results. The novelty of the proposed two stage predictor lies on that the backpropagation ANN is employed as a second order predictor, that is as an error predictor of the non-linear signal analysis stage application. This novel two stage predictor is evaluated through an extensive experimental study.

**Keywords:** prediction, non-linear signal analysis, diode, chaos, time series, correlation dimension, prediction, neural networks.

## 1 Introduction

Time series forecasting, or time series prediction, takes an existing series of data and forecasts the future data values. The goal is to observe or model the existing data series to enable future unknown data values to be forecasted accurately.

A novel two-stage time series prediction method is presented in this paper and is applied to the prediction of a chaotic signal produced by a diode resonator chaotic circuit. This circuit, being quite simple, illustrates how chaos can be generated. We have selected Multisim [1] to simulate circuits since it provides an interface as close as possible to the real implementation environment. In addition, complete circuits implementation and oscilloscope graphical plots are all presented. While non-linear signal analysis methods have been quite extensively studied and applied in several systems presenting chaos, chaotic time series prediction for electronic circuits is a field not too deeply investigated so far. Chaos has already been recognized to be present in electronic circuits [2]-[5]. Some preliminary investigations on such time series prediction have been performed by the authors in [6]. The present paper aims at developing efficient predictors for such chaotic time series. To this end, the classical

P. Perner (Ed.): ICDM 2007, LNAI 4597, pp. 329–338, 2007.

nonlinear signal analysis (i.e [7]-[8] ) has been involved as a first stage of the proposed predictor, while back-propagation neural networks have been employed in the second stage to enhance first stage results, being a second order predictor for the first time in then relevant literature. An extensive experimental study shows that the proposed predictor is very favourably evaluated in terms of accuracy with the classical nonlinear signal analysis methodology.

## 2   The Non Autonomous Driven RL Diode Circuit

A non autonomous chaotic circuit referred to as the driven RL-diode circuit (*RLD*) [2-4] shown in Fig 1.

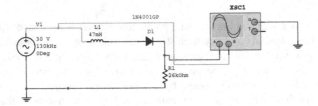

**Fig. 1.** RL-Diode chaotic circuit

It consists of a series connection of an ac-voltage source, a linear resistor $R_1$, a linear inductor L1 and a diode $D_1$ type 1N4001GP, that is the only nonlinear circuit element. An important feature of this circuit is that the current i (or the voltage across the resistor R) can be chaotic although the input voltage V1 is nonchaotic. The usual procedure is to choose a parameter that strongly affects the system.  We found that for $V_1$=30V RMS and input frequency f=130 KHz, inductance L1=47mH, the response is a chaotic one. The results of the Multisim simulation are shown in Fig. 2. The RL-diode was implemented and the voltage oscillations across the resistor $V_{R1}$ and its phase portrait V1 vs $V_{R1}$ are shown in Fig.2.

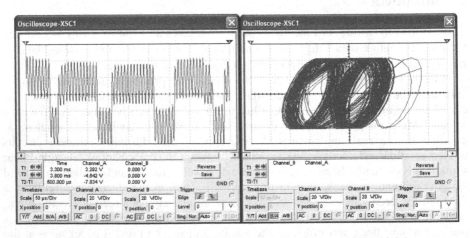

**Fig. 2.** Time series $V_{R1}$ (t) (left) Phase portrait of $V_1$versus VR1 (right)

# 3   The Proposed Novel Prediction Methodology

## 3.1   First Stage: The Non Linear Signal Analysis Process

Time series prediction takes an existing series of data

$$x_{t-n}, \ldots, x_{t-2}, x_{t-1}, x_t \tag{1}$$

and forecasts the future

$$x_{t+1}, x_{t+2}, \ldots \tag{2}$$

data values. Taking into account this point of view we could interpret the data produced by the RLD circuit as a non-linear chaotic time series. The goal is to observe or model the existing data series to enable future unknown data values to be forecasted accurately.

To evaluate the resulted time series, the method proposed by Grasberger and Procaccia [7,8] and successfully applied in similar cases [9-11] has been applied in order to define the first stage of the proposed predictor. According to Takens theory [12] the measured time series were used to reconstruct the original phase space. For this purpose we calculated the correlation integral, for the simulated signal, defined by the following relation [13].

$$C_m(r) = \lim \frac{2}{(N)(N+1)} \sum_{i=1}^{N} \sum_{j=i+1}^{N} H\{r - (\sum_{k=1}^{m} |x_{i+k} - x_{j+k}|^2)^{\frac{1}{2}}\} \tag{3}$$

for $\lim r \rightarrow \infty$ , where
N........................is the number of points,
H........................is the Heaviside function,
m is the embedding dimension

In the above equation N is the number of the experemental points here N=16337, $X_i$ is a point in the m dimensional phase space  with $X_i$ given by the  following relation [12]

$$X_t = \{V_{R1}(t_i), V_{R1}(t_i+\tau), V_{R1}(t_i+2\tau) \ldots V_{R1}(t_i+(m-1)\tau)\} \tag{4}$$

The vector
$X_t = \{V_{R1}(t_i), V_{R1}(t_i+\tau), V_{R1}(t_i+2\tau) \ldots V_{R1}(t_i+(m-1)\tau)\}$, represents a point  to the m dimensional phase space in which  the attractor is embedded each time, where $\tau$ is the time delay $\tau = i\Delta t$ determined by the first minimum of the time delayed mutual information, $I(\tau)$ [13-16]. In our case, because of sample rate $\Delta t = 4.8 \times 10^{-7}$ s, the mutual information function exhibits a local minimum at $\tau = 6$ time steps as shown at Fig .3.

We used this value for the reconstruction of phase space. With (3) dividing this space into hypercubes with a linear dimension r we count all points with mutual distance less than r. It has been proven  [7-8] that if our attractor is a strange one, the correlation integral is propotional to $r^v$ where v is a measure of the dimension of the attractor, called the correlation dimension. The correlation integral C(r) has been numerically calculated  as a function of r from formula (3), for embedding dimensions m=1..10. In Fig 4 (upper insert)  the slopes v of the lower linear parts of these double logarithmic  curves give information characterizing the attractor.

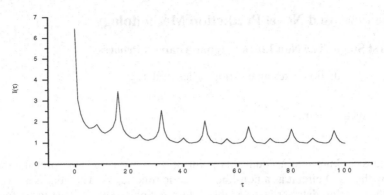

**Fig. 3.** Average Mutulal Information vs time delay τ

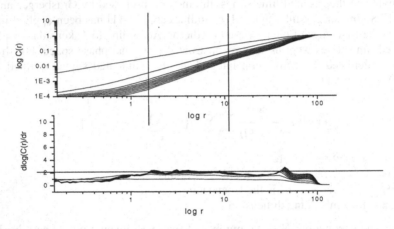

**Fig. 4.** The correlation intergral C(r) vs logr, for different embedding dimensions m (upper insert). The corresponding slopes and the scaling region (lower insert).

In fig 4 (lower insert) the corresponding average slopes v are given as a function of the embedding dimension m It is obvious from these curves that v tends to saturate, for higher m's , at non integer value v=2.11 with this value of v the minimum embedding dimension could be $m_{min}$=3 [13]. So the minimum embedding dimension of the attractor for one to one embedding is 3.

In order to get more precise measurements of the strength of the chaos present in the oscillations we have introduced the Kolmogorov entropy. According to [13] the method described above also gives an estimate of the Kolmogorov entropy, i.e. the correlation integral C (r) scales with the embedding dimension m according to the following relation

$$C(r) \sim e^{-m\tau K_2} \qquad (5)$$

Where $K_2$ is a lower bound to the Kolomogorov entropy. From the plateau of fig 5 we estimate $K_2$=0.11 bit/s.

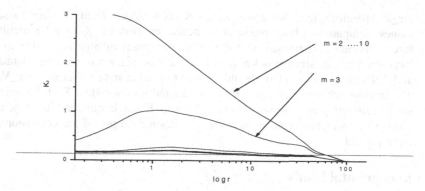

**Fig. 5.** The Kolmogorov entropy vs log r for different embedding dimensions

## 3.2  Second Stage: The Back-Propagation ANN as a Second Order Predictor

The proposed novel algorithm to enhance non-linear signal analysis prediction is as follows:

1. To predict point $V_{i+1}$, we determine the last known state of the system as represented by vector $X = [V_i, V_{i-\tau}, V_{i-2\tau}, V_{i-(m-1)\tau}]$, where m is the embedding dimension and $\tau$ is the time delay.

2. With optimum values of delay time and embedding dimension m we then search the time series to find k similar states that have occurred in the past, where "similarity" is determined by evaluating the distance between vector X and its neighbour vector X' in the m-dimensional state space. So k close states (usually nearest neighbours of X) of the system that have occurred in the past are found, by computing their distances from X.

3. We used a fixed size of nearest neighbours K (calculated for optimizing prediction performance in the training phase). if a state $X' = [V'_i, V'_{i-\tau}, V'_{i-2\tau}d, V'_{i-(m-1)\tau}]$ in the neighbourhood of X resulted in the observation $V'_{i+1}$ in the past, then the point $V_{i+1}$ which we want to predict must be somewhere near $V'_{i+1}$. This is the main concept of nonlinear signal analysis of first order approximation.

4. It is reasonable to calculate $V_{i+1} = (\Sigma q_k V'_k)/\Sigma q_k$ where $q_k$ the distance between current state X and neighboring state $X_k$, whereas $V'_k$ the corresponding prediction from $X'_k$ vector (from the training set). The above sum is considered for all X neighbors

5. Our proposition to enhance prediction results is to write down $V_{i+1} = (\Sigma q_k V'_k)/\Sigma q_k + error\_V_{i+1}$, where $(\Sigma q_k V'_k)/\Sigma q_k$ is the first order prediction and $error\_V_{i+1}$, is the prediction error to be minimized provided it is calculated properly. Therefore, it is a second order approximation proposal to predict such an error. This $error\_V_{i+1}$, could be calculated through a suitable neural network as an error predictor. This is exactly the main concept of the proposed novel methodology.

6. Suppose err_k the corresponding prediction error measured through the above procedure for each neighboring state $X'_k$ of given current state X above (out of the K neighbours of X). This err_k is known through the training set, since for each $X'_k$ in the training set we can calculate its corresponding K neighbours from the training set, and then, estimate, using step 5 above, the associated

err_k. Therefore, for k we construct all K such err_k. Then, we feed these K values as inputs to a back-propagation neural network of K-L1-L2-1 architecture. This network, trained with the conjugate gradient algorithm, due to the large training set, since it is known to be the best algorithm for large data sets and ANN architectures [18], should be able to predict state's X error error_$V_{i+1}$.

7. The training set needed for step 6 is constructed for each state X of the training set by estimating all corresponding err_k of its K neighbours and its associated error_$V_{i+1}$ , which of course serves as the desired output of the corresponding input pattern

## 4   Experimental Study

We have used a simulated  time series from RLD  circuit with $V_1$=30V RMS and input frequency f=130 KHz and we predict the voltage V across the resistor.

We use locally linear models to predict the one step and the multistep procedures. That is, instead of fitting one complex model with many coefficients to the entire data set, we fit many simple models (low order polynomials) to small portion of the data set depending on the geometry of the local neighborhood of the dynamical system. [17].The general procedure is the following: To predict point $V_{i+1}$, we determine the last known state of the system as represented by vector $\mathbf{X} = [V_i, V_{i-\tau}, V_{i-2\tau}, V_{i-(m-1)\tau}]$, where m is the embedding dimension and $\tau$ is the time delay.

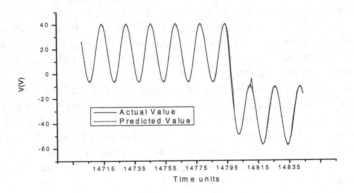

**Fig. 6.** One step prediction

So we use as a delay time the value of $\tau$=6 as before. From previous analysis the correlation dimension for RLD circuit is found v=2.11. With optimum values of delay time and embedding dimension m=3 we then search the time series to find k similar states that have occurred in the past, where "similarity" is determined by evaluating the distance between vector X and its neighbour vector X' in the m-dimensional state space. So k close states (usually nearest neighbours of **X**) of the system that have occurred in the past are found, by computing their distances from **X** as explained in section 3 above.

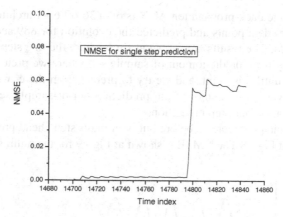

**Fig. 7.** Mean squared error of our predictor normalized by the mean squared error of the random walk predictor for one step prediction

The idea is to fit a map which extrapolates **X** and its k nearest neighbours to determine the next value. If the observable signal was generated by some deterministic map $M(V_i, V_{i-\tau}, V_{i-2\tau}, V_{(i-(m-1)\tau)}) = V_{i+\tau}$, that map can be recovered (reconstructed) from the data by looking at its behaviour in the neighbourhood of X. Using this map , an approximate value of $V_{i+1}$ can be obtained. We used a fixed size of nearest neighbours k=36. Now we can use this map to predict $V_{i+1}$ In other words, we make an assumption that M is fairly smooth around X, and so if a state $X' = [V'_i, V'_{i-\tau}, V'_{i-2\tau d}, V'_{i-(m-1)\tau}]$ in the neighbourhood of X resulted in the observation $V'_{i+1}$ in the past, then the point $V_{i+1}$ which we want to predict must be somewhere near $V'_{i+1}$. [17]. We have employed both the one step and multistep ahead prediction methods. In the one step ahead prediction, after each step in the future is predicted, the actual value is utilized for the next one –step prediction. In contrast, the multistep prediction is based only on the initial k states.

The calculated performance is otherwise known as the Normalized Mean Squared Error (NMSE) is calculated by (5-1),

$$NMSE = MAX \left( \frac{\sum_{i=1}^{NP}(\tilde{V}_i - V_i)^2}{\sum_{i=1}^{NP}(\overline{V}_i - V_i)^2}, \frac{\sum_{i=1}^{NP}(\tilde{V}_i - V_i)^2}{\sum_{i=1}^{NP}(V_{i-1} - V_i)^2} \right) \quad (5\text{-}1),$$

where $\tilde{V}_i$ is the predicted value, $V_i$, the actual value, $\overline{V}$ is the average actual value, and NP is the range of values in the prediction interval.

From (5-1), it can be seen that NMSE is the mean squared error of our predictor normalized by the mean squared error a random walk predictor. By definition, the minimum value of NMSE is 0. At that value, there is the exact match between the actual and predicted values. The higher NMSE, the worse is our prediction as compared to the trivial predictors. If NMSE is equal to 1, our prediction is as good as the prediction by the trivial predictor. If NMSE is greater than 1, our prediction worsens. With values of $\tau=6$, m=3 we achieved the minimum NMSE.

The second stage back-propagation ANN is of a 36-60-60-1 architecture.

We used 14700 data points and predicted the evolution for 889 succeeding dimensionless time steps. The results are shown at fig 6 where the one step ahead predicted values are coming from prediction out-of-sample set, where we pretend that we know the data only up until this point, and we try to predict from there, while the one step ahead predicted values are coming from prediction out-of-sample set. The NMSE is shown at fig 7 for the one step prediction.

We use the same procedure as before but with multi-step ahead predictions. The results are shown at Fig - 8 The NMSE is shown at Fig - 9 for the multi step prediction.

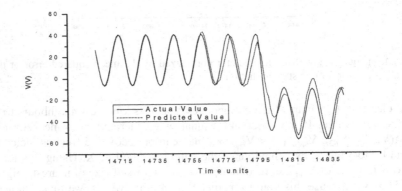

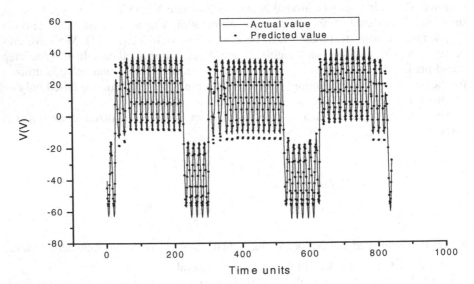

**Fig. 8.** Multistep prediction, Actual and predicted time series for 10 time steps ahead for the total set of points and the unknown time series (lower insert, in detail)

In comparison, when a first stage only predictor is used without the proposed neural network of stage 2, on average, for the 889 unknown data points we have achieved

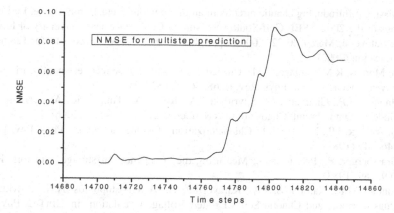

**Fig.9.** Mean squared error of our predictor normalized by the mean squared error of the random walk predictor for multistep prediction

8.5% worse performance in the one-step prediction for the NMSE and 7.8% worse performance in the multistep prediction experiments. Therefore, the proposed methodology is worth evaluating it further in larger scale experiments.

## 5  Conclusions and Future Trends

We have proposed a novel two-stage time series prediction scheme based on nonlinear signal analysis methods and a novel error prediction back propagation ANN trained with the conjugate gradient algorithm. Applying the methods of non linear analysis in the time series produced by the chaotic simple RLD circuit we found that the strange attractor that governs the phenomenon is a Lorenz type attractor with a correlation dimension v=2.11 who is stretching and folding in a 3 dimension phase space. This is also evident from the one step ahead and multistep successful predictions with the use of the correspondence strange attractor invariants as input parameters, and the efficient ANN model introduced in the second stage of the proposed predictor.

We believe that for a detailed understanding of chaos in the *RLD* circuits these results must be combined with the reverse-recovery effect and all of its nonlinearities. The proposed prediction methodology might be applied successfully in other chaotic time series too, since it is quite general. This is, also, a future target of the authors.

## References

[1] Lonngren, K.E.: Notes to accompany a student laboratory experiment on chaos. IEEE Transactions on Education 34(1) (1991)

[2] Matsumato, T., Chua, L., Tanaka, S.: Simplest Chaotic Nonautonomous Circuit. Phys. Rev. A 30, 1155–1157 (1984)

[3] Azzouz, A., Hasler, M.: Orbits of the R-L-Diode Circuit. IEEE Transaction on Circuits and Systems 37, 1330–1339 (1990)

[4] Aissi, C.: Introducing chaotic circuits in an undergraduate electronic course. In: Proceedings of the 2002 ASEE Gulf-Southwest Annual Conference,The University of Louisiana at Lafayette, March 20-22, 2002.Copyright © 2002, American Society for Engineering Education (2002)

[5] de Moraes, R.M., Anlage, S.M.: Unified model and reverse recovery nonlinearities of the driven diode resonator. Phys. Rev. E. 68, 26–201 (2003)

[6] Hanias, M.P., Giannaris, G., Spyridakis, A., Rigas, A.: Time series Analysis in chaotic diode resonator circuit. Chaos Solitons & fractals 27(2), 569–573 (2006)

[7] Grassberger, P., Procaccia, I.: Characterization of strange attractors. Phys. Rev. Lett. 50, 346–349 (1983)

[8] Grassberger, P., Procaccia, I.: Measuring the strangeness of strange attractors. Physica D 9, 189 (1983)

[9] Hanias, M.P., Kalomiros, J.A., Karakotsou, C., Anagnostopoulos, A.N., Spyridelis, J.: Quasi-Periodic and Chaotic Self - Excited Voltage Oscillations in TlInTe2. Phys. Rev. B. 49, 16994 (1994)

[10] Mozdy, E., Newell, T.C., Alsing, P.M., Kovanis, V., Gavrielides, A.: Synchronization and control in a unidirectionally coupled array of chaotic diode resonators. Physical Review E. 51(6), 5371–5376 (1995)

[11] Abarbanel, H.D.I.: Analysis of Observed Chaotic Data. Springer, New York (1996)

[12] Takens, F.: Lecture Notes in Mathematics 898 (1981)

[13] Kantz, H., Schreiber, T.: Nonlinear Time Series Analysis. Cambridge University Press, Cambridge (1997)

[14] Aasen, T., Kugiumtzis, D., Nordahl, S.H.G.: Procedure for Estimating the Correlation Dimension of Optokinetic Nystagmus Signals. Computers and Biomedical Research 30, 95–116 (1997)

[15] Fraser, A.M., Swinney, H.L.: Independent coordinates for strange attractors from mutual information. Phys. Rev. A. 33, 1134–1140 (1986)

[16] Fraser, A.M.: IEEE transaction of information Theory 35, 245 (1989)

[17] Kononov, E.: Virtual Recurrence Analysis, Version 4.9 (2006), (email:eugenek@ix.net.com.com)

[18] Haykin, S.: Neural Networks, a comprehensive foundation, 2nd edn. Prentice-Hall, Englewood Cliffs (1999)

# Using Disjunctions in Association Mining

Martin Ralbovský[1] and Tomáš Kuchař[2]

[1] Department of Information and Knowledge Engineering,
University of Economics, Prague, W. Churchill Sq. 4, 130 67 Praha 3, Czech Republic
martin.ralbovsky@gmail.com
[2] Department of Software Engineering, Faculty of Mathematics and Physics
Charles University, Malostransk nm. 25, 118 01 Prague, Czech Republic
tomas.kuchar@gmail.com

**Abstract.** The paper focuses on usage of disjunction of items in association rules mining. We used the GUHA method instead of the traditional *apriori* algorithm and enhanced the former implementations of the method with ability of disjunctions setting between items. Experiments were conducted in our Ferda data mining environment on data from the medical domain. We found strong and meaningful association rules that could not be obtained without the usage of disjunction.

**Keywords:** Association Mining, Disjunction, GUHA Method, Ferda.

## 1 Introduction

Association rules mining is an important technique widely used in the KDD community [8]. Most of the tools nowadays use the *apriori* algorithm, or its modifications [1] [2]. The algorithm searches for frequent (or large) itemsets with given minimal *support* and then calculates *confidence*. We will refer to this algorithm as to classical association mining. Its authors considered only the conjunctions (and possibly negations) of items.

Yet sometimes it is feasible to examine disjunctions of items. Consider following example: Medical expert wants to find associations between beer consumption and other characteristics of a patient (blood pressure, level of cholesterol, body mass index...). The examined data contains information about consumption of three different types of beer: light 7 degree beer, drought 10 degree beer and lager 12 degree beer[1]. It is likely to happen that the number of patients drinking 7 degree *or* 12 degree beer is higher then the number of patients drinking 7 degree *and* 12 degree beer. More formally, from the rule $A \to B$ one can get rule $A \to B \lor C$ easily than the rule $A \to B \land C$. For semantically close entities[2]

---

[1] This categorization of beer is traditional in the Czech Republic and represents the weight percentage of mash in the end product. 7 degree beer contains about 2% of alcohol, 10 degree beer about 3 to 4% and 12 degree beer about 4 to 5% of alcohol.
[2] Drinking of different types of beer is semantically close characteristics of a patient.

P. Perner (Ed.): ICDM 2007, LNAI 4597, pp. 339–351, 2007.
© Springer-Verlag Berlin Heidelberg 2007

one can therefore use disjunctions and mine for rules with higher support (and possibly other characteristics).

The aim of this paper is to present an enhancement of classical association mining with the possibility of disjunction setting between the items. One cannot use *apriori* for disjunctions, because the algorithm searches for frequent itemsets by binding items to already known itemsets (of length *k*) with conjunction to form itemsets (of length *k+1*). We used the older GUHA method instead, which mines for modifications of association rules. The generalization enables disjunctions between items and had several partial implementations before the personal computer era. We created a new implementation in our Ferda tool and conducted experiments with medical data using more strict requirements for rules than *support* and *confidence*. Meaningful rules have been found; these rules could not be found without disjunction usage and have interesting characteristics that should be subject of further research.

The paper is structured as follows: Section 2 explains the GUHA method and its relation to classical association mining. Section 3 states a brief history of tools implementing the GUHA method leading to our Ferda tool. Section 4 describes conducted experiments. Section 5 draws fields of further research and finally section 6 concludes the work.

## 2    Principles of Association Mining with GUHA

### 2.1    The GUHA Method

GUHA method is one of the first methods of exploratory data analysis, developed in the mid-sixties in Prague. It is a general mainframe for retrieving interesting knowledge from data. The method has firm theoretical foundations based on observational calculi and statistics [4], [5]. For purpose of this paper let us explain only the basic principles of the method, as shown in Figure 1.

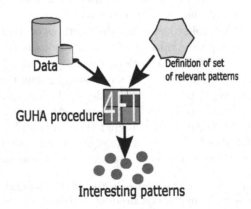

**Fig. 1.** The GUHA method

GUHA method is realized by GUHA procedures such as 4FT procedure to be described, located in the middle of the figure[3]. Inputs of the procedure are data and a simple definition of a possibly large set of relevant patterns, which will be discussed in detail in the following section 2.2. The procedure automatically generates all the relevant patterns and verifies them against the provided data. Patterns that are true are output of the procedure.

Although GUHA is not in principle restricted to mining association rules, the most used GUHA procedures mine for generalized association rules, as defined in [12]. Section 2.3 introduces 4FT, procedure for association rules mining used in our work. Comparison study between the classical association mining and mining using GUHA can be found in [6].

## 2.2   Definition of Set of Relevant Patterns

This section shows how set of relevant patterns is defined in association rules mining with GUHA. We use the term attribute in the sense of *categorial attribute*, i.e. attribute with finite number of values.

**Definition 1.** *Let $A$ be an attribute, $A = \{a_1, a_2...a_n\}$ and $\alpha \subset A$, $\alpha \neq \emptyset$. Then $A(\alpha)$ is a* **basic Boolean attribute**.

**Definition 2.** *Each basic Boolean attribute is a* **Boolean attribute**. *If $\alpha$ and $\beta$ are Boolean attributes, $\alpha \wedge \beta$, $\alpha \vee \beta$ and $\neg\alpha$ are* **Boolean attributes**.

The above stated definition was introduced in [12] when formalizing association rules. *Boolean attributes* are used as antecedents or succedents[4] in GUHA procedures, as will be described in section 2.3. Our Ferda tool is the first program to enable full *Boolean attribute* definition including disjunction and recursion. Example 1 shows us creation of *Boolean attributes* from the beer consumption example from the introduction.

### Example 1
The examined data includes three attributes: **beer7**= {**no, low, high**}, **beer10**= {**no, low, high**} and **beer12**= {**no, low, high**} for consumption of 7, 10 and 12 degree beer respectively.

Examples of *basic Boolean attributes* are **beer7(no)**, **beer10(no, low)** or **beer12(high)**[5].

---

[3] Even though we present only one GUHA procedure in this work, there are five more procedures working above one data table implemented in Ferda and also two relational procedures under development.

[4] In classical association mining called consequents.

[5] Obviously, not all the subsets of an attribute are meaningful to verify. Our method allows user to define special subsets such as subsets with a given length, intervals, cyclic intervals or cuts for ordinal data.

**Table 1.** 4FT contingency table

| M | $\psi$ | $\neg\psi$ |
|---|---|---|
| $\varphi$ | a | b |
| $\neg\varphi$ | c | d |

Table 1: 4ft table

Then we combine *basic Boolean attributes* with logical operators to form a rule:
(**beer7(no)** $\vee$ **beer10(no, low)**) $\wedge$ $\neg$**beer12(high)**,
which is an example of *Boolean attribute*.

### 2.3   4FT Procedure

Classical association mining searches rules in form $X \longrightarrow Y$, where $X$ and $Y$ are sets of items. Procedure 4FT searches (in the simplified form) for rules in form $\varphi \approx \psi$, where $\varphi$ and $\psi$ are *Boolean attributes* and $\approx$ is a *4ft-quantifier*[6]. Relation $\varphi \approx \psi$ is evaluated on the basis of *4ft table*, as shown in Table 1.

A *4ft table* is a quadruple of natural numbers $\langle a, b, c, d \rangle$ so that:

 − a: number of objects (rows of $M$) satisfying $\varphi$ and $\psi$
 − b: number of objects (rows of $M$) satisfying $\varphi$ and not satisfying $\psi$
 − c: number of objects (rows of $M$) not satisfying $\varphi$ but satisfying $\psi$
 − d: number of objects (rows of $M$) satisfying neither $\varphi$ nor $\psi$

*4ft-quantifier* expresses kind of dependency between $\varphi$ and $\psi$. The quantifier is defined as a condition over the *4ft table*. By the expression **strict quantifier** we mean that there are no rules that satisfy the quantifier in the usual case. Occurrence of such quantifier means a very strong relation in the data. In the following sections we present three quantifiers used in our work, the *founded implication, double founded implication* and *founded equivalence* quantifiers[7]. This part of the paper was greatly inspired by [11], where detailed explanation of the most used quantifiers can be found.

### 2.4   Founded Implication Quantifier

The founded implication is basic quantifier for the 4FT procedure introduced in [4] and is defined by following condition:

$$a \leq Base \wedge \frac{a}{a+b} \geq p$$

Here *Base* and $p$ are threshold parameters of the procedure. The *Base* parameter represents absolute number of objects that satisfies $\varphi$. In our work we will use

---

[6] The more complex form includes another *Boolean attribute* as a condition In our work we do not mine for conditional rules, therefore we omit the more complex definition.
[7] There are many other quantifiers invented and implemented for the 4FT procedure.

relative *Base* representation, $\frac{a}{a+b+c+d}$. So, the *Base* parameter corresponds to the *support* and $p$ to the *confidence* parameters of classical association mining. When using the 4FT procedure with *founded implication quantifier* and constructing *Boolean attributes* only with conjunctions, we get the same results as if using classical association mining. Quantifier can be verbally interpreted with the expression *tendency to.*

## Example 2

Association rule *Patients that drink 12 degree beer tend be overweight* is an example of rule we can found with *founded implication*. This rule can be formally written as **beer12(high)** $\Rightarrow_{p,Base}$ **BMI(overweight)**, where $\Rightarrow_{p,Base}$ stands for *founded implication.*

## 2.5 Double Founded Implication Quantifier

The *double founded implication* quantifier enriches the *founded implication* with symmetry feature. Symmetry means that when $\varphi \approx \psi$ is valid, when $\psi \approx \varphi$ should be also valid. The quantifier has also threshold parameters *Base* and $p$ and is defined by following condition:

$$a \leq Base \land \frac{a}{a+b+c} \geq p$$

Again, we will use the relative representation of *Base*, $\frac{a}{a+b+c+d}$. We consider *double founded implication* a *strict quantifier*. However, we wanted to use the quantifier in our experiments to question the possibilities of disjunctions. The most suitable verbal expression for the quantifier is *relation of equivalence.*

## Example 3

The sign for *double founded implication* quantifier is $\Leftrightarrow_{p,Base}$. The rule **beer12 (high)** $\Leftrightarrow_{p,Base}$ **BMI(overweight)** with the *Boolean attributes* from example 2 can be verbally interpreted as *Drinking 12 degree beer is in relation of equivalence with being overweight among the observed patients.*

## 2.6 Founded Equivalence Quantifier

The last presented quantifier is the *founded equivalence*. It is a stronger quantifier than *founded implication* in terms of equivalence; ability of two entities to attain the same logical values. The condition for the quantifier is

$$a \leq Base \land \frac{a+d}{a+b+c+d} \geq p$$

For *founded equivalence*, we will also use the relative representation of *Base*, $\frac{a}{a+b+c+d}$. The fraction $\frac{a+d}{a+b+c+d}$ means the proportion of objects in the data matrix having $\varphi$ and $\psi$ both equal to 0 or 1, to all objects. Similarly, *Base* and $p$ are threshold parameters for the quantifier. As well as *double founded implication*, the *founded equivalence* is considered to be a *strict quantifier*. Quantifier can be verbally interpreted as *equivalent occurrence.*

**Example 4**

The sign for the *founded equivalence* quantifier is $\equiv_{p,Base}$. Generalized association rule **beer12(high)** $\equiv_{p,Base}$ **BMI(overweight)** can be translated to verbal form as *Consumption of 12 degree beer and being overweight has equivalent occurrence among the observed patients.*

# 3    GUHA and Ferda

We would not achieve results presented in this work without 40 years long research of the GUHA method and development of tools that implemented individual GUHA procedures. This section acknowledges achievements made by researchers and developers in the past and briefly describes history that lead to the state-of-the-art Ferda tool. See [3] for more information about history of GUHA method.

The development of first GUHA procedure started in 1956. In modern terminology, it mined for association rules with given *confidence* with one item as a antecedent and one item as a consequent [3]. The results, published in [4], were clearly ahead of their time, long before terms like data mining or knowledge discovery from databases were invented.

First GUHA procedure to consider disjunctions was the IMPL procedure introduced in [5]. The procedure mined for rules in form $CONJ \Rightarrow DISJ$, where $CONJ$ and $DISJ$ are elementary conjunctions and disjunctions[8]. $\Rightarrow$ is an *implicational quantifier*[9]. The implementation of the procedure [13] [15] used for the first time the bit string approach[10]. The input data were represented by strings of bits, which dramatically increased performance of the procedure.

The LISp-Miner tool[11] started in 1996 and contributed greatly to the level of contemporary GUHA tools by implementing six GUHA procedures and implementing coefficients - generation of special types of subsets of an attribute [14]. GUHA procedure 4ft-Miner implemented in LISp-Miner is predecessor of procedure 4FT introduced in this work. 4ft-Miner does not allow construction of *Boolean attributes*, it constructs *partial cedents* instead and until very recently it did not allow disjunctions. *Partial cedent* is a restricted non recursive *Boolean attribute*, more details are to be found in [14].

Ferda started as a student project to create a new visual environment for the LISp-Miner system [9]. In the first version, creators used the LISp-Miner GUHA procedures. The second version of the system, implemented in work [10], uses the bit string approach and enables full definition of *Boolean attribute*. It is the first modern tool (runs on personal computers) to implement disjunctions and recursion of *basic Boolean attributes*. The procedure 4FT implemented in Ferda

---

[8] Elementary conjunction is a conjunction made from one element subsets of an attribute.

[9] There are formal classes of *4ft-quantifiers* defined in [12]. *Implicational quantifiers* are one of the classes.

[10] Also known as *granular computing*.

[11] See http://lispminer.vse.cz

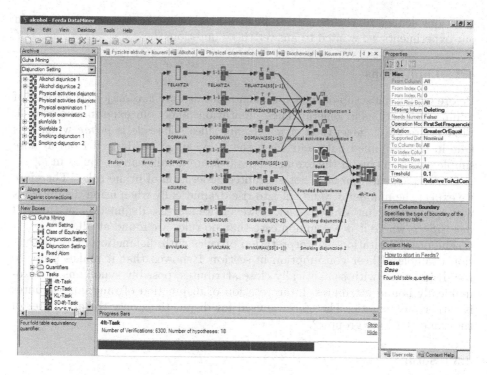

**Fig. 2.** Ferda environment

is the most generalized version of the original ASSOC procedure defined in [5]
The user environment is shown in Figure 2.

## 4   Experiments

In order to test the possibilities of disjunctions of items, we carried out experiment, which consisted of testing number of analytical questions. We chose the
STULONG data set, introduced in section 4.1. The limitations and criteria that
led to the experiment setup are described in sections 4.2 and 4.3. Performance is
discussed in section 4.4. We found interesting and also some unexpected results
which are summarized in section 4.5.

### 4.1   STULONG Data Set

We decided to use the STULONG medical data set for our experiments. The data
set contains data about longitudinal study of atherosclerosis risk factors. There
are two main reasons to choose this data set. First reason is that STULONG is
relativelly known among KDD researchers – it served as the examined data set
for three ECML/PKDD Discovery challenges. There are meaningful analytical

questions defined on the data set to be examined, which is the second reason. In our experiments we wanted to answer these questions[12].

## 4.2 Limitations

Before explaining setup of the experiments, let us note two major limitations of mining disjunctions in general. These limitations affect our experiments as well. First limitation is generation of *non prime* rules. The rule is *prime* when it is true in the examined data and when the rule cannot be derived from a more simple rule also true in the examined data. More details can be found in [5]

Our implementation does not guarantee generation of prime rules. Therefore we expect the number of valid rules to rise dramatically when using disjunctions with quantifiers that are not *strict*. However, we may use disjunctions with *strict quantifiers*, where it is a common case that no rules are found at all.

The other limitation is interpretation of rules with disjunction. The motivation example of beer consumption in section 1 showed that it makes sense to use disjunctions with semantically close attributes, possibly synonyms or taxonomically bound attributes. Interpretation of disjunction of random attributes is rather problematic. Therefore we used for disjunctions only the attributes of the same attribute groups[13].

## 4.3 Setup

From above stated limitations we concluded a setup for experiments. We answered 15 analytical questions concerning relations between significant characteristics of patients' entry examination[14]

1. *What are the relations between social factors and the following characteristics of men in the respective groups:*
   (a) *Physical activity at work and in free time*
   (b) *Smoking*
   (c) *Alcohol consumption*

---

[12] EUROMISE: The STULONG Project http://euromise.vse.cz/stulong
The STULONG Project is partially supported by project no.LN00B107 of the Ministry of Education of the Czech Republic and by grant no.2003/23 of the Internal Grant Agency of the University of Economics, Prague. The STULONG study was carried out at the 2nd Department of Medicine, 1st Faculty of Medicine of Charles University and Charles University Hospital (head Prof. M. Aschermann, MD, SDr, FESC), under the supervision of Prof. F. Boudík, MD, ScD, with collaboration of M. Tomečková, MD, PhD and Ass. Prof. J. Bultas, MD, PhD. The data were transferred to electronic form by the European Centre of Medical Informatics, Statistics and Epidemiology of Charles University and Academy of Sciences (head Prof. RNDr. J. Zvárová, DrSc).

[13] Groups of attributes, i.e. *physical examination* are defined in the STULONG data set.

[14] The analytical questions can be found at http://euromise.vse.cz/challenge2004/tasks.html

   (d) *BMI*
   (e) *Blood pressure*
   (f) *Level of total cholesterol, HDL cholesterol, triglycerides*

2. *What are the relations between physical activity at work and in free time and the following characteristics of men in the respective groups:*
   (a) *Smoking*
   (b) *Alcohol consumption*
   (c) *BMI*
   (d) *Blood pressure*
   (e) *Level of total cholesterol, HDL cholesterol, triglycerides*

3. *What are the relations between alcohol consumption and the following characteristics of men in the respective groups:*
   (a) *Smoking*
   (b) *BMI*
   (c) *Blood pressure*
   (d) *Level of total cholesterol, HDL cholesterol, triglycerides*

The experiment consisted of two steps. The first tried to answer the questions without usage of disjunctions. The second step used the task settings from the first step and allowed disjunctions of length 2. We applied the *double founded implication* quantifier with settings $p=0.9$, $Base=0.1$ and the *founded equivalence* quantifier with settings $p=0.9$ and $Base=0.1$. Below stated are the goals of the experiment:

1. Show the difference between using and not using disjunctions.
2. Use disjunctions with *strict quantifiers*.
3. Find interesting rules that contain disjunction.

### 4.4  Performance

It is shown in [14] that the 4FT procedure operation time without disjunctions is approximately linear to number of rows of the data matrix. Moreover, the bit string approach takes advantage of fast instructions in the processor, which makes running times acceptable for most tasks. When using disjunctions, the operation time rises due to the fact, that search space is not reduced by adding conjunctions decreasing *support* of the rule. However, practical experience shows that there is no need to be concerned, because the running times are acceptable.

In our experiment we used a Pentium M 1,7GHz processor with 1 GB of RAM and Windows XP. We noted the running times of tasks designed to answer proposed analytical questions. Without disjunctions, minimal running time was 0.310 seconds, maximal running time was 2.543 seconds and average running time was 0.829 seconds[15]. When using disjunctions, minimal running time was 0.370 seconds, maximal running time was 345.997 and average running time was 38.9 seconds. In the maximum case, procedure constructed and verified almost 8 million contingency tables.

---

[15] Performance tests between the 4FT procedure implemented in Ferda and LISp-Miner can be found in [10].

## 4.5   Results

After conducting the first step of the experiment, we found 0 rules for 14 of 15 analytical questions and one rule for question 3.(b). This result confirmed our presumption, that *double founded implication* and *founded equivalence* are *strict quantifiers*. When using disjunctions, we found minimum 1 and maximum 185 rules per analytical question. Although we agree that number of rules found is not a good metrics of measuring performance of new data mining technique, we think that the shift from zero rules found to non-zero rules found is significant.

Let us consider the significance of the rules. In order to reduce the amount of rules presented, we consider for simplicity only the analytical question 3.(b). We may limit our analysis, because all the rules found show similar characteristics. Possible rules answering the question were presented as examples throughout the article. Moreover, a rule for this analytical question was found during step one of the experiment.

$$Beer7(No) \Leftrightarrow_{p=0.986, Base=0.968} BMI(Normalweight, Overweight)$$

is the rule found without disjunction usage. It can be explained by the fact that 7 degree beer is very rare and it was mainly used for hydration of manual workers in extremely hot working environment (glassmakers or metallurgists). Therefore majority of population did not drink this type of beer.

**Table 2.** Rules found

| Antecedent | Succedent | DFI | FE | Base |
|---|---|---|---|---|
| Beer10(No) ∨ Beer12(No) | BMI(Normal weight, Overweight) | 0.929 | 0.932 | 0.931 |
| Beer12(No) ∨ Wine(Yes) | BMI(Normal weight, Overweight) | 0.906 | 0.909 | 0.909 |
| Beer12(No) ∨ Liquor(Yes) | BMI(Normal weight, Overweight) | 0.905 | 0.908 | 0.909 |
| Beer12(No) ∨ Alcohol(Occasionally) | BMI(Normal weight, Overweight) | 0.902 | 0.904 | 0.904 |
| Beer12(No) ∨ BeerDaily(<1 liter) | BMI(Normal weight, Overweight) | 0.946 | 0.948 | 0.948 |
| Beer12(No) ∨ WineDaily($< \frac{1}{2}$ liter) | BMI(Normal weight, Overweight) | 0.9 | 0.903 | 0.903 |
| Wine(No) ∨ WineDaily($< \frac{1}{2}$ liter) | BMI(Normal weight, Overweight) | 0.951 | 0.951 | 0.951 |
| Liquor(No) ∨ LiquorDaily(<1 dL) | BMI(Normal weight, Overweight) | 0.923 | 0.924 | 0.924 |

Table 2 shows rules found with disjunction usage. The rules were valid both for *double founded implication* (DFI) and *founded equivalence* (FE) quantifiers. Numbers in these columns represent actual values of quantifiers, $\frac{a}{a+b+c}$ for *double founded implication*, $\frac{a+d}{a+b+c+d}$ for *founded equivalence* and $\frac{a}{a+b+c+d}$ for *Base*. According to high values of both quantifiers and also to the high support of the rules (the *Base* parameter), we have found very strong rules containing disjunctions. Despite the initial concerns about interpretability of rules with disjunctions, the rules can be easily interpreted and comprehended. We are aware of the fact, that the rules do not show any surprising relations[16]. Yet they show strong relations in data, where almost no relations without disjunction usage was discovered.

To conclude the experiment, all three goals from section 4.3 were reached. We showed the difference of mining with and without disjunctions by getting almost none rules without disjunctions and more rules with disjunctions. We managed to use *strict quantifiers* and we also found interesting rules containing disjunctions. The experiment also raised many questions about further development, some of which will be discussed in the following section 5.

## 5    Further Research

There are several directions to improve disjunctions using in association mining. This section explains the directions in more detail. The first direction is optimalization of disjunctions verifications. We showed in section 4.4 that average running times for average size tasks is acceptable. However there is still room for optimizing. As was stated before, one cannot apply pruning used with conjunctions. Solution can lie in ordering of *basic Boolean attributes* according to their support. However the ordering itself can be a significant performance problem.

Another direction is to implement generation of prime rules only. The theory about prime rules is explained in [5], [12] includes information about deduction rules, which can be used when checking prime property of an association rules.

When evaluating results of our experiments, we came acros an interesting coincidence between values of quantifiers, mainly the *Base* and *p* values of *double founded implication* and *founded equivalence* quantifiers. A natural question occurs whether this is only a coincidence or if it is some kind of functional dependence. The quantifiers are known for years, yet without disjunctions we were not able on any data to mine a reasonable amount of rules to show the coincidence[17]. Examination of quantifiers as functions $f : \Re^4 \to \Re$ by finding functional extremes with the aid of calculus is another direction of further research, which would answer the question of coincidence or dependence between quantifiers.

*Boolean attribute* was presented in the article. The attribute can reach values *false* or *true* (0 or 1). *Fuzzy attribute* can also be defined, reaching values from the interval $\langle 0, 1 \rangle$. Then fuzzy *4ft tables* can be constructed and fuzzy quantifiers can be defined[18]. [7] is the inspiration for this direction.

Last, but not least direction of further research is cooperation with domain experts to evaluate usability of rules with disjunctions. We mined over medical data and presented association rules comprehensible to non medical experts. Presenting the rules found to the medical experts provides valuable feedback for us.

---

[16] This may be a problem of mining association rules in general.
[17] This corresponds to considering the quantifiers as *strict*.
[18] Naturally, some of the existing quantifiers could not be used.

# 6   Conclusion

We present an enhancement of association mining with the possibility of setting disjunctions between the items. The classical *apriori* algorithm was not suitable for disjunctions. Instead older GUHA method was applied. The 4FT procedure is used, which mines for rules in form $\varphi \approx \psi$ where $\varphi$ and $\psi$ are *Boolean attributes* and $\approx$ is a *4ft-quantifier*. *Boolean attribute* is a recursive structure, where disjunction can be used. 4FT procedure was implemented in our Ferda data mining tool.

Experiments were conducted to show the usability of disjunctions in association mining. We tried to answer number of analytical questions from the STU-LONG medical data set containing statistical information of atherosclerosis risk factors. We applied *double founded implication* and *founded equivalence* quantifiers, which are considered to be *strict*, that is to return no rules in most cases. The experiments showed difference between mining with and without disjunctions and found strong interpretable rules containing disjunctions in the data. The experiments also showed some issues, which should be subjects of further research.

## Acknowledgements

This work was supported by the project MSM6138439910 of the Ministry of Education of the Czech Republic, project IG407056 of University of Economics, Prague and by the project 201/05/0325 of the Czech Science Foundation. We acknowledge the contribution of our research colleagues Jan Rauch and Daniel Kupka for valuable comments and reviews.

## References

1. Agrawal, R., Imielinski, T., Swami, A.: Mining association rules between sets of items in large databases. In: Proc. of the ACM SIGMOD Conference on Management of Data, pp. 207–216
2. Agrawal, R., Mannila, H., Srikant, R., Toivonen, H., Verkamo, A.: Fast discovery of association rules. In: Fayyad, U., Piatetsky-Shapiro, G., Smyth, P., Uthurusamy, R. (eds.) Advances in Knowledge Discovery and Data Mining, pp. 307–328. AAAI Press, Menlo Park (1996)
3. Hájek, P.: The GUHA Method in the Last Century and Now. Znalosti. In: Conference on Data Mining, Brno 2006, pp. 10–20 (in Czech) (2006)
4. Hájek, P., Havel, I., Chytil, M.: The GUHA method of automatic hypotheses determination. Computing 1, 293–308 (1966)
5. Hájek, P., Havránek, T.: Mechanising Hypothesis Formation - Mathematical Foundations for a General Theory. Springer, Heidelberg (1978)
6. Hájek, P., Holeňa, M.: Formal logics of discovery and hypothesis formation by machine. Theoretical Computer Science 292, 345–357 (2003)
7. Holeňa, M.: Fuzzy hypotheses testing in framework of fuzzy logic. Fuzzy Sets and Systems, 149, pp. 229–252

8. KDNuggets Polls: Data mining/analytic techniques you use frequently. www.kdnuggets.com/polls/2005/data_mining_techniques.htm
9. Kováč, M., Kuchař, T., Kuzmin, A., Ralbovský, M.: Ferda, New Visual Environment for Data Mining. Znalosti, Conference on Data Mining, Hradec Králové, pp. 118–129 (in Czech) (2006)
10. Kuchař, T.: Experimental GUHA Procedures, Master Thesis, Faculty of Mathematics and Physics, Charles University, Prague (in Czech) (2006)
11. Kupka, D.: User support 4ft-Miner procedure for Data Mining. Master Thesis, Faculty of Mathematics and Physics, Charles University, Prague (in Czech) (2006)
12. Rauch, J.: Logic of Association Rules. Applied Inteligence 22(1), 9–28
13. Rauch, J.: Some Remarks on Computer Realisations of GUHA Procedures. International Journal of Man-Machine Studies 10, 23–28 (1978)
14. Rauch, J., Šimåunek, M.: An Alternative Approach to Mining Association Rules. In: Lin, T.Y., Ohsuga, S., Liau, C.J., Tsumoto, S. (eds.) Foundations of Data Mining and Knowledge Discovery, pp. 219–239. Springer, Heidelberg (2005)
15. Rauch, J., Šimåunek, M.: GUHA Method and Granular Computing. Proceedings of IEEE International Conference on Granular Computing (2005), http://www.cs.sjsu.edu/~grc/grc2005/index.html

# Author Index

# Lecture Notes in Artificial Intelligence (LNAI)

Vol. 4304: A. Sattar, B.-H. Kang (Eds.), AI 2006: Advances in Artificial Intelligence. XXVII, 1303 pages. 2006.

Vol. 4303: A. Hoffmann, B.-H. Kang, D. Richards, S. Tsumoto (Eds.), Advances in Knowledge Acquisition and Management. XI, 259 pages. 2006.

Vol. 4293: A. Gelbukh, C.A. Reyes-Garcia (Eds.), MICAI 2006: Advances in Artificial Intelligence. XXVIII, 1232 pages. 2006.

Vol. 4289: M. Ackermann, B. Berendt, M. Grobelnik, A. Hotho, D. Mladenič, G. Semeraro, M. Spiliopoulou, G. Stumme, V. Svátek, M. van Someren (Eds.), Semantics, Web and Mining. X, 197 pages. 2006.

Vol. 4285: Y. Matsumoto, R.W. Sproat, K.-F. Wong, M. Zhang (Eds.), Computer Processing of Oriental Languages. XVII, 544 pages. 2006.

Vol. 4274: Q. Huo, B. Ma, E.-S. Chng, H. Li (Eds.), Chinese Spoken Language Processing. XXIV, 805 pages. 2006.

Vol. 4265: L. Todorovski, N. Lavrač, K.P. Jantke (Eds.), Discovery Science. XIV, 384 pages. 2006.

Vol. 4264: J.L. Balcázar, P.M. Long, F. Stephan (Eds.), Algorithmic Learning Theory. XIII, 393 pages. 2006.

Vol. 4259: S. Greco, Y. Hata, S. Hirano, M. Inuiguchi, S. Miyamoto, H.S. Nguyen, R. Słowiński (Eds.), Rough Sets and Current Trends in Computing. XXII, 951 pages. 2006.

Vol. 4253: B. Gabrys, R.J. Howlett, L.C. Jain (Eds.), Knowledge-Based Intelligent Information and Engineering Systems, Part III. XXXII, 1301 pages. 2006.

Vol. 4252: B. Gabrys, R.J. Howlett, L.C. Jain (Eds.), Knowledge-Based Intelligent Information and Engineering Systems, Part II. XXXIII, 1335 pages. 2006.

Vol. 4251: B. Gabrys, R.J. Howlett, L.C. Jain (Eds.), Knowledge-Based Intelligent Information and Engineering Systems, Part I. LXVI, 1297 pages. 2006.

Vol. 4248: S. Staab, V. Svátek (Eds.), Managing Knowledge in a World of Networks. XIV, 400 pages. 2006.

Vol. 4246: M. Hermann, A. Voronkov (Eds.), Logic for Programming, Artificial Intelligence, and Reasoning. XIII, 588 pages. 2006.

Vol. 4223: L. Wang, L. Jiao, G. Shi, X. Li, J. Liu (Eds.), Fuzzy Systems and Knowledge Discovery. XXVIII, 1335 pages. 2006.

Vol. 4213: J. Fürnkranz, T. Scheffer, M. Spiliopoulou (Eds.), Knowledge Discovery in Databases: PKDD 2006. XXII, 660 pages. 2006.

Vol. 4212: J. Fürnkranz, T. Scheffer, M. Spiliopoulou (Eds.), Machine Learning: ECML 2006. XXIII, 851 pages. 2006.

Vol. 4211: P. Vogt, Y. Sugita, E. Tuci, C.L. Nehaniv (Eds.), Symbol Grounding and Beyond. VIII, 237 pages. 2006.

Vol. 4203: F. Esposito, Z.W. Raś, D. Malerba, G. Semeraro (Eds.), Foundations of Intelligent Systems. XVIII, 767 pages. 2006.

Vol. 4201: Y. Sakakibara, S. Kobayashi, K. Sato, T. Nishino, E. Tomita (Eds.), Grammatical Inference: Algorithms and Applications. XII, 359 pages. 2006.

Vol. 4200: I.F.C. Smith (Ed.), Intelligent Computing in Engineering and Architecture. XIII, 692 pages. 2006.

Vol. 4198: O. Nasraoui, O. Zaïane, M. Spiliopoulou, B. Mobasher, B. Masand, P.S. Yu (Eds.), Advances in Web Mining and Web Usage Analysis. IX, 177 pages. 2006.

Vol. 4196: K. Fischer, I.J. Timm, E. André, N. Zhong (Eds.), Multiagent System Technologies. X, 185 pages. 2006.

Vol. 4188: P. Sojka, I. Kopeček, K. Pala (Eds.), Text, Speech and Dialogue. XV, 721 pages. 2006.

Vol. 4183: J. Euzenat, J. Domingue (Eds.), Artificial Intelligence: Methodology, Systems, and Applications. XIII, 291 pages. 2006.

Vol. 4180: M. Kohlhase, OMDoc – An Open Markup Format for Mathematical Documents [version 1.2]. XIX, 428 pages. 2006.

Vol. 4177: R. Marín, E. Onaindía, A. Bugarín, J. Santos (Eds.), Current Topics in Artificial Intelligence. XV, 482 pages. 2006.

Vol. 4160: M. Fisher, W. van der Hoek, B. Konev, A. Lisitsa (Eds.), Logics in Artificial Intelligence. XII, 516 pages. 2006.

Vol. 4155: O. Stock, M. Schaerf (Eds.), Reasoning, Action and Interaction in AI Theories and Systems. XVIII, 343 pages. 2006.

Vol. 4149: M. Klusch, M. Rovatsos, T.R. Payne (Eds.), Cooperative Information Agents X. XII, 477 pages. 2006.

Vol. 4140: J.S. Sichman, H. Coelho, S.O. Rezende (Eds.), Advances in Artificial Intelligence - IBERAMIA-SBIA 2006. XXIII, 635 pages. 2006.

Vol. 4139: T. Salakoski, F. Ginter, S. Pyysalo, T. Pahikkala (Eds.), Advances in Natural Language Processing. XVI, 771 pages. 2006.

Vol. 4133: J. Gratch, M. Young, R. Aylett, D. Ballin, P. Olivier (Eds.), Intelligent Virtual Agents. XIV, 472 pages. 2006.

Vol. 4130: U. Furbach, N. Shankar (Eds.), Automated Reasoning. XV, 680 pages. 2006.

Vol. 4120: J. Calmet, T. Ida, D. Wang (Eds.), Artificial Intelligence and Symbolic Computation. XIII, 269 pages. 2006.

Vol. 4118: Z. Despotovic, S. Joseph, C. Sartori (Eds.), Agents and Peer-to-Peer Computing. XIV, 173 pages. 2006.

Vol. 4114: D.-S. Huang, K. Li, G.W. Irwin (Eds.), Computational Intelligence, Part II. XXVII, 1337 pages. 2006.

Vol. 4108: J.M. Borwein, W.M. Farmer (Eds.), Mathematical Knowledge Management. VIII, 295 pages. 2006.

Vol. 4106: T.R. Roth-Berghofer, M.H. Göker, H.A. Güvenir (Eds.), Advances in Case-Based Reasoning. XIV, 566 pages. 2006.

Vol. 4099: Q. Yang, G. Webb (Eds.), PRICAI 2006: Trends in Artificial Intelligence. XXVIII, 1263 pages. 2006.

Vol. 4095: S. Nolfi, G. Baldassarre, R. Calabretta, J.C.T. Hallam, D. Marocco, J.-A. Meyer, O. Miglino, D. Parisi (Eds.), From Animals to Animats 9. XV, 869 pages. 2006.